Shadow of the Third Century

A Revaluation of Christianity

BY

ALVIN BOYD KUHN, Ph. D.

". . . the tyranny exercised over the human mind in the name of religion."—H. H. MILMAN, *The History of Christianity* (p. 461).

"From the very beginning it was a tradition of *faith*. . . . In all strictness the Gospels are not historical documents. They are catechisms for use in common worship . . . that and no other is the content they announce; that and no other is the quality they claim."—ALFRED LOISY, *The Birth of the Christian Religion* (p. 12).

ACADEMY PRESS

218 WEST JERSEY STREET   ELIZABETH 2, N. J.

To

ALL THOSE
WHO KNOW THAT TRUTH
ALONE WILL FREE US FROM THE
TYRANNY OF INDOCTRINATED PIOUS OBSESSIONS
THIS
VOLUME IS
SINCERELY DEDICATED

CONTENTS

v

PREFACE

In the mountains of Virginia a few years ago the minister of a sect of religious addicts, standing in his pulpit, released a rattlesnake and provoked the reptile to strike him twice in the arm. This, it was announced, was to prove that the power of faith in God was able to overcome the power of the serpent's poison. Lamentably all that was proved impeccably was the failure of arrant faith in God to overcome human folly, when goaded to feverish pitch of fanaticism by irrational religion.

Some years before that the author saw the cinema dealing with the Easter (rather pre-Easter) rites of the Penitentes, or Flagellantes in New Mexico, in which on Good Friday they marched up to a hilltop lashing each the one in front with knotted ropes upon bare backs, to a cross on which a victim in human form was savagely put through an ordeal simulating the crucifixion and well-nigh actually murdered. The reflections of the beholder of this eccentric monstrosity of religious pietism were centered upon the agency that could have brought to birth in normally sensible human beings such outlandish and insufferable perversions of religious motivation. Obviously it was a product of the Christian religion, for every motive and feature in it sprang from a Christian principle or practice. What should one think about a religion that could generate such appalling prodigies of fanaticism?

Back in 1837 there broke out in New England and spread west as far as Ohio a wave of religious frenzy that threw the land into a furore of excitement and swept people into its maelstrom of insane force like leaves in an autumn gale. It originated in a single bit, or several bits, of calculation based on a literal interpretation of figures in the Bible by a rather fine young Vermont schoolteacher and local lay preacher. Young Miller took some numbers given in *Daniel, Ezekiel* and *Revelation* and with a little arithmetical manipulation, by two distinct methods, deduced that the date of April seventeenth, 1843—six years ahead—was the "day" set by Biblical prophecy as the "Day of the Lord," that dreadful day on which the crack of doom would shatter the heavens and all the world would be dissolved with fervent heat

vii

at twelve o'clock midnight. The village preacher began spreading his arithmetic in Sabbath discourses about the countryside; excitement took hold; the Boston ministerium put him on for great evangelistic campaigns; and leading divines fell in with the extravaganza. As the six years sped by, the closer approach of the "Day" swelled the hysteria to ever expanding proportions. Hundreds disposed of all their properties; and on the fatal night all sought the nearest mountain top, hilltop, treetop or rooftop (following a Biblical admonition) to be nearer the heavens.

When the night passed calmly and dawn broke the deluded fanatics were left deflated. Miller scratched his head, and also scratched pencil again on paper, with the result that he announced that he had made a miscalculation, and that the final day of earth was to fall on the succeeding October fifteenth. The pitiable farce was again gone through. Then Miller and his chief aides quarreled over who was to blame; and one more dire instance of the derationalizing power of the religion known as Christianity, taking its Holy Scriptures as literal historical record, had grievously marked its dark blot on the stained pages of world history.

Not a century since at least the tenth A.D. but has heard the lusty preachment of the repeated claims that events then transpiring were the literal fulfilment of Old Testament prophecy, to which the nineteenth and twentieth centuries have added the prophecies alleged to be indicated by measured dimensions in the halls, corridors, chambers, passages and stairways in the great pyramid of Gizeh. This rage is upon the world with more abandon and fanaticism in this twentieth century than ever before, and probably has materially influenced international movements, particularly in Germany and England. Thousands blare forth their excitable predictions, presenting for proof the texts of Scripture, twisted by a heated imagination into meanings fitted to the preconceived construction and sublimely insensible of the fact that others in every preceding century have with the same far-strained "plausibility" interpreted the fulfilment of ancient "prophecy" in the events of their time. Always Bible and pyramid "prophecy" is being fulfilled *now*. If we can reincarnate and be back in the twenty-fourth century, we will doubtless witness the same asinine procedure. It will be just as easy to match prophecy with current event then as now and in the past. Thus another weird frenzy of Christian origin runs its course in each century.

A schoolgirl in this New Jersey city a few years ago reported to her parents that her teacher in the public schools had asked her to take her turn reading the prescribed ten verses from the Scriptures in the day's opening exercises, and handed her an edition of the Bible that was a non-Catholic one. The parents, Roman Catholics, were so incensed at the thought of a Protestant Bible having touched the hands of their child that they visited the teacher, poured out their indignant feelings upon her and laid complaint with the School Superintendent. This sample of narrow bigotry is also a product of the religion called Christianity.

And so, stated simply, this book has been written to tell the truth about a religion that has produced such obviously irrational behavior. The story needs telling all the more for the reason that it has never been told in its bald straight factual truth, and because heaven and earth have been called upon to prevent its being known ever since the third century. It is in the main truth that has been suppressed, buried, its evidences destroyed, its documents changed, with a story far other than the true one substituted in its place and promulgated with every device of propaganda. It aims to take its place as the true history of the origin and spread of what has been named the Christian religion.

It is eminently desirable to say at once, before its first page is read, that the work is *not* an attack upon Christianity. So far from being hostile to Christianity, it is in all likelihood the first book in centuries that is written in support and defense of Christianity, striking forceful blows at every influence inimical to Christianity. It stands unqualifiedly as the courageous champion and crusader *for* Christianity, a Christianity that is so sorely needed at the present epoch to save a still savage world.

In spite of this protestation the essay will sound to many like the most scathing denunciation and blaspheming of what they have believed to be Christianity they have ever read. Many will lay the book down with the indignant query whether the author has never been able to see a single item of good in the whole long history of the faith. It is admitted here that emphasis in the work has been placed upon the idiosyncrasies, foibles, follies, cruelties, fallacies, impostures and falsities, the horrifying list of evils that are an integral part of the record, and are not denied. The intrinsic and sincere reason for this accentuation is the consideration that while it is assuredly not the whole story, it is that part of the story which has to be known if any true evaluation of the place, function and further utility of this religion is to be appraised in the modern generation for future history. If a tool of culture is not known *thoroughly* it will not be used skilfully. The truth of the Christian religion is not and can not be known unless that truth is known in its organic wholeness.

It has to be asserted here that one who thinks he has the true history of the Christian religion, but does not know what is here revealed for the first time, is sadly in error. What happened to Christianity and in Christianity in those two direful centuries, the third and fourth, is not only an essential part of the whole story of Christian history; it is in fact the indispensable key to any right understanding of the entire history. It is a daring venture to assert that the full truth about Christianity's rise and spread has never yet been told, and that a given work makes that disclosure for the first time. This work risks that venture. It is *the* key to the last two thousand years of world history.

As to the other side of the story—the good which it is claimed to have done in the world—let it be said once and categorically in this Preface, so that it need not be reiterated at every new turn throughout the whole book, that Christianity has wrought much of what we believe we can call "good" in its history. Since it has ruled the world of the West for sixteen hundred years, and automatically numbered among its adherents practically all the greater characters in European and American history, a religion numbering in its following such a body of high-minded people could not help but contribute much "good" to general society. If any religion has in its enrollment strong spiritual characters, or masses of commonly decent people, along with rogues, it will register a good influence. Even a bad religion can not utterly corrupt upright people. And even evil itself invariably generates incidental good, unintended good, thrown off as a by-product by evil action. The very perpetrator of evil learns something, if only by his punishment or through his conscience. So it is put down here in indisputable terms: Christianity has caused, registered, produced or generated much good in the world.

What is insisted upon, however, is that a view which is blinded to see only good in this faith is an unbalanced and hence an untrue view. The work is undertaken in its main purpose to disabuse the general mind of a host of prepossessions and conventional notions about Christianity which are simply not true. And it is in the pursuit of this laudable objective, as part of the effort to fight a battle *for* Christianity that we are under the necessity of republishing what to many will, regrettably, seem like a virulent assault upon Christianity itself. Even at that many readers will for a time at least feel that we are pursuing the paradoxical course of trying to build up Christianity by knocking it down. It must be seen, however, that what we are building up *is* Christianity, and what we are knocking down is something else that for the good of mankind sorely needs to be stricken down.

The work sets out to prove that what has passed under the name of Christianity is not and really has never been Christianity at all. The thing accepted for Christianity has turned out to be something else very unlike it, a frightfully deceptive false substitution. Thousands have found it in every age unacceptable, repelling, repugnant to every instinct of logic and sanity. Among those who have found it inhospitable and insufferable to their natural instincts of both reason and good were Emerson, Lincoln and Edison, in the American scene. Now, as in the days of its foundation it is, as a popular religion, maintained by the less intelligent majority and disdained by the truly learned and intelligent, who sanction it in a patronizing way as being good for the ignorant, but hardly adequate for themselves. Its popular vogue is deemed useful to the orderly status of society, as it tends to hold the masses to a tolerable measure of self-restraint from criminality and a fair level of human decency.

No apology, but a word in extenuation of the presentation of so large a quantity of quoted material is in order. The citation of a hundred passages from authors and historians was absolutely imperative in the case of a work which takes a stand on nearly every point in radical opposition to all conventionally accepted beliefs. A position that flies so directly in the face of all general opinion must call to its support the weight of a formidable array of authority. Only by marshaling the evidence in fairly impressive volume and quality can the real strength of the case be demonstrated. The material cited is at any rate a republication of data which are vital and valuable in themselves and should be more generally known. It is a part of the truth which so badly needs republication at this time.

The author wishes to repudiate the suggestion that he is inspired by a hostile animus against Christianity. He confesses to a natural "animus" against bigotry, superstition, narrow hatreds, persecution, tyranny, war, murder, slaughter, lying and sickening hypocrisy, the more so when they are perpetrated in the name and under the disguise of "holy religion." Since *Christian history is in the main a record of these horrible things,* he is free to express his dislike of them. But these things are no part of a *true* Christianity, and so it can not be charged that he is prejudiced against that which is true Christianity.

It needs only to be said that if he has filled his volume with material that sounds scurrilous in ordinary Christian ears, he has not invented the data, but taken it nearly all from Christian writers! Nothing he has said is really half as virulent as the statements of the Christian apologists themselves. He has refrained from using language to characterize the evils of Christianity as brutally frank and realistic as he finds the historians of the religion themselves using. Let it be remembered that he has made only the scantiest reference to the unspeakable horrors of the Spanish Inquisition, when the love of Christ in Christian hearts drove the ecclesiastics to tear limbs from quivering bodies or burn them at the stake, for conscientious conviction of honest truth-seeking. A thousand pages could be added to the record of the profligacy of the priesthood, the forgery of documents, the immorality of the clergy and laity, the economic subjugation of the peasants under churchly feudal land ownership, the never-flagging draining of money from the poor and the abuses which drove at last the northern half of Europe out of the fold in rebellion. The work is not an effort to stigmatize Christianity as it could be stigmatized, but an attempt to rewrite the history of its upbuilding on false bases, to delineate the nature of its falsification of the truth and its utter misinterpretation of its Scriptures, and then to trace the evil psychological consequences of this warping of mind on the life of the West. In the prosecution of this intent it became necessary in an incidental way to introduce a meager portion of the truly horrendous data of Christianity's record of evil influence.

It is distinctly and directly avowed that the book itself, and more particularly its strictures on religion as an influence less beneficent than philosophy, have been launched with not the remotest reference to the world's political situation at the time of writing, when supreme world conflict is being waged between two great groups, the one bent on suppressing religion, the other standing on a religious platform entirely. Odd as it may seem, the book has not been motivated by any agreement with, allegiance to or support of the party hostile to religion. The position taken is in no sense opposed to religion *per se;* it only holds that religion divorced from philosophy is inadequate to man's highest needs and will prove a treacherous and eventually dangerous guide in life. The writer stands for religion sanified and stabilized, intellectually enlightened, by philosophy and science. He stands against the use of religion to hypnotize the masses. He dislikes the religion of ignorance, when honest priestly leadership could so easily make it a religion of intelligence. The international implications of the analysis must be considered by those wise enough to discern their proper relevance. This may be said of any worth-while work on philosophy or religion. It is in no sense a propaganda work, but a challenge to general intelligence.

The effort has been made to eliminate footnotes entirely, the sources of the many citations being inserted in the text itself. It is desirable to say, however, that in many places in the work the author has openly stated, or possibly hinted, that many points, problems, questions and mysteries formerly or still baffling the world of religious scholarship, have found resolution in clear light. Particularly where it was asserted that the secret esoteric science of interpreting Scriptures composed in the ancient arcane language of symbolism had been rehabilitated and a reinterpretation of the Scriptures had been made on the basis of this new insight, the statements standing without further elucidation will naturally arouse inquiry or provoke challenge. To meet this inquiry and challenge, it simply needs to be said that the material which will be found to support the hints made in this respect has already been published in the author's earlier work, *The Lost Light,* or perhaps in its companion study, *Who Is This King of Glory?* The present work often alludes to the error of interpreting the Scriptures literally and historically, and gives the reader to understand that they can be and now have been interpreted properly on the purely allegorical and mythical basis. Obviously every scholar and every intelligent reader will bristle to this epochal statement and demand that we produce this product of might and magic, or reveal where it has been done. It has been done in *The Lost Light* and *Who Is This King of Glory?* We could not keep interjecting this information throughout the course of the book. So it is given here.

THE PATH TO THE GATE

"The vice of a soul is ignorance; the virtue of a soul is knowledge."
—HERMES.

"I do not see any sin in the world, but I see a great deal of ignorance."—GEORGE SAND.

"It is also acknowledged that ignorance and delusion in regard to the gods is irreligiousness and impurity, and that the superior knowledge in respect to them is holy and helpful: the former being the darkness of ignorance in regard to the things revered and beautiful, and the latter the light of knowledge. The former condition will cause human beings to be beset with every form of evil through ignorance and recklessness, but the latter is the source of everything beneficial."—IAMBLICHUS, *The Egyptian Mysteries* (p. 13).

"Now had commenced what may be called, neither unreasonably nor unwarrantably, the mythic age of Christianity. As Christianity worked downward into the lower classes of society, as it received the rude and ignorant barbarians within its pale, the general effect could not but be that the age would drag down the religion to its level, rather than the religion elevate the age to its own lofty standard."—DEAN H. H. MILMAN, *The History of Christianity* (p. 500).

These are a few excerpts culled from a collection that could fill pages and they may prepare the mind of the reader for what is to come in the body of the essay. Dean Milman's history of Christianity is a particularly sound and sane evaluation of the influences that engendered and conditioned Christianity throughout. If what he says here is true, the position and conclusions of the work here presented must be conceded to rest on highly accredited and substantial foundations. For, in substance, the contention of our work is that Christianity evolved and took historical form as the result of a corruption of high wisdom already extant, and not as the promulgation of new light and wisdom previously unknown. There is solid ground for the thesis that the religion which can be successfully foisted upon popular acceptance is never anything but the corruption of more exalted understanding and truer wisdom. Baldly stated, the thesis here to be vindicated is that

Christianity only gained the favor and held the allegiance of the masses of the populations of the West for centuries because it succeeded in accommodating its message to the prevalent levels of general unintelligence. In doing so it inevitably distorted its truths into ludicrous caricature and baneful forms of error and falsehood.

CHAPTER I

PRIMEVAL CHRISTIANITY

Voltaire once remarked that it might be a very fine thing if Europe some time decided to try Christianity. He was intimating, of course, that there had never been a serious undertaking anywhere in the Christian world to put into practice the Christly code of ethics as set forth in the Sermon on the Mount. He was assuming that Europe knew well enough what Christianity was, but lacked the moral strength to put its cardinal principles to work.

It is suggested here that the philosopher would have made a far more pertinent observation if he had said that it might be well if Europe at some time really learned what true Christianity was. This essay ventures to go beyond Voltaire and make the assertion that not only had Europe never tried Christianity, but that it never had it. Not only had the Occidental world never tried living its professed and dominating religion of Christianity, but never at any time in its historical period had it even possessed the true religion to which the name of Christianity had been attached. Failure of Christendom to put its nominally accepted religious systematism into living operation in its centuries of historical life was not mainly due to its want of moral stamina, but stemmed, as this work will assert, from the simple fact that it did not *have* the Christianity that should have gone with the name. Cutting many a Gordian knot of entangled debate and likewise cutting a straight path through a jungle of theological presuppositions, this work will begin with the bald bold declaration that the Western world of Europe and America has never held true Christianity in its possession, has never had knowledge of it.

"There is no such thing as a religion called 'Christianity'—there never has been such a religion. There is and always has been the Church."— Hilaire Belloc, *The Great Heresies*, p. 246.

If these assertions embody substantial truth, the obvious inference must be that the West, while under the illusion that it possessed and even implemented Christianity, in reality possessed something else that was believed to be Christianity, but was not. Its highly vaunted religion bore the name of Christianity, but strictly was at no time real Christianity. That grandiose system which it presented and promulgated under the name of Christianity was at best but a feeble, nay even a wretched caricature of the real structure that the name connoted. What is now to be expressed for the first time in all the history of religious disputation is that this assumed corpus of cultural influence was at no time truly Christian at all. It carried the name and it enacted the presumptive role which the name prefigured. But it was not Christianity. It was something else. What that other thing was it will be the burden of this work to announce clearly and unequivocally.

The prime purpose of the essay, it must be uncompromisingly asserted, is therefore to redeem Christianity from the onus of every kind and degree and weight of obloquy, disfavor, rejection, neglect, scorn, hatred, misrepresentation and denunciation to which it has been subjected by virtue of its mishandling by the parties that so falsely caricatured it in posing as its advocates, champions and sainted heads. The aim is to so restate the true character and message of Christianity that such a virulent denunciation as that leveled at it by the German philosopher Nietzsche will be totally disarmed of its force and pertinence and rendered innocuous by being shown to be utterly wide of the mark of truth. If the object in view is measurably achieved, the result will be the exoneration of Christianity from the entire mass of opprobrium loaded upon it by the irreligious, the atheists, freethinkers, secularists, the profane of every ilk. The objective, admittedly ambitious and daring, is to rehabilitate Christianity in its pristine virtue and splendor and thus to vindicate it against the violence of attack and volume of discredit which it suffered through the ignorant zealotry of those proclaiming themselves its friends, as well as from the frontal hostility of those openly declaring themselves its defamers. The high design is to restate the system that alone has just claim to the name of Christianity and to demonstrate by contrast its superiority and magnificence as over against that hetero-Christianity which by one of the most amazing demarches of all history, came to masquerade in its vestments and under its name. It is desired to establish the extraordinary fact that the system of proclaimed faith and dogma, ceremonial and government, historically known as Christianity never has been real Christianity at all. If the project is measurably successful the very desirable object will have been attained of showing that the volume of attack

2

that has been at times heavy and damaging has fallen out of bounds, since it was never leveled against true Christianity but hit hard against a pseudo-Christianity that for the most part richly merited the obloquy thus poured upon it. The blows of attack fell upon the masquerading system which, while it was never Christianity, yet stood disguised as such and therefore in line to receive the brunt of many assaults of hostile forces.

The gist of what will constitute the introductory datum is to be found expressed with wholly unexpected frankness and conclusiveness in a statement of the sainted Augustine, who has often been given the title of "Founder of Christian Theology." This citation from his writings virtually could stand as the "golden text" of our work, as it is a concise epitome and summary of the central theme. Its reproduction in this connection and at this juncture of world affairs could well become the solvent of most of the tragic misunderstandings responsible for the present world confusion. It will stand in the present work as the firing of the opening gun in a battle that will be waged from now on to unseat from its throne of power in the domain of mass consciousness that weird and fantastic delusion of literalized and historicized Scriptural myths which has steeped the minds of untold millions in doltish superstition over so many centuries under the name of Christianity. It is by no means an indulgence in extravagant fancy to assert that it is world-shaking in its implications. Here it is:

"That which is known as the Christian religion existed among the ancients, and never did not exist; from the very beginning of the human race until the time when Christ came in the flesh, at which time the *true* religion, which *already* existed, began to be called Christianity."—*Retractt.* I, xiii.

This astonishing declaration was made in the early fourth century of our era. It can be asserted with little chance of refutation that if this affirmation of the pious Augustine had not sunk out of sight, but had been kept in open view through the period of Western history, the whole course of that history would have been vastly altered for the better. It is only too likely the case that the obvious implications of the passage were of such a nature that its open exploitation was designedly frowned upon by the ecclesiastical authorities in every age. It held the kernel of a great truth the common knowledge of which would have been a stumbling-block in the way of the perpetuation of priestly power over the general Christian mind. It would have provoked inquiry and disarmed the ecclesiastical prestige of much of its power.

3

For what is it that the Christian saint actually says? It stands as hardly less than a point-blank repudiation of all the chief asseverations on which the structure of Christian tradition rests. Every child born to Christian parents in eighteen centuries has been indoctrinated with the unqualified belief that Christianity was a completely new, and the first *true,* religion in world history; that it was vouchsafed to the world from God himself and brought to earth by the sole divine emissary ever commissioned to convey God's truth to mankind; that it flashed out amid the lingering murks of Pagan darkness as the first ray of true light to illumine the pathway of evolution for the safe treading of human feet. All previous religion was the superstitious product of primitive childishness of mind. Christianity was the first piercing of the long night of black heathenism by that benignant gift of God.

Augustine shatters this illusion and this jealously preserved phantom of blind credulity. From remotest antiquity, he asserts, there has always existed in the world the true religion. It illuminated the intellects of the most ancient Sages, Prophets, Priests and Kings. It built the foundation for every national religion, whose tenets consisted of reformulations of its ubiquitous ageless principles of knowledge and wisdom. It went under a variety of designations: Hermeticism in ancient Egypt; Orphism in early Greece; Zoroastrianism in Persia; Brahmanism in India; Taoism in China; Shintoism in Japan and China. In no matter what garbled and perverted form, even tribal religionism fostered it. Mystery cultism dramatized and ritualized it in many lands. Social usages, all the round of annual festivals, chimney-corner tale and castle ballad, countryside legend and folk-lore carried it down the stream of time. Always it existed among men; never was it not present in the world. Hardly ever apprehended at its real value, its representations badly misconceived, its import warped and travestied at every turn in popular practice, it yet existed and came down to Augustine's day. He who had been reared early in the cult of Mani, with all its arcana of esoteric explication of cosmogony, anthropology and theocracy; he who later sat at the feet of Plotinus and from him transmitted to the new faith that took the name of Christianity, which he was later to espouse with such ardor of soul, its mighty doctrine of the Trinity— Plotinus' three fundamental hypostases, the One, the Oversoul and the World Soul—this man was not hesitant in saying that he and his brethren in the new movement were only giving a new impetus to this age-old system of arcane truth, and for the first time called it— after the new Greek term provided by Hellenism for the central element of all true religion, the Christos—Christianity. It was as if he said: this sublime religion has existed in the world from the beginning; it has borne many names and been exploited in varied forms. But it is our merit that we at last have given it the highest name it ever bore, Christianity, the religion of the Christos, the divine principle in all men.

So thought the devout saint in the fourth century. True was his statement—in part. For alas! and again alas! the newly promulgated religion into which he had gravitated, that had indeed drawn every single item of its theology and its ritual, of its symbols and its festivals, from that antique code, had already, even as he wrote, so far lost or perverted every facet of that ancient light that it stood as a grotesque caricature, indeed even a flat inversion, of the resplendent system of archaic truth. In fact the movement which he was helping to start on its course, and which he called the "true" religion, "already" existent, was farther from being a continuation of that extolled earlier heritage than almost any other reformulation of it known to history, the direst and most tragic corruption of it in all the ages. Indeed, had he really possessed the full and profound rudiments of that earlier lore, he would have been keenly aware that the new development he was so unctuously leading, so far from being a straight perpetuation of that great tradition, was almost its total negation and obliteration. He would have known that, instead of being a new presentation and re-vivification of that venerable wisdom-lore, the cult of his espousal was even then the surety of its death. Before he himself passed off the scene, in the late fourth century, the religion of his fervent love had already devastated the structure and prostituted the venerated message of that antecedent cultus, leaving it a meaningless jargon of inscrutable creeds, empty formularies, uncomprehended rituals and Scriptural books, over which it was doomed to wrangle in witless futility but fierce venom of theological disputation for two full centuries and to settle finally into a truce without peace that has lingered on in silent but smoldering hatred of parties ever since.

Had the great saint who fled to God on the rebound from his youthful excesses of passions of the flesh, ever fully opened his eyes to the significance of what he was promulgating with such hot passion of his soul, he would not have failed to see that the new wave of religionism had little right to the august Hellenic name which it had laid hold on, and which it had already degraded. He might have known that his new cult, so far from republishing and reanimating that ancient tradi-

5

tion of sacred philosophy, was destined to smother and virtually extinguish that very fire of living truth, which half in discernment and half in blindness he so sweepingly claimed to be the content and corpus of the new faith that Constantine had secured from further persecution. Instead of reenlivening this *true* Christianity of the past, hoary with the veneration of ages of wise men, to continue its mighty service of beneficence to later times, the movement that seized upon the holy name of Christianity actually brought that benignant service to an end. Instead of lifting the world out of heathen darkness into the light, this rabid movement put out the great light that had so long shone and plunged the Occident into Cimmerian darkness. And in that darkness it still lingers and gropes its uncertain way after eighteen hundred years.

For with the hatred of books, learning and philosophy already in full swing, the fell hostility of the new popular evangelism to anything savoring of culture and erudition had already swept out the arcane literature, and its frenzied course had not stopped until it had sent up in flames the most precious collection of books in the world at any time—the great Alexandrian library. Nay, even beyond that its furious besom swept on to the obliteration of all past heritage in the final act of closing out the last of the great Platonic Academies in the Hellenic world. And with this gesture of insolent triumph in the desolation of golden truth it could not itself comprehend, it extinguished the last candle-flicker of a luminous torch of wisdom-knowledge that had been kept steadily and brightly burning in brotherhoods of cultured students for the guidance of the race from most archaic times.

After Justinian's order to close up the last Platonic school in the sixth century came the Dark Ages. And this period of benightedness, be it observed, extended precisely over the area covered by the spread of this spurious faith, and continued to throw its pall of ignorance and gloom upon this part of the world during the time of its dominance. Carrying its own darkness with it as it went, it yet has had the incredible effrontery to call itself the light of the world, and to charge other cultures with generating the forces of darkness. The antecedent religions which it supplanted in northern Europe in the seventh, eighth and ninth centuries, the Celtic, the Druidic, the Teutonic and Norse, all in turn suffered the extinction of the ancient gleam of true philosophy which these nations and civilizations still cherished, when the devastating hand of fanatical pietism closed upon and crushed them. When the lurid persuasions of frenzied ignorance imagine themselves

6

to be the benignant light, all true light must hide itself till the black fury has swept past. For never can darkness comprehend the light. And still the shadows linger and the West still gropes in worse than half-darkness to find its pathway to blessedness.

A thousand volumes stand on library shelves bearing the titles of histories of primitive Christianity, the origins of Christianity, the formative influences in the Christian movement and the general narrative of the rise and growth to world power of this "Christian" religion. But this work will advance the thesis that flouts nearly every word in all those books in its direct asseveration that neither the history of Christianity as Augustine envisaged it nor that of the Christian movement has ever yet been written. Histories stand on the shelves, but nowhere yet has the true history appeared. It has virtually never been known; it is still buried in the wrack and debris of the past. There parades in its stead the library of tomes purporting to be that history, but they miss the mark of truth by many a league. Every volume of it is based on a mass of unfounded assumption, weirdly travestied misstatements of old truth and uncouth perversion of exalted wisdom. It is an incredible mélange of misconception and misrepresentation, adding up in the end virtually to outright falsehood. Every history of Christianity has missed the real truth of its subject, and the field is thus open for this work to present as much of that truth as it is possible to crowd into the space of a single volume. All salvation from world ills of the present awaits the first writing of this true history of Christianity. It should mark a distinct epoch in world annals. It is enough of penance and karmic retribution for half the world to have had to pay the huge penalty of nearly two thousand years of injurious ignorance, with its long train of deleterious consequences, for having been denied the true knowledge of the influences that so misshaped its life over many centuries. And not until this incubus of wretched error and arrant superstition is lifted off the common mind of the great West will there be the possibility of an advance to freer life on a higher level.

Every attempt to write Christian history hitherto has been doomed to miscarriage from the start by its being based on presuppositions and acceptances not a single one of which could be certified as veridical truth, but all of which in the total amounted to a nearly complete tangle of falsehood. It has been constructed and still rests on an insecure and untenable platform of fiction, fantasy and falsity. So blunt and challenging a statement could not be made unless the all-sufficient

7

data were at hand to support it. This corroboration will be furnished in the body of the work. That it has not been discerned, evaluated at its supreme worth and assembled before is the most damaging evidence to the stultifying force of fifteen centuries of Christian influence, and the heinous attestation of the blindness of general religious research.

Every historian of Christianity has approached his task with mind firmly set to rationalize a host of traditional conceptions which he had never had the acumen to see were themselves but the fictionalized formulations of the very movement that he essayed to delineate. His objective vision was from the start beclouded and wrongly focused on its theme through being conditioned by the very aberrations of view which the movement he set out to historicize had afflicted him with and thus vitiated his effort to envisage it correctly. He lacked the insight to correct these basic maladjustments of view before using them as lenses through which to get the properly focused picture. In short he used the glass of a badly distorted perspective supplied to him by the very movement which had created such an instrument for the conscious purpose of preventing its true picture from being seen. The rules and standards by which he presumed to judge and appraise—and applaud—Christianity were those narrow presuppositions, claims, assertions and predilections, not to say prejudices and jealousies, which were generated within the sphere of motivations which produced Christianity itself, and which wholly lacked the balance and true perspective to afford the historian the proper criterion of appraisal. The norms and standards of Christian criticism, when applied to a comparative evaluation of this system with others, have ever been found narrow, insular, in short disastrously bigoted and sectarian. It has remained for three centuries of nearly futile Christian missionary effort —itself motivated by an egregious sense of superiority—and the late acceleration of world communication, bringing distant peoples in closer touch and thus breaking down old barriers of misunderstanding, to open the eyes of discerning Christians to the provincial insufficiency of their traditional belief in Christianity's unique status of excellence and to reveal the shortsightedness of their norms of judgment.

The time is therefore ripe for the rectification of all the misjudgment that has gone into the inditing of the rows of books on Christian history. How could that history be fair, true and honest when its very bases, its fundamental theses, were weakened by error and mired in misconceptions? There is actually sufficient ground to warrant the statement that every thesis upon which the conventional historian rested his judgments and his interpretations was false and erroneous. Hardly any argument advanced for the glory of Christianity could stand on material true as fact. Perhaps no other religion has ever come so near to being based wholly on fiction, fancy and lurid imagination. Allan Upward goes so far in one of his books as to assert that Christianity has the unique and unenviable distinction of being founded completely on a web of falsehoods. If this be demerited as a snap judgment, what is to be made of the sincere verdict of a capable and fair-minded scholar like Gerald Massey, who was forced to an equally harsh conclusion as the result of forty years of assiduous and intelligent research in the Egyptian backgrounds of Christianity, every item of his "bias" being generated by data before which his mind had to bend in the direction of truth? And many another investigator, who was able finally to wrench his mind free from the suffocating hypnosis of age-old tradition, which exalted and condoned everything Christian and deprecated everything Pagan, has been overwhelmingly persuaded that what has been put forth uninterruptedly over eighteen centuries as the truth about the faith stands at gross variance from what he reads in the actual account. He sees that there has been uniform and prolonged deception, hiding of the record and subterfuge. If he will be at pains to pursue his researches to the limit of assiduity and persistence, he will be further awakened to the painful realization that, with one story standing on the record, quite another has been foisted on the world. If the history reader's integrity of critical judgment can hold fast and his sense of true values remain uncorrupted, he will eventually be unable to escape the inquiry why in this instance the true history of a movement acclaimed to be the greatest in earthly annals has stood on the books as one thing of a certain character, but has come out to the public as something radically different. And he will finally have to yield to the disquieting conviction that this has not happened by sheer natural tendency, but that it has been a development that took its course under the imposition of a pressure whose force must be reckoned as little less than titanic. And unpleasantly the accumulation of reflections on the extraordinary circumstance will bring him face to face with the long deferred but at last unescapable conclusion that the universal popular rating and estimate of Christian history has been designedly promulgated and perpetuated through what he is constrained to characterize in the end as deliberate and conscious conspiracy.

9

Only when the process of enlightenment on this exceptional phenomenon in world history has reached its culmination in established conviction is the investigator so far freed from the trammels of conventional studentship and prejudiced postures of understanding that he can orient his mind to the position of detachment necessary to undertake a dispassionate examination of the history in question. In one degree or another this reorientation of approach, conditioned to the peculiarities of the problem, is a necessary operation preliminary to this particular study. In hardly any other case is it so completely a necessity as in the investigation of the genesis and career of Christianity. For here in most extraordinary measure this preliminary conditioning of mind provides the only resource for unearthing the full truth in the story. Unless the student begins by divesting himself of the unconscious obsession of the mass of allegations, persuasions and indoctrinations in the shadow of which all Christian history has been fashioned and colored, and begins to subject to criticism that body of predilections itself, he is doomed to fail in his quest. Indeed so-called Christian history amounts in the bulk to little more than the flaunting of these same chosen asseverations, since that history has had little other aim than to vindicate these persuasions.

The reviewer of a book on religion by Profs. Frieze and Schneider of Columbia University in the *New York Times* some years ago frankly expressed his skepticism about the value of such compilations of tribal custom, belief and ritual until some one could come along and give us some interior light on the basic significance of all such things on a world pattern of common meaning, adding that such a compendium was now badly needed in view of the fact that still, as in his school days, the study of comparative religion in the colleges and seminaries was only utilized as the occasion and excuse for orthodox apologists to impale ever deeper on the student mind the claimed superiority of Christianity over all other cults. This was a sagacious observation, amounting in essence to a charge that Christian studentship had never subjected world faiths to a fair and adequate comparative evaluation. This again is to say that Christian protagonists posed as trying other religions before a prejudiced judge and a conditioned jury and under the terms of a code of values expressly framed to exalt its own system and deprecate every other.

The present epoch may well be marked in history as notable for its bringing to an end this farcical exhibition of the narrowness of mind to which factional religion can reduce its devotees. From roughly about

1930 the bars of bigotry were so far let down that Christian universities began to admit the actual scrutiny of Oriental religions into their classrooms and to give courses on such religions that were not quite the travesty they had been in all previous time. Ancient and Oriental, even tribal religion, is being given something resembling an honest investigation and its values are being assessed on a more realistic basis of fairness. Occasional tribute of high spiritual merit and quality is accorded these non-Christian religions by Christian leaders and publicists. But these gestures are still accompanied, if not motivated, by a noticeable spirit of condescension, as exhibiting something in the way of a superior's gracious and magnanimous tolerance.

The claim that the true history of the genesis of Christianity has never yet been written is founded squarely on the demonstrable fact that the numberless accounts purporting to be such true histories of the movement have blinked, ignored, missed and suppressed the most significant data in the case. In all cases the essential relevance of the data was missed because all but a few of the historians were totally ignorant of the relation between Christianity and antecedent religious influences, most particularly those stemming from ancient Egypt, in the light and bearing of which alone a true account could be framed.

It is perhaps no overstatement at all to assert that no history has ever been written less objectively than that of the Christian movement. It has been not only colored, but actually constituted by subjective elements at every turn. From the very start facts were ignored and disdained, or twisted into false shape for partisan purposes. Ancient documents of great significance were misconstrued, tampered with and mutilated, and always wholly misconceived as to their real import. Other documents were piously fabricated out of pure fancy and foisted upon the gullible as true narrative of holy event. And finally every interpretation was rendered in strict and unfailing accord with a monstrous bias of fanatical religionism generated in heavy ignorance. This statement, which will be reprobated as false and rejected as the mere venting of a violent hostility to Christianity, will be found confessed and reiterated in work after work of the cult's own authorities. If it kindles resentment it will only be because current belief has been left uninformed by a tacit conspiracy, and the few students who do encounter the unpleasant data shrug their shoulders—for the good of the faith and the faithful.

Whatever there is of sinister character in this situation lies in the fact that the general mass of the people have been and still are kept in deep ignorance of the truth of the history of their own faith. A conspiracy of silence provides its own ground for an active suspicion of its motive. Things true, honest and honorable have no reason to fear knowledge. Christian clergymen seldom—indeed as regards certain chapters of their ecclesiastical history, never—preach or teach the truth as their own books present it. The sinister element inheres in this secrecy, which has been cast like a dread shroud over the period of Christian beginnings. Generally a noble institution takes pride in commemorating its origins, heralding its founding events and honoring its first pioneers. Christianity glorifies its martyrs, of course, and speaks eulogistically of some few of its Fathers' names sanctified by tradition of holiness. But anything resembling a truthful survey of its early centuries, taking due account of all the influences contributing to the rise of the faith, has really never been undertaken. Sermons seldom memorialize the events of that period.

Reluctance in this direction must be generated in the theological seminaries, where the difficulties of presenting the record to the average congregation must become realistically obvious to the young clerical student as he reads it. And beyond doubt this reluctance is massively increased when the candidate assumes charge of his first pastorate and gets a view of his flock in the pews. In the end, and from age to age it proves to be so much easier and pleasanter if ministerial conscience can be quieted—which a little sophistry can readily achieve —to let the sleeping dogs of historical knowledge lie unawakened, rather than stir them up with data that could so readily set them growling and barking. After all, the work of the Church and its ministry is to promote the glory of God, and that work can best go forward without let and hindrance if the burden of a past record which is neither edifying nor helpful is not flung about the neck of present effort. It is the tactic that sidesteps endless disturbance and obviates the necessity of strenuous sophistry in "explanation." It is the easier course to let the unsavory annals of the early centuries lie practically unknown to the laity, leaving the writhings of apologetics to the leading encyclopedias and histories where the unfortunate chronicle can lie buried in reasonable innocuousness. Thus it is that a record which, when attention is called to it, proves astonishing beyond all belief, has during the present age escaped general notice and provoked no challenge.

Yet the honest mind asks for an answer to the question why the Christian Church has held for centuries a policy of nearly total silence about its early history. And the more persistent student sadly comes to doubt whether the same disingenuousness that silenced the history will provide a fair answer. It will be one of the motives of this work to unfold the hidden reasons for that secrecy, showing them to be the same as those which in the distant beginning distorted the entire movement out of true character and then sought to cover its iniquitous work by book destruction and documentary fraud on a scale unknown elsewhere in all history. It will be found that the original perversion of high archaic philosophy has sealed the lips and checked the pens of all later historians, muting as well the pulpit voice. *The truth of Christian history has been suppressed.* A fuller revelation of that history, tremendous in its scope and its documentary attestation, will be the nub of effort in the present work. The possibility of inditing this true history inhered in the fact that the research was undertaken with a mind free from former bias of indoctrinated belief and alerted to discern the relevance of many data commonly misconstrued or ignored. A working acquaintance with the Greek, Hebrew and ancient Egyptian languages facilitated the discovery of much that proved vital to correct understanding. The reading of ancient documents which still, in spite of mutilation and corruption, carry the full story to any capable intellect, opened up the wide vista of long lost truth.

In a detective mystery story the telling clues are so often revealed by the culprit's own measures at concealment. It is not to be denied that zest was lent to the search by the discovery of obscure clues of this nature. The trail of unbelievable skulduggery is only too easily followed through almost the entire history of ecclesiastical Christianity. Investigators had missed truth before because they were not cognizant of the fact that a conspiracy had existed and operated over a span of centuries, and they were therefore caught by its maneuvers. Once its connivance became known a thousand clues for the unearthing of salient fact came to view.

It is believed that some confusion may be avoided in the work if resort is had to a slight innovation in attaching a name other than Christianity to that wave of popular and ignorant zealotry that came to be known by that designation. It seems clear enough that a distinction in name should be made between a true Christianity that was *not* popularized in a historical movement in the early centuries and a false "Christianity" that was so developed and popularized. It will serve the interests of explicit reference throughout the study if the two are sharply differentiated by a difference of name. To this end it

13

has been deemed well to use the term "Christianity," as generally as circumstances will allow, to refer to that immemorial *true* religion which Augustine declared had always existed, and to apply to the movement which sprang to life in the first and second centuries A.D. the more properly suggestive name of "Christianism." It will not be possible to adhere to this differentiation undeviatingly throughout, as the name "Christianity" will often have to be used to refer to what should in truth be called "Christianism." But the occasional apt use of the new term will help the reader to keep the reference clear as to which of the two systems is under discussion. This may appear to some readers as an arbitrary and unwarranted shift of meaning, intimating by inference that the movement known as historical Christianity had no right to its name, that its name was a misnomer. The assumption of error in introducing a change of name for Christianity itself constitutes a strong item of evidence as to how far common understanding has been misguided from true direction. For the entire work will establish on the solid ground of verity the conclusion already announced, that the historical faith known as Christianity has no sound claim to the title, since it is in fact far from being true Christianity. Hence this essay will take the first step toward the correction of a great historical error by shifting the name from the improper object of its designation and assigning it to that declared *true* system of wisdom-knowledge which organic ecclesiasticism almost wholly stamped out after the third century. The use of the term "Christianism" will emphasize for the reader the spurious and truly un-Christian character of much that appertains to the system of Christianity, and this recognition is necessary if there is to be a restoration of Christianity to its place of high service in the crucial state of the world today.

The impregnable warrant for this shift of terminology and its challenging implications will be demonstrated in the body of the work.

The primary task envisaged, then, will be to trace the currents of influence that carried the previous high system of true religion, that Augustine insisted was true Christianity, down into the murky depths of a debasement and a distortion that would make the name "Christianism" appropriate to it. It is not a groundless asseveration but an unassailable fact of history, and one of the most tragic, that the religion that started under the name of Christianity in the first century did not long retain its original character and substance. Irrespective, for the moment, of whether it changed for the better or the worse, the simple fact is that it changed, and that radically. No argument can dispute

14

the assertion that it was not by any means the same religion in the fourth century that it had been in the first. Beginning as a more or less sincere effort of genuine, if ignorant, religiousness, it had plunged rapidly down the grade of deterioration until in the fourth century it had completed its dire transmogrification into Christianism.

As only one item offered in evidence of this assertion, the provable fact is that it had begun as a cult springing wholly from Pagan origins and motivations in the first century, and by the fourth it had utterly turned its back on Paganism and repudiated every hint of generative connection with it, loading it with contumely from that day to this. A second evidence of the fact is that a whole list of books that stood in favor in its eyes at the start and for some time thereafter, were condemned and violently repudiated within less than two centuries. A third proof is found in the later refutation of several doctrines that had held high place in the initial period. Another evidence is the tremendously significant fact that nearly all the original groups that had participated in the upbuilding of the new movement and were in fact its pioneers and leaders, had, even before the fourth century, been pronounced heretics from the true faith and reviled as such by the parties that had swept in and grasped control of all policies. Still another, and again one of transcendent import is the fact that the mystical-allegorical mode of interpreting the sacred Scriptures in use at the inceptive state of the new impulse had by the fourth century been wholly supplanted by the literal-historical approach to the meaning. These and still other marks of sweeping change will be treated in detail in their proper place in the development.

The odd circumstance about these changes is that, while in the eyes of the revisionists they were regarded as steps forward to a higher religion, they can in every case be demonstrated to have been those very things that sadly transformed true Christianity into an ungainly Christianism.

The forces which pressed upon the early Christian movement to turn it from what it was at the outset to what it became within two hundred years will be the chief objects of investigation in the introductory part of this work. Their close scrutiny and accurate determination will in fact form the main substance of the plot of the book. Their clear envisagement and delineation are what has been wanting in Christian histories. They will supply the very essence of what has been missed by all former surveyors of the scene. They make up that portion of the history of Christianity that has never been written. They will therefore contribute to the narrative its most important elements. Their presentation will provide that new light that will permit vision to resolve the obscurities and uncertainties of former blindness and to integrate phenomena in their true relations.

In the first place it has to be remarked that these forces have not been observed and scrutinized adequately for the simple reason that the savants refused to see that drastic change had taken place, and they therefore saw no necessity for discovering and charting the influences that had caused it. These influences were never isolated for observation. So it has fallen out in the historical sequel that these tendential pressures whose consequences have so banefully afflicted world culture have never been searched out and analyzed. Their reproduction here will supply the "missing link" in the fruitful study of Christian history. The undertaking involves a renewed survey of the early-century field and a new marshalling of the data presented, with the production of some new data, but more particularly with the diagnosis of the available material under the light of a new and more veridical insight. The warp and woof of the threads of fact will be given pattern and significance hitherto unperceived.

True perspective upon the movement of Christianity has been impossible for all previous historical visioning because of the salient fact that a traditional misjudgment of the background and environmental influences from the bosom of which Christianity sprang has pitifully and ruinously beclouded all correct estimate of the genius of Christianity itself. The result has been almost a complete failure to measure aright the forces which produced the new faith. There has invariably been a misreading of the data, with a consequent missing of the vital import and the inevitable distortion and caricaturing of the picture of truth.

This unfortunate circumstance sets before us the task of reconstructing the picture of the formative processes in more truthful perspective than has been done before. The enterprise involves primarily a more realistic viewing of the relation of Christianity to its Pagan antecedents, environments and sources. It is here that the prospect of the most vital rectification of view is to be opened out. This portion of the terrain has been mulled over with great assiduity by numerous spokesmen for Christianity, and the present effort to throw its data into a new orientation, so as to upset entirely the conventional theses will involve the whole matter afresh in violent controversy. But it is at such a cost that old obsessions are to be dispelled and a fairer understanding

16

gained. The colossal weight of the factual data and documentary testimony to be adduced in support of the amended view can be relied upon to break down at last the barriers of purblind prejudice and to let in the benignant light of truth upon a period and a section of history that has, for the West, been shadowed for centuries by the dark malignancy of triumphant error.

CHAPTER II

THE SHADOW OF THE SPHINX

The starting point, then, is the universally proclaimed insistence of the Christian Church that the world, before the coming of Christianity, was enveloped in "heathen" darkness. It had never enjoyed the benison of the proclamation of real truth from God, the fount of cosmic Intelligence. Over the antecedent centuries it lay wrapped in spiritual benightedness, no messenger from above ever having been sent to proclaim the knowledge of the one true God, no Word of true enlightenment having flashed into the gloom. God had not hitherto bestirred himself to vouchsafe to mankind any inkling of its relation to him. The world lay in mental nescience and moral depravity, relieved by no intermediation or provision on the part of Deity, who thus suffered mankind to grope on without evidence of his providential interest, until about the year 12 B.C. he caused his only Son to be born into the world in a miraculous fashion to bring the people the first ray of true light and to provide the first means ever available for their salvation. This is the gist of what has been taught to every child of the millions born in the past sixty generations in the Western world and is still taught over that area. Suddenly, after centuries of inactivity, God awakened to the realization that his mundane children needed his attention. Onto the scene came the Savior, crowning his otherwise completely unknown life of thirty-three years with an active career of teaching and wonder-working, covering, allegedly, three years, and ending his short life with an ignominious crucifixion on a cross at Jerusalem.

Through the force of this traditional indoctrination no Christian child in twenty centuries has ever held any other belief than that the body of sacred literature declared to be the supernal message of this cosmic visitant was the first flashing out in blank darkness of sublime truth and surpassing wisdom, transcending illimitably the crude efforts of Pagan antiquity to find true knowledge. It has served the interests of the Christian establishment to have this belief prevail over the area of its domination throughout its long period of regnancy.

It needs no argument to demonstrate how tragically erroneous this indoctrination has been, for history itself has pronounced the verdict. It is now clearly enough seen as a baseless and deceptive canard. Still lingering addiction to the belief is now sternly rebuked by the data of scholarship and criticism, all of which establishes the sharply disillusioning fact that *neither the reputed world Savior nor the religion he is asserted to have founded presented a single new or unique item of truth*. In broad statement every word this divine Emissary uttered and every act he performed can be matched by material that was hoary with age in the literature of the Hebrews or of the Egyptians. And every doctrine promulgated by the Church that sprang to being ostensibly on the basis of his life and work can be identified with its prototypal forms in most of the antecedent literature all over the world. The very narrative of this Messenger's life in Judea is to all intents and purposes a fac-simile of the mythical biography of some fifteen to fifty previous figures of Sun-gods and Avatars of the ancient world. Indeed the biographical history of Apollonius of Tyana, as written by Philostratus, is a more or less faithful replica of the life of Jesus in the Gospels. And Apollonius was born in the year 2 A.D., while Jesus, as the date is now rectified by the findings of authentic historical record, could not have been born before the period of the governorship of Cyrenius (now changed to Quirinus) in Syria, as it was during his tenure of the Syrian consulship under Rome that *Matthew* states the world tax was levied by Augustus Caesar that brought Joseph and Mary to Bethlehem, so that prophecy might be fulfilled in the Savior's birth in that town of Davidic descent. And this doubtful Quirinus is recorded as having reigned in Syria between the years 13 and 11 B.C. Herod, who, as the Gospel states, attempted to kill the infant Christ, was dead at the date of 4 B.C. The Church no longer disputes the necessity of shifting the date of its Founder's advent on earth from four to thirteen years earlier.

But this shift alone writes the verdict of error across thousands of pages of books which have hitherto based critical conclusions as to the authenticity of the events of Jesus' life on the claim of the correctness of these dates. How nearly this emendation of date comes to overthrowing the entire edifice of the case for the very existence of the Galilean few have realistically envisioned. It shakes the whole structure of Gospel historicity so violently that in the opinion of many scholars it now lies completely in ruins.

The Rev. John Haynes Holmes, minister of the Community Church in New York City, about 1945 preached and printed a sermon entitled *Christianity's Debt to Judaism—Why Not Acknowledge It?* In it he stated that Christianity derived, first, its Founder, Jesus of Nazareth, from the Jews; secondly, it drew some five-sixths of its canonical Scriptures—the *Old Testament*—from the same source; and, thirdly, everything that its Founder said and did, as well as the titles, office and function he filled and the character he bore, were already extant in the *Talmud,* the *Mishnah,* the *Gemara* and the Haggadoth of the Hebrew writings. No voice has arisen to refute any of these epochal assertions. But so steeped is the general mind in accepted traditionalism that an announcement sufficient in its purport and involvements to signalize virtually the falsity of every basic tenet on which Christianity rests goes practically unnoticed. Apparently not ten people recognized its absolutely crucial implications, as they in effect write the death warrant of the system posing as Christianity. And now it will have to be seen how many will grasp the critical significance of the further revelation that Christianity gave to the world nothing but a terribly mutilated and disfigured copy of ancient Pagan literature. For such, the sequel will determine, is what Christianity will be shown to have done.

The age-long assumption that Christianity arose like a Sphinx out of the shadows of heathen nescience and flashed its bright beams upon a world buried in aeonial darkness has had the unfortunate result of tearing it out of its proper generative setting amid the influences that bred it. The forces that pressed upon it in its birth have not been accredited with the due measure of formative power which they exerted upon it. Even when their influence has been weighed by the historians, as in Milman's, von Mosheim's and other leading treatments, a biased view inveterately blocks all possibility of giving full consideration to their values in the rise of Christianity. Historians have apparently been stolidly set against giving to the religions surrounding Christianity at its inception the weight which they obviously exerted upon the new faith. This reluctance or stubbornness has come from the fact that these scholars had never opened their minds with sufficient dispassion to examine the data which clearly revealed derivation of Christian principles from Pagan sources. As a matter of fact the affectation of Christian scholars for many centuries has been an inveterate disinclination to submit their Christianity to comparison with "heathen" cults at any time. In want of adequate comparison and comprehensive study, as well as of symbolic and analogical genius to carry it on with any chance of success, the connecting links between Christianity and its prior antetypes were never discerned with competent clarity to bring forth decisive conclusions. Once the presumptive superiority over its rival cults was spread universally in Christianity, it was offensive to the pride of Christian consciousness to degrade its heaven-blessed ordinances, rites and doctrines by subjecting them to comparison with the earth-born and bemired heathen observances and superstitions. It at one stroke divested of their divine halo the ceremonials that stood aureoled with celestial beauty in the minds of the faithful. It seemed like a sacrilege to break the spell of mystic holiness springing from the belief that the sainted doctrines and rites had been instituted from heaven. To relegate them to the province of merely human, and that Pagan, derivation and conception was to shatter their seductive force irremediably. Religion has ever been jealous of the human and earthly motivations.

So the ecclesiastical power has shunned comparative religion until now when the pressure of open inquiry is forcing it to face the conclusions of study and to find new apology for them. Such apology, it can be expected, will be specious and clever enough. The false Christianism withstood the devastating advance of modern physical science with bitter opposition during three centuries, as the positive light of knowledge threatened to overthrow the postulates of religious faith. Secular discoveries of new truth menaced the haunting dogmas of revelation until, the rack and the stake having failed to stop the tide of empirical research, a judicious compromise and reconciliation had to be effected with it. Now again the Church, finding itself periled from the side of profane research into comparative religion, but unable to stem the tide by murder and excommunication, will have to meet with whatever resources of subterfuge and evasion it can the disclosure of its own origins from Chaldea, Greece, Judea and old Egypt. For the voice of the Sphinx is being heard in the land and the budding leaves and the singing birds of a new springtime of revived human understanding in religion, herald the end of a winter of bigotry and delusion. It is safe to predict that orthodox religionism will not come off unscathed in this encounter as it has done in its conflict with science. For the revelations of Christian derivation from Egypt will undermine its foundations, which, all its advocates agree, rest upon the Gospel witness to the historical life of Jesus of Nazareth. And that life, as an event of the first century, and those Gospels, as original literary productions of the late first century, both are challenged by the identity of their data with the allegorical "life" of Horus of Egypt in the *Book of the Dead*. It is not too strong an assertion to say that those Gospels, as the biography of a man who lived in the first century, are tottering. Christian historians and exegetists are themselves dismantling the once solid fabric of the structure. Science forced Christianism to shift its position on many of its dogmas and minor tenets. But comparison with archaic Egyptian systematism will cut so deeply at the very roots of the tree of faith that its leaves and branches must wither.

The same Dr. Holmes later preached and printed another sermon entitled *Akhnaton of Egypt: The King Who Discovered God*. In it he expressed his own—and by inference all other Christians'—amazement at the fact that some seventeen centuries before Christ, back there in the Nile country, this young king, even though he died in his early thirties, had reformed the prevailing religion of his land by ousting the corrupt rule of the priesthood and reinstituting a system of worship and spirituality so high and pure that its obvious equality with the best in Christianity becomes to us today a mystery of the most inexplicable and challenging nature. How, the New York clergyman asks, can we account for this ancient king's establishment of a religion essentially on a level with highest Christianity, when the world at the time is asserted to have been enveloped in Stygian darkness? To attempt an answer to his own question the modern clergyman has to pull Akhnaton entirely away from his time, his background and his heritage. He surmises that Akhnaton had somehow worked his way by a special and exceptional genius through error and ignorance to a clear apprehension of monotheistic Deity and its fatherhood of man. It appears to be entirely beyond the reach of his understanding to recognize that already then, as ever since, the exoteric priesthood had buried an already existing true esoteric religion under a bushel of uncomprehended outer forms and fables, which no doubt were, as now, taken literally, and that the king, who, like Julian of Rome centuries later in much the same situation, had penetrated to the inner spiritual core of these Mysteries, decided to give back to his people the true mystical teaching, which thus received the emphasis it had been denied for centuries previously. It is all too easily seen what Akhnaton labored to accomplish then, for it is a replica of what clear-visioned esotericists have tried to do in more than one instance in history, when the corruptions of sound esoteric understanding had destroyed the beauty, the sanctity and the uplifting power of high truth. It was one of the efforts which seem to have to be repeated time and again in history, to break through the icy incrustations of dogmatism reduced to dead delusion and to clear the way for growth of the spirit in new freedom.

It is indeed a testimony to the total want of astuteness on the part of modern theologians that, in spite of Augustine's declaration that the true Christianity had been in existence from remotest antiquity, Christian scholars continue to express surprise when, as in the case of Akhnaton's campaign to bring that archaic true Christianity out from under the stultifying influence of a debased priesthood, they run across the evidences of the existence of something higher than the corrupt popular superstitions of exotericized religionism. They remain blind to the manifestations of this phenomenon in the past of old Egypt because they remain singularly blind to the import of an identical situation visible under their eyes at the present day. For once more the very esotericism that Augustine lauded is struggling to emerge from another period of obscuration under the despotism of an appalling deadness of literalism that has buried it since the third century, and to assert its profounder culture in the milieu of modern shallowness. Such blindness demonstrates with great cogency the incapability of modern insight to evaluate at its true worth such an outburst of intrinsic cultural enthusiasm as that which brought the remarkable awakening known as the Italian Renaissance in the fourteenth century. The causes which led to that magnificent rebirth of refined study, and then the diabolical forces which in turn conspired to crush it out after two hundred years, should be restudied with the utmost care, for they would prove instructive to the highest degree.

It has never been seen as the ultra-significant fact it is, that the Renaissance was engendered by the discovery and dissemination of old classical Greek and Latin literature, restoring to functional power the enlightening influences of symbolism and allegory and the analogical method, and that it was indeed this very magic of symbolic intimation that went far to implement this notable and fairly dynamic revival of the "true religion" of Augustine's vision. The "lesson" of this circumstance and phenomenon is that obviously the immemorially true religion of primordial times had embodied itself pretty completely in the philosophy and mysticism of the great Greek nation at its peak of Platonic excellence, with the pointed implication for the world of today that the rehabilitation of that lofty mansion of ennobling conception would be the most direct measure to inaugurate another sorely needed rejuvenescence of the jejune religious life of this age. If a Christian has still to wonder why the renaissance of Greek literature performed for fourteenth century Italy what centuries of Christian influence had failed to accomplish, he need only to heed the following passage from B. A. G. Fuller's splendid *History of Philosophy* (Introduction, p. 5 *ff.*):

"It is under the influence of the splendid pagan tradition of the good life as a harmonious development of all the faculties and exercise of all the functions with which nature has endowed man, that Greek ethics made its great contribution of sanity to moral theory."

Supplementing this notation there should be instituted an analysis of the dire forces which caused the Italian Renaissance to die out after two glorious centuries. For they were the same forces which emerge to the surface and dominate human action the moment the aggressive power of a diviner glow of light and knowledge diminishes and commonplace stolidity blankets the field of everyday consciousness. This condition constitutes the deadliest menace to the life of the world. "When vision fails, the people perish." If this Biblical declaration were taken as very actual truth and not a mere glow of poetic uplift, the world might more rapidly advance to happier days.

The indebtedness of Christianism to ancient Egypt will be outlined at length at a later place in the essay, but it will lend support to Augustine's broad assertion of the existence of an ancient universal true religion to cite a passage such as the following from von Mosheim's well accredited history of the early centuries of Christianity (Vol. I, p. 383):

"Long antecedent to the coming of Christ, there were to be found, not only amongst the Egyptians, but also among the Jews, *who copied after the Egyptians* (as is placed out of all question by the Essenes and Therapeutae), as well as in other nations, certain persons who made it their study by means of fasting, labor, contemplation and other afflictive exercises, to deliver their rational souls, which they considered as the offspring of the Deity unhappily confined within corporeal prisons, from the bonds of the flesh and the senses, and to restore them to an uninterrupted communion with their God and parent. This discipline arose out of that ancient philosophy of the Egyptians, which considered all things as having proceeded from God, and regarded the rational souls of the human race as more noble particles of that divine nature."

24

This passage has been chosen for citation at this early stage of the work because it puts the stamp of highly accredited authority upon several of the primary data on which our basic arguments rest. It testifies, first, to the previous existence of high religious philosophies which are at once seen to be germinal in Christianity. Second, it certifies that religious disciplines which certainly set the pattern for those later followed by Christianity, derived from ancient Egypt. And, third, it establishes the extremely important detail, which has been so insistently ignored, evaded and flouted, that the Jews "copied after the Egyptians." The reader will not be permitted to forget this latter point as the study develops. There has been great reluctance to take this item into account, as to accede to it means practically to trace Christianity itself back to the Egyptians. It was flouted just because its implications are potentially so menacing to orthodox constructions. Even after Dr. Holmes had preached his sermon expressing most courageously Christianity's positive debt to Judaism, and it was represented to him by the author of this work that both Judaism and Christianity owed everything they possessed to the Egyptians of old, he proved as recalcitrant to this larger datum as many readers had been to his representation of a shocking bit of unpalatable truth.

Some strength is added to the point of Christianity's indebtedness to previous systems by a brief statement from George P. Fisher's book on *The Beginnings of Christianity* (p. 177): "Christianity introduced no new element in the constitution of the soul." Indeed it lost all knowledge of those constitutive elements of man's divine nature which the Pagans had dealt with, by recognition of which the human being was the better enabled to guide his evolution judiciously.

If Augustine stands as the founder of Christian theology, no less surely is Eusebius the founder of the Christian ecclesiastical system, as well as being perhaps its most important early historian. It is indeed a notable circumstance that these two prime instigators of the Christian movement inscribed each a statement which in essence and in effect practically negate all the basic claims of the religion they extolled and instituted. Eusebius' remarkable statement adds corroboration to Augustine's and the two must stand together as a challenge to all Christian assertion throughout the ages. Had they been kept steadily before the eyes of the world, Christianity might have been spared its catastrophic miscarriage. Eusebius' affirmation is taken from the seventy-second chapter of Nathaniel Lardner's great work on Christianity:

"That the religion published by Jesus Christ to all nations is neither new nor strange. For though, without controversy, we are of late, and the name of Christians is indeed new; yet our manner of life and the principles of our religion have not been lately devised by us, but were instituted and observed, if I may say so, from the beginning of the world, by good men, accepted of God; from those natural notions which are implanted in men's minds. This I shall show in the following manner: It is well known that the nation of the Hebrews is not new, but distinguished by its antiquity. They have writings containing accounts of ancient men; few indeed in number, but very eminent in piety, justice and every other virtue. Of whom some lived before the flood; others since, sons and grandsons of Noah; particularly Abraham, whom the Hebrews glory in as their father and founder of their nation. If any one, ascending from Abraham to the first man should affirm that all of them who were celebrated for virtue were Christians in reality, though not in name, he would not speak much beside the truth. For what else does the name of Christian denote but a man who, by the knowledge and doctrine of Jesus Christ, was brought to the practice of sobriety, righteousness, patience, fortitude and the religious worship of the one and only God over all? About these things they were no less solicitous than we are; but they practiced not circumcision, nor observed Sabbaths any more than we; nor had they distinction of meats, nor other ordinances, which were first appointed by Moses. Whence it is apparent that they ought to be esteemed the first and most ancient form of religion which was observed by the pious about the time of Abraham, and has been of late published to all nations by the direction and authority of Jesus Christ."

Here is a flat declaration from the founder of Christian ecclesiasticism that Jesus did nothing more than republish the religion of the ancient Hebrew patriarchs. What then becomes of the claim that Christianity was a wholly new revelation brought to earth by the only Son of God about the year 30 A.D.? Eusebius fully agrees with the manifesto of Augustine. This work will assemble a vast body of other material supporting their pronouncements. It has been too dangerous for the Christian Church to pronounce its founders in the right, or to convict them of error. It has simply not faced the issue raised by their forthrightness and candor, which at least in the case of Eusebius was so generally wanting.

But if this statement of Eusebius is considered perilous to the claims of Christianity, it is as nothing in comparison with another sentence of his which falls with the force of a veritable atomic explosion upon the whole Christian system. If this statement of his is true—and it has everything to support it, little or nothing to controvert it—it stands virtually as a death sentence to Christianity. In a moment of extreme

26

frankness and speaking in reference to the Essenes or Therapeutae, the esoteric cultists who had flourished for ages in Palestine, he wrote in chapter seventeen of Book II of his famous *Ecclesiastical History* the following amazing utterance:

"These ancient Therapeutae were Christians and their writings are our Gospels and Epistles."

Then the Epistles of Paul and the Gospels of *Matthew, Mark, Luke* and *John* were old, old documents taken from the Essenian libraries and foisted upon a credulous rabble as new writings of the first century. For we turn to the *Encyclopædia Britannica* and under the article "Essenes" we read that "they preserved in their libraries the books of the ancients and read them not without an allegorical interpretation." What becomes of the Christian faith if it is true that those Gospels and Epistles, with an unhistorical and purely typal figure of Jesus the Christ in them, were in Essene libraries from a very remote period?

From a book called *Astral Worship* (p. 92) we take a passage which adds further strength to the assertions of Augustine and Eusebius:

"As further evidence that modern Christianity is but a survival of Eclectic philosophy of the ancient Therapeutae, we have another important admission by the same historian (Eusebius) who, in quoting from an apology addressed to the Roman Emperor Marcus Antoninus in the year 171, by Melito, Bishop of Sardis in Lydia, a province of Asia Minor, makes that apologist say, in reference to certain grievances to which the Christians were subjected, that 'the philosophy which we profess truly flourished aforetime among the barbarous nations; but having blossomed again in the great reign of thy ancestor Augustus, it proved to be above all things ominous of good fortune to thy kingdom.'"

So Bishop Melito adds his testimony to that of Augustine and Eusebius, and scores of data from other sources, hints and admissions encountered here and there, build up a formidable case. It all points with practical decisiveness to the truth of the assertion that Christians of any intelligence during the first two centuries at least did *not* regard their movement as the bearer of the first light into a world of heathen darkness, but only the republication of very ancient truth.

There is another item which is by no means inconsiderable in this connection. It is a statement which is mentioned by George Hodges in his work, *The Early Church* (p. 158) and is well known as a fact. He states that the account of the life of the Cappadocian saint Apollonius of Tyana was read by the Neoplatonists "as the Christians read the Gospels." The significance of this is found in the consideration that the Neoplatonists in all likelihood read such a work as a typal or allegorical representation of the incarnational life of the divine principle, the Christ, in man, and perhaps regarded it as a more faithful dramatization of that life than the Gospels. This would tend to show that intelligent men of philosophical interests in that period, in so far as they were acquainted with the Gospels, did not take them to be the biography of a historical personage. Along with this possibility it is significant that the Emperor Septimus Severus is said to have had busts of both Apollonius and Jesus in his chapel. What can this signify but that it was common belief that the legendary accounts of the "lives" of both Apollonius and Jesus were on a par for historical value? And if not for historical value, then both equally treasured for their allegorical pertinence. The almost certain truth of the matter is that, as always, the "rabble" took these accounts to be veridical biographies of living men, some believing Apollonius to be the true divine Son of God, others crediting that high honor to Jesus; while the men of philosophical acumen understood both to be type figures in spiritual allegories dramatizing the life of the divine principle in fleshly body.

And it should not be overlooked in this debate that we have that most notable statement of Irenaeus, Bishop of Lyons, France, in the second century, one of the early writers for the Christian movement, in which he says that there were in existence in his day not only the four Gospels later canonized, but a multitude of Gospels! Now the very momentous reflection arises as to this, that if the multitude of Gospels out of which the Council of Nicaea finally decided to select and canonize four, were all documents dealing, as they presumably did, with the biographical career of the man Jesus, written by authors having data to contribute to the narrative of his life, surely every such document would have been presumed to be of practically inestimable value and would not have been suffered to fall into oblivion. Let us imagine what would be considered the value of the sudden discovery *now* of ten or twenty, or even one, of those other Gospels, which would assumedly contain some data about the life of Jesus not found in the four chosen. Can any one inform us why new or additional data about Jesus would be less sensationally valuable to the Christians at the end of the second century than new data is to the American people coming to light now about Jefferson, Washington or Lincoln, or to the English-speaking world is the new material written by Boswell that has just come to hand? A multitude of Gospels about Jesus floating around, four chosen and the rest consigned to oblivion, when every item about this cosmic Savior of the human race, every additional saying of his, every move and adventure, would have been of priceless interest and value! Has the Christian authority kept Irenaeus' statement in its general oblivion because to publish it and face its implications would suggest the terrifying inference that *none* of the Gospels then extant could have been taken as the actual biography of the living historical Jesus? Indeed the only conclusion possible in the case is that many copies of that mythical dramatization of the life of the incarnate Soul of Divinity in human flesh—the Logos made flesh and dwelling among us—were extant among the Mystery groups and the philosophical schools. And what does that imply? Nothing short of the horrendous truth that *none* of them, including the four chosen, was the veritable biographical account of *any* living person! The intelligent knew they were not, the "vulgar" presumably took them to be such actual biographies; and when numbers counted more than quality and intelligence, the Church took the fatal step of canonizing the popular beliefs.

Is it, too, without significance that even Jerome thought that the *Gospel of the Hebrews* was the original of the *Gospel of Matthew?* Among the "multitude" of documents then known were such as the *Gospel according to the Twelve Apostles, The Gospel of the Egyptians* and the *Gospel of Peter.* Can any one estimate the value of a Gospel written by Peter if this disciple had ever written an authentic one?

Augustine gave out another pronouncement which cannot but be held to have some bearing on this debate. He says in Greek: "We come down to Moses, the ocean of theology out of which all rivers and all seas flow." How are we to reconcile the apparent inconsistency exhibited here? For certainly in his books he makes no other than Jesus the fount of all theological light and truth. We know that there were groups of early Judaic Christians who eulogized Moses as the prime originator and mouthpiece of all arcane wisdom of old. No doubt it will be explained that Augustine made Jesus the fulfiller of Mosaic prophecy. And perhaps he uttered this eulogy of Moses in his younger days when he was concerned with occult philosophies and before he had lost his soul in rhapsodies of love for the crucified Galilean.

Another challenging reference comes to us from Irenaeus. According to him (b. i, ch. xx, i) the Marcosian and Valentinian Gnostics were in possession of many Gospels. He says, "their number is infinite," and amongst those apocryphal works was one entitled *The Gospel of Truth (Evangelium Veritas)*. This scripture, he says, "agrees in nothing with the gospels of the apostles." (Irenaeus, b. iii, ch. xi, 9.) Gerald Massey comments by saying that this gospel is probably the one referred to by Tertullian, who says the Valentinians were in possession of "their own gospel in addition to ours." (Tertullian, *De Praescrip*. 49.)

And Massey has presented a point of the greatest import which, carrying danger with it, has of course been discounted by orthodox scholarship. It is dangerous because it hints forcefully at the ancient Egyptian origin of all "gospels." Here was the most learned and intelligent element in early Christianity, the Gnostics, in possession of a Gospel on which they staked their very high position, called the *Gospel of Truth*. If it came from Egypt, the original word for "truth" would have been *Maat*, the goddess of truth, often written *Maatiu*. Massey steadily affirms that this is the original form of "Matthew." All the slurs and slights which he has received from orthodoxy may not be able to prove him wrong.

At any rate it must be again asked what this conflict as between one party's Gospels and another's can mean in reference to the life of a man claimed to have lived from 1 to 33 A.D. Was the point of argument between the parties over the question whether certain Gospels gave a truer account of his life than others? Whether certain eyewitnesses were more authentic and credible than others? But if Gospels were not fought over on these grounds, but on some other questions of true spiritual preachment of a general nature, then all Gospels lose their validity as biographies of a living personage! And be it remembered, beside this Gnostic Gospel with a name that certainly appears to be of Egyptian origin, there was that other Gospel, so prominently referred to and detested by the orthodox parties, *The Gospel of the Egyptians*. The fine Gnostic Christians had of course their own wonderful Gospel, *The Pistis Sophia,* which traces to Egyptian backgrounds beyond all question. The voices of the old Egyptian gods speak volubly in such documents in the hands of early Christians.

Massey furnishes abundant data to refute Irenaeus' claim that Gnosticism had no existence prior to Marcion and Valentinus. He asserts—what is clearly evident—that the Suttites, the Mandaites, the Essenes and Nazarenes were all Gnostics, and that all these sects antedated the cult of "the carnalized Christ." He brings out a strong point when he says that the alleged heresy of the Gnostics, which they claimed had originated in the second century, the first century being carefully avoided, long antedated that period. All the facts make it evident that the unintelligent early Christians, who had unwittingly made a literal adoption of pre-Christian types and believed they had been historically fulfilled, were then for the first time becoming conscious of the cult that had preceded theirs, the members of which held *them* to be the real heretics. Gnosticism, avers Massey, was no birth of a new thing in the second century; it was no perverter or corrupter of Christian doctrine divinely revealed, but the *voice of an older cult* growing more audible in its protest against a superstition as degrading and debasing now as when it was denounced by men like Tacitus, Pliny, Julian, M. Aurelius and Porphyry. For what could be more shocking, Massey poses, to any sense really religious than the belief that the very God himself had descended on earth as an embryo in a virgin's womb, to run the risk of abortion and universal miscarriage during nine months *in utero,* and then dying on a cross to save his own created world or a portion of it from eternal perdition?

And what is to be done with such a datum as that supplied us by perhaps the most eminent of the modern German Biblical exegetists, Johannes Weiss, in his great two-volume work on primitive Christianity, when he says that "the 'breaking of bread' in the early Christian Church was originally not a commemoration of the death of Jesus"? He arrives at this concluson even without the corroboration of ancient Egyptian books, in which the division of the divine bread of Christ into fragments, so that each mortal might share his allotment, was a cardinal figure of the dramatic and allegorical presentation, wholly without historical reference. Likewise is it of no critical significance that Weiss can write such a passage as the following (*The History of Primitive Christianity,* p. 2):

"Worst of all we underestimate the fact that certain fundamental principles common to all types of Christianity, the faith in the Messiah, the worship of Christ, the Sacraments of Baptism and the Lord's Supper, the tradition of the words of Jesus and information about his life, a whole series of Christian expressions, and likewise the modification or adaptation of Jewish and Old Testament points of view and ways of thinking, had been produced by the primitive community and *were found already in existence by Paul himself.* One of the most important tasks before modern criticism is a thorough examination of the contribution of the primitive community to the origin of Christianity. Can such a task be accomplished?"

Whether Weiss is referring to the primitive *Christian* community exclusively or using the term in a broader sense, is immaterial, since it can be shown, and will be in this work, that there is not a single phase of religious formulation mentioned in this list of his that any "primitive community" would not have derived from universal traditions running from time immemorial in all those Eastern lands. What is impossible is that a "primitive community" of countryside peasants in Judea formulated a whole body of sublimely true spiritual conceptions entirely new in the development of religious ideas in the first or any other century. Well does he say that the most important task before modern criticism is a thorough examination of the contribution of the primitive community to Christianity. Can this task be accomplished, he asks, apparently with considerable doubt of its possibility? Precisely that is the task which this work has set for its accomplishment. There never would have been much difficulty in the execution of that task had not all strategic approach to its achievement been thrown into knotted entanglement and confusion by universal subscription to the legend that one little "primitive community" suddenly about the year 33 A.D. received from the skies of heaven and the hands of a heavenly visitant a wholly novel and the only true book of religious truth ever to come to man on earth. This essay proposes to set the task free from this obscuration and to trace the sources of the heritage of whatever high truth any primitive community might have possessed in the early centuries. The voice of the Sphinx, no longer hiding its eternal riddle, but proclaiming it abroad since the finding of the Rosetta Stone, discloses the primal source of every single doctrine, rite, character and allegory to be found, all debased and disfigured to crude literalism, in Christianity. This book proposes to accomplish the all-important task Weiss sets before scholarship.

In a book entitled *The Relevance of the Prophets,* the author, R. B. Y. Scott, writes:

"In Babylonian literature and to a greater extent in Egyptian literature, are to be found writings similar to the Hebrew prophetic records."

Yet this same writer says later in his work that

"The Old Testament is characterized by the historical quality of its thought, as distinguished from a mythological, metaphysical or mystical approach to reality. It is built round a history, and an interpretation of that history which becomes an interpretation of all history."

If this author had weighed carefully the implications of his first statement here cited, he would have seen that the very identity of this alleged Hebrew history with Babylonian and Egyptian "history" that
assuredly is *not* history, but spiritual drama and allegory, would have
saved his plunge into the error of his second statement. The long-lost
truth is that the sage ancients most astutely designed remarkable myths
and allegories which were to stand as a completely true paralogism of
actual history, and that ignorance mistook these sagacious constructions later on for veridical objective history.

Seconding this view is H. H. Rowley (*The Relevance of the Bible,*
p. 39), who says, referring to the Old Testament:

"It is more concerned with enduring lessons of history than with history
itself. . . . And the message of the Old Testament writers was also the
expression of timeless principles which are of abiding value to man."

What Rowley says here has been fairly well apprehended by religious
thinkers, but what has not been realized is that the timeless principles
were enunciated by ancient sagacity by means of allegory and drama,
rite and symbol, rather than by "history," and that their abiding value
for man in no way depended upon their being allegedly exemplified
by but one group of specially chosen people, in the sense that man
would never have known them unless they had been so demonstrated
to him in this particular "history." And what is still farther away from
being known is that the supposed "history" contained in the Old Testament is, for the most part, not actual history at all, but arcane allegorism sadly mistaken for it.

One can wonder if the present Christian world has sufficient insight
to react intelligently to the republication today of a single scrap of
quotation from the ancient Scripture of the Persians, the famous *Zend-
Avesta:*

"You, my children, shall be the first honored by the manifestation of
that divine person who is to appear in the world: a Star shall go before
you to conduct you to the place of his nativity; and when you shall find
him, present to him your oblations and sacrifices; for he is indeed your
lord and an everlasting king."

By intelligent reaction to this amazing citation is meant the discernment that would certify the purely allegorical character of the Gospel
story of the Star of Bethlehem. The Christian rejoinder is of course
that the actual event of the Star's appearance and conduct in the year
1 A.D. did occur in fulfillment of the Avesta's prophecy. This appears

sufficient in the naive mind to cover the case. But competent research and study has a way of dissolving most of the encrustations that harden in the naive mind, and its conclusion in this matter would be that the Gospel story of the Star is simply a later reprint of the earlier Persian allegory. The likelihood of the truth of this explanation is so strong in the minds of Biblical exegetists today that many of them have ceased to regard the story as historical and class it in the category of legend. So prophecy was fulfilled in legend!

Likewise in the *Gospel of the Infancy* (Ch. 1, v. 10) it is said that the Star even entered the stable: "And behold it was all filled with lights greater than the lights of lamps and candles, and greater than the light of the Sun itself." The reader will decide to be his own judge as to whether this is history or allegory.

There is strong meat for capable digestion in the statement of Frederick D. Kershner, who, in his book *Pioneers of Christian Thought* (p. 69), says that "the Gnostics were the founders of Christian theology in the full sense of the word. For ten or more decades they dominated the field of religious thought." What, then, have we here? Two mighty considerations that strongly contest nearly all Christian claim. The Gnostics unquestionably brought out very ancient Egyptian religious systematism, which makes the highest and dominant Christianity for over its first hundred years purely an Egyptian product. And the second item is equally discomfiting, for it is the fact that this noblest expression of the earliest Christianity was in another century ostracized as heretical! Kershner even says that the books of the New Testament were *not* considered by the generality of Christians as on a par with those of the Old. This again argues for old sources as against new revelations. And Farrar quotes St. Augustine as saying that "many of the dogmas of the Catholic faith acquired precision from the studies necessitated by the assaults of heretics." It took the "heretics" with their profounder philosophical understanding to help orthodoxy maintain some semblance of rational consistency!

An observation by Joseph Warschauer in his *The Historical Life of Christ* (p. 99) is suggestive of non-historical possibilities also. He builds up on good authority the claim that the Biblical Hebrew term *bar nasha,* "the Son of Man," refers to man generically and not to Jesus, individually. And yet this same author and nearly all others reject with instant decisiveness the thesis that this same generic reference is to be understood universally throughout the Scriptures in such phrases as the Son of God, the Lord Jesus Christ, the Savior, the Redeemer, as representing the divine elements in the common constitution of man, and not one man alone. Why limit the claim of generality to one phrase only, and deny the reference to other phrases used in the same connotation?

And what becomes of the boasts eternally made in Christian pulpits and books that the wholly new revelation of Apostolic Christianity came into the world in the first century with so powerful a light that it dispersed all the darkness of an ignorant and barbarous heathenism, when the truth is, as admitted by all intelligent historians, that if Christianity had not in the third and fourth centuries been amended, rationalized and saved by Hellenic Pagan philosophy and Paul's Mystery cult contribution of Gnostic mysticism, it would have perished altogether? This item will receive expanded treatment later, but it is mentioned here as a weighty argument on the side of the development of Christianity out of long-existent backgrounds.

When the early Christians thought they were announcing a religion of virgin truth, they were but raising an echo, faint and hollow, of the voice of the Sphinx.

CHAPTER III

WHEN VISION FAILED

The gist of the story here to be unfolded is the narrative of a great and catastrophic failure of vision at a most critical point in world history. The major thesis of the presentation is that Christianity emerged to existence and grew to power as the outcome of a dire blight that fell upon the mental and spiritual life of the mid-Eastern world in the centuries immediately preceding its upspringing. The theme to be developed is that Christianity took the form it did in consequence of a decay and degeneration of enlightening knowledge, and not at all from the dynamic energization engendered by a new release of light and truth unknown before. Forces that are held in restraint or die of atrophy when the hot glow of new enlightenment drives to noble activities, emerge to dominate the course of action when the high impulses and motivations sink into desuetude and the counsels of sage understanding fail to guide the conduct of men and nations. In the view to be elaborated here Christianity was the consequence of such a relapse from former high uplift and such an emergence of less noble expressions of the human psyche.

In very brief form of statement the position to be taken and defended is that Christianity was the outcome of a defection of human interest away from the splendid Greek philosophy of the Periclean or Platonic period. This pronouncement will unquestionably be met with the same adverse reaction as that which actuated Tertullian in the early fourth century to cry out in substance: Philosophy! What has philosophy to do with the Gospels and the resurrection? What has Plato to do with Jesus of Nazareth? But it is this blindness of Tertullian that most piquantly dramatizes for us today exactly the main clue in the proper historical analysis of the genesis and character development of Christianity. Failure of intellectual insight, crass myopia both mental and mystical, was the factor that prevented Christian leaders from seeing that relation of kinship between Homer, Plato, Proclus on the one hand and the Christian movement on the other and that therefore set the stage for sixteen hundred years of benighted religionism. The answer that is designed here to be flung back in the teeth of Tertullian is that, most unfortunately for the world ever since, Greek philosophy *had all too little* to do with the Gospels and Jesus of Nazareth and that the Dark Ages were the result of that failure of connection between the two things. The undertaking here will be aimed to restore that fatal break of connection which became the cause of the most lamentable calamity to afflict mankind in the historical period. The book itself will constitute the ringing answer to Tertullian's challenge which has lacked a spokesman for all the intervening period. When the true story of how and why the loftiest wisdom the world has ever known, Greek Platonism generally speaking, had in the minds of Christian zealots like Tertullian *nothing* to do with the Christian upsurge has at last been fully told, a new light of understanding will be thrown over the field of history of the last two thousand years. The African Bishop's indignant question has never had its competent answer, and it is the purpose of this work to give it.

Yet, oddly enough, history itself has given a decisive answer, although, like so much that history speaks to us, it has not been caught or recognized. Tertullian's own Church came up with the answer when in the early Middle Ages it turned back to found its whole theological structure on this same Greek philosophy that the Bishop of Carthage had so violently repudiated. For about two centuries the Church developed its theology upon the principles discovered in Plato's *Timaeus* and later for some eight centuries it built still greater strength into its system through incorporating the elements of Aristotle's *Metaphysics*. In the centuries of its most intellectual activity the system of Christian ecclesiasticism itself proclaimed what Pagan philosophy had had to do with the Gospels and with Christianity. And thus by its own record and action the Christian Church advertised to the world its disbelief in its own original claims, since it exactly reversed its former position by turning to those very philosophies it had so viciously declaimed against at the time of its inception. *It turned to Pagan literature to find authoritative support for the alleged preachment of its heaven-sent Christ.* Now as history records them, the Church's own acts shout so loudly that the world can not hear what it says. Had a true Christianity that could have boasted of its affinity with Greek philosophy prevailed in and from the third century, this institution would not have been thrown into the ungainly and ridiculous position of both condemning Pagan philosophy out of one corner of its mouth and using it as authority for its own doctrines out of the other.

It was strictly because Christianity early lost its intellectual link with antecedent systematic thought and its own primal motivations that it drifted off its true course of search for the light and was in so short a space disastrously involved in the shoals and quicksands of a degeneration so profound that after sixteen centuries the Western world still finds itself enmired in the bogs of absurd and impotent theologism. So bizarre, so irrational and so irrelevant to the normal life of the world has Christian theology indeed become that to all practical intents and purposes the Church that fought for centuries over its metaphysical abstrusities has at last dropped it out of its program! Sociological and humanitarian themes are the subjects of Sabbath sermons in most pulpits; theological doctrines are kept almost completely in the background. What seemed worth tearing each other limb from limb for in the fourth century is not even deemed worth a Sunday sermon now. The fourth-century controversies settled nothing then, and the great subjects of conflict are still so hazy, indefinite and vaporous that pragmatic sense has counseled leaving the dogmas and creedal statements untouched.

When ignorance comes to the front, it is its most characteristic trait to parade itself as knowing more than the wise. This phenomenon is manifested so voluminously in the run of events that crowded fast in Christian history after the movement had been given security, gained state control, grown arrogant and—pushed out all its philosophers. The poor but pious devotees, finding themselves sitting in the offices of elders, deacons, priests and bishops, began to regard their faith as wondrously superior to all the cults that Roman policies of tolerance and indifference had permitted to flourish in the Empire. Their exuberant confidence is found reflected even in their modern historian, Canon Farrar, who in his *Lives of the Fathers* (Vol. II, p. 503) writes to make the usual fulsome claim of the superiority over, in this case, Manichaeism:

"The Manichaeans freely used the name of Christ, but it was with them the mere adoption of a symbolic phrase. Their Christ was not the Christ of the Gospels. He was to them the spirit of the sun, the light-spirit from the pure light-element of God; not 'very man,' but only clothed with a corporeal semblance. Christ on the cross meant to them nothing but an emblem of the sufferings of every soul which strives to become free."

38

Perhaps no passage could be found in a random search that would better illustrate the change that is here claimed to have occurred in the early Christian movement. A chapter could hardly do justice to what a full analysis of the passage and its implications would bring out. In a word, then, it has to be asserted that a Church which in a short run of years had so far drifted from a basis of true apprehension as to condemn as outlandishly pagan a cult still seeking to identify the Christ as a divine light-principle within the heart of every mortal, and as to declare it to be a poor and crippled doctrine which made the Christ on the cross an "emblem of the sufferings of every soul which strives to become free," had in this very stand proclaimed itself sunk into a veritable morass of heathenism deplorable beyond measure. The passage cited from Farrar irrefutably proclaims the cult whose belief it expresses as being more pagan than the Pagan system it inveighs against, since it is assuredly more pagan to deny that the Christ spirit of light from God did become "very man" in its incarnation in all men, than, as with the Manichaeans, to assert that most majestic concept. The hybrid Christianity of the after-period out-pagans the Pagans at every turn.

Further food for reflection is found in the continuation of Canon Farrar's discussion, when he goes on to assert that Augustine, in failing to "regard the Old Testament as a progressive but incomplete and imperfect revelation," missed the true conception of this basis of exegesis, and strengthens his assertion by saying that Augustine "was less strong as an expositor than as a dogmatist," an observation which could be well supported in reference to all the Christian Fathers and leaders with the exception of Clement and Origen and the Theodore presently to be mentioned. Farrar continues:

"The historic method of viewing revelation, though distinctly intimated in the magnificent proem of the *Epistle to the Hebrews* and in other incidental utterances of the greatest Apostles, remained enveloped and only partially understood by the Church, from the time that the narrowed Western theologians succeeded in crushing Theodore of Mopsuestia and the school of Antioch down to the day of Nicholas of Lyra, who died in 1340."

What Farrar intimates here is that a broader view of the "historic method of viewing revelation" which prevailed at an earlier time in the Christian movement, was soon supplanted by a "narrowed" view held by Western exegetists. It will be a part of the task here contemplated to refute even this assumed broader view of historic revelation as far as it is based on Farrar's—and most other Christian writers'—understanding of it in what they take to be the exemplifications of it in the Old and New Testaments. But at any rate we have the Canon's expressed declaration that an earlier broad view was replaced by a later narrow one, thus admitting the chief thesis advanced and defended herein.

And then the eminent churchman, writing less than a hundred years ago, climaxes his paragraph with a sentence which could well stand as the digest of our first two chapters and a brief compendium of the whole study. Says he (Vol. II, 508):

"The triumph of Latin theology was the death of rational exegesis."

So true is this extraordinary pronouncement that had its pregnant implications been discerned and fully considered as a gauge of weighing conclusions in historical study over the centuries since the early day, both Christian history and world history would have moved forward on a higher level of spiritual culture than was unfortunately the actual case. But the involvements of the Canon's true statement are too radically sweeping, too challenging for the truth of it to be openly accepted and taken to heart. It says something too luridly glaring for common knowledge. It explodes too much dynamite in the face of all who would have to confront its challenge. It is far too damaging an admission.

For what does it say? Nothing short of the fact that when the Christian movement passed from the Eastern Mediterranean lands of its genesis and was captured by the churchly authority in the more westerly Roman domain, it suffered a "sea change" which left it completely transformed into something far other than what it was at the outset. The actualities and concomitants of this transfer have never been rationally or realistically envisaged.

The fall of true Christianity came with and through this transposition of its sponsorship and custodianship. When the new fervor of religionism was transported from East to West, it passed from the guardianship and fostering care of a race and a civilization that was still bathed in the genial afterglow of the brightest light of philosophy that had radiated abroad to the world from human genius, and came under the blighting influence of another culture that in the main lacked capacity for spiritual enlightenment, the while it manifested in high degree the talent for world organization. This factual item is all that is needed to explain the grounds of Christianity's remarkable temporal success and its sweeping career of acceptance in the history of the West. Given the most exalted spiritual character by its provenance from the milieu of lofty Greek philosophy, it was taken up by the race gifted in extraordinary measure with the power of empire building and by it structuralized into a firm organic body of such coherence that it conquered the Western world. Had it remained in Syrio-Judaic environment, it would have shared the fate of Manichaeism, Neo-platonism, Mithraism, Docetism, Gnosticism and the Zoroastrian faith: that is, it would have been carried on to become a cult of the inner spirit among limited segments of the population in the Hellenic world, and later been swallowed up, along with the cults of esotericism named, by the all-conquering sweep of Mohammed's fanatical dervishes.

It escaped this fate by enlisting the more Western populations who, with their instinct for world domination, welded it into the organic structure of the Roman world empire, so that it stood as a solid embodiment of power even when the political frame of that structure was dismantled by the Northern hordes. No such measure of perpetuation and salvation could have been provided for it in the East. There it might have remained, along with Neoplatonism and Alexandrian syncretism, a cult of the esoteric philosophers. But it would never have set its leaders on the thrones of world political power nor caused humbled emperors of great nations to stand barefooted in the snow all night to receive the Pontiff's apologies in the morning.

But the transfer to the West and the gain in world power thus achieved, so far from crowning the religion with the glory of victory and spiritual transcendence, became on the contrary the march to a defeat so utter and catastrophic as to have reduced it for centuries to a hollow mockery of truth and a beguiling hallucination of the Western world. For in passing from the hands of the Hellenic peoples with their genius for philosophy into the hands of the Romans who lacked that same genius, but who could organize it for world conquest, it, so to say, gained the whole world but lost its own soul.

The precious soul it lost was what Farrar calls "rational exegesis," but was in fact much more than that. It was the entire sense to interpret the ancient heritage of religious philosophy and its Scriptures spiritually, mystically, in a manner, in short, which is the characteristic that Eastern Christianity has ever displayed to distinguish it from Western Christianity and mark it as infinitely superior thereto.

At a further point it will be debated whether it would have been for the better historically if the Christian movement had remained in the East and retained its high character as a spirito-mystical cultus for philosophers and religious intellectuals than to have followed the course it did, to become a religion of shallow and banal exotericism turning every hieroglyph of spiritual and metaphysical significance into ribald literalism and historic absurdity. The point to be placed on record here is that by the transfer from a philosophically gifted race to a worldly-minded one, it gained dominance in the world at the expense of its true message of intrinsic uplift and illumination for mankind, which at the time the Roman race was intellectually incapable of assimilating and digesting. It would never have been a Hellenic theologian who would have cried out in bitter exasperation: What have Homer and Platonic philosophy to do with the Gospels and Jesus? Amazingly it was Paul who made a complete turning of the tables on the Western Tertullian. Reared in the intellectually stimulating Hellenic atmosphere of mystico-spiritual philosophy, he practically demonstrated in fifteen *Epistles* in the New Testament canon that it was the Gospels that have little to do with a true religion of Christos, with true Christianity! For no intelligent theologian has ever claimed that Paul's lofty spiritual Christianity was in any way whatever the product of the evangelism that the Gospels represent as developing into Christianity. Paul's Christianity has nothing to do with the Christianity that is assumedly based on the Gospel history. Proof of this is to be found in the historic fact that the promulgators of the Gospel evangelism both openly and covertly arrayed themselves in opposition to Paul and *his* Christianity. When Paul journeyed to Jerusalem to meet for the first time the members of the Apostolic group there, he would not have been received by them at all if it had not been for the intercession of Barnabas. The controversy between the factions and the theologies of Paul and Peter is well known. It is only by virtue of some internal predicament not historically clarified that Paul's writings did not come under the ban and stigma of "heresy" which fell with the force of a scourge upon the Gnostics, Ophites, Docetists, Ebionites and other esoteric Christian groups, who, incidentally, almost without exception purveyed a brand of Christianity more legitimately entitled to the name than did "orthodox" Christianity itself. Leading theologians of the Church, when constrained by the force of the factual data and their own counsels of sincerity, have with more or less hesitation and reluctance admitted that Paul's Christianity stemmed from sources of spiritual interest other than the movement allegedly historicized in the Gospels. The great Apostle obviously did not carry the banner of the Nazarene's evangelical crusade, but promoted the Egypto-Hellenic system of spirituality with such glowing power that it was found desirable to incorporate his letters in the canon along with the body of literature that carried the sweep of the pietistic surge of Gospel Christianity. And, to summarize a mass of quotable material, many theologians have asserted that but for Paul's contribution to evangelical and Apostolic Christianity of his volume of Graeco-Alexandrian Platonism and rational mysticism of the philosophic schools, the movement inspired ostensibly by Jesus the Avatar would have died out before the end of the first century. It was Paul's writings that redeemed it from its first status among cultured people of "an execrable superstition" and a rating of ignorant fanaticism generally.

Yet this factor that saved it from ignominy and oblivion is still harshly decried by most "orthodox" spokesmen! So far has unschooled pietism carried mortals away from balance and rationality.

Farrar was right, and more tragically right than he dreamed! The triumph of Latin theology was the death of rational exegesis. More than that, it came close to being the death, as it certainly led to the dearth, of rationality itself. Its effects soaring far beyond mere exegesis, it was the death of the highest moral and spiritual upreach that this globe has ever known; the death of philosophy, with its piercing insight into the nature and structure of man's life in the cosmos, his origin, his evolution, his destiny in glory; the death of reason in the counsels of religion; the death, by surrender, of the human critical intelligence to the narcotizing power of "faith"; the death of wisdom, knowledge, understanding, killed by the ravaging plague of fanatical zealotry unknown before in world history. In short the triumph of Latin theology was the death of true Christianity itself. It was the birth of a fatuous and fatal Christianism, which has ever since hounded, persecuted and with savage ferocity exterminated every individual or group that strove to revive the lost Christianity.

Furthermore the triumph of Latin theology brought to birth and growth in the mind and heart of Western man elements of fiendish savagery which had found expression in no other religion anywhere and which have scarred with disfigurement the face of Occidental history. The triumph of Latin theology warped the minds of its devotees into such a state of irrationality that they could find ample excuse for any barbarity deemed necessary to uphold and extend it. It provided the justification for brutal inhumanity. If this should not take rank as one of the direst calamities in world life, it would be hard to think of one more monstrous.

The connection of theological cause with murderous result is direct and immediate. It was the Latin theology that crushed Gnosticism in the Church, and what this has meant for Western history can best be seen if we scan a passage from Kershner's work, *Pioneers of Christian Thought* (p. 87). It must be remembered that Marcion was one of the greatest of the Christian Gnostics. Kershner is speaking of him:

"If his teaching had prevailed there would have been no *autos-da-fe,* no Inquisition and no burning of heretics by either Catholics or Protestants. It was the triumph of the imperialistic God of Tertullian and Augustine which led to most of the later horrors in the history of the Church. The idea that the Deity could do anything which he himself regarded as unjust or cruel seemed unthinkable to Marcion, but this was not the case with his opponents. . . . It was the common belief of the period, at least in orthodox circles, that the joys of Paradise would be enhanced by the possibility of witnessing the torments of the damned. Augustine has a great deal to say about this somewhat gruesome topic . . . but neither Augustine nor Tertullian represented anything unusual from the orthodox point of view. A God who could condemn little children to the unending flames of perdition simply because some of their remote ancestors disobeyed his commands represents an ethical ideal which was later to write history in the torture chambers of Torquemada, the flames which consumed the bodies of Huss and Servetus and which broke Jean Calas on the wheel only two centuries ago. Marcion's theology at the worst would never have permitted such things as these . . . his moral sense was sound and the world might have been better off if his heresy had prevailed."

It is the instinct of intelligence to view with charity the unfortunate aberrations of moral conduct and motive in human life, but indeed a charitable attitude toward this chapter of historical manifestation is difficult to maintain. Even an attempt to place it in a somewhat more favorable light ends in sorry satire, as Kershner adds (p. 103):

"The Spanish Inquisition arose primarily because a tender-hearted monk wanted to save the wicked from eternal torture of perdition by tormenting them a little in this world to the end that they might abjure their heresies and be saved."

If the monk's heart was so fiercely consumed by the love of Christ and his fellowmen that he could bear, perhaps with holy joy, to see their limbs torn from their bodies and their writhing in flames because he held a certain set of intellectual propositions to be true and they held a contrary set to be true, then we have at last isolated for unmistakable examination the cause of human cruelty, or the inhumanity of man to man that has made of so much of the history of the race a red glare of lurid fiendishness. When holy men turn to murder and glut their pious souls in a revel of it, the fault must lie in their *minds*. Socrates and Plato arrived finally at this conclusion at the end of their dialectical quest of a lifetime; Voltaire saw it when he declared that men's hearts are bitter because their *minds* are dark. This work will urge that the only salvation of humanity in its present or any future juncture is to cultivate philosophy instead of religion; and here, silhouetted for us against the wall of history in clearest outline, is the justification of that view. If it is true, as Voltaire shouted to us, that men will continue to commit atrocities as long as they continue to believe absurdities, then it is of primary concern for this race of thinking creatures to make the utmost effort to determine what is absurd and what is sanely true. This at last brings us to the final point of determination between good and evil, the location of which is to be found in the pursuit of philosophy. It is the theme of our volume that in the third century the Christian religion or its exponents turned from sense to absurdity and therefore, by Voltaire's prescription, committed atrocities. Argument may dispute this terse summation, but history attests its truth.

Mankind on the whole has learned distressingly little from history. The history of Christianity in the Hellenic world in brilliant contrast to its history in the Roman world should have fixed in the human mind a lesson and a truth that would have set the race on the royal road to a high humanism, if not spiritual culture, far in advance of any progress it has made since Plato's day. Put summarily, it is seen that Greece, which cultivated philosophy and exalted Christianity to the level of a lofty philosophical system, imbuing it with the light of a nearly divine genius for rational conception, rendered it an instrument, on the whole, of refined culture and general beneficence. The Roman West, however, which flouted philosophy and for the rational cultus substituted the violence of faith and religious fervor, converted that same Christianity—if indeed it could be considered the same—into an instrument of appalling devastation, virtually dehumanizing its hallucinated adherents. Here on the blackboard of history stands outlined the vividly limned scenario of perhaps the most important lesson mankind has to learn. It points straight to the moral that in philosophy, and not in religion, or at any rate not in a religion rendered desolate of philosophical enlightenment by rabid emotionalism, is to be found the golden secret of the culture that will indeed save humanity from the Egyptian bondage under the dominance of its rampant animal nature. With the advantage now of a fifteen hundred years' retrospect, it is possible to understand why the closing of the last of the Platonic Academies in the Hellenic world was immediately followed by the plunge of the West into the long night of the Dark Ages. The tidal sweep of irrational religionism over Europe reduced to the dimmest glimmer the brilliant lamp of Greek rational philosophy, which had flamed out so gloriously but a few centuries before. In this epochal instance the replacement of a rationally cultivated religion with one that with rank crudity of mind flaunted its hatred of philosophy before the world presaged the Avernal descent of the West into a Plutonian underworld of lower human motives and passions from which the light of its upper world of diviner persuasions was shut out.

The vast extent of the gulf existent between the heights of philosophical rationalism and the depths of unintelligent religionism can be most realistically sensed when one reads a passage from Plutarch's *Morals* (Vol. I, p. 13) and then thinks of the early Christian contempt for books and study. He writes:

"But learning alone of all things in our possession is immortal and divine."

And then he adds, speaking of the education of the child (*Ibid.,* p. 17):

"Yet I would have him give philosophy the preeminence of them all . . . whence it follows that we ought to make philosophy the chief of all our learning. . . . There is but one remedy for the distempers and diseases of the mind and that is philosophy. For by the advice and assistance thereof it is that we come to understand what is honest and what dishonest, what is just and what unjust; in a word, what we are to seek and what to avoid."

For consummate wisdom this passage from Plutarch stands unexcelled. The cultural salvation or exaltation of the human race will lag until the day when the religious elements so strong in consciousness are brought under control and ordered in harmony with the principles of understanding structuralized by philosophy. There is not room here for a dissertation on psychological science, although it properly belongs to the context at this point. But modern psychology is close to demonstrating that the grasp of a sound philosophy is a prime requisite for the retention of sanity. Indeed it has already done so. Like man's body, his mind can only maintain its health when nourished with proper

46

food and enough of it. Infinitely more delectable than the pleasure of feeding the body is the joy of feeding the mind. Plutarch's asseveration that there is no remedy for the distempers and diseases of the mind but philosophy should come at this exigency in world life as the answer to all those problems which so critically confront the province of education today. Philosophy should be at once restored to its kingly place in every curriculum, but philosophy as the sages of antiquity understood it. Philosophy is the science of meaning, and there is no escape from the recognition that what life means to a mortal is what it will be to him. The sudden rise today of the science of semantics is a good sign of better things, for it centers value again on meaning. The soul for whom the multitudinous events of life have little or no meaning is a lost soul. It has not found itself and knows not wherefor it exists. Its range is limited to sense and feeling and it is as a rudderless barque tossed helplessly about on the sea of events. It can steer no course and is a pitiable victim of life instead of being its king. That is the reason the god powers incubating in man are called the King.

It is cheering to note that at least one modern philosopher and one psychologist have caught hold of the great truth of Plutarch's statement. William E. Hocking, Harvard philosopher, has written (*Science and the Idea of God,* p. 42) that "there is no cure for mental disease without consulting the *total meaning* of the world." And a splendid elaboration of the theme is presented in Chandler Bennitt's fine work, *The Real Use of the Unconscious.* It is desirable to adduce this datum and to array strong authority behind it because it will shortly become the corner stone, as it were, of the central argument of the whole work. The Christian faith has drilled into the consciousness of thousands of millions of Western humans that only belief in the existence and personal ministrations of a man born one day into a mortal body will free humanity from bondage to low animal instincts. Tragedy has befallen those same billions because Christianity did not reckon with the ultimate truth of what Hocking adds: "It is only the meaningful that sets us free."

The great Christian exegetist Harnack mentions the fact that Christianity never exerted any appreciable influence on Neoplatonism. If Christianity was the great new light of the world, it is an entirely justifiable question why these profound thinkers and men of superior wisdom did not recognize its real claims. The significant answer doubtless is that it so utterly lacked all appeal to the intellectual interests of a philosopher that it brought nothing into his world worth his attention.

47

Since such great issues for human happiness depend on this relation of philosophy to religion, some further elaboration of the theme will not be amiss. Spinoza justly ranks as perhaps one of the three greatest philosophers; he came to close grips with the problem and arrived at conclusions extremely germane to our discussion. The highest virtue, he says, is for a man to act according to his nature, but that is to act only in terms of adequate ideas. If man's nature—aside of course from his animal part—is to be intelligent, then the supreme virtue is to act according to reason. True virtue then rests on true understanding. (This is precisely the conclusion reached by Socrates and Plato.) And the endeavor to understand is the promise and the basis of arrival at high virtue. This in the end is equivalent to man's innate instinct and desire for self-preservation, as his developing intelligence is the supreme necessity as well as instrument of his ability to prolong his existence.

Virtue is to act according to the laws of one's own nature; knowledge of those laws then is a first condition of right action. This knowledge is gained by acting and noting the consequences. If one is to act best, *all the difficulties of knowing the truth must be faced*. (This is the last truth humans like to accept, for inertia eternally prompts the desire to acquire truth by the least effort.) And what he brings out in another observation should stand as a signal of caution to those who plunge into religious emotionalism: the force of the emotions is not determined by the accuracy of the idea which arouses them, but by the vivacity with which we imagine it! This is of mighty import in the study of religious psychology, for the force of emotion has ever been assumed to prove the philosophical rightness of the idea that stimulated it. The sad realization that faces us here is that we can be emotionally aroused by totally false ideas. World history bears sorrowful attestation of this fact. Part of the task here is to show beyond cavil that Christianity itself swept to power through the force of emotions that were engendered not by true philosophical conceptions but by wretchedly erroneous ones.

The actual practice of ethics, declares Spinoza, is in a balancing of the emotions. What factor is present or available to determine the true balancing? Obviously only the faculty provided by God for this very purpose, the reason, which in turn must be based on intelligence or knowledge. To know the modifications of the mind in the emotions involves a profound knowledge of the nature of things. The emotions which make for true good are understood only as the nature of the mind itself is understood, and mind is determined by the nature of the intelligible universe of which it is a part. This is why the ancients insisted that religion had for its prime activity and highest aim a "knowledge of the gods," for these "gods," be it understood at last, were the graded modifications, as Spinoza would call them, of God's total and universal intellectual being or Mind. To know anything the mind of man must know God, concludes the philosopher, because, man's mind being a fragment of the Mind of God, to know one's own mind is to know God, or that portion of him.

It is therefore extremely important in life to perfect as much as we can the intellect or reason. In this alone does the supreme happiness or blessedness of man consist. For blessedness is nothing else but the intrinsic satisfaction of mind which arises in degree and power and intensity in exact proportion as the fragment mind of the individual encompasses its union with the cosmic Mind of God. Wherefore the ultimate aim of a man is to be guided by reason, the faculty by which he is brought to conceive adequately both himself and all things which can come within the scope of his intelligence. Inasmuch, then, as the intellect "is the better part of us," it is certain that if we wish to seek what is truly profitable to us, we should try above all things to perfect it as far as we can. Our highest good indeed should consist in intellectual perfection. Then comes that final summation of his magnificent dialectic which got for Spinoza the well-won title of "the God-intoxicated philosopher": since man is perfect or the reverse in proportion to the nature and perfection of the object which he loves above all others, he is necessarily most perfect and participates most completely in the highest blessedness who loves above all else the *intellectual knowledge of God,* the most perfect being, and delights keenly in it. This echoes the ancient Psalmist's rhapsody on the blessedness of "delight in the law of the Lord."

Spinoza's clear delineation enables us to set forth in vivid consciousness the defective foundations and faulty structure of the Christian system. To be a true religion, ministering to the highest good of humanity, a system must basically and centrally cultivate man's philosophical genius. But this was the very element that Christianity abominated. The assiduous cultivation of the intellect in order that the Ego may know the thrill of bringing to actual consciousness in itself the glorious might and majesty of the divine Thought, was the thing it hated and abolished. The seizure of some sort of overpowering emotional afflatus drove the people in the cult to the point of despising death and the lion's rending claw; but it was not the joy of the expanding power of the rational mind. That swelling sense of godhood in man could never drive its rhapsodists to endure, much less to gloat over, the infliction of pain and torture upon others. It would inspire compassion and tolerance, pity and help, toward those so blunt and blind as not to be able to awaken the superior faculties by which the blessedness is won.

Nearly all Christian writers including the ablest have committed themselves to the stand that Christianity won a great triumph and saved itself from early decay by its rejection of Gnosticism and its mystico-theosophic programs. If Kershner's prognosis is true, as is indeed likely, then the ostracizing of Marcion's Gnostic systemology bought victory at the price of the horrific Inquisition and the blood of more Protestant martyrs in a single nation, the Netherlands, than the whole number of Christian victims in the Roman persecutions. If to die by unholy decree of barbaric ruthlessness for one's faith—the Christian faith—is close to celestial blessedness, why are not the hundreds of thousands of Dutch Protestants, French Huguenots, the Albigenses and Waldensians haloed with as much sentimental glorification as those Christians whom Nero burned and Galerius tortured? It is a fair question. But it will never have an honest answer. The rigid ecclesiastical system will perhaps never discern truly or acknowledge openly the ruinous price it has had to pay for its rejection of Gnosticism, which came close also to costing it the loss of Paul's redeeming contribution. Kershner is right: had Marcion's Gospel been held to, there could not have been a Spanish Inquisition.

By its repudiation and ejection of all philosophical components it both then and later has had to suffer the humiliation of admitting that it had so impoverished itself on the intellectual side that it had to come begging for the enlightening help which Greek intellectualism could supply to it to escape haunting oblivion. Again and again concrete history has turned with grim irony but poetic justice to administer condign and humbling retribution to the cult that sanctified ignorance and strangled the divinest instinct in man, the delight in knowledge, the joy of intellectual understanding.

In his *The Beginnings of Christianity* (p. 160) George P. Fisher says significantly that it was the natural sequence of the stagnation of philosophical speculation after the productive period was over, and of the mutual conflict of the various systems that Greece developed schools of skepticism and cynicism. And it is out of skepticism and cynicism, or just the vacuum of philosophical nescience, that there arises a fell

50

religionism of pietistic fervor, irrational belief and sheer faith. To fill this abyss many resorted to the highly dialectical rationalism of Neo-platonism, Fisher says, calling it a form of mysticism which, while it afforded a refuge to the believing, yet perplexed the minds of shal-lower capacity. Naturally this most exalted system of rational philoso-phy perhaps ever expounded proved too recondite for all but a very few.

Some particular manifestations developing from the suppression of philosophy in early Christianity are noticed by Fisher. The play of forces in the two systems of Stoic philosophy and Christianity brings out some sparkling contrasts. We can account, he says, for the "elevated philanthropic expressions of men like Seneca," the Roman Stoic philos-opher, and for the broader spirit of Stoic lawyers, by a "providential development within the elements of heathenism itself." Not often are such flowers laid on the grave of heathenism. So even heathenism held hidden springs of spiritual power that Christian pride likes to claim for its system alone. But Fisher is hard put to account for the remark-able fortitude, serenity and general imperturbability that was one of the most magnificent characteristics of the Stoic ethical life. So, to give Christianity the argumentative victory he has to pronounce this su-preme attainment of the Stoics a subtle form of selfishness. The Stoic composure in the face of the hard blows and the rugged ways of life is only an affected indifference which gains subjective tranquillity by ignoring moral values. But in the Christian system "there is no repres-sion of natural emotions." History well and voluminously certifies to the correctness of the latter observation, for there never was philo-sophical stability enough in Christian practice to check the common sweep and sway of the most elementary passions. But it is well to note the play of narrow jealous churlishness accorded to virtue by Christian apologists when displayed by any group or cult outside its own pale, in Fisher's invidious ruse of saying that when a Stoic philosopher gains inner peace and poise it is only a selfish disregard of moral obligations, but when a Christian wins an interior calm it is the very benediction of heaven pouring down upon his upturned soul.

Instructive it is, too, to note what Fisher says regarding the Stoic aim to establish a durable kingdom of peace and fraternity on the foundations of a people practicing philosophic discipline by cultivation of Stoic fortitude and control. Such a community as Zeno and Seneca dreamed of did not and could not arise, says Fisher, until the kingdom of Christ was established on earth. Then these "obscure aspirations

51

and grand but impossible visions" became a reality! Does Fisher ask us to understand that the advent of the personal Christ in the first century established the "kingdom of Christ" in human society, and that there has been the reign of Utopia since that epoch? If so, one has to ask him where it is. Only lately nations long dominated, or shall it be said long sanctified by the influence of this "kingdom of Christ" in the form of the faith assumedly founded by the Christ himself, came close to exterminating each other in savage ferocity. And this was the result of the Christian virtue of not repressing natural emotions, in this case those of greed for power and the afflated insanity of military prowess. If the Christian Utopia has become a reality over these two thousand years of historical record, it is little wonder that men have given up on Utopian dreams.

Fisher says that Stoicism aimed to find the sources of strength and peace within the individual himself. But even this bouquet thrown to Paganism is somewhat wilted by the doubt whether this virtue does not let Christ down by managing to get on to fortitude without imploring his help and giving him the credit.

Again the laurels of disputation have to be placed on Christianity's brow in discussing the Stoic virtue of self-purification. The Stoic philosopher gains it by way of the selfish and unsocial path of mystical contemplation, hugging its raptures all to himself, while the Christian pursues it by the daily practice among his fellows of all the virtues. By what right, it must be asked, does Fisher decide for us that the Stoic does *not* carry the products of his lofty contemplation into his daily practice? His implication that he does not is entirely an unfair assumption. Surely he who meditates on high virtues is the one most likely to practice them. The sad fact is, also, that the record shows how lamentably the Christian populations in those early times did *not* practice the common virtues.

Next to be expressly noticed is Fisher's statement (p. 185) that in Cicero's time and in the century that followed, faith in the immortality of the soul was mostly confined to men imbued with the Platonic influence. This, the greatest boon and blessed assurance to brace man in his mortal struggle, was the possession mostly of men under the high influence of the Platonic philosophy.

What then must be thought of the thinking processes of the man who wrote this, when only five pages ahead of it he asks: What were the actual resources of philosophy? What power had it to assuage grief and to qualify the soul for the exigencies of life and to deliver it from the fear of death? The philosophical heathen had no source of consolation in bereavement! The philosophy that postulated the immortality of the soul left the mind cold and comfortless! He cites that in some of Cicero's letters there is nowhere the slightest reference to God or to a future life. From all of this we are to conclude that when a Pagan holds a philosophy of the soul's continuity of life and posits the existence of God, it is a cold abstraction and utterly futile, but when a Christian holds the same principles in his abounding faith they irradiate him with celestial beatitude. For what else can be made of such sophistication and casuistry?

Excuse for introducing such matters of seemingly picayune controversy is offered in the design of this work to demonstrate pragmatically that the errors and falsities inwoven in the Christian system have reduced the human mind in the West to many manifestations of imbecility and dementia. It is a legitimate procedure, then, to put on display by such animadversions the prostitution of even the scholarly mind of Christian apologists to forms and modes of disingenuousness and chicanery. A large portion of almost every theological writer's work is made up of such jugglery of the processes of logic and misrepresentation of facts to give victory to biased views.

But Fisher gives us some data about the status of philosophy in the Roman period that carry their own significance. He writes (p. 186):

"In the second century, along with the revival of ancient religion and the restoration of political order, philosophy played a more important part as an educator among the Romans than it had ever done before. There had been not only a popular dislike of philosophers, but also a strong prejudice against any absorbing devotion to philosophical study. . . . For political reasons partly, from a sense of the dangerous tendency of philosophical thinking, philosophers had been repeatedly banished from Rome in the course of the second century; but after the death of Domitian philosophy not only gained a toleration, but often received an effective personal patronage from the Emperors. There was still a popular antipathy from the supposed uselessness of studies and discussions of this nature and from the Pharisaical character of many who were devoted to them."

The human instruments of great power over the life of imperial populations which must be regulated and dominated have always had reason to fear philosophy. It tends to kindle such enlightenment among its students as makes them rebellious against the repressive measures of tyranny and the regimentation of mass conduct at a base level. Emerson has told us that when a thinker is let loose traditional institutions and vested interests tremble. So Rome had banished its philosophers. This was in the second century, he says, just when the emotional surge of the new Christian faith was gaining initial force. The populace continued to hate philosophy; but it is safe surmise that when men of deeper discernment began to see a new danger arising, greater than any presented by philosophy, from the menace to the state inhering in the wild fanaticism of the Christian rabble and their complete non-conformity with traditional religious customs, they deemed it a point of wisdom to disseminate the precepts of a philosophy which would strengthen the general loyalty of the citizenship toward the state and discourage disobedience. Both benevolent governors and tyrants have found it judicious, as saving militia and police, to utilize religion as a sedative and narcotic to lull popular grievance to quietude and innocuousness. But when, as in this case, religion itself grows fractious and threatening, there must be a resort to violence—and this measure was seen in the persecutions—or to the gentler persuasions found in philosophy. Thoughtful and instructed minds have always regarded philosophy, or at any rate a profounder studentship, as an antidote to fanatical religionism. Today it is the cry that sounder education must be employed and vastly extended to insure democracy against the ills arising from inadequate instruction and incompetent thinking. It must have been much the same discernment that induced the leaders in Roman life in the second century to bring back the banished philosophers and give intelligence its chance to cure the crazy religious distemper manifesting so dangerously. This was almost certainly the motivation behind the sudden and glorious outburst of ancient sagacity under the name and form of Neoplatonism, engineered by Ammonius Saccas, Numenius, Plotinus and their associates. For it came in the second century. But the sorrowful destiny of the world brought it about that this time religionism won its most decisive battle against philosophy, the rueful outcome being fifteen hundred years of Dark Ages, from which there has not yet been emergence.

Further insight into the strange workings of scholarly minds obsessed with the Christian persuasions is had in another excerpt from Fisher's book (p. 189), where he says that when we look back upon the ancient philosophy in its entire course we find in it nothing nearer to Christianity than the saying of Plato that man is to resemble God. It is not often in religious polemics that an outright denial of the factual truth of a statement has to be made, but it has to be done in this case. Fisher's declaration is glaringly, outrageously untrue to fact. The amazing truth is that Platonism and ancient philosophy in general, on its esoteric side, of course, is infinitely nearer to true Christianity than historical Christianism ever has been. Scholars like Massey, Higgins, Mead and others and the researches of men like Dr. Ray Knight and Wendell Harris in England have found every single formulation in doctrine, creed, rite and symbol of the Christian system to be a derivative of former Pagan institutes. Not only were all these antecedent constructions near to the nature of Christianity; they were that true Christianity itself. This is what Augustine and Eusebius told us. Fisher is completely turned around in his view: it is Christianism that is not near to the real Christianity. Pagan philosophy was near to Christianity in every facet, for it is the source of all Christianity.

Then Fisher observes that on the path of speculation the Pagan conceptions of God are hopelessly defective and discordant. He asks how in this case the soul is to break the fetters of evil and attain to its ideal. This question, he insinuates, can not be met by Pagan philosophy, but Christianity meets it through the revelation of God in Jesus Christ. Through Christ—the living man—the divine ideal is brought near to humanity in all his purity and love, and not merely to a coterie of scholars, but to the humble and ignorant. (Even this form of statement carries the tacit implication that the purity and love of divine Christhood had been brought to at least a coterie of Pagan philosophers, which is just what is asserted here.)

A later treatment will meet the challenge of this specious argument advanced here by Fisher and again and again by nearly all other Christian protagonists. It must be passed over at this place with the sententious remark that by the time low Christian mentality had converted the body of arcane wisdom, its rites, symbols and allegories, into a form "simple" enough for the concrete apprehension of their interior import by the uneducated rank and file of the "humble and ignorant," they had made such hash of it that it has ever since been totally incomprehensible and unintelligible to any one, but to the untutored masses most of all. It is a profound discernment never yet clearly enough perceived, that when the high abstruse conceptions and recognitions which tax the genius of an Aristotle or a Spinoza to formulate clearly to the understanding even of the most capable minds are converted by adroit maneuver into a form assumedly readily comprehensible to untrained simple minds, the value has long disappeared. This strange claim is true, because to make it intelligible to naiveté of mind it has to be brought entirely from the realm of abstract metaphysical conception down into the world of concrete things, in other words, vicariously represented by a physical symbol. And then ensues the tragedy that the naive mind takes the symbol for the reality, since its power to see beyond the symbol to a metaphysical reality is feeble. So that to simplify it is to falsify it for the simple-minded. That is the process, which for the discerning and competent, ends in intensified cognition of meaning, but for the unintelligent ends in actual falsehood. For the symbol is not the reality. It is a helpful tool for those trained to use it; it is the cult of falsity to the ignorant.

By the time the Pagan doctrine of the birth of Christhood in man had been put forth for lowly mental grasp as the birth of a baby on December 25, year one, it was no longer true, but fatally misleading. By the time the crucifixion of divine mind power on the cross of existence in the fleshly body had been concretized and historicized as the agony of a quivering body of human flesh on a wooden cross, it was no longer true. By the time the dismemberment of the unit power of Christhood, with the giving of a portion to each human for his divine transfiguration from within had been made "comprehensible" as the actual breaking of a loaf of bread into fragments, it was not true. By the time the descent of the Monad from the Logos of divine intellection into the water of the human body had been "clarified" and "simplified" to poor mental capacity as the baptism of a man in the Jordan River, it was a delusion and a snare to uncritical thought. Instead of enlightening him it would hallucinate him, because his ability to lift it from the concrete to the spiritual sense was non-existent. And by the time the incarnation doctrine had been "made plain" as the descent of God's radiant being into the physical corpus of one man, so that simple minds could see it, it was an outright mockery of truth.

The entire claim of Christian partisanship is that this religion alone made the entire body of recondite doctrine clear and simple to the humble and the ignorant, by presenting to mankind God's revelation of the whole of his nature in the living character of Jesus. But this is precisely the low form in which a doctrine of infinite reach and complexity had to be revamped in order to win the interest, because it could thus reach the physical senses, of people incapable of abstract conception, who were the ones Christianity chose to arouse to emotional extravagance, disdaining the philosophers. But true esoteric vision sees that this is to risk the almost certain danger of wrecking the whole system for just those lowly ones it is designed to enlighten. It risks turning truth into untruth because undisciplined mentality can not lift the symbol or the personification back to the metaphysical world where alone its truth is liberating. Crude conception ends by taking the concrete images for the factual substance of truth.

The glyphs, symbols and personifications used by ancient sagacity to structuralize for human thought the realities of the noumenal world are like the specie and legal tender issued by a government for general representation of value among the people. In and of themselves they are worth little or nothing. Their true value inheres in the fact only that the government has real gold in its secret coffers to guarantee their worth in current usage. A limited number of the holders of a valueless currency may, with determination and persistence, redeem them for their intrinsic value in the treasury. So it is with esoteric truth. Its real value is hidden away from the multitude in the secret vaults of mystical consciousness, really in a higher dimension of consciousness, generally inaccessible to the common man. The myths and allegories, rituals and dramas, are issued to the people at large to represent the golden meaning lying in the mystery treasure chests of mystic realization. They have not that golden treasure in themselves, but are token money, carrying the promise of full payment of face value to any one who will carry them back to the capital and demand the golden truth itself. They are false and fictitious money, not meant, however, to deceive and cheat, but to promise true gold to him who will redeem them. So long as *faith* in their representative and redemptive value remains firm, they serve well the purposes of real money. The possibility of tragedy and crash comes when the people *en masse* forget that it is fictitious token money and that its only safety and stability are assured by the continued existence of that gold in the treasury of the spiritual king of consciousness. With that certitude pervading the common thought of the masses, the beneficent circulation of the false coinage of myth and symbol can be continued.

But the floodgates of disaster are quickly opened when the ecclesiastical government issues an unlimited quantity of worthless specie in the shape of creeds, formulas, symbols and rituals, with no accompanying promise or assurance that they are intellectually and mystically redeemable in the upper philosophical treasure house of the Church. And spiritual poverty has stalked through the homes, the streets, the temples and the schools of Christendom because the governing Church has issued for seventeen centuries a fictitious currency of dogma and Scripture that it could not, and still can not redeem in true value. Pagan wisdom employed myth and symbol to enrich its students and devotees; Christian blindness has used them to perpetuate the poverty of its followers. As Milton wrote:

"The hungry sheep look up and are not fed."

The Christian Church gave out a fictitious mythology and the people can not redeem it.

This analysis limns with the greatest possible fidelity the process which led Christianity on the downward path to exoteric miscarriage. It must be seen as the very truth that it was the one thing that Christianity eternally boasts of—its making high truth simple for the simple —that involved it in the darkness of the Middle Ages.

Some little realization of what a ferment began to brew among the common masses when the effort was made to mitigate religious extravagances by the sobering reflections of philosophy is gained, if one reads what the great Christian historian, Dean Milman, has to say in his *History of Christianity* anent this subject (p. 291):

"The nature of the Deity, the state of the soul after death, the equality of mankind in the sight of Deity; even questions which are beyond the verge of the human intellect; the origin of evil; the conversion of the physical and moral world, had become general topics; they were, for the first time, the primary truths of a popular religion, and naturally *could not withdraw themselves from alliance with popular passions.* These passions, as Christianity increased in power and influence, came into more active operation; as they seized persons of different temperaments, instead of being themselves subdued to Christian gentleness, *they inflamed Christianity,* as it appeared to the world, into a new and more indomitable principle of strife and animosity. Mankind, even within the sphere of Christianity, retrograded to the sterner Jewish character; in its spirit, as well as in its language the Old Testament began to dominate over the Gospel of Christ."

This is a well-told story of what happens when a religion ventures on the hazardous undertaking of purveying supernal truth and the revelation of the inner light of reason and knowledge to "the humble and ignorant." Dean Milman dramatizes it for us as it happened in early Christianity. What is more banal and dispiriting than to listen to efforts of the "common people" to give expression to their crude ideas of what the virgin birth, the immaculate conception, vicarious atonement, forgiveness of sins, the Christ's death on the cross for the salvation of man, the miracles, the flood, the Jonah-whale allegory, the star of Bethlehem, the crossing of the Red Sea (now the Reed Sea in modern Bibles!), or any of the Biblical constructs mean to them? To hear the common run of popular intelligence set forth its crude conceptions of these high verities in still cruder language is an affliction to any emancipated mind. Its revelation of lamentable misunderstanding and bizarre notions is nothing less than painful. Nothing is truer than Milman's statement that the preachment of an unphilosophical Christianity generated popular passions, with no balance wheel of philosophical knowledge to hold them in restraint; and that these passions seized upon the multitude and "inflamed Christianity," making of it a bundle of mistaken principles which turned sincere people, misled by error, into a group of fanatics breeding animosity.

Milman rightly says that under this influence "Christianity retrograded," and whether to explicitly Jewish modes of character it matters not. The important fact is that it retrograded; and it suffered this fate when the rabble laid desecrating hands on the esoteric philosophy and rested not till it had reduced every noble principle of that exalted union of intellectual and mystical experience to a crude literalism, in order that the most stupid might hug to his heart the concrete illusion, the physical shadow of metaphysical realities.

When the movement had sunk to the lowest point among the ignorant multitude, it became impossible to instruct the following of the Church in the nature of the Christ as a spiritual love in the heart and piercing intelligence in the mind. The desperate situation called for a desperate expedient; the strategy of ignorant priestcraft saw its advantages, the crass stupidity of the vulgar whom the Church had gathered under her wing promised its sweeping success. Demons must have exulted in hellish glee while angels wept: for the crafty resort was to the strategy of giving the people the Christ as a man. People impervious to lofty ideas and conceptions can not be led to worship such tenuous things; *a man* at least could engage their imagination and hold their superstitious loyalties. So the Christ became Jesus.

When the bewildered human of no enlightened instruction can discover no rock of salvation within the dark alleys and unclean streets of his own interior consciousness, he will be cheered—and deluded—by the assurance given him in his childhood on impressive authority that there once was a man in history to whom he can resort when in mental and moral defeat. Such an inculcation, emanating from an institution haloed with the prestige of ages, made impressive by the embellishments of gilded beauty of temple, music and ceremony, is well calculated to sweep the ignorant world of average people. This is the victory that Christianity won. It is only the philosopher, who can free himself from its hypnotizing seductions without at the same time throwing overboard in violent resentment—as does the atheist—the prime and priceless metaphysical values that are travestied to nonsense by gross literalization, who is likely to escape from a life-long obscuration of his rational mind.

One of the prominent items of analysis in this study is the downright assertion that Christianity registered a movement of degeneracy from something truer and higher than itself in the beginning. Since this bold assertion will be neither gladly received nor accepted at all if left to rest upon the single authority of the author's pen, the support and agreement of noted Christian authorities must be arrayed behind it. Hear, then, what no less a noted and accredited spokesman for Christianity than Dean Milman says to this same effect (p. 288):

> "Yet the admission of Christianity, not merely as a controlling power . . . but as the animating principle of barbarous warfare, argues at once the commanding influence which it had obtained over the human mind as well as its *degeneracy from its pure and spiritual origin.*"

Barbarism, he says, had absorbed into its own life the Christian passions, yet remained barbaric, not becoming Christian. It thus employed Christian motives for barbaric ends. This was the fountainhead of the military Christianity of the Middle Ages, a modification of the pure religion of the Gospel, directly opposed to its genuine principles, yet apparently indispensable to the social progress of European man, as through it the Roman Empire and the barbarous nations of the North were destined to blend together in the vast European system before they could arrive at a higher civilization and a purer Christianity. Christianity has ever shown a ready disposition to compromise with dominant barbaric forces, or to temporize in devious ways with unmanageable influences, so as best to stabilize its continuing regnancy over the popular mind or further its prospects. It has more often and more consistently followed the lead of social and secular movements than led them with the superior light of a spiritual beacon.

CHAPTER IV

THE VEILED LIGHT

The causes of the translation of Christianity into the baneful Christianism can not be expounded without a brief survey of the religious field in the ancient day. That world was motivated and dominated by elements of human psychology in the domain of what is known as religion which are so different from those prevailing in later days and at present that failure to take them into account will vitiate every attempt to write the true history of the rise of Christianity. It is the incapacity of modern exegetists to apprehend and give due value to these elements that has rendered both false and worthless nearly all the histories of early Christianity. We have never had the truth about Christianity because it can not be written unless these true keys to competent understanding are utilized. It is impossible here to cover this ground with any promise of completeness. It must suffice to unfold the predominant features of the picture, the one, at any rate, which will most radically correct traditional error and guide conception to true goals by true formulas.

That chief trait of antiquity, the neglect of which has so weakened universal Christian exposition, is what might be expressed by the one word—esotericism. For modern Christian investigators it seems ever difficult, even with scores of writers expatiating on the subject, to give proper credit to the significance of the universal prevalence in the ancient world of a method of expressing religious truth which is critical at every point for apprehending what was written or spoken. And even where the principle is admitted to have been employed, there still is manifest a disposition to minimize or ignore its influence in the task of interpretation. Writers shy away from it as deftly as they can or shun it outright.

But there will be no profit in the study of ancient religious tomes, they simply will not yield their meaning, until their construction on a basis determined by esoteric principles is given full consideration in the rendering. Esotericism imposed a peculiar methodology upon the writing of all religious books, and to attempt to interpret them without reference to the specifications of this methodology is to insure gross failure. So habitual is it in the modern age for the discoverer of new or precious truth to blare it from the housetops of publicity that it seems quite impossible to believe that an age existed in which truth, new or old, was sedulously disguised and concealed from the world at large. What is called democracy today will find it an egregious aberration of human conception to hold that all truth is *not* equally the right and privilege of all people.

But ancient sapiency envisaged the matter from a different angle. Profound knowledge, the essential ground for wisdom and enlightenment and the power that goes with their possession, it was held, was only for those who could win it by individual merit, who could demonstrate the capacity for it and the moral quality to refrain from misuse of it. Invidious as this may sound in plebeian ears, it was only for a special class. That class, however, was not one marked and distinguished by any exterior or adventitious circumstances, such as wealth, physical power or social position. It was a class distinguished by its ability to fulfil the terms and conditions on which alone life can bestow any of its bounties, namely the essential moral and spiritual qualifications by virtue of which a truly higher culture can be attained by mortals. Intellectual capacity, spiritual culture are after all not privileges to be handed out to all in a nation like the vote or pensions. They are the happy possession of him alone who qualifies with the requisite development of the capability to experience and express them. Until such necessary credentials are furnished it is both fatuous and dangerous for those who may dispense religious influence to impart it indiscriminately to the masses.

Such at all events was the ancient attitude toward spiritual and mystical religion. Supernal wisdom, high truth, the arcana of knowledge, were not to be thrown out recklessly to the untutored, the stolid masses. Such treasures were to be held in secret brotherhoods, to be imparted only to those undergoing test and discipline. The privilege of being entrusted with the extraordinary mysteries of the knowing adepts was granted to those who had undergone the experience of initiation, the word meaning "beginning," since their exalted status was considered the beginning of man's divinization. High knowledge was therefore the possession of a class which formed a true aristocracy of culture and learning based on intrinsic internal and not mere external qualifications of fitness. This class was generally discerning enough to know that true culture and mystical uplift can not be imparted gratuitously to the "vulgar," for they will be certain to misconceive wretchedly and misapply disastrously the vital secrets. No class, group or individual was excluded from opportunity; but measures were taken to safeguard a thesaurus of dynamic truth against vitiation and misuse.

The chief of these measures was the cryptic form and method of inditing the sacred tomes of archaic lore. Here an ingenuity was resorted to that has confounded and egregiously, even ludicrously, misled all Christian research and effort at exegesis down the centuries to this very day. Truth was inwrought into the inner structure of a variety of modes of representation, such as myth, allegory, drama, parable, fable, number graph and finally astrological pictograph. The method had the multiple advantage that it offered truth in actual verity, but in such form that it would be missed by the unqualified and possibly apprehended by those worthy to handle it. Likewise it presented it in forms calculated to impress it indelibly upon the memory, for the books containing it were written with a view to its very desirable preservation against total loss or extinction. All folk-lore had the primary design of perpetuating, especially by impression upon the sensitive and retentive memory of the childhood of each successive generation, the outward types and structures of inner truth. Even if uncomprehended in one age, the norms and forms covertly expressing the inner essence of verity would be carried forward in outer memory, until in the end their inwardness of meaning might be realized. Such are the Greek and Egyptian myths, the Chaldean astrologies, the legends, folk-*Maerchen,* the body of traditions of wise things that have floated down from earliest days, to the interior meaning of which the world, after too many centuries of stupid blindness, is beginning at last to awaken its torpid understanding.

It was the adoption of these measures of crypticism for the high purposes just expounded that led to the mystifying of the ignorant and supposedly learned alike, and finally to the consummation of the most sweeping catastrophe to culture and world sanity known to earthly history. It opened the pathway to the transformation of Christianity into the errant Christianism. Designed to safeguard wisdom from the vulgar who would outrage it, while imparting it by subtle indirection to the worthy, it ended by missing its goal in both these directions. For there came an age when the stable conditions under which this program could continue to be carried forward with normal success were abrogated by extraordinary developments. Unprecedented circumstances arose to plunge the even operation of the factors involved into a violent welter of forces which ultimately found expression in the upgrowth and prolonged sway of the new religion of Christianism. It is a breath-taking story of the direst cultural debacle and world tragedy. Christianity, soon degenerating into Christianism, came as the result of the breach in the walls of the esoteric policy made by a ferment of ignorant zealotry and misguided religionism. Previously impervious to violation from this side, influences conspired in the first centuries of the Christian rise to traverse its beneficent possibilities and subvert its operation to ruinous outcome.

A combination of weakness within its own structure and violent assault from without overwhelmed its inherent natural strength and violated its true sacredness by traducing its structural integrity to nonsense. Almost for the first time in the life of the world, the secret sanctities of its wisdom were invaded by barbarian crudity and its treasures of sacred science were wantonly torn out from the sanctum of arcane holiness and exposed recklessly to the degrading embrace of the vulgar populace. Christianity came as the outcome of a miscarriage of wisdom due to the intellectual desecration by the religiously crazed multitude of the subtleties of the esoteric method in Scriptural composition. Through misapprehension of cryptic language the entire meaning of the Bibles was warped out of all semblance to true intent and distorted into a system of the veriest falsehood ever to find lodgment in human thought. And this falsehood, being conjoined with and itself engendering one of the most devastating outbursts of fanatical pietism in the annals of history, swept the Western half of the globe with the awful besom of its blind fury for sixteen centuries.

From causes generated in the very beginning of the change that broke down the inviolability of the esoteric regime in religion, it has become the inveterate policy of orthodox Christianism to inveigh against all esotericism. Since Christianism was itself bred by a revolt of uncomprehending religionism against esoteric restriction, inevitably the perennial attitude of that cult has been one of continued disfavor. It is necessary, therefore, if the discussion here is to reveal new elements of historic causality, that a full and comprehensive analysis of the counter claims in this question be undertaken, with a view to arriving at a more just and balanced evaluation of the mooted theme than has been the case hitherto.

The ancient Sages, proficient in religious philosophy and with lofty wisdom, regarded esoteric secrecy in religion as a prime fundamentum for the true culture of the spirit-soul in man. Christian proponents have countered this position with general claims of its inadequacy and iniquity. Can a profounder inquiry or broader survey determine on which side lies the truth in the controversy? It is asserted here that the Pagan contention is the correct one because it is in harmony with every aspect of a more competent understanding of the psychological, spiritual and anthropological issues involved; and the essay will be made to uphold that assertion.

It should need no assemblage of arguments to validate the general claim that the highest wisdom, the most profound motivations of culture and virtue, the most delicate sensibilities of beauty and goodness, the deepest intimations of abstract intellectual intuition can not be communicated to brutish men or absorbed and appropriated by them even when put in the simplest form before them. No envisagement of the potentialities of cultural education can fail to take into account the vast abysses of difference in receptive capacity between the demonstrably capable and potentially educable, and those hopelessly doltish and imbecile. Between the bright and the stupid there are, of course, infinite grades of capability and stolidity. A system of education aiming at general discipline of all levels seeks to adapt the training to the varying potentials of each grade. Modern educators are largely unaware that the religious instruction of the schools of arcane wisdom of early times was very closely graded in relation to the differentiated strata of intelligence and moral character. Long periods of probation were imposed on the learners and further courses of tutelage and testing were laid down for fulfilment before admission to the highest degrees of instruction was opened. At any rate it is indisputably known that the ancient hierophants of the Mystery Schools divided their body of teaching into at least two broad segmentations. They had their Greater and their Lesser Mysteries.

Never has this distinction been handled in Christian history with the attention it deserves and the perspicacity and candor needed to canvass it rightly. It has been slurred over, disdained as unimportant and altogether slighted. It too patently suggests that the Christians were working in the systemology of the Pagans or copying their procedures to be given its rightful emphasis in the Christian purview. Its discontinuance in the new faith after some two centuries is looked upon as another advance away from heathen error to Christian rightness.

The truth of the matter is far other than this easy explication. It was indeed an advance away from Paganism, but one not moving from error to right. It was both a part and an evidence of the disastrous turn from living Christianity to a degenerate Christianism. In breaking down all distinction between truth for the cognoscenti and simple religion for the multitude, Christianity took one of the most fatal steps in its march to depravity. It meant, in short, that it was no longer going to hold itself as a system of high truth that could fulfil the demands of philosophic minds for rational religion, but that it had decided to let philosophy go and use faith alone as its appeal to the unenlightened. It intimates what has not been known to be the sad truth that the new cult early decided to abandon any attempt to move with the intelligentsia and to make its bid to the rank and file of the downtrodden masses groaning under the yoke of Rome. Little did it realize how truly, in another sense, this move would, centuries later, subject it in unwitting but none the less thorough bondage to another tyranny centered at Rome.

Indeed it has been the boast of Christianity that it provided a religious provender to nourish the masses of lowly humanity, whereas Paganism had offered a hyper-mystical and profoundly rationalistic philosophy that must necessarily be limited in its service to the minority segment of the studious and the learned. Christianity therefore provided spiritual food for mankind at large, while Paganism reached a mere fringe of the population, the intelligentsia, leaving the host of "common people" spiritually unnourished. This is claimed as the outstanding merit, even the glory, of Christianity.

But this is a point that is not proved by the mere stating. It is a glory, no doubt, to supply to the ruder stages of human development a regimen of religious faith and elementary indoctrination that will serve the interests both of those masses and the general welfare. But it is surely nothing glorious to have fed these simpler folk with an incredible diet of fables, fancies, fictions and falsities that in the end subverted their divine potential of reason under a mass of irrational beliefs that enslaved them to fanatic bigotries and incredible superstitions for generations. The tragic truth about Christianity's purveying the food of simple truth to the humble masses, and enriching the down-trodden multitude with a precious faith is the historic fact that it fed these masses not on truth simplified, but truth contorted into horrendous untruth. What was fed them turned out to be downright

66

falsehood. The lamentable weakness of most exoteric teaching is in the fact that it comes out as gross error, the dead ghost of truth.

If one holds to the historical tradition, it is apparent that even the Christ used the esoteric method in his spiritual instruction. A passage from Joseph Warschauer's *The Historical Life of Christ* (p. 88) runs:

"The disciples would not have asked him why he taught in parables, because they knew quite well; the parable is a concrete way of teaching, *eminently suitable for simple folk,* who formed the bulk of our Lord's audiences, and easily comprehended by them; they liked parables precisely as children like stories and are best reconciled to moral lessons when they are in story form."

Warschauer speaks of the esoteric methodology in Scriptural writing as

"a product of the same tendency which in Judaism was unable to read any Old Testament passage in its plain meaning, but allegorized even the most obvious statement."

This brief sentence is worth a moment's analysis. It is ill-conceived and illogically expressed. His words "plain meaning" are quite ambiguous, unless they are taken to say that narrative of stories in the Old Testament carried a purely physical literal sense and no other. If Jephthah took an oath to sacrifice the first person he saw after his return and this happened to be his daughter, well then, that is what happened, is what we must assume that "plain meaning" means. But if it be supposable that the original writer of that story designedly framed it to express a great spiritual or cosmic fact, then its "plain meaning" is not to be found in its having happened on given days. If Jesus fell into the literary spirit and technique of his times and used allegory and parable, why is it not entirely legitimate to assume that much if not most of previous Scriptural writing and teaching was done according to the same method and pattern? Warschauer does not stop to ask why the Jewish exegetists were so enslaved to a "tendency" to see everything as allegory. And here is the crux of the discussion. It was more than a tendency; it was universal practice, the established method of the sages and prophets.

Galilean peasants may have liked to listen to children's stories from the Nazarene, but

"A later generation arose which looked for hidden meanings and thought these picture stories of Jesus, with their homeliness and raciness, specially full of hinted secrets; why, then, these people asked, should he have communicated his teachings in the shape of such dark riddles?"

And it is one of the facts of most tragic moment for all humanity that all Christian theological scholarship since those days of Judean history has been stumped with this same question. This work is dedicated to the task of giving that question competent answer.

Warschauer adds an instructive sequel to this situation. This "later generation" he speaks of was not satisfied with lakeside parables, but wanted more "history" about Jesus. Let the Christian world of today take note how they went about getting it! Says Warschauer:

"Within the following thirty years, however, the desire arose, as it could hardly fail to do, for fuller knowledge of the Lord's origin; and, the want being once felt among the faithful, *imagination set to work to fill the gap.*"

The situation with which this problem is concerned is not merely one that touches the early days of Christian development; it is the ubiquitous problem of culture in humanity at all times. Can high truth ever be safely given, or really given at all, to the masses? The answer is contingent; it depends upon the state of development of those masses. If their level of intelligence is fairly high, a commensurable degree of understanding can be imparted to them. If it runs low, only a little can be absorbed. Obviously one must rest with the assertion that a mind can assimilate only that measure of apprehension which its developed capability potentially qualifies it to take in. To offer it higher ranges, demanding more expanded powers, is to waste effort.

The vindication of the esoteric method is integrally bound up with the whole problem of culture in the human race at any time. Much apologetic is summoned to the justification of the modes and procedures that brought Christianity forth in its formative days. They are presented as "special" conditions. But the conditions prevalent then can hardly be claimed to have been in any pronounced way different from those which affect the progress or state of culture in any civilized age or nation. Always and inexorably the agencies and gauges that set the marks of true culture, or conversely defeat it, are at bottom the intelligence quotient or cultural capability of the age or the folk concerned. Perhaps one age differs little from another, except in the ratio of intelligence in the cultured minority to the ignorance of the masses. The latter element, sadly enough, remains all too deplorably constant; the state of the age's culture fluctuates with the brilliance or decay of sound intelligence in the cultured minority. The comparative

68

dominance of minority influence, or its submersion by reason of its own default of superior attainment or its suppression by the outer tyranny either of the masses or of despots, is perhaps the basic criterion of the relative status of culture in any age. But in all ages there is the inevitable yawning gap between the stolid mental inertia of the masses and the alert mercurial genius of the emancipated and the spiritually adventurous, those who "face the morning."

Perhaps no citation could more bluntly state the case for this analysis than the passage from *Sallustius on the Myths.*

"They also represent the activities of the Gods. For one may call the world a myth, in which bodies and things are visible, but souls and minds are hidden. Besides, to wish to teach the whole truth about the Gods to all produces contempt in the foolish, because they cannot understand, and lack of zeal in the good; whereas to conceal the truth by myths prevents the contempt of the foolish, and compels the good to practice philosophy."

What the ancient philosopher is setting forth here is that all objective things, the world and all things in it, physically objectified to the senses, are the phenomenal images of noumenal concepts, all things visible being the concrete reproduction, and therefore the actual material presentation of the ideas of a cosmic consciousness that framed them in thought. Such being the case, the grandest and noblest, the most transcendent activity of intellect is to discern the frame and content of the original cosmic Mind. The art or science of such an activity for the human mind was, as is obvious at a glance, an enterprise that fell within the capability of only the most cultivated intellects. It lies quite beyond the reach of "average" humanity. It was a heavy task even for the most capable among the philosophers. The knowledge of the basic principles constituted the true esotericism, whose prime claims to the title of science consisted in just this development or consciousness of the relation between the seen things of the objective creation and the noumenal principia that generated them in the high counsels of divine Thought.

It is not hard, therefore, to grasp the essential dialectic of the necessity for esotericism, and for the use of the myth and allegory as its indispensable tools. The most stirring truths within the scope of human apperception come not through the power of pure intellect alone. To be sure, they are an intellectual product, or they would not be registered in consciousness at all. Yet they arise from the mind afflated, as it were, by an access of rich coefficient of mystical vividness and with touches of sensibility of nearly ineffable moving power and beauty. The

69

clear mental picture generates exalted *feeling* beyond the power of language to express. The only way in which mind can attempt to embody the concept so as to give it the dynamism to awaken in another mind these overtones of mystic afflatus is to structuralize it in the form of myth or allegory. The essential utility of the myth inheres in the fact that it copies and preserves in a dramatic formulation the precise frame of the mental concept which is its apprehensible subject matter. The inspection of the myth will always revive the representation of the idea; and the dramatic form of its rehearsing furnishes the added stimulus to receptive minds to experience as much as possible the mystic feeling reactions that are latent in the suggestive power of the concept. In plainer statement, the myth or allegory clearly reformulates the central idea, and its dramatization—rather than its staid expression in mere words—subtly supplies the incitements to the mystical ebullition of feeling elements that is the sublime accompaniment of the clear mental vision of liberating truth.

Gerald Massey, in his *The Natural Genesis* (p. 134), announces the great revelation that *mythos* equals *Logos,* and he hits the mark of fundamental truth about this mystery of ancient science when he writes:

"The essential character of a true myth consists in its being no longer intelligible by a reference to the spoken language."

It calls upon the suggestive power of a visual construction to strike the soul with more dynamic force than can be generated by mere words.

It takes no sharp analytic discernment to see that such exercise of cultural proficiency or genius is not the habitude nor the capability of the mass mind. True culture then must subsist necessarily at the level of capability which manifests the susceptibility to both the more delicate and more profound modes of spiritual consciousness. It must be able to apprehend esoteric modes of representing truth. The intellectual incapacity of the multitude makes esotericism inevitably the method both of preservation and of secret communication of high truth, wisdom, mystic beauty among those who can appreciate it, utilize it for the forwarding of evolution and treasure it safe from the hands of uncomprehending boorishness that would defile it.

It is thus at last clearly revealed that there were two prime motives behind the esoteric method: first, to preserve truth in the world; second, to safeguard it against vitiation.

Another modern scholar of great eminence in the field of ancient religion, Sir Gilbert Murray, comes forward with a sagacious statement on the myth, or rather its kindred device, allegory. In his celebrated work on *The Five Stages of the Greek Religion* he writes (p. 199):

"I have tried to sketch in outline the main forms of belief to which Hellenistic philosophy moved or drifted. Let me dwell for a few pages more upon the characteristic method by which it reached them. It may be summed up in one word—allegory. It is applied to Homer, to the religious traditions, to the ritual, to the whole world."

Then he adds:

"Allegory is not the frigid thing it seems to us. . . . The Hellenistic age did not wantonly invent the theory of allegory. Allegory may make the emotions sensitive. . . ."

It would be a happy circumstance if the citation from Murray could end here, for what he says so far is markedly true. His phrase, "make the emotions sensitive," confirms what has been said here to the effect that the myth or allegory impresses the idea it pictures upon consciousness with enhanced force because it envelops it in an aura of mystical sensibility, springing from the power of drama. A myth is an abstract conception dramatized. It concretizes an abstraction to the inner eye of thought, giving it a new and more vivid power to stir the feelings. He who can dramatize abstract truth is the leader of man to his divinity.

But—the great British scholar disappoints confidence in his perspicacity when he concludes the uncompleted sentence above with the utterly mistaken assertion that allegory, while making the emotions sensitive, "certainly weakens the understanding." Sad comment on this maladversion is that, medieval and modern ignorance being what they are, Murray's statement is only too lamentably true. The myth or allegory has weakened—rather has failed to enlighten and strengthen—the understanding. But, along with all others, the scholar ascribes this failure to the nature and function of the allegory. In sharp contravention of this it must be asserted here that this is quite wrong. *Default is not in the allegory; it is in the ignorance and blindness* that for centuries have shut off the esoteric sense of ancient Scripture from academic perception. Sterility of imagination and poverty of conceptual insight in orthodox circles have kept the scholarly eye from viewing the allegories with the penetrating rays of rational understanding. The myths still stand in all their ancient majesty of near-divine illustrious-

71

ness. Modern eyes still gaze upon them and still find them dull and opaque. All that is needed is a new lens of higher power to bring out their wondrous beauty and by this achievement to reintegrate Christianity.

A monumental work packed with challenging data is Godfrey Higgins' *The Anacalypsis*. The sane views presented therein should not be missed (p. 446):

"When all the curious circumstances have been considered, an unprejudiced person will, I think, be obliged to admit that the ancient epic poems are oriental allegories, all allusive to the same mythos, and that many of those works which we have been accustomed to call histories are but allegorized representations of mythologies on the secret doctrines of which I am in pursuit, and which have been endeavored to be concealed and perpetuated for the use of the elect, the initiated, under the veil of history— to which, as the first object was the doctrine or mythos, the *history* in each case was sacrificed or made subservient."

It is best to let Higgins go on with the story (p. 622):

"And I contend that it is philosophical to hold in suspicion all such histories, and unphilosophical to receive them without suspicion. . . . *The mythos has corrupted all history*. Who can doubt that the Argonautic expedition is a recurring mythos? . . . As Virgil has told us, new Argonauts would arise from time to time."

Comment that might be added here is that, while it is but too sadly true that the mythos has corrupted all history, as Higgins puts it, he doubtless would have agreed that it was only the abject failure of the human mind in the mass to comprehend what might be called the *mystos* behind the *mythos* that led to the vitiation of the true purport of ancient "history."

Indeed it is a question whether the ancients, at least until the writing of Herodotus, had any conception of history as it is held in view today. So we subjoin another most pregnant citation from Higgins, which, coming from this conscientious seeker after truth, should bear with great weight upon the counsels of modern scholarship (p. 616):

"After giving the subject all the consideration in my power and a diligent examination of ancient documents for many years, I have become quite convinced that almost all the ancient histories were written for the sole purpose of recording a *mythos,* which it was desired to transmit to posterity—but yet to conceal from all but the initiated. The traditions of the countries were made subservient to this purpose, without any suspicion of fraud; and we only give them the appearance of fraud *when we confound them with history*. This is the case with all early histories. They were all anciently composed; or, if written, they were *written in verse* for the sake of correct retention by the memory and *set to music* for the same reason. They were all the same nature as the *Iliad* and the *Aeneid*. The most ancient of the ancients had nothing of the nature of real histories. Real history was not the object of their writing, any more than of Virgil's or Milton's. Herodotus was the inventor of history."

These words should be framed in gold on the walls of every library and classroom. They are reprinted here because they ring out the truth so long smothered by indoctrinated folly. The real mystery is history itself, and the *mythos* is the only true key to it. When we throw away the myth-key we can not read the history!

When a man who spent his substance and his life in honest research has at last come to conclusions such as these, they deserve recording (p. 366):

"How can any one consider this striking circumstance and not see that almost all ancient history and epic poetry are mythological,—the secret doctrine of the priests *disguised in parables,* in a thousand forms? Mr. Faber, Mr. Bryant and Nimrod have proved this past doubt. . . . Our priests have *taken the emblems for the reality.* The lower orders of our priests are as much the dupes as their votaries. The high-priests are wiser. Our priests will be very angry and deny all this. In all nations, in all times there has been a secret religion; in all nations and in all times the fact has been denied."

Higgins here says in words what this work will say in total effect. Another trenchant passage runs as follows (p. 386):

"No doubt every division of the universal religion had its secret and sacred writings as well as the Jews, only they were never made public and they were lost. Those of the Jews were made public by Ptolemy. The Athenians had a sacred book called *The Testament,* to which they believed the safety of the Republic was attached." (Spinette on *Hierog.*, 123.)

Higgins expresses surprise that there could be any person of intelligence who would not see that

"almost every part of *Genesis* is enigmatical or a parable. The system of concealment and of teaching by parable is the most marked characteristic of the religion. I suspect that there is not a sentence in *Genesis* which is not consistent with good sense *if its true meaning could be discovered.* I feel little doubt that such a passage as that of God wounding Jacob in the thigh, and his failing in his endeavor to kill Moses at an inn, are wholly misunderstood. . . . The *Genesis* was considered by most if not all of the ancient Jewish philosophers and Christian Fathers as an allegory. For persons using their understanding, to receive it in a literal sense was impos-

73

sible; and when we find modern Christians so receiving it, we only find a proof that with the mass of mankind *reason has nothing to do with religion,* and that the power of education is so great as in most cases to render the understanding useless."

Two things need accentuation in this passage: the Bible would make mighty and sublime sense *if its true meaning could be discovered;* and, in the main, *reason has nothing to do with religion.* Both these theses will receive elaborate consideration farther on.

General corroboration of Higgins' radical position is not wanting in other writers. There is a categorically direct statement in a fine analytic work of an eminent authority on the Orphic Religion, Prof. Vittorio D. Macchioro, formerly of the University of Naples. His work is entitled *From Orpheus to Paul,* and is a discerning survey of the influences that this essay is undertaking to delineate more fully. His insight into the nature and design of the myths is exceptionally clear. He writes (p. 218):

"But there is no denying that only by means of myth does our experience become concrete and communicable. . . . Myth, therefore, is necessary for religious history . . . it cannot be dispensed with, since the divine, the mysterious, the ineffable cannot be expressed except by imagination, that is, by myth."

He follows this with the very pertinent observation, so necessary in enabling the mind to preserve its aplomb in its judgment on the myths, that "hence it is not the myth which is of consequence, but the idea it serves to express." The steadying and sanifying force of this notation is found in its pertinence to the inevitable tendency of scholars unfamiliar with the ancient habitudes of expression to swing away in disgust from the myth when they fail to pierce through its outer veil to its intelligible message for reflection, and reject it as valueless *in toto.* He is aiming to halt the wholly catastrophic sweep of the scholarly belief that because the myth, *per se,* is ignorantly concluded to be childish nonsense, it is to be thrown out on the rubbish heap of "ancient superstition."

He aims to stress the true manner of approaching the myths, which is to expect nothing but sheer fiction in the form and matter of the story itself, but to penetrate through its factitious disguise to catch the form of splendid verity which the features of the story are designed by subtle indirection to portray. The catastrophe which befell the world as the result of the loss of the acumen necessary to read the esoteric sense of the ancient myths is attributable largely to the sheer impotence of genius on the part of scholars of the later time to realize that the ancients really did *not* "believe" their myths. The sapient original formulators of these constructions never could have dreamed that an age would come so steeped in mental lethargy that it would suppose the great myths were to be taken as narratives of veridical happenings, that they would be thought to have been written as "true stories." Concocting these great dramatic depictions, an ancient sage might well have jocosely remarked: "I hope no one will ever think we believed these stories!" What did transpire in the course of history was, *mirabile dictu,* that in default of the ability to interpret the myths in their interior primary meaning, they have stood for all these centuries as insoluble riddles, baffling and perplexing the brains of all scholars who do not like to think that men of the mental stature of Plato and Plutarch actually "believed" them, but who still do not see how they fitted into a picture that is all over tinted with the aura of the profoundest intellectual genius. The boasted modern world of scholarship is still at a loss to know how to throw away the myth as a narrative while yet holding on to it as a legitimate and truly scientific mode of inciting the human spirit to its most edifying apperceptions of sublime verity. This task is still one of the mightiest of the cultural problems challenging the modern world, which must handle it capably before it can claim to be on a level with the ancient conceptive genius.

Perhaps it might be said that to general modern conception meaning-value disappears in the myth; whereas to ancient usage the true essence of meaning-value is preserved in the myth, there for any mind discerning enough to catch it. It is true, of course, that when the esoteric underlying purport is not apprehended, and the story stands in its naked form, opaque to interior view, all meaning disappears, or rather simply does not appear. To the modern the myth remains a crude and crass formulation just because he can not supply a glass of adequate spirit-ray vision which would enable him to see it as objectively transparent, but inwardly meaningful.

Then Prof. Macchioro follows along to a practical conclusion of his well-conceived elucidation, in observing that

"the only way to deliver Christianity from this imposition is to transform theology into mythology, that is, to cease to consider it from a religious viewpoint as a sort of knowledge and to view it in the light of the history of religion as a complex of symbols by means of which man realizes his faith."

In the train of this thoroughly sound suggestion he pronounces a great and sweeping truth, which will fall with the shock of a completely outlandish assertion upon orthodox minds, that

"there is really no essential difference between theology and mythology; their content is the same. They differ in that theology involves faith and implies truth, whereas mythology makes neither religious nor philosophical presumptions. The reduction, then, of all theology to mythology is tantamount to delivering oneself from all religious presumption and to inquiring into the origin and history of theology in the light of philology."

He might have better concluded: "in the light of universal truth detached from religious influences"; although he is correct in attributing to philology a central influence in the evolution of general philosophical science.

He is driven by the convincing force of his keen discernment to the magnificent position where he views precisely what this work designs to present as one of its chief conclusions, viz. that

"from this reduction of theology to mythology arises what seems to some a great danger, to others a great hope, the hope for a possible reintegration of Christianity. The history of Christianity has been a long process of disintegration. From the Apostolic Age down it has shown a dispersive tendency, a tendency to divide, dissolve into churches, sects and heresies. This centrifugal tendency is remarkable in a religion which had its center in a person and ought therefore to present the greatest unity. The whole sad history of Christian disintegration takes its rise from the theory of the cognitive function of theology.

"But with the reduction of theology to mythology the reintegration of Christianity becomes possible. The dogma-concept may be replaced by the dogma-symbol, which permits harmony in difference. Hence the great importance of every inquiry into the mythological origins of theology. . . ."

When another will speak our piece for us, as Macchioro here so eloquently does, it is desirable to give him the floor. The first pages of this volume announced that a leading motive inspiring this work is the "reintegration of Christianity," and this eminent authority in an important field of religion points the way to this reintegration in precisely the same direction as is here advocated. Doctrinal theology—who can deny it?—has brought about endless schism, sectarian hatreds and vain wastage of strength. To replace its hazards with the luminous essence of meaning of the symbol and the myth, which can generate in each individual as much of the light of eternal truth as he is capable of cognizing in any case, thus permitting each one to abstract from every doctrine whatever it can mean for him, without contradicting

76

what it means to another, this, as Macchioro so well affirms, would be to end Christian disunity and conduce to what is at this writing the insistent cry of an alarmed Christian leadership—namely Christian brotherhood. This is plainly indicated for any one who is conversant with the truth of historical Christianity. Yet, as will here be demonstrated, even this logical consummation will remain an impossibility until the intelligence and genius needed for the reinterpretation of the language of myth and symbol is once more awakened.

Nothing is more obvious to the honest investigator than that the way for Christianity to return from division to unity is to return to the unity all religions had in the remote period of the Golden Age. If no one else ever assembled the proof of this, Godfrey Higgins did. His wonderful *Anacalypsis* should be required reading in every Seminary.

"Proof that what the Eclectic philosopher Ammonius Saccas said was true abounds, viz. that one universal and very refined system originally pervaded the whole world; which only required to be divested of meretricious ornaments, or the corruptions with which the craft of priests, or the infirmities of men, had loaded it in different countries, to be everywhere found; that in fact in the Christian and Gentile systems there was fundamentally no difference." (*Anac.*, p. 477.)

"But one thing is clear—the Mythos of the Hindoos, the Mythos of the Jews and the Mythos of the Greeks are all at the bottom the same; and what are called their early histories are not the histories of man, but are contrivances *under the appearance of histories* to perpetuate doctrines, or perhaps the history of certain religious opinions, in a manner understood by those only who had a key to the enigma. Of this we shall see many additional proofs hereafter."

Higgins affirms that this universal refined system (Augustine's *true* religion) needed only to be divested of its figurative ornaments to be clearly apprehended. He says it was put up in cryptic form, but that those who had the key could read it. What is needed, then, is obviously the recovery of the lost key. The Rosetta Stone made this possible and the possibility is now being realized. The one path to Christian reintegration is now being reopened. As Macchioro says, it is the return to myth and symbol, *competently handled.*

That the return to myth and allegory will have to be fought for against denial and opposition is evident from what many Christian writers have put forth on this subject. One such statement is at hand and can be inserted here as an example of hundreds more.

"And the universal prevalence of sacrifice among the heathen nations seems to imply that sacrifice was in some way a natural expression of man's

77

sense of his relation to God. The hypothesis of a primitive revelation, the remains of which lingered among all the peoples of the world, and which expressed itself through sacrifice, is precarious. It certainly can not be proved; and to explain sacrifice by it must leave the origin of that institution involved in the same and hypothetical condition." (A. B. Davidson, *The Theology of the Old Testament,* p. 312.)

The universal prevalence of just one feature, such as sacrifice, might not of course "prove" a universal primitive revelation, though it in itself is a strong hint. But there are other evidences without number that do point to it. The remains of a primeval religion, found to be identical all over the world when carefully and with the proper keys compared, attest the original unity of religions. This blindness and imperviousness to a great idea on the part of modern scholars must be broken through if the truth is to be recognized. It is critical for the future of mankind.

Dean Milman's allusion to the matter in much the same spirit should not be passed by. He is speaking of the term, Logos or Word.

"By the Targumists, the earliest Jewish commentators on the Scriptures, this term had already been applied to the Messiah; nor is it necessary to observe the manner in which it has been sanctified by its introduction into the Christian scheme. From this remarkable uniformity of conception and coincidence of language has sometimes been assumed a common tradition, generally disseminated throughout the race of man. I should be content with receiving it as the general acquiescence of the human mind, in the necessity of some mediation between the pure spiritual nature of the Deity and the intellectual and moral being of man, to which the sublimest and simplest, and, therefore, the most natural development, was the revelation of God in Christ." (*History of Christianity,* p. 46.)

Evidence of the inadequacy of this dodging is found readily enough in the certain fact that all the "remarkable uniformity of conception and coincidence of language" was a phenomenon in the world long before God had made a revelation of himself through Jesus of Nazareth, and therefore must be explained on other grounds.

In Milman's great *History of Christianity* (p. 28) there is found a very striking passage which admits the most of what is asserted here regarding the myths, and adds strength to the contention that the one indispensable feature of the myths that is the nub of the entire debate over them is that they be thoroughly comprehended. It goes without saying that an allegory is of no utility for enlightenment unless that which it allegorizes can be grasped in full. All the rage of savants against the myth must be seen as directed against a thing they do not understand. The aversion and hostility will vanish away the moment clear apprehension reveals the wondrous light buried under the bushel of dramatic stratagems. Milman prefaces his pronouncement with the statement that the nearer a people approach to barbarism, as in the childhood of the race, the more earthly are their conceptions of deity, and the moral aspect of the divine nature as conceived by man seems gradually to develop with the progressive unfoldment of the human mind. This deepening conception of moral and spiritual values, he says, is a prerogative of the higher classes; "the vulgar are left to their stocks and stones," their animals and reptiles. In republican Greece the intellectual aristocracy of the philosophers, blessed with superior and interior insights, rarely dared to let their greater understanding be known, "but concealed their more extended views behind a prudential veil, as a secret or esoteric doctrine" and disarmed suspicion by studious conformity with all the national rites and ceremonies. Much of the entire motivating principle of all esoteric polity is hinted at here.

But Milman then adds the significant declaration that "yet nothing was needed but to give a higher and more extensive sense to those types and shadows of universal wisdom" to make them instruments, not of intellectual mystery and bafflement, but of luminous cognitions. For he says that this clearer impenetration of the myths would have been

"an improvement which the tendency of the age manifestly required and which the Jews themselves, especially in the Alexandrian school, had already attempted by allegorizing the whole annals of their people and extracting a profound moral meaning from all the circumstances of their extraordinary history."

And no one can possibly conceive how remarkably this extraction of ethical and spiritual meaning from their Old Testament "history" altered the entire meaning of this people's cherished literature who has not read the *Zohar* and other haggadic books of the Jews.

From Milman's history we cull another passage revealing again the ubiquitous use of the mythicizing principle in ancient religions. Speaking about the Alexandrian syncretism he says (p. 48):

"The poetic age of Greece had long passed away before the two nations [Greece and Egypt] came into contact; and the same rationalizing tendency of the times led the Greek to reduce his religion, the Jew the history, of his nation, to a lofty moral allegory."

One is impelled to ask why, then, are not Greek religion and Hebrew history read as "lofty moral allegory" and not as veridical factuality?

Can it never be comprehended that at least in the case of the Hebrew "history" in the Old Testament, the narrative *was* a lofty moral allegory, highly illuminating as such and ludicrously asinine as reputed veridical history? Failure of later ages to read both Greek mythological religion and Jewish history as lofty spiritual apologue can be put down as one of the most directly causative factors in the general stultification of world sanity that has bred the unending run of calamitous events in Occidental history over two millennia.

In lieu of an allegorical rendering of Scriptures we are asked to read them in their "plain meaning," as Warschauer put it. The astonishing fact—which the literalists ever overlook—is that millions *have read* the Scriptures in their "plain meaning" and thrown their Bibles down in disgust and bafflement. The "plain meaning" of Holy Writ is so far from being "plain" or yielding its "meaning" that there never has been agreement on what the meaning is and in simple truth the meaning is still unknown. As an instance of what is meant by our statement, there are the two verses, fifth and sixth, of the twelfth chapter of *Judges* in the Old Testament, in which the judges in Israel were ordered by God to put to the sword on one day forty-two thousand Ephraimites because they could not pronounce the word "shibboleth," but instead said "sibboleth." The literalist would assure us that the meaning is that, like the battle of Gettysburg or Hastings, it happened. But the final meaning of this *as an event* would be that God and man have both done idiotic things. And it is calamitous to implant such an idea in human heads. Even as an event it has no "meaning." But magnificent meaning comes to view if it is taken as allegory, meaning which it is not calamitous to implant in mortal minds.

Julian, the nephew of Constantine, whose ungracious task it was to try to resuscitate a dying philosophical world, and who met the arrow of death for his pains, clearly saw that

"the ancient myths are the only ways in which the human mind grasps and represents to itself a true religion too high and too pure to be envisaged except in the images they present, or to be approached except symbolically through the sacraments and ceremonies they prescribe."

In his book *Christ in the Gospels,* Burton Scott Easton says (p. 1) that

"from the very first, however, there was probably some tendency to treat the parables allegorically and to search for recondite meanings; a tendency that rapidly grew to impossible dimensions; we already find Mark treating the parables as puzzles and setting forth the appalling theory that Jesus used them to conceal truth, in order to keep the Jews from being converted."

Apart from the dialectical question that arises on the perusal of this passage as to what other possible function a parable can be conceived to exercise than to represent a truth allegorically, it is pertinent to remark that had Easton been familiar with the innermost motivation of the ancient mythological method, he would not have rated as an impossible over-development of allegorical tendency that which was the essential *raison d'etre* of the method itself. If it ran into impossible dimensions, that was because it ran into ignorance in its handling, as it always has done sooner or later. For it was precisely to keep undeveloped groups from getting precious truth into their hands when they could not get it into their heads. Easton says that "Mark is not held up as a model of historical precision. . . . Mark's story already contains palpable allegorical elements." Likewise he asserts that the "naive character of John's historical writing is still more clearly seen in the subsequent scene." (*John* 6:22-26.)

Many of the second and third century Christian rites, he says, "have long defied explanation." (Where is Warschauer's "plain meaning" then?) "No one knows why oil was poured into the baptismal water or why a candle or a staff of olive wood was dipped into it." Here surely is allegory, not only in printed words, but enacted in dramatic reality. And the default of Christianity is seen in this admission that no one after two thousand years of Christian dominance knows why oil was poured on the baptismal water and the symbolism of the candle in religion, when every initiate in the Pagan societies knew a book of such things thoroughly.

And well this author sees the dilemma in which Christianity finds itself through its usage of many forms which it even now cannot explain. For he writes (p. 76):

"We have not only to explain the appearance of certain ceremonies in Christianity; we have to explain their almost universal acceptance."

The modern philosopher-educator John Dewey, in his *The Quest for Certainty* (p. 15), says in discussing Aristotle's contribution to the history of thought:

"This core of truth in effect, was embroidered with myths for the benefit of the masses, for reasons of expediency, namely, the preservation of social institutions. The negative work of philosophy was then to strip away these imaginative accretions. From the standpoint of popular belief this was its chief work, and it was a destructive one. The masses only felt that their religion was attacked. But the enduring contribution was positive."

What Dewey means by stripping away the imaginative accretions from Greek religion is not clear. If Aristotle stripped away the Greek myths he did it by fully explicating them in straightforward fashion. What the popular religionists resented, as Dewey intimates, was that Aristotle elucidated their hidden purport in such a way as to rob them of their literal reference, for this is the reaction that an allegorical rendering of Scriptures always produces from the populace.

But in this deduction of Dewey's lurks a discernment of verity in man's world of being that is among the most fundamental visions of truth that mortal mind can catch. The philosopher expounds this more explicitly in the next passage (p. 16):

"Logic provided the patterns to which ultimately real objects had to conform, while physical science was possible in the degree in which the natural world . . . exhibited exemplification of ultimate immutable rational objects."

This principle of understanding puts the proper foundation under the whole edifice of the mind's effort to structuralize truth on the basis of his living contact with the objective reality of the world. Man can know only as life teaches him, and he is taught only by his experience with the world. If his contact with life and the world gave him no true conceptions of enduring and dependable verity, then the real world would not educate him in truth, but would misteach him in the end. Life would betray him. And we have Wordsworth's assurance that

"Nature never did betray the heart that loved her."

So we have G. R. G. Mure, in his work on *Aristotle,* saying (p. 171, note) that "reason apart from its object has no character." Dewey continues the discussion by saying that Greek thought never made a sharp separation between the rational perfect realm and the natural world. Greek thinking accepted the senses, the body and nature with natural piety and found in nature a hierarchy of creations leading degree by degree to the divine. The soul was the realized actuality of the body, as reason was the transcendent realization of the ideal forms contained in the soul. The senses included within themselves forms which needed only to be stripped of their material accretions to be true stepping-stones to higher knowledge.

It needs to be proclaimed as with a trumpet that this wholly salutary truth of the great Greek philosophy was one of the items of priceless knowledge that was corrupted into the frightful conception of the sinful character of the world and the body, in that sweep of Christian ignorance which devastated the whole area of natural human delight in sensuous existence to the infinitely tragic wreckage of millions of lives.

Dewey, commenting on Spinoza's ideas, says that Nature is naturally, i.e., rationally knowable and that knowledge of it is such a perfect good that when it enlightens the human mind, all lesser and otherwise disturbing objects of distraction and passion fall away or are easily subordinated to control.

The further expansion of this theme, so deeply inwrought with the causes of Christian decadence, is demanded if only by the stubborn rejection by modern thinkers of the ancient method of analogy. For it was the discreet use of this device that enabled ancient Egyptian and Greek thought to hold itself in such sane and constant touch with reality.

So, then, says Mure, in his *Aristotle* (p. 230):

"The eye for an effective metaphor is in fact a mark of genius and unteachable. And in devoting most space to illustrating that form of metaphor which depends upon analogy,—as when old age is described as 'Life's sunset'—he means perhaps to mark the manifestation within the poet's imaginative world of that hierarchic order of analogous stages which pervades the whole Aristotelian universe. The last and least important element in tragedy is spectacle."

Matching what the ancient sages declared was the last and least important thing in their spiritual Scriptures,—history.

This again stresses the great truth to which general modern thought is almost totally a stranger, that poetry, philosophy, conceptual realization of meaning are more important than the record of man's actual doings. Current thought feels itself secure only on the ground of historical *fact;* it is ever uncertain and insecure when dealing with poetry and philosophy. It does not trust them; they are too thin ice and may let the skater crash through. The paradoxical fact is that *history is the least secure ground to stand upon* and is constantly letting all skaters down into bogs and quicksands. The thing that proves this is history itself. Hegel saw this clearly enough. A clever version of this sad fact has been put in the statement that the only thing we have learned from history is that we have learned nothing from history. This is of course hyperbole, but still largely true. It has taken the race thousands of years to formulate a few of the most rudimentary lessons of history into ordained norms of future behavior. Ignorance eternally blunders ahead without heeding the garnered wisdom of the ages, for if it did it would not be ignorance. Mighty is the utterance, then, of the great Aristotle (*De Poetica*):

"Hence poetry is something more philosophical and of graver import than history, since its statements are of the nature rather of universals, whereas those of history are singulars."

Mure corroborates what has been advanced herein earlier that "the Romans lacked any metaphysical genius." He adds that "the rebirth of Aristotelianism in Europe determined the whole course of Medieval and modern culture." Few will quibble over this statement; and if true it places beyond debate the ground-claim of this work, that it was the displacing of Greek rationalism out of the early Christian movement that led to the debacle of the Dark Ages.

Then John Dewey (*The Quest for Certainty*, p. 133) states most luminously the case for the principle on which the greatest of the ancient sages based their fathomless wisdom, the principle of the uniformity of truth in all the worlds, at all the levels. A living expression of truth at any level was at once a replica of the same truth at any other grade. Modern science has not yet recovered this priceless item of ancient sagacity. If it had, it would not go on scorning "analogy." This truth validates analogy. Empirical investigation can only confirm sensually what analogy teaches ideally. If analogy was loyally cultivated, the mind could know beforehand what investigation and discovery will bring to light. Says Dewey:

"The meaning which one event has is translatable into the meanings which others possess. Ideas of objects, formulated in terms of the relations which events bear to one another, *having common measures,* institute broad smooth highways by means of which we can travel from the thought of one part of nature to that of any other. In ideal at least, we can travel from any meaning—or relation—found anywhere in nature to the meaning to be expected anywhere else."

This is grandly stated and if it were given its full sweep of influence in the realm of thought, would go far toward inaugurating another Renaissance in intelligence.

Then comes a passage from Dewey's pen which for momentous truth is worthy, as Carlyle phrased it, of being "written on all walls," certainly those of all libraries, seminaries and halls of culture (*Ibid.*, p. 151):

"A solution was found when symbols came into existence." "The invention or discovery of symbols is doubtless by far *the greatest single event in the history of man*. Without them no intellectual advance is possible; with them, there is no limit set to intellectual development except inherent stupidity."

Inherent stupidity is still and always man's most frightful danger; but with such a gleam of intelligence alight in the mind of even one modern thinker, the torches of all others might be enkindled to burn with a new flood of light. Alas! It is so far from being seen and applied that one of the main contentions of this work, the asseveration that the sacred Scriptures are written in a language of myth and symbol, and that the Christian religion threw away and lost the very soul of their meaning when it mistranslated this language into alleged history instead of reading it as spiritual allegory, will be disputed raucously even when all the mountain of evidence is piled up before the eye.

Perhaps nothing could be more fitting than to place by the side of Dewey's epochal statement one from Spinoza which falls little short of it in vital import for human knowledge. It is significantly corroborative of the relation between nature and the minds of the sentient creatures that grow up in her lap. Says the great author of the *Ethics:*

"Man's greatest good is the knowledge of the union which the mind has with the whole of nature." This well accords with Prof. Hocking's statement that the only cure for a sick mind is to understand the meaning of the whole of life. The philosopher utters this sententious truth; the poet echoes it in his metered rhyme. For Wordsworth sings:

"To her fair works did nature link
The human soul that through me ran;
And much it grieved my heart to think
What man has made of man."

Christianity, wretchedly directed away from its first connections with high arcane philosophy, was the influence that tore man out of his intelligent kinship with Nature and set him, in weird aberration of religious zealotry, over against Nature and Nature over against him, in a fictitious hostility that drove him to such unnatural extravagances of conduct as to have blighted all possibility of happiness for ages.

85

A. B. Davidson, in his work *The Theology of the Old Testament* (p. 514), has a quite discerning statement to the effect that the acquirement of a familiarity with the Scriptures is not easy; that it takes the labor of a lifetime; for the reason that the Bible is a literary work written in the language of life and feeling, and not in that of the schools, whether of philosophy, theology or science. One has, he says, to extend all his sensibilities and bring himself *en rapport* with its varied genial, subtle, enraptured human-divine presentations, making the necessary deductions from a hyperbole, calculating the moral value of a metaphor, if one is to feel the sentiments expressed. But two positions, he concludes, are to be firmly maintained:

"First, that Scripture has a meaning and a view of its own on most moral and religious questions; and not more than one view really . . . and, second, that the meaning of Scripture is capable of being ascertained from Scripture alone, and ought not to be controlled from anything without."

All of which is a somewhat indirect way of affirming what is contended for here, that the Scriptures are basically esoteric. But of great value is Davidson's claim that the Bible has but one single meaning. For no idea is more generally prevalent than that one can go to Scripture and find it sustaining any one of many diverse and even opposing theorizations. It is commonly averred that it is possible to find support for almost any thesis of interpretation in the language of the text. This is a good occasion, therefore, to put forth the definite assertion that when the Scriptures are read with the true esoteric keys to their cryptic signification, they mean one thing only, and that definitely, consistently and incontestably.

In his *The Beginnings of Christianity,* George P. Fisher (p. 253), speaking of Philo's amalgamation of the Greek and the Mosaic systems in his profound syncretism, says that the Jewish philosopher effected this quite harmonious unification of two great systems commonly considered quite divergent, by the "flexible" method of allegory, the interpretation being that of an occult sense which underlies the literal wording.

It will be well, however, to counterblast an observation which Fisher makes in reference to "the mythical theory," which to him as to nearly all other orthodox writers, is such a prickly thorn in the theological side. He says (p. 464) that "the mythical theory is wrecked upon a variety of difficulties which it cannot evade or surmount." Wreckage has come, but it was not, as he assumes, inevitable. Alluding to the

86

growth of the myths and legends that obviously had to be called in to provide an explanation for the admittedly purely-poetic and decorative part of the Gospel narrative,—adduced by so many Christian apologists—he says that

"there was no time for a cycle of myths of this sort to arise before the date of the earliest written Gospels. The circumstances, especially the presence of the Apostles, the recognized guides of the Church, would render it impossible."

And more to the same effect. A full refutation of this utterly unfounded view will be produced in the course of this work. In the briefest form of rebuttal now, it is to be said that it shows blindness on the part of this writer to assume that the cycle of legends had only a few years in which to develop to general knowledge and value. What a sound study of comparative religion brings to light now is that these same legends, a vast cycle of them, were no sudden development in any age, but were of immemorial antiquity. The birth of any Messiah would have been lavishly embellished with these legends. Categorically, the "mythical theory" is *not* wrecked upon a variety of difficulties, for these vanish in a scheme of utter and splendid intelligibility when the mind brings to the task acumen enough to pierce their diaphanous veil to the light shining behind it.

From our own Emerson comes the sententious observation that "a good symbol is a missionary to convince thousands."

A modern writer of keen discernment is Thomas L. Masson, who in a work he calls *Ascensions* says (p. 194):

"There are many things beyond the power of words to convey, which can only be indicated by symbols which are understood by the few and reinterpreted for wider circles."

Warrant for citing this excerpt is found in the notation it contains to the effect that it is the business and function of the few at the summit of the intellectual coterie who can grasp recondite esoteric significance, to exercise their best ability to pass on to the next grade below them in intelligence as lucid a rendering of the deeper import as possible. In turn this group must do its best to convey the subtle meanings to the rank next below it, and that in turn to the one below, and so on down to the lowest. It is in this transmission that the inner sense is lost, being supplanted sooner or later by a more easily apprehensible literal one, thus making false "history" out of true allegory.

87

Proclus in his majestic volumes *On the Theology of Plato* (Vol. I, p. 57) writes:

"Socrates, therefore, . . . narrating the types and laws of divine fables, which afford this apparent meaning and the inward concealed scope, which regards as its end the beautiful and natural in the fictions about the Gods. . . ."

Here there is an open declaration that the myths about the Gods are fictions, but that they hold an "inward concealed scope" of meaning.

Another modern, the eminent psychologist, C. G. Jung, in his *Modern Man in Search of a Soul* (p. 189), says:

"It is therefore to be expected of the poet that he will resort to mythology in order to give his experience its most fitting expression. The primordial experience is the source of his creativeness; it cannot be fathomed and therefore requires mythological imagery to give it form. In itself it offers no words or images, for it is a vision seen as 'in a glass darkly.' It is merely a deep presentiment that strives to find expression. . . . Since the particular expression can never exhaust the possibilities of the vision, but falls far short of it in richness of content, the poet must have at his disposal a huge store of materials if he is to communicate even a few of his intimations. What is more, he must resort to an imagery that is difficult to handle and full of contradictions in order to express the weird paradoxicality of his vision."

It is significant for moderns that this sharp discernment can be brought to the support of our thesis from perhaps the most eminent exponent of the great new science known as psychoanalysis.

The association of mythology, symbolism and natural imagery with poetry has long been an integral item of studied culture. It is inexorably based on that oft-stated but never completely realized parallelism between the logoic structure of intellect and that of the world, the order and harmony of the inner conscious process being matched by that of the outer material universe. In short, man's and God's thinking can and should correspond, and will do so when man's thought arrives at rational perfection. God's thought being manifested in the formations of the living outer world, man's ratiocinative processes must reflect the logicality of natural events in the objective sequence. The interrelationship of details in the outer will be matched by the similar unimpeachable concatenation in the intellect. Hence when in his stage of inadequacy man's logical effort fails to bring him to complete clarity of insight, he may look out to the phenomena deploying their meaning everywhere in the natural world and haply light upon some link of connection that will supply a missing element in the thought problem. If nature is a living key to all truth, man must pick up that key which he has disdained since ancient days.

All this was understood by Aristotle, so that he could affirm that poetry is ever truer than history. For it presents, in its imagery and natural analogies, paradigms of eternal truth, whereas history is a hodge-podge of approximations of struggling but still imperfect beings, trying to harmonize their lives and deeds with aims that seldom envisage these paradigms with any true discernment whatever.

The Harvard Santayana, in a work on *Plato and the Spiritual Life,* has a most penetrating analysis of the psychological basis and necessity for esotericism in religious writing. After making the clarifying observation that the distinctive object of spirit "is not pure Being in its infinity, but finite being in its purity,"—an extremely pointed and important delineation—he goes on to say that the elevations of consciousness attained in high moments of vivid clairvoyance, when the spirit has seemed to be united and identical with the Supreme Being, can never be adequately reported across the bridge from those high mounts to the cognitive mind. "Words cannot render what has been seen, nor would it be lawful, perhaps, to reveal it." This is entirely in the same sense as that in which Paul in *II Corinthians* tells of the man he knew who was caught up into the third heaven "and there did witness such marvelous things that it is not lawful that a man should speak of them." And the Church that Paul founded has fought the claims of esotericism down the ages!

Santayana's fuller elucidation of this experience must not be omitted (*Ibid.,* p. 76):

"The saint pulls his ladder up with him into his private heaven; and the community of the faithful, on whose sturdy dogmatic shoulders he has climbed, must not be deprived of the means of following his example. Hence any dissolving culmination of the religious life must be kept a secret, a mystery to be divulged only to the few whom the knowledge of it can no longer scandalize or discourage. Besides this prudence and this consideration for the weaker brethren there is a decisive reason for silence: the revelation has been essentially a revelation of the illusion inherent in all language, in all experience, in all existence. It can not be communicated save by being repeated. . . . Silence is therefore imperative, if the mystic has any conscience."

This is to affirm again that when the whole gods of enraptured mystic perception of divine states come, the half gods of stodgy traditional formal dogmatisms go, and that, ventures Santayana, would not be good for the cause of established religion. It is likely that Paul's regarding it unlawful to spill out the wine of spiritual intoxication was due to his deep sense of its sheer incommunicability to any one not having experienced the like. Scores of hints in his *Epistles* intimate his recognition of the ineluctable necessity for esotericism. He speaks several times of the mystery of knowledge and of divine revelations in the secret place of inner illumination, as if he had been conversant with such elevations more than once. Plotinus' comment on his having been four times lifted beyond the boundaries of our common consciousness into a world of enchantment amid spiritual and cosmic realities is well known. The testimony of saints, mystics and contemplatives is voluminous. Even ordinary life testifies to sudden upliftings in which the veil is rent and consciousness rides the steeds of a higher dimensional freedom into realms of gloriously expanded being, where magic is the natural.

Whenever at any rate the seer, descending from the mount of vision with the glory of his ecstatic uplift still glowing on his features, attempts to communicate his experience to another on the common level, his only chance at possible success lies in his resort to allegory and symbol. We have been accustomed to the assertion of this from the side of philosophy, religion and poetry. How immensely significant it is, then, to hear it in our modern day also from the side of physical science! Sir James Jeans, in his work *The World Around Us* (p. 318), comes forward with this amazing declaration:

"When we try to discuss the ultimate structure of the atom we are driven to speak in terms of similes, metaphors and parables."

This comes near to saying that even the concrete world, in its ultimate impingement on consciousness, dissolves into mystical states and modes of being, and any communicable method of portrayal of it must resort to the basic intimations that spring spontaneously to man from his contacts with the living world.

Higgins (*The Anacalypsis,* p. 480) adds heavy weight to the motives for esoteric secrecy when he says that the custodians of mystery teaching desired to retain in their own hands the keys of knowledge. He avers that they instituted a solemn fast to commemorate the day on which they believed the LXX translation was finished, this as a penance for their great national sin in having permitted it to be translated by Ptolemy and therefore made public. Higgins says that "this is the last proof which we possess, and a decisive proof it is, of sacred writings concealed, and also of their forced exposure."

This final statement is indeed "proof" of the main thesis here advanced. If the full truth could be known, it is next to a certainty that the open publication of the sacred books of the ancient sages and semi-divine hierophants of a genuinely esoteric secret wisdom, was never contemplated by the creators of the arcane myths and allegories. The *Holy Scriptures were not originally designed to be given out to the world*. This came rather by mischance. Their ultimate publication is to be attributed to developments that came through influences beyond their control; it escaped their jealous guardianship. This work ventures to discuss whether from this fortuitous circumstance more evil has not come than good.

It has been declared on esoteric authority emanating allegedly from the spiritual hierarchy of the world, that the near-divine custodians of the true teaching never permitted any but the most superficial of the esoteric doctrines to see actual print, the method of instruction and transmission of the inner and higher wisdom being the oral one.

Yet it seems clearly apparent that there is enough, even though indirect, mystic intimation, allegorical disguise and mythic form in those great documents of Greece, Egypt, Chaldea and India to support the belief that the books of the great wisdom were at last given to the outer world. It is the contention of this dissertation that it was the wider dissemination of the arcane literature that gave form and character to the Christian movement.

CHAPTER V

WISDOM IN A MYSTERY

The next task is to establish the fact that the allegorical method was in practically universal vogue throughout the ancient days and that the first and most rational thinkers in the Christian movement were entirely committed to the representation and interpretation of spiritual and Scriptural truth through the medium of allegory. The ancient sages composed the Scriptures as allegories; and the highest Christian intelligence accepted and expounded them as such. Gibbon asserts that both Origen and Augustine were among the allegorists. He could have added Pantaenus and Clement, indeed the whole Alexandrian school.

Guignebert's work of splendid scholarship, *Christianity Past and Present,* will yield much material in later sections. On p. 148 he states that entrance into the early Church was complicated through the tendency to elaborate the ritual which develops as soon as a religion begins to be systematically propagated by a true clerical class. "We must take into account," he says, "the fear of the unsound brother *who might misuse the Mystery* if he were admitted to it without due formalities. Precautions are accordingly taken to avoid this profanation."

But after showing that the Mystery registered so much importance, he commits the inconsistency of saying that the arcanum of the Mysteries amounted to little or nothing. Why then should even the ignorant Christians have taken so much precaution to avoid its profanation? But it is true enough that the Mystery importance dwindled along with its meaning as the wave of ignorance flooded rapidly over the early movement.

From the *Orpheus* of G. R. S. Mead we draw a statement that fixes the fact of the wide prevalence of the esoteric method in religion, with its adjuncts of training in the interpretation of the myths, symbols and allegories (p. 24):

"The perfection of the highest virtue and the opening of the real spiritual senses constituted the highest degree of the Mysteries; another and most important part of the discipline was the training in the interpretation of myth, symbol and allegory, the letters of the mystical language in which the secrets of nature and the soul were written, so plainly for the initiated, so obscurely for the general; without these instructions the mythical recitals and legends were unintelligible."

We have quoted Sir Gilbert Murray as saying that Greek religion was bound in with "a romantic, trivial and yet very edifying mythology." No one can miss the fact that Greek religion was deeply grounded in mythology. But once more must be registered the pitiable confession of modern savants that the Greek myths have been too much for them. Be it said with the utmost positiveness that those marvelous myths are the products, not of infantile groping, but of consummate dramatic genius, and the mind that holds them to be trivial has simply never been awakened to the hidden purport of these constructions, to see the wonderworld of glowing beauty therein. This negative note from Murray is all the more difficult to comprehend because in another passage he speaks of "the widespread and almost incredible error of treating Homer as primitive." Why this gap in rating between the myths and Homer? The *Iliad* and the *Odyssey* can fairly be claimed to belong to the myths, or to the mythic period and instinct. And surely he did not rate these greatest of epics as trivial.

What Higgins has found out about the Homeric poems is worth noting (*The Anacalypsis*, p. 542):

"The poems of Homer I consider to have been originally sacred Asiatic songs or poems, adopted by the Greeks, and that for perhaps many generations they were unwritten [A school history says that they were held in the memory of the Greeks for five hundred years before being written down.]; and as they related to the cyclic mythos, they would in the principal part suit every cycle. . . . They were like the plays of Aeschylus, each an epic, but all combining to form the history of the cycles to those who were initiated. . . ."

Returning to Macchioro's fine work *From Orpheus to Paul*, there is found an assertion of the plain fact which must be hammered home to the intelligence of modern scoffers at the status and influence of the ancient Mysteries. It shows that these brotherhoods and the disciplines they enforced stood at the peak of culture in the ancient world. To have reached the highest degrees was the certification of the topmost refinement and spiritual unfoldment. Says he (p. 203):

"Nothing was more usual or honorable for a man of the cultured class in Hellenic times than to become acquainted with the Mysteries. In the Hellenistic Age religion as well as literature showed the deep influence of the Mysteries."

And he shows how this stream of refinement would have touched the mind of St. Paul:

"Nothing is more reasonable than to think that a cultured man like Paul, born in a great center of culture, gifted with a peculiar intellectual grasp and a vivid curiosity about religious experience, should feel attracted to Orphism."

It will be refreshing, as a new baptism in the waters of truth long neglected, ignored, repressed, for the world of modern Christianism to face the fine truth about these Mysteries, penned, not by a hostile mind, but by one of the most highly accredited of Christian historians, the English scholar, von Mosheim. In his great two-volume work on the *History of the Christian Religion* covering the first three and a quarter centuries, he writes of the Pagan Mysteries (Vol. I, p. 18):

"None was admitted to behold or partake in the celebration of these Mysteries but those who had approved themselves worthy of such distinction by their fidelity and perseverance in the practice of a long and severe course of initiatory forms. The votaries were enjoined, under the peril of immediate death, to observe the most profound secrecy as to everything that passed: and this sufficiently accounts for the difficulty that we find in obtaining any information respecting the nature of those recluse practices and for the discordant and contradictory opinions concerning them that are to be met with in the writings of various authors, ancient as well as modern."

Here is the rebuke to many a quibbling snarl of Christian scholarship at the Pagan Mysteries. He continues by assuming, in the dearth of positive record, that perhaps "in these brotherhoods some things were done in the highest degree repugnant to virtue, modesty and every fine feeling"; but

"it is probable that in those of a more refined cast, some advance was made in *bringing religion back to the test of reason,* by inquiring into and exposing the origin and absurdity of the popular superstitions and worship. There might, therefore, be some foundation for the promise usually held forth to those who were about to be initiated, that they would be put in possession of the means of rendering this life happy, and also for the expectation opened to them of entering upon an improved state of existence hereafter. However this might be, it is certain that the highest veneration was entertained by the people of every country for what was termed the Mysteries; and the Christians, perceiving this, were induced to make their religion conform in many respects to this part of the heathen model, hoping that it might thereby the more readily obtain a favorable reception with those whom it was their object and their hope to convert."

These lines have stood in print in a highly respected and accredited work by a Christian protagonist for a century or more of the modern age, but in open defiance of their forthright and truthful assertion as to the high character and reputable status of the ancient Mystery Brotherhoods, Christian writers have gone on in a dismal drone of reprobation and denunciation of these institutions in book after book. It is all too evidently but part and parcel of that inveterate disposition to besmirch with one taint or another everything Pagan or pre-Christian, a disposition which, the more it is encountered in reading Christian literature, the more clearly it is seen in its true light as at base a sheer disease of the Christian mind. When the spokesman for a religion that by its own claim inculcates love and charity, plus forbearance of one's enemies, must endlessly vent the spleen of sheer jealousy over every laudable thing connected with a rival, till even a rival's clear virtues must be made to appear as sins, one has before the eye the certain marks of what is named bigotry and pusillanimity.

It is doubtful if even the cautiously laudatory statement of von Mosheim is quite true and just in every particular. He, too, must not lose the chance to throw in, almost as an "aside," his animadversion that charges the Mystery cults with gross immorality. This is not the time or place to take up the controversy over the comparative immoral character of Pagan versus Christian rites and conduct. But it is little short of certain that, as in the case of the rituals in Buddhistic and Hindu ceremonies which employed phallic emblems and sex symbolism with high and pure mystical significance, certain items and appurtenances of the Mystery ritualism have been grossly misconceived and misconstrued. The actions of unworthy participants can debase the purest ceremonial. No brief need be held for the stainless "purity" of the Mystery cults. With a fair court to hear all the evidence—a privilege which has hardly ever been accorded the case—it is beyond doubt that the Mysteries of the Pagan religion would not suffer by comparison with the moral tone of Christian behavior both in the early days and since. Indeed a decision of Omniscient Judgment would almost certainly give the Mysteries a whit the better in the verdict. This statement must not be taken as a snap-throw of biased conjecture; it is only too well grounded on a mass of data of Christian history lying close at hand, which there is no room to present here.

Since, then, the Mysteries propagated the science of spiritual development and incorporated all the motions of the mystical experience of the soul's attunement to divine nature in myths, allegories, symbols and dramatic representations, the Mysteries can be considered to have been the originating source and propagators of the mythical science. It is clearly evident, as has been seen by a few of the more astute of the Christian scholars, that the sacred writings, done in myth and allegory, were just the ultimate transcription of the oral ritual forms and locutions from memory to paper. This at once accounts for the mythical and allegorical character of all this ancient literature; and it thus solves a problem which has taxed the brains of generations of scholars to the breaking point. More than a few writers have seen and stated that the body of the myths was a literary deposit from the rituals of the ancient festival celebrations. The myths came to be produced and finally precipitated into writing as a kind of gloss on the dramatizations in the mystic rites. Space forbids our citing the authorities that would corroborate this pronouncement.

Thus it happened that the early literary productions of nearly all races fall into the mythical form, as Higgins has so strongly asserted. Therefore it is not surprising to hear another writer on ancient things, Zenaide A. Ragozin, in his *The Story of Chaldea* (299) say:

"A race that has no national epos is one devoid of great memories, incapable of high culture and political development; and no such has taken a place among the leading races of the world. All those that have occupied such a place at any time of the world's history have had their Mythic and Heroic Ages, brimful of wonders and fanciful creations."

And he supplements this with the fine observation that (p. 297)

"Thus in the tradition of every ancient nation there is a vast and misty tract of time . . . between the unpierceable gloom of an eternal past and the broad daylight of remembered, recorded history. There all is shadowy, gigantic, superhuman. There gods move down yet visible, shrouded in a golden cloud of mystery and awe; there by their side loom other shapes as dim, but more familiar, human yet more than human—the Heroes, Fathers of Races, founders of nations, the companions, the beloved of gods and goddesses, nay, their own children, mortals themselves, yet doing deeds of daring and might such as only the immortals could inspire and favor, the connecting link between these and ordinary humanity—as that gloaming, uncertain, shifting but not altogether unreal streak of time is the borderland between Heaven and Earth; the very hotbed of myth, fiction and romance."

This marginal area between heaven and earth for the mortal race is comparable to the childhood period of humanity, before methodical plodding written record of happenings is kept, and when of course the imagination glows with the idealistic coloring which suffuses the consciousness in childhood. But that which the period has handed on as written record of its life need not be "a vast and misty tract of time" to intelligent interpretation of its myths and is so only because of the arrant stolidity of the modern mind, which closes itself off from all possible chance to read the myths aright.

Lundy, in his *Monumental Christianity* (p. 178) comes to grips with this question of the status and meaning of the myths in very cogent manner:

"If the mythos has no spiritual meaning, then all religion becomes mere idolatry, or the worship of material things. But we have seen symbols of Oriental Pagan religions which indicate a supreme Power and Intelligence above matter; and also how early Christianity abhorred idolatry. Apollo, as a mythical type and the Good Shepherd as a reality, then, must mean something more than mere material light and guidance."

If Higgins is correct in saying that mythology has corrupted all history, it will be necessary to give more heed to the statement made by Allan Upward in his book *Divine Mystery* (p. 215), where he says:

"On the surface the Israelite legend is an attempt to find in the national history an illustration of Zoroastrian theology.'"

This broad statement would demand a small voiume to substantiate it in its essential truth. But it is an item of the lost understanding attested by a mountain of data from many sources. Not only did the Hebrew people attempt to structuralize their past history to fit the model dramatizations of the theological systemology, but many another nation did the same thing. No work of ancient study so clearly and convincingly sets forth this operation as *The Anacalypsis* of Godfrey Higgins, cited herein. To this end the formulators of the religion of every nation worked to redact their objective history and their national geography into the form and nomenclature of the models provided by the mythos, and, most strangely of all, the astrological mythos. Place names and historical events were contorted into the nomenology and type-graphs of spiritual experience in the mythos, first placed on the constellations of the heavens and later transferred to earth and interwoven into the geography and history of one nation after another. *The Anacalypsis* presents over eight hundred pages in substantiation of this general assertion.

Gerald Massey indeed states that "the chart of Judea looks like a copy of the scenery in Amenta, the Egyptian 'underworld' or place of dead souls, actually our earth itself as it would be if the land had been originally mapped out by the immigrants from Egypt. Amenta and the Aarru-Paradise, with its heaven on the summit of the mount, have been repeated at innumerable sacred places in the world." Massey is emphatic in claiming the astrological origin of indeed all religion. Says he (*The Logia of the Lord*, p. 4):

"Astrologically, every religious dogma the world over may be traced to and located in the zodiacal signs of the Sun."

And trenchantly he carries this to the Gospels, as to which he says:

"The truth is, that the earliest Gospels are farthest removed from supposed human history. That came last, and only when the spiritual Christ of the Gnosis had been rendered concrete in the density of Christian ignorance!"

That the sacred Scriptures of the ancient day were in that time taken allegorically and not historically is well attested by one fact alone of nearly decisive weight. In speaking of the Essenes and the Pagan Sibyls, Higgins (*Anac.*, 576) says:

"Almost every particular in the life of Christ as detailed in the Gospels is to be found in the Sibyls, so that it can scarcely be doubted that the Sibyls were copied from the Gospel history, or the Gospel history from them. It is also very certain that there was an Erythraean Sibyl before the time of Christ."

This intimates that the copying must have been done when the Gospels were being put in written form. The Sibyls were undoubtedly first; previous does not copy later.

The *Encyclopædia Britannica* (Article "Jews") says that "the varied traditions up to this stage cannot be regarded as objective history." Yet it goes on to say that these narrations cannot be treated from any modern standpoint as fiction. If a thing is neither history nor fiction, what, one must ask, can it be? To this pertinent query only esotericism holds the answer. Nowhere else can it be found. The only literary production that is neither history nor fiction is allegory, myth. It is truth that is not, or not yet, historicized. It is truth in the ideal, the abstract, the eternal possibility of actualization.

Pliny, referring to the Essenes, remarks:

"The Essenes had already existed several thousand years and one of the best ascertained facts concerning this sect is that they possessed secret holy writings of their own, which they guarded with special care."

Again the *Encyclopædia Britannica,* in its article "Midrash," says that

"the tendency to reshape history for the edification of later generations was no novelty when *Chronicles* was written (about the fourth century B.C.). Pragmatic historiography is exemplified in the earliest continuous sources."

Midrash was just this tendency to see romantic sense in the narratives in the old written tradition, the article emphasizes.

"The rigid line between fact and fiction in religious literature which readers often wish to draw, cannot be consistently justified, and in studying old Oriental religious narratives, it is necessary to realize that the teaching was regarded as more essential than the method of presenting it. 'Midrash,' which may be called useless for historical investigation, may be appreciated for the light it throws upon forms of thought. Historical criticism does not touch the reality of the ideas, and since they may be as worthy of study as the apparent facts they clothe, they thus indirectly contribute to history. In any case, while the true historical kernel of the Midrashic narrative will always be a matter of dispute, the teaching to which it is applied stands on an independent footing, as also does the application of that teaching to other ages."

This discussion in the *Encyclopædia* is a truth that needs constant re-emphasis among moderns. It can not be taken otherwise than that the article is trying with a bit of circumlocution to say that the Midrashic literature of the Jews is spiritual allegory masked in the guise of Hebrew history. Useless for historical investigation—and this should be driven home to all students—it still conveys a profound message that concerns and illumines all history. But it is silly to say that the teaching was regarded as more essential than the method of presenting it. Where, except perhaps in poetry, is this not the case? It makes a flourish over a point where no point is in question. Yet the observations made are of great moment, because their important findings have been made crucially significant by their neglect and flouting.

Among those who have joined in the chorus of flouting the allegorical method is a figure no less eminent than Canon Farrar, who in his *Lives of the Fathers* (p. 384) says:

"But when we clearly scan the somewhat vague and mysterious references of Clement, his 'tradition' seems to be ultimately nothing more than the application to Scripture of that allegorical method which he received from Pantaenus, as Pantaenus had probably learned it from the writings of Philo, and as Philo and his teachers had borrowed it from the Stoic method of interpreting Homer. So far as we may judge from Clement himself, the method was absolutely valueless. It did not even furnish any criterion by which he could draw a deep line of distinction between the Scriptures and Apocryphal writings; and when he came to apply it practically, the results to which it led him were untenable and even absurd. Clement's Gnostic was supposed to be able to interpret Scripture in a higher and more 'spiritual' way than the ordinary believer. The Scriptures were the common possession of all Christians, but the *illuminati* of orthodox Gnosticism were supposed to read in them meanings undiscernible to the vulgar eye. In point of fact the allegorical evolution of so-called 'spiritual' interpretation was so far from being a valuable method, that it became the favorite camping ground of all heretics, and the least assailable bulwark of their manifold aberrations."

This lengthy passage is introduced because it so frankly presents the element to be dealt with in this section and because it furnishes perhaps the most glaring example of that horrific stupidity that caused generation after generation of Christian scholarship to gaze upon the body of ancient allegorical depiction of truth and never once register a single ray of comprehension of what mighty value lay *en masse* before them. Every single assertion of Farrar's misses the point by miles and becomes a downright untruth. The result of the handling of allegory by Clement and even the more learned Origen were admittedly not what they might have been in more competent hands. Nevertheless the allegories of the Bible (and allegories they are, from Adam and the tree and serpent to Jonah and the big fish) were only "untenable and absurd" because even Clement lacked the technical skill properly to bring out the abstruse cryptic sense. The "interpretation" of allegory by rash champions and expositors has often been little short of horrendous in its miscarriage of true sense. More must be said about this presently.

To show that in Christian understanding of the origins of their own religion there is by no means certified knowledge of vital points, it will be well to follow Farrar's arraignment of Clement's allegorism with another eminent Christian historian's view of the more famous and more widely discussed allegories of Clement's very distinguished pupil and successor, the great and learned Origen. "Origen's allegories" have ever been a thorn in the flesh of orthodox exegesis and theological history, for his deep learning commands the respect, while it at the same time baffles the exegetical ingenuity of all the theologians.

The situation has left them non-plussed and defeated. Reluctance to condemn perhaps the greatest originator of Biblical analysis restrains them from too severe opprobrium on his work. So the tack is always to praise cautiously and with reservation, or to censure mildly and with commendatory side remarks—to straddle the issue and save Christian "face." But on the whole, while it still falls far short of seeing and registering the *truth* of the matter, von Mosheim's treatise on Origen's allegories is far fairer than most others. In his great *history* he writes (Vol. II, p. 167):

"Certainly he would have had no enemies if he had merely affirmed what no one then called in question, that in addition to the sense which the words of Scripture convey, another sense latent in the things described is to be diligently sought for. This will be manifest if we consider who were the men that inveighed so bitterly against Origen's allegories after he was dead: I refer to Eustatius, Epiphanius, Jerome, Augustine and many others. All these were themselves allegorists, if I may use that term; and would undoubtedly have condemned any man as a great errorist who would have dared to impugn the arcane sense of Scripture, or to censure the deriving both doctrines and precepts and the knowledge of future events, from the narratives and laws contained in the Bible. There must therefore have been something new and unusual in Origen's exegetics, which appeared to them pernicious and very dangerous. Otherwise they would have regarded his system of interpretation as beautiful and perfectly correct."

It is thrilling to have the historian thus set the stage for the revelation of this extra something that Origen insisted on in Bible reading, but which the orthodox Fathers could, or dared, not accept. And well can we understand now why they dared not go along with their too deeply and occultly discerning fellow-exegetist! To accept and endorse his mode of interpreting Holy Writ would have written the death warrant of their world-conquering Christianity! For his method would have read out all the "history" in the Scriptures and read in nothing but the "spiritual" sense. So, says Mosheim (Vol. II, p. 168):

"The first and chief was that he pronounced a great part of the sacred books to be void of meaning if taken literally, and that only the *things* indicated by the words were the signs and emblems of higher objects . . . he turned much of the sacred history into moral fables, and no small part of the divine precepts into mere allegories."

What a picture this presents! Here was *the most intelligent* of all those "Fathers" of the Christian faith standing for what he knew to be the true character and high spiritual purport of the arcane Scriptures that his Church had taken up from ancient Pagan sources and had adopted and put forth as the literary vehicles of their sacred tenets. From his teaching at the hands of Clement, who received it from Pantaenus and he, in common with all the Alexandrian school, from the chief ancient purveyor of it all, Philo Judaeus, he was fully conversant with the secret tradition of literary esotericism that pervaded all the ancient world, in the light of which the Scriptures were to be translated *never* according to the letter of the words, but in a mystical spiritual relevance, by which a far profounder and entirely sublime anthropologico-cosmic meaning could be caught by a mind instructed in the proper manner of detecting such underlying significations. Origen, let it be repeated, well and surely knew this. And, in the spirit of one truly Christian, that is, seeking to develop all aspects of the science of the cultivation of the Christ-in-man, he aimed to strengthen the growing movement with which he had allied himself with the true and only profitable, indeed only possible, distinctive method of deriving spiritual light and sustenance from the selected Scriptures of his Church.

And not only did Origen know this semi-secret methodology in Biblical science, but there is no doubt that the other intelligent leaders of the movement were as well acquainted with it as he. There are many proofs of this, the foremost being that most of his associates followed him, including Ambrose and even Jerome, until the latter was, so to say, jerked up short in his tendency to do so by the embittered outcries of the ignorant majority leadership who had by now been completely dominated by the wholly literal and historical thesis of interpretation. Naturally, not too many followed Origen, at any rate not enough to give his method any general acceptance. The esoteric method tends ever to be a prized possession of a limited few. But all those in the tradition of esotericism understood and accredited Origen's style of approach to Bible meaning.

It was a, nay *the,* critical epoch for Christianity. It stood at the cross roads. If it could have risen to the high point of appreciation and acceptance of "Origen's allegories," the fate of Christendom, of the world, would have been determined for all time to work out to a more elevated culture than the one historically extant. For the decision would have enabled it to meet every contingency of future history with a vastly greater power of discriminating intelligence than it ever to this day has commanded in the ranks of either its laity or its clerical hierarchy. But alas, the acumen needed to see the sound bases and the actual rightness of Origen's position had already been extinguished; and he was left as the last true Christian exegetist, bleating plaintively in the wilderness of plebeian ignorance, hoping that his voice might still be heard by enough to hold the inner citadel of a spiritual understanding of the sacred books of soul science. But again alas, he was doomed to disappointment; and with the suppression of his voice and his influence, the last hope of saving true Christianity from a swift and final descent into the mires and quicksands of an impossible and ruinous literalism and historization of its holy Scriptures was swept away. Origen went down into repudiation and rejection among his own brethren, so that he was hardly dead until it was a foremost accusation brought against others of the Fathers, such as Jerome, that they had let Origen's teachings, and predominantly his "allegories," influence their beliefs and teachings. And within three hundred years of his death the Second Council of Constantinople anathematized him and threatened with a curse and excommunication any one found owning or reading his writings. His great work of comparative texts, the *Hexapla,* was destroyed. Origen held out to the new movement the chance to redeem itself from its early tendency to reject the esoteric doctrine in favor of bare historical literalism. But once more alas, the insight to descry the true advantage and justness of this course had been blinded by pietistic zeal and sheer ignorance, and the chance to save Christianity for truth and sanity was gone for at least sixteen hundred years.

Paul's message and contribution tended to restore the religion to true position; and a little later Dionysus the Areopagite strove to re-introduce the deeper spiritual modes of apprehension. And several centuries later another outstanding figure arose in a bleak epoch of Christian history to redeem the movement from its smothering by literalism, in the person of Scotus Erigena. Both wished to irradiate Christianity with the restored light of Platonic philosophy. In their cases and some others the light of true meaning of theology flared out in a limited circle of esoteric cultists, but of course never reached the masses with any effective impact. A blanket of intellectual stolidity settled down over the world of Christendom with the defeat of Origen and there it has lain ever since. Not only has the priesthood done nothing to lift it, but indeed it has designedly cultivated and perpetuated it. And we have the odd but tragic spectacle of Origen's own Church, in the person of such a learned scholar as von Mosheim, not to say many others, holding up to ridicule the authoritative claim of a man like Origen that their Scriptures held a higher and more mystical meaning than would be apparent to the mind of a lout or a simpleton.

Origen was striving to uphold the method of interpretation by which they could glorify their own Scriptures with a meaning far more edifying than the simple literal narrative. Christianity stood at the parting roads of its destiny, the one with the signboard marked "To Literal Degradation," "To Darkness," "To Bigotry," "To Persecution" and "To Murder"; the other "To Spiritual Insight," "To Refined Culture," "To Humanitarianism" and "To Intelligent Understanding"; and it chose fatally the one to the left. Christianity rejected the true spiritual meaning of the Scriptures, even when offered to it by its most learned Father. But man singly or collectively must pay for his choices ignorantly or intelligently made. And for sixteen hundred years this religion has been meeting the evil consequences of that choice against Origen. A religion which has never ceased to claim that it is the highest spiritual system in world history definitely rejected the higher spiritual in favor of a ludicrous and debasing literal interpretation of ancient books of supernal wisdom. And five-sixths of all its theological effort ever since has as a consequence had to be devoted to the impossible hopeless task of reconciling the crudities and inconsistencies of a literal and historical rendering of books that were clearly only allegorical, with the demands of fact, of logic and of common sense.

This is the appropriate place at which to register a vigorous protest against the use by Christian writers of one single little word which they have so sedulously let creep into their denunciations of the allegorical method. Times without number one finds them declaring the method ineligible and a failure for the reason that it reduced the text to "mere" allegory. Or they aver that it left the Bible "nothing but" allegory, or "only" allegory. To one who has enlightened his mind with the understanding of the full dynamic power of allegory and the knowledge of its absolutely indispensable utility in bringing out the one true and exalted meaning of the Scriptures, to the displacement of the tawdry outcome of the literal-historical rendering, the word "mere" as a fit adjectival companion of "allegory" becomes the spur to a quite justifiable exasperation. Not only does it reflect all too clearly the crass ignorance that has dealt so unjustly with the most elevated mode of human edification, flouting the everlasting appeal of poetry and symbolism, but it testifies also in a most repugnant way to the cheap trickery of a false insinuation to damn a noble thing with a slimy slur. It deserves the sharpest reprobation.

For it casts on allegory a totally untrue and unmerited slander. One has no more right to speak of allegory as "mere" allegory than to speak of poetry as "mere" poetry, or beauty as "mere" beauty or a picture as a "mere" picture. After all a thing is entitled to the right to be called whatever it is without slur or stigma. Either a thing is what it is or it is something else. The writers' resort to calling the esoteric Bible meaning "mere" allegory is their disingenuous way of advertising their contention that it is not allegory at all, but real history. Many, with Origen, have claimed with strong foundation that it is not history at all, but allegory. So the "mere" must go in to discredit the claim. It has no right there whatever. Either the Bible is allegory or it is not. And if, as is indeed the case, it is allegory, or was originally so, then allegory it is and not "mere" allegory. To besmirch allegory with the "only" or the "mere" is to discredit a noble thing, the transcendently utilitarian thing allegory truly is. Had real knowledge of the grandeur of allegory continued in the Christian Church, its spokesmen could have kept saying for centuries that the Bible is a work of beauteous and splendid allegory, and thus saved themselves the chagrin and opprobrium that must now descend upon them when it is recognized at last that those Scriptures, now so falsely misread as factual history, are in solid truth the sublimest of allegories and a hundredfold more illuminating as such.

The way is cleared, then, to meet and refute another claim of the Church apologists that has been put forward again and again to excuse their failure to discern the true serviceableness of Origen's allegories. One writer after another has vented the allegation that Origen's method, while perhaps attaining some measure of success in the most spiritual illumination of Bible texts, in the main ran out in an extravaganza of untenable, strained, unnatural and often clearly ridiculous meanings. To these critics it seemed no doubt honestly conclusive that the allegorical method swept away all solid substance and reality from the text and left only a thin gossamer tissue of metaphor and mystic notions, quite too tenuous to hold up the sword of a conquering world faith. It swept away, too, the one central keystone of the whole Christian edifice, the historical reality of Jesus, although Origen does not seem to have carried his thesis so far as to reject, except possibly by implacable logical inference, the actual existence of Jesus, or to reduce him, as Smith, Drews, Robertson, Dupuis and the Tübingen school in Germany undertook to do, to the status of a mythical personification.

When Origen had done his best to lift the Scriptures into the lofty atmosphere of a spiritual sense, that atmosphere proved to the critics and to the laity then and since to be of too rare and thin a substance to support the strength of robust piety and whole-hearted devotion. It seemed to release the meaning, not on the solid ground of earthly reality, but in the misty clouds and shimmering vapors of "mere" senti-mentality and dreamy unreality. It dissolved the Christian rock of Holy Writ into the atomic dust of mere metaphor. In revulsion from the unsubstantial and hollow Pagan mythicism and the shadowy sense of symbols, the new Christian faith, that was to carry the hopes and pietistic yearnings of the lowly masses, was destined by the necessities of the case to throw out in grand impatience these glittering append-ages that culture professed to toy with, and demand the stanch real-ism of a historical factuality to stand upon and abide by. And so it was—indeed.

Hence the time is ripe to utter the words that will put in its true light for the first time the reason why, even when advocated, sup-ported and with his best endeavor utilized by the most learned of the Church Fathers, Origen, the true key to the Scriptures totally failed to win recognition and adoption by the Christian movement. Others have essayed to render the Scriptures according to the allegorical method and with the keys it provides. Let it be acknowledged here frankly that the method has never, so far as the present writer is aware, achieved a measure of success that at all proved its merit or its possibilities. It is here and now asserted that this failure does not prove the inadequacy or the potentiality of the method, but does prove the incompetence of those endeavoring to employ it! This explanation has never been offered before, and the whole Christian academic world will shout to controvert it. Nevertheless the assertion now has solid grounds of evidence to stand upon that it lacked in all the centuries until the present.

It has to be admitted, also, in the light of a far more perfect insight into the subtleties and profound intimations of the marvelous ancient language of symbolism, that Origen, while sufficiently astute in catch-ing some portion of the true spiritual sense of the old tomes of wis-dom, still was far from qualifying as an adept and sure interpreter in this field. It is clear enough that if the redactor is not equipped with a practically perfect knowledge of this great symbolic and ana-logical science, his effort is bound to run out in gross misreading amid some partially true rendition. This, it is now seen, is the case with

Clement and Origen. Much chaff remained clinging to the golden wheat of their sifting. He did not succeed by more than a meager percentage. He was on the right track, but stumbled along and did not ever reach the final goal of full esoteric meaning. It is true, as the orthodox charge, that if the claims of the allegorical method rest on Origen's real accomplishment in this province—or that of many others since—the method would lack vindication. But present studentship, building upon the great results of the discovery of the Rosetta Stone in 1796, the consequent translation of the religious literature of old Egypt, the epochal analyses of this revealing material by Massey and Higgins, and the revival of the genuine theosophic philosophies of the Orphic and Hermetic, the Pythagorean, Platonic and Neoplatonic systems of arcane wisdom, promises soon the cultivation of an interpretative competence that will redeem the holy Scriptures from their absurd sense as objective histories to the full glory of their ineffable transcendence of meaning as spiritual allegories. With the perfection of this new-found but age-old science of symbolism, veritably a new era in religion is dawning for the world. The wisdom sorely needed to solve distressing world problems awaits the consummation of adeptship in this mightiest of sciences.

The inveterate recalcitrancy of the orthodox scholastic mind to the obvious realities underlying and making necessary the allegorical method of interpretation is difficult to understand. Farrar in his *Lives of the Fathers* (Vol. II, 443) says that the key to Origen's allegorical method of interpretation was not the right one, and the text was entirely contorted from its original sense; but it took the world one thousand years more to learn the true principles of exegesis! Farrar has not deigned to tell us when these true principles of exegesis were regained, who recaptured them and how religious books have been reilluminated by the new flood of light that their application would release. In spite of the freedom to indulge in "higher criticism," the method of exegesis is still the literal-historical one, although one notices that orthodox interpreters of Scripture, at places where the context renders what Warschauer calls the "plain meaning" obviously absurd, are forced to declare it to be allegory. They have no hesitation in declaring the text material to be allegorical when it suits their purpose and no other resort is possible. This is manifestly disingenuous.

Likewise Fisher's reference to the Greek myths in another place is too intriguing to be passed by. He says it is natural to ask how the Greeks could ever have given credence to the myths, some of which attributed gross immorality to the gods, while continuing to venerate these unprincipled deities! How could men adore, as just and good, beings to whom they imputed deeds of treachery, lust and cruelty? He suggests that men could have supposed the gods to be privileged to indulge licentious whims in a realm of divine freedom above the laws that bound lowly humans. He is even generous enough to think that it was "not an impure fancy chiefly, but circumstances attending the growth of mythology in the form in which it was cast by the poets had led to the creation of these offensive stories." But we in turn find it natural to ask Fisher how *he* can now give credence to a fairly long list of equally offensive stories exhibiting treachery, lust and cruelty, not to say gross sexuality, printed in his own Biblical Old Testament. Is it too much to expect that men like Fisher can ever be brought to understand that no intelligent Greek ever "believed" those myths? They had sense enough to know that the myths were not made to be believed; belief was not asked. What *was* asked was understanding; grasp of a subtle recondite and splendid meaning obscurely hinted at in the form and structure of the fabrication. None but the grossly ignorant and stupid in Greece could ever have "believed" those myths; and it is not spleen but simple truth to assert now that only the ignorant and unimaginative really "believe" the narratives assembled in the Old Testament. But, tragically enough, there came a time when high intelligence in Greece failed and all but the few philosophers and initiates in the Mysteries did "believe" those stories. And it is the purpose of this book to show that this blight of intelligence swept on until it deadened the minds of Hebrews and Christians to the point where they came to "believe" the myths that composed their own Scriptures. And with that came the Dark Ages.

Referring to Apollinaris, Farrar states that "this teacher seems to have confirmed Jerome in the allegorical method of explaining Scripture."

In a work on *Philo* (p. 33) the author, Norman Bentwich, says that the Jews also studied philosophy and began to talk in its technical catchwords; then to reinterpret their Scriptures according to the ideas of philosophy. This will be done by any group that holds long enough to the pursuit of philosophy of the ancient world to begin to see that the true and correct, at any rate meaningful, interpretation of Scripture can be made with no other keys. Bentwich follows this on the next page with a fine analysis of the ancient situation that made esotericism an indispensable usage. Nowadays, he says, the Bible is the holy book of so much of the civilized world that it is somewhat difficult for us to form a proper conception of what it was to the civilized world before the Christian era. We have to imagine a state of culture in which it was only the book of books of one small nation, while to others it was at best a curious record of ancient times, just as the code of Hammurabi or the Egyptian Book of Life is to us. The Alexandrian Jews were the first to popularize its teachings, to bring Jewish religion into line with that of the Greek world. It was to this end that they founded a particular form of Midrash—the allegorical interpretation, which is largely a distinctive product of the Alexandrian Age. The Palestinian rabbis of the time were on the one hand developing by dialectic discussion the oral tradition into a vast system of religious ritual and legal jurisprudence; on the other, weaving around the law, by way of adornment to it, a variegated fabric of philosophy, fable, allegory and legends. Simultaneously the Alexandrian preachers—they were never quite the same as the rabbis—were emphasizing for the outer world as well as for their own people, the spiritual side of the religion, elaborating a theology that should satisfy the reason, and seeking to establish the harmony of Greek philosophy with Jewish monotheism and the Mosaic legislation. Allegorical interpretation is based upon the supposition or fiction that the author who is interpreted intended something "other" (*allo*) than what is expressed. It is the method used to read thought into a text which its words do not literally bear by attaching to each phrase some deeper, usually some philosophical meaning. It enables the interpreter to bring writings of antiquity into touch with the culture of his own or any age; the gates of allegory are never closed, and they open upon a path which stretches without a break through the centuries.

This picture drawn by Bentwich has the merit of being accurately delineated. Again and again in the course of history groups of students and thinkers, breaking through the prison bars of heavy orthodoxy to discover the delight of reveling in the intoxicating wisdom embodied in the arcane philosophy of the past, have formed centers to cultivate and republish the golden knowledge of old. The schools of Pythagoras and Plato were such centers. But the one that shone brightly for a long period was that which flourished at Alexandria. Here intelligence was keen enough and learning profound enough to hold the level of study and understanding at a high pitch. Here, then, was the birthplace of much of the arcane literature that strove to perpetuate and transmit the esoteric wisdom in its allegorical dress. Here were the great brotherhoods of mystic cultism, with their academies and libraries. Here the pursuit of a wisdom that knew no bounds of national character, but was truly catholic and ecumenical, served as a bond to unite Jew and Greek, Arabian and Chaldean in the fraternity of a truly unifying depth of understanding. It was a center where in the interests of a knowledge that transcended all earthly demarcations all men of deep penetration could find a brotherhood of the spirit. But for the infusion into it of elements of philosophical lore emanating from Alexandria, the young Christian movement would not have survived the third century. Fisher lends corroboration to this general assertion when he says, "It was at Alexandria, under the peculiar influences that belonged to that great meeting-place of the nations, that Jewish thought underwent the most serious modifications." Of those modifications Christianity was shortly to receive the effect. Here Philo formulated his system, which in Fisher's words,

"was an amalgamation of Greek philosophy with the Old Testament theology, a combination of Plato and Moses, the tenets of which he considered to be in many points identical. The Greek Sages, he held, were borrowers from the Hebrew teaching. This interpretation he effected by the *flexible method of allegory,* his theory being that an occult sense, open and discerning, underlies the literal and historical meaning of the Scriptures and is to be accepted with it."

Pantaenus, Clement and Origen labored and perfected their product in this same Alexandria; is there need to ask why they strove to engraft onto the budding Christian movement the branch of learning that would insure to this movement at least the deeper and saner interpretation of the holy Scriptures?

Massey brings to our attention a point of keen discernment in this connection: he notes Origen's observation that if the Law of Moses had contained nothing which was to be understood as having a secret meaning, the prophet would not have said, "Open thou mine eyes and I will behold wondrous things out of thy laws" (*Psalms,* 119:18), whereas he knew that there was a veil of ignorance lying upon the heart of those who read and do not understand the figurative meanings. And he tells Celsus that the Egyptians veiled their knowledge of things in fable and allegory.

"The learned may penetrate into the significance of all Oriental mysteries, but the vulgar can only see the exterior symbol. It is allowed by all who have any knowledge of the Scriptures that everything is conveyed enigmatically."

In the *Pistis Sophia,* the Egypto-Gnostic Gospel, Jesus is represented as asking: "Do you seek after these mysteries? No mystery is more excellent than the seven vowels, for they bring your soul into the Light of Lights. Nothing, therefore, is more excellent than the mysteries which ye seek after, saving only the mystery of the seven vowels and their forty-nine Powers and the number thereof."

Perhaps this excerpt from a document that was wholly one of allegorical fabrication will well serve to illustrate the exasperation and impatience with which the orthodox exegetists react to the ancient method of esoteric writing. This would be a sample of what the theologians claim runs out into empty nonsense. What can the seven vowels and the number forty-nine hold in the way of meaning comparable to the concrete personality and the living love and the resurrection of Jesus Christ, they ask. Away with this abracadabra of letters and numbers and give us the solid verity of the Gospels! How can the harlequin prestidigitation of magic numbers save our immortal souls? Away with your Pagan mummery!

Aside from the facts that the number seven is the basic number of the constitution of the solar system and human life, as well as an absolutely essential key to the meaning of the Christian and other Scriptures, there is no answer to this impatient query of the theologians.

The most modern of eminent Egyptologists, the American William H. Breasted, in his *History of Egypt,* says of the Egyptian beliefs (p. 60) that they were

"fused into a complex of tangled myths . . . neither did the theologizing priesthoods ever reduce this mass of belief into a coherent system; it remained as accident and circumstances brought it together, a chaos of contradictions."

Breasted is probably right in saying that the priesthoods never reduced the mass of the myths in Egypt to a coherent systematism, although, had they done so, ancient secrecy would have kept the evidences of it largely out of sight. This is a point, incidentally, which modern investigators seem to leave entirely out of account in their search for archaic survivals.

Even today the status of the most enlightened study of ancient Egyptian religion and its lore is so muddled that it is well described by what Herder is driven in a kind of baffled irritation to write about it:

"If there is a province of literature which is a mire, and where a host of learned men were all deeply sunk into the mud, it is here."

The noted British Egyptologist, E. A. W. Budge, not to mention others, has given expression again and again to the same baffled irritation. The truth is that barring Massey, whom they have shelved into oblivion, modern scholars are miles away from discerning even the rudimentary bases of what those ancient seers and sages in Egypt were writing about. And this spells disaster for all human culture, since it is in that "mire and mud" of old Egypt's depth of wisdom that all the keys to the interpretation and understanding of the Christian religion and its still sealed Bible lie as yet undiscovered.

The Alexandrian school was, so to say, on the trail of this recondite treasure hidden under the sands of Egypt, and there must have been the general legend that ancient Egypt had been the fountainhead of a surpassing wisdom, though the stream might have disappeared again into the sands; for it seems that every noted thinker of the Hellenic world was drawn to visit Egypt with the thought of gaining there the fundamentals of a supernal knowledge. The debt owed to Philo Judaeus, born almost at the very year of the beginning of the Christian era, for his work in developing the principles of the Egyptian system into a code of elucidation of the mass of Scriptural material then extant, is immense. Philo's work proves that the basic principia for a harmonization of seemingly widely diverse currents of religious expression are present and available in this desperately baffling meadow of old Egypt's lore. Norman Bentwich, previously quoted, has so well expressed this (*Philo,* p. 40):

"To effect the true harmony between the literal and the allegorical sense of the Torah, between the spiritual and the legal sides of Judaism, between the Greek philosophy and revealed religion—that was the great work of Philo Judaeus."

In following the path cut through the tangle of ancient cryptic allegorism, symbolism and dramatization by Philo, world culture might have saved itself from plunging into a mud and mire infinitely worse than any allegedly prevailing in ancient Egypt, into which the popular movement of Christianity gave it the final push. But alas, not even the great talent of an Origen was sufficiently sharpened to carve out the statue form of radiant beauty all overlaid with the accretions of ignorant misconception.

Far on down the run of the ages, some eleven centuries later, Europe was to feel some thrill of the inward delight of the human mind when stirred by the wind of the spirit, as thought is moved by the magic power of symbols and allegory to vision and understanding. For suddenly there flashed into the deadened soul of Europe the light and glory of the Italian Renaissance of the fourteenth century. In that irradiation of the ancient glow old Egypt had a rebirth, destined to be short-lived and to miscarry, but still a rebirth. Though it sank again to dimness in two centuries, it was glorious while it lasted, and did perpetuate its liberating influence in instigating the Reformation which came a little later.

Obtuse to the essential values of real culture, the modern age has never properly assessed the force, the significance or the spirit of the Renaissance. If it had ever caught the power and meaning of the wave of intelligence that was wafted over the soul of the Italian world of the fourteenth century, it has lost it again. Culture can be won and lost again. Its rise to realization in the vision of one people or one age does not automatically guarantee its permanence. Like its greatest natural analogue, light, it flashes forth to brightness and dies away again. Like all things of the spirit, it bloweth where it listeth, and one can not be sure whence it cometh or whither it goeth.

But one can be sure that the Italian Renaissance came from the revival of ancient classical literature and that it went on to give the shackled soul of Europe its first pure breath of intellectual freedom it had drawn since the suffocating mantle of ecclesiastical tyranny had settled down upon it ten centuries earlier. It opened the door for stifled human beings to step out again into the pure free air of mental liberty. And with that release from captivity the European mind began its modern adventure into the realms of true science, the knowledge of truth that liberates from all bondage.

Such was the power to awaken the dormant human soul latent in classical literature of ancient peoples! And what was the dynamo and transmission vehicle of that power? *Nothing less than symbol and allegory!* The Christian Church smothered allegory when it denounced Origen in the fifth century; the Renaissance more than vindicated "Origen's allegories." It revealed what that Church might have done for true human culture had it exploited the germ of truth and power implicit in the system of Biblical interpretation he propounded.

Although perhaps not catching the *full* sweep of the significance of the spirit of the Renaissance, the author of the history of that epochal denouement, John Addington Symonds, has clearly recaptured and adequately depicted the part played in it by the esoteric dynamism of myth and symbol. What he says on this theme should be burned into the consciousness of all educators. From his *The Renaissance in Italy* (p. 54) we take the following:

"The culture of the classics had to be reappropriated before the movement of the modern mind could begin: before nations could start upon a new career of progress, the chasm between the old and the new world had to be bridged over."

Then Symonds launches into a keen analysis of the particular habitude or posture of the mind demanded of the human being for the apprehension of true cultural elements, which exhibits more discernment of the basic factors required than any we have seen. For its worth in this connection it calls for entire reprinting (p. 67):

"The meagreness of medieval learning was, however, a less severe obstacle to culture than the habit of mind, partly *engendered by Christianity,* and partly idiosyncratic to the new races, which prevented students from appreciating the true spirit of the classics. While Mysticism and allegory ruled supreme, the clearly defined humanity of the Greeks and Romans could not fail to be misapprehended."

"Poems like Virgil's Fourth Eclogue were prized for what the author had not meant when he was writing them; while his real interests were utterly neglected. Against this mental misconception, this original obliquity of vision, this radical lie in the intellect, the restorers of learning had to fight at least as energetically as against brute ignorance and dulness. It was not enough to multiply books and to discuss codices; *they had to teach men how to read them,* to explain their inspiration, to defend them against prejudice, *to protect them from false methods of interpretation.* To purge the mind of fancy and fable, to prove that poetry apart from its supposed prophetic meaning was for its own sake, and that the history of the antique nations, in spite of Paganism, could be used for profit and instruction, was the first step to be taken by these pioneers of modern culture. They had, in short, to create a new mental sensibility by establishing the truth that pure literature directly contributes to the dignity and happiness of human beings. The achievement of this revolution in thought was the great performance of the Italians of the fourteenth and fifteenth centuries."

It may not be realized at this moment; but another revolution in Western thought of exactly the same kind and through the same pathway must be consummated at the present epoch if civilization is to be saved. All over again scholars must be taught how to read the classics, how to purge the mind of fancy and fable or, better, how to read ancient fancy and fable so as to force them to yield the bright gold of eternal truth. All over again must be cultivated, if not created all afresh, a "new mental sensibility," so that the mind may be able to divest itself of the consequences of the traditional false methods of interpretation of the written treasures of wisdom and free itself from conventional trammels to be able to eat the fruit off the forbidden tree of knowledge.

If a new faculty was needed for medieval scholars to read the classics and catch their inner message, a still higher potential of human genius is demanded now if at last the full and emancipating purport of the whole body of ancient arcane wisdom is to be recovered and utilized for dispelling the fogs of lingering religious superstition and ushering in the brighter day of rational salvation.

Speaking of the labor of the Renaissance scholars over the new-found Greek and Latin manuscripts, Symonds writes (p. 52):

"Through their activity in the field of scholarship the proper starting-point was given to the modern intellect. The revelation of what men were and what they wrought under the influence of their faiths and their impulses in distant ages with a different ideal for their aim, not only widened the narrow horizon of the Middle Ages, but it also restored self-confidence to the reason of humanity. Research and criticism began to take the place of scholastic speculation. Positive knowledge was substituted for the intuitive guesses of idealists and dreamers.

"But how was this effected? By long and toilsome study, by the accumulation of MSS, by the acquisition of dead languages, by the solitary labor of grammarians, by the lectures of itinerant professors, by the scribe, by the printing press, by the self-devotion of magnificent Italy to erudition."

"By long and toilsome study," "by devotion to erudition," "by the acquisition of dead languages"; these footprints of the Renaissance mark the road that must be trodden again if humanity is to mount once more up the slopes of Pelion and Parnassus toward the summit of Olympus. In short Christendom, for its salvation from decadence, must revive the dead language of ancient symbolism and devote itself to the toilsome study—thrilling, however, if the lost keys are recovered from Egypt—of classical erudition and the thorough reindoctrination of its mind with the mighty wisdom of ancient philosophy.

Poetry, Symonds says, is instruction conveyed by allegory and fiction. Theology itself, he most discerningly glimpses, is a form of poetry; even the Holy Ghost may be called a Poet, inasmuch as he used the vehicle of symbol in the fashion of the prophets and the *Revelation* of St. John. The poet wraps up his meanings in delightful fictions—and the mental lout takes these for real. Though the common herd despises the poet as a liar, he is, in truth, a prophet uttering his dark speech in parables. How foolish, then, are the enemies of poetry, sophistical dialectitians and avaricious jurists, who have never trodden the Phoebean hill because it does not glitter with gold!

"Far worse is the condition of those monks and hypocrites who accuse the divine art of immorality and grossness, instead of reading between the lines and seeking the sense conveyed to the understanding under veils of allegory." (p. 96)

He alludes to Boccaccio's work as containing "a full exposition of the allegorizing theories with which humanism started."

"While we regard this change from creative to acquisitive literature, we must bear in mind that these scholars who ought to have been poets accomplished nothing less than the civilization, or, to use their own phrase, the humanization of the modern world." (p. 55)

What can be more significant than this next paragraph (p. 112)?:

"The study of Greek implied the birth of criticism, comparison, research. Systems based on ignorance and superstition were destined to give way before it. The study of Greek opened philosophical horizons far beyond the dream-world of the churchmen and the monks; it stimulated the germs of science, suggested new astronomical hypotheses and indirectly led to the discovery of America. The study of Greek resuscitated a sense of the beautiful in art and literature. It subjected the creeds of Christianity, the language of the Gospels, the doctrines of St. Paul to analysis, and commenced a new era for Biblical inquiry . . . we are justified in regarding the point of contact between the Greek teacher Chrysolaras and his Florentine pupils as one of the most momentous crises in the history of civilization . . . since the reawakening faith in human reason, the reawakening belief in the dignity of man's desire for beauty, the liberated audacity and passion of the Renaissance received through Greek studies their strongest and most vital impulse."

No words could be more thrillingly significant for modern man than those of Symonds, for we are made by fate to be witnesses at this moment of another denouement perhaps even more significant than the fact of a group of Florentines taking their first lessons in the Greek language from Chrysolaras. For the modern world of study has just had its first lessons in an even richer language than that of Greece, one destined to open out a wider and more fruitful field of knowledge questing than that of Greece, magnificent as that was. The Renaissance, like the Reformation, could go only a few steps along the road to full illumination without the primeval light of old Egypt's sun of intellect. Even the glorious lamp of Greek philosophy has not yielded, and can not yield, its full radiance until it is refilled with the oil of ancient Egyptian sapiency.

We can not forego the pleasure of sharing with the reader Symond's vision of the new era that the Renaissance opened for Europe (p. 13):

"Petrarch opens a new era. He is not satisfied with the body of medieval beliefs and intellectual conceptions. Antiquity represents a more fascinating ideal to his spirit. . . . The Revival of Learning, begun by Petrarch, was no mere renewal of interest in the classical literature. It was the emancipation of reason in a race of men, intolerant of control, ready to criticize accepted canons of conduct, enthusiastic in admiration of antique liberty, freshly awakened to the sense of beauty and anxious above all things to secure for themselves free scope in spheres outside the region of authority. Men so vigorous and independent felt the joy of exploration. There was no problem they feared to face, no formula they were not eager to recast according to their new convictions.

"Meanwhile what gave its deep importance to the classical revival was the emancipation of the reason consequent upon the discovery that *the best gifts of the spirit had been enjoyed by the nations of antiquity*. An ideal of existence distinct from that imposed upon the Middle Ages by the Church was revealed in all its secular attractiveness. Fresh value was given to the desires and aims, enjoyments and activities of man, considered as a noble member of the universal life, and not as a diseased excrescence on the world he helped to spoil. Instead of the cloistered service of the *Imitatio Christi,* that conception of the union, through knowledge, with God manifested in his works and in the soul of man, which forms the indestructible religion of science and the reason, was always generated. The intellect, after lying spell-bound during a long night, when thoughts were as dreams and movement as somnambulism, resumed its activity, interrogated nature and enjoyed the pleasures of unimpeded energy. Without ceasing to be Christians . . . the men of the Revival dared once again to exercise their thought as boldly as the Greeks and Romans had done before them. . . . The touch upon them of the classical spirit was like the finger of a deity giving life to the dead."

Florence, he says, "borrowed her light from Athens, as the moon shines with rays reflected from the sun. The Revival was the silver age of that golden age of Greece."

Movements of true advance in human history are sometimes lured ahead by the attractiveness of higher light and beauty; sometimes they are pushed, as it were, from behind by the repulsion of ugliness and baseness. Was there any of the latter motive in causing the Renaissance? Symonds presents a picture of conditions that would seem to answer affirmatively:

"Christianity, especially in Italy, where the spectacle of the Holy See inspired disgust, had been prostituted to the vilest service by the Church. Faith was associated with folly, superstition, ignorance, intolerance and cruelty. The manners of the clergy were in flagrant discord with the Gospels, and Antichrist found fitter incarnation in Roderigo Borgia than in Nero. The corruption of the Church and the political degeneracy of the commonwealths had quite as much to do with it as the return of heathen standards. Nor could the Renaissance have been the great world-historical era it truly was, if such demoralization had been a part and parcel of its essence. Crimes and vice are not the hotbed of arts and literature; lustful priests and cruel despots were not necessary to the painting of Raphael or the poetry of Ariosto."

If the statement of Symonds that the best gifts of the spirit had been enjoyed by the nations of antiquity is true, half of our ground hypothesis for the message of this work is fully substantiated by eminent authority, and half of all the claims of the Christian religion are nullified.

The thrill of sensing again that joyous exuberant outburst of the human spirit from the restraints of a strangling Church is so keen that one would fain linger with it. But it only remains to ask what killed it. Again Symonds has the answer (446):

"What remained of humanism among the Italians assumed a different form, adapted to the new rule of the Spaniards, and the new attitude of the Church. To the age of the humanists succeeded the age of the Inquisition and the Jesuits."

"There was not enough time for students to absorb antiquity and pass beyond it, before the mortmain of the Church and the Spaniard was laid upon the fairest provinces of thought." "The infamy of having rendered science and philosophy abortive in Italy, when its early show of blossom was so promising, falls upon the Popes and princes of the last half of the sixteenth century." (p. 396.)

The shadow of that third century is long. The same stultifying force that had withered the bloom of ancient Greek philosophy was at hand to exhale the same blighting breath of dark bigotry upon the new spring growth of arcane wisdom in the fourteenth century. It is no less stealthily active at the present epoch to fetter the wings of free thought.

As Symonds has told us how iniquity oozed from every pore of the ecclesiastical system when the dark forces of pietism snuffed out the tender growth of enlightenment in the later period, so Farrar tells us how iniquity likewise ran rampant when the same forces killed philosophy at the earlier time (*Lives of the Fathers*, Vol. II, 674):

"The story of the iniquities with which Chrysostom had to grapple . . . is one of the saddest and most deplorable among the many sad and deplorable narratives which deface the ecclesiastical history of the fourth century. It exhibits the prevalence among bishops and clergy of an almost inconceivable amount of greed, worldliness and disorder."

Chrysostom took spirited action against these abuses within the fold of Christ and got himself roundly hated for it. Such was the corruption among even the Bishops that Ammonius had his ear cut off to disqualify himself from being appointed a bishop. He was called by the Greek name *parotes* because of the severed ear.

Synesius, Bishop of Ptolemais, "but of doubtful orthodoxy," because he was a great Kabalist, wrote: "The people will always mock at things easy to be misunderstood; it must needs have impostures." "A spirit," he said, "that loves wisdom and contemplates truth close at hand, is forced to disguise it, to induce the multitude to accept it. Fictions are necessary to the people, and *the Truth becomes deadly to those who are not strong enough to contemplate it in all its brilliance.*"

"If the sacerdotal laws allowed the reservation of judgments to the allegory of words, I would accept the proposed dignity on condition that I might be a philosopher at home, and abroad a narrator of apologues and parables. . . . In fact *what can there be in common between the vile multitude and sublime wisdom?* The truth must be kept secret, and the masses need a teaching proportioned to their imperfect reasoning."

What history reveals in all too concrete realism of the havoc and devastation wrought by the policy of giving out to the "vile multitude" the "apologues and parables,"—what this same Synesius elsewhere calls "the fables of our religion"—without teaching them that these constructions were but the fictitious vestments of truth only to be brought to living reality within the confines of the human consciousness, and not to be taken as the narrations of historical events, is the most appalling of all real stories. In world annals it should be called The Story of the Great Deception.

CHAPTER VI

MILK FOR BABES

It would seem as if the subject of esotericism could be dismissed at this point. As a matter of fact it has by no means been adequately dealt with in its vital connection with the catastrophic deterioration of Christianity into Christianism. The whole chance to understand the development of Christianity lies in a complete grasp of the fundamental relation of esotericism to culture in general. As Christianity was the world's most signal and massive movement away from esotericism to the wide dissemination of a popular faith, all the elements of true comprehension of the course it took are deeply buried from sight. Into the depths and intricacies of this situation the probing for historical truth must be made.

Esotericism, as has been seen, is an ineluctable necessity and a perfectly natural condition inherent in the evolution of human genius, based on the inevitable differences of capability and attainment subsisting between highly and less highly evolved mortals. It is an earned privilege of those who have developed high capabilities and opened knowing faculties, to acquire wisdom and enjoy its satisfactions and boons. These blessings are not the hap of those who have not yet paid the price to possess them. Even this simple rationalization has been made a matter of unacceptability by the quirks of Christian erraticism, for it became almost a basic conviction of the early fanatical devotees of the cult that the rudest and crudest members of society were equally entitled to the largesse of divine favor and the gift of intelligence to understand the mysteries of faith with the studious and the philosophical. Indeed it became a pious legend that the height of blessedness was in proportion to the depth of ignorance. The Gospels appeared to exalt the lowly to the disparagement of the wise and cultured. To tear down the mighty from their seats and exalt them of low degree became a kind of shibboleth of the new movement. An ignoramus with God in his heart could excel the philosopher. But it was a mistaken presumption and it led to disaster. The obvious differences in intelligence quotient can not be ignored. Dearly has the world paid for Christianity's exaltation of ignorance in those formative days.

Christianity made a momentous choice in its second and third centuries, and that choice was to throw in its lot with the lowest and meanest ranks of society in the world of the day, as against the elite and the intelligentsia, against instruction, philosophy and the cultus of higher learning. Its history is a long and horrifying record of the results of that choice. All Occidental event since then has been a dark shadow bearing the shape of the structure of unwisdom that prompted and executed that choice. Not only did it deliberately make that choice, but it has endorsed and sanctified it, indeed gloried in it, ever since. Christianity, its proponents said, is so much the nobler religion just because it ministers to the humble, the simple and the unlearned, while the esoteric cults of the Pagans reached only the few intellectuals. This claim, and its implications, must now be the theme of many pages.

No better place to begin could be found than in a passage from Chrysostom (*Homily* III on I Cor., 1:10). He glories in the ignorance of the twelve Apostles, so often lauded as plain "fishermen," and the more glorious for it.

"Rather, let us charge the Apostles with want of learning; for this same charge is praise. And when they say that the apostles were rude, let us follow up the remark and say that they were also untaught and unlettered and poor and vile and stupid and obscure. It is not slander on the Apostles to say so, but it is even a glory that, being such, they should have outshone the whole world."

Facing the sobering fact that almost certainly these twelve personages were simply dramatic-allegoric personifications of the twelve signs of the zodiac, themselves being symbols of the twelve powers of divinity to be unfolded as the adjuncts and essences of the Christ nature itself, as many great sages declare them to be, and that they were never living men at all; but assuming their factual existence for the sake of argument, we may agree with him of the "Golden Mouth" (the meaning of "Chrysostom") that the twelve were ignorant simple fishermen. But we are not so ready to agree with him that "they outshone the whole world." This is a fine sample of what an early Christian, in the exuberance of his hypnotized faith, could bring himself to imagine and assert.

It chances that there comes to hand at this moment a passage from no less a responsible historian than Guignebert, who, in his fine history of Christianity, has this to say in almost direct contradiction to the rhapsodic exudations of Chrysostom's golden, but fanciful eloquence about the twelve haloed fishermen. Dealing with the legends about the work of the Apostles in different countries, he writes (p. 61):

"But it is to be feared that not one of them is true, and, in fact, apart from the early chapters of the *Acts of the Apostles* (which we possess only in the form of a second-hand adaptation of the first edition), there exists no information really worthy of credence about the life and work of the immediate Apostles of Jesus . . . *their immediate and direct inflence upon the history of Christianity is practically negligible.*"

Other writers comment on the odd fact that following the commissioning of the twelve disciples and then the seventy by Jesus to go forth and evangelize the whole world, either they met with no success worthy of record, or no record of it was made; in either case the score marks another total miscalculation of a practical move and its expected results to be tallied against the reputed omniscience of the Cosmic Logos in the person of the Nazarene. So far as history knows, the great command of the Son of God to eighty-two men to go into all the world and preach a gospel that, unknown to them, was already a common esoteric possession of all nations and already prescribed in sacred books the world over, was entirely a futile gesture, making at no time enough impact on the life of the times to win a single notice from any historian. Yet every pious Christian has in his imagination pictured these doughty and sanctified missionaries as valiant pioneers of the first true world faith, haranguing multitudes on hills and lakesides and swaying them to conversion by thousands. Incidentally there are scholars, not a few, within the pale of orthodox Christianity, who regard even the *Acts of the Apostles* as a spurious work.

We have the word of such a fine historian as Guignebert that the disciples "were, it must be remembered, Jews in mean circumstances and without culture." And Guignebert considers how extremely unlikely it would be for any one born and reared a Jew, even an ignorant fisherman, to regard it as less than actual blasphemy against the Deity to conceive of the Divine Infinite, "which he dared not name lest he should seem to be putting restrictions upon it, as being enclosed within the narrow confines of a human body." If Jewish reverence for the majesty of Deity was so great that it was regarded as gross impiety to utter the ineffable name of Yahweh, how unthinkable would it have been for one to believe that this Cosmic Deity would come to earth in the humble flesh of a mortal creature! Guignebert suggests that had any one come and told the twelve that Jesus was an incarnation of God, at first they would have failed to catch his meaning; then they would have cried out against it with horror. But, he says, they could have made sense of what Paul told them concerning Jesus, i.e., that he had been a celestial man and even the incarnation of the Spirit, the *Pneuma* of God. Yet, one has to wonder, what would such fishermen know about the *Pneuma* of God? What were they likely to know about the literary method of allegory, myth and drama?

In committing itself wholly to the religionizing of the untutored masses, Christianity inevitably and irretrievably aligned itself with the interests of ignorant pietism and sheer faith as against those of intelligence and philosophical reflection. As said, the gap between these two nodes of human consciousness, or two worlds of conscious dimension, is of immense width and yawning impassability. The choice pledged the movement to concentrate all its force upon the glorification of pure religious "faith" as against bookish intelligence or study and its fruits in understanding. If stress on the intellect and its findings was to be reduced to the vanishing point, then all emphasis had to be increased proportionately on sheer pietism and the emotional elements. Fervor of belief and devotion to the things fixed for credence and worship would come to be the badge of sanctified membership in the body of Christ. Zeal carried to fantastic and fanatic lengths would be the character-mark of the early Apostolic and evangelical Christianism. And such is what history records.

So at one fell swoop Christianity sank down to make itself at home on the level of the lowest classes of the Roman Empire. At one stroke it set its destiny by an alliance with the undergrades of humanity. For a time indeed, while still motivated by much respect for the Pagan policies and principles, it made a sincere effort to retain in its message a distinction between the esoteric teachings for the wiser and an exoteric form of parabolic instruction for the less capable. An enlightening view of this effort is gained from what Fisher tells us in his work already cited (p. 360):

"Among the Jews, in the later period of their history, prior to the birth of Christ, many pseudonymous works were composed. This was true mostly of the Alexandrians, but not of them exclusively. . . . At first and often this was a literary device, no deceit being intended. It early led, however, to intentional fraud. The same practice passed into those Christian circles where Judaism and Judaizing influences were potent. A distinction was made between esoteric and exoteric doctrine, between what the enlightened may hold, and *what it was expedient to impart to the people*—a distinction which had its prime source in the Alexandrian philosophy. Under the cover of this false ethical principle, writings were fabricated like the Sibylline oracles and the Pseudo-Clementine Homilies. But pious frauds of this nature were possible only where there was a defective sense of obligation to truth. They are utterly repugnant to a sound Christian feeling; nor is there ground for supposing that in the ancient Church, generally speaking, they were regarded otherwise than as at present. Speaking of one of these fabricated books, *Acta Pauli et Theclae*, Tertullian says that 'in Asia the Presbyter who composed that writing, as if he were augmenting Paul's name from his own store, after being convicted and confessing that he had done it from love of Paul, was removed from office.' This act is indicative of the judgment that would be formed of such an imposture by Christians generally at that time."

History has found it can not be so lenient in its judgment on the vast body of "pious frauds" perpetrated by the early Christians as Fisher is here. If the presbyter fabricated an *Acts of Paul and Thecla* for the love of Paul, likewise the Inquisitors murdered Protestants later for the love of Christ. This should illustrate for us—and we need this illustration—what "love" can do when not instructed by intelligence.

Fisher's statement gives us the first evidence introduced here that the religious movement which was so soon to scorn all esotericism itself started out with the institution of distinction between the milk for babes and the meat for strong men. This singular fact is so generally unknown that testimony to support it must be presented.

We have the strong direct statement of Origen himself that the Mysteries were perpetuated in the Christian Church as they had been in the Pagan societies. In his *Contra Celsum* (Bk. lcvii) he says:

"But that there should be certain doctrines not made known to the multitude, which are revealed after the exoteric ones have been taught, is not a peculiarity of Christianity alone, but also of philosophic systems, in which certain truths are exoteric and others esoteric."

The point to be noted is that an exoteric-esoteric differentiation *was* a peculiarity of Christian practice, according to Origen.

Now let us listen to the exhortations of St. Cyril of Jerusalem in his *Fourth Catechetical Lecture,* in which he speaks of the esoteric doctrine thus:

"To hear the Gospel is indeed permitted to all; but the glory of the Gospel is set apart *for Christ's genuine disciples only.* The Lord spake in parables to those who would not hear; but privately explained these parables and similitudes [i.e., analogies and nature symbols] to his disciples. The fulness of the glory belongs to those who are already illuminated; the blindness is that of unbelievers. These Mysteries the Church communicates to him who is going out of the class of catechumens. Nor is it customary to reveal them to the heathen; for we do not tell to any heathen the secret Mysteries concerning the Father, and the Son and the Holy Ghost. Neither do we openly and plainly speak of them among the catechumens, but only in a covert and secret manner, so that the faithful who know them may not be injured."

One can be pardoned a smile of gracious indulgence to an overweening presumption on the part of the sainted Cyril when he says that they, the Christians, do not communicate the mystery of the great doctrine of the Trinity to the heathen, if one happens to be aware that it was from a "heathen" philosopher himself that the Church drew its doctrine of the Father, Son and Holy Ghost! It was imparted by the Neoplatonic philosopher Plotinus to Augustine, his pupil, being based on his "three fundamental hypostases."

And St. Basil the Great, in speaking of certain rites of the Church appertaining to baptism and the Eucharist, which he claims were received by tradition from the Apostles, says expressly that they were guarded in reverent silence and dignity from all intrusion of the profane and uninitiated, so that they would not fall into contempt. (*De Spirtu Sancto,* C 27, pp. 311-12, Lepsiae, 1854.)

There must be entered in this chronicle the gist of the statements made by Clement of Alexandria in his *Stromata* (Bks. I, c. 12; IV, c. 22; V, cc. 9, 10; VII, c. 17). Here he speaks of the necessity of hiding in a mystery the wisdom which the Son of God had brought; of the hindrances which there were in his day to his writing about his wisdom, lest he should cast pearls before swine; of the reason why the Christian mysteries were celebrated at night, like the Pagan ones, because then the soul, released from the dominion of the senses, turns in upon itself and has a truer intelligence of the mystery of God *hid for ages under allegory and prophecy,* but as now revealed by Jesus Christ, and which St. Paul would only speak of among such as are perfect, giving milk to babes and meat to men of understanding; and of those mysteries as entered upon through the tradition of the Lord, i.e., by means of Baptism and Divine Illumination.

From many authorities it is demonstrated that there were three general classes of Christians, graded according to their proven development, in the primitive Church, viz. the Catechumens, the Competentes and the Illuminati, or Mystae, or the Faithful. The names indicate the order of rank. It can not escape observation for its great significance that the name Mystae given to those considered "illumined," was taken directly from the designation of the initiated in the Orphic and Eleusinian Mysteries of the Pagans.

What Clement says receives confirmation from a statement in Lundy's *Monumental Christianity* (p. 82) which is very germane:

"But for all this there was something mysterious about the Eucharist as related to the Incarnation and Resurrection of Christ, and his union with the Church, which could only be appreciated by the highest exercise of faith, and therefore none but the faithful were admitted to the high privilege of its participation. No explanation of it is given by the Fathers; no explanation appears on the monuments. It still remains where the Lord left it, a profound mystery, like the union of soul and body, spirit and matter, God and man, Christ and his Church."

If there are those who linger under the impression that the sacramental offices of the Christian fellowship were from the start and ever since open to every humble member of the laity, here is the evidence that the truth was otherwise. And it is part of the voluminous and authoritative body of evidence that the religion began in the full spirit and practice of *esoteric understanding*. The influences that led to the discontinuance of the practice are those same that brought in the entire deterioration of the original spiritual power of the movement.

In Massey's brochure on *Paul the Gnostic Opponent of Peter* (3), there is a statement eminently worthy of reproduction:

"At the same time, as Irenaeus tells us, the Gnostics, of whom Marcion was one, charged the Apostles with hypocrisy, because they 'framed their doctrine according to the capacity of their hearers, fabling blind things for the blind according to their blindness; for the dull according to their dulness; for those in error according to their errors.'"

At first sight this passage would seem to reverse the sides or positions of the contending parties in the controversy. Here it is the Gnostics, who certainly stood for the method of true esotericism, this being indeed almost the foundation of their system, who charge the non-esoteric apostolic Christians with dividing the word according to the capacity of those to whom it is preached—in other words, practicing esotericism. But the wording of Irenaeus' passage makes it clear that it was not a genuine esoteric technique that the Gnostics were accusing the Christians of practicing, but a disingenuous one, as it were, deliberately departing from the truth to give simple minds something concrete instead of a mystery to be grasped spiritually. This is exactly what Celsus and other cultured critics of early Christianity record of the practices of the Church: the leaders and instructors imparted to their catechumens and ignorant laity every sort of plausible or miraculous concoction of fancy to explain the mysteries of the faith, when they found their protogées sitting in stolid incomprehension of an attempted elucidation of trinitarian, eucharistic, or other aspects of the imparted theology. A little later, and practically ever since, it is clear that those who essayed the role of instructors or expositors, were as dark about the inner meaning of those dogmas as their pupils. When the blind attempt to lead the blind, the ditch by the side of the theological road will have many visitors or inmates.

Perhaps not too much blame is to be attached to a resort to fabrication in the face of solid incapacity for the appreciation of subtler aspects of spiritual experience or cosmology. It is the fact of such fabrication that needs recording simply for the truth itself. Its elucidation can come afterwards. It is the common temptation confronting priesthood, indeed all higher instruction anywhere in the cultural field, when low capability is to be enlightened, to find simplification in some sort of "easier explanation." But the fact is, the tendency was carried on to such a degree of recklessness that Celsus exclaims at one place that even nursemaids would blush to be caught telling such lurid falsehoods and fairy tales to their infantile charges. The rule that apparently governed the degree of arrant profligacy with which the treasures of truth were thus thrown around was: the duller the catechumens, the more weird and fantastic the "explanation." One does not need to look beyond the present epoch to find the similar procedure in things religious. It is a common phenomenon of all times. Christians should be the last people to snarl at esotericism, for their early leaders used the method, and in ways that were considered decidedly advantageous to the interests of the faith.

But what can be more revealing and more authoritative, because written in secret and in confidence, than the statement in a letter written by Saint Gregory Nazianzen to his friend and confidant, St. Jerome, in which he said:

"Nothing can impose better on a people than verbiage; the less they understand the more they admire. . . . Our fathers and doctors have often said, not what they thought, but that to which circumstance and necessity forced them."

The sainted Bishop's own words relieve us of the necessity of charging the hierarchy of early Christianity with deliberately forging fabrications designed to impose on the gullibility and ready credulity of their simple followers. This item of historical fact, however, should be remembered when one reads of the eternal boasts of Christianity that its consummate merit and glory was that it gave *truth* to the humble and lowly. This work is aimed to show that the sort of "truth" it imparted to the ignorant, instead of blessing them, bound them in the chains of a tenfold deeper dungeon of ignorance and superstition.

There is a hint in the *Clementine Homilies,* a work that brings to light some of the salient features in the opposition of the Petrine party to Paul. Peter's faction held Paul almost as a Gnostic and hence a heretical enemy of the true evangelistic faith. They even accused Paul of having been converted by a false Christ, i.e., the mystic Christ of his Damascus vision and not the man Jesus. So far did this obsession creep into their minds that they even ventured to suggest that he was the Antichrist, the arch enemy of the Crucified, and that he would be the author of some great heresy expected to arise in the future. Peter is said, therefore, to have declared that Christ instructed his disciples not to publish the one true and genuine Gospel for the present, because the false teacher must arise who would publicly proclaim the false gospel of the Antichrist, that was the Christ of the Gnostics. The true Gospel was confessedly "held in reserve to be secretly transmitted for the rectification of future heresies." Massey says they knew well enough what had to come out if Paul's preaching, proclaimed in his *Epistles,* were widely broadcast. It was Paul whom they had reason to fear. Justin Martyr never once mentions this real founder of Christianity, never once refers to the writings of Paul. Strangest of all things is that the book of *Acts,* which is mainly a history of Paul, should contain no account of his martyrdom or death in Rome. Paul's writings seem to have been withheld for a whole century after his death. There is intimated here a holding back of "the true Gospel" from the world at large. It shows the prevalence of the esoteric motive in early Christianity.

Even in connection with the Gospels themselves there is evidence of the operation of the esoteric principle early in the life of the new faith. It is found in such an item of data as that which comes directly from Jerome himself, the translator of the *Vulgate* into Latin. Writing to the Bishops Chromatius and Heliodorus, he complains that "a difficult work is enjoined, since this translation has been commanded me by your Felicities, which St. Matthew himself, the apostle and evangelist, *did not wish to be openly written.* For if it had not been secret, he (Matthew) would not have added to the evangel that which he gave forth was his; but he made up this book sealed up in the Hebrew characters, which he *put forth in such a way* that the book, written in Hebrew letters, and by the hand of himself, *might be possessed by the men most religious,* who also, in the course of time received it from those who preceded them. But this very book *they never gave to any one to be transcribed,* and its text was related, *some one way and some another.*" (St. Jerome, V. 445; *Sod, the Son of the Man,* p. 44.)

What is this but the expression of reluctance on the part of a student of esoteric things to give out to the public literature hitherto always held inviolably esoteric? There is more than a hint here, too, that such Gospels as Matthew's had not been recently written, but had been handed down from generation to generation of men cherishing these writings as secret manuals of truth not to be given to the multitude.

Lundy records that the secret discipline of the primitive Church seems to have formulated two or three classes of catechumens, in different stages of advancement and fitness for admission into the Christian assembly. Origen thus testifies, he says:

"The Christians having previously, as far as possible, *tested the souls* of those who wish to become their hearers, and having previously instructed them in private, when, before entering the community, they appear to have sufficiently evinced their desire towards a virtuous life, introduce them then, and not before, privately forming one class of those who are beginners and are receiving admission, but who have not yet obtained the mark of complete purification; and another class of those who have manifested to the best of their ability their intention to desire no other things than are approved by Christians; and among these there are certain persons appointed to make inquiries regarding the lives and behavior of those who join them, in order that they may prevent those who commit infamous acts from coming into their public assemblies, while those of a different character they received with their whole heart, in order that they may daily make them better. And this is their method of procedure, both with those who are sinners and especially with those who lead dissolute lives, whom they exclude from their community." (Bk. III, c. 51, Origen.)

And Lundy goes on to say that in Tertullian's day, somewhat later than Origen's, "the heretics," meaning the general run of Pagan and semi-Christian sectaries,

"made no such distinction between a catechumen and a believer; for he says, 'They all have access alike, they hear alike, they pray alike—even heathens, if any such happen to come among them. That which is holy they will cast to the dogs, and their pearls—only false ones—they will fling to the swine. Simplicity they will have to consist in the overthrowing of discipline, attention to which on our part they call finery.'" (Tertullian: *Praes. Adv. Haer.*, c. 41.)

There is hardly a greater anomaly in history than to find Christians accusing Pagans of disregarding, while they held fast to, the program of esoteric systematism, for by and large it was the Pagans who held to it and the Christians who disregarded it. It could have been a time and a particular group in which the rigid distinctions holding generally in Pagan esoteric practice had been relaxed, while the Christians were still working in the tradition of careful gradation.

Then Lundy points us to a document called *The Apostolic Constitutions,* in which is laid down the catalogue of doctrinal items in which the catechumens were to be instructed. A glance at this list reveals at once that the instruction imparted to these candidates ran deeply in the channels of what would have to be called the esoteric studies in theology, including such mysteries as those of the knowledge of the unbegotten God, his only-begotten Son, and the Holy Ghost; the order of creation, the course of Providence and the dispensations of God's laws; the divine motive in world creation and why man was appointed to be a citizen therein; anthropology, the nature and constitution of man; God's punishment of the wicked with water and fire; his glorification of the saints in every generation; then the doctrine of the Lord's incarnation, passion, resurrection and ascension.

But then, says Lundy, there was reserve as to imparting even to the catechumens all the mysteries of the Christian faith. In other words, there was an esoteric and an exoteric doctrine. Origen thus states it in his reply to Celsus as to the *Disciplana Arcani:*

"Since he frequently calls the Christian doctrine a secret system, we must confute him on this point also, since almost the entire world is better acquainted with what Christians preach than with the favorite opinions of philosophers. For who is ignorant of the statement that Jesus was born of a virgin, that he was crucified, and that his resurrection is an article of faith, and that a general judgment is announced to come, in which the wicked are to be punished according to their deserts and the righteous to be duly rewarded? And yet the mystery of the Resurrection, not being understood, is made a subject of ridicule among unbelievers. In these circumstances, to speak of Christian doctrine as a secret system is altogether absurd."

Here is Tertullian taunting the Pagans with their flagrant violation of the esoteric practice and boasting of the Christian adherence to it.

And here is a greater than Tertullian, the most learned Origen, shouting that it is absurd to regard the Christian system as a secret one. This is pretty direct contradiction. Doubtless Origen meant to say that a system which freely taught its deepest knowledge to any qualified student, and that prepared the less intelligent for such qualification, could not be charged with being a secret cult. But the same claim could just as legitimately be made by the Pagan side. Origen had already said that esotericism was by no means a "peculiarity" of Christianity alone, but was a practice of the other spiritual cults of the time. Our effort here is to show that Christianity did in the early days of its existence continue the "heathen" practice of esoteric instruction, but failed to perpetuate it in all too short a time.

In a sentence a bit farther on, Origen clarifies his position somewhat. He says:

"Moreover, all the mysteries that are celebrated everywhere throughout Greece and barbarous countries, although held in secret, have no discredit thrown upon them, so that it is in vain that he [Celsus] endeavors to calumniate the secret doctrine of Christianity, seeing he does not correctly understand its nature. (*Contra Celsum*, Bk. I, c. 7.)

Here is the great Patristic defending the very thing that a thousand Christian protagonists have reprobated and deprecated as a practice in the Mystery Brotherhoods and the religion of the Pagans. This could be the reason why the Christian historians are so loath to admit the fact that their religion began with the same attempt to distinguish between grades of intelligence in their following and to impart to the more capable what it was deemed injudicious and impolitic to cast broadly out to the rabble. There can eventuate only good from bringing the Christian system to book on this flagrant item of its inconsistency and logical insincerity. Surely the one and only true religion will not wish to compound and perpetuate an obvious subterfuge.

Much reliance can be placed on von Mosheim's studied conclusions, at least on their sincerity. He says (*History of the Christian Religion,* I, 19, note) that the Christians adopted, in common with the Pagan nations, the plan of dividing their sacred offices into two classes; one public, to which every person was freely admitted, the other secret or mysterious, from which all the unprofessed were excluded. The initiated were those who had been baptized; the unprofessed, the catechumens. The mode of preparatory examination also bore a strong resemblance, in many respects, to the course of initiatory forms observed by the heathen nations in regard to their mysteries.

"In a word, many forms and ceremonies, to pass over other things of the Christian worship, *were evidently copied from these secret rites of paganism;* and we have only to lament that what was thus done with unquestionably the best of intentions, should in some respects have been attended with an evil result."

Without end the vociferators of Christianity's all-supreme excellence have ignored or made light of the reverence paid generally by the ancient world to the esoteric polity. This is disingenuous from the historical standpoint, since every historian knows that Christianity started out to practice and perpetuate the esoteric order of religious impartation. When it is known that the young movement so soon dropped the more cautious and secret handling of what was held to be recondite precious truth and, so to say, flung wide open the doors to all and sundry to enter the most sacred holy of holies of mystical knowledge without furnishing credentials of mental competence or spiritual qualification, the apologist for the faith is confronted with the task of excusing the change and mitigating its challenging implications as best he may. What is needed, however, is that it be explained and honestly accounted for. The difficulty of doing this without making damaging admissions which convict the early Church of being swayed by the forces of ignorance, has so far deterred the writers from a frank facing of the true situation. Within little more than a century after Origen had charged the esoteric Pagans with admitting indiscriminately the low and ignorant as well as the high and intelligent into their associations, and boasting of the Christian practice of careful segregation of its devotees into graded classes, it was the Christian Church that took the fatal plunge irrevocably into that very practice and has held to it unremittingly ever since. Indeed the fact has become one of the very proudest boasts of the Church, which heralds abroad at all times its vast humanitarian beneficence in ministering to all grades of human intelligence, without let or bar to the meanest.

One more excerpt from Higgins' wonderful old *Anacalypsis* rightfully belongs here to help round out the picture (p. 647):

"It can not be doubted that all the explanations pretended to be made of the esoteric religion by Jerome and the early Fathers are mere fables to deceive the vulgar. How absurd to suppose that when these men who were at the head of the religion were admitting that there was a secret religion for the initiated only, they would explain it to all the world! Their explanations to the vulgar are suitable to the vulgar, and were meant merely to stop their inquiries."

Here indeed is stern confrontation of a proud and boastful religion with the long suppressed and unwelcome truth. Higgins' strong charge can be shouted down with loud denials, but it can hardly be proven incorrect. The Fathers' own admissions hold it up as true. In this passage Higgins states in a few words the whole prime case of the Christian religion, its rise and spread and—failure. It is all condensed in his charge that while the Fathers confessed—and for close to two hundred years upheld—the existence of an inner profundity of meaning and a high range of mystical experience that could only legitimately be imparted to initiates and genuinely tested and accredited competents, they were at the same time spreading the forms of these inner teachings abroad to the general populace and in the process reducing the rich and sumptuous feast of wisdom to such hash and porridge as the ignorant masses could find in some way digestible. Thus came Christianism, which was the wreckage of Christianity.

What this meant in concrete result for "the vulgar" can be seen only too clearly in a statement out of Gibbon's great *Decline and Fall of the Roman Empire* (p. 502):

"The most extravagant legends, as they conduced to the honor of the Church, were apprehended by the credulous multitude, countenanced by the power of the clergy and attested by the suspicious evidence of ecclesiastical history."

The Church may with good reason applaud the axiomatic expression that it is necessary to make human life appear thrillingly romantic. For it itself managed the introduction of any amount of romantic wonder-lore into the actual history of the faith, indeed converted a mass of romantic legend into actual "history." It is presumably a function and prerogative of religion to infuse into the drab texture of ordinary life the more seductive hues of romantic allure; but it is expected to be achieved through the channels of a revelation of the actual wonder of life in its overt factuality—the mission of philosophy—and not by the sheer fabrication of fictitious stories.

More than one writer comments on the demoralizing effect of the presentation of the comedies, the mimes and the mythological scenarios, even the pictures and statues which, failing entirely to carry to the low populace their purer and higher esoteric connotations, "they had," says Fisher (*The Beginnings of Christianity*, p. 212), "the most corrupting effect upon the morals of women and of youth."

133

Von Mosheim's summary survey of the situation can be appreciated (*History*, I, 371):

"It is not, therefore, Origen who ought to be termed the parent of allegories amongst the Christians, but Philo . . . many of the Jews, and in particular the Pharisees and Essenes, had indulged much in allegories before the time of Philo [then obviously even Philo was not the prime "parent" of this device], but of this there can be no doubt, that the praefects of the Alexandrian school caught the idea of interpreting Scripture upon philosophical principles, or of eliciting philosophical maxims from the sacred writers by means of allegory, and that by them it was gradually propagated amongst the Christians at large. It is also equally certain that by the writings and example of Philo the fondness for allegories was vastly augmented and confirmed throughout the whole Christian world: and it moreover appears that it was he who first inspired the Christians with that degree of temerity which led them, not infrequently, to violate the faith of history and wilfully to close their eyes against the obvious and proper sense of terms and words . . . particular instances of it, however, may be shown from Origen and others who took him for their guide and who manifestly considered a great part both of the Old and New Testaments as not exhibiting a representation of *things that really occurred,* but merely the images of moral actions."

Here is strong confirmation at Christian hands of what this thesis consistently claims, that allegory, along with the rites, symbols, doctrines and all other appurtenances of Christian religionism were derivatives from a remote past. The origin of practically every feature of the Christian religion is buried in the far distant beginnings of civilization and culture. All claims that Christianity was a new and entirely unique religious expression in the day of its rise are sheer mental moonshine.

Von Mosheim clinches the claim of an earlier source of the use of allegory in a further passage from (p. 379) his first volume:

"Philo without doubt *imitated the Egyptians;* Clement as unquestionably followed the example of Philo; and Origen trod closely in the footsteps of both. The more recent Christian teachers, for the most part, formed themselves upon the model of this latter Father. The secret discipline of Philo consisted in the application of philosophical principles to religion and the sacred writings; nor was that of Clement ever thought to differ from it, except by those who had not sufficiently informed themselves upon the subject."

In another paragraph von Mosheim makes the categorical statement that "the Jews copied after the Egyptians (as is placed out of all question by the Essenes and the Therapeutae)." This is of great importance, as there has been an ingrained and persistent tendency on the part of

Christian writers to doubt, when not actually denying, that the Jews drew their religious fundamentals from the Egyptians. This is the pivotal datum that must be faced today.

In the larger view it is to be seen that allegorism, as an intellectual or psychological device based on intrinsic modes of inculcating an apprehension of recondite truth, occult knowledge and exalted mystical states, was an instrument employed for the preservation and impartation of such verities by the Masters of Wisdom, the seers and sages who parented early cultures, from the remotest antiquity. Its usage by the elder Tanaim and Targumists of the early Jewish systematism, learned from the Egyptians, as von Mosheim affirms, and its adoption and exploitation by Philo and then by Clement and Origen, were only incidents in the long history of its ancient dominance in the field of religious literature and oral instruction. Catastrophe, wreckage loss and insane fanaticism unrolled from the sad fact that it ended with Origen! How desperately awry of the truth must that school of belief be that has ever since heralded this most tragic of losses as its great glory and the salvation of truth! The failure to continue and perfect Origen's allegories has let loose upon Western humanity the crowning dementia of all history.

The clear grasp of all this facilitates our charting of the causes of the great gulf that quickly widened between the first real Christians, the Gnostics, and the party that usurped the place of orthodoxy a little later. Says G. R. S. Mead in his valuable work, *Fragments of a Faith Forgotten* (p. 189):

"The difference between Gnostic exegesis and that of the subsequent orthodox, is that the former tried to discover the soul-processes in the myths and parables of Scripture, whereas the orthodox regarded a theological and dogmatic interpretation as alone legitimate."

Rather Mead should have said that the orthodox clung only to the straight literal and historical sense of Biblical narration.

Philo was indeed a pillar of strength in his day and later for the support of intrinsic esotericism, and Christianity is deeply indebted to him for what little it preserved of a more abstruse spiritual inwardness of meaning. But it is folly to ignore the solid substance of the power of the allegorical method that had already built up the mighty edifice of Greek and Egypto-Greek, not to say also Persian, Chaldean and Jewish mythological religion for centuries antecedent to Philo. Philo was surely not the originator of the usage, but one of the many who, in periods of material darkness, again and again have rediscovered this recondite and cryptic key to the hidden meaning of the otherwise "dark sayings" of Scriptures that were never written to be perused like a modern book. Ancient sages used the allegorical method in a way that militated against the literal wording of Scripture so as seemingly "to violate the faith of history, and wilfully to close their eyes to the obvious and proper sense of terms and words," which is to say that they followed the allegorical usage to its only possible end, namely the discernment of a spiritual instead of a literal and objectively historical rendering. Surely one does not violate the faith of history if one stands on the allegorical meaning of what is obviously allegory, refusing to be gulled into taking it for history. But with sore distress to all mentality one does violate the faith both of history and of truth when one reads allegory and calls it history. And millions have perpetrated this violation of truth, history and sanity alike, when they assert, for instance, that such a thing as the Lazarus restoration was a historical fact and that Jonah lived three days and nights in the belly of a great fish, or that forty days of rain elevated all the oceans to the highest mountain tops.

Even in a modern *History of Philosophy* (B. A. G. Fuller, p. 269), one finds such an item as the following, which corroborates all that is here contended for:

"Not only Plato and the Neo-Pythagoreans, but the earlier thinkers, contemporary Stoics and even Skeptics, had all in their several ways guessed at the truth of which in its fulness the Scriptures were the chosen repository. Philosophers and prophets alike were all setting forth in different *allegorical* forms the same essential ideas. . . . God is so high and so removed that he cannot be comprehended, but must reveal himself indirectly *through myth and allegory* to the finite human mind."

In his *Christ in the Gospels* (p. 1) Burton Scott Easton has brought out how disastrously even a mild influence like "an apologetic motive" has warped the truth of history. He says that the attempt to mingle apologetic motives with historical material in the research is to destroy both apologetics and history. Hesitancy in this regard has been unfortunately common in what is called "reverent Gospel criticism," and the results have been nothing less than calamitous. It has carried with it in many minds the conviction that Christian reverence can be preserved only at the cost of intellectual integrity, and so has led to a suspicion—more widespread than one likes to realize—that if the Gospels are outside the circle of history, but in that of allegory, then the meanings are flung outside the pale of history altogether. In the modern world, Easton proceeds, from the assertion that the Gospels are sacrosanct entities it is only a step to the assertion that Jesus is a myth. Our responsibility, he concludes, consequently is unspeakably serious.

This is introduced to exhibit by a comparative showing how immeasurably more important and catastrophic it can be when, in addition to impugning the sheer historicity of the Gospels by lifting them up into a spiritual atmosphere rarefied by sacrosanctity, one comes to know of a surety that they are not to be read as history at all.

When we consider this in the light of a pronouncement from a modern exponent of the new-old science of Semantics, we can see how fearfully devastating can be the failure to distinguish between history and allegory. Miss Langer says (*Philosophy in a New Key,* p. 149) that it is characteristic of poetic images and figures that their allegorical nature is not recognized. Only a mind which can distinguish both a literal and a figurative formulation of an idea can differentiate the figure from its meaning. This is exceedingly cogent and true. This incapacity is the one eternal root of idolatry, which is only the taking an image in its literal factual sense and failing to catch its sublime "poetic" reference.

Nothing is more thrilling than the dawn of a new conception, she says, implying that new and dynamic conceptions break upon the mind from this very recognition of a mystic or poetically romantic sense in the image and likeness of the literal idea. And she follows this with the luminous observation that the symbols that embody basic ideas of life and death, or humanity and the universe, are naturally sacred. But naive thinking does not distinguish between the symbol and its import. It fails to see the import adumbrated by the symbol. Therefore naive thinking never divines the sacredness of symbols, although it actually worships the symbol itself. It pays a mistaken homage to the symbol, making it primal and final instead of only secondary and suggestive. And with Miss Langer's statement, combined with John Dewey's asseveration that the discovery of the use of symbols was the most important single event in human history, the case is now established on adamantine bases that Christianity's rejection of the ancient structure of myth, allegory, symbol and typology was the one root cause of the dire deterioration of human intelligence from the light of ancient divine philosophy to the horrid shadows of the Dark Ages. Christianity tore itself completely loose from the anchorage of the mind in the sage arcane philosophies of the great Masters of Wisdom, which were truly the Light of the World, and committed its lot, its guidance and its destiny to—naive thinking. And, as naive thinking overwhelmingly predominates at all times, it thus won the masses of the West, but, having won them, it had lost the light to guide them. It gave them the lamp, but without the oil and the flame, or the flash of intellectual fire to kindle the flame. The light that was in it was darkness and how great that darkness was this work will endeavor to depict.

Miss Langer quotes M. W. Urban who in his *Language and Reality* writes the discerning statement that it is a false presupposition that whatever can be expressed symbolically can be better expressed literally. This holds nothing less than the promise of a new charter of exalted conception, as well as a merited rebuke to cultural myopia. For conceptions and experiences in a higher area of consciousness often lie far beyond the reach of language. The resources of poetry, heavily drawing on symbol and imagery, must be called upon to give proper feeling tone and mystical color to the soul's intimations at these levels. And Urban proceeds to the explication of a principle of understanding that marks an epochal discernment in human insight in saying that when all is said and done, it remains true that poetry is covert metaphysics, and it is only when its implications, *critically interpreted and adequately expressed,* become part of philosophy, that a culturally dynamic view of the world can be achieved. This is the dawn of a new intelligence. Poetry is covert metaphysics because the strength of poetry is nature symbology, and in turn nature is cosmic Mind reified concretely in the universe. The poet who reads the message of nature's preachment interprets God's thoughts to human intelligence and those thoughts constitute the Logos or rational philosophy of Being.

How this recognition would affect, for instance, all Scriptural interpretation is shown in the case of such a statement as that made by Fisher (*The Beginnings of Christianity,* 421):

"The accounts in *Luke* unquestionably formed a part of his [Jesus'] Gospel from its first composition, and were drawn from a written and that a Christian-Jewish source."

Then he adds that these beautiful events recorded by *Luke* "would be unintelligible regarded as unconscious poesy." Here is precisely the point at which all Biblical exegesis, the whole science of Scriptural interpretation, has stumbled off the path of true competence. The immense fact and factor in the situation is that the beautiful allegories and poetic constructions in the Bible, along with the great myths of ancient peoples, certainly are not intelligible in the way all orthodox exegesis has persisted in taking them, namely as history. Therefore their intelligibility must be located in some other realm, and that realm is the province of allegory and poetry. All conventional exegesis has wrecked their intelligibility by insisting it be made in the wrong world of thought. Its terms are not commensurable with those of history. But they are completely commensurable with the demands of logical thought. They are to be interpreted in the world of thought and imagination, and even with mathematical exactitude, not in the world of event. Dewey's assertion that the discovery of the use of symbols is the most significant event in the life of the race does not receive its final importance until the science of symbolic interpretation is developed to perfection. Our true reading of the Scriptures still awaits this consummation. Philo, Clement, Origen labored at the task when Christianity began; Freud, Jung and the psychoanalysts are toiling at it now from the side of the subjective consciousness; semantics is working into it. *Ancient Egypt apparently understood it in all its scientific adequacy!* That ancient insight, lost already when Christianity was forming, must be recovered. The cultural salvation of the race awaits it.

It is to be noted that Fisher speaks of *Luke's* beautiful poetic legends as "unconscious poesy." This again shows failure of modern vision of truth. The myths and allegories, so far from being *unconscious* poetry, were the most masterful creations of supremely *conscious* dramatic representation of truth ever produced by the genius of man, i.e., man risen to godhood. The modern mind still deludes itself in thinking that the great ancient Scriptures were the products of primitive child-humanity. No true evaluation or reading of them is possible until this delusion is ended by the sharp recognition that they were the designed creations of the near-divine genius of enlightened maturity in the evolutionary scale. They were the perfected products of man matured, designed to be the evolutionary guides to man immatured.

It is certain that Christianity started in the tradition of esotericism. Says Frederick D. Kershner, in his *Pioneers of Christian Thought* (p. 69), speaking of the Christians:

"They produced literature that was highly symbolic and which revealed its inner meaning only to the initiated."

He says that *Revelation* "puzzles the unenlightened and gives rise to all sorts of fantastic interpretations." But he is building on a false assumption of the brilliance of early Christian mentality when he adds that "no doubt the early Christians, who understood the symbolic language, read the book with enthusiasm and drew great comfort from its pages." Neither then nor since has any Christian writer penned an elucidation of the mystic symbology of the book of *Revelation* that can be regarded as anything but a pitiable travesty of its meaning.

Miss Langer has given us some most vital statements on the myth that should be broadcast. Divinities, she says, are born from ritual, but theologies spring from the myth. The myth-making instinct does *not* belong to the *lower* phases of mental view, but comes with the dawn of philosophical thought. (This is an important corroboration of our thesis.) The myth is a fabrication out of subjective symbols, *not* out of observed folk-ways. A single higher conception, she says, can be a marvelous leaven in the heavy amorphous mass of human thought. What, then, we ask, could accrue to human uplift if the entire luminous structure of the master-wisdom of ancient sages were rebuilt for the world in all its radiant beauty?

The origin of myth is dynamic, she writes, but its purpose is philosophical. This again is a vital discernment. And she reaches the heights of clear vision in saying that our metaphysical symbols must spring from reality. We have asserted that the poet, the philosopher, the religious mystic has one kingdom to which he can resort at all times to find the concrete images of eternal truth, the kingdom of nature. There every object, form and phenomenon mirrors an image of noumenal reality, an archetypal idea, a phase of creative reality. The Egyptians, we have claimed, were adepts in the deepest knowledge of truth. We wondered if they had been close to nature or lovers of nature. At last we found Breasted saying: "The Egyptian was passionately fond of nature and of outdoor life." The missing link in culture was found.

CHAPTER VII

NIGHTFALL

The ground may now be considered to have been tolerably well prepared for the planting of the seeds of a new envisagement of the genesis and true character of the Christian movement. This new approach goes to the profoundest depths of the human psychological nature and its reaction to history. Its sources are to be located in the innermost recesses of the human psyche in its living struggle with its evolutionary problem. The terms and conditions of that problem, its relation to cosmology in the overall picture and to anthropology in the distinctly human sphere, were themselves largely swept out of general knowledge by the repudiation of previous Pagan learning, the closing of the esoteric Platonic academies, and the destruction of books and libraries. Christianity thus came close to obliterating the very keys to a more glorious understanding of its own highest message. But happily it failed; and now the supplementation of Egyptian wisdom upon the splendid rationalism of the Hellenic philosophies enables us to rebuild those basic *archai* and upon them erect the lovelier and stronger edifice of the systems of religious truth. Seen in the light of this restored wisdom, the situation that gave birth to the Christian development can be viewed with a clear discernment of its features, currents and motivations that has not been possible before.

Christianity was a growth resulting from one of the most thrilling episodes in the history of culture. It sprang to the fore as the outcome of a struggle between the forces of enlightenment and those of darkness. The universal tradition in all Christendom has had it that the new faith sprang into existence out of this conflict as the bearer of the banner of victory of the light over darkness. Alas and again alas, it was not so. It came out waving the banner of darkness as victor over the light. It all but put out the light of the world.

Light and darkness, as in the grand symbolizations of the Hermetic and Zoroastrian systems, are eternally in combat. Every human historical predicament is a phase of the battle. The rise of Christianity was an outstanding episode in the everlasting Battle of Armageddon; and it stands now clearly revealed as perhaps the most complete and smashing defeat of the powers of the light in the recorded period of the world's life. If this is doubted and flouted, it takes but one instant's consideration of a single feature of Christianity's motivation and character to silence dissent from the terrific indictment: its fiendish hatred of books and libraries and learning and philosophy, the noblest agencies of man's culture. Picture the anomaly presented by the spectacle of the Christian hosts emerging from the struggle allegedly carrying the victorious banner of the light, while with hot feet it stamped out the blackened ashes of the books of the Alexandrian library. Picture this bearer of the standard of new light that had never gleamed before, burning in 553 A.D. the books of its most truly exalted theologian, Origen, and invoking anathema on any one found owning or reading them. As Emerson said, one's actions shout so loud that one's protesting words can not be heard; and here the acts of Christian fanaticism resound abroad in such volume that its pious protestations avail not to refute the incontestable fact that its victory in the fourth century dimmed the brightest light of human culture ever to be kindled and plunged the West into the night of the Dark Ages.

Lothrop Stoddard has a book that should impress general thought more deeply than it has done. It is *The Revolt Against Civilization*. It unfolds the thesis that ignorance is ever resentful of the possession of knowledge and rebellious against the superior power which knowledge confers. Periodically it bursts out in violent upheaval to wrest the special advantages away from the intelligent groups that have used their skills to build up happier conditions of existence. It mobilizes in as nearly a concerted effort as possible that sullen disregard and covert resentment of the majority of "common people" against what an illiterate backwoodsman used to call "book larnin.'" Almost all movements of popular rebellion have been tinctured more or less heavily by this strain; but it was the Christian movement that most luridly manifested this feature in all the run of history.

The area of man's life is the battleground of this perennial conflict. The battle is that between the two antagonists, the soul and the flesh in the constitution of the individual, moved out into the collective body of the nation and the world. Says Goethe: "Two souls, alas, contend within my breast apart." As human society is the life of the individual multiplied and massed, the mighty battle between the carnal instincts of the physical man and the slowly developing divine spirit within the body is the massive waging of the warfare between these two powers of consciousness. It is the carnal mind against the god-mind in man. In Egypt it was the duel between Horus and Sut.

For a long period of early human history the animal instincts and sensual impulses reigned with nearly unchallenged dominance, motivating every act with a selfish aim. Eventually the sleeping divinity within man's breast awakened, and began to interpose the protests of its developing reason against rampant brutality. Tamed by suffering, the animal self must pay heed more and more to the soul's voice and curb its violent propensities. Extended experience finally instructs the man that the principle of reason is his only constant and dependable guide and monitor, and he brings himself to the study of philosophy, in which a complete understanding of the whole field of knowledge by which he may attain the happiest life is presumably to be found.

In order to serve mankind with a systematic code of wisdom principles for the achievement of this lordly end, ancient sages of graduate human status took pains to formulate in ever memorable fashion the principia of such a soul-science. They designed it for the guidance and eventual self-illumination of all such as would rise from animality into an awareness of the need of genuine superior wisdom. These formulations constituted the first of all Bibles and the codes of the first religions. Ancient "churches" were associations of sufficiently evolved men to undertake, consciously and intelligently, the more direct and more rapid unfoldment of the genius of divinity latent in the human constitution. Heraclitus tells us that "man's genius is a divinity." As the substance of this highest of all cultures lay deep in the domain of the mystical consciousness, truly occult and mysterious until experienced, the associations were termed the "Mysteries." There conscientiously the "wisdom of God hidden in a mystery" was to be cultivated, under the instruction of hierophants, who presumably had attained mastership in the divine cultus.

Now the point of vital significance to the analysis is that inevitably in the world situation at any time in the main human epoch, the number of those who by karmic merit and excellent progression had emancipated themselves from the toils of the animal nature to which ignorance had kept them bound until the light of reason and philosophy had dawned upon their consciousness, is always a very limited few. The truly liberated and enlightened always have formed a very tiny minority amidst the great masses of those still sense-ridden. What a

143

scant company are the philosophers in any community, in any age! How few are the light-bearers and the pioneers of any advance above the steady level of ordinary "average" mediocrity!

Thence arises the condition in human society that necessitates esotericism in cultural life. It hypostatizes an oligarchy or aristocracy of intellect and culture, as against a loose democracy of unintelligence and crudity. And the boorish "proletariat" that can not comprehend the just claims of a superior intelligence is ever resentful of the latter's posing in the seats of headship and power and is in revolt against its assumption of privilege and "nobility." Stoddard competently brings this out.

This state of affairs, ineluctably inherent in the status of human evolution, wherein souls of many variant grades of attainment in life science are traveling onward side by side, gives genesis to a series of facts, without a circumspect consideration of which no science of human history or sociology can be formulated to aid in the handling of world problems.

The first and most challenging of these concomitants of evolutionary inequality is the radical pronouncement that, as regards all questions concerned with lofty spiritual experience, intellectual discernment and the cultivation of mystical faculties necessary to apprehend the three elements of beauty, truth and goodness, it is a fearful thing to have to realize that only a limited minority of the cultured are right; the great majority are always wrong! This flouts the ordinary belief or conviction that the majority is always in the right—so dear to the presuppositions of a democratic hope. This deduction means that in such things the standards of the cultured few are more nearly *en rapport* with divine ideas and ideals and perfect norms than are those of the masses.

Hence there is always a clash between the practical ideals of the few cultured members of society and those of the mob. As the professionally cultured individual, learning a higher wisdom, attempts to align the practice of his life with its dictates, he finds himself differing from the common herd, who, if they take notice, begin to deride and denounce the "heretic." For sheer self-protection, then, and peace, the person fighting his way to clearer views from loftier peaks takes measures to conceal his "eccentric" and "peculiar" modes from the rabble, tends to draw away in semi-seclusion from its rude contacts and seeks the more inspiring association of those of his own caste. For the farther he advances in his individual emancipation through surer and wider knowledge, the more detestable become the slavish mannerisms and deadly conformities of the "average." The meaner banalities of the social and thought levels become ever more distasteful to him, until it is a crucifixion of his free-spirited soul to suffer the deadly impact of the crudities of common people. To meet a fellow philosopher is to come out of a dark prison and inhale draughts of fresh pure air.

And then comes a series of almost dismaying realizations. He finds himself in mortal danger from that mob of conventionalizers. It does not take kindly the tacit rebuke administered by the different attitude of the one who has gone beyond it to nobler things. It does not like to have its inferiority demonstrated in the open. It resents something that reveals its baseness. Or it is incompetent to see the nobility of anything that stands out in sharp contrariety to its norms, and casts at once the stigma of eccentric, queer at any one who has the moral hardihood to violate its laws. It dislikes any member of the clan who will assert his freedom from the fixed restraints and taboos and live a life of his own on liberal grounds.

And so the well-known cry of "Crucify him, crucify him!" all too readily rises. The rule of the mob is "Conform, conform. You dissent at your peril!" And since the mediocrity of general culture thus holds the whole body to only a mediocre level, missing depravity at the lower end through social fear, and nobility at the upper end through want of capacity for loftier reach, the common crowd is ever challenged by the moral and intellectual pioneer who feels in his breast the upsurge of more divine character. His independent aspiration shocks them. The war is on between him and the many.

The mass of average humanity is still under the sway of the primitive elemental instincts of the animal part of the human dual nature, the divine part not yet having been placed on the throne of the personal life. It is not yet above raging and tearing with the fury of brute savagery. It is therefore the Beast of the old allegories, indeed the Beast of the *Book of Revelation*. It is the beast in man, not yet domesticated and tamed to gentleness in the service of the coming Lord of Love. And this is the brute unfeeling force that reaches out and besmirches and defiles every creation of beauty, truth and goodness that the ardent pioneer and the philosopher struggle to embody in thought and act, in art and literature. This is the dull incapacity that takes every symbol that intimates to sensitive appreciation a sublime import and tears its mystical halo from it, to leave it a dead and empty husk. This is the stupidity that takes the fertile images of truth conceived by the genius of seers and prophets and reduces them to the bare and unlovely aspect of their literal status. This is the ignorance that in the end transmogrifies every sublime ikon of verity into an idol. For only the ignorant can become an idolator. And this is the crude power that in the final failure to discern the uplifting purport of the images, and thus at last revolting from the assumed falsity of all images, breaks into the churches and in fell fury vents its iconoclastic rage against what it believes to be the instruments of pious sham and vainglory.

And this is the dumb incomprehension that ever since history began has taken hold of every splendid construction of high spiritual genius, designed for the guidance of all aspiring souls at their level of developing intelligence, and presenting the basic principles for true understanding of man's unfolding divinity, and inexorably transformed it into something so completely divergent from its pristine sense as to render it wholly an instrument of crass stultification instead of a means of edification. There is not a religion on earth today, however high and pure in its original conceptuality, that has not been traduced from its first grandeur into a base and banal exteriorization. Not one has escaped the slimy claws of the Beast. It has dragged all alike down into the grossness of flat misconception, in a fearful metamorphosis of exalted sense over to a degrading crudity of meaning that has thwarted the true intent of all noble religions and held the masses of mankind to a low level of culture in all ages.

There comes to hand a passage from one of the ancient world's honored thinkers that puts the truth of this delineation in strikingly forceful manner. It is the philosopher Epicurus, who says:

"The Gods exist, but they are not what the *hoi polloi* [the many] suppose them to be. He is not an infidel or atheist who denies the existence of the Gods whom the multitude worship, but he is such who fastens on the Gods the opinions of the multitude."

So true is this astute discernment of the philosopher that indeed it can probably be truly affirmed that religions harbor more real infidels and atheists in their folds than are to be found outside them. Only the few enlightened and emancipated minds could be accounted free from idolatry and atheism. Certainly to build up in an ignorant mind a conception of deity that must fall far short of the truth of the divine nature is to institute the worship of false gods. It confronts man boldly with the question whether to worship a Being or Beings whose real nature is admittedly past all grasp of the finite human mind is not a gross mistake from the very outset. For the worship, and eventually the worshipper, will become molded to the likeness of the conception of the Object worshipped, and a life will be misshaped over a false pattern. Philosophers have in fact declared that for man to attempt to formulate any concrete idea of Divinity is at once to demean, defame and degrade it. Times without number Christianity has denounced the ancient Pagans for want of worship of the One True God. But this, if true, may but prove that the Pagans were more astute than the Christians, knowing the certainty of committing gross idolatry in so doing. The truth is that most lofty Pagan philosophy advised and practised a discreet silence in regard to the One. We read that they venerated the Unknowable with a befitting silence. Christianity strove in its blindness to make God a familiar Personage to all men, and in the process objectified him to as idolatrous a form of anthropomorphism as had ever been done. Intelligent Paganism revolted from such practice with a sense of violated reverence. Paganism did not essay to drag the Deity down to man's level, but in wiser fashion tried to hold man in more discreet anthropological relation to those inherent aspects and powers of divinity that are manifest and active both in nature and in man's constitution alike. It was in this spirit, mistaken for a lack of worshipful adoration of Supreme Deity, that the Buddha enjoined, "Seek not safety in any one else whomsoever outside yourselves." If religion is the expression of man's relation to God, then ancient Paganism made it, not the relation of man to a God in cosmic heavens, but to the presence of God within man's own nature and his own reach.

In its laudable, but impracticable blundering motive of giving high religion to the multitude, Christianity entrusted its destinies to this Beast. It is intended in all symbolic religion that the bestial segment of man's nature is to be made the sacrificial oblation on the altar of man's life. The numberless sheep, bullocks, heifers and pigs slain with priestly knife and burned—not too badly for convivial banqueting—upon holy altars to make a sweet savor unto the nostrils of a sensual God (if Scriptures are to be taken literally) have betokened this dramatization of the great sacrificial burning out of the animal propensities of the human constitution in the fires of suffering on the altar of the fleshly life. But in the case of Christianity the divinest elements in man's makeup were sacrificed to make the religion appealing and acceptable to man almost at his beastly level. The consecrated genius of perfected minds risen to near divinity was thrown recklessly out to the wolves, the dogs and the swine, and it was but a few years until those hordes had trodden it into the mire of low mortal meanings and motives, or degraded it with base misunderstanding. It consigned its future into the same hands that stone the prophets, crucify the saviors and starve the genius of the poet, the artist and the creator of sheer beauty, and that regard as offensive every fully righteous, loving and holy soul struggling amid its restless surgings. It raises the howl of scorn and hatred against every prophet who essays to correct its sordid *mores* or elevate the tone of its culture. It prostitutes the glory of every gleaming revelation of new truth into tawdry commonplace or distorts it into caricature.

The thinkers in the philosophical quest have always drawn a sharp distinction between "naive thinking" and what is termed philosophical reflection or "speculation." Any intelligent student in this field becomes startlingly aware, sooner or later, of the astounding fact that naive thinking is, as regards essential truth, always in error. Truth is to be found generally as a correction of naive thought, and reflection always ends by correcting common assumption. Common belief is always wrong! Education is largely a process of correcting the erroneous character of naive popular ideas.

Particularly is this true in the realm of religion. And a vital point is that priestcraft has found it on the whole profitable to refrain from emancipating the laity from the errors of the naive viewpoint. They remain more pliable in that state. And deeper reflection tends to lift the thinker out of the ranks of the docile and faithful, and to breed independence and non-conformity.

Need we ask for more valid testimony to the fixity of the general level of indurated belief of the naive mind in human society than this statement from Gibbon in his famous work? (p. 418): "But the practice of superstition is so congenial to the multitudes that, if they are forcibly awakened, they still regret the loss of their pleasing vision." The common mind shrinks from the ordeal of the birth-pangs of new and larger view.

The history of religions has been the invariable story of the degradation of a pristine lofty teaching in the course of time at the hands of later incompetence. No religion has remained the same or carried the same message that its dynamic founder embodied in it. There is a succinct delineation of the inevitable process of deterioration, once the generative power is withdrawn, in Joseph Klausner's valuable work on *Jesus of Nazareth,* reflecting the Jewish viewpoint (p. 213):

"It never yet happened that there were parties and teachings or systems, where in course of time they did not deteriorate, and their teachings become corrupted by certain of their adherents who had no higher motive than honors, power and gain. In every system, as time goes on, the secondary comes to be regarded as primary and the primary as secondary; the most exalted idea has associated with it disciples who distort it and transform it. . . . This happened to the Law of Moses in the time of Jeremiah, *to Christianity not long after Jesus,* and to the teaching of the Buddha two hundred years after its propagation."

And Thomas Taylor, the luminous genius who saw and registered the profundities of the great Platonic and Neoplatonic wisdom as no other scholar has ever done, illustrates this process of degradation in a phase of historical development that vitally concerns this study. From the Introduction to his great work on *The Six Books of Proclus on the Theology of Plato,* one of the two or three greatest books in all the world, Taylor shows how that mighty system of enlightenment was rendered mute while a world went down into darkness (p. x):

"No objections of any weight, no arguments but such as are sophistical, can be urged against this most sublime theory which is so congenial to the unperverted conceptions of the human mind, that it can only be treated with ridicule and contempt in degraded, barren and barbarous ages. Ignorance and priestcraft, however, have hitherto conspired to defame those inestimable works [of the Neoplatonists] in which this and many other grand and important dogmas can alone be found; and the theology of the Greeks has been attacked with all the insane fury of ecclesiastical zeal and all the imbecile flashes of mistaken wit, by men whose conceptions on the subject, like those of men between sleeping and waking, have been turbid and wild, fantastic and confused, preposterous and vain."

One could readily transfer this indignant voice of Taylor's disappointment and disgust over what orthodox religion had done to mutilate the noble body of Orphic Wisdom and apply it with undiminished force to the similar situation in Christian theology. Indeed the statement covers practically the same deterioration in the same general movement.

But nothing could be more specifically corroborative of this argument than the excerpt from the pen of a modern historian of philosophy. It clinches the point to be driven home at this stage of the development of our theme. It is from the *History of Philosophy,* by B. A. G. Fuller (p. 95):

"The untutored mind is naive and soft-headed. In its operation it scarcely distinguishes fact from fancy, dreaming from waking. It swallows everything it is told. Hence it is forever shying at shadows, growling at reflections, pursuing will-o'-the-wisps and clinging to phantoms. Now and then it may happen to lay hold of a truth, but it does so at random, on irrational grounds and with no sense of the difference between the real and the illusory."

And from D. F. Strauss' well-known and much-debated *Life of Jesus* (Vol. II, p. 49) we take this notable statement:

"Simple people, says Origen, in their simplicity, think it is a light matter for the universe to be put in motion or for the heavens to be rent asunder; but those who think more profoundly on these matters see in these superior revelations how it is that chosen people believe in their watchings, and more particularly in their dreams, that they have had evidence by their corporeal senses, while it has simply been a movement in their minds."

At first sight this might seem to be out of reference to naive thinking. But in the religious field the tendency of the "simple-minded" people to reify the substance of their visions and dreams and to entify the symbolic personages of dramatic allegory has made an immense contribution to the vague mass of crude "belief" that helps to solidify these ruinous fixations of naive thought in the world at any age. The disposition of hosts of people to mistake their inner dreamings and haphazard guessings for objective reality in the outer world has been a foremost cause of popular corruption of true religion. True beyond cavil is Plutarch's analysis of the stultifying influences of "popular religion." Fuller (op. cit., p. 265) puts it as follows:

"But a godly life can flow only from a right knowledge of the divine nature and from immediate communion with it."

Words like these are worthy to be framed in gold and hung on all walls, for they hold the correction of aberrations in true religion and philosophy.

"Atheism is therefore the worst thing that can befall a human being."
"Equally bad is superstition, which is exemplified by the unworthy stories and ideas about the gods current in the popular theology, and by the fear, the cringing before their power and the distrust of their will, *engendered by the traditional religion*. Indeed the orthodox notions are bound to sow and foster atheism."

This will sound like atheism itself to most pious religionists in the orthodox parties of today, yet it is indubitably a true statement. For the weird and turbid mélange of ideas that arise in the masses in their efforts to make sense out of an unintelligible theology breaks down assurance in the end and breeds infidelity. Most of those who desert religion do so when they take one step above the naive stage and begin to reason.

It might be appropriate to insert here with at least general endorsement John Dewey's strong assertion (*Quest for Certainty,* p. 308) that

"the pride of the zealously devout is the most dangerous form of pride. The pride of those who feel themselves learned in the express and implicit will of God is the most exclusive."

It is fair to say that such pride is not a peculiarity alone of naive thinkers and the unintelligent orthodox. It surely is characteristic of those groups, however, in large measure. It takes pretty competent philosophical education to break it down into a wider humility.

Hodges, in his *The Early Church* (p. 68), speaking of Celsus, learned Jewish critic of Christianity, writes that "he disliked them for their poverty and ignorance. They seemed to be presumptuous and impertinent people who undertook to be teachers, having never learned."

Guignebert, one of the greatest of Christian historians, speaks of the "superstitions which vex the shallow minds of men." And this French historian gives us a passage which is most pertinent to our discussion (*Christianity Past and Present,* p. 207):

"Simple folk are doubtless accessible to all forms of suggestion. . . . Their religious sensibility is more quickly stirred and reacts more profoundly when it is under the will of group contagion, and then they usually show themselves so incapable of regulating it that they very often put the theologians to embarrassment . . . they constitute, therefore, a disturbing element in the Church . . . in ferment and *always unstable,* nevertheless, nothing frightens them worse than the prospect of change in their belief. . . . For a man to accord to any creed whatever his reasoned and well-considered assent, he must experience an ordinary need for reason and reflection; he must also be accustomed to reasoning. Experience proves that this habit is not common, but presupposes an educated man and a daily schedule which from time immemorial has been the precious privilege of a minority; even smaller in the fifth century than it is today. The majority of men may indeed find that they possess within themselves a religious life in principle, but it ferments in their consciousness as a vague yearning; they prove incapable of organizing it, just as they remain impotent to organize their minds. Of themselves they do not succeed in unifying either their intellect or their moral ego. The necessary light and direction come to them from without, usually in the form of statements of a metaphysical kind which can not be verified. It matters little that they are neither very coherent in themselves nor easy of justification, provided they be clear and decisive. But if they are to be classified with the Truth they must not vary by a hair and issue from one authority worthy of confidence—or at any rate deemed so—in which they shall find unwavering support. . . . For this reason simple-minded faithful souls in Augustine's day, and he along with them, willingly believed that the Church represented a divine institution established to teach unerringly and to preserve intact the eternal truths revealed by Christ and by the Holy Spirit. . . . The reality of the religious thought and life enclosed in that setting varies infinitely from age to age and milieu to milieu, for the passage of time modifies the reason of educated men as it does the impressionableness of the ignorant."

All of which, coming to us from out the long-considered lucubration of a deep-thinking, fair-minded scholar, intimates to us very concretely that the general mass of untutored people at any time will always follow the trend of the most conspicuous religious influences brought to the fore and embodied in the ministrations of religion that most largely confront their attention. When inner reflection and more studied and balanced reason does not offer resistance, the commonalty of men will follow the most popular trend, or the psychologically strategic seductions of a sly and deft propaganda.

And how the true inner sense of spiritual doctrines went into complete eclipse under the general ignorance early in the history of Christianity is brought out curtly by Guignebert (op. cit., p. 212):

"The general intellectual apprehension of Christianity falls rapidly away into obscurity. The formulas which churchmen go on repeating *without really understanding them* themselves, only serve as a mask for an unbridled immorality and a faith really uncouth and incoherent; a gross syncretism in which Teutonic superstitions mingled with those native to the soil, really count for more than the Christian dogmas."

And the low potential of general intelligence exerts a strong pull also to drag the clergy down to its mark. For, says Guignebert (p. 215), speaking of the period of about 500 A.D.:

"In those days, too, the large majority of the clergy are miserably ignorant and share in the profligacy of the age. . . . Scarcely anywhere save in the heart of the monasteries . . . in the sixth and seventh centuries does the light of intellectual culture and theology even flicker."

Indeed early in its history Christianity had already sunk so low under the downward pull of mass ignorance of its lowly and uncultured addicts that the Greeks called the new religion "atheism." (Sir Gilbert Murray, *The Five Stages of the Greek Religion,* p. 19.) And

152

so quickly had the popular ignorance committed to oblivion the real meaning of doctrines and rites that Murray asserts that whatever of reality there ever had been in the ceremonies had "apparently by classical times faded away." This fatal depravity shows the quick and devastating work of the Beast.

Never should be missed the plain reminder of Herodotus, the father of objective history, to the effect that it is always intelligence that elevates one people, age or epoch above another. Says he (op. cit., I, 60): "The Hellenic race was marked off from the barbarians as more intelligent and more emancipated from silly nonsense." And nothing in the end but intelligence will avoid silly nonsense.

And it would be a pity to omit another keen and trenchant thrust of Guignebert, when he tells of the ignorance of the laity at a later epoch (pp. 222-3):

"Unfortunately their credulity also was unbounded and they became attached by preference to the most indifferent rites and practices, because those best agree with ignorance and thoughtlessness."

And so it resulted that the Christian dogmas, which, says Guignebert, had been formulated by keen Eastern minds, had by the tenth century—certainly long before, as the light went out as early as the third—"proved incapable of penetrating tenth-century minds." If, then, he argues, the veritable core of Christianity inhered within those dogmas, the contemporaries of Otto the Great or of Hugh Capet had to content themselves with a mere semblance of Christianity.

Anent our earlier asseveration that nearly all the facts of religious history are caricatured into untruth in the mass mind, Guignebert, in refuting popular ideas regarding the growth of the authority of the Popes in Rome, says (p. 227): "The truth of history is widely different from this decidedly biased theory." This statement could be applied with generally similar aptitude to nearly every major theory about the Christian religion and its history. Popular ignorance has misconceived almost every single item of theology and history alike.

At several places Guignebert openly affirms that Christianity was adapted for the lower orders, and thus enthroned the tyranny of ignorance in the Western world. He makes it clear that it spells woe to any religion to entrust its destinies into the hands of the simple folk. Such people never merit the prerogative of setting the higher guiding light before a civilization. Their proper and beneficent function is to abide as steadily as may be by a general norm of decent *mores* and maintain them as pure as possible. However they are to be hailed as sovereign lords in a democracy, it is they who wreck every noble culture and demean it to a vulgar level. It is they who wrecked Christianity and doused the ancient gleam.

The ignoble work of mass mentality in world history is seen when one studies the tribal religions of the backward nations of the earth. Scholastic sense has gone all awry in estimating these crude forms and practices as primitive outgrowths of child-minded conception. What they are in truth is the unintelligible wrack and debris of very ancient constructions of sage allegorical skill. As Massey affirms, all the insanity in them is in *our* assumption that these long-descended forms represent real beliefs originally. They stand as vivid markers to our intelligence of what stupid handling of sacred emblems and rituals in total ignorance of their symbolic meaning can do to traduce an initially fine representation of verity into a mummery of nonsense.

It could be a matter of at least casual and incidental interest to introduce here the amazingly frank confession of the eminent English Egyptologist, Budge, as to our paucity of sound knowledge about ancient cultures. In *The Gods of the Egyptians* (Vol. I) he asks:

"Is it true that the more the subjects of Egyptian religion and mythology are studied the less we know about them? The question is, however, thoroughly justified, and every honest worker will admit that there are at the present time scores of passages even in such a comparatively well-known religious compilation as the *Book of the Dead* which are inexplicable, and scores of allusions to a fundamentally important mythological character of which the meanings are still unknown."

This confessed ignorance of what are now known to be the immediate sources of all that Christianity holds is the price centuries have had to pay for the Christian repudiation of "Origen's allegories." Had Origen expounded the mystic and cosmic significance of the Egyptian myths of Osiris, Isis and Horus, of Hathor, Atum, Kepher and Shu, and had succeeding theologians retained the insight to follow, perpetuate and uphold such elucidation, Western history would have taken a far happier journey than it did. But already in Origen's day the mighty scrolls of the hieroglyphics had lain in oblivion, uninterpretable, for some eight hundred years. Origen can hardly be blamed for his inability to measure up to adeptship in the deep art of a luminous grasp of the cryptic reading of the myths and allegories inherited from Egypt, for he lacked the true keys which only that ancient system of code principles could supply. Thirteen centuries later the same important keys were still lacking to the Reformers. For those ancient runes still defy the best intelligence of Western minds to fathom their mysteries of meaning, and will do so as long as the secret clues that only Egypt could furnish are missing. Now at last those keys and clues are available, and the near future is waiting to be glorified by the completion of the unfinished Protestant Reformation by the release of a flood tide of illumination radiant beyond all possible calculation. The true Period of Enlightenment for Christianity and the end of the Dark Ages are at hand.

If this sounds like the ebullition of extravagant fancy, let the reader contemplate another amazing admission from this same renowned Egyptologist, and speculate on the possibility that what is here advanced supplies a hidden clue to the explication of a fact that has perplexed Christian minds and undermined Christian pride over all the centuries. Says Budge in the same passage:

"And at last when his [Osiris'] cult disappeared before the religion of the man Christ, the Egyptians who embraced Christianity found that the moral system of the old cult and that of the new religion were so similar, and the promises of resurrection and immortality in each so much alike that they transferred their allegiance from Osiris to Jesus of Nazareth without difficulty; moreover Isis and the child Horus were straightway identified with Mary the Virgin and her Son, and in the apocryphal literature of the first few centuries which followed the evengelization of Egypt, several of the legends about Isis and her sorrowful wandering were made to center around the Mother of Christ. Certain of the attributes of the sister goddesses of Isis were also ascribed to her, and like the goddess Neith of Sais, she was declared to possess perpetual virginity. Certain of the Egyptian Christian Fathers gave to the Virgin the title 'Theotokos,' or 'Mother of God,' forgetting apparently that it was an old translation of *nefer mut*, a very old and common title of Isis."

Here is the background for an understanding of our assertion that the lost literature of Egypt holds the explicatory or exegetical secret keys to Christianity and its Scriptures. For in the full blunt truth the latter are only a prolongation and revamped republication of the same old Nilotic system, with the keys lost. The early Christian Fathers, in their unintelligence, presumed that their misshapen keys would unlock the doors of mystic mystery. Their incredible mistake committed their world to chaos and ineradicable bigotry. The Rosetta Stone offers the lost key to a lost world; but after translation must come competent interpretation, and even on top of that must be regained what Symonds called a new mental sensibility to catch what interpretation has completely missed till now. This accomplishment promises the coming dawn of a new revelation, which is of course nothing but the recovery of a lost old revelation. Happily it is near at hand.

The *Catholic Encyclopedia* more than once admits that the history of Catholic ceremonials "affords numerous parallels for this Christianizing of Pagan rites." But its sponsors and editors have never had the discernment to recognize that one would therefore have to go back and investigate the genesis and meaning of those antecedent Pagan rites if the Christian usage of them was to be rationally apprehended. The inevitable claim is that the Christians took hold of old heathen practices which the Pagans followed, *but never themselves understood,* and at last placed the true and rational interpretation upon them. But this presupposes the preposterous and impossible assumption that the Pagans, steeped in densest mental and spiritual darkness, had in all their rites hit upon formulations and procedures that were later by the Christians found to express true, sublime and authoritative significance. In total ignorance of such significance and by blind chance the Pagans had developed the forms and types of the most exalted verities, which the Christians could adopt and find expressive of the divinest realities. On such baseless and fantastic foundations do most Christian "explanations" of many challenging facts rest.

We can well see the impossibility of upbuilding a religion of truth to benefit all ranks of mankind—as Christianity claims to be—on the naive thinking and poor intelligence of the lower orders—as Christianity claims to have done—if we listen to what that prodigious thinker of the later European period, Immanuel Kant, wrote in his *Die Religion:*

"It ought not to be made a condition of Salvation to believe that there was once a Man who by his holiness and merit gave satisfaction for himself and for all others; for of this the reason tells us nought; but it is the duty of men universally to elevate themselves to the Ideal of moral perfection deposited in the Reason, and to obtain moral strength by the contemplation of this Ideal. Such moral faith alone is man bound to exercise and not historic faith."

Truer words than these were never spoken, and no one in this case could allege that they do not embody the conclusions of the most prolonged and conscientious thinking of one of the greatest of human minds. Shallow thinking can not be charged against *this* declaration. Kant finds that the Gospel narrative of the Jesus life can not be accepted on a basis that makes it in any way a substitute for the need of man's salvation through his own reason. Not a few other notable scholars have reached the same conclusion. Now the Egyptian literature discloses that Kant is right; the Gospels are not histories, but rescripts of old allegorical and dramatic mystery representations—falsely turned into "history." And the Christian Fathers, Clement, Origen, Eusebius, Augustine and others corroborate this dictum by statements that drop from their pens when the truth escapes them at unguarded moments.

Kant further stresses the query whether one must not fully make allowance, as one reads the Gospels

"for the desire on the part of Jesus' biographers to conform these incidents to texts of the Hebrew Scriptures; and hence each reader must judge for himself whether he is being treated to facts or to this process of conformity."

And this observation of the great German philosopher epitomizes a view which has been forced upon the attention of most Christian historians and exegetists open-minded enough to face what is unescapable in a study of Scripture. There will be occasion to revert to this view and its weighty involvements in a later chapter.

Kant also enlarges upon the odd fact that Jesus so woefully lacked defenders at his trial and death, when he had personally benefited so many.

As showing the gullibility of the populace in religious matters, we have Gerald Massey's opinion, founded on a life-time of devoted study in Egypt, that

"The ancient wisdom in the Hebrew books has been converted into a spurious specie and passed off on the ignorant and unsuspecting as a brand new issue from the mint of God."

Humiliating and repugnant to swollen pride as such an assertion proves to be, it has now to be accepted as positive truth. No redemption of a decadent religionism can be achieved until this is known.

We may agree or disagree with the pronouncements of two ancient historians, but both ascribe the vogue of deliberately cultivated religion to motives that are far from holy and spiritual. Says Polybius (VI, 56):

"Religion would perhaps be unnecessary in a commonwealth of wise men. But since the multitude is ever fickle, full of lawless desires, irrational passions and violence, it is right to restrain it by the fear of the invisible world and such tragic terrors. Whence our ancestors appear to have introduced the notions concerning the gods and opinions about the infernal regions, not rashly or without consideration. Those rather act rashly and inconsiderately who would expel them."

And Strabo is even more direct (Lib. I, p. 19):

"It is impossible to govern a mob of women, or the whole mixed multitude, by philosophical reason and to exhort them to piety, holiness and faith; *we must also employ superstition with its fables and prodigies.* For the thunder, the abyss, the trident, the torches, the serpents, the *thyrsi* of the gods, are fables, *as is all ancient theology;* but the legislature introduces these things as bugbears to those who are children in understanding."

Here with brutal frankness is laid bare the shrewd politic design behind what has often been declared by astute students to be the world's oldest and greatest "racket." If we demur to its correctness, we still must admit that what was doubtless intended to be something immeasurably higher and nobler in its origin and conception has almost generally sunk to this status in its motivation. High purposiveness has been lost along with high understanding, and a grand culture vouchsafed by the gods to men has been dragged down into the mire in which the Beast wallows. But Polybius and Strabo remind us forcibly what may be and has been done with the symbols and rites and Scriptures of a lost sublime religion, when knowledge of their meaning has long been extinct, and when the open gullibility of the crude masses offers tempting opportunities to crafty and none too conscientious priestcraft. If there is greater general indifference to religion in the modern age and Western world, it is doubtless due to the fact that broader education of the masses has awakened them to this insincerity of the motivation behind established religions. They are catching on to the "game" and are beginning to resent being played upon in the role of gullible dupes. But in their reaction they will sweep out the cultural good of religion along with the evil of it. The problem is to eradicate the evils due to ignorance and preserve for a redemptive culture the intrinsic good, the high intellectual and enlightening content that was swept away with the tide of fanatical pietism that brought in the Christian movement. This work will point the way to that achievement.

Von Mosheim says (Vol. I, 21) that the Egyptian priests had a sacred code of their own

"founded on very different principles from those which characterized the popular religion, and it was studiously concealed from the curiosity of the public by wrapping it up in characters the meaning and power of which were only known to themselves."

This system, so sedulously kept from the multitude, he suspects put nature as causative principle in the place of the Deity, while the multitude was allowed to ascribe all things to Deity. Children can readily be led to accept a Deity as the universal creator; philosophers come around to the view that the creative power is Nature, which they may accept as the arm or instrument of Deity.

Again the susceptibility of the "vulgar" is seen to have tempted the duplicity of the priesthood when one takes at its real, if hidden, worth such a statement as that made by Farrar (op. cit., Vol. II, 367), when he says:

"In the practice of the vulgar Christianity became an idolatry enriched by myths."

To this should be added, of course, the reflection that if Christianity had not impoverished itself by discarding and flouting the myths in the first place, it need never have fallen to the mean status of becoming an idolatry, and then regaining some of the lost wealth by recovering the myths later. This exactly matches the situation in the processing of modern wheat flour: the millers sifted out the bran, the germ and some vital mineral elements from the grain till it was a lifeless product. Now they have had to put back into it the elements they had left out.

George Hodges, in a sensible work on *The Early Church,* speaking of the Mystery religions, writes (p. 22):

"They led their disciples on from grade to grade till they were taught at last a doctrine too sacred to be told to the common world."

And this simple true statement from a scholar out of the ranks of the modern theological milieu is expressly contradicted, denied, smudged, vilified by ecclesiastics and spokesmen of the Church, even by such a renowned investigator as Renouf, who declares that the Mystery groups had no inner secret teaching worthy of being considered either secret or mysterious.

We have then perpetually in the world a condition which in the end exerts a greater determining influence in the practice and conduct of religion than any other single factor. On the one hand we have the general run of average and subnormal humanity, deprived of opportunity to become enlightened, or by virtue of their low stage in the scale of evolution incapable of it; and on the other the very limited number of the mentally elite and truly illumined, or potentially fitted for the finest culture. How to preserve and to use the body of the highest and deepest wisdom garnered by previous mastership has been the perennial problem confronting the cognoscenti and illuminati down the ages. Various motives can be seen to have dictated the policies pursued at different times in history. True humanitarian wisdom prescribed the segregation of the profoundest elements of knowledge among a tried and proven few, not from motives of selfish enjoyment or unwillingness to admit the many into the arcana, but strictly because it was considered a risk of debasement of noble truth to cast it out to the undisciplined multitude, a very great danger to society itself. A thing so intrinsically precious was not to be cheapened by common spoliation. This motive resulted in the institution of esotericism both in the substance and the content of oral and written knowledge, and in the method of impartation or instruction. The instruments used were myth, allegory, symbol, drama, number, letter and star picture, in a wide variety of combination and cryptic reference. Says G. R. S. Mead in his *Orpheus* (p. 60):

"These myths were not only set forth in verse and prose, but were also represented pictorially and in sculpture in the Adyta of the Temples."

The danger is suggested in his next sentence:

"And though it can be argued that in a pure state of society, in which the nature and interaction of divine powers could be taught, such myths could be understood without damage to morals, nevertheless in a degenerate age, when the meaning of these symbols was forgotten, grave dangers arose, and the insanity of phallicism inculcated its virus into the community."

"Myriads on myriads of enigmatical utterances by both poets and philosophers are to be found, and there are also whole books which present the mind of the writer veiled, as that of Heraclitus *On Nature,* which on this very account is called 'Obscure.' Similar to this book is the *Theology* of Pherecydes of Samos. And so also the work of Euphorion, the *Causae* of Callimachus and the *Alexandra* of Lycophron."

Clement of Alexandria cites the various styles of writing practiced among the learned Egyptians: (1) the Epistolographic; (2) the Hieratic, which the sacred scribes practice; and finally (3) the Hieroglyphic, divided into two modes: (a) literal and (b) symbolic; which is further described as being of two kinds. "One speaks literally by imitation, and another writes as it were figuratively, and another is called allegorical, using certain enigmas."

Clement leaves no doubt as to the rule of the esoteric method in ancient literature:

"All, then, in a word who have spoken of divine things, both barbarians and Greeks, have veiled the first principles of things and delivered the truth in enigmas and symbols and allegories and metaphors and such like tropes."

And he concludes with a fine statement which should clear up all lingering intransigence on the part of moderns as to the importance of myth and allegory:

"Now Wisdom, hard to hunt, is the treasures of God's unfailing riches. But those, taught in theology by those prophets, the poets, philosophize much *by way of a hidden sense*. I mean Orpheus, Linus, Musaeus, Homer and Hesiod and those in this fashion wise. The persuasive style of poetry is for them a veil for the many."

The survey of this field, so important in the knowing, so fatal in the ignorance of it, should not omit a citation from the *Zohar* of the Hebrews (iii, fol. 152*b*):

"Each word of the Torah contains an elevated meaning and a sublime mystery." "The recitals of the Torah are the vestments of the Torah. Woe to him who takes this garment for the Torah itself. The simple take notice only of the garments or recitals of the Torah. They know no other thing. They see not that which is concealed under the vestment. The more instructed men do not pay attention to the vestment, but to the body which it envelops."

Echoing these destiny-fraught words of the Hebrews one might cry now: "Woe to the age that takes the testaments of ancient wisdom for literal history!" For woe *has* come to every age since esotericism was dragged down into desuetude in those fatal third and fourth centuries of the Christian era, and precisely because the intelligence that would have read the wondrous truths hidden in the mysteries of spiritual exaltation and a symbolic language that alone can impound the substance of those exaltations, was crushed out or hounded with murder.

But the condition that led wisdom to resort to the subtleties of esoteric method led to exactly what the scribes of Christendom have been eager to cry against as the bane and the weakness, the failure and the evil of esoteric Paganism. It brought into existence the very evil that Christianity prides itself upon so lavishly for having expunged: the aristocracy of intellect, the snobbery of exclusive knowledge. Christianity preens its feathers on having taken into its bosom the masses of the downtrodden under-elements of the population of the Roman

Empire and ministered to their religious needs, masses whom the exclusive cults of the Mystery Brotherhoods allegedly deemed beneath their notice.

And so the essay must deal with the involvements of this outcome of esoteric polity. If there is ample ground for the unassailability of esotericism, then there must be equally unassailable bases for the validity of an aristocratic grouping of parties, a limited minority of those who are versed in knowledge, as over against the great body of the untutored, whom the writers on ancient history like to term the "vulgar."

As it was the claim of glory for Christianity that it gave the true religion to the poor and downcast, so of course it was the kindred effort of the religion to cry up the futility and failure of the Pagan groups composing the elite and the intelligentsia. Having cast its lot with the humble and the ignorant, the new religious ferment ineluctably came to espouse the cause of ignorance and to take arms against the interests of learning and intelligence.

CHAPTER VIII

HATRED OF PHILOSOPHY

In his *The Beginnings of Christianity* (p. 180) Fisher rants against "the aristocracy of philosophical thought; the notion of an oligarchy of philosophers." Learning held exclusively in the ranks of those who have by righteousness and virtue earned it from life, savors too readily of what the Gospels have held up to scorn as "Phariseeism," which the Christian mind has been conditioned to hold in contempt and load with contumely. And of course the plea of the great Plato that was still ringing in the ears of the intelligent of society in those early centuries, that the state should be presided over by philosophers, finds little acclaim in Christian thought. For the Church had turned in bitterness and implacable hostility against all philosophy, and perhaps still looked for a returning Jesus to set up the millennial kingdom on the throne of theocratic universalism in Jerusalem.

We'll have none of philosophy or philosophers in our glorious religion of the spirit, was Tertullian's irate outburst. Our religion is not for the few haughty scholars; it is for all of God's simple children. And it seems as if his idea must have included the thought: the simpler the better. The Church should be reminded of his words today:

"What indeed has Athens to do with Jerusalem? What concord is there between the Academy and the Church? . . . Away with all attempts to produce a mottled Christianity of Stoic, Platonic and dialectic composition!"

The truth is that Christianity went on to become just about the most "mottled" and variegated religion in history, since it had to make endless compromises and adaptations to every variety of religious system that it encountered in overrunning Europe. Indeed it began as a most motley aggregation of widely differing cults, and, as will be shown, very shortly introduced elements from surrounding religions.

Fisher enlarges on the assertion he makes that in Christianity God in all his love and compassion for sinful man is brought near "to the apprehension, not of a coterie of philosophers merely, but to the humble and ignorant." As hundreds of other apologists make exactly the same assertion, we have here the text for a discussion which does not seem ever to have been undertaken in a completely dispassionate and critical spirit, and which, therefore, stands in need of just that sort of treatment. For to handle it in the simple and naive fashion of the Christian defenders is at a glance seen to be dangerously fatuous. No one writing in this mood—which is too easily seen to be the result of sheer bias—has had the perspicacity to catch the patent asininity that is only thinly hidden beneath the surface of this thought situation. For the very presumption in the thesis that represents God as being more devoted to the welfare of the economically and mentally lowly masses than to his more intellectually grown children, by that very token argues that he is more lovingly interested in ignorance than in intelligence. It shows him favoring the former and rewarding their failings more than his more capable offspring. It tacitly but logically presupposes that God will love you more if you are poor and stupid than he will if you are intelligent. To win his best blessing you should forego all deeper study, remain in childlike nescience and receive that outpouring of divine benignancy and beatitude which the All-Father prefers to bestow on babes, while the wise of the earth philosophize in vain. It does not impugn the genuine rationality of this point to realize that within modest limits book-study and mental gymnastics may end in befuddlement of mind and a certain stultification of vision, and that an attitude of simple expectancy on the part of untrained minds may invite some of the clearer perceptions that fall to naive thinking. It is true enough that the endless disputations of philosophers have too generally yielded little of sound or practical value and failed to decide momentous issues for human understanding and assurance. But if this much-labored opinion of Christian writers is in any remotest sense held to as real truth and fact, why, then, has the movement in actual performance declared it to be baseless? If deep and life-long study of its theology really yields less than the instinctive intuitions of child-like faith, why, one asks, has the institution of Christianism seen it to be desirable to establish thousands of theological seminaries and academies? If faculties of school-bred philosophers are a treacherous source of useless maundering over abstrusities that only befuddle the simple mind, why have them? They are highly expensive. Why not let the babes in wisdom teach the simple faith of Christ from their cradles and play-boxes? Evidently the Christian movement itself distrusted the maxim of simplicity, except to use it as appealing sentimentality when that approach could gain a point with the masses, because it itself reverted to the despised Pagan habit of study of philosophy and the discipline of the intellect. And not only that, but it took up the very systems of Pagan philosophy that were as a stench in the nostrils of Tertullian and other Fathers, and built its later edifice of rational theology upon them!

We hear again and again that Christianity was a "religion of the heart," in sharp contrast to Pagan philosophy, which was all mind and no heart. Hear Fisher dissertate on this (p. 541):

"The contrast between Christianity as a religion of the heart, *accessible to all,* and regarding with special compassion the poor man and the outcast, and the creeds of philosophy, which gave precedence to the 'wise and prudent' and created an *intellectual oligarchy,* provoked a contemptuous estimate of the new faith on the part of those of whom Celsus is a representative. It is scarcely a matter of surprise that Christian societies, made up, as at first they were, almost exclusively from the humbler class, should be suspected of meeting for purposes of conviviality and debauchery, and that even rumors of hideous crimes such as were often imputed to the Jews in the Middle Ages, should be propagated concerning them."

If we recall the simple fact that the Christians of the early days were at about the level of present-day Salvation Army intelligence, we shall have no difficulty in understanding the low estimate put upon the Church by Celsus, Pliny, Seneca, Suetonius and other cultured minds of the day. But here, as always, the emphasis is on the contrast between the poor, who have heart feelings, and the few who have cultivated intellectual interests in religion and philosophy.

That this was a tremendously impelling motive for the inception and growth of Christianity should not for a moment be overlooked. It is one of the truest keys to the comprehension of the influences that combined to give Christianity its initial impulse.

And it is of more than common significance because it is a question that still agitates controversy in religious circles. To the ubiquitous question, which is the true or the surer guide for religious faith, the intellect or the heart, in what B. A. G. Fuller, in his *History of Philosophy,* calls the "soft-headed" sentimentalism that so largely makes up conventional religionism, the religion of the heart gets the affirmative vote. But in the opinion of "hard-headed" thinkers, emancipated from the traps of naiveté, the intellect would win the decision. It will do to say here that a greater judge than any people's opinions has already pronounced an irrefutable and unassailable verdict: which is, that religion of the heart, feelings, emotions, dispositions, devotions, when not regulated and guided by sound intellectual judgments, has proved itself to be the most frightfully devastating scourge known to history. The debate is closed; the jury, written history, has spoken: the heart is never safe to trust until it is directed by something more securely anchored to verity than feeling. That something is studied intelligence.

And again the hollowness of the Christian glorification of its interest in the poor and humble is glaringly exposed by the implication, as in the case of God's imputed favoritism for ignorance as against learning, that God has once more shown himself partial, this time to man's emotional nature as against his intellectual endowment. It is an around-the-bush way of intimating that God has rated feeling in rank and value above intellection, with the sly side hint that he would deprecate the mind of his creatures, while giving greater glory to their emotions. As a matter of fact the verdict of the greatest thinkers has never failed to place the intellect above the feelings. As far as the best human perception goes, Christianity thus finds itself on the losing side of a centuries-old controversy. It lost everything but the fanatical idolatry of emotion-ridden zealots by choosing to follow the glorified hegemony of the heart,—and that uncorrected by the intellect—instead of that of mind and heart combined in philosophical stability.

Speaking of the constituency and personnel of the first church congregations, Fisher says (pp. 576-7):

"They were made up mostly of the poor and obscure, who were drawn to embrace the Gospel by an inward need, and whose low position in the social scale was a standing ground of reproach against the new religion from the side of its adversaries. Moved thus by spiritual hunger, and by no motive of self-interest, they laid hold of the priceless boon offered them in the Gospel with all sincerity and earnestness."

This is, as far as it goes, a complete and comprehensive description of the genesis of Christianity. It is the true statement of what took place. Yet it is too simple and too partial to cover the whole case. It leaves the matter standing somewhat in false light, because it needs further qualification and interlining. It glorifies or sanctifies "inward need" and "sincerity and earnestness" when these are manifested by people who sought refuge in the cult of Christianity. These qualities are not so lauded when they are similarly the expression of people who did not resort to Christianity for satisfactions.

166

One must live long and study closely if one is to learn that "sincerity and earnestness" are by no means a sure badge of rectitude or even good intent. Certainly they have never in history been a sure badge of intelligence. People do very little without generally sincere and earnest motives. These qualities do not present guarantees of the good of what they motivate. The Inquisitors, now looked upon as worse than ferocious beasts of cruelty, no doubt were sincere and certainly were earnest. Most inhuman savagery can claim the activation of the two generally laudable qualities. Nearly all bigots are sincere and earnest, to the point of repulsiveness. What this volume is aiming to substantiate is precisely the human fact that a body of normal people of humble station and low intelligence, hungry, as all humans intrinsically are, for a saving religion, laid hold of a body of high ethical and spiritual wisdom and, incapable of interpreting it in its esoteric sense, corrupted it through ignorance into a corpus of belief, the obvious literal preposterousness of which has wrecked a world.

Even Fisher has to pause a moment, pulled up short by his sudden remembrance of how deficient were these early devotees of the new popular faith (p. 580):

"If they disclosed dark features of human imperfection, they at the same time give one a glimpse of the mighty power of that new religion [which we now know was not new in a single feature] which was laying hold of the poor and untutored, and was beginning its work as a leaven in the midst of a corrupt and decaying world."

What our intent here is to present for the first time is that the very movement that Fisher takes to have been a beginning of the rise of true light out of surrounding darkness was itself basically the clearest evidence and manifestation of the darkness, and indeed a movement downward to greater darkness, or at least further blind groping in the murks. Surely it was no beginning of a tide surging back to the light. As it moved on it sank ever deeper into darkness and crystallized the works of darkness into a hard mold that held the fluid spirit of mankind bound in unbreakable incrustations for two millennia. A movement that can be truthfully so described is no movement toward the higher star of truth.

Says Guignebert in his work previously cited (p. 150) in speaking of the Creed:

"In the first place it was the work of ignorant folk who obviously can scarcely take in anything above ordinary inventions and inflations."

But he adds, these simple folk can make nothing of their venerable formulas and rolling phrases of ancient cosmogony without some help from the Greek schools.

"Accordingly they apply them [the principles of Greek philosophy] to the premises of the faith and to the suggestions which they draw from the religious sentiments of the ignorant."

Guignebert says (p. 165) that not only the learned despised the ignorant Christians; they were disliked by the bulk of the common people as well. If this is in any measure the strict truth, it would seem to place the Christians as the lowest of the lowly, even below "the common people." This fact should forsooth open the eyes of good Christian people today who go on under the bland assumption that those early Chrisitans were the misguided, vilified and persecuted embodiments of the highest godly virtue and holy courage. It is clear, that, as writer after writer admits, they were the very dregs of society. Like Chrysostom, many spokesmen for the faith have abstracted glory from this very lowliness, counting it the prime evidence of divine ordination that wisdom came not through the learned, but through the spiritual ferment amid the lowliest. What this hallucinated infatuation has cost the world is beyond calculation.

And how narrow and self-hallowing this arrogance of ignorance, this pride of mental poverty, as Dewey calls it, can become is shown by Guignebert's statement a few pages farther on (p. 170) that the early Church,

"as depository of divine truth, she saw in every pagan an agent of the Evil One, and the mere idea of equality of treatment with Paganism for herself was like an outrage which necessity alone could force her to tolerate."

The dictionary definition of this attitude is "bigotry."

Celsus doubtless spoke with a jeering sharpness in his famous description of the personnel of the early Church, or the Church at his time, the third century:

"It is only the simpletons, the ignoble, the senseless—slaves and women-folk and children—whom they wish to persuade to join their congregations or *can persuade* . . . wool-dressers and cobblers and fullers, most uneducated and vulgar persons . . . whosoever is a sinner, or unintelligent, or a fool, in a word, whoever is god-forsaken (*kakodaimon*), him the Kingdom of God will receive." (See Glover's *Conflict of Religions in the Early Roman Empire*.)

Says Edward Carpenter in his *Pagan and Christian Creeds:*

"The rude and menial masses, who had hitherto been almost beneath the notice of Greek and Roman culture, flocked in" and became "a source of weakness to the Church and a cause of dissension and supersition."

Von Mosheim says that

"By far the greater part of those who embraced the Christian religion in this its infancy being men of mean extraction and wholly illiterate, it could not otherwise happen but that a great scarcity should be experienced in the churches of persons possessing the qualifications requisite for initiating the ignorant and communicating instruction to them with a due degree of readiness and skill."

Guignebert says that side by side with the aristocracy of birth, the aristocracy of intellect for a long time refused its adhesion to the Christian faith, and often indeed it pretended to treat it as beneath its notice. The intellectuals are not drawn toward the rabble's emotional religion; they preserve a superstitious reverence for Hellenism. Why he should let an unfounded slur slip into his sentence here in calling a deep reverence for Hellenism "superstitious" is hard to fathom. It presents once more attestation of the palsy to which the virus of an indurated Christian bias will reduce the best of orthodox minds. Thousands of scholars and truth-seekers have found the Greek philosophy most highly elevating and most brilliantly illuminating to their minds, and they would justly resent having their admiration for it called "superstition." In it they have found themselves farther from superstition and closer to divine light than in any other field of truth they have searched through. It has become the fixed habit of Christians to snarl and snap at all things found in Paganism that would obviously have to be deemed worthy of praise.

Concomitant with the praise of ignorance in Christian apologetics must of course come the calumniation of the exclusiveness of Platonic philosophy. We find Hodges saying in *The Early Church* (p. 88):

"But the essential weakness of Neo-Platonism was in the narrow range of its appeal. It addressed itself to cultivated people and among them to such as had the temperament of the mystic. It was right in its insistence upon a supreme good beyond sense, beyond reason, beyond reality; but when it endeavored to explain what that supreme good is, the plain man could not understand it."

Tedious as is this citation of examples of stupid misconception, it is a work that must be done if we are ever to make our way out of the brambles and thickets of asinine misjudgment in which the accumulated nescience of generations has entangled the minds of the commonalty of men in Christian lands. Statements like this of Hodges are still accepted as conveying the truth, and consequently still hold minds in perverted ideas. It is certainly a most reprehensible error on the part of a man posing as a scholar to ascribe weakness to the Neoplatonic system because its appeal was to such height of intellectual capability that only a limited minority could provide the credentials to appreciate it. Neo-Platonism is not a weak system, but perhaps the strongest for light and truth ever held by mankind. It is noble beyond anything coming out since its day. Its revival is a crying need today if civilization and culture are to be saved. It still exalts and illuminates the finest minds beyond what Christianity has been able to do. This churchman argues that the limited range of its appeal proves the weakness of the system. This is a blind stab at an argument and it misses truth and hits a great untruth. In this case at any rate the limited range of appeal is not the weakness of the system, but sadly proves the weakness of the human masses. When has the highest culture ever had a wide appeal? As sensibly should he rail against fine music or fine art, because their appeal is only to connoisseurs. Good music is forsooth to blame because the vulgar disdain it and will have their "popular" songs instead! Just so surely did early Christianity disdain high Platonic philosophy and swing away in an abandon of lower excitability to the "jazz" philosophy of weird apocalyptic fervor and the cult of a personal divine Savior that swept it down to the level where only the meanest could find an elemental instigation in its message.

Then in Hodges' next words we read the solemn dirge of true Christianity (p. 88):

"The Emperor Justinian closed the doors of the Academy at Athens and the seven philosophers, who alone represented the Neoplatonic faith, took their books and sought the hospitality of the East."

It is a legitimate question whether this was not the saddest, most rueful day in world history. It was the last flicker and final out of the Lamp of Ancient Wisdom.

Hodges himself helps us to see how the darkness thickened when the light was withdrawn. He says (p. 89):

"Origen was a fellow-student of Plotinus in the school of Ammonius Saccas. The perception of God *in all honest thought* was, indeed, confined mainly to the Greek Fathers. The Latins were of another mind. Tertullian, contemporary of Clement and Origen, hated all philosophy and poetry. This was in part by reason of his temperament, but also in equal part by reason of his ignorance."

This is further corroboration of the claim that Christianity, as developed in the Roman West, bore little of kinship in spirit and rationale with the higher Christianity that was enwombed in the Hellenistic East. It is by no means only geographical and historical differences and external influences that caused a Greek Christian ecclesiastical system to arise and take its course in independence of a Roman Christian system. The two were not really born of the same stock and parentage. Or if the Western stemmed from the primitive Eastern, it did not long maintain its parental heritage and characteristics. It soon became a wayward and degenerate offshoot, abandoning philosophy and rationalism for an arrant emotional pietism that could only save itself from frenzied excesses by being held to the restraints of disciplined reason. These failing it, it plunged down into that abyss of irrational faith that swept it on to its long career of unparalleled inhumanity.

An odd reference to the ills arising from "intellectual aristocracy," this time not as between Pagan philosophical oligarchy and Christian simplicity of faith, but between a class of intellectual nobility in the Church itself and the common unschooled laity, is found in Guignebert's comment on the amazing effort of the Church philosopher Scotus Erigena to reintroduce into Christianity those esoteric elements drawn from Platonism and Pythagoreanism, or from Neoplatonism, which the Church had by the fifth century so completely cast out. Says the historian (p. 220):

"Scotus Erigena indeed took good care to emphasize the difference between his theology, which was, he said, *vera theologia,* as well as *vera philosophia,* and the popular beliefs. As a matter of fact, the doctors who join with Gottschalk, Rabanus Maurus and Hincmar in the dispute over predestination or the effects of the consecration of the Eucharist, *take no interest in the ordinary believers,* nor do these ordinary believers take any interest in them. And although this aristocratic isolation of Christian thinkers with regard to the mass of Christians is nothing new, it is none the less disturbing. Not only will it favor the theological virtuosity which plays with empty words and juggles with abstract ideas so remote from all religious experience and concrete reality, that it is so much lost time, but it will also turn the 'intellectuals' of the Church aside from their real duty, which is to instruct and enlighten the ignorant, to safeguard them from themselves and the suggestions of their milieu, and to make them better people."

Some items here need to be noticed. Erigena's conception that true theology is identical with true philosophy is precisely what this essay proclaims and endeavors to validate. Religion fell into debasement when it divorced itself from philosophy, as will be argued presently. Again, Erigena took care to let no one labor under the delusion that high spirito-mystic and rational theology was the message the Church held for the unteachable masses. He stood true to the esoteric tradition. Next, it can be admitted, with Guignebert, that the aristocratic isolation of the intellectuals can become a priggish and snobbish thing, distracting the learned from their duty to the common people in the way of real instruction, for the mental delights of true philosophy can become absorbing and enthralling to a competent mind. But as to this danger, a bit of practical wisdom could dictate a safe handling of the situation. After all somebody must devote their entire time to the business of loving truth and seeking to formulate it organically. Woe to that society that will pull its intellectual aristocracy away from its consecrated effort to keep the vision of truth glowing brightly and put them to teaching the semi-capable and the idiots. True esotericism contemplates the existence and function of liaison grades standing between the glowing light at the top, able to catch its clarifying gleam and qualified to transmit it on to the lower ranks. The Lesser Mysteries are to be formulated in the image of the Greater, but come forth as reflections in a medium of lower intelligence, which will be able to comprehend nothing falsely, but all as truly as its lower capacity will permit. Ancient esoteric competence knew that "learned doctors" can not impart their profound intellectual sensings directly to the multitude. The best they can do is to pass it on to a select group of proven competence, who may in turn impart it as successfully as may be to the grade below them. True understanding of recondite learning must proceed from the few on the summit of the mount down grade by grade until its light will at last reach the lowest. But it is inevitable that it should lose some of its luster at each step of descent. The very sons of God lost a degree of their divine soul-light as they descended plane by plane from the empyrean into mortal flesh. The great Greek-Egyptian wisdom gave this out as one of the noble truths. Christianity has lost it or violently contorted it into a bizarre doctrine of the "fall" of the angels, with little left in it of its basic anthropological significance. Thus high knowledge loses its clarity and brilliance at every step of descent from its gleam in a philosopher's mind to its murky obfuscation in the dull minds of the unthinking. The multitude sees through a glass darkly, or in a mirror blurred by ignorance; the thinker has a more polished glass. If it is not so then all academic learning is an impertinence—as indeed the early Christians fatuously considered it!

Another worthy historian of the religion notices this intellectual oligarchy, which held the skirts of its deeper learning above the dust of the lower mental ground. Dean Milman says (op. cit., p. 36) that

"The unity of the Deity becomes, not the high and mysterious creed of a privileged sacerdotal or intellectual oligarchy, but the common property of all whose minds are fitted to receive it; all religious distinctions are annihilated; the jurisdictions of all local deities abolished. . . ."

Many writers simply say that Christianity made the higher truth the common property of all, and place the period there. But Milman was not off his guard, to be caught in so errant a statement. He saves himself by adding, "whose minds are fitted to receive it." If Milman supposes this to have been the merit of Christianity, then it was still more meritorious in Paganism. For the Pagans built instruction solidly upon the condition of fitness to receive it, and the Christians shortly abandoned all such care and tossed the pearls with utter profligacy to the mangy dogs.

Milman remarks upon the "remarkable union between the highest reason and the most abject superstition which characterizes the age of Imperial Rome," noting that "every foreign religion found proselytes in the capital of the world."

Overlooking the fact, which might have surprised Milman had he known it, that many of these cults, as the Mithraic, the Orphic, the Isiac, the Dionysian, the Bacchic, the Manichaean and others, instead of inculcating, as he supposes, arrant "superstition," were in fact teaching in general those same high and esoteric truths which the best Christianity had essayed to incorporate into its system, but soon had to abandon because of the ignorance of their people, there is nothing to be wondered at in the fact that great Rome harbored groups perpetuating the secret wisdom that Christianity was so soon to dishonor and to murder by turning it loose upon the ribald multitude. New York City, no doubt London and Paris, present a similar situation today. The pertinent comment is that the "remarkable union" between highest reason and the most abject superstition does not exist. The two are incompatible. High reason abolishes superstition. The gloomy fact is that there is so much superstition and so little sound reason in the many cults flourishing now as then. The gap between true intellectual aristocracy and wild fancies of the "vulgar" is no less yawning now than it always has been. But there can readily be found learned esoteric societies and ignorant cults side by side in any city at any time.

One can not let go unchallenged another excerpt from Milman's *History*. He is commenting on Cicero's statement about the imperial Roman state religion of Paganism and writes:

"The education itself, by which, according to these generally judicious writers, the youthful mind was to be impregnated with reverential feelings for the objects of national worship, must have been coldly conducted by teachers conscious that they were practicing a pious fraud upon their disciples, and perpetually embarrassed by the necessity of maintaining gravity befitting such solemn subjects, and of suppressing the involuntary smile which might betray the secret of their own impiety."

This could be the theme of an extended rebuttal that could wax vehement in ironical sallies. Already we have noted Celsus' vigorous allegation that the early pious Christians flooded their catechumens with such concocted stories of holy miracle as any nurse-maid would be ashamed to tell to children. Now we have the modern historian charging the Pagan teachers of youth with imparting such baseless fables that they had difficulty in keeping sober countenance. But surely it is invidious for any Christian to accuse another religion of perpetrating "pious fraud" upon its youth, when every Christian chronicler has sadly to narrate the glaring fact of the commission of the same or far worse "pious fraud" by centuries of Christian teaching without a parallel in any other religion. Indeed pious fraud is a perennial characteristic of Christian history, a motive found active in every period of its existence. One has but to peruse such a careful and documented work as Joseph Wheless' *Forgery in Christianity,* for a mountain of proof. One can not read Gerald Massey's life-long studies without being depressed with the prevalence of insincerity and chicanery at every turn. A hundred sources add to the conviction.

No brief, of course, is made here for Pagan failings. The teachers may themselves already have lost the esoteric sense of the mystery allegories and myths; the representation of these things had no doubt already in Paganism become caricatured. It probably has to be considered a sad fact that hardly at any time has the high and luminous conception of the great science of esoteric truth and allegorical adumbration of it held true and clear for an extended period. The vision of truth and its figures is caught once and again by a perspicacious mind or a group; it flashes for a time and is gone again. It has to be recaptured over and over again, and can not be made a permanent possession simply by being published broadcast. If the efforts of Pagan teachers to impart some degree of clear comprehension of ancient rites and symbols is any more ludicrously pathetic than the attempts of the average teacher of a Sunday School class in the ordinary Christian Church to explain to her protégés such a doctrine as the Trinity, the Virgin Birth, Vicarious Atonement, the Immaculate Conception and the other items of theology that young minds conjure up questions about, they must have been ribald indeed.

And after all there is a wide gap between the effort to give to children the venerable constructions of sage wisdom, which hold the promise of a priceless emancipation of the mind when finally comprehended, and the conscious attempt to put over on gullible children a code of what must be known to be symbols and nothing more, with the fell assertion that they are historical realities and the allegories are actual historical events. One is a necessary stage on the road to final instruction; the other is unpardonable and heinous. If anything could excel in the criminality of pious fraud the entire cycle of stories and fabrications, including whole "Gospels" and "Epistles" that have had to be styled *Pseudepigrapha,* that have been invented and foisted on gullible generations to uphold the transmogrification of spiritual allegories into alleged history, it would be a nefarious perpetration indeed. The Pagan teachers of youth need only have experienced difficulty in keeping a straight face of sober gravity, if they were knowingly passing off the myths and fables of their religion as historical events. Whether guilty of that procedure or not we have not the data to pass judgment. It is quite more than likely that they left that comic performance to the Christians.

There is a decided hint as to the incapacity of the masses for response to more cultured presentations in Fisher's remark that "tragedy interested only a minority of cultivated persons." The Greek comedy and the Roman plays of the same order had a large measure of popular favor. The subjects of the comedy were borrowed largely from the licentious stories of Greek mythology. But the pantomime gradually usurped the place of almost everything else in the dramatic line.

The art of expression through movement and gesture was carried to a marvelous perfection. The dances were beheld with an enthusiasm which knew no bounds, and the mimes were commonly of an unchaste and even obscene character. The "vulgar" then as now, and now as then, will flock to their amusements; divine philosophy, then as now, was wooed by the few. Is it a criterion of judgment on Christianity's historical influence that after twenty centuries this phenomenon of social and cultural life in Christian countries manifests to about the same degree?

There is significance also in Fisher's stating that "human rights and human equality were the vague theories of a few philosophers." If it is the philosophers who have stood for human rights, implying their recognition of the "dignity of the individual," Plato was unquestionably right in saying our kings should be philosophers. But Christianity threw out the philosophers; is it possible as a logical inference then that Christianity is largely responsible for the denial over so many centuries of individual human rights, and that such rights are dangerously jeopardized again today?

According to Fisher (p. 219) the depravity of the population was so great in the first century that "the noblest men took refuge in Stoicism," if they did not try suicide. At all times thoughtful and observant men, in later life, despair of achieving human betterment dreamed of hopefully in youth's more ardent idealisms, and adopt a stoical attitude of mind. The low predilections of the "multitude" are perhaps more painful to cultured people today than even in the time of Rome's decadence.

Fisher uses this datum to prepare the way for his assertion that Christianity was about to flash into this gloom with its superior radiance, and he draws the picture of the disparity between the two. This disparity between heathen and Christian society, which he says can not be denied, is mainly due to the fact that under the heathen regime the objects of worship were the imperfect creatures of human fancy— meaning the gods—and worship was itself largely sensuous, while under Christianity the objects of religious faith correspond to the true ideal of perfection, and worship rises to an unseen world.

Things exactly like this have been written all through Christian history, and no one in all that time has dared to say they are not true. Now positive refutation can be made. It is not true to say that the gods worshipped by Paganism were the imperfect creations of human fancy. The truth that at last, after centuries of Christian suppression, comes to an awakened intelligence is that the Pagan gods were the creations of near-divine sagacity to embody in personified form the attributes of the divine nature for the everlasting enlightenment of mortal men. If untutored and unimaginative folk could not see through the figurism to the cosmic reality prefigured by the personification, they would entify the characters, but would still be moved in salutary ways by their conception of them as deities. The last degradation of the typism came when Christians turned the divine figures entirely into the status of humans, making actual human beings out of them, as in the case of the Christ, the Logos and the twelve facets of Christly divinity. Not too far did Christianity fall clear of actually turning God himself into a benevolent venerable human Patriarch. Indeed to the general run of more ignorant Christian people the conception of him stands not more than a step or two above an actual anthropomorphization. If less intelligent Pagan mentality accepted the gods as personal entities instead of abstract, though actual, creative forces, they at least kept them in the superior worlds. It remained for Christian ignorance to sink them to the abject level of living humans. Far more truly did the Pagan gods picture the "true ideal of perfection" for man than the character and career of the Galilean has done, seeing what an eccentric picture comes to form when the Christ-allegories of old Scripture have been transmogrified into the supposed biography of a living man. Ancient peoples never lacked the true picture of ideal perfection, for it was presented in every nation from the earliest times. From the picturization every grade of intelligence would draw that level of understanding which would best minister to its cultural needs. It could miscarry to ruinous consequences only if its representations should be completely reduced to human character. This last stage of the degeneration was achieved in Christianity.

Kershner in *Pioneers of Christian Thought* (p. 105) says of Plotinus that his philosophy was intended for intellectual highbrows only and he cared nothing about the common people. The very form of such a statement savors badly of disingenuousness. It intimates the philosopher's scorn and contempt of the common people. But this is in truth an unfair assumption. No one believes that a man so wise as Plotinus, one of the world's three greatest thinkers, despised the common people. In fact he surely knew they were as much and as truly the sons of God as was a philosopher. But he also was wise enough to know, as any philosopher knows, that the system of dialectical rationalism by which he was able to discern and to represent for the human mind the

177

principles of deific wisdom could hardly be comprehended by the masses. He wrote for them no more directly than does any university doctor in philosophy now. The art and genius of the philosopher can not be exerted upon the common people directly. They must affect the grade at his own level first, and then percolate down to the underlings in mentality. A Pagan philosopher must be slandered at all costs, and so Plotinus has to be gratuitously slandered with the charge that he cared nothing for the common people. No sincere philosopher but hopes that his high work may touch and eventually liberate the common people from some of their burden of victimization by false conceptions. But inasmuch as they would probably stone him if he labored with them to change their errant popularized misconceptions at first hand, he keeps to his ivory tower while they work in the fields.

But Farrar (*Lives of the Fathers,* Vol. I, 384) comes forward with the assertion that this attempt to draw any distinction between the religion of the vulgar and that of the initiated, as though an ordinary amount of knowledge sufficed the former, while something different, secret and superfine was needed for the latter, is "an error and a dangerous evil." He says that so far as Clement (and he should have added, Origen, too) used language which seems to lend any sanction to such an hypothesis, "so far he lent countenance to a tenet which became a fatal source of spiritual pride and usurping tyranny." The answer to this must be a direct denial of its truth. The "spiritual pride" which naturally accrues to any person developing lofty and elevating mystic and intellectual insight and understanding can be entirely justified and honest, for it is a pride that walks with its sister humility. It takes due countenance of its own splendid reality, but leads to no disdain of those who as yet lack it. With complete charity in its view of the humble and unenlightened, with even intense pity of their darkened state, it yet knows no way on the mental side to bridge the gap between its position and that of the multitude. It will do what can be done to instruct unwisdom; but what it will not do is to prostitute its vision of reality, its dynamic and emancipating realizations, to a form of untruth to beguile the benighted commonalty. No more would it do this, to win popular applause, than would a Beethoven produce modern "jazz." It was Christianity that followed the fatuous dream of obliterating the difference between religion for the vulgar and philosophy for the initiated, and with disastrous consequences this work essays to delineate.

Christian exponents do not hesitate at any time to institute comparisons between their principles, practices or dogmas and those of the Pagans, and always to the disparagement of the Pagans. If this matter of "spiritual pride" is thus submitted for comparison, it is obvious that superiority lies with the Pagans. For always has Christianity flaunted to the world an egregious pride in its spiritual attainments. Its pride, however, was in its sanctified devoutness and pietism, rather than in its rational insights. And we can be reminded here of what the modern thinker John Dewey has told us on this score: "that the pride of the zealously devout is the most dangerous form of pride." The pride of those who feel themselves learned in the express and explicit will of God is the most exclusive, he expounds. This hits Christianity more directly than it does Paganism, surely.

Farrar, discussing Augustine's high tributes to Platonic philosophy— he having been a pupil of the Neoplatonist Plotinus—says it is surprising that he should express such rapturous admiration of the truths that had been long commonplace with Plato and the Stoics, with Cicero and Seneca. But what seemed so admirable to him was his observation that the loftiest morality of the greatest heathen thinkers had become the ordinary heritage of the most uninstructed Christians. "What had been a rare heroism had become an everyday belief, so that

> Each little voice in turn
> Some glorious truth proclaims;
> What Sages would have died to learn,
> Now taught to cottage dames."

One can take a kindlier view of such a presentment, or a stricter view. The Christians were wrought up to a high pitch of fanatical frenzy; the unrelenting driving motivation was pietistic zealotry. Under its goad and lash the human spirit may manifest in unintellectual people extraordinary heroisms and insights. One does not deny these things. What we assert to be the point of sanity in all this is the full recognition of the fact that fanatical zeal in ignorant people does not discredit the sage reflections and insights of philosophical study. The Christian argument almost contends that pious frenzy is far superior to intellectual contemplation. We contend that history sides with our argument in disproof of this. Severe personal or national crises always bring out latent heroism in common people. Novelists write up these things. And no deep-thinking person will quite accept

179

the dictum that all the common proselytes to the new faith suddenly put into daily manifestation the highest virtues of the philosophers. This claim is itself an offspring of a similarly overweening pious presumption. Guignebert says that it was to the Gentiles of the lower orders that the Christian preachers addressed themselves. It was among this class that the consoling and all-leveling doctrine of the humble brethren had the best chance to be well received. The historian says that until the time of the Antonines the more enlightened never formed more than an infinitesimal minority in the Church: "slaves and day laborers constituted her main force. . . . Christianity continued to find its recruits especially among the *humiliores*." After that period the new faith came in contact with philosophy, and the results were incalculable.

To controvert the endless catalogue of major and minor aspersions and slurs which Christian writers have flung at Pagan institutions would take volumes. Lecky, in his *History of European Morals* (Vol. II, p. 15), makes a statement which can serve as a pretty generally comprehensive conclusion on the whole discussion. He gives the Christians credit for advancing beyond the Pagans to a higher humanitarianism in several respects; then he says:

"On the other hand they rank immeasurably below the best Pagan civilizations in civic and patriotic virtue, in the love of liberty, in the number and splendor of the great characters they produced, in the dignity and beauty of the type of character they formed. They had their full share of tumult, anarchy, injustice and war, and they should probably be placed, in all intellectual virtues, *lower than any other period in the history of mankind*. A boundless intolerance of all divergence of opinion was united with an equally boundless toleration of all *falsehood and deliberate fraud* that could favor received opinions. Credulity being taught as a virtue and all conclusions dictated by authority, a deadly torpor sank upon the human mind, which for many centuries almost suspended its action, and was only effectually broken by the scrutinizing, innovating and free-thinking habits that accompanied the rise of the industrial republics in Italy. Few men that are not either priests or monks would not have preferred to live in the best days of the Athenians or of the Roman Republics, in the age of Augustus or in the age of the Antonines, rather than in any period that elapsed between the triumph of Christianity and the fourteenth century."

The main point sought to be established here is that in what Lecky calls "intellectual virtue" the Christian movement was the expression of a deterioration that carried to the lowest mark in all history. Lecky's well-deliberated statement asserts nothing less than that the Christian

ferment palsied the human mind with the deadliest blight it has suffered in the civilized historical period. Albeit it is still contended that
it was the glory and praise of Christianity that it ministered to the
humble, it must be realized that there was something intrinsically
wrong with a mental ministration to lowly minds that would set them
in bristling enmity to that which proves to be an even more dynamic
ministration to minds of vaster capability. This study is largely directed
to the investigation of the forces and influences that converted the
Christian populace, as the ferment spread, into haters of philosophy
and learning. Logically and naturally the antagonists of pious zealotry
would be assumed to be irreligion, apostasy, atheism, moral evil in
general. But here we face the odd situation that the enemy that
Christian fervor bore down upon was a thing ranking at the very
summit of human estimation—rational philosophy and intellectual
transcendence. Christianity set itself from the start in bitter hostility
against the highest rated cultural influence in the world! The religion
claiming to be the purest, best and noblest in history attacked the
purest, best and noblest element in human culture. This adduces a
damaging refutation of practically all Christian claims. It is at the
very least a startling anomaly. Christian protestations fall smitten with
a fatal nullification under the blows of the logic of this historical
item. That system will approve itself best and noblest which upholds
the best and noblest and antagonizes the worst and meanest. History
often turns anomalous and paradoxical, it works out in quirks that
are often quixotic and chimerical. The only escape from the devastating logic of this situation is for Christianity to claim that the intellectual philosophy against which it bred hatred was itself degenerate and
below the best. And to that claim there would be advanced by no
means a complete denial. The allegation is unquestionably true in
partial degree at least. A fatal dry-rot had by the first century spread
through the ranks of esoteric philosophical culturists. It had prepared
the ground for an outburst of popular superstition such as Christianity manifested. There had been steady degeneration in and under
the sway of Pagan systems. Vision had failed, understanding had flick-
ered to low ebb, the noble grip of "divine philosophy" on leading
minds had relaxed, and superstition crowded in as true comprehension
of mystical realities faded out. Once more had human insight, sharpened to extraordinary keenness in one of history's great periods of enlightenment and uplift, dimmed away to dullness and obtuseness in

the ebb of a great cycle. The magnificent Greek philosophy came as the expression of human genius when its light and power flared out at their highest; Christianity came as the expression of that human genius when its light and power had burned down to their dullest embers.

CHAPTER IX

FROM RELIGION TO PHILOSOPHY

The matter of the antagonism of the low Christian personnel against philosophy and all learning may have far deeper involvements than those suggested by merely historical incidence. There may be the apprehension of a natural or at least inevitable hostility between good motive activated in uncultured minds and similarly good motives activated in minds given to prolonged and profound reflection and keen analytic thinking. Lothrop Stoddard's book, *The Revolt Against Civilization,* has been quoted as establishing that there arises always an animosity on the part of the uncultured populace against the aristocracy of intelligence. It might be readily attributable in part to the envy of the possession by the learned class of that which gives its possessor decided advantages. Again it may be seen as part of the general reaction of those occupying inferior status and privileges against those enjoying the fortunes of a superior rank. Poverty looking across the great social gulf that has too generally separated the mansion from the hovel, comes to hate all the evidences and appurtenances of superiority. This would include its preoccupation with cultural objects such as philosophy. That which social superiority flaunts in the face of penury as an exclusive possession or activity will breed envy and hatred. It may cover the ground of explanation of the case in early Christianity to consider it in this light.

At any rate the point is deeply inwoven into the texture of a larger situation which must now be the subject of searching analysis. It becomes necessary to deal with another aspect of the relation of religion to culture, one that has the greatest need of being acutely diagnosed and brought into clearer focus. Continued study accentuates more and more dramatically the ineluctable fact that this cleavage and disparity of wisdom between esoteric students and the masses practically marks also the division of human thinking and feeling between philosophy and religion. It pronounces almost with final decisiveness the judgment that it is the prerogative of the learned to possess and enjoy the blessings of philosophy, while it is the lot, if not the necessity of the masses to be limited to religion and sustained by its assurances and promises. This view at once sets philosophy and religion sharply over against each other in a distinction of rating, quality and value. As opposition will be registered to the formulation, it must therefore be studied more deeply.

The distinction in most minds between religion and philosophy is generally quite vague. It is thought commonly that a man's religion takes in his philosophy; that, broadly speaking, the two are about one and the same. This may be true to a minor degree. For fruitful discussion succinct definitions are demanded. Philosophy is that which a mind holds to be the truth it can apprehend of the meaning of life and the world. It is a mental enterprise or accomplishment. It is a body of intellectual conceptions embodying one's understanding, true or otherwise, of the nature and meaning of life.

Only very loosely, however, can it be called one's religion. That comes into the scene when the philosophical activity of the mind generates something that attends or follows it in another segment of psychic functionism. That new element is the disposition to consecrate oneself more or less completely, in an area beyond the domain of mere intellection, to the intellectual view adopted as a philosophy. It emerges when there is a transferal from the abstractly mental view over to another realm of the psyche's activity, wherein that which is first thought upon in the abstract generates the individual's action in the concrete. It engages the psychological elements of mystical or emotional feeling and the final commitment to overt action. It brings to active operation such psychological energizations as those covered by the words devotion, consecration, allegiance. It is a disposition psychologically assumed to act in loyal accord with the principles or maxims that have been adopted as true and good in the philosophical purview. So religion can be tersely defined as philosophy emotionalized—as perhaps conversely philosophy might be said to be religion rationalized. When people stand ready to fight—or die—for their settled convictions, or consecrated to live loyally for them, that surely constitutes their religion. If a person entertains—as one really must—ideas about the meaning of life, but is totally indifferent about supporting or witnessing for them, he may be a philosopher, but is hardly a religionist.

People unused to critical distinctions in commonplace thought, generally confuse the two in one broad reaction in consciousness. They have come to certain beliefs about life and their commitment or loyalty to them follows as automatically as a muscular action follows a nerve impulse. The mental and the emotional components of the double operation do not get distinguished; or do so only in the case of the philosopher. The actual case is found to be that people mingle their philosophy and their religion in one motivation. In some the mental or philosophical interest predominates more or less completely; in others it has little say, the emotional or actualizing motivation ruling the life.

But this failure to classify the two elements in different compartments for the purposes of determining the basic issues involved in the mind's adoption of and consecration to a given philosophy is seen to be fraught with catastrophic consequences. It introduces a feature of the situation that becomes critically momentous for all human culture. It concerns the matter of *the truth or falsity of one's philosophy*. If religion is the individual's psychological attachment to a set of beliefs about the world of life, it matters quite decisively, for weal or for woe, whether the attachment, the devotion, the sacrifice, is rendered to principles that are true or that prove to be false. Modern psychology of the psychoanalytic stamp is firm in its pronouncement that attachment to an erroneous belief, or failure of attachment to a sound creed, is fatal to the normal balance or sanity of the mind. It is thus a discovery, or at all events a thesis now demonstrated by the overwhelming evidence of clinical and empirical investigation, and is to be rated as one of the most momentous scientific findings in ages. The eminent psychologist C. G. Jung declares after years of clinical study and practice that a mind not balanced, or as they say, integrated by a positive philosophy grounded in reason will break down in psychotic disease.

In the light of this epochal disclosure nothing could be clearer than that the most critical element in the entire problem of the life of culture is the content of the philosophical code adhered to. This conclusion apparently flies in the face of the most general opinion, which inclines to think that in the domain of religion it is not the intellectual content of one's belief that counts most for the good life, but the strength of the disposition to piety and devoutness. It is the psychological attitude of sincere commitment to a program assumed to be right and good, and not the system of rational theology, that constitutes the substance of the religious addiction. So firmly and extensively has this persuasion become established that the whole study of religion as theology has fallen into disrepute and practical desuetude among all the laity. And in a broad sense it is true to say that theology weighs so lightly in the counsels of modern religion that it has been relegated almost out of sight, with a more "practical" application of the religious spirit taking its place. Ordinarily church folk know little or nothing of the theological principles on which even the sect they adhere to rests, or on which it took its rise as a dissent from some former faith.

Our averment, then, that the theology, which is the rational formulation of the grounds for a given faith or religious adherence, is of far more vital influence for the good life than the sheer force of religious persuasion or afflation of religious feeling, should come as something of a challenge to conventional thinking. It is confirmed as true by the simple logical consideration that if health and sanity hang on the issue of what one understands or fails to understand truly as to the plan, purpose and meaning of life, then the final good of all psychic culture is a matter of how true or how false are the ideas that form the framework of one's philosophy. This throws the onus of the problem back upon that side of it that the unthinking masses abhor, because they are virtually incapable of understanding and therefore of handling it. "The common herd" even of piously disposed people resent it when religion is made a matter of the mind and its knowledge or its thinking power. To it true religion must ever be sheer pious inclination, goodness of "heart," no matter how inadequately interwoven or intermixed it is with the follies of undeveloped intellection.

The ultimate criterion, however, is located in the perception that is inescapable, that, as psychology scientifically proves, the decisive factor in the life of culture is not the measure of one's psychological devotion to a commitment, that is to say, one's religion, but the measure of the truth of the commitment itself, that is, what one understands about the total meaning of life, or one's philosophy. Prof. Hocking's statement that there is no cure for mental disease without consulting the total meaning of the world is most relevant here. People have *en masse* generally accepted the idea that the force of one's consecration to pietistic interests was the certain gauge of a true religion. But this is a delusion which happily is now exorcized both by reason and empirical psychology. The decisive thing is not the volume, vigor or vehemence of the element of devotion, but the harmony with truth and reality of those conceptions to which the loyal sacrifice is being emotionally made. Is it not significant that mental sanatoria always have a larger percentage of inmates who are there by reason of weird religious idiocies and fanaticisms unbalanced by any intellectual restraint, than are admitted for any other cause? The egregious misconception that still sways common thought is that the devoutness is the sure pledge of goodness and righteousness, when in direct contrariety to this the truth is that the crucial element is not the fact or the force of the devotion, but the rightness or falsity of the philosophical principles to which the devotion is paid. It is not by mere chance that religion has found a synonym in the word "devotion." Religious exercises are commonly termed "devotions." "A life of devotion" means a religious life, not specifying at all *to what* the devotion is to be directed, other than just—religion.

Ages of sad miscarriage of good intent could have been obviated and culture kept sanified, if there had been held constantly in view the discernment that the nobility of religion lay not in the sheer fact or fiat of "devotion," but was at all times to be determined by the criteria or the trueness or goodness, falsity or folly of the objective upon which the devotion was to be lavished. In brief the chief determinant in the issues of the life of religion was not the attitude of piety, but the nature of the mental objects upon which the piety was to be expended. And this finding for good and all constitutes philosophy as the prime and ultimate element of decisive value in the religious quest. Philosophy gains the verdict as the final arbiter of good in the life of devotion. And there is implicit in this conclusion enough dynamic significance to generate a sweeping revolution in the world's present religious life.

Piety and devotion are still accorded a high rank as noble and laudable attitudes. But it must now be recognized that their nobility and worth are to be judged finally by the philosophical rectitude of the intellectual objectives upon which they are showered. The sorry record of history which shows the pitiful wreckage and devastating power of devotions *wrongly directed* toward *unholy ends,* is sufficient attestation of the soundness of the judgments here adduced.

It comes back, then, to the dictum of truth that those who have not earned the benison of philosophy must linger on under the sway of the forces of religion. Religion inexorably is for the multitude; the intellectual aristocracy have earned the right to philosophy. Religion must perforce be as a boon and a support for those many who have not climbed to the heights from whose summits the beauteous land of philosophy can be glimpsed in all its fine enchantment. Religion is ever for those for whom pious disposition must serve, because they have not cultivated the intellectual perspicacity to understand wisdom hidden in mysteries. The only element that can end religion or the need of it is knowledge. With all thy getting, get wisdom, get understanding. For then one can release oneself from the bonds of pious fealty to trusted revelation or authoritative dictum and rest in blessed understanding. It is impossible that man's highest beatitude, namely peace of mind, can come until it rests on positive inner understanding. Ye shall *know* the truth and it alone shall set free.

It has been more or less vaguely sensed by capable thinkers that religion represents the failure or default of knowledge, or of philosophy; but it has not been bluntly stated, owing to the hypnotizing mental palsy exerted by the common regard for pietism. Mankind has ever tended to bow before devoutness, as if a devout man were sacrosanct by his closeness to Deity, or as if he touched influences under which all men have been taught to bend as to the presence of Deity itself. From the crushing force of this obsession only knowledge of the truth, or philosophy, can emancipate one. Lacking the enlightenment of knowledge and understanding, the human being has no recourse but to fall back upon the strength believed to flow from faith, hope, prayer, belief and the effort to win the support of an unknown Providence.

Echoes of the drastic thesis here propounded are to be heard in more than one modern work on religion, philosophy and psychology. Already has been noted Miss Langer's statement that the myth-making instinct belongs not to the lowest order of mentality but to a lofty philosophical capability and that philosophical thought is the last reach of genuine religion, its consummation and finally its dissolution. For as Scripture so well expresses the great truth here under discussion, in the finale of human perfection *faith is lost in sight*. And faith is religion and sight is philosophy. So religion must ultimately be swallowed up and disappear in the luminous apocalypses of philosophy.

If this relative view of religon as handmaiden to philosophy were widely recognized it would at one stroke reorient man's idea of religion to a new conception, so as to change it completely from a tyranny in the mental domain to an agency of liberation. It would open all blind eyes to the vision of religion as a thing to grow through and beyond, instead of a force to be enslaved to through life. The realization that religion is to serve but as a support for humanity through the period of its childhood ignorance and a crutch to be cast aside, or a scaffold to be torn away when the edifice of philosophy has been erected, would edify human life to such an extent that all existence would be cheered and brightened immeasurably.

Several of the strongest expressions on the subject are discovered in a strong work, *Psychology and the Promethean Will*, by William H. Sheldon. He writes (p. 69):

"The inability of the undeveloped mind to tolerate and *intellectualize* conflict constitutes the deepest bafflement of civilization."

If one can not rationalize the flow of events to see how beneficence is working to its divine ends through their incidence one becomes the hapless and helpless victim of outer circumstance. This is equivalent to saying that one is condemned to the greatest unhappiness. Sheldon's dynamic utterance restates the proposition that the "undeveloped mind," from the sheer fact of its undevelopment, is not equal to the task of bringing life under the eye of understanding, and must therefore abide on the lower levels where religion takes on predominantly the cast of dependence upon a Power deemed gracious enough to hear cries and pleas. Religion becomes then essentially a cult of worshipful rites and ritualistic techniques, inciting to emotional states found adaptable to the effort to throw the human self upon the mercies, tender or harsh, of the Power assumed to be dominating life. It is sycophantic, it is servile, showing in ugly form the character and quality that Nietzsche so furiously resented and anathematized in Christianity.

Au contraire, philosophy, by fortifying the mind with a knowledge of the laws which are seen to be the ordained will of Infinite Beneficence, inspires the mortal with the high spirit of adventure in winning benefit through obedience to these ordinances. The very knowledge that such obedience will bring the blessings that prayer must beg for obviates for the thinker the need for pleading. "All the things that thou canst desire are not to be compared unto her," asserts *Proverbs,* in its majestic tribute to wisdom, understanding. Fawning at God's feet still implies the worshipper's uncertainty, doubt, fear and helplessness, the basic elements of religion. Knowledge, the coefficient of philosophy, removes the uncertainty and the insecurity, and generates the happy consciousness that salvation lies within one's own grasp.

There is a citation of some length from Sheldon's work which so pointedly expresses what is here asserted that it is hard to pass it by (p. 199):

"The churches are filled with thousands of individuals who have bought a cheap religion and have promptly become a dead weight. They call themselves religious and in the eyes of the observant young they pass as the religious population. The influence they wield is labeled religion, and *it produces fearful confusion*. That is what makes it necessary to devote such a study as this almost altogether to the definition of elementary concepts, and that causes half or more of the men and women I know whose opinions are worth while to feel that the wisest course is to *abandon the concept of religion altogether,* to leave it to those people who have cheapened it, and to let them wallow in it until it disintegrates entirely, in the meantime replacing it, if possible, with better-built psychological concepts. The contempt for religion *created in the best minds* by the loading of religious institutions with people whose . . . development seems to have come to an abrupt end when they joined the Church, constitutes one of the poignant perplexities of our culture. In *something* they must ground a faith, for *it is by faith one must live after selling out the chance to grow a mind*. Whatever substitute may in time appear for the present formulary religion, this will likewise become the source of the faith of kind but unintellectual souls, and then it, too, will be in the same sense a cheap religion."

These are words of trenchant truth and they stand almost as if written to buttress the points here projected.

Sheldon (pp. 187-189) writes luminously about the Christian suppression of the Promethean element in human psychology. Space to cite all this splendid material corroborative of our theses is lacking, but it would be a virtual revelation to those steeped in the lethargy of pious ignorance, with critical faculties silenced by religious hypnotizations.

But the inviolable authority of our presentment needs no merely literary confirmation, however impressive. Its rightness is established beyond cavil or debate by the collective experience of thousands of people of education who, having passed in youth beyond the period of naive religious indoctrination in lifeless orthodox formulas, and having reached by study an emancipation from earlier crudities of belief, finally come to the point described by Sheldon where they see it is far better to drop the religious pretence altogether. All these liberated minds, when they cut the umbilical cord that tied them to the inanities of youthful Sabbath pietism, find themselves experiencing a release and freedom as from a devil's own curse of conscience, that amounts to a complete regeneration of the buoyancy and health of mind and body.

Not to be missed is Sheldon's pungent statement (p. 70):

"In the past religion has bound minds together effectively *only at a low level of intellect*. It is a vital question whether men can find a way of using religion as a cohesive and protective force in binding together minds determined to intellectualize conflict and so to achieve a common purpose at high levels of self-understanding."

Precisely this is the confirmation and the ground of our dictum that minds can be bound together at high levels only by philosophy. Religion is for the benefit of minds that can not reach to the plane of intellect. Philosophy comes in with its light of reason and understanding to lift minds out of that lower realm up into the place where man's divine dowry of rational conception can illumine the way. Surely man must call upon some benignant Power to take him by the hand and lead him aright as long as he does not kindle that true light that must be set aglow within his own being. For until he lights up that lamp, he dwells in comparative darkness. Religion is thus seen to be the kindergarten of the human evolutionary school system; philosophy comprises the upper grades, the college, the post-graduate degree.

The infinite pity of it all is that the ministrations of religion for the greater part are not at all what they are believed or hoped to be, guiding lights to simpler minds who must be helped to tread their way in the semi-darkness till they find the inner light. All too generally they are not truth simplified, good milk for babies, but tragically sheer delusion and infatuation, milk gone sour. This is the risk and the unfortunate outcome whenever esoteric formulations are given forth to the multitude without the possibility of the true sense being at least in some measure kept alive. So Sheldon comments most discerningly (p. 57):

"Even in modern times individuals find *in delusion* a short cut to wholeness. The cry is still raised that the magic formula has been found, and always there are unhappy thousands eager to ring the echo to the cry. . . . Any new religion, however cheap, gives a sense of character for a little time. The human mind is forever lured by an easy way; by some short cut; some *salvation by faith alone,* which is *salvation by dissociation of the intellect.* Yet to try to achieve character through mere intensity of the wish is like solving a puzzle by throwing half of it away."

These again are words of keen insight and tremendous import. Sheldon is here passing an intelligent and perfectly just sentence of condemnation upon the hundreds of cult religions that are set up by self-proclaimed leaders of groups, with which our present age is so thickly beset. All advertise the same magic formula for a quick jump at the goal, of course for compensation. Pitiably the multitudes plunge or nibble at the old bait. It will be shown that Christianity arose as just one of such cults of a former age, when the content of the preachment might have varied somewhat from present forms, but when spiritual hunger and uncritical naiveté and unbelievable gullibility united to produce fantastic religionism with the same sad consequences as are witnessed now.

So notable are these characteristics of religion that of late years the consensus of the highest thought has been that religion, which formerly (as still too largely) was considered a high motivation, sacred in itself, is no longer to be held in this lofty regard as a noble emotion, but is coming to be seen as virtually a thing of mental and moral weakness, in the view that it is in most of its activations really a cowardly retreat in the face of reality, the refuge of a weak soul, an escape from the brunt of the battle of life. Religion has come to be classed by astute criticism as one of the several "escape mechanisms," which include most of the forms of mystical experience. People who for one reason or another—now being sought and tabulated by psychology—lack the spiritual hardihood to face valiantly up to life's battle, seek refuge and surcease in religious fantasy of one sort or another.

The description is true in the main, but can be too broadly applied. It can even be argued that to a certain degree such refuge-seeking is justifiable, is a beneficent provision of life to enable its developing children to stand the gaff and hold firm under pressure. It can be thought of as a salutary measure on the part of the universal will to gain its ends for its creatural embodiments by permitting them to bend to the strain instead of breaking under it. Even in military science a retreat may in its proper place be a part of winning strategy.

In the large view, however, it must be considered a failure to fight, to play the life game with valor. It too generally betrays a surrender, a retreat in rout. It is the ostrich act of hiding from the horrid reality.

The justness of the view is to be determined by the character of the religion in which refuge is taken or escape sought. And the criterion is again the measure in which that religion is steadied by philosophy, or left to run the gamut of emotional, that is, religious states. This observation, then, opens the door to the consideration that perhaps no other religion in the world has stood to its votaries as the temptress to escape life's strain and pressure of stern realities as the Christian has done. Other religions have held forth equally with the Christian the promises of divine help and salvation, succor in time of distress, from a Deity or deities. Except in the most abject forms of idolatry, in which this Deity might have come to be anthropomorphically personalized, the ideal of Deity was in the form of some Power or Intelligence that at best had to be superinduced to act within the sphere of the votary's own life. The manipulation of psychic or devotional states within the individual's own area of consciousness was a necessary part of the process of obtaining divine attention or favor. One had to put oneself in certain conscious attitudes to invite the providential interest. The matter was still largely—and the more in proportion to the intelligence, the less in the ratio of the ignorance—a subjective operation, and the agency of help was within the sphere of the worshipper's mind.

Christianity, on the contrary, offered its followers an actual living person in history, a man talking, eating, doing things that John Smith might do daily. The religion of the Nazarene offered the Nazarene, and in profuse largesse of Scriptural promise, invited all mortals to come and freely throw all their burdens upon his shoulders, as he could bear the infinite load. Buddhism indeed invited the weary mortal to take refuge in a divine sanctuary of power and protection and con-solation; but it was a refuge in the Law, not in a living man. The Law had still to be learned and made operative within the directive purposiveness of the recipient of salvation. It was still subjective. Even when the *Bhagavad Gita* exhorts the devotee to "seek refuge in Me," it is still not a historical man speaking, but the voice of an impersonal Force to which the humble aspirant must himself lend an ear.

But Christianity invites the believer simply to surrender himself and his personal fight and call upon another man in history to win for him. It is the only religion that has embodied the saving grace of Deity in a living personal human being, and made divine Power to be implemented through an individual homo. And every last resource of language has been drawn upon in thousands of sermons, books and theologies to enforce on all believers the idea that a Christian could apply for help to this person, allegedly having lived in Judea, in the same realistic sense in which one could apply for help to an employ-ment bureau or government relief board. No possible conceivable effort or method has been overlooked in the straining to make this saving individual as realistic and humanly concrete as could be done. Every tensing of psychological muscle was exerted to have people pray to this man as if they were addressing him in fleshly presence. This invitation and persuasion are unremitting to the present hour.

The seductive disarming force of such a maneuver in religion is beyond imagination or calculation. Millions of struggling humans, distraught over their ill-fortune in the rugged going in life's journey, and unintelligent, have inevitably been enticed by this temptation. The call to cast all their burdens upon him, indeed his own "Come all ye that labor and are heavy laden, and I will give you rest," is powerful to the point of virtual hypnotization of all critical opposition. In Christianity, then, there is the most potent psychological force ever exerted upon the masses of humanity to dodge the hard fight and seek an easy refuge in a haven located outside themselves. It has been a phenomenon, demonstrated in limitless volume over centuries, to the boundless confusion, misery and disappointment of Western man.

The escape into religion is a hollow delusion. It is an escape from one cell of the prison of ignorance into another, with less possibility there of the mustering of real strength to get out. How can one escape into a condition which is itself a house of bondage? The etymology of the word "religion" is very suggestive as to this. It is from the Latin *re,* "back," and the stem *lig,* "to bind or tie." It is therefore a binding the mind back to either the basic source and reality of life, from which in its pilgrimage through the elements it has traveled far from base, or in a less noble sense, a binding back to the trammels of earth and sense from which man is expected in the course of his evolution to free himself. If it is taken in the first sense of a binding the fragment of consciousness to the divine or cosmic whole, then in its ultimate reference it becomes not a binding but a freeing force, for only in perfect union with God is there freedom. The perfected alone enjoy "the liberty of the Sons of God." All life short of that is slavery, as Paul says, to "the elements of the world."

There is no escape into religion and no escape out of it until one graduates into the upper grade of philosophy. If the world of intelligence can catch the idea that religion constitutes a grade in the cosmic curriculum, and one that is to be as quickly as possible passed through by the scholar, the stern face of human history can relax into a softer mien. Like a grade in the public schools, religion should be considered in its true function as a way station that exists not to hold its pupils, but to pass them on to a grade above it. The fatal blunder, to which there has apparently been no awakening in the circles of religion itself, has been in thinking that the human soul can be perpetually lodged in the religious house by the wayside. As Hopper says in his *The Crisis of Faith,* man is a viator; he is on his way; he is bound on a long journey. But religion would catch and hold him to its "binding back." Religion is reluctant to bid him God-speed on the longer path. Religion would shield him, caress him, mother him overlong to the detriment and eventual atrophy of his own powers. It is the fond mother that can not tolerate the thought of seeing her child step out from her nurturing home and care, to wage his battles out in the purlieus of an evil world. She is fearful of letting the believing mind of the youthful soul become subject to the critical assaults of rationalism on trusting faith, such as it will encounter when it delves into philosophy.

The outcome of the discussion on this point should be the firm hypostatization of a completely new view as regards religion. It should be categorically realized that as long as religion serves merely as a harbor of reliance and dependence on God viewed as a Power exterior to man's own spirit, it is in truth a form of escape from that necessary meeting with reality as it presses closer and closer upon the living soul, and as such it is a retreat, a childhood protection, a hugging the shelter of home in reluctance to brave the adventure in which the soul must overcome the world to win its crown. It is the coddling of a soul not yet strong enough to make its own fight. And in so far as it ties the initiative, the adventurous spirit of man down into grooves of complacent security and mediocrity, it is indeed a binding back of the wings of the soul, as Plato so graphically dramatizes it.

How ingloriously religion can bind people back to fixed anchorages in its indoctrinated dogmas and shibboleths is indicated by John Dewey (*Philosophy and Civilization,* p. 54), when he says that in large part religion is "hopelessly at the mercy of a Frankenstein philosophy which it originally called into being to be its own slave."

And how tightly one of these fixations of theological ideology can bind the free soul of him who accepts it can be seen if we note how even Guignebert interprets the doctrine of the saving office of Jesus in Christian systematism. He says that Jesus' death becomes clearly intelligible in the light of the theological formula that through it all men were provided, in a way that had never been opened to them before, with a means of their salvation. All men had crumpled under the weight of their sins. They were unable to right themselves and face the divine light. But Christ had come to offer them the required means; he took their guilt upon him and expiated their sins through his death of ignominy. Then, that they might share in his accomplishment and find grace in the day of judgment, it was expedient first of all to effect a union with himself through faith and love. What a monster Frankenstein this dogma is bound to become to any soul that takes it in its historical reference to a man living in Judea two thousand years ago, instead of entirely to a process of transfiguration of his mind by its union with the higher mind of the Christos developed to ruling power within his own consciousness, is surely apparent to any thinking person.

As to this particular doctrine an observation in passing is noteworthy. Hodges in his work on the early Church brings out the fact that Marcion, the eminent Gnostic, upheld a spiritual interpretation of Scripture in opposition to a religion debased and materialized, holding that the humanity of Christ was only in appearance, that Christ could not have taken on our material flesh which is essentially evil. Along with this it is most interesting to note what Charles B. Waite in his *History of the Christian Religion to A.D. 200* says as to the part that this same Marcion played in the formation of Christianity. Waite says that beyond question Marcion's gospel was the original from which the four canonical Gospels were afterwards fabricated by the later Christian plagiarists. He also tells us that pure Christianity has suffered no greater loss than that of the writings of Marcion, the great theological thinker of the second century, compiler of the first complete Gospel, collector of the Epistles of Paul, editor and publisher of the first New Testament. While the elaborate work against him written by Tertullian, who called him a "hound," has been preserved, and the work of Epiphanius, who bestowed on him the euphonious appellation of "the Beast," the writings of Marcion have perished, except such as are found in the references and citations of his adversaries. His works have shared the common fate of those of the heretics of the second century, none of which in their original form have been permitted to come down to us. Waite asks, significantly, why.

Sir Gilbert Murray essays to define the difference between religion and superstition by saying that superstition degrades its worshippers by turning its beliefs into so many statements of brute fact, on which it must needs act without question, without any respect for others or any desire for higher and fuller truth. It may be only an accident, though an invariable one, he asserts, that all the supposed true facts turn out to be false. Superstition is the belief in and action predicated upon false assumptions. But in religion, he says, you know that the truth you draw from it, however precious to you, is a truth seen dimly, and perhaps seen by others better than by you. It is time to add on our part that in philosophy you see truth with the dark glass mediumship removed, all things standing clear at last.

Perhaps the entire truth of the situation under discussion here is to be arrived at through the realization that essentially the conflict that eventuated in the production of Christianity was not so much a conflict between Christianity and Paganism as it was simply a conflict between ignorance and learning, between uncultured religious emotionalists and a minority group of esoteric philosophers. With the masses on the side of the former, the religious ferment won out and philosophy went into eclipse. This is evident beyond contradiction if only from the fact that the Gnostics, the more intelligent party that would have held the religion in line with high philosophical interests, were turned out as heretics. Gibbon states that the Gnostics were "the most cultured, the most learned and most worthy of the Christian name." Mosheim, too, says that slender indeed must be the acquaintance with the writings of antiquity of any one who would contend that the followers of the Gnostic ideas were men of low status or errant minds. Many of them, he says, had by their continence and austerity of demeanor acquired a reputation for sanctity and won the love and veneration of the multitude. It might be instructive to compare this statement of the historian with what the Emperor Julian is impelled to report on the Christian party. In his work entitled *Arguments Against the Christians* (p. 41) he speaks of what comes to light "when we begin to explore the monstrous deeds and fraudulent machinations of the evangelists." And Julian was in a position to know whereof he spoke. The Christian scene in the early centuries presents the anomalous picture of those perpetrating egregious fraud and vandalism in the field of sacred literature casting out as heretics the most cultured, learned and worthy from their community. And this anomaly has been defended, mitigated and condoned ever since.

The honest writings of the philosophers, the Gnostics and many of the learned, such as Porphyry and Celsus, were destroyed by the fanatical Christians; we have left only what the rabid Christian historians, Tertullian, Eusebius, Epiphanius, Hippolytus and others deemed best to write for the advantage of the Church. Gibbon is sure he has ample grounds for saying that

"The gravest of the ecclesiastical historians, Eusebius, himself indirectly confesses that he has related whatever might redound to the glory, and that he has suppressed all that could tend to the disgrace, of religion."

Gibbon has been joined by a veritable chorus of historical assent to the accusation that Eusebius is untrustworthy, and the others almost equally so. The result of the literary vandalism and the dishonest nature of Christian writing have, as Massey so clearly shows, caused the true evidence of the rise of Christianity to lie buried out of sight for a thousand years. The evidence is only now being recovered and pieced together to form the true picture.

Pertinent here is the observation of Manly P. Hall, popular present-day exponent of ancient esoteric philosophy, that

"Philosophy is the least degree of intellectual illusion . . . the least degree of mental error, since all other forms of learning contain a greater percentage of fallacy."

A statement made by Joseph Warschauer in his *The Historical Life of Christ* should be included here. He says it seems likely that the view which located the coming kingdom in the heavens or which spoke of the descent of a heavenly Jerusalem was confined to the thoughtful and better educated strata rather than spread among the masses. The latter, no doubt, he assumes, held their hope in the most concrete shape,—the overthrow of Rome and a revival of national political independence under a scion of the old Davidic dynasty. This is almost certainly the truth, and it shows, if the showing were needed, what historical hash the "popular mind" can and will make of esoteric spiritual truth and the allegories that have been devised to dramatize it. Warschauer suggests that the idea of a non-physical, non-historical Christ came in from Persia. It did not have to come in from any particular country. The esoteric tradition of a spiritual, in contradistinction to a human personal, Christ was already present, but held back from popular corruption in the hands of the few esotericists. It had to come out rather than come in. But catastrophe for general human interests has ever attended its coming out when that dissemination amongst the incompetent and uncritical masses eventuates in its mutilation and reduction to falsity. Such, we assert, was its fate at the hands of the Christian agitation. It was wrecked by ignorance.

B. A. G. Fuller, whose splendid new *History of Philosophy* has been cited herein already, ventures to say that wise men can do without religion and even flout the gods. They have risen above the need of or certainly the dependence upon such supports. But it is hazardous to claim that a wise philosopher flouts the gods. The truth of the matter is that he can well disregard the gods, as Epicurus also said, which the common people worship. Surely he discards all notions of the popular anthropomorphic deities. But he has gods of his own conception to whom he does not fail to pay the profoundest homage. But such gods are not those the people know about, for they are the personified cosmic powers of mind and matter, the faculties and energies of Universal Being.

Then Fuller places the philosopher far above the needs of religion on another count. The clear knowledge he possesses enabled the philosopher to free himself from the despotism of two giant fears which afflict the religious mind. In elucidating Epicureanism, Fuller states it was the view of this philosophy that men are haunted by two great fears which quite thoroughly inhibit all effort to gain mental imperturbability, or what the Stoics called *ataraxia,* that is, settled peace of mind and soul. The first of these supernatural and superstitious terrors is the fear of what may lie beyond this life, and the second is the fear of being spied on by the piercing eye, and punished by the interfering hand, of the gods. Thus, the Epicureans claimed, religion, by instituting these two fears alone *is the arch-destroyer of human happiness.* A philosopher fortifies his mind with a positive knowledge that obviates these fears. Therefore the loss or suppression of this philosophical knowledge has thrown the masses back upon religion, from which, in want of intellectual assurance, they are driven to seek consolation in sheer faith and hope. Fuller says that some of the grandest and most dramatic passages in Lucretius, exponent of Epicurean philosophy, are devoted to reciting and depicting the evils that follow in the train of the mind's surrender to religion: the cringing before the supernatural; the sense of being spied upon by the gods; the uncertainty of what the gods may decree; the dread of what may befall after death. Men enlightened by philosophy finally awake to this situation and disentangle themselves from its psychological toils. But crafty men catch at it as offering wide opportunity for cajoling the masses into easy dominance. Since it yields such prime advantage to a ruling class through keeping the populace docile and submissive to harsh conditions, its perpetuation becomes an objective of a dominant commerical, social or political ruling hierarchy. This comes to view in what Guignebert says in his fine history, in speaking about the syncretistic religion of the Roman world when the Empire succeeded the Republic (p. 114):

"Educated men no longer have any faith in it, but they respect it in public and, when forced, take part in its rites. They do this because they continue to believe religion obligatory upon the common people, whose dangerous appetites and instincts it holds in check."

Here is the theme for whatever vituperation any one feels inclined to pour forth upon the hypocrisy and duplicity of designing demagogues and leading citizens, who privately place themselves above the need of religion, but help to support it because it tends to make more secure their position of easy privilege in the social or secular world.

In line with this supercilious and insincere attitude is the remarkable utterance of Synesius, Bishop of Alexandria, in the fourth century:

"In my capacity as bishop of the Church I shall continue to disseminate the fables of our religion; but in my private capacity I shall remain a philosopher to the end."

Celsus has given us some idea of what those "fables" of early Christianity really were, and a perusal of some of the fictitious "Gospels" and "Epistles" that were invented to impress the heathen will give us more. But could any words more vividly convey the truth of what is here contended, that the "people" are to be fed on religion, with all its seductive technique of fable and falsity, while one who has respect for his own integrity of mind will hold on to philosophy?

The popularization of a profound esoteric wisdom or deep subjective mystic perceptions necessarily, then, can be effected only by way of a conversion of philosophy into religion. What stands in the philosophic mind as an enlightening conception emerges in the less intelligent mind as the basis of an emotional reaction. Fuller traces this subjugation of philosophy to religion as operative early in the life of Christianity.

Pliny believed that man worshipped best when he deified himself. He was convinced that the great head of all worlds pays little or no heed to human affairs. Can we have any doubt, he asks, that the divine nature is polluted by such a disagreeable and complicated office? This challenges us to imagine what we impose upon the Eternal when we ask him to turn his attention to all the entanglements of petty and trivial human relations. Pliny ridicules the superstitions of his age.

Lecky observes in his *History of European Morals* that the love of truth in most men is so languid and the reluctance to encounter the strain of mental understanding is so great that they yield their judgments without an effort to the current of conventional ideas, withdraw their minds from all critical opinion or research and "thus speedily convince themselves of the truth of what they wish to believe." Then he asserts that "an elaborate process of mental discipline with a view to strengthening the critical powers of the mind, is utterly remote from the spirit of theology." For this reason, he says, the growth of an inductive and scientific spirit is invariably hostile to theological interests. These statements of Lecky place side by side two strands of analytic thinking: the flaccid, languid temper of the common mind in its attitude toward truth; and the repugnance to mental discipline in the spirit of theology. Are these two manifestations related and if so, how? May the connection not be found in the reflection that since the common mind can not be reached and influenced by the deeper abstrusities of theology and the attempt to instruct it through theology would only confuse and disturb its settled trust in authority, theologians have deemed it wisest to let the sleeping dogs of their doctrinal principles lie? If it had proved historically possible for ecclesiastical power to utilize the abstrusities and subtleties of theology to bind the multitude of common people in loyalty to its program, we may be sure theology would have been developed as a popular weapon of religion. Evidently the languid interest of common man in theology and his obtuseness in grasping its niceties of meaning led to the great silence on the subject.

In view of all this analysis one is not surprised to hear John Dewey saying (*The Quest for Certainty,* p. 254): "With the expansion of Christianity ethico-religious traits came to dominate the purely rational ones." This was the process of the supplanting of philosophy by religion at work.

There will be vehement challenge to the direct statements and the obvious implications of many things adduced in this chapter, to the effect that philosophy fortifies the human mind with the certitude of knowledge, while religion leaves that mind in the darkness of doubt and hope. Philosophers of the present day will demur to the positiveness of these asseverations. They will say they have not found that certitude in philosophy, and that religion provides, on the whole, surer grounds of confidence than does philosophy. But our reference is to ancient, not modern philosophy; the philosophy that Plutarch was so conversant with, as he expounds and dilates upon its dynamic cogency for the human mind in the following passage (*Morals,* II, p. 369):

"The true philosophy is of a quite different nature; it is a spring and principle of motion wherever it comes; it makes men active and industrious; it sets every wheel and faculty a-going; it stores our minds with axioms and rules by which to make a sound judgment; it determines the will to the choice of what is honorable and just; and it wings all our faculties to the swiftest prosecution of it. It is accompanied with an elevation and nobleness of mind, joined with a coolness and sweetness of behavior, and backed with a becoming assurance and inflexible resolution."

One man's sheer laudation does not, of course, end all controversy. But what this one man—seconded, however, by many others—says has in its support the tremendous volume of evidence of similar character, all of it the outcome of the severest of all proofs,—the pragmatic test. The men of ancient days who conned this arcane wisdom, as well as thousands in later times to the present, add testimony to Plutarch's encomium. It *has* given the mind this elevation, this insight and this assurance. It is at this moment working its benignant magic of enlightenment and purification of life upon hundreds in the contemporary period, and with such force and satisfaction, such joy and delight in the mind, that it is having a veritable rebirth after thousands of years of obscuration. It carries the evidences of its own rightness, its own trueness, with it. But it must be cultivated with deep love before it yields its fruitage of certitude. There *was* a primeval revelation; it was not mere speculation; it was the voice of perfected understanding of graduates from the human school. Pythagoras and Plato had recaptured it; Plotinus, Philo, Proclus and Plutarch basked in its sunlit brilliance; Augustine had caught its reflected gleam and testified to its immemorial existence. If civilization is not to perish in the twentieth century it must be made to glow again.

CHAPTER X

TO FAITH ADD KNOWLEDGE

The subdivision of the theme that falls next in place is the obvious perception that the line of cleavage that marks the boundary between religion and philosophy likewise becomes the frontier between faith and knowledge. A synonym universally employed where a substitute word for "religion" has to be used is just this word "faith." A cognate term for religion is faith. As set forth in our thesis, religion presents faith as its main constituent, and it is for the most part simply an attitude of faith, a want of knowledge being humbly if not often aggressively confessed. It is that source of trust to which the individual soul must look for assurance and peace when the certitude of knowledge is wanting. "Faith" is close to being the literal description of what religion generally is—faith and belief.

On the other hand, philosophy so deeply rationalizes, as Sheldon says, the facts which life presents, and so well catches the marvelous correspondence between the order and harmony of straight thinking and the order and harmony of things, that it lays the solid foundation for the mind's certainty of knowledge, which is the only enduring ground for peace and blessedness in this mortal life.

The vast abyss of difference in authority and vitality between the two, faith and knowledge, or religion and philosophy, is to be discerned when it is reflected that in the case of faith the reliance is placed upon the beneficence of powers outside the self, while in the case of knowledge, it is localized entirely within. The disparity is so immense that there never should have been a question as to which is the more desirable element. The reign of faith is attended with all the mental hazards that spring from lack of certitude: doubt, vacillation, dread, worry and fear, not to mention constant dependence upon the unknown and unpredictable whim of the trusted Deity. There is no relaxing a tension of expectancy, either of good or evil event. Hope is the final basic reliance.

One is aware that Christian writers, so often transgressing the rules of dictionary exactitude, stretch the meaning of "faith" until they make it embrace almost what is really full knowledge itself. It is made to consist virtually of such a force of inward conviction, through mystical persuasions, that it is a form of knowledge itself. But this is disingenuous, an evasion and breach of intellectual honesty. If faith *is* knowledge, then it should be called knowledge.

The whole matter is brought to a sharp focus by St. Paul, who obviously does not telescope faith into knowledge. For he writes: "To your faith add knowledge." Clearly the Apostle is here saying: Faith, brethren, is good—as far as it goes; but it is not enough. It will hold you forever in the kindergarten. If you would grow in grace and in the favor of God you must increase your knowledge. Faith alone will never develop your divinely desired prerogative of conscious cooperation with the will of Deity. It will help you as a child, but when you become a man you must put away childish things and learn to stand in the consciousness of your participation in the intelligent mastership of your own evolution.

This opens the way for the presentation of an item in the current preaching of Christian clergy that should long ago have been seen in better light. Every year records the delivery of thousands of sermons on the need in the world of more faith in God. The cry is that irreligion is rampant, engendered by want of trust in Providence. Men are wild and reckless in their own base conceits and lawless graspings, because they do not recognize the influence of God in the world. Faith is the power that would anchor man more safely to divine beneficence.

The upshot of this unremitting emphasis is that for centuries the Christian mind has been conditioned to the idea that faith is the very pinnacle of spiritual virtue. It is considered to be the peak of Christian attainment, the summit product of the Christian life.

This is an egregious and hurtful misconception, since it throws the scheme of values quite out of proper focus. It places emphasis on the wrong end of the scale of values. It regards as a consummate achievement a feeling that, on the contrary, is an elemental reaction of childlike naiveté. It places at the top of the ladder the rung that actually is the very first and almost automatic step at the bottom. In fact faith in God is almost as inevitable and automatic as breathing. It is as unfailing as an instinct. It is present *a priori* and is not the product of cultivation.

For what can the human being do but trust in the goodness of life?

Any other posture of mind toward life would be an anomy. If life is going to be hostile to man, then trust will avail nothing. Man *must* assume that life will be benignant to him. There is nothing he can do *but* trust it. Therefore faith, instead of being the climax of growth in man's closeness to God, is the very first and most naive of the virtues. It is almost pre-virtuous, a spontaneous inevitability. It is the first, not the last, in the gamut of virtues. Virtue begins with it and then proceeds to advance from it to higher aspects of development.

St. Paul clearly discerned this status because he begins his ordered series of Christian qualities, taken obviously in the scale of their rank, with faith. "To your faith add virtue and to virtue knowledge." Faith is not the crowning glory of spiritual growth, but its first childlike beginning. This is a vastly needed correction of uncritical religionism.

When the Christian Church, in its violent revolt against the intellectual side of religion, repudiated the importance of knowledge in its system, it was by sheer necessity forced to fall back on faith. Faith, with its sister hope, enters when knowledge leaves. The mind must, of course, start its quest with the confidence that infinite treasures are there to be gained. But this confidence will be replaced or swallowed up as the treasures are unearthed.

Gibbon points out to us one danger that can all too readily flow from the perpetual exercise of faith, when not supported by data of critical thinking and knowledge. It lays the person open, he says, to an excessive and perilous expectancy, generating gullibility:

"The primitive Christians perpetually trod on mystic ground, and their minds were exercised by the habits of believing the most extraordinary events. They felt, or they fancied, that on every side they were incessantly . . . confronted by visions, instructed by prophecy and surprisingly delivered from danger, sickness and from death itself, by the supplications of the Church. The real or imaginary prodigies of which they so frequently conceived themselves to be the objects, the instruments or the spectators, very happily disposed them to adopt with the same ease . . . the authentic wonders of the evangelical history. . . . It is this deep impression of supernatural truths which has been so much celebrated under the name of faith; a state of mind described as the surest pledge of the Divine favor and of future felicity; and recommended as the first or perhaps the only merit of a Christian."

This places behind the analysis made here the support of Gibbon's forceful logic and historical vision, at the same time that it also cites from history itself the actual evil consequences of the substitution of faith for understanding. But he concludes with a corollary observation that again confirms our delineation of the Christian habit of belittling everything Pagan, the better to exalt everything Christian. He adds:

"According to the more rigid doctors, the moral virtues, which may be equally practiced by infidels, are destitute of any value or efficacy in the work of our justification."

The better sanity in Christian minds should years ago have seriously set itself to the task of analyzing the sort of dialectical aberration that could have driven pious people to the invidious position of deriding even their own best virtues when practiced outside their own fold. Again and again one finds Christians denouncing as vices the identical traits or qualities which in their own practice were extolled as supreme religious virtues. We are almost asked to think that virtue practiced by Christians is virtue, but practiced by Pagans it is a vice.

When religion is reduced from an interest engaging the whole man, his spiritual, intellectual, moral and physical qualities, and exercised only in the narrow area of "faith," as so nearly describes the situation in early Christianity, it becomes the parent of many forms and expressions of untoward and harmful reaction. Faith may be never so valiant and perpetually recharged by pietism, but it will not serve to instruct, to enlighten, to guide and to save from irrational venture. It leaves the devotee bereft of arms and armor which he *must* have to travel securely and avert evil hap. It still and always spells the lack of intelligence. It needs no logic to certify the fact that faith can never supplant knowledge or supply its want. It forever leaves the ignorant person open and subject to the errors that knowledge would enable him to avert. The Church has held its millions in the cradle stage by decrying knowledge and asking them to rely on faith.

In actual world life a religion based on faith is pretty nearly always confined to people of lower and median rank, the intelligentsia for the most part having "risen above it." An immense proportion of those who in childhood go through the customary mill of indoctrination in orthodox groups, leave that early faith as soon as they attain the power to think freely and study historical culture. Nearly all students cast off the puerile reverence for the churchly authority. Thinking, based on a wider range of data, which is only obtained by study, is the accomplishment of the intelligentsia only. It is dialectically necessary, then, that religion should be the cherished interest of the masses, since it is accepted on revered authority and held on faith.

A vivid picture of what the Christian religion became in the sight of men with minds equipped and balanced by philosophy is presented in Hodges' delineation of Celsus' antipathy to the Christianity of his day. In his *The Early Church* (p. 68) he recounts Celsus' disgust over the personnel of the Church on account of their impertinence, which was in exact proportion to their ignorance:

"He was disgusted with their insistence upon confession of sin, and the pride which they seemed to take in having no health in them; they spoke like worms in the mud. . . . As a philosopher intent on the pursuit of truth, he resented the doctrine of faith, which was offered, he thought, as an easy way to attain that which the student gains with labor and difficulty; it puts the ignorant on an equality with the educated; it leads only to illusion."

"Do not examine; only believe": this, he said, was the Christian principle, to be abhorred of all philosophers.

Massey sums up a long series of citations from the eminent literary figures of the Roman world who expressed their contempt of Christianity. He says: "The 'primitive Christians' were men whose ardor was fierce in proportion to their ignorance."

The indifference, antipathy and harsh judgments of the learned of the day toward the early faith have puzzled Christian publicists not a little. Hodges gives expression to this perplexity, when, speaking of Marcus Aurelius, he says (op. cit., p. 65):

"But the blindness of the Emperor was shared by all the eminent men of the day. The most important movement in the history of man, which was speedily to take possession of the Roman Empire and to build a new Rome upon the Bosphorus, and thereafter to dominate the progress of civilization and to save out of the wreck of barbarian overthrow the books of the very men who were writing at that moment in utter ignorance of the meaning of this struggling and depressed religion—this movement began and continued with no attention from the wise and the great. They either overlooked it or regarded the Christians as an insignificant Oriental sect."

In the second century they were made the subjects of satire by Lucian.

This passage of Hodges assumes that in this case the ignorant were wise and the wise were ignorant or blind. The dull and stupid saw with eagle eye what the learned missed. On the whole there is plenty of cause for disturbance and alarm in such a statement as Hodges here makes. It is an ominous event if brainless people in the year 33 A.D. or at any time could descry the cosmic and epochal significance of a religious ferment among the ignorant classes while the *truly* wise and great missed it entirely. There is something wrong in the way Hodges draws this picture, something that Hodges, wise and learned as he is, missed seeing. It is important that he and we alike see what is wrong there. He errs, first, in saying that the movement received no attention from the wise and the great. It had plenty of their attention, as witness what they said of it and the Emperor's persecution of it. Again, it had their attention because they at least took notice of it sufficiently to read its low character and to pronounce severe judgments against it. "A monster superstition," exclaims Pliny. "A pestilence," cries Suetonius. "Exitiabilis superstitio" (Destructive superstition), says Tacitus. "Certain most impious errors are committed by them," says Celsus, "due to their extreme ignorance, in which they have wandered away from the meaning of the divine enigmas." (Origen: *Con. Celsum,* Ch. VI.) Which statement, comments Massey, "is as true as it is temperate." Porphyry adds his contemptuous opinion and wrote his critique of the movement, a work that surely would have been immeasurably valuable had it not been destroyed by the fell ferocity of hatred of philosophy and its literature.

If Hodges fails to understand why Marcus Aurelius, one of the world's truly eminent philosophers, should have paid little attention to Christianity except to persecute it and otherwise disregard it as beneath his notice, he must find it difficult to see why a great and profound thinker should despise a crude and fantastic religious ferment among a small group of enthusiasts upon whom he must inevitably look down with pity and compassion. His persecution of them was no doubt motivated by his sense of duty toward the state, which was being menaced by the Christian agitation and departure from certain loyalties to the nation.

It may help us to see what Hodges fails to see if we look at what he himself says some pages farther on (p. 154). And when we hear him say this, we have to wonder how he can call Christianity "the most important movement in the history of man," seeing by and large that its effect upon the Occident as a whole differed little from its effect upon the world of the Roman Empire, which he describes as follows:

"There is plenty of other evidence, however, that the internal conversion of the Roman Empire to the Christian religion had effected no visible improvement in the common morals. *The world was worse,* rather than better. Out of its besetting temptations men fled to save their souls.

"They fled from the world, which in the first century was believed by the Christians to be doomed and liable to be destroyed by divine fire before the end of the year. . . . They fled also from the Church, which they accused of secularity and hypocrisy. Many of the monks were laymen who in deep disgust had forsaken the services and sacraments. They said their own prayers and sought God in their own way, asking no aid from the priests. They were men who had resolved never to go to church again."

And Hodges wonders why men of profound intellectual attainment and spiritual culture paid little attention to this movement among the rabble crowd, fanatical and already repulsive in its corruption and hypocrisy. The attention they did give it was inevitably to hold it up to derision and reprobation, mingled with pitying condescension. But as its furies spread they were in time brought to the resolve to put out by severe measures a pestilential mania of ignorance and frenzy that threatened the stable government of the world. Hodges heralds as the greatest event in history the smothering of true ancient light under the blanket of low superstition which brought no improvement, but on the contrary rendered life so evil that even from the portals of its own temples earnest men fled in disgust. Luther was to experience the same disgust and loathing of an evil thing as he descended the steps of a Christian temple at a later period. Perhaps the rise and spread of this religion *was* the most important event in world history. But the time may be at hand when happily a truer discernment will assuredly see that it was by no means the most beneficent event in that history. This work frankly presents a ground for belief that it was pretty nearly the most tragic event of that history. With the rise of critical thought, the advantage of a longer perspective and the privilege of untrammeled judgment, studious minds are calling into question whether the advent of Christianity was the most important event in history in the sense of an advance of the human spirit toward the light. Certainly any event which, along with much incidental good, has brought into manifestation a long train of evils, such as bigotry, slaughter, persecution, wars, divisions breeding hatred, mental confusion and delusion beyond measure and a host of ills never yet charted, must be considered important. But no one can longer claim that it is gloriously important. Millions of intelligent people in Oriental lands believe it was the most horrendous calamity in all history. On its evil side the wish might be that it were less important.

Hodges remarks that Ambrose, Bishop of Milan in the fourth century, read Origen and Plato. The two Gregories, Basil and others of the more intelligent leaders at that period had discernment enough to see what wells of truth the ancient heritage of knowledge contained, and knew what Origen was aiming to keep alive in Christianity. But it was becoming more hazardous to read and quote these Pagan sources of theology, and Jerome was severely taken to task for nibbling at the same table.

In view of the fact that Christianity has always claimed that it was the hordes of northern barbarians descending upon Greece and Rome that put out the light of learning and superinduced the Dark Ages, it is at least one item of interest to know that it was a Christian mob which burned the Alexandrian library, priceless beyond calculation; while the Goths, though destroying the temple of Diana at Ephesus, spared the library at Athens. Also, as cited by Higgins in *The Anacalypsis* (565), "St. Gregory is said by John of Salisbury to have burnt the imperial library of the Apollo." (From Forsyth's *Travels,* 134.)

It is indeed a fact looming large in relevance in Christian history that, as Guignebert says (p. 201), the influence of the Eastern, or original philosophical Christianity, upon the Christianity of the West "since the beginning of the Middle Ages has been very slight." This is evidently the result of the substitution of faith for the knowledge that philosophy supplies. Guignebert gives us an item of data here that speaks most significantly on this point. He says that out of the five hundred years from the death of Constantine to the end of the dispute regarding the images, i.e., from 337 to 843, two hundred and forty-eight of them, or nearly half of that period, were spent in open and avowed schism between the Eastern churches and Rome.

We find Guignebert testifying authentically to the broad claim here made that philosophy was discredited and pushed out, displaced by ignorant faith. Speaking of conditions in the fifth century, he says that the intelligence quotient of both priests and laity had fallen to so low a point that an uncouth compromise could be made between Church dogmas and "Teutonic superstitions." Since neither dogma nor Norse mythology was understood in its true occult sense, it was possible to join them in a common handling without too obvious discrepancy. F. S. C. Northrop, in his recent fine work, *The Meeting of East and West,* calls the modern practice in Protestantism of repeating set phrases without knowing their real meaning "idolatry and hocus-pocus."

Here again is common unintelligence drowning out all capable intellectual perception, and thereby reducing religion to simple faith, which, however, always will cling tenaciously to the traditional customs of the past. What Guignebert calls Teutonic superstitions, however, are to be truly recognized as ancient Norse mythological forms and usages, esoterically understood doubtless by the inner circle of the hierophants, but long ago gone meaningless among the common people.

What "simple faith" did to Christianity as early as the sixth century is again ably portrayed by Guignebert. It brought the religion down exactly to the level of those Pagan practices from which in horror the early Fathers had labored to rescue their people. He writes (p. 216):

"By a strange turn of fortune Christianity now tends to become actually nothing more than a collection of legends and sacra . . . and consequently to resemble that ancient Olympian Paganism whose poverty of dogma and morals, lack of deep capacity and childish ceremoniousness it had formerly inveighed against so bitterly. This was the foundation and not the completed Patristic Christian tradition, upon which the *popular religion* practiced in the Middle Ages was reared. In the sixteenth century the Reformation will try to uproot it, and will only partially succeed."

The gist of this really momentous passage is that whenever a religious movement surrenders itself to the influence of common standards of the masses, it sinks at once to the level on which an unintelligent herd tendency to follow custom in complete blindness and automatism rules all practice. But again correction of the historian's imperfect opinions must be introduced for the sake of truth. Olympian Paganism was not in poverty of either dogma or morals, did not lack deep capacity and was not lost in childish ceremoniousness, as he asserts. When we at last rise to the height of ability to comprehend the subtleties of the ancient legendary mythology, we shall know that these apparent puerilities of the great Greek race were the outward vestures of profound verities.

In support of this assertion we have the declaration of no less a scholar than Sir Gilbert Murray that he begins to feel that the great works of the ancient Greek imagination are penetrated habitually by religious conceptions and postulates which literary savants like himself have not observed or understood. And this more discerning scholarship, he adds, while harder, rarer and less popular, is perhaps the most permanently valuable work, and certainly needs to be defended at this juncture of history. The effort to do just this is the basic warrant and "apology" for this volume.

Murray gives further powerful support to the claims here adduced, when he says that the whole noble effort of the Greeks to enlighten the barbarian nations after Alexander's conquest failed. This must be noted as one more failure of culture when esoteric wisdom attempted to reach and uplift the servile masses. The great Platonic philosophy failed; the Pythagorean failed; the Mysteries failed; the Orphic and Hermetic philosophies failed; the great Neoplatonic effort failed; Alexandrian eclecticism and syncretism failed; Mithraism, Manichaeism, Gnosticism, Therapeutism, Essenism, all failed; failed, that is, to reach beyond the ranks of the limited intellectual aristocracy and to precipitate lasting beneficial effects upon the stolid masses. Philosophy of course never fails; it is human appreciative and perceptive capacity that fails philosophy. And in the same way and to the same extent Christianity failed, even when it was given some chance of success by its incorporation of the Hellenic systems of wisdom teaching through the *Epistles* of Paul and the "Johannine" writings. It failed as culture always must fail when it casts its pearls indiscriminately to the untamed appetites of the Beast. What is most notable in all this is that Christianity is the ebullition and ferment that came like froth to the surface when deeper knowledge had vanished.

We see one other disastrous outcome of the preachment of simple but uncritical and unintelligent faith to the common people in a result pictured by Guignebert (p. 221):

"They are drawn to the conviction that the Lamb himself is the occupant of the altar during the Mass, and that the consumption of the bread and wine constitutes a genuine sacrifice. Christ is sacrificed anew at every Mass, as he was upon the Mount of Calvary."

This throws on the historic screen the devastating mental effects of the attempt to impress simple folk with the realistic sense of what should clearly be told is drama and nothing more. But the citation is worth its space, if only because it prompts the observation anent its last sentence that if every reenactment of the Mass really crucifies a living being, the Christ, as an existing conscious entity, all over again, one surely is warranted in asking the Christians why in the name of mercy and humanity they do not put an end to this melancholy act of sadistic gruesomeness. Christians surely claim that Jesus is still a living personality, and hears prayers and suffers crucifixion. The Mass crucifies him again every time. What kind of a religion is it that knowingly goes on perpetually murdering its Redeemer over and over again? Might not psychology find that there is some true basis for the surmise that this repeated killing of the Christ has so blunted Christian hearts that they found it easy and emotionally stimulating to kill their dissenting fellowmen by the thousands at a later time?

But where could there be found a more direct and powerful condemnation of simple faith as against knowledge than in the statement from Erigena's *De Divisione Naturae,* a work developing again the Neoplatonic system? There the outright assertion is made that "Christian faith is an obstacle to the progress of knowledge." If Medieval European history does not fully prove the correctness of this declaration of the Platonic Christian reformer, proof would indeed be hard to find. But it is difficult to perceive the almost stunning paradoxical truth of this remark by Erigena unless one has had the background of Neoplatonic wisdom with its splendid illumination of the soul, to silhouette vividly against its light the feeble consolations of sheer pious faith.

Guignebert comments on the deadening force of those pronounced dogmas of the ecclesiastics which the blind and subservient faith of the laity enabled authority to impose on the Church. Without knowledge to divine or to understand an elevated import in the doctrines or ordinances, worship degenerated to a meaningless automatism of habit. Religion went into dead formalism. For to act without meaning is close to the last stage of human irrationality and inanity. And with intelligence completely reduced to a nullity under the power of faith, there was neither chance nor room for the free spirit, which had been the dynamo of driving power at the inception of the movement, to exert its active and purifying influences. In fact, once a code of dogmas had become crystallized in the organization and been deified by authority, the activations of a free spirit became a menace to settled orthodoxy. And when spurts and sallies of such free inquiry were made in any century, they were forthwith and summarily beaten to earth.

All too diaphanous is the unsoundness of a religion which can so reduce the normal sense and balance of human beings, not all of whom can always be rated as doltish simpletons, as to drag them to the sorry pass of forgetting their divine dignity and accepting their categorization as worms in the sight of Deity. Some egregious stultification of the sense of normal human worth must be superinduced upon average minds before so unworthy a self-humiliation can be inflicted. A system of "faith" that ends by abasing the natural human being to the level of the worm has little on which to ground its claim to being the highest religion in the world. And this *is* the religion that has most loudly asserted its claim that it more than any other has exalted the dignity, the divine worth, of the individual.

Again let truth have its hearing on another aspect of this theme. Here is the Church whose arrogant boast it is that it tore religion out

of the hands of the few cold-hearted aristocrats of intellect and gave it
to the mean and lowly, to their infinite benefit. Yet Guignebert paints
a picture of the revulsion of the "common people" against this same
Church in the later period in Europe. He is speaking of the groups
that again and again voiced their disapproval of the dead dogmatism
of the Church, and asked for the privilege of giving free vent to the
strivings and afflations of the spirit in the individual life, unrestricted
by ecclesiastical dogmas (p. 290):

> "Down below the agitation of these people . . . hostility to the estab-
> lished Church was evidently strong. Not only did these groups no longer
> believe that she was fulfilling her divine mission, but they saw in her the
> main obstacle to the advent of that era of happiness to which they looked
> forward."

Even those who gave religion to the poor and simple will find that
these beneficiaries will not forever receive with complete docility a gift
that leaves them hungry and unnourished. Even the worm will turn.
And eventually the divine principle in all mortals, no matter how
overlaid and stifled by ignorance, will not everlastingly accept without
rebellion the characterization of infinite meanness. Now and again
among the "common people" is born an uncommon spirit, a soul that
rises despite obstacles to an understanding and a vision, and who may
open the eyes of his lowly fellows to the poison of their imposed diet.
The poor can at times even bite and mangle the hand that holds forth
the spiritual diet of "worms." In 1260 there arose in Germany, Holland, Hungary, Flanders, all eastern France, following their first uprising in Italy, an order calling themselves Flagellantes or Penitentes.
They marched in bands through the towns and villages of these countries chanting hymns and lashing each other for the space of thirty-
three and a half days, as they regarded this as the period of time necessary to effect the purification of their souls. On their way, says Guignebert, they massacred Jews and displayed their feelings toward the
clergy by robbing the Church of its possessions and abusing the pos-
sessors. "Wild fanatics like Tauchelm in the Netherlands . . . or Eon
de Loudeac, who gave himself out to be the Son of God, are by no
means rare."

The free human spirit finds or takes many strange ways of manifesting its independence when it is too long and too rigidly held in
conformity to express forms and formulas. Tyrants have often learned
this lesson when it was too late. The Christian Church, which arose
as an outburst of the free, but unintelligent expression of the feelings

of lowly people, eventually became the crystallization of such a rigorous despotism in the kingdom of thought that its own devotees could no longer brook in silent submission its ecclesiastical thraldom, and so it was rent violently asunder in the sixteenth century. Good simple folk lack the capability of discerning recondite aspects of truth and the abstractions of philosophical understanding. But they are not to the same degree incapable of sensing gross falsities, which the course of events has a way of bringing to open sight after a time. Hypocrisy and deceit will show their hand in due time. Time often teaches what brain alone can not discern. The people can at times be wisely led to take up arms against humbug and dishonesty.

Still to be examined on the theme of faith versus knowledge is the patent truth that life and evolution inexorably demand of the individual, as a *sine qua non* for his advancement to the goal of glory, something more than sheer faith. As Paul showed, that something is first goodness, or virtue, and then the prime requisite, knowledge. Nature would be unjust if she dispensed without discrimination her blessings equally to those who have through toil and suffering met her terms of capability and to those who have not so earned them. The ineluctable truth is that man will not receive any grade or quality of benison until he has evolved the ability to command it. In this sense life bestows nothing gratuitously. All her benefits are freely held forth to all; but only he who knows how can take them. This is the fundamental meaning of the word "king." Seen in its German etymology, he is the one who "can." Part of Nietzsche's abhorrence to Christianity was engendered by his observation of the working of one of the basic theological dogmas of the religion,—its emphasis on a practically unlimited largesse of blessing from God on no more substantial ground of merit than simple "belief." Such an unmeasured generosity of Deity introduced chaos into the philosopher's ordered world, where precise law rules. Effects must stand in exact relation to adequate causes; and the Christian doctrines of the forgiveness of sins, the vicarious atonement and the inexhaustible reservoirs of God's infinite mercy and grace, dismantled the philosopher's conception of cosmos. Such religionism naturally repels the thinker. If the philosopher finds in his own life that salvation from life's ills is only won by dint of his keen search and capture of truth and his obedience to natural law, he is loath to accredit a system which claims that a few hours of maudlin emotionalism will win eternal bliss.

A pertinent reflection of Milman is most apropos here (p. 29):

"When man becomes more acquainted with his own nature, the less he is satisfied with deities cast in his own mold." This is indeed a trenchant deduction; and we need look little farther for an elucidation of the hold of anthropomorphic theory upon the masses. Educated men become more realistically aware of the subtleties and shallowness of their own motivations, as well as of their sincerities. But the lower masses remain naive and unsuspecting, credulous and susceptible. The deeper thinker will accept no God in his own image, however magnified to cosmic stature. The thinker has won his way to freedom from ready credulity; the uncritical man has not, but must accept what revered authority hands out to him.

Milman plunges without hesitation into the tremendous question under discussion in a passage (on page 32) of his great *History of Christianity*. It is a notable statement and commands our attention, since it badly needs competent answer:

"Philosophy, as a substitute for religion, was still more manifestly deficient. For in the first place it was unable, or condescended not, to reach the body of the people, whom the progress of civilization was slowly bringing up toward the common level; and where it found or sought proselytes it spoke without authority, and distracted with the multitude of its conflicting sects the patient but bewildered inquirer. Philosophy maintained the aristocratic tone, which, while it declared to a few elect spirits alone, it was possible to communicate the highest secrets of knowledge, more particularly the mysteries of the great Supreme Being, proclaimed it vain and unwise to attempt to elevate the many to such exalted speculations."

Here is the old cry: philosophy failed the masses. It ministered only to the needs of the aristocratic few. But it is time the weak points of this stricture on philosophy be examined. To call philosophy a substitute for religion is, to begin with, a false premise. Philosophy can be called a substitute for religion only in the wholly admissible sense in which it can be said that maturity is a substitute for childish immaturity, or a good meal is a substitute for an empty stomach, or education a substitute for ignorance. Milman's use of the term "substitute" is in the sense that religion is an adequate and perfect element, while philosophy as an alternative is an impliedly inferior replacement. In the proper sense philosophy substitutes vaster understanding for religion's groping faith, and the sooner the substitution in this sense is made, the better. As Miss Langer has said, philosophy is that upper realm of vision and knowledge in which the activations of religion are absorbed and finally dissipated, like smoke and steam in the pure upper air.

It is not a deficiency or defect of abstruse speculation and reflective thinking that they are not readily communicable to the mass level of mind. It is their nature, yes, even their utility and their beneficence that they can not be. It is time that just rebuke be administered the criticism thrown eternally at esotericism and intellectual aristocracy for their "deficiency" in not being something which by their nature and description they have no right to be asked to be.

A syllogism might more pointedly bring out the illogicality of the argument which is used to prove the "deficiency" of philosophy. The first or major premise would be: (a) *Esoteric philosophy is abstruse and highly recondite.* The second or minor premise would be: (b) *The masses are incapable of grasping abstruse and recondite philosophy.* The conclusion would be: (c) *Therefore esoteric philosophy is defective.* This is the unsound upshot of all this diatribe of Christian writers against ancient esotericism: it makes the stupidity of the ignorant the criterion of the good of esotericism. The masses are dumb and recusant to every higher advance or enlightenment, until higher genius discovers and demonstrates it. One does not call higher mathematics defective for being beyond the reach of the common mind. It is time we stop belaboring esotericism for not being something other than what it by nature is.

Then when the question arises as to supplying the needs of the lower ranks of society, let wisdom guide the discussion into proper channels. Failing that guidance history has taken hold of the situation and fed the "vulgar" multitude on religion, with philosophy only vaguely hovering in the background in the guise of a little known theology.

The tragedy of this actual working out of the problem is, as has been stated, that the multitude has never been fed on truth simplified, to be grasped by that level of capability, but truth turned into utter falsity, through the mistaking the images of truth for its actual substance. When spiritual complexities have been dramatized in fable, allegory and myth in order to stimulate the imagination through concrete picturizations, the sad outcome has been that, in the incredible density of their minds, the people fail to see the principle depicted and take the dramatization for the truth itself.

Of course philosophy condescends not to reach the body of the people. For the people have invariably treated it as did the dogs and swine of the Biblical metaphor; they snap at it and turn and rend it, trampling it in their filth. Christian insistence that philosophy failed because it did not transfigure the common mass of people is a most damning indictment of its own defective insight into the authentic and realistic conditions that are basic for high human culture.

And what is more: when the actuality of history is studied without bias, and the conspicuous consequences of the Christian effort to cast arcane philosophy to the *hoi polloi* over twenty centuries are fully tabulated, it is seen that their allegedly noble attempt to take the mysteries of truth to the masses has eventuated in the unparalleled darkening of the human mind, the loss of all true sense of the arcane books of wisdom, the hallucination of the millions, the dupery of all ecclesiastical rulership, and the befouling of history with the most frightful inhumanity of man to man in world annals.

In the same strain runs the exceptionally frank tribute to the high quality of the esoteric philosophy taught at Alexandria and its later degeneration. Kershner says that it had become less philosophical, "more and more spiritualistic and fanatical," until it was finally overwhelmed by the Mohammedan sweep in the seventh century. "Paganism and the old Greek culture had flared up in one final magnificent expression in the teachings of Plotinus and his Neo-Platonist companions." Then, referring to Plotinus, he writes (op. cit., pp. 105-7):

"His philosophy was intended for intellectual highbrows only. . . . Like most of the Hellenes he appears to have despised Christianity, looking upon it as a vulgar superstition fit only for slaves and the lower classes of workmen. Naturally enough the philosophy of Plotinus appealed to the higher classes, especially at the Roman court, and during the latter part of the third century it loomed up as a most formidable rival of the Christian teaching.

"It possessed attractive features for the upper class intellectuals, but it had no word for the down-trodden masses of the Empire, and therefore failed in the competition."

Then follow statements that are too singular to be missed:

"Neo-Platonism allied itself with the old Pagan cults in a last effort to prevent the inevitable. . . . But the new faith had the power to deal with facts as they are, while the other cults lived only in a world of dreams. The gray era of the Middle Ages was at hand."

Kershner is here graphically depicting the most tragic turn of events in world history and treats it as a turn toward the light! That the magnificent enlightenment glowing on every page of the great Neoplatonic system was doomed to "inevitable" extinction under the thickening pall of mental incapacity expressing itself in the new Christian movement should be termed by a man posing as a scholarly exponent of religion as a "world of dreams" and set over in disparaging contrast to "things as they are," reveals pitiably the incomprehension of the Christian mind about true history. Had the philosophy of Plotinus conquered instead of Christianity, there would not have been at hand "the gray Middle Ages." One of the "dreams" out of his philosophy Plotinus gave to Christianity itself, the "dream" of the Trinity. We are indebted to Lecky for a view of *some* at least of the "facts as they are" which it pleased Christian ministers to deal out to their gullible followers. Says he in Vol. II of his *History of European Morals* (p. 223):

"It was the custom then, as it is the custom now, for Catholic priests to strain the imaginations of young children by ghastly pictures of future misery, to imprint upon the virgin mind atrocious images which they hoped, not unreasonably, might prove indelible."

He speaks of incredible, grotesque, horrible visions reportedly seen by Christian monks of the pagans suffering torture in hell, with literal fire and all the lurid realism. They fed to children the stories of demons punishing the wicked and pictured the impending destruction of the world.

"Mr. Hallam, *The Middle Ages*, Ch. IX, Part 1, speaking of the legends of the miracles of saints, says: 'It must not be supposed that these absurdities were produced as well as nourished by ignorance. In most cases they were the work of deliberate imposture. Every cathedral or monastery had its tutelar saint, and every saint his legend, fabricated in order to enrich the churches under his protection, by exaggerating his virtues, his miracles and consequently his power of serving those who paid liberally for his patronage.' No impartial person can doubt its essential truth."

"The religious history of several centuries is little more than a history of the rapacity of priests and of the credulity of laymen."

"But legends of this kind . . . must not blind us to the fact that the period of Catholic ascendancy was on the whole one of the most deplorable in the history of the human mind. . . . A crowd of superstitions, attributed to infallible wisdom, barred the path of knowledge, and the charge of magic or the charge of heresy crushed every bold inquiry in the sphere of physical nature or of opinions . . . true inquiry had been cursed by the Church. A blind unquestioning credulity was inculcated as the first of duties, and the habit of doubt, the impartiality of a suspended judgment, the desire to hear both sides of a disputed question, and to emancipate the judgment from unreasoning prejudice, were all in consequence condemned. The belief in the guilt of error and doubt became universal, and that belief may be confidently pronounced to be the most pernicious superstition that has ever been accredited among mankind. . . . *Not till* the education of Europe passed from the monasteries to the universities, not till Mohammedan *science and classical freethought and industrial independence broke the scepter* of the Church did the intellectual revival of Europe begin."

"The monasteries diffused, wherever their influence extended, habits of credulity and intolerance that are the most deadly poisons to the human mind."

"It is difficult to look upon Catholicism in any other light than as the most deadly enemy of the scientific spirit. . . ."

This incredible recital could go on for a hundred pages; it is thrown in here only to present actually what the Christian "power to deal with facts as they are" brought forth.

It would seem unnecessary to heap up additional confirmation of the conlusion that a religion of faith will stifle reason and reduce the believer to a bondage under his emotional states; but we have before us further testimony to this fell force in the case of a man as intelligent as the canonized Augustine. When a leader of his potential capability surrenders his mind to mystical forces, one can be certain that the mass of common people will be surer victims of the same tendency. Says Joseph Wheless in his *Forgery in Christianity* (p. xvii):

"The proudest boast today of the Church for its ex-Pagan Saint Augustine is that: 'as soon as a contradiction [between his philosophy and his religious doctrine] arises, he never hesitates to subordinate his philosophy to religion, reason to faith.' (*Cath. Ency.* ii, 86.) So this great ex-Pagan Saint of the Church surrenders his reason to faith and avers: 'I would not believe the Gospels to be true, unless the authority of the Catholic Church constrained me.' " (Aug., *De Genesi.*)

Faith had done its baleful work all too well. We can see Plotinus' justification for appearing to be neglectful of the ignorant in a passage from Guthrie's translation of the works of Plotinus (p. 18):

"Not a single word or similarity of expression in the *Enneads* betrays any acquaintance with the Christian formulations, nor does Plotinus anywhere betray that his doctrines had arisen in opposition to or imitation of Christianity; he utterly ignores it. And the reason of this is plain; for the Christian usually belonged to the lowest and most unphilosophical classes with a few exceptions; and it seems almost amusing to think of a man so deeply read in philosophy as Plotinus or Ammonius Saccas were, should borrow all their best doctrines from unphilosophical sources."

He asks how so "barren a source could furnish the acknowledged rich results of Neo-Platonism."

In his *Christianity Past and Present* (p. 476) Guignebert sets forth the justification which the Church has advanced for its practice of feeding the multitude on the porridge of simple faith and materialized conceptions:

"The pretext by which the worst practices can always justify themselves, i.e., that they edify those who take their religion simply and who would never become attached to it if it were not brought down to their level; God will always be the gainer as far as their *intention* goes, at any rate."

The skulduggery of this subterfuge can not be expounded in a paragraph. But in quite succinct form let it be said that God can gain nothing from anything that does not edify and elevate man; for the only way that man can contribute to the glory of God is by the increase of his own portion of deity, the spark of divine mind implanted within the core of his own nature. If that is not made to shine brighter, God is not the gainer. The Church that holds its millions to a low level of intellectual development and makes no effort to cultivate a truly higher vision is depriving God of his only chance to be glorified through man.

The Church received its exalted and central doctrine (at least the one it fought over with tigerish fury for two centuries) of the Trinity from Plotinus. But the consequence of its failure to follow his philosophy is that not in eighteen centuries has it ever had the true exposition or understanding of that doctrine. Its explicit and comprehensible meaning is not known to anybody in the Church to this day. But at least one high churchman in the modern day has testified that his own most luminous comprehension of Christian theology has come from his extraordinary interest in the philosophy of this same Plotinus. This is Dean Ralph W. Inge, long primate of Westminster. His two fine volumes on the philosophy of Plotinus amply testify to this.

Paganism had itself run the gamut of bitter experience in having endeavored as best it could to impart the myths and allegories, the symbols and emblems of supernal verities, to the populace. Time and again the outer types of representation had become agglutinized in the general mind as realities in themselves. The ignorant are ever ready to take the shadow for the substance. The result is always that the multitude turn these precious truths into the agencies of hallucination.

It is going to demand a whole new orientation of method in education to hit finally upon the right course to be pursued, so that untutored minds can be furnished with forms that really simplify truth without transmogrifying it into blank error. It will always require considerable deftness in elucidation. But the proper procedure will always have to be based on a grounding of instruction on nature-forms. The ancient Egyptian science of analogical paralogism, or nature symbolism, must be revived and made the cornerstone of a new semantic pedagogy. Then a skill must be developed, *the technique being happily already envisaged,* to effect the transfer of meaning and reference from the nature symbol over to the conscious domain where mystical and spiritual realizations are born. But the one sane method will have to be the representation of supernal truth over the image and pattern of natural truth.

In regard to the excessive credulity engendered among the Christians by the preachment of faith and the condemnation of philosophy Lecky tells us (op. cit., I, 384) that

"Lucian declares that every cunning juggler could make his fortune by going over to the Christians and preying upon their simplicity. Celsus describes the Christian jugglers performing their tricks among the young and credulous. The most decisive evidence we possess, however, is a law of Ulpian directed, it is thought, against the Christians, which condemns those 'who use incantations or imprecations, or (to employ the common word of imposters) exorcisms' . . . that when the Laodicean Council in the fourth century forbade any one to exorcise, except those who were duly authorized by the Bishop, these miracles speedily declined. . . ."

The history of the Church would supply a thousand illustrations of the follies of wild belief and superstitious practice that are bound to take form and find expression when people are fed on faith and their minds left to starve for rational nourishment. A full recounting of the evils of a faith religion would cover the history of a hundred great and lesser movements of religious ferment in the Western world down to the present.

Religion in general has been the horrifying story of one rampant delusion after another. Most dismal of all is the survey of the multitudinous aberrations of sound human mentality venting their expression without end in the pale of orthodox Christianity itself. Rebound from disgust and disillusionment met with in one outburst has often precipitated unintelligence over into another equally wretched at the other extreme. Thus the student of religious history passes over the endless train of cult movements, every one of which sprang from the failure of true philosophical insight at some point of its formulation. And over all hovers the dank and clammy atmosphere of the mass persuasion that any movement inspired by a sodden heavy pietism is therewith sanctified and must command holy respect. When men assemble to pray, let the secular world keep silence. And the story of how slyly men garbed in black have utilized the reverence for pietism toward the attainment of their own very secular ends is one that also has never been written.

The Christian charge that the Pagan philosophers cared nothing for the mental upliftment of the masses is controverted by the evidence. Who more than Socrates strove to take his logic to men on the street corners of the world? Printing was not at hand to make universal dissemination possible. But Plato formed his school, as did Pythagoras before him, as centers of light to all who could come to study. Paganism had schools whose instruction is still the guiding light of human thought. Christianity closed them, and put out their light. Let there be an end of the base slander that Paganism cared nothing for the people. The power that closed these centers of radiation of intellectual light later, of course, established its own schools. But the instruction imparted therein aimed straight at the extinguishing of the light that has been the primal mind dynamo of the human race.

There was never a time when the priceless boon of esoteric truth was withheld knowingly from any who could furnish the requisite credentials; and these were fixed by nature and not accorded by the teachers. The philosophers simply used the discretion of intelligence in recognizing the inevitable limitations of the recipients, and in adapting methods of instruction to the capabilities of the learners. The leading and more intelligent Christians themselves strove to keep higher knowledge from its lowest ranks, until all caution and prudence were swept away by the inrush of the masses seeking salvation on terms falsely proclaimed as quite too facile.

The fall of culture from high to base levels is always marked by the shift from philosophy to religion and in religion from knowledge to faith.

All this can be seen in clearer perspective by reflection upon a master statement by Sheldon in his *Psychology and the Promethean Will* (p. 26).

"One of the first and most vital concerns of man is the maintenance of integration between feeling and intellect. It is a need fully as imperative as the need of food, and to meet this need is the true psychological function of religion."

This is a truth of supreme import. A religion that fails to nourish the thinking soul of man fails even as a religion, much more as a philosophy. Calamity follows in the wake of failure to apply this truth. Its mighty sanity has been flouted by the religion that abandoned, nay, scorned and berated the intellect and worked on feeling alone. But that religion was, for its own salvation, forced to take up again and again the intellectual systems of the very Paganism it charges with being a mental aristocracy and a failure to meet human needs. How idiotically its own history confutes its monotonous claims!

What a fresh breeze of sanity blows through the utterance of Rabelais who (*Gargantua,* I, 52) puts the gist of all our long exposition in the pith of a single sentence:

"The greatest dream of the world was to regulate itself by the sound of a church bell and not by the dictates of common sense and intelligence."

The Christian "faith" is the paramount demonstration in all the world's life that to try to dominate humankind by a religion divorced from philosophy is to take the path leading straight to wreckage. History records that fearful wreckage.

And again the irony of history grimaces tantalizingly and vengefully at the institution that tore its people away in hatred of philosophy and thus loosed upon them the whole Pandora's brood of superstitions, wild beliefs and pious addiction to supernatural expectations. For this monster Frankenstein has turned to master its creator. Or so says Guignebert (op. cit., p. 476):

"The official Church is dominated by the letter and by superstition; she has become incapable of holding her own effectively against them, and she no longer seems to believe that any attempt to do so is to her interest."

And so all the shining glory acclaimed to itself by the Christian religion for having gone out into the highways and by-ways of the world and given holy and comforting religion to the outcast and despised of men, is turned by the wand of the ugly fairy in the tale of history into the ignominy of having debauched a world with ignorance and folly.

CHAPTER XI

THE GREAT EBB-TIDE

At last, then, the long-buried truth emerges to view. Christianity was not a movement generated by a wholly new revelation of light—much less of the first light—kindled out of heaven to end previous earthly darkness. On the contrary it was a popular sweep of violent reaction that dragged truly sacred esoteric wisdom out of its adyta and inner sancta and purveyed it wholesale to the people at large. However heroic in its motive to disclose secret knowledge to the poor, it was historically fatal in its consequences. For it contravened, ignored and violated the inexorable ordinance of life, that man can appropriate only what he has won and can utilize beneficently only what he can handle with the sure precision of intelligence. Christianity's much-lauded gift of religion to the submerged groups ended by perpetuating and deepening that submergence for seventeen centuries.

The ignorantly manufactured tradition that Christianity arose from a sudden outburst of new light in the heathen gloom is one of the most outlandish fabrications in the course of all human errancy. The claim of such an origin for this religion flies in direct contradiction of all the implacable laws that govern the evolution of movements in human society. The notion universally purveyed by Christian writers is that the religion sprang from no roots grounded in the past and owed nothing to the past. This is asserted to be true in spite of the fact that many books, as shall be noticed, do admit the adoption of much Pagan or antecedent material into the Christian constitution. For even when such appropriation is admitted, the position is still always maintained that the Christians converted what it borrowed into its first relevant meaning and utility, and thus redeemed it from a senseless vogue among the heathen to a high usage and import. The dogmatic plea is that Christians took up some of the old forms and doctrines of Pagan usage and for the first time invested them with the dignity of a true meaning and a dynamic good force. Assertions to this effect abound.

This is another of those many canards invented by the Christians that are as baseless as they are disingenuous. It is sadly enough true that the light of inner significance of most of the ancient Mystery practices and formulae had gone out or dimmed low before Christianity had its inception. But that the new religion, which soon agitated the popular mind, took up features whose esoteric sense had vanished and restored to them that lost deeper significance, is as bald a falsehood as ever insinuated itself into the most depraved minds.

The astonishing truth is almost the direct contrary of this. For the most part it was the Christians who, inheriting past forms and liturgies, pushed out of focus or lost utterly every last vestige of a nobler esoteric interpretation and substituted for that truer understanding their own gross literal or historical rendering. At any rate, when the body of ancient mythic and ritualistic presentments had passed through the wringer, so to say, of the process of revamping at Christian hands, it emerged stripped bare of any remaining esoteric significance. The charge that the Pagans had enacted rites and mouthed doctrines in entire ignorance of a noble sense behind them, and that the Christians elevated all this material to lofty sublimity and saving intelligence, is quite the opposite of the truth. It has been shown that the very effort made by Origen, Clement and to some degree Augustine, to do something in this direction, was violently repudiated by the Church; and similar efforts have been summarily smothered ever since. The most determined search is unable to find any authentic evidence that Christianity at any point instituted any improvement over Pagan things. Rather at every turn it registered a movement from intelligence to ignorance, from better to worse, from lofty conception to degradation.

The attempt to set forth in clear light the generating causes of Christianity—more properly of course, Christianism—requires the making of a preliminary survey of the status of affairs in religion and culture prevailing before its birth. For this movement took its rise immediately out of the play of forces operative at the time and was not the product of a revelation from spiritual heavens. It is the assumption that it was a new effulgence of celestial light that has prevented the attempt to explain it on the usual grounds of historical influences at work in background and environment. It was as definitely an earth-born surge of religious feeling as any in history. Indeed it was less heaven-born than most, in the sense that a stir engendered among the ignorant is less "divine" than one generated in the upper ranges of intelligence.

Assuredly Christianity grew out of the religious situation of its day and its past. That situation must be scrutinized with a regard to its actualities and a scrupulosity of truth-telling apparently not accorded to it before.

The background screen against which it is all to be thrown is, of course, the rule of the esoteric spirit, the true custodianship of culture, as outlined here. Intelligence and a passionate love of truth for its own sake, or "divine philosophy," as the Greeks denominated it, exercised its rightful hegemony over the field of thought, sending its benignant rays as far down from the apex of eagle-eyed apperception as it was able to penetrate into the area of the general mind. Veiled in myth, allegory and symbol and other arcane forms, and kept in pretty strict secrecy, it reached only a select group of the best qualified. Nevertheless the inveterate bent of the masses to ape or respect the aristocracy of wealth, position or intelligence provided a bridge, narrow enough, no doubt, by which some of the aura and the benison of culture could pass down to the masses. In the face of Christian statements to the contrary, it must be affirmed that the cultivation of esoteric wisdom by the intellectual aristocracy in the Pagan world did not leave the masses in such destitution of sane and balanced views of religion as has always been alleged. General standards of thought and understanding were high, much higher in such a land as Greece, than they were when philosophical interests got out of hand, slipped from the control of the few and ran their rampant course among the people. At least it is evident from history itself that while the Hellenic philosophical culture dominated the scene, there is not to be found anything comparable to the emotional extravagances of religious pietism and violence of religious fanaticism that came with the Christian upsurge. If, as is recorded, as many as thirty thousand people assembled to witness certain of the dramatic representations produced in celebration of the festivals of the Eleusinian Mysteries, it is an evidence that the influence of the "few intellectuals" was both powerful and edifying generally. All, of course, depended upon the mental development of the people themselves, as to how far and how beneficially the arcane wisdom propagated by the secret brotherhoods could penetrate and leaven the mass mind. It is legitimate to contend that if the so-called upper class of society is highly enlightened with a true and elevating philosophy, the people beneath cannot utterly fail to be benefited. A society which can produce Platos and Aristotles must itself be permeable by their light. When vision does not fail, the people will not perish. Christianity, this work claims, was produced by a force and a spirit that found expression and character under the influences that prevailed when vision had failed. That failure of vision, its causes and consequences, must now be canvassed.

Christianity surged forth when a lamentable and tragic recession of a high tide—perhaps the very highest tide in the period of known history—of a philosophical culture that is still the brightest glory of human civilization, had reached the nadir of its cycle. Among the most informing of all studies should be the effort to account for the failure of high development after touching the apex of its advance. In the dearth of exact knowledge of this phenomenon, resort must be had to the broad principle that human culture, like everything else in the life movement, advances cyclically, rhythmically, or in waves. It rises high and sinks back. Its crests form and break at a given point. They do not run steadily in the same form. Like the surf on the beach, they gather their forces, take their form, spend their energy in one climactic surge and die away. Rhythmically another follows. The streets of Athens are devoid of groups listening to Socrates now. The studios of Florence harbor no mighty artists or humanists now. The inns of London toast no Shakespeares, Dr. Johnsons, Boswells, Goldsmiths. Wordsworth laments England's need of a Milton. Even Concord is silent without the oracular voices of Emerson, Thoreau and Hawthorne. Cultures surge to heights, then recede. Brilliance does not reproduce itself. Culture is not static. What is to be adduced here for its weighty import is that Greek philosophy came at and as the culminating point of perhaps the highest tide of uplift in human culture, and Christianity came at and as the lowest point of the recession of that wave.

If it is possible to ascertain and delineate the particular features that conduced to the lofty development in the Age of Pericles, as well as those that were in manifestation when the Hellenic light declined, it should be done. What lighted that lamp, and why did it not burn longer, or continuously? Here indeed is the crux of the matter. The world is condemned because it did not receive the light when it came. Equally it is worthy of blame for not having kept the lamp trimmed and burning, once the flame was kindled. The world is always clamoring for new light. This is silly, seeing that it has not held the great light it so abundantly received of old. The glory beamed once and again. But the blind and fatal stupor of the human mind has dimmed it, lost it. There is no surety that if a Christ comes to give light to the world, the world will either accept it or retain it. It has been given and renewed again and again, only to die out as often. A significant saying of the Lord in the Hindu books is: "As often as piety and religion decay among men, I send my messenger to revive them."

The great age of crowning glory in philosophical culture came with Pythagoras and Plato, flared in the sky of human thought and died out in the succeeding age. Six hundred years later, when the darkness had settled again over the Hellenic world, the spiritual custodians made a supreme effort to rekindle the Platonic flame. Forth again flared the gleam in brilliance even perhaps surpassing its original glow, in the school of Ammonius Saccas, in the writings of Plotinus, Iamblichus, Porphyry, Proclus, in the esoteric successors of Philo. Neo-Platonism gave the world its light again. If there is a hierarchy of spiritual counsellors that exercise some supervision over the periodic cultural revivification of the world, it can be reasonably assumed that this outburst of Platonic esotericism in the third century of the Christian era was the deliberate engineering of an effort to stop the horrendous blighting of all deep wisdom by the Christian uprising, which was with sickening speed closing all minds to the impact of the spiritual mystery teaching, as it descended from the lofty apprehension of myth and allegory to blunt dead literalism of the Scriptural word. But too late it came, and the horrid debacle crashed to its full ruin. The ignorant masses had begun their march, and the voice of esoteric sanity could not make itself heard to halt them. Down into the Dark Ages plunged the Western world. The story of this chapter must be the descent of human culture from Platonic heights to Medieval depths. This great world cataclysm has hardly ever been made the subject of intensive, or at any rate, enlightened study. Gibbon's great history is a sidelong approach to it. Christianity of course has resented his truthful exposition of its own low character, its disingenuous motivations and its fanatical violence.

But the dismal rescension of culture after Plato has not gone unnoticed. It is descanted upon by numerous investigators, if in far from exhaustive and discerning treatment. But one of the most astute of modern scholars has immortalized a phrase that was hit upon by him to express the salient idea that describes the fatal decline. Readers in this field are well acquainted with Sir Gilbert Murray's famous descriptive term for it: the failure of (Greek) nerve.

In its broad connotations it well characterizes what is set forth here.

But its breadth of meaning needs delineation to more specific particularity. What is it that Sir Gilbert wishes us to understand in his word "nerve"?

It is indeed a well-chosen term. It connotes such qualities as courage and self-reliance to fight out the issues of life's battles. Its most central concept, however, is that it embraces this resolute facing of life's struggle in reliance upon the resources within the scope of man's own nature and constitution, without falling back upon extraneous aids or depending upon what might be called a subsidy from a Power entirely outside man's prerogative. To keep this stout "nerve," philosophically speaking, was to fight the good fight in the might of his human wisdom, guided and enlightened by the diviner wisdom germinally resident and potentially perfectable within his own sphere of consciousness and direction. This "nerve" held men fast to the high and true philosophical ideal of waging the Armageddon battle of their evolution on the terms set as conditions by life and Deity themselves, demanding the exercise that would bring the unfoldment of those inner potentialities of insight and knowledge that must govern the growth of the whole man in the end. Not to use them, but to let them lie untried and unproven, while looking helplessly outside for help, when God had placed that sword of the spirit immediately within man's own constitution, was to fail both man and God at the only point at which God's supernal power stands within man's actual reach and influence. To abandon, or to fail in, this resolution to stand and battle with the weapons God had provided for this express contingency, and to surrender the battle-front and retreat in admission of helplessness, and then in servile mood to call upon external powers to save oneself, is what the scholar meant by the loss of nerve on the part of the Greek world. It is a notable and only-too-true analysis of the rueful epoch. It was this demoralization of the human courage and élan inspired by Greek philosophy that prepared the ground for the upspringing of the fantastically degenerate Christianism.

This failure of nerve, not only in Greece but everywhere, should be the subject of the keenest research by all students of human currents. For it draws the rough sketch of the nature of every deterioration or backsliding of religious culture. It announced the prime criterion of all culture, since it defines culture to be the exercise, growth and perfected beneficent use of the divine powers potential in man. The moment, then, that the central intelligence in the human being falls so short of competent knowledge as to give over the resolution to employ and deploy the resources providentially made available within his reach, and to run to sources of help allegedly available outside his sphere of initiative, there is the failure of nerve and the end of self-culture. Man in such deplorable state resigns the lordship of the only god who can save him, and sinks in abject surrender to the mercies of elementary powers and the forces of nature. Indeed Paul tells us that before we had risen in evolution to the point of consciousness of our own mastery of the forces drawing the chariot of our advance to deity, "we were in bondage to the elementals of the earth" and of the air, or the "elements of the world." The divine gift of a spiritual soul linked in with our mortal components was to lift us above this subservience and helplessness under nature's laws, to give us conscious command of our own growth through the awakening powers of the free spirit of truth which should lead us into all truth. Once developed and set to its task of rulership, this Holy Spirit, or Paraclete, man's eternal Comforter, dare not be surrendered. For man to do so is for him to surrender his divine to the power of the elemental nature in him. For it is the cosmic prerogative of the divine to rule the natural.

In the realm of such mental cultures as religion and philosophy, it is to surrender understanding and knowledge to emotion, the possibility of wisdom and sure guidance to faith. And this surrender is what crept like a palsy over the area of the Hellenic world after Plato. With philosophy in decadence, there was nowhere available the sufficient knowledge to fortify men with the courage to stand in the might of their divine donative and front life with yeoman heroism of the spirit. Man surrendered his divine sword and ran in fear and rout to God—the God not in his own selfhood, but the God in remote "heavens." In conformity with the usual outcome of unintelligent religionism, the devotees abandon earth as the place where vital values and salvation can be won, and look and flee to heaven. The flight of religion from earth to heaven for the realization of supreme values has with never an exception marked the divorcement of religion from philosophy, of faith from knowledge. And perhaps no short description can so well delineate the decline and fall of true religion as this shifting of the locale or point of focus of true values in the spiritual life of man. Not to wage life's engagement but to flee it for the happier land beyond the tomb, becomes man's objective. This of course paralyzes further initiative and wilts the budding flower of the soul's life.

The prime objective of originally sound religion was to focus the battle for values here in the world and inside the conscious human sphere. A religion of decadence, made violent with undisciplined emotion and bereft of philosophical knowledge, always distracts man's vision from its true objective here. Thus all such arrant religious upheavals sidetrack man from the proper road of his evolution, leave him to wallow in the mire of his own wild propensities and stagnate his upward drive to divinity.

It is true that Murray does not paint the same picture of the failure of nerve as is here done. He sees it as a failure of hope and confidence in Greek people to achieve the better earthly life through national governments and mundane institutions. He sees it as the disillusionment of the philosophers in their dream of such realizations and their consequent retirement from the collective outward effort into the solitary seeking of spiritual comfort and contact with God in the depths of their own retreats and their own souls. It represented to Murray an abandonment of communal effort in society to institute the perfect state—such as Plato's Republic—and to elevate man as a whole and outwardly, and a withdrawal in despair from this enterprise to the seclusion of the life of contemplation. It was a dereliction from all social brotherhood to the single chance of saving oneself.

But all this is only a further extension of what our thesis presents. It was still a shift of the heft of aim and endeavor from earth to heaven, the heaven in this case of man's own mystical nature. Our delineation took the shift to the heaven of expectation beyond the earthly scene. For Christianity did later transfer the locus of divine realization from earth entirely, teaching its devotees to abandon hope of it here and court it assiduously for the life to come. The failure of nerve was real enough both in Murray's analysis and in ours.

The downfall of Christianity came in the form and features of a surrender of philosophy to religion. It is a parallel phenomenon in the life of a nation, race or an age to a similar manifestation in the life of an individual. Indeed it is the reduplication on a collective scale of a change of attitude that nearly every person goes through in his intellectual growth in a life-time. In youth the mind looks forward to the dreams and possibilities of actual worldly achievement. Plans are made to accomplish many things. Ideal goals are set as attainable. It seems to youth that ideal programs of reform and advance can be carried through to success if only people will unite to effect them. A philosophy points the way and charts the principles of right action. The mind stakes all on such a philosophy and loyalty and sincerity commit the individual to action for it.

But age changes the tune. Hope, confidence wane as time goes on and the exhibitions of the stolidity, the weakness and treachery of humans in the mass weigh down the sanguine spirit. At last courage is shattered by doubt, fear, disappointment; the stout heart quails, the "nerve" fails. The individual surrenders the fight and falls back on God, his private refuge.

We are witnesses of this turn back to religion of one after another notable person, not to mention thousands of lesser ones. It is quite accurately and scientifically described as an aspect of a real "second childhood." Middle manhood makes a valiant effort to achieve success under its own power, on its own resources. The effort being generally thought a failure, and personal strength waning, the individual reverts back into the mental trust in a higher power that was the native instinct of childhood. Then it was unconscious, now it is not only conscious but rationalized. If the child leaves his Father's house on migrating to earth and forgets his paternal home after childhood, he just as naturally turns back to it as he nears the end of his journey abroad. It is the homing instinct, a divine nostalgia.

In the Periclean Age the soul of Greece ventured heroically to achieve the good life by means of its own great genius and insight. It had picked up the true keys from Egypt; it strove with courage and clear vision to chart the course of action that would achieve the good life among humans generally. No historical effort to this end was ever better grounded.

But it was like the high moment of inspiration of the artist, the poet, the diviner of beauty. It could not be sustained at high pitch overlong. The delicate poise and harmony of the elements of body, mind and soul requisite to channel smoothly and powerfully the forces of such an exaltation can not be held indefinitely. New souls enter who change the rhythm and precipitate discords. The glow of genius, the flame of the divine, dies away, to be replaced by a lower and less beautiful expression. The tension is too high to hold long. The soul takes refuge again, for a time, in mediocrity.

So the great age of philosophy, of divine illumination, faded out after Plato. The mid-East world, the Hellenic peoples, saw the light grow dim. The divine child of Christly genius was again to be threatened with being devoured by the Apap reptile of brutish ignorance and dull human inertia. Sut was to win another victory over Horus. Satan was to grin mockingly at the Christos, on earth's mount of temptation.

And what might the dragon of darkness breed in the time of his triumph? What monstrous prodigy of diabolic frenzy might it now generate? What hybrid offspring of the incestuous mating of faith and folly might it not bring forth like the horrid minotaur, fathered by animal passion and mothered by natural instinct?

The decline of erudite philosophy took the divine principle out of the human compound and left man to wallow in his own bootless groping, or to throw himself abjectly on the mercies of an external Deity. Man threw up his hands, abandoned his job of self-evolution, ignored the god within his own being, and ran helplessly like a child back to the heavenly Father. Vision had again failed and the people were destined to perish in an age of darkness. For the monstrous product of the union of faith and ignorance was to come forth in the form of a misshapen creature, whose brutal power over the Western millions for twenty centuries was destined to derationalize the human mind with morbid hallucinations beyond belief.

In a notable passage in *The Natural Genesis* (Vol. II, p. 497) Massey asks how it was that the religion of the ignorant overturned and superseded that of the learned. He attributed it chiefly to the secrecy and exclusive guardianship of the arcane wisdom.

"The religion of mystery was doomed to die of the secrecy in which it had been self-enshrouded. It was buried alive with its own seal on its own mouth. It was an unpublished religion."

This factor played some part, no doubt; it deprived the people of an assumed good and irritated them. Still, secrecy has not killed the Masonic Order, and the Christian ecclesiastical system has maintained its place and influence largely by keeping its Scriptures and its history and its most esoteric polity a secret from its own members. Secrecy is only a facet of a more adequate answer. The fuller analysis reveals that finally the intelligence failed that might have kept arcane knowledge alive in the philosophical schools and academies. There is required almost as much genius to perpetuate a flashing message as to originate it. The Platonic, the Orphic, the Hermetic wisdom is shining in the pages of books in dusty shelves at this moment. Alas, the vision to discern it and evaluate it is wanting even now. *Philosophia,* the love of wisdom, is grievously lacking. The Bible itself, a tome rich in cosmic and anthropological truth, is in unbounded circulation at this day; again alas, it is still a book sealed up by the ignorance of even the theologians who pose as its expounders. The mere existence of great truth in print does not by any means guarantee its assimilation by the world, its circulation in the veins of the body of world consciousness.

Massey's reason is convicted of inadequacy by what he himself says in the next sentence—that

"the new sect put forth the same dogmas, doctrines, tenets under the same types, accompanied by the same rites and ceremonies . . ." and thus "became the first publishers of the ancient religion with a new interpretation of the Christ made flesh. The Gnostics did try to say, with the suppressing hand on their mouths, 'You are only publishing our secrets with a lying gloss put on them'; but this slight protest was unheard amidst the loud clamor of the fanatically ignorant."

He has said that the arcane wisdom of the Gnosis died, or killed itself, from the self-imposed lack of publication and dissemination. Then he tells us that the new sect of Christians came along and published it; and that, he claims, killed it. It is a weird logic that holds that a system died both from publication and non-publication. The thesis proffered here is that its publication *with a false interpretation attached* killed it. What Massey rightly has in mind, no doubt, is that the failure to publish it with the true esoteric interpretation, by which alone its continued beneficent influence could be prolonged, led to its falling into desuetude for want of supporters and propagandists among those qualified; whereas, on the other hand, its publication "with a lying gloss put upon it" by the ignorant literalizers of spiritual representations beyond their comprehension, did kill it, by reducing it to inane nonsense.

This republication or broadcasting to the world for the first time of the literature of the wisdom hitherto held in secrecy was the generating cause of Christianity. This is almost certainly the first time since Massey's books that this item of history has been advanced in any work essaying to print the truth of Christian origins. But it is a declaration that needs an immense and elaborate assemblage of precise and authentic data to substantiate it and vindicate it against the denials that will assail it. Even before the ink of the statement has dried, it must be added, as a necessary qualification, that it was the republication of the arcane or secret wisdom, not by any means in its true form of either presentation or comprehension, but *pitiably caricatured and mutilated by incompetent interpretation*—with a lying gloss put upon it—that generated the sweep of erratic religionism that became Christianity.

We have indeed the sharpest and most instructive contrast here be-

235

fore us between two movements pushing forward at nearly the same time, the one proceeding with a start of about two centuries over the other, but then overlapping it; the first, Christianism, the second, Neo-Platonism. Both published essentially the same doctrinal system. This will be vociferously denied, to be sure; yet it is the truth, and has been seen, hinted at or openly admitted by many religious historians. The reason it has not been clearly evident to all is that the one—Christianism—presented it in grossly garbled and misshapen form, as it had already been corrupted by vulgar unintelligence. As given out by the Christians, its resemblance to its pristine form as Neo-Platonism is almost completely obliterated. In fact its mutilation and disfigurement had already progressed so far that the general historian is hardly to be censured for not knowing that the one was the hybrid child of the other. This work will add accumulated data to prove this contention, namely that Christianity was a reissuance or resurgence of Platonic systematism, but so frightfully mangled by misconception of its interior message and its cryptic language as to be unrecognizable in its lineage.

The two systems really dealt with essentially the same body of ancient wisdom. The one gave out a marvelous elaboration of the loftiest conceptualism possible to the human brain; it could be received in its high truth only by the best-disciplined minds among the people. The other gave out the mere husk or shell of the mighty philosophy and the dynamic ritual that dramatized its impelling truths; and it became, as we shall see, the inciting motivation of the most rabid religious fanaticism. The massive instruction or moral of this datum or episode in history has not been caught at any time. Its sensationally enlightening lesson should be grasped now and never lost again.

But it will still be pointed out and jibed at, how abjectly the publication of Neo-Platonism failed the world, and how triumphantly Christianity swept in to reach the masses whom Neo-Platonism could not help. The jibe and the boast are precisely the two things which this work is designed to reveal in their bald falsity. It is the aim here to show just what the *apparent* failure of Neo-Platonism, and the *apparent* rampant triumph of Christianity actually meant to the later course of history in calamity and woe. The matter is simply one of point of view as to the value or the significance of this failure and this triumph.

It is the wholly unique view here advanced with challenging data as proof, that this "failure" of Neo-Platonism and its resultant outcome in the upsurge of naive Christianism—in spite of much incidental good attributable to the latter in its history—constituted the direst catastrophe in the historical period. It can be readily shown that the same default of high mentality that led to the desuetude of Neo-Platonism, or its failure to lead the succeeding ages in culture, was the source-spring of nescience that produced the monstrosity of misguided zealotry known as Christianity. The absolutely intimate, even indissoluble interrelation between the failure of Platonic revival and the outburst of pious but unphilosophical religiosity in the third century, is the prime text of this book, and needs infinite recognition and attention. For it determined the whole texture of succeeding history and has cast its gloomy shadow even down upon the events of today. No one can comprehend the meaning of events in the world today—and religion is the open or hidden (usually hidden) cause of most events—who does not know the truth of what occurred back in those first centuries, when not even the more open republication of the sanctifying truths of the sublimest wisdom known to man availed to stop the swift rush of human thought from noblest balance and vision down into the veriest idiocy, turning its cryptic myths and dramas and a symbolic language into the fantastic parade of alleged history. This is the unspeakable tragedy we would depict.

Even when later the arrant absurdities of literal interpretation drove the defenders to Hellenic philosophy for saner elucidations of its Scriptures and creeds, it remains that the touch of popular religionism on the body of the esoteric arcana transformed it into a terrible caricature and travesty of its real self.

The anomaly of all history is that Christian writers have harped interminably upon the fortunate escape of Christianity from the threat of being dominated by this same Hellenic esoteric philosophy, and so losing its power to sweep the masses into hysteria and dementia. Likewise they have with equal unanimity pictured the dire fate of Western civilization if the Greek wisdom systems—later made the basis of Christian doctrinism itself, and now prized by high-bred academic thinkers as the summa itself of human sagacity, and even exalted by such churchmen as Dean Inge—had come to dominate the thought-life of Europe, instead of the faith-cult of a deadly regimen of ecclesiastical power. Nobody can say what history would have been under changed influences. One can only surmise with some flourish of logic. But at that it would be hard to find a system, still determining the psychological destinies of millions, so tied in the knots and tangles of contradictory claims, logical inconsistencies and impossible historical averments as is this one called Christianity.

What external causes in Greek history combined to diminish interest in the lofty sallies of the Hellenic mind must be left to the investigator of such things. It will always be a question whether the causes of decay inhered in the wisdom systems themselves, in the impact of outer events, or in the deterioration of human quality after Plato. The great tide that lifted the Greek intellect to a mountain peak of lucid vision swept on by, and left the world to sink back in a sorry state of deflation and jejune philosophical interest. The Dark Ages had begun in the twilight following the bright day of Plato's reign. But it was five hundred years before the dusk darkened into the night that gave birth to the dementia that then fastened itself like an obsessing mania upon the West for another direful two thousand years.

If this pronouncement seems too strong, it is enough in the main to justify it with the simple irrefutable historical fact that the ecclesiastical power that this darkened outlook generated absolutely clamped a chain upon the free use of the rational mind of the Western world for at least a millennium and a half. This is a statement of historical fact freely made by many a professor in great universities in Europe and America today. An additional proof of its correctness is the single fact that in the brief period since the Occidental mind has liberated itself from that strangling tyranny, it has made advances in science and general knowledge incomparably vast in comparison with all the gain made during the sixteen hundred years of the ecclesiastical despotism. Indeed that despotism had completely stagnated the course of European thinking. The free mind was stifled by the enforced rule of uncritical belief in imposed dogma. For that monstrous tyranny stood with club in hand ready to beat down every reappearance of independent thought action or any publication of solid scientific fact that would give the lie to its rigid dogmas based weirdly upon a literal interpretation of the Scripture.

The investigation requires us to look now at a world carried far down, by the time of the first century A.D., in the deep trough of the receding wave of Platonic uplift. There we must seek to locate the immediate productive causes of the Christian faith. It demands careful scrutiny, and much of the data has been obliterated.

When the great light of esoteric understanding had been almost completely extinguished the Hellenic world lay in a state of defenselessness, easily to be seduced by any religious appeal that might be made to it. A keen rationalistic philosophy is the only, or the final, guardian power able to save people from falling a prey to irrational religious inculcations, and this steadying gyroscope was now in nearly total abeyance. The whole population lay fatally vulnerable to the influence of whatever cult fever might seize them at any moment.

This situation, however, is by no means unique in world history. A replica of it is extant at this present epoch. The complexion of things in this field of human interest differs little from one age to another. In any age there is found a vast and weird diversity of all sorts of religious cults, each expressing some phase of doctrinal or mystical or ceremonial infatuation. This is as true of New York, Los Angeles and London today as it was in Alexandria, Antioch, Ephesus of the first century A.D. Christianity itself started out not as a movement of a single group, but as a ferment among a large number of different cults. There was a wide variety of divisions among them, including several diversifications of the Gnostics, who are accredited to the Christian movement, even if heretically classified. Plotinus in his *Enneads* expends his scathing reprobation upon cults or cultists of a number of semi-philosophical, semi-mystical groups that remind one of such organizations of today as Christian Science, New Thought, Unity, Divine Science, Spiritual Science and the like. Each had doubtless caught some prominent aspect of philosophy and emphasized it to the exclusion of other necessary elements. This tendency to magnify one facet of truth into a whole philosophy led to that limitation of view which breeds bigotry and intolerance. Here has always lain the danger of religious ideologies and convictions. A half-vision of truth entails almost certain bias, disproportion, error and wreckage. In the systems of the great seers like Plato and Aristotle the principle of disproportion was indeed the fatal factor, the wrecker of all true happiness and justice. Socrates came to define the good life as that in which all the elements of consciousness, indeed all things, were held related to each other in a certain exact measure and proportion. The golden mean between the two extremes was the path of wisdom leading to virtue and to happiness. Every doctrine must be balanced in that poise between under- and over-emphasis that alone guarantees its rightness. Perhaps this is what—at last—the crucifixion of the Christ between two thieves can mean in its profoundly abstract sense. The force pulling on each side of any true view or position always steals something away from the truth. It robs the truth of its just measure and balance. This may mean little to the unreflective mind, but it is something that every deep-thinking philosopher comes to realize, as Socrates did, namely that the truth always stands balanced on that narrow ridge between too much and too little. As courage is the golden mean between recklessness, as excess, and cowardice, as deficiency, so true religion is the golden mean or exact balance between fanatical devotion, as excess, and spiritual deadness, as deficiency. Virtue is devotion to good determined by intelligence and restrained from both extremes by the exercise of the utmost delicacy of understanding. All decisions fall at the mid-point between pro and con. People are unconscious of the operation of this principle in daily life, yet it is the nub of all decision, all action as between right and wrong, prudent or reckless.

The shrewd student comes at last to evaluate all historical movements in the light of this basic law. Nearly all historical events can be appraised as the result of the reaction of masses or individuals from excess in one direction to excess in its opposite. History is mostly a record of the swing of the pendulum first too far toward excessive zeal, then too far over to its curbing. Life, so to say, gathers too much steam, then reduces it too sharply. The philosopher is he who strives to hold the balance even between the two pulls. This is why Plato dramatizes the chariot of life, driven by the noetic principle of higher intelligence, as being drawn by two horses. To keep the two at exactly even pace was the condition of "happy motoring," failure to do so the menace of wreckage or the penalty of no advance. Weak people, undeveloped souls, do little but swing helplessly back and forth from violent action to equally violent reaction. The philosopher essays to disregard the strong pulls in either direction and to hold the balance between them. He calls upon reason, or his diviner faculty, to stem and curb the rabid throes of his emotional nature. This epitomizes the moral side of the great Greek philosophy, which, asserting that in man there are the two natures, the animal-human and the divine-human, exhorted the wise man to exalt the divine to rulership over the human, so as to hold all elements in balance.

Transferred to the area of religion this high philosophy would dictate the control of emotionalism by divine reason. Lacking its presence and operation, religious movements have been just the procession of one emotinal flare after another. The virulence of the infatuation or hypnotization runs in exact proportion to the deficiency of philosophical knowledge. The less philosophical a movement is, the more religious it is.

The world after Plato's day was filled with a mélange of religions that closely parallel those endless divisions of cults and sects found today. One springs from another in reaction or sharper differentiation. Each had sprung from the independent leadership of some one vigorous thinker. People become the sheep that follow some likely shepherd. But the leader—where did he pick up a system that would attract a following?

Answer to this leads into the field of our proper searching. The truth is that each formulator of a system had made some contact, deep or shallow, with antecedent preachment. He had found brilliant light shining in some ancient document, and saw that it would revitalize current low thinking. The real sources, then, trace back and back. Always research brings one face to face with the existence of a primeval revelation or initial wisdom. Tradition postulates its having been vouchsafed in remote times from demi-gods to men. The Scriptures speak of it as having been an original dictation of God to "holy men of old." This comports perfectly with the occult tradition, if it is envisaged properly; meaning that "holy men of old" could embrace such exalted figures as Pythagoras and Plato, Hermes, Orpheus, Zoroaster, Krishna and the Buddha. The question whether the dictating God was deity in some anthropomorphic shape or just the evolved divinity within the minds of such men, is not too important. The presupposition that "holy men of old" were humans evolved to near-divine status far better satisfied the human zeal for concrete understanding and provides a way viable to reason. Any other elaboration falls beyond human conception as to modus and agency.

It is predicable then that all the various schools stemmed by one line of successive propagation or another from a revered system of high truth delated to early humanity. This, it can surely be assumed, is that "true religion which already existed" from farthest antiquity, that Augustine averred came to be called Christianity in his day. These clarifications are vital elements in the long-lost story of the true origin of Christianity. It exemplifies how a unity of organic thought in the minds of demi-gods can and will be broken up into an endless diversity of segmentation as it passes through multiple minds of less and less keen vision. The gods see truth whole; limited human mentality sees it only in parts. Religions are thus the facets of one primeval religion, some so badly distorted out of relation to the structural entirety as to be hardly phases of truth at all. It takes profound and luminous focus of intellectual sight to integrate all rays into the full original brilliance. The merging of all colors back into the white light demands the most

241

rapid movement of thought sustained at high frequencies. The average human never possesses this heightened power. His religion, therefore, will always represent a partial view. He does not see life truly because he does not see it whole. It is the work of philosophers to see things not separately, but as elements related harmoniously in a transcendent unity of structure, as Kant so firmly insisted.

What, then, was Christianity at its start? True history can now be written. It was a conglomerate loose grouping of a number of various cults out of the total number of such in existence in the first century. The chief binding or unifying force subsisting between them was their tendency to emphasize a popularization of the varied tenets in the interests of mass edification as distinct from Mystery cult exclusiveness. It was a movement inspired largely by resentment and revolt against the "intellectual aristocracy," as before noted. It was a trend, in itself laudable when rightly envisaged, to extend more widely the participation of the common people in the deeper spiritual wisdom held in custody by the intelligentsia who handled the Mysteries.

It can be granted without too much dispute that by this time the Mysteries had fallen to a low state of knowledge, refinement and purity. Naturally the receding wave of the grand Platonic uplift had brought deterioration into the personnel and intelligence of the Mysteries. They were bound to suffer some of the impact of the general depravity setting in upon the Hellenic world. Degradation may have crept in to reduce to revolting status some of the mystic rites of symbolic and dramatic character. Phallic symbolism and ritualism dramatizing creative process, such as formed part of Buddhistic ceremonialism in the Orient, can all too easily lose its elevating influence and slip into actual sensuality. Positive evidence on this score is none too conclusive, though the Christians leveled charges of the sort against the Mysteries. At any rate a popular revulsion set in against them and popular leaders denounced them. Then a movement began to take form to drag the arcana of the Mysteries out to common knowledge and to make the emblems and rites "understandable" to the people. Here is where catastrophe was invited. The terms on which alone Mystery doctrine and ritual could be made "comprehensible" to simple minds, or the forms in which it would become understood, would be fabricated through the process of a conversion of all its allegory and drama into ostensible objective fact and the taking of Scriptural literature as history. This in the course of time was done, and no one has seen it, studied it and traced its processes and its calamitous effects more clearly than Gerald Massey. Nothing less than epochal in importance are these words of his which describe this tragic miscarriage of human intelligence. He is expatiating upon the consternation which struck the early Christians when the evidences began to come to view that the religion they had believed was a wholly new revelation from God was already in the books and practices of the ancient Pagans. The excerpt is taken from a brochure of his entitled *The Logia of the Lord, or Pre-historic Sayings Ascribed to Jesus the Christ* (p. 4):

"Never were mortals more perplexed, bewildered and taken back than the Christians of the second, third and fourth centuries, who had started from their own new beginning, warranted to be solely historical, when they found that an apparition of their faith was following them one way and confronting them in another—a faith not founded on their alleged facts claiming to be the original religion and ages on ages earlier in the world— a shadow that threatened to steal away their substance, mocking them with its aerial unreality—a hollow ghost of that body of truth which they had embraced as a solid and eternal possession! It was horrible! It was devilish! It was the devil, they said, and so they sought to account for Gnosticism and fight down their fears of the phantom terrifying them in front and rear; the Gnostic ante-Christ, who had now become their Anti-Christ. The only primitive Christians then apart from or preceding the Christianized pagan Church of Rome, were the various sects of Gnostics, not one of which was founded on an historical Christ. One and all were based on the *mythical* Christ of the Gnosis, and the mythical Messiah— Him who shall come because he was the Ever-Coming One, as a type of the Eternal manifesting figuratively in time. Historic Christianity can furnish no sufficient reason why the biography of this personal founder should have been held back; why the facts of its origin should have been kept dark; and why there should have been no authorized record made known earlier. *The conversion of the myths* and of the Docetic doctrines of the Gnosis *into human history* alone will account for the fact. The truth is, the earliest Gospels are the farthest removed from the supposed human history. That came last and only when *the spiritual Christ of the Gnosis had been rendered concrete in the density of Christian ignorance!* Christianity began as Gnosticism, continued by means of a conversion and perversion, that were opposed in vain by Paul. The mysteries of the Gnostics were continued, *with a difference,* as Christian. . . . The first Christians built on secret doctrines that were only explained to initiates during a long course of years. These mysteries were never to be divulged or promulgated [and were not] until the belief in historic Christianity had taken permanent root. We are told how it was held by some that the Apocrypha might only be read by those who were perfected, and that these writings were reserved exclusively for the Christian adepts. It must be obvious that the doctrine or knowledge that was forced to be kept so sacredly secret as that, could have had no relation to the human history, personality or teachings of an inspired founder of that primitive Christianity supposed to have had so simple an origin. . . .

"Now there is plenty of evidence to show that these sayings which are the admitted foundations of the canonical Gospels, were not first uttered by a personal Founder of Christianity, nor invented afterwards by any of his followers. Many of them were pre-extant, pre-historical and pre-Christian."

(It is going to be difficult to overthrow the logic and implications of this forthright passage when we recall Eusebius' admission that the Gospels were old books of the Essenes.)

Need there be excuse for citing this long passage? It came in because it testifies on factual ground to the conversion of sublime mystical figurism into impossible history. But it presents such a lucid pictograph of the situation and development that is to be re-pictured here, that it should be welcomed by those who believe that truth is worth having. This life-long student of the Christian Scriptures in relation to their unquestioned Egyptian sources pours out the incontestably established convictions of his knowledge to emancipate a world from baseless hallucinations. It is small wonder that his prodigious works have been permitted to go out of print, and that every copy that finds its way to old bookshops is bought up as soon as discovered, some by eager sincere students, others by persons who will see to it that it never reaches the public again.

It is well to hear, then, his summary analysis of what this conversion produced for human society (*Luniolatry*, p. 2):

"There is nothing insane, nothing irrational in it, when considered in the light of evolution, and when its mode of expression by sign language is thoroughly understood. *The insanity lies in mistaking it for human history or Divine Revelation.* Mythology is the depository of man's most ancient science, and what concerns us chiefly is this—when truly interpreted once more, it is destined to be the death of those false theologies to which it has unwittingly given birth."

Massey himself carried that process of reinterpretation, which simply required the reconversion of alleged history back to allegory and then the elucidation of its mystical connotation, far on toward its completion; and others are now consummating his noble effort. It is the most important work being done in religion today.

The primitive Christians, of the group that fathered so-called Apostolic and evangelical Christianity and declared all other groups heretics, thought in their ignorance that they were putting forth a new religion of transcendent light. Massey well pictures their unbounded dismay when they found the evidences pouring forth that they were only revamping old Egyptian religion. Their consternation at this discovery was the incentive that drove them on to destroy all the books of ancient arcane science that would betray the tell-tale similarity and the true source. They could not well scorn and scoff at Paganism when they found they had its own substance and paraphernalia in their hands. They could not condemn it when it was that which they themselves were exalting.

What actually happened, the thing that to Massey himself as to all others had seemed incredible and impossible when first suggested for consideration, but which his evidences left him no alternative but to accept—the complete metamorphosis of figurative depiction of esoteric truth into alleged history—is well described by Higgins (*Anacalypsis*, p. 33):

"These doctrines have been, like all the other doctrines of antiquity, gradually corrupted—incarnated—if I may be permitted to compose a word for the occasion.

"Sublime philosophical truths or attributes have become clothed with bodies and converted into living characters. Perhaps this might take its origin from a wish in those professing them *to conceal them from the vulgar eye;* but the cause being forgotten, *all ranks of society at last came to understand them in the literal sense,* their real character being lost; or perhaps this incarnation might arise from a gradual pulling away of mankind from a high state of civilization, at which it must have arrived when those doctrines were discovered, into a state of *ignorance,*—the produce of revolutions, or perhaps merely of the great law of change which in all nature seems to be eternally in operation."

How completely this expresses the form and content of the analysis here presented!

And can one refrain from printing Higgins' frank and fateful conclusions from this phenomenon (*Anac.,* p. 50)?

"That the rabble were the victims of a degrading superstition I have no doubt. This was prdouced by the knavery of the ancient priests, and it is in order to reproduce this effect that the modern priests have misinterpreted the doctrines of their predecessors. By vilifying and running down the religion of the ancients they have thought they could persuade their votaries that their new religion was *necessary* for the good of mankind; a religion which in consequence of their corruptions has been found to be in practice much worse and more injurious to the interests of society than the older one."

Few even of those who have been forced by their studies to this devastating and disheartening conviction, have had the openness to state it and front the storm of vilification that it would evoke. Yet it has been the conclusion, the unmistakable discernment of nearly every scholar who has covered the ground of the proper investigation of the ancient field. Massey and Higgins, like Renan, Strauss, Robertson, Smith, Drews, Dupuis, Brandes, Mead and others have been charged with narrow prejudice. If the body of convictions to which one is forced by the overwhelming and harrowing record of violence, fanaticism, bigotry, slaughter, imposture and forgery is to be termed prejudice, then prejudice must for once be held both warranted and eminently desirable. None of the alleged traducers and critics of Christianity, any more than the present writer, began the study of Christian history with any other feeling than that of good will, if not even of high approval, of the Christian religion. If the study has generated a prejudice, it is because a shocking history has had to be weighed justly in the student's scale of judgments.

We have cited Allan Upward's forthright assertion that the Christian religion is the only one that has been completely founded on falsity. If intelligent men of sterling character have come to hold prejudices against Christianity, it is because they would confess to a "prejudice" against a record of fiction, fancy, fatuity, insincerity and knavery unmatched in human annals. "Prejudice" of this stamp might be essential to the salvation of humanity. If open-minded scholars come out of their study of Christianity with a decided bias, or frank hostility, they must have encountered facts in their researches that superinduced such an attitude. These scholars have been "prejudiced" because they have first been horrified, disillusioned and frightened by what they have seen. It may spell calamity now and in the future that there is too little of this "prejudice."

Christianity started out with what uninstructed zealots thought, or were led to think by designing priests, was a wholly new religion of celestial truth passed straight down from heaven itself, but which soon proved to be a conglomerate mass, one might say mess, of pre-existent Pagan material, contorted out of all recognition as esoteric wisdom and presented in the light of "history." It was composed of scraps and crumbs of that one "true religion" proclaimed by Augustine as an already existing Christianity since Adam. But alas, the want of ability on the part of any Christian, since even Origen failed, to perform with these scraps and fragments a reconstitution of the original structure of meaning, such as Cuvier could do in reconstructing the form of a mammoth from a tooth, a jaw or a leg-bone, doomed the new movement that went forth to save mankind with inadequate tools, to condign failure. The net result was to enmire the human reason in a mélange of piety, zeal, weird belief, doubt and expectation of the speedy end of the world that made the immediate and succeeding history of the West a nightmare of tragic ineptitude.

CHAPTER XII

CRUMBS FROM THE TABLE OF THE GODS

In the life of culture the conversion of figurative speech and ritualistic allegorism over into veridical history is the incredible fact of mightiest import for the world in two thousand years. It strikes one as a thing past all belief. It is impossible to credit as a factual occurrence unless one has given years of study to detect its subtle evidences. As Higgins has so well said, it took place in a long and gradual process. Yet the evidences are neither subtle nor vague after all; they are open, glaring, breath-taking. In the end, instead of being difficult to discover, they are ubiquitous; there is nothing else to be seen. There is no other way to explain what happened, what has come to pass. It provides the only formula that enables one to fit together the facts as they stand into consistent rationalization. It must have occurred, since no other eventuality can explain the situation as it exists. To prove it finally it is only necessary to take the ostensible "history" that was precipitated and molded out of the mythologies and dramas, *turn it back to its original mythico-allegorical relevance,* and one has reconstituted the structure of primeval thought out of which all religions and philosophies took their rise. Then turn it all again back to "history" and one is immediately foundered in the mires of events that can only be admitted to the pale of history by being accepted as miracles. They become such unlikely happenings that it is impossible to include them in the common category of real history as man knows it. They get into history only by the doorway of miracle. And that is precisely what the mind could assume as likely to be the case when the extraordinary mechanism and strategies of allegory must be made to fit into the Procrustean bed of believable event. Allegory becomes a fantastic personage when dressed up and paraded in the garb of history. This has been the origin of the supernatural in Scriptural literature, the force of dementia that lifted the Book from a manual of righteousness to a fetish of prodigies before which reason bowed in abrogation of its prerogative.

So the great Scriptures became intriguing records of God's arbitrary decisions and unpredictable performances, and lost their power as dramatizations or poetic structures portraying the realities and the scheme of man's life and the modes of his evolution from animal through human to divine status. They became wonder-books of God's greatness and his whimsical capricious dealings, not with man as a whole, but with an alleged "chosen people" whom he had selected to be the special objects of his favor and his interest. And this interpretation has wrought the unspeakably costly demolition of man's complete confidence in law both natural and moral, as the fixed axis of the universe, and substituted for it his belief that his safety is to be won by cajoling a capricious Deity who transcends—and flouts—his own laws.

All the various cults and systems of religious character bore, it can be assumed, a more or less clear, precise and authentic segment of inheritance from Augustine's primeval "true religion." It can be presumed that the more esoteric ones carried a closer and more complete approach to the original integral representation of it, the exoteric and popular ones a more partial and diffuse copy. Such unquestionably was the case, for it has ever been so. A popularized religion must necessarily be less an integer of meaning than an esoteric one.

The item next in sequence to be noted—and stamped indelibly forever henceforth upon the minds of Christian people—is that Christianity was not in the remotest sense a move of more knowing people away from or in opposition to any form of Pagan religion, but on the contrary was just a slightly new, if new at all, alignment, combination or expression of Pagan culture itself! It was in no sense—even when it had conquered all rival interests—the end of Paganism, as is universally believed. It was composed of nothing that Paganism had not already furnished,—except an infinitely more impossible miscomprehension of Paganism's material, which it appropriated and built up on. It was nothing but more Paganism, but a reformulation of it on principles never hitherto brought forward to rationalize—rather to derationalize—its tenets. It was Paganism refurbished with a "lying gloss." It was Pagan philosophy, misappropriated, misconceived, misapplied. It was a legitimate enough offshoot of Pagan culture, but an offshoot malformed and disfigured. So far from being anti-Pagan, it was entirely Pagan, but not good Paganism. It was Paganism run out into foul corruption and inane nonsense by the disfiguring power of ignorance. It was Paganism purloined from the sancta of the Mysteries and thrown out to the multitude to be mauled and pilloried in the most atrocious despoliation of high truth ever seen.

The item that would have given scholars the adequate basis for a correct answer to the inevitable question as to how the religion could have arisen and spread so quickly had there been no new Messenger, is now to be dealt with. Failure of scholars to grasp this answer has permitted the old assumptions to stand unchallenged and to control all belief. Scholars have failed to discern it because the presence of the "history" obviated the need to trace any other origin of Christianity. The destruction of documents added to the difficulty. Nevertheless the data in evidence are open and plain and—overwhelming.

The millions who have lived and died in the Christian faith have never doubted that the religion had its beginnings as a result of the presence and preachment, the miracles and phenomena, of a great divine man who came in the flesh to give it its initial impetus and fix its supernal character. How, they have asked when faced with a contrary view, could the mighty sweep of Christian piety have gathered conquering force if there had been no figure of outstanding personal power to start it? Surely Christianity had its Founder and also its nuclear inception from a little band of consecrated and transfigured men who had gathered about him and seen the many demonstrations of his divine messengership. Movements do not originate out of the air; they must be implemented and empowered by some leader. Ideas do not propagate themselves; they are advanced by men whom they have inspired to heroic action. Surely the great Christian upsurge could not have taken form and developed power except from the driving force of a dynamic preachment by a dynamic personality.

Viewed superficially and without a knowledge of the detail of actual history appertaining to the event, this is the belief that stands fixed in the general mind of Christendom. That it is a completely false belief, wholly unsupported by the data of history, is the claim of this work. *It did not need the presence or the preachment of any man to generate it.* It took form naturally and spontaneously out of the elements existent at the time and place of its birth. It did not spring from the introduction of anything new from without or above; *it was the inevitable product*—perhaps better to say by-product—*of what was already extant* to precipitate it. It came not as the release of new unction from on high, for it required the presence and operation of but one element in the situation to produce it. The world today may well recoil aghast at the pronouncement of that one word; for it is—ignorance! Given what was on the ground in the form of venerable ancient schools of secret wisdom on the one side, and the untutored populace on the other, the one thing that alone could leaven the masses with a ferment of religious enthusiasm of the form that did come to manifestation was ignorance. With every necessary prerequisite for such a development provided by the features of the situation, it is the simple truth, as Lecky has stated it, that "Christianity floated into the Roman Empire on the wave of credulity that brought with it this long train of Oriental superstitions and legends." But this is but a preliminary hint of what is to come in the way of more specific corroboration. That the Christian faith was launched by "men whose ardor was fierce in proportion to their ignorance," as Massey put it, is as clear as any historical fact can well be.

But one of the most nicely accurate views of what happened in those fateful early years, that fixed the character of history from then to this very moment, is given in words of momentous gravity by G. R. S. Mead in his *Fragments of a Faith Forgotten,* where, speaking of the "rape" of the Mystery schools and their esoteric doctrines by the new upheaval, he writes (p. 113):

"The new method was *to force out into the open* for all men a portion of the sacred Mysteries and secret teachings of the few. The adherents of the new religion itself professed to throw open 'everything'; and many believed that it had revealed all that was revealable. This was because they were as yet children. So bright was the light to them that they perforce believed it came directly from the God of all Gods—or rather from God Above, for they would have no more of gods; the gods were straightway transmuted into devils. The 'many' had begun to play with psychic and spiritual forces let loose from the Mysteries; and the 'many' *went mad for a time and have not yet regained their sanity."*

If the story of Christianity's rise had to be condensed in a dozen lines, this passage would tell the story better than any other that could readily be found. Indeed the last sentence alone carries the gist of it all. It is the direful account. If it is denied to be the true story of the rise of Christianity, it is at any rate a true account of what occurred in immediate connection with that upheaval. And it *is* the record of the popular ferment that brought in Christianity.

If the modern student needs either confirmation of Mead's analysis or an instructive parallel of the same set of circumstances, he has but to look at what he finds before him in his world now. The situation is paralleled unbelievably. Beginning openly—after centuries of hidden existence—some sixty or seventy years ago, there were launched a number of movements, notably modern Theosophy, with a concomitant revival of Rosicrucianism and kindred forms of occult and esoteric systematism, all tracing far descent from the same ancient body of teachings that the rampant early Christians pilfered from the Mysteries of old. And again we are called upon to witness the scramble of the "many" for these pearls of truth, and the exhibition of the various degrees of "madness" by many of these cults is one of the marked features of the modern scene. So Mead's following sentence must be noted (p. 115):

". . . in things religious there is no middle ground among the uninstructed. They fly to the opposite pole. Therefore when the new impulse seizes upon people, we are to have a breaking down of old barriers and a striving after a new order of things, but at the same time a wild intolerance, a *glorification of ignorance,* a wholesale condemnation; a social upheaval, followed by a political triumph. One thing, however, is acquired definitely, a new lease of life for *faith.*"

Here we have before us accurately analyzed the "makings" of such a religio-socio-political upheaval as that on the wings of which Christianity floated in upon the early Roman Empire. (In the case under consideration, it must be noted that while the final political denouement was fondly envisaged as the earthly consummation of the whole program of faith, it signally failed to come to realization, the whole hyper-fervid frenzy collapsing at its very height with the destruction of Jerusalem by Titus in A.D. 70.)

Mead's analysis states our case with great clarity. He notes expressly that fatal "glorification of ignorance" and hatred of philosophical rationalism which we have asserted as prevailing and sweeping the movement on like a torrent into violence and boundless fanaticism. Also he marks in it the same surrender of intellect to faith.

Fuller (*History of Philosophy,* p. 256) adds strength to Mead's point of view:

"The revival of the Orphic-Pythagorean religious cult was incidental to a rising tide of religious interest and fervor that was creeping into the Roman world from the near East as early as the second century B.C., and that four hundred years later had completely engulfed the Empire."

This is a key statement in the wake of the one from Lecky given above. A hundred other authors would fall in line with similar testimony. The facts are indisputable. Christianity came up from the masses almost, it might be said, as the backwash of the great surge of a lofty philosophical movement that about that age of the world had crept in from the ever-mystical East. It can be described as a backwash because it was the repercussion, the secondary impact, following the first impingement of the inrush of Oriental psycho-spiritual philosophies. The first impact of mystical religious preachments falls upon the more intelligent classes, who can supply a fair measure of the acumen necessary to distinguish the higher values of the religious experience. These classes can hold it in a fair degree of balance and sanity. It can among them give rise to the cults of profound philosophical interest, such as those that flourished so markedly in the great cosmopolitan center of Alexandria. But when in the course of a little time the profounder contents filter down to the nether strata of society, they become inevitably the source-spring of such irrational agitation as Mead has described. This is the backwash that sets in following every pronounced religious stirring; and our work is to show conclusively that Christianity was the product of that great popular repercussion from an extraordinary migration of Oriental religions of spiritual and mystical dynamism into the West.

To some extent Christianity was the product of the most profound of esoteric teachings; yet at the same time it is the least esoteric of religions. The true description of it is that it sprang from esoteric sources, but emerged as the most exoteric of all. It was built on and from the material of religious systems that proclaim as their core of truth the existence and saving activity of a divine principle, a veritable Son of God, in the heart of every human; yet it was the system that supplanted the predication and central importance of this divine principle with a historical Jesus. Schools teaching the essential divinity of a portion of man himself existed prolifically when Christianity arose. If not directly out of one or another of them, or from an eclectic or synthetic amalgamation of a number of them, Christianity stemmed forth into existence. Nearly all the early contributors to the cult's more enlightened tenets at first were themselves members of the several Hellenic or Egyptian Mystery Schools. As many writers do actually assert, internal evidence points to the fact that Paul himself had been a member of the Eleusinian, Dionysiac or Bacchic Mystery schools. Augustine had been a Manichaean before embracing the "faith of Christ"; Tertullian joined in with the Montanists, who rather felt that Montanus was the Messiah-Avatar rather than Jesus of Nazareth. Justin Martyr was not averse to parading the identity of Old Testament "prophecy" with the oracles of the Sibyls. Ammonius Saccas is said to have been "converted" to Christianity after launching the great Neo-Platonic release of hidden truth. It was Plotinus who gave Augustine the true significance of the Trinity doctrine. Such instances can be multiplied. Christianity was beginning to take form out of the elements that were extant and in ferment in those early days.

Important as evidence at this point is the statement found in the famous letter of the Emperor Hadrian to Servianus. It puts beyond question the intimate connection of some of the most intelligent early Christians with the Pagan Mysteries. Says Hadrian:

"Those who worship Serapis are likewise Christians; even those who style themselves the Bishops of Christ are devoted to Serapis."

Even this one bit of authentic testimony puts to rout the universal Christian belief that Christianity arose in entire independence of, or in revolt from, antecedent Pagan systems. It stemmed from religious soil enriched with the accumulated deposit of age-old growth.

Indeed when the movement first began it had little or nothing to distinguish it from other sporadic outbursts of religious expression among Pagan groups. It bore few of the characteristics which marked it later as distinctively the Christian religion. Its minor divergences were in no sense anti-Pagan; they were simply divagations from basic principles, just as all schismatic movements in any religion are. But within an all-too-brief period of time there was to come a nearly complete reversal of position, a wholesale turn-about that was to lift the new cult out of the family of Pagan religions altogether and bring it under a classification that has ever since been sharply set over against them. For the bright hall-marks of Pagan religionism were esoteric secrecy, symbolic representation of mystical truth and the spiritual nature of the gods. The new rabid movement was soon to fly completely off the solid ground of every one of these basic fundamenta. From esoteric secrecy it flew over to popular dissemination of the arcana; from symbolic representation it flew to the letter of the myth or the allegory or the symbol; and from the spiritual nature of the gods or the Christos it leaped clear down to a God in the form of a man of flesh! In so doing it quickly ceased to be Pagan and became strictly anti-Pagan, carrying unfortunately the revered name of Christian with its apostasy.

As the more capable minds which early in the movement had grasped and adhered to the esoteric nature of their doctrines passed off the scene and their place was taken by men of cruder intelligence, degeneration rapidly set in. The allegoric-mystic meaning of Scripture, dimly as it may have been caught by the first leaders in their attempt to popularize the cryptic message of the Gospels, was soon reduced to the wholly litero-historical rendering, and the mental havoc was in full cry. The fogs and mists that were to deepen into the dismal murks of the Dark Ages were gathering their gloom.

The first, or more intelligent reaction to the invasion of Eastern spiritual ideas, soon gave place to the second. With the latter, Christianity was metamorphosed from itself into something else,—Christianism.

Much of our thesis is upheld by what Fisher says in his work already cited (p. 374):

"The Church, including the Apostles themselves, was to be enlightened gradually as to the real import of the Master's teaching by the influence of the Spirit, and by the gradual course of Divine Providence. Especially is this true of His prophetic utterances, which offered glimpses of particular ends and under symbolic forms of the future of his kingdom, the full meaning of which time alone could unveil."

If this says anything important it is that the simple-minded second-century agitators of a popular ebullition of religious feeling, handling esoteric material they had not the acumen to understand any more than a fifth-grader comprehends the propositions of Einstein or the quantum theory, were at the beginning wholly ignorant of the inner significance of the treasures they were bandying about, and would have to wait the slow education of time and its lessons to write out for their crass faculties the hidden purport of their own documents of creed and dogma, rite and symbol. That even two millennia of developing history since then have not brought the expected enlightenment to the deluded followers of the simple fishermen of Galilee prints large, very large, the doleful ineptitude of the early expectations and of such apologetic reasoning as Fisher's.

Could anything, now, be more corroborative of the exegetical position here defended, as well as more devastating to the opposing orthodox views, than this surprisingly frank and revealing statement from Fisher (op. cit., p. 458):

"The full blaze of truth would not have enlightened, but have dazzled and misled, those who were not prepared, by previous training, to recognize it. . . . The minds of men, even of the Apostles, must by degrees be educated up to the apprehension of truth, which clashed in many of its features with their traditional ideas."

Chrysostom declared that these simple fishermen "outshone all the world"; but Fisher thinks they were far behind, and had to be gradually educated up to, what intelligent men then already knew. It is well to note these disagreements, discrepancies and inconsistencies.

It is not acrimony, but simple truth, worthy, however, of notice, to say that had our pen put down in our own words the gist of this paragraph of Fisher's, it would have been received with ill grace, sullen resentment and positive denial. But a Christian partisan proponent has written these lines. At that it paints the same picture that we have just exhibited from Mead's brush. Light had come into the hands of people who were no more than children in intellect and, as it first dazzled and blinded them with its effulgence, so it later afflicted them with madness and frenzy, as its uncomprehended mysteries and unbalanced philosophies drove them into wild excesses of passionate zeal.

At first, no doubt, a few of the more enlightened, in all likelihood out of the more charitable motive of guiding the ignorant proselytes gradually into a deeper glimpse of the inner esoteric purport of it all, kept in with the movement. But for this intelligent minority fringe it would have quickly gone the way of a thousand minor emotional surges and revivals among the "many" in all history. Through these learned esotericists, however, as Guignebert says, it made a link with Hellenic philosophy, that same philosophy that men like Tertullian were to revile and berate as having nothing to do with the faith of the man Jesus—as ironically enough it most certainly did not, except by errant misconception and confusion of the two by stupid presumption of knowledge; that same philosophy that in spite of its scorn by the dumb leaders was to come to the salvation of the rabid faith that sneered at it, and thus provide its only link of appeal to the interests or intelligence of thinking men ever since. There is potency enough in the statement that without the introduction by the Gnostics and others like Ammonius Saccas, Plotinus, Clement, Origen and even in part by Augstine, of the rational elements of the great Hellenic philosophies, as Christian writers themselves assert, the new religion could not have kept its hold on the world's attention for more than a generation or two.

Guignebert traces with what can be considered general accuracy the gradual development and progressive amalgamation of the currents running in the whirling maelstrom of early Christian agitation. He says (op. cit., p. 118):

"Naturally, however, open as the Christianity of the post-apostolic age would be to influences of such a nature through the fluidness of its dogmatics, and flexible as it would have been rendered by the Pauline and Johannine speculative thought, it had not foreseen these developments nor did it possess any means of sifting and more sharply defining them. For this reason their first efforts to work them over were marked as much by disorder as by intenseness. Some time necessarily elapsed before the main body of the membership, always tardy in arriving at a clear consciousness of the real situation, sensed the fact that they were driving the faith in two very different directions. . . . The one movement tended to borrow from Hellenistic culture all of its ideas that were capable of rendering the early Christian doctrine at once more profound and more beautiful. [Let it be noted that Christianity had to borrow from Greek philosophy to become both more profound and more beautiful!] It is evident that this process of assimilation cared little about scrupulous exactitude, and neither did it always find itself in complete accord with logic or reality. The same was true of its documents. . . . It only sought to establish a working agreement between the elements of its fundamental postulates and the most important principles of Greek thought."

It will not be time ill spent to pause for a brief examination of what lies before us in this exhibit. The world has been asked to believe that the Christian movement was the dissemination of a body of divine revelation first and uniquely proclaimed at a given time almost from the skies by a divine Avatar or Messiah-Christ, persisting intact amid other and opposing religions, and finally winning the world. Is there anything remotely suggestive of all this in the historian's true picture? Instead, we find this divinely promulgated faith "borrowing," "assimilating" and with almost reckless disregard of "scrupulous exactitude" and out of all accord with "logic and reality" accommodating itself to Hellenic philosophy. Indeed it had to go a-begging to this Hellenic learning even to come upon the deeper import of its own "postulates," and only by the aid of Platonic wisdom did it come to find its own material of dogma and doctrine, both more profound and more beautiful than its own offering. Here is the disclosure of error in a tradition that ought to shake a world of religious fetishism and blind belief out of its delusions. That a host of passages of such similarly epochal revelations of mangled truth have been written and read, and nothing done to align general understanding with the facts as they stand, is harrowing evidence of the hopelessness of trying to shake religious hypnotizations out of their lethal obsession of the common mind.

Guignebert has conjectured that Paul changed the apostles' ideas of the Christ by telling them that he had been a celestial hierarch and was on earth as an incarnation of the Spirit, the Pneuma of God. One has to ask where simple fishermen would have learned about the Pneuma of God. Such a datum goes far to prove that these simple "fishermen," loudly boasted of as children in mental culture, either were not historical men at all, or that they were somehow in the intellectual grade and attainment of university wranglers, familiar with abstruse and recondite philosophical technical terms, the Holy Ghost having worked a miracle by inspiring untutored men with divine knowledge.

And how does Guignebert know that Paul told the twelve fishermen anything? The historical existence of both the Galilean Jesus and the twelve disciples is questioned on the most solid of grounds,—lack of actual evidence and the implications of a host of "internal" evidences contradicting it. No Christian historian examined in much reading has claimed that Paul ever contacted or apparently ever heard of the man of Galilee, and therefore it is unlikely that he ever told the disciples—if they did exist—anything in person.

Then Guignebert characterizes the second wing of the Christian movement, the first having been described above:

"The other movement, known to Christianity from the second century and possibly even earlier, sets out from a different starting point. It, too, seeks to inflate the too simple confession of faith of the early days and to excavate deeper foundations for it. It can accomplish this purpose only by combining it with beliefs and theories *borrowed from its surroundings*. But in the first place it shows no discrimination in its choice, which settles upon numerous features widely different in nature: The Olympian paganism, Orphism, diverse Oriental religions, systems of philosophy—*everything is gathered into its net*. In the second place it takes no interest in reconciling what it borrows with the historical data or even with the traditions of the faith. Instead, it pretends to possess a special revelation of its own, which it uses to justify most anomalous combinations of ideas that constitute real syncretistic systems, in which true Christianity appears as only one more element. It becomes almost unrecognizable as part of a complicated cosmogony and an abstruse system of metaphysics, neither of which owes anything of value to it."

If this is a true historical record—and nobody has found warrant to dispute it—there is here again a disclosure of unrecognized truth that confutes all common belief about the early history of Christianity. Finding its first professions of simple faith too bodiless, too ephemeral, too subject to the flows and ebbs of pietistic fervor, too much an emotional surge with little of doctrinal rock to which to anchor its barque, Christianity sought to find firmer mooring by appropriating and tying in with itself the more stable structure of the great Hellenic philosophy. But such was the want of discerning intellectual power in its ranks that it grasped almost anything within reach amongst the religions it brushed against in its environment; it levied toll at once on Greek, Chaldean, Hebrew and Syrio-Egyptian ideologies and, says the narrator, appropriated their elements without discrimination. Nor does it attempt, he adds, to reconcile them after borrowing them. Could anything testify louder than these facts to the utter absence of any power either of apocalyptic divine revelation of supernal truth from heaven above, or even of human acumen in the way of an effective systematization of existent fragments, in the movement of Christianity? What a scenario it all projects on the screen! Groups lifted to near frenzy by religious afflations, feeling that their height of zeal for the kingdom of God gave them the right to claim any and all expressions in the religious domain as inclusive under the all-dominating tidal sweep of their wild ebullience!

All this makes it a proven case that Christianity was by no means a particular specific system of principles and teachings—never for centuries a system of anything at all in the realm of organic thought structures—but instead was only a mass fervor, spurring its intoxicated partisans on to excesses of emotion and aberrancies of every sort and degree. The unbounded faith in Christ and abject surrender to him carried them easily over the widest abysses of logical inconsistency and even enabled them to spurn the truth of fact. They reached out to claim and appropriate everything in sight, until the little core of their own nest-egg contribution—the Christ made flesh in one man—becomes but one element in the large accumulation of their borrowings. Christianity is thus seen to be nothing but a hodge-podge assortment of scraps from prevalent religions around it. Historical testimony strengthens at every point the thesis that Christianity was a direct product of the soil of already existent religious systems and in no sense a new implantation from the heavens.

It is alluring to go on with Guignebert as he limns the picture of the early development still more in detail:

"To put it differently and perhaps preferably, the inflations borrowed from Hellenistic culture they had selected and fitted into the system were treated as properties of these postulates even in that wonderful School of

Alexandria of which Origen was the pride, which completed the master-piece: the metamorphosis of Christianity into a revealed and perfect phi-losophy."

What again glares at us from out this statement? This Christianity which allegedly came full-blown in its cosmic perfection from God through his Son—this Minerva-wisdom from the cleft brow of Jove, this finished system, first-born light amid heathen darkness—in reality was so anemic that it had to be kept alive only by forcible transfu-sions of virile blood of truth from surrounding Pagan philosophies! Whatever may have given it its initial impulse, it ended shortly by being jumbled in a mélange of already existent systems perfected by the genius of the Greeks. It is therefore categorically concluded that Christianity was, as here contended, simply the conglomerated reori-entation of some prominent elements of ancient religious cult teach-ings, given a most unfortunate and ruinous distortion of meaning and reference by ignorant miscomprehension. *That is the essence and gist of all Christian history of origins, and any one who attempts to rep-resent it in terms inconsonant with this analysis is laboring amid phantoms.*

For still further enlightening detail another step with Guignebert is profitable (121):

"The ritual development of Christianity advances step by step with the dogmatic, and by the same process. It began with very simple practices, *all taken from Judaism:* baptism, the breaking of bread, the imposition of hands, prayer and fasting. Then a meaning more and more profound was assigned to them. They were amplified and *gestures familiar to the Pagans* added; they were loaded with the larger interests, for example, embraced in the rites of the Greek and Oriental Mysteries, and thus charged, as it were, with the ancient formidable power of magic. This work was insti-tuted as soon as the Apostolic faith was transported from Palestine to Greek soil."

While this excerpt is pretty definitely corroborative of our position, it still is necessary to register dissent from one of the historian's asser-tions in the passage. He falls into the inveterate habit of Christian the-orists in thinking that the more penetrating insight of the Christians took over practices and forms used by the Pagans in total incompre-hension of their inner significance and imbued them with truer and deeper meaning not known before. This assumption has been advanced times without number and rests on no evidence anywhere discover-able. It is simply the product of Christian determination to leave no laurels resting on the brow of Paganism. The truth is as nearly the exact contrary as could well be. The truth, out at long last, is that the Pagans had possessed—and admittedly at one time and place or another already lost—the true esoteric import of all the rites, symbols and rituals of the arcana of the Mysteries. They administered them with splendid understanding until such time as that subtle and elusive mystic essence of apprehension had effervesced and vanished. If not known to every ancient hierophant or mystagogue or psychopomp or his candidates in instruction, this inner core of meaning was presented and preserved in Plato and Pythagoras, and the abstruse philosophies of Orpheus and Hermes Trismegistus. Whatever high cryptic meaning inhered in the insignia lay in the hands of the Pagans, and never came to the surface again with the Christians. It was finally in Christian hands that every last vestige of true interior sense at spiritual or mystical levels was utterly swept aside and indeed violently negated and cast away. It is time this purely conjectural presupposition that Christianity took the empty shells of Pagan belief and clothed them—as Daniel Webster said that Justice John Marshall did with the skeletal form of the American constitution—with the flesh and blood of real meaning and power, should be tagged for the brash and unfounded falsehood that it is. Christianity it was that despoiled every doctrinal symbol, the crucifixion, the temptation, the baptism, the transfiguration, the eucharist, the "miracles" and every parable of its golden meaning in Paganism. *And it is therefore back to Paganism that we have to go to recover every treasure of light that Christianity bartered away in its purchase of the favor of the masses.*

And can the next paragraph from this candid writer be passed by (p. 121)?

"It is sometimes very difficult to tell exactly from which pagan rite a particular Christian rite is derived, but it remains certain that the spirit of pagan ritualism became by degrees impressed upon Christianity, to such an extent that at last *the whole of it* was distributed through its ceremonies. . . . Moreover, the power of the clergy was singularly enhanced by the almost exclusive right which they very early acquired, despite some faltering objections of ordering and dispensing the magic power inherent in the rites known as sacraments."

Again there is ground for astonishment for what is here revealed bearing on the refutation of age-old Christian claims. In every Christian history the pure power of the Christ in the heart of the believer has been set over against the claims of Pagan spiritual magic, the one divine in its purity, the other infernally diabolical. Yet here is the intelligent chronicler of that history asserting that the Christian priesthood actually built up its claims to be the wielders of divine unction or magic by taking over the rites of Pagan origin. It is here given to us by a Christian narrator that magic inhered in the Pagan rituals before the Christian priesthood claimed that all spiritual power flowed from the fountain-head in Christ, a historical person. Obviously it has been the interest of priestcraft ever since to hide these historical anomalies.

Again comes the statement, already corrected, that (p. 123):

"This order of clergy presides over the rites which more or less directly borrowed from Judaism or the pagan Mysteries, though entirely re-adapted to Christian uses and reinvested—the chief of them at any rate—with the magic mysterious power which the secret cults of Greece and the Orient had rendered familiar to the men of those days. Nevertheless Christianity became a real religion, the most complete of them all, because it has taken the best they possess from all of them."

Here again is the record of borrowing from outside and readapting to Christian uses. And again must protest be made against the subtle insinuation that Christian re-adaptation baptized the borrowed practices with a new spirit of light and power. If, however, by re-adaptation Guignebert means that, in total ignorance of the true inner import of the magical rites the Christians contorted them over to fit their own new and literal readings of the Scriptural allegories, dragged them from their lofty mystical reference down to suit the predication of the carnalized Jesus and his ostensible biography in the Gospels,—yes, sadly enough it is true that they effected such a drastic re-adaptation. It was precisely that re-adaptation that ruined true Christianity; it was that reorientation of all truly Christian meanings which constituted the betrayal of Pagan religion to ignorance and misuse. But it is categorically denied that this transferal of meaning from the world of spiritual consciousness to a supposed living personality implemented the first infusion of true meaning into these things. What is affirmed is that the readjustment of their substance to a new view utterly subverted all true sense which they formerly bore for knowing Pagans.

As to Guignebert's vigorous final assertion that Christianity became the best and most perfect of all religions because it appropriated the best of all of them, and presumably synthesized them all into a perfect organic whole, this must be viewed as another of those wholly gratuitous predications that flow so unctuously from the pens of Christian apologists. It is so obviously not true, because history records that it was at

Alexandria that the highest and most enlightened project of syncretism of religious systems was effected, never in Palestine.

But Guignebert says (p. 123) that this religion of Christianity, so syncretistically constructed, declares itself invulnerably exclusive; it stands rigidly aloof from any other religion, even though this stiffness subjected it to the severest of perils, particularly because it challenged the animosity of the State as well as that of the civil community. Should one ask why, the conventional answer would doubtless be forth-coming that Christianity held something that no other religion had,— the precious all-sanctifying grace of God manifested uniquely to the world in the person of his only-begotten Son, sent to earth to pay the ransom for sinning man. Their possession of this item of transcendent blessedness warranted their collecting the best truth out of all the sur-rounding faiths, but *closed the doors to fellowship with any of them.* Indeed this singular outcome proves the narrowness and not the broad-ness which should flow from true syncretism. It negatives the thesis of sound syncretistic principles. It might be supposed that the blessed possession of more knowledge and assurance of God's grace would generate in its fortunate beneficiaries a far wider graciousness of fel-lowship in the spirit of sharing its benignant treasure—which never loses by being lavished abroad—than the empty-handed heathen could have exhibited from their poorer store. From those who are the more lavishly endowed and blessed more is to be expected. Yet what do we see? Fuller tells us in his *History of Philosophy* what we see, and the story runs counter to what we would have a right to expect from the divinely commissioned Christian movement. He writes (p. 328):

"The new growth, however, differed in one vital respect from the old. The service of the ancient gods was one of *perfect philosophical freedom.* As long as their existence was not denied—and even that could be safely challenged save in religiously hidebound communities like Athens—free-dom of criticism and speculation was untrammeled by interference from priest or populace. Heresy was as yet a thing unknown." [It even ran to unbounded philosophical licence, he adds.] "Still such licence was prefer-able to the straits in which philosophical speculation now found itself. Christianity was founded on *revelation. . . .* But now the true version of the nature and the constitution of reality, which in the past had been sought by the use and tested by the standards of reason, was made mani-fest once and for all to all mankind by God, speaking at sundry times and in divers manners by the Hebrew prophets and in these latter days by Christ. There was no gainsaying the content of this revelation, however repugnant to reason it might seem. Even to question it was heresy, and heresy might mean death."

And the inevitable conclusion, which writes a historically damning count in the whole indictment of Christianity, follows:

"Under Christianity, then, the status of philosophy was reduced in theory at least to that of a slave. She was deprived of her essential activity of inquiring freely into the nature of the Real and of fearlessly publishing the conclusions drawn from her investigations. Her task, none the less menial for the greatness of the cause into whose service she was impressed, was to expound and defend the content of revelation in terms acceptable to the intellect as far as this was possible."

As ruthlessly as Russia today (1949) lays hold on philosophy and art and science and reduces them to a servitude to the cause of its world control program, did Christianity drag philosophy into captivity in the service of its cause deemed holy and beneficent. So, affirms the careful historian, did it reach out, appropriate what it felt it could utilize of the treasures of contemporary religions and bend them to its service. If history should ultimately decide that fifteen centuries of total silencing of the truth-searching instinct of the human mind exerted in free inquiry has not been too costly a price to pay for the sycophancy of philosophical investigation to an alleged "revelation" that was itself only the corrupted version of earlier spiritual genius, then we may hail the capture and degradation of "divine philosophy" by the bigoted Christians as a victory for faith and zeal. But this is to accede to the proposition that intelligence and light can be harnessed to the chariot of ignorance and darkness.

This painting of the picture throws Christianity's capture and enslavement of philosophy in the third century into true perspective for the first time. Historian after historian has seen this development, included it in his account, and more or less cursorily dilated upon it. Scarcely one of them has paused to comment on it as being perhaps history's most doleful tragedy and most calamitous human failure. Inasmuch as the genius of the race has advanced immeasurably further in knowledge and discovery in the two centuries or less since it has been liberated from the throttling hand of ecclesiastical fanaticism than it was able to do in some fifteen centuries under that allegedly holy thraldom, the bald inference is that Christianity has held back human progress by just that many centuries. Even this glaring object-lesson of history is blinked at and kept from natural emphasis.

The truth is that Christianity was just some more nibbling at the same feast of primal wisdom from which all systems had drawn their first nourishment, but in this case the nibbling was done not by capable philosophers and men of balance, but by illiterates, in the main, who plunged into a wild scramble to grab at it for the sake of the rabble. And this rabble could do nothing but rend it into meaningless shibboleths of miscomprehended phraseology as soon as it laid its defiling hands upon it. At one time or another later on more knowing minds did labor to coalesce the scattered fragments picked up in the wild melee of early ignorance into some approach to dialectical coherence.

And it will be instructive to record another evidence that Christianity—the simple faith of the apostolic fervor—had virtually changed character in the years following its initial impulsion, so as to become something quite other than it had been at the outset. Guignebert gives us a pointer to this effect that should not be missed or left out of account:

"Contemplate the Christian Church at the beginning of the fourth century and some difficulty will be experienced in recognizing in her the community of Apostolic times, or rather we shall *not be able to recognize it at all.*"

A community of simple unction of the spirit (or of the emotions so easily mistaken for the spirit) had by this time, through its efforts to meet and hold its own with one or all of the cult systems hemming it around on all sides, become so complex a mixture of all these elements as to bear little resemblance to what it was when little groups of pietists had first launched it into the currents of religious unction of that day.

We turn to Lundy, author of a valuable old work, *Monumental Christianity,* and find him corroborating our position, yet saying particular things that need to be challenged. We can agree with him when he says that treatises on Christianity "do not deal as they ought to do with the simple facts of an *entire primitive Christianity before* Protestantism and Romanism had existed." That is what the work here projected aims to do. But how he can be half right and half wrong in the same sentence is shown when he says that

"these religions were all, indeed, systems of idolatry, perversions and corruptions of the one primeval truth as held by such patriarchs as Abraham and Job; and yet these religions contained germs of this truth which it became the province of Christianity to develop and embody in a purer system for the good of mankind."

How true he is in saying that the various separate systems, in their exoteric or more public and popular developments, were all perversions and corruptions of that one primeval truth (with the necessary correction that Abraham and Job were not historical but allegorical type figures in the ancient mythic representations), we here attest. It can be said without too much risk of error that all religions at all times since that primeval revelation have been just such more or less drastic perversions and corruptions of its pristine grandeur and truth by incompetent human understanding. So then those that were on the scene when Christianity arose were in this category. Some were more crassly distorted than others; a few, the esoteric, possibly held to the arcane truths pretty closely, thus being less corrupt. But how wrong Lundy is in asserting that it became the province of Christianity to "develop and embody" the "germs of this truth" "in a purer system for the benefit of mankind" we most vigorously proclaim. Since it faced the opportunity, it might be considered the "province" of Christianity to knit up the frayed strands of the great primeval truth into a potent system for the true edification of mankind. But, as he intimates that this is what Christianity did, it is the duty of truth-telling to say that this is just the thing it failed to do. It never did tie together the loose and tangled threads of the pattern into anything remotely resembling the original unity and beauty. Origen saw what was to be done and tried his hand at it. This, the closest effort in the right direction, was savagely attacked and beaten down. It lost the keys to this very secret and therefore left the design of consistent wholeness still irrationally disjointed, with the constituent parts wildly jostling each other in any thinker's sane reflection. It is one of the oddest of the quirks of history that the very nub of Christianity's failure should be put forth as the rock of its success! It levied tribute on all the Pagan cults in a way that Guignebert asserts bore no relation to an intelligent systematism at all; and ended by covering all Paganism with its blanket of universal condemnation, giving no thanks to previous systems for its wholesale pilferings; even in the long run denying the Pagan sources of much of the material it had made off with. This whole chapter of its history has been marked with complete insincerity, if not outright misrepresentation and coverage of facts. Perhaps it can be granted that Christianity did bring out the principles of the hidden wisdom for the intended edification of the populace. But the tragedy that resulted sprang from the fact that it offered cryptic Mystery teachings to the lowly in a form that turned their beneficent potentiality into a darkening of the mind through the conversion of luminous allegory into ridiculous history. Proofs of this will come later.

It is singular that this author, a man of fine analytic mind, could err so egregiously in some particulars of the situation as in this passage and another to be cited, when in between he writes one of the most keenly discerning reviews or surveys of the period, completely in harmony with our exegesis (op. cit., p. xvii):

"It is a most singular and astonishing fact, sought to be developed in this work, that the Christian faith, as embodied in the Apostles' Creed, finds its parallel or dimly foreshadowed counterpart, article by article in the different systems of Paganism here brought under review. No one can be more astonished at this than the author himself. It reveals a unity of religion, and shows that the faith of mankind has been essentially one and the same in all ages. It furthermore points to but one Source and Author."

If these words, inspired by their author's clear momentary vision of the virtual identity of all ancient Pagan systems and their common "Source," had been recognized as *truth* and sculptured in enduring stone on the front portals of all temples in all Christendom, there is no question but that world history would have proceeded on a course of felicity engendered by the fellowship of faiths instead of being disfigured by the division of mankind into groups expressing mutual acerbity.

And it must be entered on the record here that if there was one influence which more than any other tended to obliterate the marks and memorials of that fundamental unity and homogeneity of all religions, and hence to foster disunity in this greatest of all arenas of human communion and fellowship, that influence was Christianity. For this was the religion that in a passion of bigotry and fanaticism flung itself upon all the great literary evidences of the derivation of its own and others' forms and doctrines from that supernal Source and Author of light, and wiped them out of existence. Ever since that woeful day also its churlish temper has fostered religious division and separativeness to an inordinate degree.

Then follows Lundy's overweening and insupportable claim that

"Christianity is simply the full development of the old Patriarchal faith of the world, as Abraham and Job and Melchizedek held it, the complete realization and efflorescence of the one primitive religion given to mankind."

267

Already refuted, this claim needs only the comment that Christianity was no development of that aboriginal gift at all, unless rank dismemberment and despoliation of a faith of all its true sense and organic unity is what is taken to constitute development. It is a gain in knowledge to record Lundy's affirmation that the primal religion was a unity of all elements of religious truth. But no facts warrant the statement that Christianity even at its best was the crowning "realization and efflorescence" of it. With infinite reluctance it has to be said that on the contrary it was the corroding and catalytic influence, the express *de*florescence of that primitive wisdom, by its transferal of mystic realizations into the empty husks of literal events.

Lundy later states (p. 202) that Christianity degenerated by association with Paganism:

"The Church had now placed herself under the fostering care of the secular power, which was yet half-Pagan; what wonder is it that she degenerated with such frightful rapidity as to be almost overwhelmed by Mohammedanism by reason of her dissensions, corruptions and weakness? . . . Was the weakness borrowed from a distant Oriental Brahmanism? Or was it inherent in the Christian community itself?"

Is it not quite illogical to lay Christian degeneration at the door of its association with the Paganism from which it had drawn all its basic principles—save, of course, its transformation of the Christos spirit into a historical man? Rather can its deterioration be traced to its ignorant misconception and mishandling of the body of esoteric teachings it had picked up and then completely turned into the instruments of derationalization. Only so far as a measure of this same tendency to stupid literalism may have crept into the Mystery interpretations and vitiated their received message could Paganism have been a party to the corruption of Christianity. It was Christianity's own default and defection from the esoteric side of Paganism that led to its degeneration, its dissensions, corruptions and downfall.

Great light shines for us in G. R. S. Mead's studies and findings as announced in his *Fragments of a Faith Forgotten*. To rebut the claim advanced by Guignebert and Lundy that Christianity effected the syncretism of the old Pagan systems into a true and the best religion, we have asserted that that was not the case, but that the great work of syncretism was done by the Hellenists at Alexandria, some Christian, others non-Christian. Mead's conclusions are strong evidence in support of this thesis (p. 118):

"It was the Alexandrian school of Christian philosophy, of which the most famous doctors were the same Clemens and Origen, which laid the first foundations of General Christian theology; and that school owed its evolution to its contact with Grecian thought."

Then Mead outlines the succeeding development so well that his brief statement could stand as an epitome of general Christian origination (p. 118):

"Now Christianity in its *popular* origins had entirely entangled itself with the popular Jewish tradition of religion, a tradition that was innocent of all philosophic or kabalistic mysticism. . . . As time went on, however, and either men of greater education joined their ranks, or in their propaganda they were forced to study themselves to meet the objections of educated opponents, wider and more liberal views obtained among a number of Christians, and the other great religious traditions and philosophies contacted the popular stream. All such views, however, were looked upon with great suspicion by the 'Orthodox,' or rather that view which finally became orthodox. And so as time went on, even the very moderate liberalism of Clemens and Origen was regarded as a grave danger; and with the triumph of the narrow orthodoxy and the condemnation of learning, Origen was himself at last anathematized."

It would be hard to tell the story of this early period in Christian development better and more succinctly.

Guignebert says that the arcana of the Mysteries exerted little or no influence upon Christianity. Others have stated the same thing. If so it is easy to understand. The Pagans understood more or less clearly (admittedly often less) the inner subjective reference and significance of the dramatic rituals; the Christians did not. Naturally a movement is not influenced by what goes beyond it and is alien to it. Also Mystery meaning was esoteric and secret. It did not spread abroad beyond its own membership. It is no derogation of Mystery ritual that it did not severely affect Christianity. This is a point that has long needed decisive reorientation.

Guignebert well says, however, that the several stages marking the Christian initiations undoubtedly reflect the gradations in the Hellenic Mystery ratings of its members. The Creed, also, he says, was the work of "ignorant folk," incapable of abstruse conceptions. The germs of Greek thought continued to exert an influence upon all those who had been edified by it before they yielded to the seductions of the Christian faith. These men, he says, can not, however hard they try, renounce altogether the remembered elucidations given out in their esoteric studies in Greek philosophy. Accordingly they fall back on these to expound the dogmas, such as those of the Trinity and Trans-substantiation, when they are challenged by the stupid arguments of the ignorant, who have construed a wrong sense out of every doctrine.

In line with the arguments of other writers already noticed, we find George Hodges, in his work already cited, *The Early Church,* advancing the theory that the Pagan cults had used the "corn myth," or death of the seed in the ground over the winter and its germination in the spring, and had built their religion largely upon it. They had lifted the natural phenomenon into a spiritual significance. This would be a trite statement, hardly calling for repetition if it were not that this lifting of a fact of nature to a higher sphere of meaning has been expressly denied by so many expositors. But this beneficent apotheosization of meaning, he adds, "touched only a few of the people."

Here once more is the old charge: Paganism failed because it edified only a few more advanced minds. Yet after nineteen centuries of Christian effulgence of divine light, one may go across any Christian country and ask all farmers what there is of high spiritual illumination in the fall and spring phases of his activity, and not a soul will know what at least the instructed Pagan could have intimated lay hidden in the "corn myth." So that Christianity has not succeeded where Paganism has failed.

On the opposite side Hodges records for the Pagan devotee his belief that "there was a divinity for every act of life from birth to death." This could eventuate in odd superstitions, to be sure; but the good of a reverent attitude toward all nature and secular things, the constant feeling that the deific power and purpose are at work in the total world, can surely be admitted to be a more religious attitude than a sharp mental cleavage between things specifically sanctified and things commonplace. Emerson has said that the true essence of the doctrine of the Omnipresence is to see the miraculous and the divine in the common. A religion that brings its people to regard the whole of life and all things as being instinct with divinity must surely be rated higher than one which attributes sanctity to only a few things in special buildings and on particular days.

Hodges highly lauds the eclecticism, the syncretism and the spiritual mysticism of the Pagans that has been so generally berated by apologists as the influence detrimental and hostile to Christianity.

Guignebert repeats that Christian dogma, liturgy, discipline were not the outcome of any spontaneous generation, but on the contrary were the product of a syncretism "from Oriental surroundings—from

Israel, from the Mystery Religions and from Hellenistic philosophy." Little by little the new cult absorbed these elements, thus preserving all that was living and lasting from what the Graeco-Roman world contained. This process went on, he argues, slowly until the day when the Pagan cults disintegrated through the defluxion of their strength drained off by Christianity. If all this is so, it clinches the contention that Christianity was simply revamped Paganism. The crucial thing about it, however, never to be forgotten henceforth, is that Christianity did not revamp Paganism to a perfection or rationale or purity never manifested before, but virtually dismantled it. This assertion is a complete *volte face* in historical exposition of Christian origins.

Guignebert says that "the Christian faith, Oriental in its origin and mystic and excitable, was foreign to all that Roman customs regarded as a religion."

This is a true statement of the historian, but his implied conclusion that Christianity was a religion markedly characterized by elements of Greek wisdom and spiritually too deep for the Roman masses, is hardly as true. Or it is true in the specific sense that its myths, rites and symbols, which even the Christian masses never could understand, would also be too far above the Roman populace. The probable truth is that these things were not understood by either the Christians or the masses. If Origen, the very apex of intelligence in the Christian communion, could not entirely regain their true esoteric significance, the masses surely could not.

The truth of this position is further attested by consideration of the work, the position and the final repudiation of the Gnostics in early Christianity. They it was, of all the Christian groups, who attempted to structuralize the Christian system on a philosophical basis. Hodges says (op. cit., p. 73):

"Gnosticism arose from an honest desire to make Christianity a consistent intellectual system, to provide for it a theology which should appeal to men of learning and reflection. Such men were beginning to come into the Church, bringing their intellectual habits with them. They were somewhat dismayed at the informality of the Christian thinking, and undertook to introduce into it the element of order."

"But most of the Gnostics were honest and earnest men. They believed themselves to be . . . fighting over again the splendid battles which St. Paul fought."

These Gnostics, men of philosophical keenness, were not the last to be dismayed by the "informality," which must be taken as a euphemism for gross illogicality and complete unintelligibility (due to the conversion of allegory into "history") with which Christian doctrinism has struck and dismayed the minds of disciplined thinkers.

But Christianity rejected these fine men and ended by casting them out branded with the stigma of heresy. These are the men who would have made Christianity a system adequate to satisfy the innate hunger of cultivated minds for high truth, without at the same time deluding the populace with caricatured untruth. That these lowly masses eventually did adopt it is evidence that it was not too high or profound for popular choice, as against its chief rival, another religion of esoteric depth, Mithraism.

Gnosticism was so esoteric and recondite that Marcion, the great Gnostic exegetist, held that, since spirit is so directly in opposition to debased matter, "the humanity of Christ was only in appearance," and that "Christ could not have taken on our mortal flesh, which is essentially evil." Marcion was carrying a doctrine to its extreme and illegitimate application in this case, since there can be no incarnation without the embodiment of spirit in the flesh. But such questions would hardly be matter of household debate among the people.

But again Hodges says that the Christians were dumbfounded by the cropping out of many "coincidences" and similarities between their faith and Mithraism. They were disconcerted to find that their "new religion" was not novel.

Massey's grave charges are seconded by a writer, J. R. L. Morrell, in his work *Spiritism and the Beginnings of Christianity* (Foreword):

"It is a strange and amazing history that I have to tell, but it is true . . . every word of the charge which I make. It is an account of the deliberate and malicious corruption of the most ancient and honorable religion in the world. It involves the interpolation and destruction of a vast literature and finally the ruin of one of the greatest civilizations ever known, to cover up the crime. And so successfully was this work of interpolation and destruction brought about that few people of the present even suspect the colossal humbug that was played upon the world.

"The accusation which I make is that those religious beliefs constituting what is known today as the Christian religion do not owe their origin to the teachings and practices of a Jewish itinerant named Jesus Christ, but came into being in quite another manner, and actually existed before the time he is supposed to have lived. Indeed it is a matter of grave doubt among profound scholars whether any such person ever lived, or as to whom he may have been if he did live."

The orthodox publicists have refuted these various claims as to the pre-Christian existence of Christianity, yet with more in the way of sheer assertion than competent documentary or historical evidence.

There is a school of opinion which holds that the mythical Jesus of the Gospels was the shadow character of a real personage whose birth was in the year 2 A.D., namely Apollonius of Tyana. His *Life* by Philostratus comes close to being a parallel of that of the Gospel Jesus. It is claimed that he was the living prototype of both Jesus and Paul, inasmuch as his biography runs much like that of Jesus, while oddly enough Paul addressed his letters to churches in precisely those places where Apollonius had traveled and founded religious societies studying Hellenized spiritual philosophy. Likewise Paul's name in the *Acts* has been associated with a mysterious Apollos; and still again Apollonius' personal attaché, Damis, seems to match well enough Paul's companion and personal friend Demas. A growing body of opinion holds that Apollonius was the flesh and blood reality behind the uncertain and in many respects decidedly unsubstantial historicity of both Jesus and Paul.

What is claimed to be convincing proof of the pre-Christian associations before the first century is to be found in the Jewish philosopher Philo, born close to the year 1 A.D. But such evidences are neither more sensational nor more definite than the general fact now largely conceeded that Christianity built up its creeds and dogmas, rituals and practices upon what it drew from antecedent Pagan cults. Early churches were Essene temples and Orphic temples and monasteries throughout the Eastern world.

A definite testimony is the charge of Hierocles, a learned Pagan statesman, that the priests plagiarized the Gospels from the writings of Apollonius of Tyana, the "original Gospel" of those days. When one reads that "the proclamation of Hierocles was destroyed by Eusebius," and that the latter in a work against Hierocles threw discredit on the claims for the derivation of the Gospels from Apollonius' writings, one must wonder where the truth lies—in view of Eusebius' *well*-known reputation for twisting the facts to make them tell a story favorable to Christianity.

When it is stated that Philostratus' *Life of Apollonius* was based upon original MSS in the possession of the cultured Empress Julia Domna, there seems to be ground for the authenticity of the claims of Hierocles. Assertion is made that Philostratus' work on the great Pythagorean philosopher has suffered greatly at the hands of Christian redactors and been much caricatured, "the real truth being obtainable only by careful scrutiny." If Christian scribes and partisan zealots could show a record for probity and honesty in the handling of old MSS, the claims for the Apollonian background of the Gospels and *Acts* might be heavily discounted. But in view of a record notorious and well-nigh incredible for tampering and mutilation of documents and the invention of whole "gospels" out of fancy, the situation can well merit cautious conclusions.

Apollonius at the age of twelve studied at Tarsus! This was Paul's city, one of three basic centers of Hellenic culture. The name Apollos, in the *Acts,* is said to be given as Apollonius in the *Codex Beza,* found in a monastery in France by a Huguenot soldier.

Morrell points out the strange feature of Jesus' being suddenly and without any events leading up to it, recognized and accepted "throughout all Syria." His inference from this is that only Apollonius could have fulfilled this role and character, since it was in Syria that he had founded the many "churches." The writers have always wondered, not too loudly, how and when it was that Paul could have been in Syria and Asia Minor and have so quickly founded a list of growing congregations to whom he wrote his *Epistles.* The autochthonous growth of these "Christian" communities so early in the history of Christianity is indeed a phenomenon that has never been satisfactorily explained. Particularly that society at Antioch, where the "brethren" were first called Christians, indicates stubbornly that the movement that came to be included under the general term "Christian" was a concurrent activity among groups on the ground and functioning before the advent of a heavenly Savior and his life of thirty-three years and his death could have been in any way a determining element in their formation.

The clear implication of these and concomitant facts in the historical scene in the first century and antedating it is that almost beyond dispute there were associations and brotherhoods practicing cult programs constituted of elements of Oriental, Jewish, Graeco-Egyptian and Chaldean esotericism, which little by little, starting at Antioch, came to be subsumed under the general name of "Christians," adopted from the Greek term *Christos,* meaning, like *Messiah,* the "anointed." This name would be appropriate to all of them in virtue of their all having made the Christos-in-man the central or basic teaching in their systems. The Gnostics, Docetists, Elkasites, Ebionites, Ophites, Therapeutai and even Nazarenes and Christianoi, later denounced as heretics, all accentuated this note even in the pale of early Christianity. Indeed there is every reason to believe that the wing of the Christian movement that was stirred into activity in the Syria and Asia Minor sector by Paul's preaching had not the slightest connection with the Palestinian apostolic Christianity; nor had it anything doctrinally or theologically in common with it. There is no sound reason for their inclusion in the movement that later appropriated the name of "Christian" and made it historical. There is a total dearth of data which would establish the claim that these Syrio-Asian "Christians" promulgated their religious movement with the remotest reference to the Galilean Jesus as founder of their faith. The "Lord Jesus Christ" whom they expounded was the spiritual Christos within the heart of all men, and not any historical personage. For the former is what he is with St. Paul himself.

There is not room to make this an elucidation of data from comparative religion. But it may impress readers unfamiliar with the endless run of such parallels to be confronted with at least one item of identity between Christian legend (taken for history) and ancient Egyptian allegorism. Horus, the perennial Christ of Egypt, as a babe was laid in a manger in a scenic reconstruction of a stable, and an image of his mother Isis was placed beside it. Also Hermes, Egyptian Logos figure, was born in a cave, son of Zeus and Maya (Mary), and represented as a child wrapped in swaddling bands and laid in a manger.

Images of the Christ have been found much resembling those of Apollo, Greek Sun-God, and of Orpheus, mythical divine teacher.

Morrell's summary is that

"Christianity is but a combination of Pythagorean spiritualism with the essential features of Pagan supernaturalism, in which every trace of the original spiritualism has been distorted or suppressed; and the symbols greatly exaggerated and interpreted literally as Christianity."

Is it not singular that so many men have been inexorably led to the conclusion that Christianity is ancient Paganism with its Scriptures literalized?

The outcome of this sweep from Hellenic philosophical Christianity over to practical Roman ecclesiasticism is well stated by Guignebert (op. cit., 180):

"In reality, however, the Church is passing through a crisis of growth. The outcome of her 'growing pains' will be an orthodoxy which will perpetuate the victory of the mass over the individual, and will lay the foundation for the necessity of intolerance in God's name.

"The formula prescribed settled down into a tyranny, the initiative native to religious sentiment grows feeble and personal enthusiasm renders one suspect of heresy. Henceforth doctrine will take control of faith, an event of capital importance in the history of the Christian life."

How Christianity made its synthesis of diverse elements borrowed from Pagan creeds is well limned by Guignebert (p. 181):

"Side by side with the data of the Apostolic faith are fundamentally dissimilar religions and philosophical ideas borrowed from the complex surroundings in which Christianity has been living its life, and a union is effected betwen them by arguments very similar to those in use by Greek sophistry, concealed beneath more or less ingenious formulas, but at bottom empty and deceptive. In this work the influence can be specially traced of the aristocrats of the intellect, the men of letters and the philosophers whom the faith has won over. I must repeat that in adopting Christianity these men have not divested themselves either of the substance or even more particularly of the method and forms of speculation which they had hitherto used."

It is a pity that too much quotation prevents the reader's having every word of a splendid analytic passage from Guignebert's history. It shows so clearly how the process of borrowing by Christianity originated and continued on to its final stages. He reminds us that while the people at large appear submissive to the clergy and ready to accept their dicta, they are far less passive than they seem. In them, ultimately, rather than in the work of the priests, will be found the determining causes of the changes by which Pagan backgrounds of the common life transformed Christianity. The common people do not reflect or reason, but still they are sensitive to the effects of change or innovation. Their faith is intense and spontaneous, becoming habitual and automatic, and its exploitation in religious ceremonial must continue to yield them its inflations and expansions. They have been accustomed to find these exaltations, however illogically baseless, through the means of their forms of Pagan inheritances. They will cling persistently, therefore, to the time-honored, custom-bound rites and beliefs of ancestral origin, and will make these the nucleus of their Christianity. The human birth and existence of the Christos must be seen as a miracle; the worship of Mary must take on the color of goddess veneration, and the adoration of Saints helps to keep alive the sense of polytheism. Legends of Pagan heroes are woven into the construct of

276

thought and feeling. It is easy for them to fit into their church worship the imagery and splendor of the Pagan ceremonies, with the comforting sense of magic and mystery.

Naturally, Guignebert is frank to admit, all this faces the clergy with some embarrassing problems, calling upon all their ingenuity for adjustments or compromises. But, cost what it may, these maneuvers are made and they succeed tolerably. The accommodations found necessary are "clarified, sifted, arranged and finally imposed upon the theologians who had to adjust themselves to them as best they might."

"Thus by a sort of unintentional collaboration of influences of somewhat diverse origin, yet convergent in their effect, a religion very different from the Christianity that we caught a glimpse of in the beginning of the third century acquired shape and form in the fourth, and has become practically mistress of the Roman world when the fifth century opens."

Then he carries the religion thus transformed by the necessity of adapting its original program to the inveterate fixations of Pagan religion into its medieval period and notes how it was further vastly oriented by the forces governing its development. And it is a picture in contrasts that should be missed by nobody.

These, he writes, are the features of the Christian religion in the Middle Ages: it is universalist in temper, bent on warfare; exclusive, violently intolerant, especially to the Jews; bustling with summary dogmas which "set reason at defiance", flourishing elaborate rites, which exercise a mighty and mysterious potency, an arm of power never to be ignored; cluttered up with numberless special "devotions" addressed to a catalogue of Virgins, specialized Saints; directed by a clergy in strict control of the conscience of the laity, who are being herded more and more under the direct authority of one sole center and kept in line by an army of monks and a quibbling troop of acute theologians. If we look at this scene and then compare it with the religion of the Galilean prophet, meek and lowly, who came to announce only the "glad tidings" of the coming of the Kingdom and to galvanize heedless hearts in readiness to receive it, "it is difficult to discover what these two have in common." Stage by stage the gospel of Paul, the Gnosis of Origen, the theology of Augustine, the faith of the Crusaders, and at last Thomism, this religion has built a bridge across the centuries that linked the humble Galilean's simple preachment with the panoply of regal world power. And, concludes Guignebert,

"It is no less true that the triumph of the Church in the course of the fourth century was rendered possible only by the failure of the early faith, of that which we may call the faith of the twelve."

But what does all this show? A picture so different from what the body of communicants of this religion have been led to construct in their imagination that the republication of the truth would be shockingly unacceptable. Instead of presenting from the first a firm and well-defined compact body of truth given by the Messenger of God to illumine a world groaning in heathen blindness, and holding this gleam steadily before the world right down the centuries, till finally its brightness won the masses to rejoice in its comforts, there is the record of a surge of zealotry amid the ignorant masses, a ferment of fanatical pietism, carrying its contagion to the down-trodden populace of the Roman Empire, winning by its very abandon of devotion, gaining power through numbers, intriguing more learned people to join it and then strengthening it by the introduction of philosophical elements to hold the more intelligent, and then when political expediency had gained its recognition from the State, at once becoming arrogant and tyrannical, and going on thence to execute in regal glow of power its original frenzied purpose to conquer mankind.

And all its victories can be considered won by accommodations, surrenders, compromises, intrigues and finally by violence and slaughter; never shining as one clear single light of truth and wisdom, but a power sinuous, insidious, sycophantic and fickle, changing form like a chameleon, fastening its clutch upon the sensibilities of the gullible masses by mingled ministrations of faith, beauty, art, subtly intertwined with the psychologies of fear and intimidation, particularly of the young. If this is the form and the program which had to be taken to bring mankind in the West from darkness to blessedness, it is nevertheless a horrendous spectacle and a procedure shocking to sincere minds.

CHAPTER XIII

WISDOM IS MUTE

The people of the Church, says the historian, more especially after the persecutions had ceased, could relax from the high tension of witnessing for God in the heroic spirit of martyrdom. The Christian could live a normal life and, without the spur of the challenge of consummate sacrifice, his high-pitched consecrations could be deflated, from sheer want of incentive. He was left to sink back into an acceptance of and by the world and a compromise with its spirit, terms and obligations.

"In other words the mystic struggle which primitive Christianity undertook against life had ended in complete defeat. In fact the Church accepted and acquiesced in it, and was content to transform the ideal which contains the very essence of the primitive faith and indeed constituted her own *raison d'etre* into a theme for pious meditation."

Her own numerous converts, while giving her success and power, were themselves a large factor in her spiritual defeat. For these people were let into the Church too hastily prepared and were for that reason less capable of keeping in check the basic force of the ordinary low-level sensual nature of average man, the formidable antagonist of true religion.

So, avers Guignebert, the "triumph of Christianity," culminating in the fifth century with the silencing of Paganism was, when regarded from a deeper point of view, *"a triumph in appearance only."* Indeed, so far from Christianity having changed and conquered the Roman Empire, it was the Empire that absorbed Christianity, is this astute critic's verdict.

"Far from having transformed the Graeco-Roman world, Christianity was really absorbed by it and applied to its own atavistic needs and customs in the whole domain of both mind and body."

After some centuries the Church was to learn that the stolid mass mind and its staunch rock of collective feelings, its fixed habitudes, its impregnable solidity and stolidity of traditional inheritances, its immalleability, its intellectual inertia, can be a massif against which even the waves of a turbulent religious upheaval can dash themselves in futility. The storm subsides, the thunder and lightning pass, and the cliff stands as unmoved as before. Not much was Paganism changed by the sweep of the besom of pietism; it was Christianity that came out of the cauldron changed almost beyond recognition. And so far was Paganism from being extinguished that nearly two thousand years from Christianity's founding era whole nations of Europe long dominated by a Christianity that seemed as secure and ordained as the sun, suddenly threw off the shackles of this religion that had never been a native growth from their own soil but an unnatural grafting from without, and hurled it with the virulence of a pent-up curse completely out of their life. Paganism had been a more natural, indigenous growth, connecting the social and the mental life of the peoples with their natural habitat and their very hills and vales. Early religions had always connected the manifestations of Deity more closely with nature itself. Christianity came in as an exotic importation, foisted upon them by force and violence, or the persuasions of expediency. That in hundreds of years it was not able to entrench itself with real strength in the life of its subservient nations so as to be able to withstand a sudden modern revolt against its despotism indicates how shallow and extrinsic had been its hold in the antecedent years. Guignebert puts the responsibility for the hollowness of Christianity's "triumph" and the evil consequences following its real failure squarely on the doorstep of the Church.

With the fall of the Roman state power in 476 A.D. the Church, just because her power is invisible and intangible and is therefore rooted in superstition, remains the one structure that will maintain organic unity and a semblance of authority in the dismantled West. Innate reverence even of so-called barbarians for things outwardly paraded as sacred effected for the Church and Christianity a safety which it was quick to enhance and buttress into actual power. But this very security, with its great advantages, rapidly became the means and alluring opportunity for her development in a direction farther and farther away from the spiritual unction of her primeval idealism and plunged her deeper and deeper into the stream of secular and political concerns. Thus her utter metamorphosis of character and mission is completed.

Guignebert reaffirms that Christianity must always be remembered as essentially an Oriental product—

"an edifice for which Judaism provided the foundations, and all the materials of the superstructure were obtained from the Hellenistic world in which Greek and more accurately Eastern (Asiatic, Syrian, Mesopotamian, Iranian and Egyptian) influences were mingled, from the time of Alexander. The Western world was prepared for Christian permeation by the propaganda done on their own behalf—on the long commercial routes or in the camps—by various Oriental religious Redeeming cults, such as that of Isis and the Great Mother (Cybele) of Phrygia, of Mithra and others. But it took no part itself in the formation of the new religion. It gulped it down whole, as it were, and after assimilation by it, Christianity became more massive and stricter."

It could not, he says, either grasp or express in the inflexible Latin of its day the

"subtle fluid cultures of Greek thought, the foster-mother of early theology. It became hard, crystallized and encrusted in fixed modes of legalistic determination. In this spiritual poverty and barren sterility the needs of the people sought means of self-expression by utilizing the ancient cults and inflating the old myths. But again these can not adequately supply the spiritual vacuum and fail."

The old mythic forms fail because they

"are too narrow a framework to be an adequate setting for ideas which are constantly growing and for which they were not designed."

These final words are cited so that they may be rebutted. Condensing pages of dissertation already given herein, let it be asserted finally that myth is only as narrow as the unintelligence that misapprehends it, and that there are practically no basic ideas, deep and luminous as life itself, which the myths have not been designed to dramatize and illuminate, when a capably receptive mind of clear vision is at hand to interpret their recondite sense. But solutions will never be found for the riddles of mythology and allegory when the requisite insight into the esoteric depths of the near-divine genius that formulated those myths is totally wanting and a prejudice of nescience defeats the will and aspiration of the mind to encompass true discernment.

Guignebert makes the venturesome assertion—mistakenly, as we have shown—that Christianity was the first to succeed in making this syncretism because it stepped in to profit by the preparatory work of its Jewish antecedents, which had put into its hands "a fundamental monotheism and an exclusiveness, intolerant, to be sure, but at that

281

time also salutary." Certain ancient nations, or their initiated priest-hoods, had needed no syncretism, because they had the entire won-drous structure of divine-human truth virtually intact. It had not yet become fragmented by schism and ignorance. Later, when it had thus been in part dismantled, efforts of more knowing ones had to be made to reintegrate it. But so far was Christianity at any time from making a perfected syncretism of it all, that it carried its disintegration to the lowest stage of ruin imaginable, and has never yet brought into any degree of harmony with each other the monotheism (which it must be said was by no means an attainment of the Jewish religion alone) of the Hebrews with the polytheistic elements of the Greek and Ori-ental cults.

That a harmony between these two seemingly so diverse conceptions is at all possible is even yet not contemplated by Christian thought. Monotheism contemplates God as One; polytheism contemplates that organic Oneness from the point of view of man who can see the One only in his manifold constituent parts. Christianity has wrought in-calculable mischief in the realm of the human mind by ascribing divinity to life in its conceived Oneness; but denied divinity to life in its component divisions and segments. It is as if we should consider the human body as worthy of the highest veneration and care in its wholeness, but scorn and deny the separate organic parts and functions. This has brought about in Christendom as almost in no other religious segment of the globe that sharp distinction between things "holy" or "sacred" and things secular and profane, which has made the Western nations a race of people who feel no nearness of the divine in the commonplace, but set aside only an hour or two a week in a feeble consecration to something gropingly sought after as "spiritual." Chris-tianity has never mustered the philosophical acumen to discern that in casting out the rational polytheism of the Oriental religions it was con-demning the West to a rule of real "paganism" hardly ever matched in Eastern civilizations. Admittedly ignorance can misconstrue poly-theism into crude forms of nature worship, fetishism, animism and a pantheism wanting in balanced comprehension. But just as fatally can ignorance fail to make anything of monotheism. God as One must remain perpetually an abstraction, called indeed the Unknowable. God as One is the Infinite, the Absolute, the Unmanifest. The God that man *can* know through life itself is the living universe, which he contacts through his endowment of sense and reason. God, the

Monon, man can only wonder about; it is with God, the polytheistic whole of organic being, that man must deal.

If Christianity had at any time mastered the profound cosmogonic and anthropogenic principles by which the ancient sages such as Orpheus and Hermes had expounded the truth about God in his multiple expression in the universe, and had understood that man's approach to God is through the logical synthesis of this multiplicity, the Occidental world would never have become either so distinctively secular-minded or so lawless.

Guignebert brings out the odd fact that Christianity's two main antagonists in the days of its inception, Neo-Platonism and Manichaeism, were of Oriental origin like itself; they took rise out of the same general trends of thought as it did; they were nourished by the same religious sentiments and deal with the same religious matter, and were products of the same religious crisis as that which generated Christianity. They took form at the same time in the second half of the third century. Neo-Platonism proclaimed the Christos as divine principle lodged and to be developed in human consciousness; Mani proclaimed himself to be a spiritual descendant of Jesus, one of the messengers of God who had preceded him. But the Jesus he speaks of is more akin to the "Lord Jesus Christ" or the Christos of Paul and the Jesus Aeon of the Gnostics than referable to the Galilean. This is itself a notable, indeed a tell-tale fact.

What, then, made the difference between Christianity and the two others? Again the sad answer has to be—ignorance; ignorance on the part of the rabble that followed the Christian groundswell. Neo-Platonists were men of the highest contemplative culture and studiousness. Manichaeans were about at the same level. But the Christians were those, mainly, who were readily instigated to despise books, learning and philosophy with a flame of fury that consumed the Alexandrian library and the priceless volumes of the arcane truth. The two great philosophical rivals of Christianity held the ancient body of sage wisdom to its high standards of intellectual appreciation. Not so Christianity. It took the lower road of adaptation of mythic representation and abstruse principia to the crass mind, thus wrecking the organic beauty of the structure and enslaving the thought of its devotees to idolatrous conceptions and materialized entifications.

That the orthodoxy established in the fourth century did not wholly eradicate the seeds of Neo-Platonism and Manichaeism is indicated by many developments in the succeeding periods. Paul's proselyte, Dionysius the Areopagite, was soon to base a new presentation of esoteric philosophy on the Neo-Platonic structure and see it assume some prominence. A little later came Scotus Erigena, who repeated a procedure of much the same sort. And on down in the Middle Ages there were the Albigenses, whose system of powerful philosophical strength was, according to Guignebert, "a Christian adaptation of Manichaeism." Indeed the Church has had almost constantly to wrestle with recurrent upsurges of interest in the ancient philosophical deposit by individuals or groups. Guignebert deprecates Augustine's "unworthy twaddle derogatory of" these cult philosophies "current in Christian circles."

But when the scholar asserts that Christianity supplanted these two noble philosophies "because it could express their own tendencies better than they could themselves," and also express them with a harmonization of their differences so as to render them capable of "answering the needs of all the various classes of men who were seeking spiritual sustenance for themselves," dissent must be registered. That Christianity was, or is, capable of inculcating the profound principia of the Neo-Platonic philosophy better than the Greek academies or the Alexandrian syncretists could do it, or indeed that it could ever fully apprehend and apply to the edification of its own people the precepts of that exalted system, is a claim that any competent scholar would not seriously consider supportable. At any rate history holds the disproof of the assertion. Christianity not only did not exploit Neoplatonic wisdom to any appreciable degree, but indeed suffered it to pass out into near oblivion. It never urged or abetted a revival of interest in it, but in case after case when an attempt was made to revive it, including the preaching of Nicholas of Cusa and of Giordano Bruno, stamped any recrudescence of it out like a fire in forest leaves. Among the Church's exploits that helped give it "victory" certainly was not that of applying or expressing Neo-Platonism (or Manichaeism) better than they could do it themselves. But what they could and most certainly did do "better," was to reduce a few of the basic fundamenta of those systems into a caricatured form which could delude the mass mind into the belief that spiritual essences were historical figures, and thus generate superstitious notions and irrational passions.

Guignebert affirms rightly, however, that in condemning Origen and his writings and methods, "they inadvertently shut themselves off from the main highway for their speculative thought and the path that it had been following for more than a century." Even in Augustine's work, he argues, was epitomized the whole Christian thought of the fourth century, and it was "interpreted, cleared up and put in good order by the profound, though not always visible, aid of Platonic principles."

Then our chronicler really extends himself in a genuine laudation of Augustine's work, which, since he has assured us it was largely a product of Platonic systematism, is well worth noting in full:

"His doctrine constitutes a landmark, erects a ledge, as it were, in the increasingly steep climb upwards of the faith. For this reason it can be said with equal exactness that all the Medieval evaluation of Christian theology in the West originated with St. Augustine. He is the founder of the mysticism of the Reformation as well as of the Middle Ages, and he is an inspiration to Protestantism as he was to the Medieval Church. . . . His doctrine is looked up to as the supreme authority by the doctors of all schools. . . . Finally his opinions upon certain essential points of the faith, on grace and on predestination, for instance, or upon the connection between reason and revelation, from his times to our own, have supplied the grist for all the discussions of the theologians. His dread statements also on the necessity of punishing the sacrilegious furnish the justification in advance, of all the later Medieval intolerance and the Inquisition."

This last sour note is made still more astringent by the next tribute, which says that

"No one contributed more than he toward the adoption of the opinion that a decision of the Church is a truth against which human reason is not qualified to rebel, and that the worth of Holy Scripture itself is due to the guarantee and the interpretation given it by the Church."

Who can say to what degree this influence from the far-off fourth century is responsible for the feebleness of the democratic spirit that is threatening to let arrogant dictators and cliques crush out again for ages the human rights and liberties won by centuries of heroic sacrifice?

Guignebert tells how the ignorant thronged into the early Church and how the clergy, aiming at numbers and letting down all bars of qualification, admitted men who knew little of Christianity save a few formulas or phrases. These people, he says, in making connection with the new movement, had forgotten none of their Pagan customs. They were simply forced to dress their Paganism in a Christian cloak. The ancient festivals were kept as holidays and celebrated in the country districts; and the Church can only neutralize their effect by turning them to account for her profit. It is thus apparent that in adopting

Christianity, the Roman population were trying on a garment that was a misfit and uncomfortable, and that the wearers had to cut it down to size and adapt it to their former habits of convenience.

It is not yet time for a summarization, but as the reader comes to the end of the long trail followed through by this renowned historian and takes some stock of what has been revealed, it is hard to avoid the realization that here has been painted the picture of a great sweeping movement in human history that leaves one stupefied with its record of weakness, deception, misguided zealotry, mental despotism and general miscarriage of intelligence and integrity that at last sickens the very soul. Critics of this Juggernaut of triumphant faith, as they see it winning by stealth, by preying on superstitions and pietism, are without exception accused of bigotry and intolerance. Yet this charge falls down, when it is realized that the alleged bigotry and intolerance of criticism has been generated by a revulsion against the bigotry and intolerance of the system they criticize. Is it bigotry and intolerance to denounce obvious bigotry and intolerance? The ultimate feeling in reaction to a study of the recorded course of this surge of human beliefs, first compounded of ancient creeds and customs utterly misconceived and jumbled together into an unimaginable association of illogical theology, then speciously made organic by the skulduggery of priestcraft, then pursuing its relentless march down through the centuries of Western struggle, crushing every hopeful revival of intelligence and enforcing its ruthless regime of faith, is at last the nauseous conviction that all sincerity has long since evaporated from its counsels, and that the whole gorgeous fabric of its pietism is the organic instrument used for the religious exploitation of mass credulity and the grandiose agent employed to regiment mass psychology. Such is the revulsion of mind arising from the endless rehearsal of the story that "piety" takes on the character of a thing to be hated and "sanctity" becomes a thing of revulsion. If historians like Massey, Higgins and others have turned bitterly critical and condemnatory of Christianity, it is because its history reeks of the things that breed this revulsion in men of mental integrity. It is little wonder that the conscience of later Europe, even in the Church itself, could no longer endure the onus of supporting such an edifice of duplicity, corruption and shameless insincerity, and broke away to demand a cleaning out of its temple. But that sally of honest resentment against deceit had not the tools (which only ancient Egypt could have furnished) wherewith to cut its way clear of the whole distortion, and went only a fraction of its way to full reformation. It is time now, and the missing tools are at hand, to carry that task the rest of its long way to complete eradication of the false principles wrought into the structure in the fourth century. And what could stir mankind today more acutely to come alive to its task of winning emancipation from groveling superstition than to meditate, and then act, upon the words of Sir Gilbert Murray, when, as the upshot of his life-long studies in the influence of religion in the world, he was moved to indite his soul's conviction that

"It is obvious indeed that most religions, if analyzed into intellectual beliefs, are false; and I suppose that a thoroughly orthodox member of any one of the million religious bodies that exist in the world must be clear in his mind that the other million minus one are wrong, if not wickedly wrong." (*Five Stages of Greek Religion*, p. 21.)

If further incentive to prompt action were needed, it can be found in his further declaration:

"But we must always remember two things about it [religion]: first, that the liability of error is enormous, indeed almost infinite; and second, that the results of confident error are very terrible. Probably throughout history the worst things ever done in the world on a large scale by decent people have been done in the name of religion, and I do not think this has entirely ceased to be true at the present day."
"The record of early Christian and Medieval persecutions which were the direct result of that one confident religious error comes curiously near to one's conception of the wickedness of the damned."

These strictures should not lose, but immensely gain, cogency by their temperate and unemotional utterance.

The general populace must go on, perforce, being led with a ring in its nose by designing ecclesiastical polity and psychologically crafty showmanship. But if there is a modicum of sincerity left in men in high places, it is a terrible obligation facing religious leaders to take rational account of the whole broad condition of the world as regards the power and function of religion. Man's folly as the result of inexperience, undevelopment and ignorance is great and tragic. But if he is still too ignorant to correct the evil, there is nothing to do but accredit it to him as the best he could do and let him take the sorry consequences as best he may. But when he can see by merely looking at the conspicuous record that his infatuation with religion is a false leading, and that the religious development in history itself reveals the utter error and fatuity of his addiction to it, there is no justification of leaders in continuing to bind the masses to *further com-*

mitment to proven folly. The logical basis of this radical statement is Sir Gilbert's observation, so obvious if people will think beyond their noses, that since there are multitudinous religious cults of differing and *opposing* persuasions, at least half of them are at once convicted of being invincibly wrong; for if two systems are opposed to each other, at least one must be in error. Man has no way of avoiding a plunge into possible error when he can not be sure beforehand whether his contemplated course is right or not. But he has a means to put an end to a course which has already demonstrated its folly. With history's black pages open before us, a continuance in this brute madness must seem to all, as it did to Murray, the wickedness of the damned.

Challenged to outline a program which would end the dementia, we would answer with the obvious application of the open lesson of history itself. The world—or a section of it—once basked in the shining light of a wisdom that the gods themselves, we must believe, designed to impart to mankind for its guidance over the precarious path of human growth to divinity. We still have the tomes of this sage gift. We see now how closely the low ebb of intelligence and the upheaval of ignorance came to obliterating the light in those two fatal centuries, the third and the fourth of the Christian day. We see how the wrong promulgation of the mere husks of this divine message turned the world from truth to its deceptive mirages. The one sane thing to do is to let go of the mirages and come back to the reality of that ancient sunlight of man's morning. The literary lamps that kept that flame alight are, happily, still in our possession and Egypt has now instructed us how to relight them. But the same folly and perpetuated ignorance persists in keeping this benignant light under a bushel. It needs but to be set on the hill. The infinite calamity of the fourth century must be undone.

If the present appalling danger of the loss of civilization is in any measure due to the world's failure to venerate God, then the single point of wisdom indicated for us is to take the word of that one nation that had the intelligence to woo the divinity of man into its most beautiful expression in all history, the one nation that was in position to judge accurately—Greece. And that nation, as Sir Gilbert points out, called Christianity atheism!

The need plainly indicated, therefore, for the salvation of the world's culture is the complete, not partial and timid, Reformation of Christianity. Unless it is brought back to the forms and meanings which it

288

(under other names) bore in the early days, it will, in its present vitiated character, continue to pollute the Western mind with ideas that constitute the genuine atheism. For it continues to hold the mind at arms' length from the final realization that the saving power of divine light must be cultivated within the individual, and was not delivered to the world and made effective for its work by one person. Piety will go on in its futile way until it is really sanctified by the knowledge that it flows from within to outer conduct, and will never be won by pleadings to sources believed to lie without. Only by such an expression can the leaven of righteousness come to pervade society.

Christianity keeps blatantly accusing Greek esoteric philosophy of having failed the masses because it put the problem of personal salvation forth in terms of its knowledge of the multiple constitution of man by which salvation was to be implemented, a knowledge which demanded something in the way of erudition and intelligence to comprehend. Christianity took the simpler way of telling the masses that a man had come and he would do the complicated work in and upon them. Even untutored fishermen could see the ineffable light of divinity glowing in his features, shining in his words and acts. But in giving to the people a Savior in the person of a single historical character Christianity unwittingly robbed the masses of the knowledge of the one path by which alone salvation can be won by the human mortal, the path of self-evolution. It set them gaping in stupid wonder and grasping in pitiable hope at the Judean paragon, utterly bereft of any realization that their salvation from animal brutishness to human-divine graciousness is a work that must be consummated in every stage of its long progress by their rousing to consciousness the divinity slumbering within their own bosoms. Christianity turned the hopes, prayers and aspirations upon the man of Galilee; and this was their tragic following of the mirage. The mirage pictures wells of life-giving water in the skies of faith and belief in this Jesus. All the while the real water of life springing up on every side out of the common experience on earth was missed. The one solid fact, as alleged, that Christianity offered—the epiphany of divine salvation to man in one person in history—was from the first moment of its presentation and ever since, the one most fatal delusion of all time.

Christianity directed the eyes of the world to two explicit places where man could look to find his divinity: in the skies; and in one man in history. Both were false; both lured man away from his true direction of aim. Greek philosophy had indicated where alone it could be found,—in the soul of the individual. By its ignorant forsaking of the Greek wisdom it condemned humanity to two thousand years—and how many more?—of wandering in the darksome cave of Plato's splendid allegory, in suffering, wretchedness and horror past the telling. It condemned him to these centuries of the continued domination of his life by the instincts of the beast in his own nature; for it did not tell him that the Christ in history can do nothing for him until he himself tames the ferocity of the beast within him. It set the King of Glory on the throne in Jerusalem; but failed to persuade its millions to set this king on his proper throne in the human mind. This was the cost and the consequence of its revulsion against Greek esoteric wisdom. When Tertullian cried, What have Homer and Virgil to do with the Gospels or with Jesus? there was no voice to answer: "They have the fate of the West for two millennia at stake. They have the one possibility of the world's escape from unthinkable tragedy to do with it."

When the cry arose that with the coming of Christianity "Great Pan is dead," there was no voice to answer: Yes, woe is the world! Great Pan *is* dead, and twenty centuries will rue his passing. When on his death-bed the Emperor Julian is reported to have said—as cited jubilantly by Christians as the evidence of victory for their faith and poetic vengeance for one who tried to extinguish it—"The Galilean has conquered," there was no voice to shout back: Yes; too true! Too true! And now the world will reap the harvest of a mental infatuation that will blight the sanity of nations for sixteen centuries!

It is by no means surprising that a system so potent for misguidance of the lower orders, so grounded on a distortion of former high enlightenment, should have been at straits in nearly every period of its career to hold its power and smooth its way against disaffection, indifference or rebellion by resort to every type of duplicity and forgery in the catalogue. It has indeed a record for such chicanery as would require volumes to detail. And such volumes have been written. Nearly every historian not too preponderantly overweighted with bias to condone or skip this aspect of its history has had to include in his narration the regrettable chapter of what has come to be known as "pious frauds"; tampering with manuscripts, forgery of interpolations in documents, not to mention the wholesale concoction of entire "gospels" and "epistles," and the misrepresentations of historians like Eusebius, Hippolytus and Epiphanius. This story is well known; it is unimpeachable and indefensible, though ably apologized for and sometimes shamelessly condoned "for the glory of God and the faith." The plan and scope of this work militates against the devotion of a chapter to rehearse this segment of Christian history. It is real enough, true enough and appalling enough to shake the whole edifice of pious sacerdotalism based on it if the whole of it was widely known. It is doubtful whether in all history any movement of such volume in either the religious or the secular field of human activity ever won and held its power over millions by such an unending course of fraud and imposture, deception and dishonesty. And when these did not work productively enough, slaughter and extinction of opponents could be resorted to. It must be indeed an atrocious career about which a careful historian, Guignebert, can print without the possibility of a charge of slander or defamation such a summary passage as the following (op. cit., p. 248):

"It is a fact that they did derive advantage thus and so persistently that the Greeks have some little foundation for saying, as they do, that the fabrication of documents is the characteristic industry of Rome. At these inventions Gregory VII, as well as Nicholas I, will himself be caught, and all the other Popes throughout the Middle Ages."

If there is any historic application of the statement that we war against the powers of darkness in the air and spiritual wickedness in high places, this subtle nest of plotting and skulduggery in the headship of this ecclesiastical conspiracy must certainly be the chief object of the reference.

"Nearly every pontificate will add its supplement of false documents to this formidable *corpus,* whence the theologians, St. Thomas Aquinas among them, will for a long period confidently derive the justification for whatever the Roman pontiffs may desire to do or to say. Much more guilty than the forgers themselves are men such as Baronius, Bellarmin and different Jesuits who, in the sixteenth and seventeenth centuries, employ their erudition and their zeal in the face of considerations of fact and good sense which admit of no reasonable rejoinder, to bolster up a body of arguments for the sake of conclusions drawn from them which they could not consent to abandon."

And if the actuality of these disclosures, which must be new and incredible to most readers of our work, is not as yet impressed duly upon minds set to believe that the religion of the Christian Church has been developed and propagated by a "Christian" regard for integrity and decency, this final shocking revelation must certainly complete the realization of unwelcome truth (op. cit., p. 251):

"About the time of Gregory VII in particular (1073-1085) the work of forging false documents and their systematic utilization, i.e., fitting them together into a body of doctrine, reached a magnitude and a degree of openness absolutely stupefying."

"Towards the year 1140 the monk Gratianus, the first professor of canon law in the University of Bologna, blends together the earlier forgeries, adds others, and constitutes a *corpus* which becomes the legal framework of the 'papal system,' and of an 'authority' beyond dispute."

The authority and power of the pontiff *thus* built up, the manipulators find it not too difficult to represent it as having been so authenticated from the beginning. They "find" documents which leave it unquestioned that the Roman bishop was the supreme delegate of divine power on earth from the very beginning. By so scheming, Guignebert asserts, "they render the Pope a service, but not Christendom."

The lust for unified power was in no wise to be deterred or thwarted. It meant nothing to the power-hungry clique that rebellion of sensible honest groups or individuals against its arbitrary seizure of the religious hegemony was registered time and again in the later Middle Ages. Mystical religion, no matter how devoted to a system, must have unbounded freedom to adventure into its unbounded field of inner experience. It can not be hedged in by legalistic or doctrinal limitations. It must be free to roam at will over the limitless expanse of spiritual feeling and psychic vision. Hence groups of "the mystical unlearned" were constantly rising to challenge the prescribed boundaries charted around the province of the mind by ecclesiastical authority. It is surely significant that even then the Papal sovereignty, growing every decade more imperious, was regarded as an evil power in the world, even by its own loyal devotees. For Guignebert says that all these revolts "are inspired by unconquerable hatred of the established Church, in recoil from the luxurious and dissolute life of the clergy, all steeped in asceticism."

Here fall in line those later movements of groups here and there to revive and revitalize Manichaeism, and the still lingering memories and secret propagations of the Neo-Platonic wisdom. First come the Paulicians; then the Catharists and then the Albigensians, people inspired with as lofty and genuine a purpose to cleanse their lives in spiritual purity as mortals can ever well be. When their growth and influence could not be stopped by churchly mandate, Pope Innocent III cut the Gordian knot of scruple or hesitation with the brusque announcement that "it is necessary that the horrors of war should bring them back to the Church." Having crushed down the free spirit of Christly aspiration in men, imperfect in its expression, but evolving through the experience permitted by freedom, the ecclesiastical power dared not suffer its grip to be loosened in the slightest. Ruthless suppression was fully justified by the necessity of maintaining unbroken solidarity of the holy faith. Order, obedience, docility, submission must be kept intact at any cost. "Christ" would understand the holy motive that regrettably made murder necessary, and would bless the sacred intent. So Europe had to go down through the valley of everlasting ignominy and the shadow of nameless terror and slaughter before the terrified conscience of men was sufficiently aroused in Huss and Luther to rise and defy the wolf-monster of frightfulness masquerading in the clothing of the Lamb of God, the gentle Jesus.

There arose after the slaughter of the Albigensians such rebellious upheavals as those of the Waldensians, the Patarini of Milan, the Beguines (Lambert le Bègue), the Beghards, the Brethren of the Free Spirit and the Brothers and Sisters of the Common Life. All of these advocated a return to the Scriptures and to the freedom of the spirit as it sought union directly with the divine nature in transports of mystical exaltation.

Let imagination try to reconstruct the state of mental unbalance and spiritual hypocrisy in which an institution posing as the earthly custodian of true religion and arrogating to itself the shepherd control of man's conscious relation to the Creator, would justify its necessity of crushing down with savage butchery the sincerest upreachings of the souls of Europe's finest people in the name and for the love of the Christ! Our work is aimed to be the history of the dementia that contorted the aspirations of men in the fourth century into this wretched slavery to misconceived ideals of good. Civilization hardly less now than at any former time is menaced by the unbroken continuity of that same dementia.

These movements, continuing to spring up incessantly, were so persistent and

"this multiform agitation was so prevalent that it harries the Church without respite, at the very time when she seems to be most completely mistress of the thought and conduct of men, and all present philosophical thought and human science in revolt against orthodox dogma and revealed cognition."

We have here, of course, the growing resentment that was to explode finally in the sixteenth century in the Protestant Reformation. One needs not a score of books to make clear the prime motivations of this revolt. It was a fight to free the human mystical propensity from the fetters of an externalized authority or formal limitations and to emancipate from any external tyranny the spirit of innermost man. It was a fight to disburden the individual of the intermediary trappings and formalities by which an ecclesiastical power had asserted its right to regulate the communion of the spirit with Deity.

It is worthy of note, comments Guignebert, that most of the weighty doctrinal heresies originating in the intellectual circles of the Middle Ages took a pantheistic turn, and were definitely the product of the old Neo-Platonic spirit rediscovered once more either in the writings of Scotus Erigena or in those of the Arabian doctors. Amaury de Bène (died 1204) drew heavily upon Erigena's *De Divisione Naturae,* a work on Neo-Platonism. The "modernists" of Paris and Oxford maintained that "the Christian faith is an obstacle to the progress of knowledge." And it is significant that while the Archbishop of Paris, Etienne Tempier, condemns 919 Averroist errors in 1277, and the Archbishop of Canterbury does likewise, we note a sort of crusade in process of organization among the orthodox doctors against the "fresh spirit of unbelief which is filtering down from the Schools to the lower classes in the form of a gross materialism, to such a degree that the Inquisition will be forced to take note of it . . . in the beginning of the fourteenth century."

Then the Church had its hands full to combat a tendency of another sort, the status and influence of which are forever a matter of indeterminate evaluation. This is the unconquerable propensity of nearly every grade of human intelligence to indulge in one or another form of what is called the "occult." It is a region of interest and experience not far removed from the mystical, indeed a close brother to it. Some aspects of its exploitation are almost inescapable in even the most intelligent minds, for the "occult" forces are just the deeper and less commonly observable influences that activate feeling and conduct from within the psyche. Even the hardest headed in the modern age dominated by the scientific mood can no longer hold the "occult" in cold disdain, since modern psychological science has itself disclosed a whole world of unconscious sources of motivation lying underneath the open area of consciousness. Investigation of psychic awareness lying beyond the possible scope of intelligence obtained through the normal channels of the senses and reason, has been taken up by the universities. Man is recognized as being an entity related to other worlds or regions of consciousness beside the one he commonly contacts by means of his physical organism. There is danger that this epochal discovery may open the door to a new vogue of license in the mystic life, and threaten science's exact procedure in obtaining knowledge. However, the tremendous authority of science in the present age gives promise that advance of new investigation will proceed cautiously in this strange domain. At least there is the fortunate assurance that the most novel phenomena encountered in the search will not again generate that rueful horror of witch-burning and devil-exorcism that blackens the escutcheon of official Christianity with one of the most wretched of its many frightful inhumanities.

The Medieval Church was surrounded and harassed on all sides by all kinds of adversaries absorbed in this interest.

"The belief in the reality of occult forces, in the value of astrology, in the power of sorcery, was a bequest from antiquity; its adepts were to be found in all the nations; folklore helped to keep it alive with its innumerable legends, and it seemed to be confirmed by a mass of those hearsay experiences which strengthen in the simple-minded and the illiterate a dogmatic faith in the absurd . . . the conquest of the Western world by Christianity had not destroyed these older heterogeneous layers of varied superstitions."

This is the historian's version, no doubt, betraying something of his personal attitude to this aspect of "religion." The tendency, indeed the inevitable bent of the human mind to hypothecate the play of forces or intelligences in our lives in the realm of the unknown is ever a thing to be reckoned with. People have experiences which do not seem explicable on any of the known grounds of causation. Beings in a world invisible may be able to reach the human consciousness by short-length high-frequency waves of mind bearing messages. Telepathy under rigidly prescribed testing has not been too successful in positive demonstration. But spontaneous telepathy has established a record that can hardly be ignored. Science has not yet mastered the basic conditions of formal success. Man is obviously a citizen of more worlds than the one he commonly moves in. Hypnotism, still a science in swaddling clothes, has revealed incredible powers of a subconscious (or superconscious) intelligence within us. Inventors have found the elusive secrets of new mechanisms in their sleep, or worked out on awaking. Writers, musicians, artists, orators bring forth productions of a genius that is by no means their own normal reach of creative power. Sir Walter Scott, Coleridge, Blake and many more have written under the "drive" of a power that actually pushed aside their own minds and dictated its own versions, even guiding their pens as by an automatism. People with no skill or technique have suddenly rendered difficult musical compositions or painted pictures of real merit.

What is of great importance in all this is the challenge that it casts before humanity in this modern day, to see that this recrudescence of interest in supernormal (falsely called for so long the supernatural) activities of the psyche in man's composite consciousness be accepted in the spirit of scientific balance, and not again turned into a holocaust of ignominious persecution. Superstition unquestionably can all too easily becloud the reaction of thoughtless people to the incidence of such phenomena. But superstition has been no less evident and surely less pardonable in the exercise of ecclesiastical power through the inhuman savagery with which innocent young girls, lads, men and women who manifested psychic abilities were sacrificed on the altar of the Church's invincible regimentation. The despicable murder of Joan of Arc is still a shuddering memory, not one whit extenuated, but rather more heavily to be resented, by her later canonization.

We can fall back on Guignebert's language to conclude this part of the story:

"It is much more certain that the authority of the Church has deeply implanted in the credulous public and in the poor brains of the deranged this lamentable aberration of witchcraft. No better example can be cited to prove the extent to which the Church has failed to prevail with her infallible verities over the prejudices and errors of all the ages, but has on the contrary submitted to them and at times *systematized and justified* them."

"The shameful sore will go on spreading incessantly, particularly in the sixteenth century . . . the evils of all kinds and especially the horrible sufferings of miserable human beings for which the Church is responsible in this way can not easily be exaggerated. . . . The Church by its obstinate persecution of magic and witchcraft has already begun to struggle against science."

Truly enough there begins then that stubborn intransigency of the churchly power against the first and then the later waves of the movement of "modern science." Science threatened to break the hold of the absurd doctrinal theologies over the stupid mass mind. It must be resisted, turned back, defeated. No one can picture the horrific realities of this prolonged fight of "holy Church" against the advance of empirical science, which seemed so likely to rend its foul pretensions to bits, who has not read Draper's work on the conflict between religion and science and Andrew D. White's two monumental volumes on *The History of the Warfare Between Science and Theology in Christendom*. One need but picture Galileo writhing as the flames of the faggot pile crept closer to his flesh, martyred for having refused to recant his announcement that the earth revolved around the sun.

There is no question but that the upsurge, in spite of all the hellish devices of persecution, of science in the seventeenth century shook the power of the religious system to its base. Millions escaped from its tyranny, those who saw in science the sure grounds of the wholly preposterous "scheme of salvation." After fifteen centuries of fearful suppression, the mind of Europe began to tear free from its mental thongs to regain again the use of the sword of reason to cut its pathway out of the jungle of killing superstitions grown to rank exuberance through ages of stifling tradition and authority imposed on childhood.

The Inquisition had failed to crush the divine spirit in man. Since even its unforgettable savageries are being condoned and even denied, it might be well to hear again Guignebert's caustic summarization of it (p. 316):

"Pronouncing secretly and without right of appeal the most terrible penalties, it constitutes one of the most horrible inventions ever conceived by fanaticism in any age."

It might be added that the same power that executed this satanic inhumanity is grasping greedily still to obtain that predominance over the modern world that will enable it again to wipe away all civil rights of the individual and tyrannize once more over the minds of the people as it did in Medieval days. The part of the world that still believes it is free had better look to its liberties. They were lost in the third century and but barely regained in the eighteenth. The monster Ignorance, or the craft of those aiming to wield its massive power, is straining at the leash to grasp again the authority it held so long. The world struggle is always the warfare between intelligence and ignorance. The almost immovable obstacle thwarting the dawn of intelligence and equally bulwarking the cause of ignorance, is the great body of untutored, unawakened, undisciplined masses. It blocks every sacrificial heroism of its hopeful liberators; it kills its emancipators, as Socrates and Lincoln, and symbolically its Christs. Religion, insinuated into the sensitive mind of childhood, is the instrument by which, even though seductively interwoven with the beauty aspects of ritual, music and art, this

297

conspiracy of pietism aims to retain its hold on the populace in every generation, and by rapid birth accretion, gain voting strength and power. While philosophy, the true emancipator, is converted into idle speculation, or is as widely neglected as possible, religion gains the day.

True democracy aims to educate all its members and thus avoid the dangers that inhere in mass ignorance. But ecclesiastical authority, which desires to wield the power of the ignorant masses, discourages education, except such as will condition the mass mind to easier susceptibility to its program and shibboleths.

One of these shibboleths of the Church is that the sense of the sacredness of life which, as Fisher says, "prevails at the present day," is due to Christianity. Doubtless pious sentimentality has spread widely the ideal of life's worth. But the mawkish and revolting insincerity of such a claim, at any rate its shocking falsity, could be seen by any one who will look. A religion which, historians estimate, has been responsible for the deaths of fifty millions of people from bigotry and persecution even before the two mammoth holocausts of modern world war, which were bred and inaugurated by the leading Christian nations, with the Church either indisposed or helpless to avert them, should be ashamed to put forth the claim that it has inculcated in mankind a sense either of the dignity (another of its arrant and preposterous claims) or the sacredness of individual life. An institution which has never stopped at murder to gain its ends should not boast of its regard for the sacredness of life.

Perhaps the whole nub of the failure of Christianity, its fall into impossible Christianism, can be seen most vividly from a glance at one of those felicitous phrases which now and then flash into a mind and epitomize whole movements in history. Allan Upward says in his book, *The New World:*

"If the foregoing pages point to any truth, it seems to be that the Divine Man is a type of the divine *in* man."

This well condenses in a phrase the cause of Christian failure. Christianity took the type figure of the divine in man for the Divine Man. It exalted the alleged Divine Man (when not using him to excuse and exculpate its atrocities), but left the divine in man to grovel in the dust, even drove its spirit down to think of itself as a miserable worm. Christianity cut itself off from all possibility of commanding the loyalty of high intelligence and maintaining a connection with sanifying philosophy when it shifted the center of gravity, so to say, from the cult of the Christ within to that of the Christ without, or from the Christ as principle to Christ as a man. Christianity stakes its all on this displacement of human incentive and location of human power. Indeed this single aberration, by which it took a stand of utter uniqueness in its day or any other day, is in the finale the one mark of character that gives it noteworthy distinction from a number of other religious cults in its time. Those other systems strove to hold the understanding of the Christos-Messiah principle to the high level of its spiritual conception. The Orphic, Mosaic, Hermetic, Platonic, Pythagorean; the Gnostic, Essenian, Docetic; the Neo-Platonic, Stoic, Mithraic, Manichaean had presented the Christ as the ray of Divine Mind born and to be reared in the consciousness of the human race.

Naturally the masses can go only a certain length of the intellectual road toward entifying this principle beyond the stage of a remote abstraction. And abstrusities leave the lower ranks cold to religion of the philosophical kind. This condition confronted the world of intelligence with a constant problem, which it sought to meet generally by methods of esoteric polity. But whether through sheer chance or by a happy hit on a device that yielded unexpected results or by shrewd connivance, Christianity at a given point in its early career suddenly presented the Christ as a man. The effect began to be magical. The untutored could lay hold of the "personality" of Jesus with a human warmth with which it could never adopt the conception of the mystical Christ. It proved a ten-strike. It caught the fancy and aroused the sensitivities of the lowly. The Christ, the cosmic Logos, had been here on earth, in Galilee, in Jerusalem, had wrought wondrous miracles, had radiated blessing and divine grace, had been wickedly murdered while still blessing his enemies, had risen and ascended in glory to the skies—the whole scenario was overpowering in its human appeal. Where philosophy passed over the heads of the common people, the Gospel story, turned from dramatic suggestiveness to realistic "history," won the populace. No religion had ever brought divinity home to man on earth in the form of palpable history. This was something the common fancy could take hold of. And it was a thing to move the humblest to awesome reverence, to love and pity, to worship and loyalty. It swept over the multitudes, lighting its emotional fires in all hearts, inciting all minds; while poor philosophy could light a glow in but a rare mind here and there. And it won the day in the Roman Empire.

But thrice blind is he who would acclaim this as a victory for culture, for civilization, for humanity. The victory of Christianity wrote defeat for mankind. It was victory of the baser, the cruder, the elementary segment of human motivation over the refined, the disciplined, the cultured and reasoned way of life. This is the party of the first part in human nature which has always been winning its victories over the party of the second part, "the Lord from heaven," as Paul names it. But Christianity is the first party in history that has ventured to call it a victory for humanity. Philosophy, learning, intelligence, mystical profundity, spiritual purity were ruthlessly suppressed and driven underground, while fanaticism, bigotry, ignorance, intolerance and fraud reigned in insolent tyranny. And a thousand Christian publicists have hailed this as the greatest, the culminating victory for humanity.

Christianity won on those terms and on those grounds on which a prostitution of refined taste in beauty, truth and goodness to meet the levels of low appreciation of rude humanity will always win those whose preferences can not rise to higher things. It ever marks a deplorable turn in mankind's upward progress when culture has to give way to mass boorishness and go in retreat to esoteric sanctuary to wait until a new and perhaps fairer trial may be adventured.

Christianity's triumph was a harrowing victory for rampant pietism over studied intellection. The third century should ever be shrouded in the memory colors of gloom and mourning, for it witnessed the disappearance of philosophical enterprise for centuries. The present hope of perpetuating the very existence of mankind in a state of culture higher than barbarism depends upon breaking this spell of psychopathic hallucination under which the Council of Nicaea has laid the consciousness of the West since its fateful meeting. What the Occident should have learned from these centuries of tragedy is that religionism not balanced and sanified by philosophy and intelligence will plunge the world in wreck and ruin.

This work is the first effort to interpret the conquest of the Roman world by Christianity as a tragedy and not a great, far less the greatest, blessing for mankind. It is designed to point the way in which effort must now and quickly be made to end the run of evil consequence following that unfortunate debacle.

Forever must be dropped the wholly spurious tradition that Christianity came as the first burst of true light out of heathen darkness. It was a new departure only in the peculiar sense that it took off from long established and familiar bases and shot out in a direction never taken by a movement of any volume before. That direction was unique because, to a degree unparalleled in any previous time, it proceeded not forward to a clarification of something vague and less defined hitherto, but went in exactly the opposite direction, from clarity to befuddlement. It took a weird turn in an unheard-of direction, because it attempted to recast its Scriptural constitution in the terms of outer history, when they had hitherto only been applicable to the life of inner consciousness. It was a movement away from the light.

Christianity had to wait for its victory until in the long course of philosophical degradation the state of general culture in the East had sunk to the low ebb at which for the first time in all history the popular apprehension of the coming of the Christ-Messiah as the birth of a spiritual motif in all humanity was finally lowered to the birth of a babe in a Judean village. And what has happened since in the name of that babe proves its calamitous character.

CHAPTER XIV

THE MYTH-GHOSTS WALK ABROAD

Christianity was in no wise new, since it was a reissuing, in the main, of ancient Egyptian lore. Says Allan Upward (op. cit., p. 222):

"When the test of emotion is applied to it, Christianity stands revealed as an Egyptian faith. Those cries of the soul that were heard in the liturgies of Osiris have passed into the Psalms of Zion and into the Christian liturgy. The pilgrimage and warfare of the soul is the theme that underlies all the astrological and all the historical allegory. The inspired prisoner who wove The Pilgrim's Progress (as he tells us) out of the substance of his dreams, has reproduced with marvelous fidelity the very incidents of the initiation ceremonies of ancient Egypt almost in the language of the *Book of the Dead*."

The same writer, standing in the Niger Valley of Africa, wrote:

"Elsewhere I trod a green hill outside a city wall, whereon a man had been sacrificed at Easter from time immemorial."

In his *The Divine Mystery* (p. 217) he says:

"In the meanwhile the originals of whole chapters of *Genesis* and whole sections of the Mosaic law have been deciphered amid the dust of Babylon. A vivid light has been thrown on the Canaan of the fifteenth century B.C. by the discovery of correspondence between the petty kings of the country and their Egyptian overlord; and it reveals the whole region at the very time assigned by the legend for the exploits of the mythical Joshua, already inhabited by a population which wrote the Hebrew language in the Babylonian script."

Little by little the historical foundations of the Christian hypothesis crumble away, leaving nothing but the original myth and allegory whose lucid interpretations will restore Christianity to its original light and power.

Joseph Klausner in his *Jesus of Nazareth* (p. 107), referring to Joseph Salvador, says:

"He finds the whole of the 'Sermon on the Mount' in Ben Sara, so anticipating Kalthoff."

"Salvador explained that much of what was told of the birth, death and resurrection of Jesus was derived not from the Old Testament, but from Oriental and contemporary Greek mythology. In this and also in explaining the genesis of Christianity from the pagan religious corporations (*thiastoi*), Salvador anticipated the celebrated writings of Pfleiderer, from whom Kalthoff drew most of his ideas."

More pointed than this is the outspoken opinion of Graetz, tne profound investigator of the German group. Says Klausner:

"Graetz frankly acknowledges that even what seems most certain in the study of the life of Jesus has only the value of an hypothesis. The sole historical fact we possess is that Christianity arose out of Essenism." He calls Christianity "Essenism mixed with foreign elements."

Klausner states that Graetz' grounds for his tracing Christianity to Essenian origins are the fact that

"John the Baptist, who paved the way for Jesus' manifestation, was an Essene in all his manner of life, and that James, the Lord's brother, who led the Church after the crucifixion, had all the habits of an Essene; and that even the entire Church . . . behaved in all respects like an Essene community."

It is doubtful if too much credit can be granted such speculations and conjectures as these, for the extreme likelihood is that all these characters are *dramatis personae* out of the old religious dramas, like the Prodigal Son. What may be well conceived to be a connection with historical truth is that the first pious Christians were a cult of much the same order and purpose as the Essenes. Graetz could be right in assuming that it started as a cult of Essenism, with much evidence tending to prove that, whatever it was at the outset, it soon mixed with "foreign elements."

The work of G. Friedlaender, *The Jewish Sources of the Sermon on the Mount,* says Klausner,

"shows with much authority that not only the Sermon on the Mount, but the entire Christian system (excluding its asceticism) is borrowed from the Old Testament, the *Book of Ben Sira, The Testaments of the Twelve Patriarchs,* Philo of Alexandria and the earlier portions of the Talmud and Midrash."

Similarly precise corroboration of our thesis is found in Klausner's saying that Abraham Geiger agrees with Graetz in thinking that in Jesus' teaching

303

"there is either nothing new or that what is new is put before us in a somewhat enervated form just as it originated during an enervated period." (From Geiger's *Das Judentum und Seine Geschichte*, p. 119.)

That Christianity was just a weird and twisted malformation of old truth by an enervated mentality in an enervated period (Cf. Murray's "failure of nerve") is the theme of this portion of our work. The astute German critics evidently inclined to this opinion.

What else would dispose another erudite German scholar, Chwolson, to say (a specially noteworthy observation) that

"rightly to understand Pauline and post-Pauline Christianity, a knowledge of the Sibylline Oracles, Philo and Greek literature generally is most important"?

Josephus and Zeller endeavor to show that the line of development from esoteric secrecy out into more general deployment came originally through Pythagorean channels.

Klausner asserts that "Christianity therefore drew from Essenism for a short time before Jesus and immediately after the death of Jesus." But what could be the meaning of "Christianity . . . before Jesus"? Christianity was not predicated as being in existence before Jesus founded it!

Klausner traces other points of resemblance between the early Christians and the Essenes. But the Essenes maintained strictly their high standards of mental and spiritual culture and lived within monastery walls and colonies. The Christians certainly did not long hold this status in common with them. In fact they soon became the antithesis of nearly everything the Essenes stood for, including esotericism, allegorism, mysticism, philosophy, study, libraries and a certain exclusiveness based on qualification. The Christians soon let down all bars, opened all doors, reached out and embraced the lowest and least disciplined of men.

The finality of Klausner's strong statement should not be missed (op. cit., p. 384):

"Yet, with Geiger and Graetz, we can aver, without laying ourselves open to the charge of subjectivity, and without any desire to argue in defence of Judaism, that throughout the Gospels there is not one item of ethical teaching which can not be paralleled either in the Old Testament, the Apocrypha or in the Talmudic and Midrashic literature of the period near the time of Jesus."

"Every single clause in 'the Lord's Prayer' is, however, to be found in Jewish prayers and sayings in the Talmud."

Since the whole position of Christianity rests on "the divinity of Jesus," it is quite pertinent to consider what Gerald Massey has to reflect on this feature. In *The Historical Jesus and the Mythical Christ* (p. 22), he writes:

"It is not I that deny the divinity of Jesus the Christ; I assert it! He never was and never could be any other than a divinity, that is, a character non-human and entirely mythical, who had been the pagan divinity of various pagan myths, that had been pagan during thousands of years before our era."

And it is brought out that the Christian Father Justin Martyr (*Apol.* ii) incautiously admits that this rite, in which bread and wine are partaken of as symbolical of the flesh and blood of the Sun-God, had been celebrated from time immemorial in the Mysteries and ministrations of Mithras.

Even such a renowned modern Christian theologian as Benjamin Bacon (*Jesus and Paul*, 77) says:

"It may help us to know that Philo, thirty years before this time had already advanced the doctrine of a transfiguration of Moses through his intercourse with God, and that Philo always makes this Moses' preparation for immortality. Describing his departure into heaven at the summons of the Father, Philo declares that by the vision of God Moses' soul and body had been blended into a single new substance, an immortal mind-substance having the appearance of the sun." (Matching the features of Jesus' transfiguration, to the letter.)

If Christians—and all others—but recognized it, there is here the complete resolution of all Christian systematism, theology and creed back into the old sun-worship of ancient Paganism. For this merging of the human into the divine in the final union, or marriage, of male spirit with female matter, is the essence of the much-derided "heathen" sun-cult worship. If Christianity had ever possessed the insight to discern the great reality concealed behind the forms of ancient sun-worship—the spiritual cosmic sun and not merely the physical solar orb— it would have maintained the high glory of the arcane sapiency of yore and spared the later world its orgies of blood-baptisms.

In his *Jesus and Paul* Benjamin Bacon, noted Yale theologian, admits that Paul clothed his teaching in "the figures of speech which he borrowed from Hellenistic religion." "He is speaking that which he knows and has seen, even if he is driven for expression to language borrowed from Hellenistic faiths." Bacon does not glimpse that Paul's background was the Hellenistic systems and not Jerusalem Christianity at all. He employed these formulae of the Mystery cults because they were the coin current among the groups seeking true spiritual culture in his day.

J. M. Robertson, who with Drews and W. B. Smith of Tulane University, some decades ago put the Christian system under a severe challenge to uphold the historicity of the Gospels, is decisive in his final assertion that

"In short, the Christian system is a patchwork of a hundred suggestions drawn from pagan art and ritual usage."

And he proclaims openly and unhesitatingly that ignorance got the upper hand, took the body of myths and turned them into the "history." Paul had set forth how that the heavenly Messiah, in his descent from the empyrean, had been stripped of his celestial glories and reduced to a state of "poverty" on earth. So, says Robertson, when the myth was altered to read as history, "Christ was turned into a poor man in the economic sense of the word, while Joseph, the divine artificer and father of the sun, became an ordinary carpenter."

The arguments advanced by Robertson, Drews, Smith and Dupuis have been countered by many Christian writers contending for the absolute historicity of the Gospels. But their protestations for the historicity are refuted by the amazing veridical situation itself: the Gospel stories that they contend can stand on their own feet as positive historical occurrences on given days and dates at given localities still pointed out to tourists, very surprisingly are found to be but copies of allegories now brought to light through the discovery of the Rosetta Stone and the Behistun Rock in Mesopotamia. If myths afloat for centuries in Chaldea and Egypt did not become concreted into alleged history, how is one to account for the fact that the actual "history" only repeats the myths? Few realize it, but the Christian system will stand or fall according to the way it ultimately decides to meet the challenge of this modern denouement. It has held off the fateful decision till now only because so few are in possession of the data that constitute the challenge.

One of Robertson's sharpest critics, T. J. Thorburn, in a work called *The Mythical Interpretation of the Gospels,* admits that it was "simple folk who formed the bulk of the earliest converts to Christianity," but does not see that this would vastly increase the probability of their misinterpreting myth as true history. He is right in saying that it is not likely that myths would be pruned down so as to be rendered acceptable to thinking people. But it was not thinking people who did accept the myths as history. They were forced out of the religion just because they could *not* accept the "fables of the Church" as history. It is not a process of "pruning down" that makes myths acceptable to thinking people, but a process of profound analysis of the elements of the myth that makes them luminous to understanding of the cryptic message they convey. The myths were accepted as history only by the fanatics who had so far set aside what reason they might have exercised and reduced their minds to that state in which the belief in the factuality of the myths became a tragic possibility. This sad collapse of reason accounts in full for the debacle of sanity in the third century and the consequent launching of a body of weird beliefs that till then had never been accepted even by ignorant people, much less by the thinking class.

The myths were extant and afloat for hundreds of years before the Christian era, with nobody, unless only the most abjectly ignorant, mistaking them for history. But finally they began to be taken for objective events. What is the only sane conclusion that properly explains such a denouement? Surely nothing but that after performing their proper service and function as myths for many ages, they finally fell upon an era of degenerate mentality so blunted and blinded that their esoteric non-historical nature could no longer be made understandable, and minds wanting in keenness at last accepted their objective historicity.

In his *Christianity and Mythology* J. M. Robertson (pp. 82, 85) writes:

"That Joshua is a purely mythical personage was long ago decided by the historical criticism of the school of Colenso and Kuenen; that he was originally a solar deity can be established at least as satisfactorily as the solar character of Moses, if not as that of Samson"—whose very name is from the Hebrew *shemesh,* the sun.

And how can such a datum as the following be ignored as of little effect upon Christian foundations, when Thorburn cites Robertson as saying:

"The cave of Bethlehem had been from time immemorial a place of worship in the cult of Tammuz, as it actually was in the time of Jerome; and as the quasi-historic David bore the name of the sun-god Daoud, or Dodo (Sayce, *Hibbert Lectures*, pp. 56-7), who was identical with Tammuz, it was not improbable on that account that Bethlehem was traditionally the city of David, and therefore, no doubt, was deemed by the

New Testament myth-makers the most suitable place for the birth of Jesus, the mythical descendant of that quasi-historic embodiment of the god Tammuz or Adonis."

As Bethlehem yields unshakable connections with myth long antecedent, likewise does Nazareth. From data given us by Epiphanius (*Haer.* xxix, 6) brotherhoods or sects of religionists under the name of *Nazaraioi* (Nazoreans) had existed in pre-Christian times. Drews ventures the likely surmise that "Nazareth took its name from the sect of Nazoreans instead of the reverse, as is admitted by so distinguished a scholar as W. Nestle." And Epiphanius gives out the startling datum that "all men called the Christians Nazoraeans" in his time. Again he writes: "The heresy of the Nazarees *was before Christ,* and knew not Christ." The Arabian name for Christians was "Nasara."

Authority supports Massey's statement that "the doctrine of the incarnation had been evolved and established in the Osirian religion at least four thousand and possibly ten thousand years before it was purloined and perverted in Christianity."

Massey's life-long pursuit of Egyptian wisdom left his mind with no escape from the knowledge that the Mosaic *corpus* of mythic literature in the Pentateuch derived from Egypt.

"A profound study of the Ritual reveals the fact that the wisdom of Egypt was the source and fountain-head of the books of wisdom assigned to Moses and David, to Solomon and *Jesus;* and also proves the personages and characters to have been Egyptian. It is chiefly the wisdom of Egypt that gives a value to the Hebrew writings."

A systematic study of Philo would clinch the correctness of these assertions.

A fair section of modern scholarship has heard these most sincere and voluminously corroborated protestations of this scholar and has treated them as so much froth and vaporing of a misguided zealot and enemy of Christianity. Outside of his mislocation of *Amenta,* the Egyptian "underworld," in the world beyond the grave instead of here on earth—a mistake made by every other Egyptologist down to the present—Massey's insight into what the religion of Egypt was presenting to the human mind was so superior to that of the more noted investigators that beside his monumental analyses their light is almost total darkness. And the day may happily be not far removed when his six prodigious volumes will be held as treasures beyond estimate, and reprinted.

Lack of space forbids unfolding the full thread of the reasoning by which he pretty clearly proves that the alleged three years of the Lord's ministry was a fallacious development from the Old Testament phrase, "the acceptable year of the Lord." In the symbolic language of ancient Scripture both "year" and "day" stand for any completed cosmic or evolutionary cycle. So the divine soul's cycle of ministry to the lower element in human nature was termed his "year." Likewise his ministry effectuated the development in man of the four prime grades of conscious power, sense, emotion, thought and spiritual will; which were poetically likened unto the course of the four seasons of the year. Then, too, this ministry was to unfold in man the full glory of twelve rays of divine consciousness, completing the twelve months. Further, as the trinitarian aspect of divine emanative energy was always prominently accentuated, by a quirk of misunderstanding hard to locate but easy to imagine, the "year of the Lord" was at some time converted into three years, and from emblemism was turned into history.

After tracing seemingly endless items of resemblance or identity between the Horus-Christ of Egypt and the Gospel Jesus, Massey ends by saying:

"The catacombs of Rome are crowded with the Egypto-Gnostic types which had served to Roman, Persian, Greek and Jew as evidence for the non-historic origins of Christianity."

The child-Horus of Egypt reappears as the mummy-babe in the catacombs.

And who can be obtuse to the pointed significance of tne item Massey now presents? "There is neither date nor history of Horus between the age of twelve and thirty years." Never have Christian theologians been able to "explain" either to themselves or to others this long and singular lacuna in the history of their Gospel Savior, eighteen years from puberty to full manhood. This bafflement was inevitable for the very simple reason that what is composed of the tenuous essence of allegory can not be explained as history.

And what can be the answer to such a challenge to every one of Christianity's historic claims as this from Massey's researches?

"The story of the Annunciation, the miraculous conception (or incarnation), the birth and the adoration of the Messianic infant had already been engraved in stone and represented in four consecutive scenes upon the innermost walls of the holy of holies (the Meskhen) in the temple of

Luxor, which was built by Amen-Hotep III about 1700 B.C., or some seventeen centuries before the events depicted are commonly supposed to have taken place."

And some day not too far distant the fateful character of Massey's concluding paragraph of his stupendous work, *Ancient Egypt, the Light of the World,* will be recognized as not the ranting of an over-wrought scholar, but the oracular pronouncement of sober and sobering truth:

"From this we learn by means of comparative process that the literalizers of the legend and the carnalizers of the Egypto-Gnostic Christ have but gathered up the empty husks of Pagan tradition, minus the kernel of the Gnosis; so that when we have taken away all which pertains to Horus, the Egypto-Gnostic Jesus, all that remains to base a Judean history upon is nothing more than the accretion of blindly ignorant belief; and that of all the Gospels and collections of 'Sayings' derived from the Ritual of the resurrection in the names of Mati or Matthew, Aan or John, Thomas or Tum, Hermes, Iu-em-hetep or Jesus, those that were canonized at last as Christian, are the most exoteric, and therefore the farthest away from the underlying, hidden, buried, but imperishable truth."

How one item of the dramatic ritual was converted into "history" can be plainly seen when the name and role of the Gospel Herod is scrutinized:

"The name of Herod in Syriac denotes a red dragon; and the red dragon in *Revelation,* which stands ready to devour the young child that is about to be born, is the mythical form of the Herod who has been made historical in our Gospels."

To strengthen this inference, already well grounded on comparative religion studies, is the additional fact that the same red dragon, or evil serpent of the lower nature in man, is in the Egyptian myths the monster Apap (Apep, Apepi) whose other name is found to be the Herut reptile! When also the name for the "dense sea" (of matter) under which the Christ aeon was said to suffer in its incarnation is seen appearing in old creedal formulae as the Greek *pontos piletos,* and we have thus the entirely non-historical origins of "Pontius Pilate" along with "Herod" in the Gospel framework, there is a clear challenge to the upholders of the historicity of the Gospels to explain how these two names, the one threatening the Christos in its infancy, the other carrying him to his death, have found their way into the story in precisely the same place, role and character as the two non-historical elements of the names!

Alluding to the Greek myth of Heracles and the Hindu one of Krishna, Edward Carpenter (*Pagan and Christian Creeds,* 245) writes these words which fall with entire agreement into the structure of theses we are establishing:

"What we chiefly notice so far are two points: on the one hand the general similarity of these stories with that of Jesus Christ; on the other their analogy with the yearly phenomena of nature as illustrated by the course of the Sun in heaven and the changes of vegetation on the earth."

On these two features—identity of construction and conformity with nature—the entire fabric of ancient religious formulations, so far as they could be embalmed in literature or representation, was solidly based. But both these absolutely fundamental generic elements, indispensable for interpretation by later ages, fell out of the purview of the Christian mind. Both went into desuetude and oblivion. And the engines of persecution were turned against any group or individual who strove, under the impulsion of the spirit of truth and the spur of true knowledge, to restore them to their proper place at the corner of the temple of understanding.

And what becomes of the raucously insistent claims of this religious establishment to the sole uniqueness of all its creeds and dogmas in the face of this pronouncement from one of its three greatest witnesses and advocates in the whole second century, Justin Martyr? He tells the Romans that by

"declaring the Logos, the first-begotten of God, our Master Jesus Christ, to be born of a virgin mother, without any human mixture, and to be crucified and dead, and to have risen again and ascended into heaven, we say no more than what you say of those whom you style the sons of Jove."

And can such an accredited item of fact in the descent of Christian doctrine from antecedent forms as the following from Massey be ignored? (*Natural Genesis,* 1-32.)

"But it is well known as a matter of history that the worship of Isis and Horus descended in the early Christian centuries to Alexandria, where it took the form of the worship of the Virgin Mary and the infant Savior and so passed into the European ceremonial. We have, therefore, the Virgin Mary connected by linear succession and descent with that remote zodiacal cluster in the sky." (Referring to the constellation Virgo.)

Here one sees a bit of the part played by the second element pointed out by Carpenter just now, the association and vital kinship between ancient religious types and external nature.

Again this feature is brought out in strong light when we consider that late summer festival known as the Assumption of the Virgin, a cardinal institute of the Catholic Church and still noticed by the Anglican and some Protestant bodies, though apparently in complete innocence of its signification! To typify the reabsorption of primal matter, the "virgin" substance, the first pure mother of life, back into the all-capacious bosom of cosmic being at the end of the cycle of manifestation or creation, the sagacious ancient seers fell back upon that demonstration of nature's energies which is the phenomenon of the physical order at the very end of the yearly cycle of the sun, when the luminary has returned to the heights of heaven after its wintry immersion in the round of "death" and limitation in darkness. There is enough of suggestion and instruction in this one doctrine alone to illumine the stolid mind of Christian dogmatism with a conception that would revolutionize the entire science of religious methodology. For the doctrine of the Assumption can have no rational resolution of meaning as long as the "virgin" is taken as a historical woman! Only as the type of matter in its first and "unpolluted" state of "virginity," allegorically considered, and standing as the figure of cosmic motherhood, can the Assumption dogma have not only sane signification, but any acceptation at all. The hollowness and total fatuity of thinking that the woman Mary was absorbed into the August skies must be apparent to any person who still retains normal faculty. Yet nature shows us every summer, in the Dog Days (the heliacal rising of the great Dog-star Sirius) how water-vapor, the natural symbol of virgin matter, *is* absorbed into the capacious expanse of the heated air and the solar rays. The ancient conception was the reabsorption of the virgin matter (Latin *mater,* mother) "into the rays of her own Son" (Sun). Here is sense and sanity; the other way leads to nonsense and insanity. Such wreckage of high typings of truth has Christianity foisted upon the world as its surpassing wisdom.

Perhaps this is the place to inject that rebuke and censure that Christian interpretative theology so roundly has earned by its age-long obtuseness, incapacity and recalcitrancy in respect to the perfectly obvious implications of comparative religion study. How the completely conclusive case for the uniformity of the myths of all lands, their descent from a common mental origin and their unanimity in proclaiming the same one body of high truth could have been ignored in spite of evidence that is more than overwhelming to every honest mind that has ever looked broadly over the field, is a thing that seems past comprehension. The conclusion is obvious that there has been present and in ceaseless play a force of deliberate obduracy adequate to achieve the determined stand against recognition of a situation that would be subversive of organic religion if honestly recognized. But the spectacle of the suppression of truth and fact is not pleasant. Sooner or later sincerity must force the issue.

And what would be the challenge to both intellect and conscience in Christendom as they confront the picture of Prometheus, the first and greatest benefactor of mankind, nailed by the hands and feet, and with arms extended, on the rocks of Mt. Caucasus, with the sobering reflection that beyond question Prometheus (Forethought, the primeval Idea), with his brother Epimetheus (Afterthought, or the manifest universe), can not be taken as living historical persons? When it is clearly seen that the continued ignoring of these items of comparative religion lead to the stultification instead of the edification of humans, one must ask how long the stubborn obstinacy generated by the fear of what such data could do to pious religious legends turned to "history" is going to continue.

Then there is a doctrine which, if it had not fallen quite into oblivion in the Christian system, would likewise trace its origin incontrovertibly to ancient Pagan forms,—the doctrine of the dismemberment of the god or the Christ node of mind upon its descent into the human flesh. As the Titans tore the body of Bacchus into fragments—later to be united again by Apollo—and the evil power of Sut dismembered the body of Osiris into fourteen pieces—to be reconstituted by Thoth "whole and entire"—so the Christ, breaking a loaf, intimated that his (spiritual) body, too, was "broken" for us, and that we in the unity of the reconstituted wholeness of our divine principle were to bring a "re-membrance" of his dismantled nature; since we are all members of his one body, and in re-membering or re-collecting our own scattered segments we resurrect him.

Edward Carpenter goes into the matter of the long-previous hope of the nations of antiquity of the coming of the Messiah-Savior. He enlarges on the item by saying that this doctrine, which is commonly believed to be distinctive of Christianity and Judaism, "comes down from the remotest times, and perhaps every country in the world. The Messianic prophecies of the Jews and the fifty-third chapter of *Isaiah* emptied themselves into the Christian teachings."

So reliable an authority as Papias emphatically declares that the Christian Gospels were founded on and originated in the *Logia,* or sayings of the Lord, remnants of such *Logia* having been found quite apart from any inclusion in the Gospels. Massey connects Matthew with the Egyptian *Mati,* or utterances of truth by the goddess of the balance, *Maat;* also with *muthoi* (*mythoi*), as the etymological ground of "myth" and "mythology." The Greek *meta* also, he avers, is cognate with *Maat,* since *Mati* in Egyptian means that perfect measure of balance between right and wrong which becomes the eventual definition of right and true. Utterances are not true unless they express this exact measure of the equilibrium between higher and lower, spiritual and material, on the line of which boundary normal evolution can alone advance.

How Christianity has spread abroad the claim that it has offered to humanity the assurance of resurrection for the souls of the deceased from the grave of rock or of earth by having based its very existence on the fact of a corporeal resurrection of the divine-human Son of God, is well known. It has staked its all upon this feature; for, says Paul, "if Christ be not risen, then is our faith vain." But again derivation and not origination of a new fact never demonstrated before, but now based on a historical reality, is indicated by the massed data of comparative religion. The soul's "death" in incarnation and its resurrection from this "death" on the cross of matter, had been memorialized in ancient systems from a distant past. The ancient Egyptian, no less than his late Christian copyist, had the assurance that he would rise from this death on the cross of incarnation, because the myths and rituals had represented Osiris as rising anew to life from his dismembered and deadened condition under the limitations of the flesh. And what the Egyptian knew that his Christian imitator did not, was that the Osiris whose death and resurrection were thus portrayed was the divine element within his own constitution and not a man perishing on a wooden cross and pushing away a rock from his hillside tomb two days later.

This same cross on which the Christian believed his personal Master had groaned in physical anguish had been an emblem in nearly every religion of the world for ages past.

Is it to be taken without significant implications that the founder of Christian theology, Augustine, naively confesses that it was by means of the Platonic system that he was enabled to understand properly the great doctrine of the Trinity, which became the bone of contention between two split sections of the Church and threatened to rend it in pieces for over two hundred years? It is hardly questionable that there is almost no clear and specific comprehension of this mystery dogma in Christian minds today, the true elucidation of it having been made impossible by the rejection of all Platonic philosophy in the third century, and the keys having been lost by the time Plato's *Timaeus* was later made the manual for a deeper survey of Christian doctrine. And the Church stands in the anomalous and ridiculous position of having to go back and call upon the resources of a system she has spurned in order to find the light to clarify her own doctrines.

Justin Martyr also had come into Christianity with the enlightenment that he had derived from Platonism. It is superfluous to mention Pantaenus, Clement, Origen, who brought to Christian exposition the luminous principles they had gleaned from Philo's work, who in turn was revitalizing more ancient wisdom in a syncretism of its profoundest expressions from Egypt and Greece with the Mosaic stream.

What becomes of the Christian claim that it alone—if the Hebrew antecedents are comprehended in its system—gave the world the conception of Monotheism, when Budge, the great authority on Egyptian studies, can write (Introduction to the *Book of the Dead,* xciv) this sentence?

"At all events the One God of the Egyptians possessed all the essential attributes of the Christian God."

And what possibilities of a needed rectification in conventional views as to the "primitive" origin of tribal religions, which it is the Christian and general academic custom to scan with the condescending interest of an entomologist studying an insect, might be opened up if the full involvements of the following passage from Budge's other great work, *Osiris and the Egyptian Resurrection* (Vol. II, p. 201), were given their due meed of attention:

"Wherever we find fetishism it seems to be a corruption or modification of some former system of worship rather than the result of a primitive faith . . . the people might forget the doctrine, and their ancestral figures, amulets, etc., would then degenerate into fetishes; authorities on modern African religions tell us that this is exactly what has taken place among the peoples of West Africa."

And this tell-tale excerpt is strengthened by the testimony of a Col. Ellis who states that there is more fetishism among the Negroes of the West Indies who have been Christianized for more than half a century than there is among those of West Africa; for side by side with the newly implanted Christianity have lingered the old superstitions, whose true import has been forgotten or corrupted.

How close this analysis comes to fitting, or in fact being a true description of, Christianity itself this work may possibly establish. If there is one thing that can be predicated and sustained by multitudinous evidences, it is that Christianity is a system of doctrines so contorted from original sense to outrageous illogicality that they are properly described as superstitions whose once truly apprehended import has become lost or corrupted.

If Massey is not penning a madman's ravings, what is to be done about the truth of such a disclosure as is contained in the following from his *The Natural Genesis* (Vol. II, p. 378)?

"The *Revelation* assigned to John the Divine is the Christian form of the Mithraic Revelation. In the Parsee sacred books the original Scriptures are always quoted and referred to as the 'Revelation.' . . . And the *Bahman Yasht* contains the same drama of mystery that is drawn out and magnified in the book of *Revelation*. . . . The personages, scenes, circumstances and transactions are identical in both. Each revelation relates to the Kronian allegory and in both the prophecy is solely astronomical."

The God Agni of the Hindu system is sevenfold in constitution. Does this hold any menace to the Christian scheme? Only if that scheme persists in claiming that it presented formulas of truth never known or understood before. Nearly every deity of Pagan religions was described as a Oneness (Monotheism) manifesting seven distinctive creative forces, like white light and its seven segmentations of color. Christianity chants its seven Archangels before the throne of God, but hesitates to give them proper place and importance in its scheme, lest it take even half a step toward polytheism. That these were the seven primary differentiations of the first Oneness is scarcely understood in Christian circles even today. And that these seven physically creative powers, called in all old religions the Seven Elementaries, when united in operation, as they are in man's own constitution as in the cosmos at large, with the Trinity of spiritual intelligences constituting the divine soul of life, give us the meaning at last of the Beast with seven heads and ten horns of *Revelation,* is likewise still a dark mystery in Christian minds. Christianity must face the humiliation of turning back and learning what the despised Pagans knew if it is to redeem its own dogmas from sheer gibberish.

Scorning astrology as heathen superstition, it will have to scan the zodiac and re-learn the symbolism of Pisces and the star Fomalhaut, in the mouth of the Southern Fish constellation, and the River Eridanus (the Jordan) which flows out of this *piscis vesica* or fish's mouth and runs clear up to the feet of Orion, and which must be traversed or "crossed" by all souls to pass over the watery course of evolution from their birth out of matter up to their deification in and as Orion, the Christ, if it is to understand why its own Founder and Savior was called by the Greeks Ichthys (Greek, "fish"), the Divine Fish, and why the twelve disciples were "fishermen," and much more of its own detail in the Gospels.

How thoroughly early Christianism was dominated by its inheritance from Pagan influences is clearly shown by Massey's statement in *The Natural Genesis* that as late as the fifth century A.D. the Pope was compelled to rebuke the "pestiferous persuasion" of those Christians who kept on celebrating Christmas day not for the birth of Jesus Christ, but for the solstitial resurrection of the sun. As has been so often admitted by its proponents, Christianity was almost wholly unable to shake its converts loose from their hereditary or ancestral customs and traditions, and had to try as best it could to interpolate its doctrinal ideas into the frame of established and unchangeable usage, the inner purport of which, as in present-day Yuletide ritualism, actually belied or negated the very principles of the new faith. It is in reality not carrying the case too far to assert that in much of its ceremonial still adhering to it from Pagan custom Christianity dramatizes meanings virtually subversive of its own accepted beliefs.

The Egyptologist Wilkinson, commenting on the role of Osiris in the Egyptian religion, as matching that of Christ in the Christian, remarks on the similarities between the two, suggesting that one has no escape from thinking that the Egyptians were aware of the promises regarding the real Savior and had anticipated the event, writing of it as if it had already taken place and constituting it a part of their religious system. If these parallels are so extensive and challenging as to lead the mind of a scholar to so firm a conviction, the fact of their virtual identity should be given the weight due so significant a circumstance. Massey has listed so many of these correspondences that for him the case for the derivation of the later Christian from the earlier Egyptian was closed past all controversy. As the vast body of evidence he has assembled would close the case likewise for his readers, it was found necessary to derogate his work and permit it to gather dust on library shelves.

Von Mosheim, who obviously felt his obligation to give the truth as investigation brought it to light, says that the monks of early Christianity, first appearing in Egypt, seem to have taken as their models of the monastic life the Essenes, the practical mystics of the Judean nation for many centuries.

"Indeed," he says, "the account given us by Josephus of the latter corresponds so exactly with the institutions and habits of the early votaries of monachism that it is impossible for any two things more nearly to resemble each other."

Even in another not too praiseworthy feature that has received scant notice in the histories the Pagans were copied. Says Mosheim (*History*, Vol. I, p. 110):

"Since it has been pretty clearly ascertained that the same spirit of vainglory which prompted ancient nations to pronounce themselves the offspring of the soil, or the descendants of the gods, found its way into the churches of Christ and induced many of them to suppress the truth and claim for themselves a more illustrious origin than in reality belonged to them."

And this historian gives the position of one of the Christian religion's greatest early Fathers, Clement of Alexandria. This renowned and learned Christian teacher says (*Stromata* I, cap. 1, p. 326) that he would not hand down Christian truth pure and unmixed, but "associated with or rather veiled by and shrouded under the precepts of philosophy." He even says that the basic *archai* of the Christ's teachings lay hid in the philosophy of the Greeks, as the edible part of the nut lies concealed within the shell. He has convinced himself that the essence of the Greek philosophy was sound, wholesome and salutary, perfectly accordant with Christian wisdom. He even goes so far as to say that the Greek system had emanated from the same divine source as had the Christian and, coming earlier, had constituted the basis of the doctrine later reissued by the Christ.

If this view, shared by his even more illustrious pupil Origen, was the intelligent and surely well-grounded conclusion of this most brilliant duo of the Christian Fathers, there is warrant for asking why this luminous understanding was permitted to go into oblivion. Was it a thing too dangerous to later pretensions? Did such truth demand suppression? What could have made the revelation of this kinship of Christian faith with Greek philosophy so perilous that it dared not be allowed to become common knowledge?

Origen was fully persuaded that the wisdom proclaimed by Christ was based upon Greek philosophy and that all Christian doctrines might be explained and vindicated by that philosophy. He even sanguinely hoped for a combination of Hellenic philosophy with Christianity. He did his part toward this laudable end by "introducing the whole of the Academy into the Church," as Bacon puts it.

Origen had here caught the view that has been recaptured now and again by men of consecrated intelligence bent on finding truth, apart from ecclesiastical pressure to condition it. In the bright flash of such insight, vouchsafed only after years of recondite study, the vision of truth discloses at last that not only might the keys supplied by the "divine philosophy" of the Orphic-Hermetic system serve to open the Scriptures to an infinitely clearer intelligibility than can be gleaned without them, but that these keys, picked up again out of the archaic presentations, being in nature astrological, symbolic, mythic, allegorical, numerological, are in fact the indispensable semantic cipher code by which alone the deeper cryptic sense of the Scriptures can be recovered at all. This recognition is that extra final reluctant step that Christian systematism *must* take if it is to restore its discredited Bible to its true place of power over the modern mind.

It is certainly a matter of pointed significance in the estimate of Christian origins to consider that Origen, as Mosheim says,

"did not aim to overthrow the ancient and simple religion of the previous ages, which he himself taught and recommended; but he wished the supervisors and doctors of the Christian Church to have a more profound knowledge, and to be able, when occasion required it, to explain rationally that simple religion."

One can feel this high-minded Patristic's inward struggle as he wrestled with the problem of how to convey esoteric and always semimystical sense of the deep Scriptures he labored over so industriously to the less capable minds of the Christian converts. The deep instructive power of the picture should not be lost on Christian thought: here was a Christian, and the most profoundly learned of all, hoping to enlighten Christian ignorance with the rays of a knowledge that on his part was wholly Pagan! The ordinary Christian of today would be bewildered by the implications of this picture; he would not understand why it was not a Christian trying to enlighten Pagans with Christian material.

Grethenbach in a work called *A Secular View of the Gospels,* comments on the fact that at the close of Jesus' ministry, after all his mighty "signs and wonders," the number of followers attached to him was just one hundred and twenty. Were the number to be multiplied by ten, by one hundred, even by ten thousand, "one might still be left in amazement at the signal failure of a divine personage to impress itself on a contemporary people; and this, too, in an age when credulity was co-extensive with ignorance, and among a people willing for and expectant of divine interposition."

This can be matched by what Gibbon (and others) has commented on as so odd a circumstance as to throw doubt on the historicity of the events recorded in the Gospels,—the fact that of the series of pre-ternatural occurrences, such as the three hours of darkness over the earth from the sixth to the ninth hour, the earthquakes and even the rending of the veil of the temple at the Savior's crucifixion, not a single mention of any of them has ever been found recorded in the books of the historians or any other persons of the age. The supposed "biography" of Jesus runs, as a phenomenon, precisely counter to that of all known historical characters: generally the record made at the very time the personage lived is authentic, full and clear, and only grows dim and legendary in the centuries following his day. With Jesus it is precisely the reverse: the record made at the time of his life is not only dim and legendary; it practically is non-existent. Nearly two centuries elapse before, so to say, the character appears on the stage in a history that has to be made retroactive to place him at the time alleged for his career. Even the four Gospels selected finally as canonical, which al-legedly were written somewhere in the latter part of the first century, do not come out into general use so as to be quoted in early Christian writings until near the beginning of the *third* century. The age in which he lived was totally silent about his existence, in spite of the cited facts that after his miracles thousands excitedly followed him and five-thousands believed and were converted. How could it be that none of these throngs of grateful and awe-struck people ever wrote letters to friends recounting the miracles or left some literary survival of the events? Only after some two whole centuries does this wonder-man and his wonder-life emerge from oblivion and then only within the limits of a narrow sectarian group. Events such as he participated in would have made him the most widely heralded figure in centuries.

There is nothing in this situation to suggest that we are here dealing with an authentic historical character, for the presentment breaks down with every historical test and tradition. There are hundreds of points which militate against its being history. We have to face the fact that a character, under various names, Bacchus, Dionysus, Tammuz, Izdubar, Mithra, Witoba, Krishna, or Horus, and standing almost as an exact counterpart or model of the Jesus personage, was already extant in the religious literature of many nations and that this figure was obviously made up into the historical man of flesh two hundred years after the period of his alleged existence. If this is history it defies all the natural and inexorable requirements and phenomena of true history.

And these "events" of his life did not fall in an age which was too illiterate, too far removed from literary activity or notice to have received adequate recording, considering the marvels alleged to have occurred. Indeed they "occurred" in an age which was exceptionally well marked for the notable work of historians, Jewish writers and the official records of the Roman government.

What would be advanced in explanation of the dearth of all literary notice of the man Jesus during his "life" and for close to two centuries following it? Only the series of theses presented in this work and in that of Massey, Higgins, Robertson, Drews, Smith, Brandes and others: that the figure was accreted out of the mythic dramatic types of the non-personal but ever-living Christ-man as divine principle coming into humanity as its Messianic Savior, and from that intellectualized form and pattern transformed by ignorant men into a living personage. Had he lived in fact, the age of his life would have carried the record; since it carried no such record, the inference is practically irrefragable that his later appearance in Christian literature was the outcome of a later reinterpretation of man for principle. This elucidation is supported by a thousand items of fact and of literature, by all the intimations of internal textual evidence and by the glaringly palpable features of the history itself. And finally it is the only conclusion completely compatible with that allegorical rendition of the esoteric purport of the great Scriptures on which the Western religion rests. For only the unqualified spiritual character of the Christ-Messiah figure which Paul preached—against fierce opposition from the Petrine wing —supplies the dialectical key to the wholly consistent interpretation of Scripture. A personal historical Savior incarnated in one mortal body, throws this interpretation into confusion. And to support itself it has to conjure up as its background and setting, its frame and accompaniment, a picture of assumed history that becomes chimerical, disjointed and whimsical, often preposterous, at every turn. And all these ill-fitting and immaterial accretions fall away and leave the structure clear and distinct, legible and intelligible, if the thesis of the historical man is not needlessly interjected to toss everything about in confusion.

Massey sums up all this contention in his statement in *Ancient Egypt* (Vol. I, p. 29) that any attempt to explain or structuralize the mythologies and religious systems of ancient nations, even of the forest tribes and denizens of the sea-isles, without resort to the nature forms and sage conceptions of the ancient Egyptians is doomed to abject failure.

But it is quite worth our while to look at the reaction of America's most eminent modern theologians to the suggestion of a thousand data like those here adduced, as an example of the complete ineptitude and apparent helplessness of mind of this age when confronted with the growing strength of the case for the non-historicity of the Nazarene. Says Shirley Jackson Case, of the University of Chicago Theological Seminary, in his work on the historicity of Jesus: if the earthly Jesus must go, how much more completely must any supposed reality of a supernatural Christ be abandoned!

As an example of twisted "logic" this declaration gains high rating. If the historical man-Christ must be let go from our theology, there would remain, he says, nothing substantial for Christian faith to build upon; man must then grope into the higher realms of mystical spirit to lay hold, if he can, on some sort of supposed "reality" in the form of a "supernatural Christ." Is it not at once obvious how completely a Christian theological mind must turn to belittle or negative even its own highest reaches of abstract conception when it is a case of discrediting a Pagan idea? Have not millions of pages in Christian books been written to postulate the reality of a supernatural Christ element with which man might inwardly coalesce his very being in rapturous rapport? Yet obviously in Case's thought, that reality is so unsubstantial, so impalpable, that Christians can not rely upon it, and must have a personal fleshly man-Savior to guarantee certitude for believers. In the finale, Christianity has put itself on record as maintaining the position that even if every son and daughter of humanity were inwardly possessed and transfigured by the Christ-light, there still is no reality to the presence of Christos in the world except as embodied in the person of the one historic Jesus! And this tacit imputation has opened the gates of tragedy for half the world.

How can the testimony of the great Egyptologist, Budge, be ignored which proclaims that a study of the texts of all periods proves the immemorial existence of the great fundamental religious ideas of the

Egyptians from remotest times, and discovers among the most prominent and pivotal features of that archaic religion the doctrine of immortality and the belief in the resurrection of the (spiritual, not physical) body? What becomes of the claim for the originality of all Christian doctrinism in the face of a massive datum of this sort? And, affirms Budge, these mighty tomes of the ancient Egyptians

"cannot be the literary product of savages or negroes; there is no evidence
to show that they are of Semitic origin, and the general testimony of their
contents indicates an Asiatic home for their birthplace."

True Christianity had its roots in the earliest gift of divine spiritual
science from gods to men in most distant periods. The claim of its total
newness is the pretension of that arrant Christianism that supplanted it.

Yet what a revelation of degeneration of high mental concept into
wrecking literalism is before us even in this statement from Budge!
He makes it an inexpugnable fact that Christianity inherited its doctrine of the resurrection from the ancient Egyptians. But what a change
has taken place in the substance of the doctrine in its passing into
Christian hands! In that recension it emerges as the doctrine of "the
resurrection of the body," as recited in Christian creeds, and this body
has been accepted as the actual physical frame of the earthly man!
Could any vitiation of lofty esoteric doctrinism be more completely
wretched than this? The Egyptian concept never asserted the re-arising
or restitution of the physical corpus (or corpse) of the defunct human.
With Paul, it proclaimed the resurrection out of the flesh of the physically deceased of the soul of the man in its shining body of spiritual
light. For it was, they averred, sown a natural body; and it was raised
in or as a spiritual body. Paul could affirm that we have a psychic and
a spiritual body, in addition to the natural physical one, because he
had studied religious philosophy anciently derived from the Egyptians, who constituted man of seven distinct bodies, held together by
radiant forces and affinities within the frame of the living mortal.
The lower three separated at death; the higher four survived and could
encompass embodiment on earth again. The latter doctrine also was
incorporated in the highest strata of early Christian belief, but, as
recorded, was ousted finally in the sixth century by the Second Council
of Constantinople, the wording of the decree being: "Whosoever shall
support the mythical doctrine of the pre-existence of the soul and the
consequent wonderful opinion of its return, let him be anathema." If
there is a reaction of indignant horror at the assertion that Christi-

323

anity, in its form as Christianism, is a degenerated offspring from Egyptian religion, the challenge of this item of corrupted knowledge must be answered.

That Case could hold to his assumption of the proven historicity of Jesus in the face of some of his own adduced data of comparative religion is difficult to see. He tells of Joshua with his twelve helpers passing over Jordan and offering the Paschal Lamb on the farther shore; of Jason with his twelve companions seeking the Golden Fleece (Lamb symbolism); and mentions that all these stories were the myths of the sun's wandering through the twelve signs of the zodiac! Had he gone further into this exploration and found that *all* the groups of twelve from the twelve reapers in the Egyptian "harvest of Amenta," the twelve rowers or sailors with Horus in the lower ship, and the twelve companions of Ra in the Ship of the Sun; the twelve labors of Hercules; to the twelve knights around Arthur's table and still other such representations of the number, were nothing but allegorical depictions of the twelve powers of divine consciousness to be evolved in the human sphere of mind by the growth of the Christ nature in man, and this divine energy being symbolized by the sun with its power to give life and light to all creatures evolving out of darkness, he might have gained the insight to discern the non-historicity of the Gospel texts, built up on ancient allegorical foundations, particularly the astrological. His failure to espy this truth is all the more surprising in view of his saying that before Paul's time forms of pre-Christian Christianity were already in existence, not only in Palestine but also throughout the Diaspora. Also it is fairly incomprehensible when we hear him state that nature-myths personifying the winter's death and the vernal revival of life were common among the "heathen mythologies"; just as if the universal prevalence of this corn-myth could be dismissed as having had no relation to the Gospel death and resurrection of a Messianic Savior, when the similar portrayals of that Avataric denouement had already been outlined over the analogy of the natural seasonal course of the sun through wintry death to summer life again in its eternal cycles. He believes he is venturing far in stating that acquaintance with these forms of dramatization was "possible and even probable" on the part of the Jews, but reveals how shallow his knowledge of ancient comparative mythology is in saying that

"evidence that these notions formed an important part in the construction of the messianic hope is scanty. Certainly a mere collection of isolated points suggesting similarities of ideas is not sufficient proof of borrowing, particularly when the Jewish literature shows so little to confirm the supposition."

What shall one say to this? What *can* one say save that the evidence he estimates as scanty is well-nigh voluminous in all Egyptian, Hebrew, Greek and even in the Gospel literature itself, and that if all this is a "mere collection of isolated points," then the house of Christianity rests on very frail foundations indeed. When in the aggregate of positive identities among scores of ancient religious fabrications to adumbrate truth he can see only "points suggesting similarities of ideas," the conclusion of scholars who have surveyed the almost limitless mass of such identities can only be that Case's observation of what is there to be seen has been myopic and imperfect indeed. When scholars are so fortunate as to uncover points suggesting similarities of ideas in diverse systems, they are usually ready to welcome them as significant clues and to follow them out to fulfilment of every intimation of importance. But this laudable instinct is non-operative when such pursuit threatens established Christian positions. In that case even a mass of most patently evidential material denoting positive identity of meaning throughout all ancient literature is to be dismissed with a slighting allusion to its scantiness. And it would, of course, never be taken into account by Christian champions that one reason for the "scantiness" of much of the Pagan literature is that it was fiendishly destroyed by Christian zealots haunted by terror inspired by the multiplying ghosts of their own teachings springing up all around them in the guise of Greek and Egyptian formulations.

Thus it has been the fashion of Christian defenders to brush aside with a sheer word assertion the evidences of Pagan origins of the faith, when the grounds for the factuality of these origins can be stoutly established by adequate examination and competent interpretative genius. Thus the Christian tradition has survived and thriven upon a determined neglect of honest critical evaluation of comparative religion material and an arrogant bluster of contemptuous reference to points in it which, if accorded full rating for their great significance, would prove menacing to settled positions and claims.

In *The Relevance of the Prophets* (p. 57) R. B. Y. Scott says that in Babylonian literature and to a greater extent in the Egyptian are to be found writings similar to the Hebrew prophetic records. Likewise there is much for any one to ponder over in such an extraordinary observation as that made by the renowned scholar Cumont when in his *Die Mysterien des Mithra* (p. 4), comparing Christianity and Mithraism, he writes:

"Both opponents perceived with astonishment how similar they were in many respects, without being able to account for the causes of this similarity."

But is this much different from the situation today when scores of sects and cults face each other across gulfs of prejudice and aloofness, yet manifest such similarities in fundamental principles that few could clearly express the points of difference? And almost no one could account historically for the near-similarity of their creeds. So Christianity stands as a whole in the same relation to other religions, expressing a vast quanta of similar tenets with them, yet unable to understand why there is this identity. The reason for this blindness is the widespread unfamiliarity with the truth of ancient religious history. Were the people at large more conversant with the true history of their religion instead of being hallucinated with a run of fables and persuasions, none of which are indeed true at all, let us imagine what would be the effect of the amended knowledge of just the one item that appears on a page of our note-books open before us, in which Kershner (*Pioneers of Christian Thought,* p. 68) makes the statement that "the Gnostics were the founders of Christian theology in the full sense of the word." With what astonishment this fact, which is provably true, would strike the minds of millions in the Christian establishment who, first, never heard of the Gnostics at all, and who, next, would have to be educated in the part they played in early Christian development, and would then finally be totally bewildered when told that although they founded the Christian theology, they were not true Christians and had to be ostracized as heretics! And if then the newly enlightened church member, recovering from the shock of such an anomalous situation, should ask why he was never told of such predicaments in the life of his religion, what might be his final reaction when told that it has not for centuries been held for his good that he and other people should know about such unpalatable oddities and quirks of Christian history? And what might conceivably happen if all rational communicants of this religion should, in the democracy of general intelligence at last come to know of this and a hundred like idiosyncrasies of Christian history?

While Tertullian was calling the Greek philosophers "the patriarchs of the heretics," a greater Christian than he, Clement of Alexandria, in his catechetical school at the Egyptian city was providing the motive power of a great stream of Christian influence that flowed forth to irrigate the age when Christianity was forming its character. How many pew occupants today would know that Clement had been initiated into the Egyptian Mysteries; and that he writes: "I have eaten out of the drum, I have drunk out of the cymbal, I have carried the kernos, I have slipped into the chamber" in his initiations in these ancient brotherhoods?

What indeed must have been the scourge of base corruption that swept a movement among people of sincerity so far beneath the level of intelligence that it turned upon and denounced the work and the contribution of those men whose profounder genius and learning had alone given stability to an outcropping of pietistic fervor lacking any appeal to thinking people! It was from Alexandria that Canon Farrar says Christianity received a powerful impress. "It was the cradle of Christian theology."

And for these eminent services, which are generally agreed to have saved a wave of unintelligent pietism from quick extinction, the two eminent philosophers who made this contribution were rewarded with suspicion, denunciation and final repudiation and anathema. The point of vast significance in the matter is that these two eminent philosophers brought to Christianity from out their store of Pagan learning those principles of philosophy and a system having nothing in common with or generically related to the movement which without their accretions stood so deficient, so naked and bleak on its intellectual side that all men of mental culture held it in supreme contempt and derision.

But, comes the rejoinder, it was Paul who saved Christianity from a quick dissipation of its purely emotional energies amongst the rabble. Many writers have so declared. To the considerable degree to which this is true, the same reasoning applies as in the case of Clement and Origen, Philo, Ammonius Saccas and even Plotinus. Paul saved Christianity with the same philosophical resources that were brought to its aid from Alexandria. And he saved it from its own poverty with the wealth of philosophical wisdom that came from the same non-Christian world of thought, and that likewise bore no cognate relation to the Christianity of the Gospels, or the Apostolic religion that those Gospels generated. For Paul, be it said, gave no place to the Gospel biography of Jesus in his contribution to Christianity; he apparently never heard of Jesus as a living person, referring to the Lord Jesus Christ only as a spiritual principle in all men, and gave it no play or place in his majestic and truly Christian documents. If Paul, Clement, Origen and others saved Christianity from vanishing, they did it with Pagan philosophy.

It can readily be seen that the motive of a few eminent Pagan philosophers in uniting with the popular religious movement was an inclination to forfend it against its own wild propensities by instilling in it the light of their higher wisdom for its safer guidance and its ultimate benefit. They aimed to lend their better knowledge to a philosophically naked, barren, destitute, lean and hungry Christianity. And as is so frequently the case in such circumstance, the beneficiary, too abject to comprehend fully and appreciate adequately the boon extended, turned shortly and cast the princely gift in the dirt and trampled it underfoot, snapping at the hand that proffered it. We know how Clement and Origen were calumniated; Paul was kept at arm's length for some years after his adoption of the faith and sullenly tolerated, while rated as the "Apostle of the heretics" by the whole Apostolic Petrine or Jerusalem nucleus of the orthodox party.

Barring the revival of Platonism by Dionysius the Areopagite and later by Erigena, this revolt against the Pauline Hellenism and Origen's introduction "of the whole of the Academy" into Christianity held the field until the Schoolmen in the tenth to twelfth centuries began to revive the Platonic and later the Aristotelian literature and apply it to the reconstruction of the faith on its intellectual side.

Remarkable indeed are the utterances on this crucial phase of Christian history by the writer of one of the most sagacious of all Christian histories, Dean Milman. He introduces the colossal figure of Paul into the story with the statement that

"to propagate Christianity in the enlightened West . . . to emancipate it from the trammels of Judaism, a man was wanting *of large and more comprehensive views; of higher education and more liberal accomplishments.* Such an instrument for its momentous scheme of benevolence to the human race Divine Providence found in Saul of Tarsus."

Late modern horror of war generated in Christian lands has thrown grave doubt over the claim that the spread and dominance of the Christianism of eighteen centuries is a scheme of benevolence engineered by Divine Providence, and not just a bad miscarriage of poor human intelligence, costing the world untold anguish for modest benefits. But Milman goes on to say that Paul's role in human history was to be so prodigious that "no event in Christian history . . . would so demand . . . the Divine intervention as the conversion of St. Paul." Milman will not allow us to construe it otherwise in human thought. "To doubt, in whatever manner it took place, the divine mission of Paul would be to discard all providential interposition in the design and propagation of Christianity." This all depends on the ultimate definition of "Divine" and "intervention." It raises the whole question of whether a divine mind interposes in special acts of fiat. Deistic thought regards all things as divine, but none in any special sense, or in dissociation from established laws of order and sequence. The mother bird bringing a worm to the mouth of the fledgling is divine, too, in most human thought.

At any rate "Paul was essentially necessary to the development of the Christian scheme," avers Milman. This is fine grist for our mill. But while the scholars blare this fact abroad, to extol the "Christian scheme," how little disposed they are at the same time to stand by the major concomitants of Paul's contribution, which consists of the Hellenic Theosophy and the cosmo-anthropological fundamentals of the great Pagan philosophies! And how little the Christians whom he immediately joined after the stoning of Stephen were prepared to welcome him into their fold is painfully evident also! Says Milman (p. 156):

"The Christians, far from welcoming so distinguished a proselyte, looked on him at first with *natural* mistrust and suspicion." "Even the apostles stood aloof." "Unquestionably it is remarkable how little encouragement Paul seems at first to have received from the party to join which he had sacrificed all his popularity with his countrymen, the favor of the supreme magistracy. . . . Barnabas alone espoused his cause, removed the timid suspicions of the apostles, and Paul was admitted into the reluctant Christian community." "But a new conspiracy again endangering his life, he was carried away by the care of his friends to Caesarea."

The stern opposition of Peter's faction to the true founder of the Christian Church is in print in the books, but the laity knows nothing of such items and blithely goes on believing that the great Apostle to the Gentiles, following his vision of light, was a devotee of the cult of the Nazarene and enthusiastically welcomed by his followers. The universally hailed apostolic promulgators of Christianity, believed to be saints of piercing insight into divine truth, stood ready to murder the man who came to them and eventually saved their ribald "system" from ignominy and oblivion! They are here revealed, by a great Christian historian, men of such boorish grossness that they would murder the first scholar who ventured to join their movement of rancor against learning and culture!

It becomes obvious that these philosophers did not join or countenance the Christian movement under any sense of need of its ministrations for themselves. In all likelihood they must have come in with the motive of contributing to it the elements that would supply its deficiencies, fill up its philosophical vacuum and as far as possible justify rationally its basic affirmations.

Guignebert goes the length of saying that Paul at first detested Apostolic Christianity. In a philosopher of his grade that would be understandable, especially when for some three years this group of enraptured enthusiasts held him off and eyed him askance. Then Barnabas broke down the impasse and Paul decided to visit the Jerusalem Christian colony.

CHAPTER XV

PAUL KNOWS NOT JESUS

The Church, says the historian, has never faced the implications of Paul's visit to Peter. The fact is, it has never faced the positive implications of Paul's contribution at all, seeing that Paul does not preach the Gospel message, but presents the magnificent conclusions of Hellenic-Egyptian esotericism, or spiritual philosophy having direct connection with prior Pagan systems and none at all with the cult based on Bethlehem and Calvary event. In fact, says Guignebert, Paul came to Jerusalem to meet the consecrated band of disciples there, to spend a fortnight with Peter and James, the brother of the Lord himself; and propounded such a Greek philosophical doctrine that he aroused a tumult and was forced to leave the city!

So far from his having based his preachment of the risen Christ upon the alleged veridical resurrection of the Galilean Jesus only a dozen years before he came to Jerusalem, Paul is affirmed by Guignebert to have drawn his theology of the death of the Savior from the several Hellenic Mysteries.

Commenting on Paul's visit with Peter in Jerusalem over fifteen days, Fisher (op. cit., p. 477) writes that this was indeed "a memorable visit, and a fact fraught with interest in its bearings on the evidences of Christianity." For these two men (assuming for the moment that it *is* actual personal history and not converted allegory we are here dealing with), as they faced each other, represented those two wings of the Christian influence that began their warfare with each other at this meeting and have prolonged it ever since. It is clash between the two most salient elements that manifest in the religious life of mankind: formal, fixed, authoritative, canonized and invested religious power on the one side, requiring only prescribed loyalty and routine observance; and on the other the free sweep of man's individual spirit in its aspiration to reach up to the divine above it or within it, unfettered by external supervision and needing no intermediary save its own bridge of intelligent communication. Fisher is right: the atmosphere of dissent that must have loomed thick in the room where these two met was ominous for Christianity, for the world. At any rate Paul came away from the fifteen days of what must have been a keenly dispiriting experience, filling his disciplined philosophical mind with dismay at the Petrine expressions of great doctrinal principles turned into unbelievable oddities of assumed "history," and with the solemn resolve to mention nothing about the Apostolic belief that the saving principle of life had come as a man. And what must have been the effect on Paul's mind of his meeting in person James, the very blood brother of the Logos of God and the Second Person of the Cosmic Trinity!

If this sounds next to blasphemous in its flouting of all traditional view, let us hear what Guignebert injects on the subject (p. 101), referring to Paul:

"Wholly indifferent to the Nazarene so dear to the Twelve, he resolved to know the Crucified alone, whom he would portray as a divine personality, in existence before the beginning of the world, a kind of incarnation of the Spirit of God, a 'celestial man' long retained in reserve, as it were, in heaven beside God, and at last come down to earth to institute a veritably new humanity, of which he would be the Adam."

There is instructive suggestion in Guignebert's saying that it was in the Syrian atmosphere that the first Gentile Christian communities were born and grew to influence. The very word *Kurios,* Lord, that figures so prominently in the New Testament, is not a Hebrew word, but comes from the Hellenic world in Asia Minor. Again the misinformed common belief of Christians everywhere that the faith of Christ spread from the Judean villages where multitudes witnessed the Christ's and then the Apostles' miracles of healing, and thence radiated out and made converts in all directions, must be sharply negatived and the real truth recorded. Not only were the "churches" found or spoken of as existing so early after the crucifixion and resurrection events in Jerusalem not the products of the missionary evangelization of either the twelve or the seventy, but it is close to a certainty that they were in existence in Syria and Asia Minor even before the climactic denouement of the Gospel scenario. There were communities not only of Essenes, but also of Nazarenes, Naasenes and Christians (Greek: *Christianoi*) in those countries before the founding of Christianity.

There is but one rational and completely plausible explanation of this startling fact: these were associations, modeled more or less closely upon the pattern of the Essenes, of brethren instituted to lead the monastic-spiritual life under conditions of fellowship and abstraction from the world, and some had taken the name of "Christian" from the central motive of their organization, i.e., the cultivation of the *Christos* in the individual consciousness. They could have had no reference to or connection with the biographical eventualities of the Gospel Jesus, although these may have been in the venerable texts as the *allegory* of the Logos-Monad of spirit made flesh in all men, and typically personified in one dramatic figure, long antecedent to the first century. They would certainly have embodied the esoteric essence of Greek philosophy in their practice of the mystical life.

All this gains credence when taken with that significant fact given in the *Acts* that it was at Antioch that the believers or brethren were first called Christians. From this tell-tale datum it becomes apparent that another devoutly but falsely cherished belief of Christian people must be overthrown, to the further discomfiture of confident Christian persuasion. It is the accepted conviction that the Christian group took from the start the title of "Christian" from the man, Christ. Nothing could be more fallacious. The name, as Guignebert declares (with others), traces back to the Greek *Christos,* the Anointed, which had never in all previous time borne a reference to a historical personage, but only to a divine conscious mind coming to manifestation slowly in mankind or in human nature.

And now the relevant fact must be faced that it was not the adherents, even the inner circle of the followers of a man Christ, who gave themselves the title of cultivators of the inner Christos, or "Christians." The title emanated from groups of Syrian spiritualists, devoted to the cultus of the subjective Christ consciousness, with no intimation of allusion to the Founder of Christianity at all. The name arose among and was applied to communities of Hellenistic philosophico-religious cultism and was only later seized upon by the Jerusalem Jewish Messiah-enchanted religionists. Antioch must have been one of the most prominent and powerful of those centers of Hellenic philosophical interest.

Again there is the strongest sort of hint that the view here enunciated is close to the truth, in a statement made by Fisher (op. cit., p. 479), since it describes precisely what would be expected to be the

333

reaction of the Apostolic party in Judea upon their learning of these Graeco-Christian (but, so to say, not Jesus-Christian) "churches" flourishing over in Syria:

"The surprising growth of the Gentile Church at Antioch could not fail to excite the attention and awaken misgivings. There the disciples first began to be called Christians, and properly, for there they first became *Christians in the full sense*—a body distinguished from the Jews. Before, they had called one another 'brethren' and had been termed by their enemies, by way of opprobrium, Nazarenes, Galileans or Ebionites. It was natural that anxieties should arise at Jerusalem when the Jewish Christians saw the rapid progress of the Gentile Church in the flourishing capital of Roman Asia."

But there is more here than meets the eye or reaches the mind of the reader. Fisher's analysis may not be the basically correct one. He makes the cause of the Christian mistrust and concern over the strong growth of their own religion at Antioch a matter of a clash of sentiment on the part of Jewish Christians between their loyalty to a purely Jewish Christianity and their misgivings about a Gentile upsurge of Christianity. This logically implies that they were all for Christianity as long as it was of a Jewish cast, but distrustful of it when taken up by the Gentiles. But this presents anomalies in the situation which Christian analysts would not like to face, if not indeed fundamental absurdities. Reason would seem to deduce from this the rather unwelcome conclusion that, if Judaic Christianity was to the founding group of the faith the one true and revealed religion, but that Gentile Christianity was to be viewed with misgiving, then Christianity was more Judaism than it was Christianity.

One of the most salient points in the platform of early Christianity was that it was to transcend all national, racial and creedal bounds and be preached to all nations as the one true faith supreme over all and transcending all. What, then, if this was the spirit and understanding of the original propagating group who had (presumably) heard Jesus command them to go into all the world and preach the tidings of great joy over the coming of the Kingdom of God to all nations, should have been to them the cause of apprehension and misgiving over the good news that the great city of Antioch had come up with a powerful congregation of Christians? What could have been lurking deep in the minds of the Apostolic religionists at Jerusalem that made them fearful of the church at Antioch? Either they had not at all caught the spirit of universality for their fanatically cherished new faith, and did not either expect, hope or dream of propagating a flame of religious unction that would sweep over a third of the earth; or they felt that what was springing up to such rapid growth over in Antioch was not the same thing as they were committed to. Out there in Syria, they heard, was a strong and advancing cultism which had taken the Greek name of *Christianoi*. It had philosophical and esoteric backgrounds and a spiritual mystical character. Could the Lord Jesus Christ they spoke of be an incarnation of God in the flesh of Jesus of Nazareth, or might he be put forth as only the spirit of truth and love, an abstract principle? Could the Antioch movement be welcomed into the fold of the incarnated and crucified Christ?

There are no doubt particular circumstances that condition the attitude of hesitation and suspicion at Jerusalem; but the fact still looms large and glaring that the spread of their cult at Antioch was none too welcome to the first propagators of the faith. This is a predicament that needs more than a merely Jewish explanation. It militates decidedly against the presumption that the founding group began their evangelizing work with the broad motive of breaking through all local or national religionism and going out to spread a pristine new gospel over all the world. It indicates that their aims were narrowly restricted to elements inbound with Jewish or at any rate a limited purview of religious interest. Why should not the Christians who were launching a new world faith rejoice unreservedly at the news that their program was gaining converts in a neighboring land? There is but one conclusion to be reached, which is that their reluctance to receive Paul, a Hellenistic philosopher, and to be joyous over the rising tide of Christianity at Antioch were due to one and the same cause—their knowledge that the Syrian brand of Christianity was by no means the same thing they were ebullient with zeal about.

The outcome clearly pointed to in this analysis is that, in so far as the alleged Gospel events furnished the first impetus to the Christian movement, that movement was nothing more than an outbreak of emotional fervor of a heavy pietistic tinge on the part of common Jewish folk who mistook the Messianic allegorism, spiritual prophecy and the divine Israelitish mission for historic reality in the objective literal sense and, being wrought up to a pitch of frenzy over the realistic immediacy of the events so prophesied, preached this body of convictions with such force and unction that they inaugurated a sweeping popular agitation, all the more durable among the illiterate because of the element of literalism that gave it apparent substantiality, while it increased its power to hypnotize uncritical minds. Philosophers are mentally critical and emotionally placid; they therefore despised the violent swing of uncritical irrational pietism; they both scorned the tide of faith and held aloof from it. Hence they were at once its enemies and its targets of hostility.

From Guignebert (op. cit., p. 87) we have this pertinent allusion to what is here under discussion. Speaking of Paul, he says:

"Since apparently he did not create, even if he was able to improve upon, those ideas peculiar to himself, the assumption is warranted that he found them outside the Apostolic Christian circle of ideas, and this could be only in a Hellenic community. It is most probable that Antioch was the one."

It is pretty substantially established on these grounds, then, that Christianity was not so much, or not at all, the product of a new cycle of either historical occurrences or revealed truths centered about or emanating from a unique character in the flesh, who came from heaven and, flouting all antecedent religious development, proclaimed all afresh out of cosmic wisdom the one first universal code of truth. What it appears truly to have been was a singular aberration of religious fanaticism springing up in the popular form it took from the conditions of the times, the locale and the distinctive qualities of mental development and status of prevalent belief, of those amongst whom the ferment originated. It arose from the play of mental-emotional forces charactered by the Jewish background of Mosaic and Messianic preachment, and then twisted into a new mésalliance and a misshapen configuration by the fantastic outcome of gross misconception of high truth which had become traduced from metaphysical reference to absurd and impossible local event. It had its origination and its motivation not from the alleged veridical events of the Gospel narrative, but from the unconscionable contortions of divine ideas given to man by deific intelligence, into the freakish predications of allegory wrenched awry into supposed history. It thus sprang, like Athena from Jove's forehead, from the fanciful hypostatization of a structure of ideal and metaphysical truths conceived in the perfervid regions of deluded belief.

Neglected and slandered as he has been, Massey is still right; he is the one investigator who on this matter of Christian origins is completely right. He had been overwhelmed with the volume and clear intimations of the evidence; Christianity arose out of the fervor that was generated by the mental disorder that ensued among the ignorant of the Roman Empire when magnificent spiritual allegory, ritualistic dramatism and symbol language were mistaken for human history. The entification of a whole assumed cycle of historical events out of the sacred allegories in the minds of deluded devotees provided the alleged factual foundation for the ferment. It rests on no other ground.

Is this *lèse majesté* against the sacred truth? Could Massey alone be right and billions of Christians be wrong? Impossible, preposterous, unthinkable, is the uprush of all reaction to the suggestion.

Yet—Paul was on the scene of the crucifixion and resurrection within a few years of those events—if they were events—and a little later passed two weeks with Peter and the Lord's brother; and in all his fervid writing and exhortation to the churches of the religion ostensibly founded by this personage, it is as if to him these things had never been. The life of Jesus had nothing to do, played no part, was of no consequence, in Paul's Christianity. His Christianity rested on those foundations on which the rising church at Antioch rested, not on the events of the Gospel narrative. His Christianity was a non-Judean Christianity, Greek and philosophical, mystical and allegorical, which was the Christianity that caused alarm and opposition when its resurgence at Antioch was announced to the little group of unintelligent devotees in Jerusalem. And this spiritual Christianity flourishing at Antioch was a Christianity that was to be known in history as "the heresy of Antioch." What does this announce but that to the fanatical deluded emotionalists at Jerusalem true Christianity was the heresy, and an utterly warped and irrational substitute was the true Christianity? And what has it meant to two millennia of human struggle in mental darkness that this misjudgment of the fishermen and their companions in delusion as to true and false Christianity has been the acceptance also of the mind of the Western world ever since?

In fact there is not an iota of evidence in Paul's fifteen letters in the canon that he is writing to churches that were built upon the premises of the Christianity of the Gospels. He is clearly writing to groups propagating the spiritual-mystic esoteric philosophy of the Greek systems of that culture in which he had been reared. His terms, as has often been noted, are those that were current coin in the Egypto-Hellenic Mysteries. His Lord Jesus Christ, even when he says "this Jesus whom we have seen," is not a man of flesh, but a divine radiation of light in consciousness. For Paul had never seen any physical Galilean Christ Jesus, but only the flashing light of an inner mystical illumination.

We have seen that one of the names by which the "brethren" were

337

designated by those who held them in derision, before they won the name of "Christians," was the Ebionites. From any Encyclopedia we learn that these were a sect of Jewish Christians who were close to the original band of Palestinian Christians. It is not odd that Irenaeus, Hippolytus and Tertullian describe them as hostile to Paul. They are also described by Epiphanius as strongly tinctured with "Essene peculiarities." Origen, however, distinguishes two sects of Ebionites, the one accepting, the other rejecting, the miraculous birth of Jesus from the Virgin. The more rigidly orthodox faction, as was to be expected, were of that remnant of the Judaizing party that had persistently attacked the doctrine and person of the Apostle to the Gentiles. This is additional testimony to the fact that Paul was out of favor among the group nearest to the apostles and disciples at Jerusalem.

Cerinthus was the most prominent among the groups of those Christians who, fleeing in the year 70 A.D. from the destruction of Jerusalem eastward to the Trans-Jordan, came in touch with the Essene monastery colonies in that region and effected a union of Christian ideas with the principles of the Essenes. The group known as the Elkasites (Elchesaits) were the product of this amalgamation. This datum is worth noting as evidence of how Christianity was acted upon and modified by surrounding influences. Additional evidence of the correctness of our analysis is that, as Fisher says, the theology of the second century Christian, Justin Martyr, "is thoroughly repugnant to Ebionism." There was too much of the Gnostic strain, so soon to be purged out of the orthodox body, in a Christianity influenced toward Essenism.

That Christianity is, as here claimed, a pitiful aberration of misconceived Judaism is evident from a thousand sources, and is testified to, tacitly at any rate, by hundreds of writers. Says Fisher (op. cit., p. 469):

"Christianity was born of Judaism: it was the offspring of Old Testament Religion."

This indubitable fact then casts the shadow of grave suspicion over the truth of the claims that Jesus established a wholly new religion, overriding all local bounds of traditional Jewish ecclesiasticism, to become a vast universal faith. That this claim is made and commonly accepted, in spite of much hedging and compromising with its outright factuality, is certified by a sentence from Milman's great history (p. 158):

"Nothing is more remarkable than to see the horizon of the apostles gradually receding and, instead of resting on the borders of the Holy Land,

338

comprehending at length the whole world; barrier after barrier having fallen down before the superior wisdom which was infused into their minds; first the proselytes of the gate, the foreign conformists to Judaism and, ere long, the Gentiles themselves admitted within the pale; until Christianity stood forth, demanded the homage and promised its rewards to the faith of the whole human race; proclaiming itself in language which the world had as yet never heard, the one, true, universal religion."

This passage could well be made the subject of a whole chapter of discussion. Considered for what it asserts that is not true at all, being sheer bombast; for what it admits that, when seen in proper perspective, is very unfavorable to Christianity; and for what it presents of elements of self-contradiction, it is indeed a very remarkable paragraph. It admits first that the disciples had *not* started their movement from the motives of compliance with Jesus' command to preach his gospel to all nations,—although all narrow cultists are invariably persuaded it is their heaven-ordered duty to impose their particular strain of religionism upon all humanity—the bane incidentally of most religion. It confesses they had a very limited prospective view of their faith. That view, he says, gradually widened, driving back the narrow horizons, Jews first, then Gentiles, then the whole world, to feel the sweep of their fantastic ambitions.

And then Milman well says that Christianity stood forth and proclaimed in language the world had never yet heard that it was the one true universal religion. Christian thought, it is to be feared, has never yet realized how terribly, how incredibly true Milman's burst of magniloquence in this sentence really is. The ghastly truth it is that never before had the world been called upon to witness, or to hear, such a proclamation of blind ignorant zealotry. Again and again, indeed almost continually, the world has to look upon religious parties, small bands of sectarian cultists, made heady as with new wine by the experience of some type of psycho-spiritualist manifestations, stand forth proclaiming that they have contacted the main line of divine voltage from the dynamo of God. And again and again the world has had to watch barrier after barrier of good sense and intelligence fall away before these movements as thousands follow the swelling tide of credulous infatuation. This tragedy is constantly being re-enacted. But alas! Milman is not right when he says that these barriers fell "before the superior wisdom which was infused into their minds" by the revelations of a divine man. It is now proven beyond cavil that the divine man uttered not a single true word that was not

339

in the Jewish-Graeco-Egyptian-Gnostic-Christian books long antedating his period. What they took for a flashing new revelation was—as they so soon found to their confusion and dismay—just the old esoteric wisdom, which they at once transformed in their pitiably incompetent intellects into frenzy-breeding literal history. The barriers, the natural or cultural safeguards with which God has endeavored to shield man against his own too ready gullibility, did not succumb in the case of the apostles to "superior wisdom," it must at last be said. They were burned away by the excess of fiery zeal that swept in like a prairie or woodland blaze, under the force of persuasions that in others were restrained and moderated by some balance of philosophical understanding. But the Christian disciples hated philosophy. Therefore they had not the salutary benefit of its rational modulators.

Time and again a sectarian group has stood forth and demanded the homage and promised its rewards to the faith of the whole human race. It is being glaringly repeated at this age as often before. Milman, with the centuries of Christian history under his eye as a *fait accompli* to lend sanction to his reconstruction of the prophetic vision of the apostles,—an instance of how the reconstruction of Christian history is colored by modern imagination—subtly casts in the assumption that this was the *one* instance in which the sectarian group in question offered in reality the one true universal religion. The gem of precious assumption thus slyly dropped into our intellectual treasure-box by Milman is that these illiterate fishermen had fully, clearly, with the highest and the profoundest intellectual rationalism, comprehended the whole system of supernal wisdom as none had ever comprehended it before; and therefore he can place them as standing before the world with this lamp of truth to demand its homage and offer its gleaming rewards.

Out of all this discussion should emerge the sane conclusion that the matter of supreme importance is the verdict to be arrived at as to why this one proclamation of narrow religious sectarianism succeeded to such a prodigious extent, while hundreds of more or less similar effusions of pietistic zealotry did not. The answer to that question is the one thing of transcendent moment to the future of the human race. That crucial knowledge is what this work is aimed to establish, on the strength of irrefragable data. The presentation of that body of data demands much space. But the matter adduced so far points to the major element in the answer, the prime fact that the legend of Messiah's coming had finally been materialized in human history and fulfilled in the birth and life of a personal Savior, and that the Scriptures were converted from a metaphysical realm of reference to external occurrence in order to uphold this interpretation, all of which directly and powerfully challenged the interest and seduced the loyalty of the lower masses.

But the very pertinent question also arises: if Christianity grew out of Jewish roots, why did Judaism repudiate it? Here is the nub indeed. Obviously they did not accept it for the very good reason that its announced Messiah had not come in the form and manner at all congruous with their ideas. Except probably among the most crudely ignorant, they were not prepared to receive the Divine Avatar or Messiah in the low character and status of a mere mortal man. This description demeaned their loftier conception of Deity's epiphany on earth to a nadir of concreteness impossible for them to accept. They could not endorse the embodiment of the second person of the Cosmic Trinity and an Aeon of the Supreme God coequal with him from the foundation of the world, in the fleshly person of a Galilean carpenter. The intelligent Hebrew would want to know how such powers of cosmic range could be housed in a single body of mortal decay. They were not prepared to look for the Logos to come walking through the streets of their villages.

What the instructed Jew was looking for in the Messiah tradition was the coming into the world of the universal spirit of divine wisdom and power, truth and righteousness, first developed to dynamic expression through their theocratic Israelitic kingdom and from them being disseminated throughout all the world. Naturally he was taken aback by the sudden announcement that Messiah had already come in the form and person of a given man in Galilee. If one has defined the word Messiah as a spirit of unified law and love animating or to animate all human beings, he will not welcome the proclamation of his presence in one single individual. It is important to recall here Guignebert's succinct statement that a Hebrew mind could not countenance the thought of the ineffable majesty of the Godhead, so sacred that he feared even to pronounce its Jehovistic name, being "enclosed within the narrow confines of a human body."

Our work could well stop with this note and make it the culminating point of the exegesis. For it strikes the key that correctly sounds forth the consummate thesis of the dissertation. If Milman can work his mind to a pitch of rhapsodic intoxication over the conception that the half-demented band of Palestine zealots were offering to the world its first true and universal religion, he does so in complete disregard of the sobering fact that this all-highest religion was offered to mankind on the terms of a predication which itself contradicted, flouted and outrageously demeaned one of the most sacred considerations of all wise sages of a glorious antiquity. All astute philosophy has agreed that to localize supreme Deity in a given concretion, even to define it in terms of human conception, is to defame it. How strongly, then, a philosophic mind would derogate the religion that presented the whole majestic Being of the Godhead in the pitiably feeble scope of expression offered by a human body! So that this surpassing boon of a true and universal religion that Milman, in a grandiose flourish of rhetoric, says Christianity first proffered to the human race, was not only not a true religion at all, but on the contrary, that which it offered as its supreme blessing, the incarnation of Messiah in one man of flesh, was itself a conception that had been endlessly scrutinized before and rejected as a base hypothesis infinitely dishonoring to the Ineffable Supreme. In brief, it is the staggering truth that the central and pivotal proposition advanced by Christianity, the one that carried its appeal with winning force to the millions of uncritical minds everywhere, was a tenet of religious speculation long regarded as so infamous and defamatory of the Godhead that a respectful silence was tacitly imposed on human thought and inquiry with respect to it. To suggest to philosophers that this unthinkable majesty of Being could not only be named, but also incorporated in the confines of a single human body, was a thought horrendous beyond belief. Could anything, then, more completely indicate the low intellectual state of a religious group that would blare abroad the message that the Divine Mind and Nature had taken residence in the body of a peasant in Judea? To think of the Logos as being made one hundred and seventy pounds of human flesh—this was unconscionable.

But if the Jew rejected with shocked reverence the personal incarnation of God in one man, this did not impugn his true interest in the Messianic idea. By no means did his rejection of any man Jesus close the door against the sane doctrine of the Advent. In truth it opened the door to his understanding of that coming in all the height and depth of its real historical denouement. For it left him free to conceive of it in the one and only way in which it can be rationally envisaged, as the birth, growth and eventual rulership of the spirit of charity in all hearts. If it was a blasphemous defamation of Deity to think of it as being cribbed, cabined and confined within the pitiable limitations of one human form, it was quite a different matter to consider the mind of Christ as coming to gradual dominance at the very core of consciousness in all men.

So Guignebert writes that, while the Hebrew mind could not accede to the recognition of the Logos-Messiah as incarnated in Jesus of Nazareth or any man of flesh, it was not the less expectant of the actual advent of a Christly motif in the lives of men and nations (108):

"But it was a proposition easy to reconcile with Paul's Christology, or, rather, closely allied to it, when the Apostle's fundamental declaration is recalled, that 'the Lord is the Spirit.' "

The Judaic religion contemplated the coming of Messiah in the form of a spiritual regeneration that would glorify mankind in a solidarity of brotherhood under the moral law that had been enunciated from Mt. Sinai; it did not envision it in the form of the birth of a babe. It realized that there is only one form in which the Christ can arrive to all men,—a new spirit in the heart and a new intelligence in the mind. The Christian pronouncement of Messiah's coming did not in any measure fulfil the Hebraic expectation of the Savior. Of that high and mystical conception the Bethlehem "event" was but a gross misshapen caricature; and was accordingly rejected.

The delusion that the Christos can come—nay, has come—to the world in the form of a historical human; that he comes singly and not collectively, is close to the most fatuous imbecility that has ever engrossed man's consciousness. Indeed Christianity must answer to the ages the opprobrious accusation that it offered the Christ mind to the world in but one man, and not in all men. That is the final summation of all the stricture that this work marshalls against Christianity. It is the ultimate focus and core of all critique of Christianity.

We have dissertated on the church at Antioch; the one at Corinth demands notice also. When Paul speaks of "the Church of God which is at Corinth," it must not be understood that he is referring to an organized congregation in the later Christian sense. It was one of those communities of esoteric students cultivating the mystical and intellectual philosophy theoretically and practically. Little did they dream of initiating a movement that would eventually establish a great priestly commonwealth and virtually rule the world. In short neither Paul nor his confreres could justly be considered as members of the historical Christian Church. They were bound together only by the

343

strength of kinship in a high mystical experience. Indeed the historian describes this fellowship as an "anarchy of full dependence upon direct divine guidance." It is "self-governing and controlled by the hazardous suggestions of the inspired." And well we know, he adds, that "the directly inspired are the natural enemies of all ecclesiastical orders."

Yet when after centuries of a far worse anarchy—rather a tyranny—of ecclesiastical power, the people under this system turned against its overweening and overreaching central control and threw off the yoke of its strangling clutch, they did so precisely in order to regain this "anarchy" of the spirit, in the effort to set up again the dynamics of communion directly with divine guidance. And all through its history the publicists of this system have advertised their intellectual insincerity by alternately exalting to the heavens this same subjective mystical communion which links the soul of man ecstatically with the divine shekinah, lauding it as the climax of Christian spiritual attainment, superior to anything in Pagan religious experience; and again condemning it,—especially when it was the experience of Pagans—as the "anarchy" of wild licence in the mystic domain. Once the powerful ecclesiastical organism was in full authority, the sublimest of subjective ecstasies, though the individual spirit melt into the very soul of God in rapturous union, but were it outside the pale of the churchly authority, had to be frowned upon. Once the Church of God held sway, all personal benison must come through its channel or be condemned. The Protestant Reformation did indeed fling a large segment of revolters free of this outrageous imprisonment. But alas! it made but the first halting steps away from the prison door and stands there uncertain whither to proceed and badly confused as to the location of its goal or its home.

Our work is designed to prove that the unsound ideas that generated Christianity contributed to induce a fearful dementia in Western mentality. What it could do to derationalize the mind of an Augustine, it would do in tenfold measure to lesser people. Says Farrar:

Augustine's "personality becomes less attractive as his episcopacy becomes more triumphant, until at last the man who sighed so ardently for Christian charity, and was so much opposed to sacerdotal tyranny, uses expressions and arguments which become the boasted watchwords of the most ruthless inquisitors and are quoted to sanction deeds so unchristian and so infamous as the brutalities of Alva and the massacre of St. Bartholomew."

Here indeed is a psychograph of great value tracing in most vivid relief the horrid warping of mind under Christian corruption. On him directly most writers of the Christian saga lay the blame for the holocaust of Medieval murder. He set up the wanton authority which later lent sanction to this sickening chapter of "Christian" history.

Out of the twisted mentalities of early Christian "saints" like Augustine, Jerome, Tertullian and others, whose consciences were captivated and racked with the deadly concepts of sin, issued that black and turbid stream of morbidity that has darkened the lives of billions in their train. We have seen how Augustine and Jerome mentally lashed themselves for having yielded momentarily to the delight of reading Homer, Virgil and other classic literature. It can be said that Christianity bequeathed to the West a sickly mind, a deranged darksome view of life and a psychopathic haunting obsession of the evil of happiness.

At this point it is more than interesting to compare two insertions standing on the same page in our notebooks. The first is from Lecky (*The History of European Morals*, p. 99):

"Religion is the one romance of the poor. It alone extends the narrow horizon of their thoughts, supplies the images of their dreams, allures them to the supersensual. . . ."

The other is from Dr. Macdonald-Bayne (*The Higher Power You Can Use*, p. 41):

"But thousands have lost their lives, many murdered in cold blood, because of crystallized concepts held immovable in the minds of many people. The secret of growth and understanding is to have a flexible mind, so that we can receive new knowledge and discard old worn-out concepts that are hindering the progress of humanity."

The juxtaposition of these two observations, both supremely wise, is next to tragic in its shocking revelation of man's pitiable victimization by his own feebleness. The romanticism of religion need, however, not be restricted to the poor. It is the one ultimate possibility of romance for the human mind, if the far reach of its influence is taken into account. It is the one avenue of escape from the deadly tawdriness of mortal things for rich and poor alike. It is the one thing that man instinctively flees to when he rises above the sheer interest in physical existence and the objective focus of interest. When the sweetness of its release of the soul from bondage to material interests is once felt, there is no delight to be cherished equal to its power to vivify the enjoyment of life itself. It is or can be truly man's savior.

But the tragic side of this noble interest comes to view in the second observation. The golden allure of the sweets of religion can so soon become a deadly Midas touch. The *Katha Upanishad* of India says, speaking of the Lord of Life, the divine soul at the heart of all consciousness, "with sharp and subtle mind is he beheld." Alas! the religious mind of man is not commonly either sharp or subtle. It is naive, dull, not keenly discerning. It does not sagaciously choose among all the alternatives and possibilities; it sees generally only what chances to come in front of it, and if there be a bit of novelty to stir interest in this segment of truth, it fastens it upon itself with eager readiness and deadly finality. The concept then takes control of the mind accepting it and molds the whole personality over its pattern. The pity is that when one mental scene occupies the stage of vision, it shuts out all the others. The price of our possession of a truth is the privation of all other truth,—unless indeed the sharp and subtle intellect can develop the power and breadth of vision to include practically all segments in a universal organic construct of meaning, in which each truth can be fitted into its proper place in harmony with all other facets. But it is only the few, the philosophers, who can manage this synthetic accomplishment. The commonalty of souls remain steeped in dormancy of intellect. They are unawakened to this keenness of perception and lack the power to hold and relate the many data together in one view. They see through a glass darkly, and see in part. As their attention becomes fixed on one part, and that out of its context in the larger whole, they are blind to what is still not in the range of vision, which, if seen, would alter even the significance of the little section that is in view. For all values are relative.

To give absolute meaning or value to a fraction of the whole, instead of relative value, is the crime constantly perpetrated by ignorance. It is the crime of naiveté. The greatest, most telling and thrilling enterprise, the highest joy open to mankind, is the growth of the power of mind to discern the relations of the knowledge fragments to the whole context of ultimate meaning. Modern psychology has come to see that the prime condition of health for the human mind inheres in its ability to *integrate* its components. This demands, as Hocking of Harvard has said, a consultation with "the *total* meaning of the world." This is the supreme lesson which education can bring to its hopeful matriculants. And for this reason it is a shrieking necessity that the ancient "divine philosophy" be restored to its place of central status in the curriculum of all education.

And all too clearly can it now be seen that Christianity's spite at philosophy, its divorce of religion from philosophy, stands as the consummate wreckage of human cultural aim. In ancient philosophy was embodied the vast knowledge vouchsafed to early races by semi-divine intelligence, which outlined enough of the cosmic perspective for the capable mind to perceive the place and part man was to fill in relation to the scope of the whole. In throwing out cosmology, anthropology, the hierarchical ranks of beings in the evolutionary gradient, the multiple spiritual, psychic, etheric and physical constituent bodies of man's nature, Christianity despoiled both philosophy and religion of their structurally regulative frame of reference. For humans to form judgments without possessing the whole of the data or some knowledge of the ultimate plan and design of Creative Mind, is to leap in the dark. This was the reason why the sagacious philosophers of antiquity made so much of the symbol of the sun and its light. They likened the luminary of day to the divine intelligence. Mind brought to the multitudinous objects of the world a light of understanding because it revealed all things standing in relation to each other and to the whole, in the same way that sunlight, by making things visible at their place in the context, gives meaning to all visible objects. Darkness prevents this vision of relationship, hence of meaning. All human ills are therefore due to imperfect mental vision, limitation of range and inability to see enough of the all to form true judgments about any part.

Had Greek wisdom not been blacked out by the surge of piety rendered unintelligent by the crushing of philosophy, the Christian cultism would not have plunged into the unconscionable blunder of building a new faith on the epiphany of divine life allegedly manifested in one historical person. For this would have been seen as an undue allocation of significance to one item of supposedly historical fact standing without relation to or support from larger segments of the context. For the race of man can never be divinized by the glow of deity shining on the face of one Avatar. The leaven must permeate the whole lump. Divinity outside of man is a glory of life; but only divinity born, reared, magnified and made king inside a mortal man will convert him into the god he is to be. The glorified life, mission and meaning of the one Christ claimed for history stands utterly out of possible harmonious relation to the total of the evolutionary scheme. It can find no niche of perfect articulation into which it alone fits. The Protestant Reformation itself established the thesis that the fragment of God in the individual can make complete union with the God of all; and in so doing it reduced to superfluous status not only the Roman Catholic hierarchical intermediacy but the similar intermediacy of the man Jesus. An external historical Jesus is rendered not only not indispensable, but not even necessary. He might be ancillary and auxiliary; he certainly is not essential. The scheme of salvation can ignore him, dispense with him. The individual soul can make its own peace with God. The High Priest of God, King of Righteousness after the order of Melchizedek, is an oversoul of intelligence within the area of the individual consciousness. Tertullian's arrant challenge to the intelligence of his day can now be reversed: instead of asking what Homer, Plato and academic philosophy had to do with the Gospels of Jesus, the proper question now is: what have Jesus and the Gospels (taken as history, of course) to do with the deification of the Christ in man? On what basis do they have a claim to be considered an essential element in the subjective kingdom and activity of the Christ in every man? How do extraneous and fortuitous "events" and personalities in an almost totally uncertified chapter of Judean history become uniquely an integrated part of the structure of cosmic and human racial evolution? Would the failure of the man Jesus to appear in history at that specific period have left man bereft of an essential stairway to heaven? Had Plato and the philosophers, even common men, no access to redeeming grace and power from the sheer fact that they lived some centuries *before* the Galilean had come?

When the fact of the developing Christhood in one and all men is framed in its proper place and relationship in and to the whole scheme of human evolution, it is at once seen that the narrow view that confines the idea of the Advent of deific mind to its unique manifestation in only one man is untenable, since it neglects the race that is to be transformed by a power that can do its work from nowhere but within each individual. This treatment almost absurdly belabors a point that should be fully clear on first view. But it has to have this excessive reiteration because of the obdurate blindness to it that has afflicted one-third of the human race with dementia and horror over nearly two thousand years.

The concluding word could be that the human effort to bring its inherent deity to conscious function and lordship of life has stood paralyzed into inanity by the Christian legend that the race is to be apotheosized by Divinity once resident in Judea. Not again will Western man take up seriously the task of consummating his deification until he realizes of a certainty that the work must be done by the function of divinity in the Western lands, not in Judea. The redeeming Christ he has been taught to look to for his salvation must be relocated, transferred from Palestine to where he lives in the West, and finally from any outward location geographically to its final location spiritually within the area of present human consciousness. The redemption of Occidental civilization depends upon this reorientation in Christian theology.

Yes, the religious romanticism of untrained, uncritical minds, combined with the stodgy inflexibility of ideas held by the masses, has written its record across the history of twenty centuries in such revolting script that the darksome pages have to be hidden from general sight, since the reading bends down the human spirit with shame and humiliation past endurance. The annals of the one true and glorious religion that was to emancipate the human mind from the blindness of heathen error should make joyous reading, from the heralded birth of the Luciferian messenger to the latest paean of churchly halleluiah. This work is aimed to tell the reason at last why, on the contrary, they make the most harrowing story in history.

Lecky descants most forcefully upon the deadly inertia, the indolence and sluggishness of the common human mind which is the immediate parent of nearly all human ills and woes. Intellectual incompetence and sheer idleness and inertia generate the moral error and delinquency that breed every evil. The human mind, not nourished by its food of truth, reason and understanding, becomes a sick mind. A sick mind bred Christianity.

Rufinus accused Jerome of a change and interpolation in a manuscript. Says Farrar:

"The anecdote, however, has its value, for it shows us the prevalence of forgery and puts us on our guard against heretical interpolations in the works of the Fathers."

This Jerome it is who frankly writes of those who visited and then left him in his desert retreat:

"Lo, they desire to depart—nay, they do depart, saying that it is better to live among wild beasts than with *such* Christians."

The full force of this fling of Jerome's pen will be caught when a chapter of treatment is given to the item of Christian asceticism and monachism. It, however, offers a foretaste of the low, almost inhuman condition to which Christians were reduced by their obsession with the legend of a historical Christ whom Paul either never heard of, though he visited with his brother, or hearing of him, resolved never to mention his existence.

CHAPTER XVI

GREAT PAN IS DEAD

The exigencies of the study demand that notice be taken of that great cry that has gone up in Christian books in their exultation over the displacement of the ancient Pagan religions by Christianity: Great Pan is dead! It is supposed to imply that the end of Paganism and the beginning of a new world era of sane and rational human understanding had been brought to pass under the benign influence of Christian truth. In its underlying implications the cry, swelling out over the world with the death of naturalism and the advent of a supernatural or divine age for humanity, is supposed to have announced the end of a period, as it were, of the world's infancy, in which it had naively believed that Nature was the God that ruled the universe under the natural law, with no place for the interposition of the benevolent will of Divine Intelligence to effect its personal work of Paternal Love.

Pantheism predicated the presence of God in all things, and thus drew the mind of man outward to reckon with him in all his works. Opponents argue that this was to demean the Supreme by making him coequal in stature with his creation. God was no greater than his works; God was in fact his world, which carried his full expression and was the garment of his being. The ancient man could worship God without lifting his eyes above the earth, its grass and trees; for nature was the living manifestation of God, embodying his life and energies. God was resident in every oak, pine, flower, bush, hill, spring and vale, in the sunshine and the rain. The Pagan needed to look no farther off than the visible world of earth, sea and sky, for God was omnipresent in all these. Therefore there was no spirituality, no metaphysical conceptuality, in the Pagan systems. Paganism, worshipping Pan as its God, worshipped the material universe.

With the coming of the divine Babe in Bethlehem a new era of human conception was ushered in, so Christianity has asserted. The advent of Jesus and the spread of the new dispensation heralded by him, changed the whole mood, mode and frame of human thinking. It shifted the focus of mankind's interest and its reliance from the God in external nature to the Supreme God in the holy of holies of spiritual realizations. It destroyed at last the superstitious beliefs in the existence of naiads, oreads, dryads, nereids, giants, ogres, demons, heroes, dragons, serpents and such creations of Pagan fancy and delusion, whose whimsies had to be placated by offerings and eccentric rites, and substituted for them the rule of a Divine Father, whose will was the moral and spiritual law, motivated by cosmic beneficence. For the law of nature administered by the presiding genii of the woods and mountains, Christianity substituted the rulership of Divine Love. The governance of life passed from the hands of the nature-gods into those of the God of all, with a mind that could understand man's problems, a heart that could sympathize with him in his tragic moments and finally a love that could enfold him in unremitting providential care.

In the language of Milman (*History,* p. 33):

"The mental childhood of the human race was passing away; at last it had become wearied of its old toys."

Before engaging in dissertation on this remarkable pronouncement it will be well to present the larger picture that Milman paints of the momentous juncture of affairs at this age of the world's life. He portrays the Pagan religions on their popular side as having run into a dead end street. The masses had been overfed on the myths and allegories of the gods and finally had found this provender nothing but husks and empty shells. Nature went on in her invariable course, turning neither right nor left to lend an ear to man's prayers and special pleadings, solicitations or offerings. The old faiths were weakening, the edifice was crumbling. And Milman asks what remained for minds enlightened beyond the poetic faith of their ancestors, yet not ripe for philosophy. How was the craving for religious excitement to be appeased when minds had turned with dissatisfaction or disgust from the old accustomed nutriment? Here, he says, "is the secret of the remarkable union between the highest reason and the most abject superstition which characterized the age of Imperial Rome."

The turning away from old lifeless forms opened the way for the entry of all sorts of new religious adventures. Rome opened its arms to Jewish, Phrygian, Isiac, Serapic, Mithraic, Neoplatonic, Pythagorean cults. Anything that was imposing, or secret, or unique, or mystical was welcomed, though the very multitude and variety of these cults rendered the general mind after a time indifferent to or palled by their presentations. Astrology and witchcraft, he avers, led captive many minds which boasted their emancipation from the popular tyranny of the old faith in the gods and nature spirits. The venerable oracles were silent, but the voices of astrologers and soothsayers were voluble, dispensing the secrets of futurity for inquisitive minds—and a compensation. Pompey, Crassus and Caesar all consulted the Chaldeans, to be told what the planets revealed of their fortunes. These hawkers of prophetic knowledge were driven out by the exertions of the state officials, but returned and, favored by popular support, defied the authorities.

The death of the god Pan was thus followed by a burgeoning forth of a whole scale of religious or semi-religious superstitions before the air was magically charged and cleared by the coming of the Gospel of incarnate Love in the person of Jesus of Nazareth.

The interim of transition from dead Pagan nature fetishism over to the full enlightenment of a historicized Christology was filled with astrological superstition and mantric divination of many kinds. With the propagation of Christianity would come the master light of a heavenly philosophy and a divine revelation buttressed, as never before in all the life of mankind, by an epiphany of actual deific power in person. This last stage would complete the historic process of ending the world's childhood and inaugurating it into its puberty and final adulthood development, as the one sole religion of eternal truth crowned the cycle of growth for the whole human race. Great Pan was dead; the Babe of Bethlehem had displaced him on the throne of the world.

So proclaim the voices of Christian oracles, and so believe the trusting devotees of the faith. But a searching critique discloses that every aspect and item of this legend is both analytically fallacious and factually untrue. Or if it at points chances to coincide with data, it still is conceived in a warped and unsound rationale.

As has been intimated at an earlier place herein, yes, great Pan, alas, *was* dead. He had been suffered to languish and die through the failure of human understanding and balanced wisdom. The instinctive human faith that nature administers the laws of beneficence with which it is man's duty to harmonize his life in a beautiful accord, was destroyed by the gradual recession of esoteric interest and dimming of esoteric insight, preparing the ground for the implanting of the idea of a personal Savior. Pan was dead; and there died with him the price-less knowledge of the necessity of man's coordination of his life with that of nature. Pan was dead; and no longer would the Mediterranean civilization stand with its feet on solid reality. Pan was dead; and the mind of Western humanity was laid open to the sweep of every wild mystical and emotional excess that can overflood it when its defenses of critical judgment based ultimately on natural law are toppled by irrational tempests. Pan was slain; and buried with him for dreary ages lay the ancient science of nature symbolism, the final reliance of all human thinking and one true guide in the criterion of truth. Gone was Pan; and gone with him the master knowledge that all perfection can be won only through the intermarriage of the two elements of man's constitution within him, the spiritual and the natural. And flown with him, too, was the knowledge that nature is the mirror of all truth, since she reflects in her modes and processes the very mind of God. Gone with the sylvan deity was the one anchorage provided by Omniscience by which alone man can tie his life and his mind to the level of balance between the two worlds of subjectivity and ob-jectivity, on the sharp boundary between which his evolution must proceed. Gone was Pan; and with his disappearance went the hope of any chance to realize more than a modicum of psychological benefit from even the false belief that a Savior-Messiah *had* come. Gone was Pan; and with him vanished every possibility of normal evolution of the human genius for two thousand years.

For the counsels of folly that rushed to take charge in his place de-creed that the last word of universal truth had been uttered once and for all by an untutored Galilean peasant, and that therefore the need of all further thinking was ended. With that usurpation of the thought power of the Western area by upstart presumption, man's greatest birth-right in existence, his power to search the world and his own soul for the living founts of truth, was abrogated at one stroke by the most monstrous tyranny that ever clamped its iron clutch upon the life of the race: he was forbidden to think! Swept away from him for ages was all that prerogative which is his by virtue of his incarnation on earth, to reflect upon the world without and his experience with it, and let his mind report the wealth of understanding that accrues to him from the adventure.

And gone with great Pan also was that intelligent conception of the nature and function of matter which had until the age of Christian degeneracy steadied the philosophies of wise men in an intellectual poise that immeasurably sweetened the daily tasks of life for the creature man. The history of the despoliation of human sanity and happiness by the persistent vogue of the doctrine of the essentially evil nature of matter in religious conception is yet to be adequately written. Its horrendous results in the devastation of human weal are beyond tabulation. It has spread its blighting shadow across the minds and deadened the happiness of millions. Had great Pan not been dethroned and outcast, never could that plague of idiotic delusion about the sinful nature of the human body and its procreative powers, which fell like a blight upon the conscience of Christian populations and sickened all the existence of soul in body for close to ten centuries, have gained its fearsome power to warp natural instinct into a nauseating morbidity.

Yes, great Pan was dead; and human delight was dead with it. A miasma of sin-sense settled down upon the imaginations of the Western millions, striking dead with its pestilential thought-poison every wholesome impulse of natural man. Matter was evil; the body innately bound in sin; to give it its pleasure would drag the spirit-pure soul down into hell. The flesh, with its goads and temptations, must be mortified, crucified. The only merit was in crushing down its appetencies. The saint was he who tortured his body most hideously.

Pan was dead; but he was dead only in the diseased minds of hallucinated simpletons. He could still exert his kingship in minds unaffected by psychopathic disorders. And he could also bide his time of exile, knowing that his day of return and triumph would come. And in the fourteenth century it came. His restoration came with the Renaissance in Italy, which foreshadowed the Reformation in Germany and the North. His reed pipes were heard once again in rustic dales and leafy bowers, as the ostracized human spirit released itself to partake of delight in nature's largesse of beauty without the haunt of a morbid consciousness of sin. And poetry, art, romance, love and beauty could once more lift mortal sense to heights of sweetness and purity.

And perhaps Pan could be laughing his satyr whinny in anticipation of the day, now realized in the giddy whirl of the cycles, when his power, scorned and vilified by priestly curse and philosophic stigma, could be demonstrated in such fearful fashion as to send his traducers, the pious religionists, reeling from the impact of the discovery of how to release his terrible swift sword of secret might buried in the atom of his despised matter. Great Pan dead? Yes, dead to those whose native powers of perception and understanding had been killed by outrageous parody of supposed knowledge; dead to a world in which the genius of divine light struggling to shine in the darkness of unintelligent moronism had been quenched by fear and madness; dead to a world that through the feebleness of human élan had stifled the wisdom that would have united Pan in blessed union with the rising vigor and sweet grace of the divine spirit growing in mankind.

But Pan was dead thus only to that segment of the collective mind that had succumbed to blind obsession of error. He was dead only for the world that with consummate folly had rebelled against his sovereignty and denied his beneficence. To them his death was a tragedy of loss, of befuddlement, of derationalization. And every century of his prolonged exile from his rightful place and office in human life and thought was an added century of a corroding canker at the core of human blessedness. And as the end of the dismal night of the Christian Dark Ages is heralded by the rising dawn of returning human sanity, perhaps the hirsute Satyr may again deign to haunt the arches of the wood and bring the sunlight of natural joy back into the sin-darkened chambers of the deluded religious consciousness.

It is necessary in this connection to deal with the repeated assertions of most publicists that Christianity came in by a natural movement of the mind of the age to supply a void in the religious life of the Roman world population produced by the failure and decay of the old Pagan cultism. It is generally argued that the new religion took hold because of the natural death of a religion that had been long imposed on a submissive world and then at last proved its insufficiency and left a people groping in an empty dusk.

It is not in the purview of our understanding to quarrel much with these broad hypotheses adduced to explain the state of things two thousand years ago. Our essay is not a brief for Pagan philosophy, but an effort to grasp and delineate the situation so that the world has the truth of it instead of wretched half-truth and outright falsity. It is not likely ever to fall within our purpose to vindicate any popular form of religion, for the excellent reason that popular religion is almost always and in all its manifestations a conglomerate of gross error and false conceptions, or at the best true doctrines atrociously warped into weird distortions. True religions are never the upgrowth of popular movement; they do not spring from the common soil. They are gifts of supernal truth and wisdom from evolved overlords of an evolution; they are handed down from the heights of vision and understanding, and are inevitably soiled, damaged and torn in pieces by the incompetent beneficiaries.

It is therefore not necessary to enter a defense, exoneration or laudation of the Pagan system of antiquity, so far as its consequences showed themselves upon the ranks of the populace and the run of history. It is not there we look for the excellence of any cultural system; except as the common ranks are affected by the cultured class above them. And on this ground it is permissible to affirm simply that if, as this work aims to show, it was under the Christian influence that the most abject vitiation of esoteric wisdom swept out to derange the mentality of a world, then the stultification of common intelligence could never have been so gross in former times under Pagan molds of thought. Also it would seem sufficient, if there must be controversy between Pagan and Christian claims, to say that if the Pagan religion reduced the mass mind to a state of rank depravity, the nadir of that downward cycle of degeneration, after five hundred years of gradual recession from the heights of Platonic glory, finally brought the cultural level to the point at which it produced Christianity. If we hold it legitimate to lay the blame and stigma of condemnation upon religious and philosophical systems for what in reality is purely *human failure,* which in most cases the highest systems could not avert, then Pagan philosophy must bear the brunt of censure for the vast cultural debacle following Plato. But that the great decline after Plato *was* human failure and not the failure of high philosophy, ought to be finally and incontestably determined by the anomaly of attributing a great cultural decline to the admittedly sublimest thought effort in world history. The point of absolute verdict in this is that it is impossible for a true philosophy to fail man; but it is possible for man to fail a true philosophy. Christians have been both heroic and vile with the same Bible and the same sword of the Christ faith in their hands. Did the same Christianity make the one man heroic and the other vile? The kind of man that wielded the sword determined the beneficent or evil influence it released on history.

Yet in its extreme application this allows no formative influence to religions and philosophies; it makes all outcomes the product of the purely human factor. Do thought systems have no power to change human nature, to elevate culture? Here, then, is the median truth: systems of philosophy are to be historically gauged by the outcome of their practice when their basic principia have been assiduously studied, fully understood and given thorough application over a sufficiently long time to demonstrate their efficacy. A system should never be held accountable for results springing from a shallow knowledge, a defective comprehension and a blundering half-way application of its principles. Such a manifestation becomes a miscarriage; it furnishes no fair test. On this standard of measurement it may be said that both Paganism and true Christianity have, as Voltaire intimated, never had a fair trial. Before, during and since Plato's day a limited few exceptional souls have fairly comprehended and practiced, or at any rate suffused their minds with the high influences of the Pagan wisdom cultures; and in that area of its application Pagan philosophy has demonstrated beyond Christian cavil and slander its transcendently salutary influence. It has *not* failed humanity when humanity laid hold of it and embraced it fully. Since that same high Paganism was also at the same time the true Christianity, so then true Christianity has likewise not failed mankind. But mankind failed both high Paganism and true Christianity when, following the Golden Age of Greek wisdom, people, for reasons that might be brought to light by deep scrutiny, failed to cultivate, to cherish, to love, comprehend truly and embrace fully the great inspiring knowledge that moved men so deeply before. Greek philosophy was no less potent for high and heroic human stimulation in one century than in another; it is again lifting thousands to new and glorious heights of vision and goodness today. What happened was that the human incentive to gain so winsome a prize and human ardor for the boon of enlightenment faded out or burned low. The causes of this failure of the *love of wisdom* are the pivotal things for the study of objective history. But, for the argument, it is wrong to blame a philosophy for untoward and woeful developments in the course of history when its principles are in no sense being truly applied at all. Neither Paganism nor Christianity is to be held blamable for results when something not even remotely resembling their true character is masquerading in their stead and flaunting their names. And this is what has transpired in the case of both. Paganism is not to be blamed for the decline of high culture after Greece's bright day; likewise true Christianity is not to be blamed for the debacle of world sanity generated by the usurping force and movement that was only a false Christianism. But what needs to be inscribed indelibly upon the consciousness of humanity is that this degraded excrescence from the body of a primal true Christianity that we have called Christianism was, like an unnatural growth on a diseased part of a tree, the product of human cultural spirit at its lowest stage of feebleness and blindness.

358

The common supposition in academic circles has been that Pagan religious conception had degenerated from Plato's time to a darkness profound and universal, and that Christianity then burst forth as a meteor of new light to break the heathen night. Nothing could be more erroneous. Christianity was the expression of that darkness at its deepest point. It was not a rebirth of light, but the eerie glow of the stirring among the buried embers of an extinguished blaze and the weird misshapen shadows dancing round about.

There is not a strand of evidence to indicate that a coterie of great new thinkers had arisen to give forth a gleaming new elucidation of truth superior to what had gone before. There is not a sign anywhere to show that a new system of understanding had been proclaimed. Christianity was a ferment of violent mental aberration engendered by a misconception of old forms of esoteric expression twisted into untruth. It was the upsurge of mingled passions bred out of a mental brew of great truths warped into ungainly deformity by crass ignorance.

Ah, but, say the faithful in the Christian tradition: a divine Messenger, a prophet sent from God, needing no schooling in Greek philosophy, came to earth and brought a light never seen on land or sea. Compared with this celestial message, philosophy was darkness. What could lame human lucubrations do in competition with the flashing glory of an empyreal revelation? What indeed had Homer, Hesiod, Plato, Virgil or Cicero to do with the Gospels? These outshone classical poetry as the sun outshines the candle.

Such at any rate is the notion that fills the heads of nearly all the commonalty of Christian people. The answer to it from the side of truth and fact is the positive affirmation that, if he lived at all—which is a possibility growing less plausible and less tenable all the time—*he inculcated not one new preachment or principle of truth;* and again, that the agitation allegedly produced by his messengership and ministry would have died out in a generation or two if it had not supplemented its meager spiritual capital by the appropriation of the very Greek philosophy with which it compares itself as the candle to the sun. Indeed the long-eclipsed truth has at length come to view; it was Christianity that reduced the sun of Pagan philosophical intelligence to the rush light of pitiable superstition.

The analysis of the situation then extant that yields true understanding is achieved through the view that sees an odd and somewhat perplexing phenomenon in human life and history: the coexistence side by side at the same time of the highest illumination of philosophy and the grossest darkness of ignorant superstition. This has been the case in known human history. An age is lauded as one of brilliant achievement, with a list of outstanding names of the greatest luster; yet at the very time there was virtual savagery in remote continents and mental depravity in the lower strata. So it was in the pre-Christian era, during the time of Christianity's inception and ever since. And along with this oddity, always the vested interests that are fostered by the traditional orthodoxies stand fast against the spread of a higher and freer philosophy that would subvert the fixed customs based half on error. Remembering always that esoteric truth is treasured only by a minority and never purveyed by the commonplace majority in its true form, we see how it was that while the sublimest wisdom was cherished in the cult of the Mysteries and the philosophical Academies, it was unknown or viciously garbled by the masses. The stumbling block that brought catastrophe was the insuperable tendency to mistake allegory for external truth. Such was the ineluctable cause of superstition then, the same as it is today and at every moment when ancient religious Scriptures have been elevated to a place of authority in the mental domain and their interpretation emerges filtered through the minds of unschooled people. Whenever these conditions provided the environment, the result has been a nightmare of undigested ideologies twisted awry into deceptive phantoms.

Fisher envisages the Pagan world as breaking up through the spread of skepticism from the higher groups down and out among the masses. This has ever been the manifest phenomenon when the grip of higher minds on an elevated philosophy has grown lax or failed entirely. When vision fails at the top it is indeed a tragic time for the world. Most cultural recessions come through this channel. Darkened minds lay hold of the esoteric manuals of wisdom and misapply their abstruse knowledge to the utter ruination of all sound meaning.

Fisher delineates the minority at the top of society as disillusioned about the Pagan religions, emancipated from the illusions which those myths perpetuated and cynical about what the common people still took seriously. This skepticism finally permeated all ranks. And as the old beliefs went out, the void was filled, as before intimated, by the invasion of "magicians, sorcerers and necromancers" and cults of foreign origin from the East. These, while they excited and fed for a time the insatiate thirst for the interests of religion, could not permanently satisfy the deeper yearning of souls for spiritual food. The soul must have some contact with the supernatural, he says. Therefore, his conclusion is, when the humble fishermen presented the person of the Son of God in human flesh, the multitudes were ready to flock to their standard.

This is near enough to the truth to be accepted without quibble, if it is remembered always that Paganism would not have failed and produced skepticism if there had been common astuteness enough to see through the outer veil of myth to the supernal and eternal truths beneath the veil. The myths have failed to perpetuate human enlightenment because of the default of human intelligence to read them aright. That really covers the whole ground of historical explanation.

Fisher need not have elaborated an analytic background to account for the drift of the mob of the lower orders from Paganism over to Christianity. The masses follow like sheep the modes of thought that become conventionalized, as people follow dress fashions. The multitude did not reason its way across the abyss from Pagan darkness to Christian bliss. It followed an insensible drift, as esoteric wisdom faded to low glim and mass tendencies of reaction set in toward the things that Christianity was soon to formulate in a concreteness never dreamed of before.

Milman, like Fisher, has expatiated upon the flocking into Rome in Paganism's last days of the "empirics," the "traders in human credulity," astrologers, soothsayers, diviners of all brands, advertising their ability to foretell the future, cure disease and generally to insure health and prosperity. "All these circumstances," he says, "were manifest indications of the decay and the approaching dissolution of the old religion" of Paganism.

If Milman is correct in this analysis, a startling conclusion leaps to the mind as to the imminent danger that confronts Christianity in the world at this present. If the vogue of cult traders in human credulity is a sure sign of a dissolution of prevalent religion, then Christianity today faces quick obliteration, for there has hardly ever been a time when this trading in human gullibility and ignorance has been so voluminous and popular as at the moment of this writing. The ready acceptance of such traffic in religion and superstition today can hardly be less than it was in the Roman Empire. As much of it is secret by its very nature, the vast extent of its prevalence is not commonly known. Milman's formula at any rate worked out so precisely in the case of modern Germany that it seems to have been well founded. After the first World War the process of decay in the age-old Christianity of Germany was so far advanced that Hitler and his group decided to dismantle it entirely and replace it with Nordic Paganism. (Russia had already dismantled not only Christianity, but religion itself.) And now an astonishing datum came to light and significance: preceding and during the time of Hitler's rise Germany, so careful reports authentically stated, was actually saturated with popular interest in all forms of the "occult," and esoteric study permeated all ranks. Astrology, psychism, clairvoyance, mediumship and all their ramifications were in almost universal vogue. And it was by no means confined to the lower orders. Unquestionably Hitler's own inner circle considered itself a select and divinely chosen esoteric group. It needs only to be recalled that every movement of Hitler's military strategy was dated to meet the time implications of the position of the planets on the astrological charts to realize the same forces that Milman classes with sorcery and necromancy, or psycho-spiritual charlatanism, are rampant in our world today. If they portend the doom of the currently predominant religion, then Christianity is soon to pass.

But what needs to be said is that these more conspicuous manifestations of religious interest in exceptional channels are by no means more violent aberrations from sane conception of religious values than is the ordinary run of orthodox Christian belief. If nothing else, they at least reveal a more vital interest in and concern with religious influences than orthodoxy ever does. They evidence a more vigorous play of religious motivation. To whatever extravagant lengths they may go, they really stem from forms of genuine mysticism and psychic potencies in the human constitution that give them a solid base of veritude. They manifest in much of their development the pure spirit of true Protestantism in the exercise of the freedom of the powers of the diviner potentialities in man's dual nature to express themselves apart from the rule of uniformity and conformity insisted on by ecclesiasticism. Therefore churchly power must frown them down, unless, as one organization has done, it is wise enough to reach out and embrace them in its own program and polity.

But they are indeed at this time a part of a great revolt against or away from Christianity, and, if the point is pressed, a trend back to Paganism. And whether it is to be decried as bad or welcomed as in a way a measure of advance for religion, depends quite definitely upon the degree of intelligence with which they are taken up, understood and employed. This is, of course, a criterion which holds for all religious evaluation, it might be interjected. Uncritical zealotry can make superstitious hash out of the sublimest spiritual truth. Ignorant belief can turn the very bread of life, mentally eaten, to poison. Ignorance always corrupts higher understanding to nonsense. Education is the only antidote. If Milman and others would recognize how vast and recondite is the study of religious psychology, with the faculties of universities themselves overwhelmed and baffled by the complexities of the phenomena and the problems involved, they would see the general populace is going to be unstable and fall into gullible acceptance or equally fallacious complete denial of the claims of the phenomena mongers.

And what they do not see likewise is that orthodox religion is itself the most direct generator of an inclination favorable to the vogue of all such things. It was orthodox Christianity that exalted the cult of miracle, of prayer, of the magical potency of physical objects, of special divine interposition, of witchcraft, necromancy, obsession of devils, demonology (turning the very gods of the Pagans into minor demons), relic worship, money favor and what not. The record of this aspect of Christianity is of proportions to fill volumes, and it should have a place in this work, as constituting palpable concrete evidence that the vogue of the thing we have called Christianism has borne its natural fruit in the derationalization of its victims. But the space is not available for the presentation of a minute fraction of the data. The sale of relics including tons of saints' bones, pieces of the wood from the cross on which the Savior died, bottles of the milk, not of human kindness, but from the breasts of Mary the mother of Jesus, mementoes picked up at "holy places" and a host of "sacred" objects of every imaginable sort were among the grounds of revolt which gave the Protestant reformers the courage to break loose from a soulless and conscienceless exploitation of the uncritical religious tendencies of mankind. It is a recital of venality and deception, of sheer premeditated fraud and duplicity that should, if known, scald the eyes of the millions of still gullible dupes of it with tears of burning shame. The space the gruesome narrative would take is saved for more instructive exposition.

The extensive quotation featured in this volume is made necessary because the critique can be seen in its rationale only as it stands related to the claims and actual statements put forth by the proponents, the drum-beaters and horn-blowers for Christianity. The sedulously nourished traditional notions of the wholly immaculate character of all Christian history have left the general Christian populations sadly unprepared to believe the incredible truth of that history. The books revealing it are buried in libraries away from the laity. Unless the facts are recited anew and on the authority of Christian writers themselves, their presentation will be put down as the expression of mere spleen and vituperation. It is not desired that the truth be widely and fully known.

A claim that needs refutation is embodied in a passage from Milman's history. He voices the oft-repeated tradition that Christianity was the influence which elevated civilization from the level of Pagan barbarism to a higher humanitarianism and cultural status. He announces his object "to exhibit the reciprocal influence of civilization on Christianity, of Christianity on civilization."

"As Europe sank back into barbarism, the imaginative state of the human mind, the formation of a new poetic faith, a mythology and a complete system of symbolic worship; the interlocking of Christianity with barbarism, till they slowly grew into a kind of semi-barbarous heroic period, that of Christian chivalry; the gradual expansion of the system with the expansion of the human mind; and the slow, perhaps not yet complete, certainly not general, development of a rational and intellectual religion."

It is important to note the admissions which here are dropped almost as inconsequential incidentals, the grave significance of which would be subversive of the chief arguments if given due notice. Milman begins the statement with the admission that *after* Christianity came in Europe there was a relapse into barbarism! This devastating confession is made and passed over as if it did not itself negate the whole of the argument in which it falls as a mere trifling incident. But the main implication is that Christianity advanced into central Europe and made an amalgamation of its barbarism with Christianity's humanitarian fundamentals. The result was a hybrid brew, a sort of heroic semi-barbarism.

Then the thesis is advanced by Milman that in his opinion "at every period much more is to be attributed to the circumstances of the age, to the collective operation of certain principles which grew out of the events of the time, than to the internal or accidental influence of any individual or class of men." He is aiming to show that Christianity was gradually to lift Europe up to moral and spiritual heights it could not have attained without it. Yet he announces that the basic principle of critical evaluation of the uplifting influence is the general strength of the human spirit reacting naturally to the impact of the circumstances of the times, rather than the power of any specific preachment of an individual or sect, and inferentially a religious system.

364

But this validates the argument we have in readiness to refute his claims for Christianity as the force that lifted Europe from barbarism to culture. It is our contention that the elevating force in the uplift was not Christianity, but the *sheer strength of the human spirit,* acting in response to events, which raised Europe to civilization, and that rather in despite of Christianity than with its help. His own further development of the case confirms the error of his "logic"; for he says (p. 37):

"Christianity, in short, may exist in a certain form in a nation of savages as well as in a nation of philosophers, yet its specific character will almost entirely depend upon the character of the people who are its votaries." (Abyssinia is cited in a note as a good example of this.) "It must be considered, therefore, in constant connection with that character: it will darken with the darkness and brighten with each succeeding century; in an ungenial time it will recede so far from its genuine and essential nature as scarcely to retain any sign of its Divine original: it will advance with the advancement of human nature, and keep up the moral to the utmost height of the intellectual culture of man."

Here is the entire plan of our critique and defense of our position handed to us gratis. It will not be necessary to contend against Milman on what Milman himself establishes. He practically admits our contention that Europe, with a long antecedent natural religion of Celtic, Teutonic, Nordic type behind it, struggled through the blighting effects of a rabidly irrational morbid religionism foisted forcibly upon it by Christian zealotry and impudence, to a final advance to "modern civilization" by the inherent force of human cultural aspiration, *lifting Christianity up with it* as it advanced. His own thesis states that Christianity invariably took the character of the influences that touched it. All general Christian claim is that it was the beacon light, the leader, the molder, the instigator of advance; Milman says it was rather the *product,* the thing molded and charactered by a power independent of it, the raw strength of the human soul struggling toward the light. Apparently he sees that he has conceded too much and hastens to retrench:

"While, however, Christianity necessarily submitted to all these modifications, I strongly protest against the opinion that the *origin* of the religion can be attributed, according to the theory adopted by many foreign writers [French and German] to the gradual and spontaneous development of the human mind. Christ is as much beyond his own age as his own age is beyond the darkest barbarism. The time, though fitted to receive, could not, by any combination of prevalent opinions, or by any conceivable course of moral improvement, have *produced* Christianity. The conception of the human character of Jesus, and the simple principles of the new religion, as they were in direct opposition to the predominant opinions and temper of his own countrymen, so they stand completely alone in the history of our race; and, as imaginary no less than as real, altogether transcend the powers of man's moral conception. Supposing the Gospels purely fictitious, or that, like the 'Cyropaedia' of Xenophon, they imbody on a groundwork of fact the highest moral and religious notions to which man had attained, and show the utmost ideal perfection of the Divine and human nature, they can be accounted for, according to my judgment, on none of the ordinary principles of human nature. When we behold Christ standing in the midst of the wreck of old religious institutions and building, or, rather, at one word commanding to arise, the simple and harmonious structure of the new faith, which seems equally adapted for all ages—a temple to which nations in the highest degree of civilization may bring their offerings of pure hearts, virtuous dispositions, universal charity—our natural emotion is the recognition of the Divine goodness in the promulgation of this beneficent code of religion, and adoration of that Being in whom that Divine goodness is thus imbodied and made comprehensible to the faculties of man. In the language of the apostle, 'God is in Christ, reconciling the world unto himself.' "

If apology is needed for the insertion of this long ebullition of turgid pious bombast, it is found in the actual need of the world today to *know* that this is one—and possibly the finest—of the hundreds of such egregious laudations of the Christian religion that have sprung out of the traditional assumptions obsessing the mind of Europe and America from those early days of obscurantism. It is worth our careful examination now, as it continues still to bind its millions of uninformed religionists in slavery to its glaring untruths. Modern man must remove from before him this false occlusion of his vision.

Already has been demonstrated herein the baseless claim as to the "simple and harmonious structure of the new faith," and the falsity of the assertion that the simple principles of the new religion "stand completely alone in the history of our race." These two magniloquent sallies of unctuous presumption are now found to be wholly baseless, flat untruth. The preachment of the Divine emissary included not one single new or higher principle, intellectual, moral, spiritual. All of his presentation was already in the Essene books. With brutal directness it must be asserted now that his message does not "stand alone in the history of our race," soaring mountain high above every other system in matchless purity, grandeur and edifying power. As fast as attention can be turned to the hundreds of identities between the Gospels and the arcane books of Egypt, so fast is the structure of assumption on

366

which Milman's grandiose flourish of fervid delusion crumbling to ruins. For Christian writers since his day are forced to transfer, one after another, the Gospel "events" in the life of this Christ from asserted history back to legend and poetic embellishment. If ever a new Avatar of sane intelligence stood, as Milman represents Jesus as standing, in the wreckage of old religious institutions and building the temple of a nobler order of human understanding, that Avatar is now standing at such a point. He is witnessing the rapid demolition and collapse of a structure erected upon the delusions of a fantastic faith inspired by piteously ignorant misconception.

After two thousand years of a course of sickening history perpetrated by beclouded intellects, he sees a climax of horrific madness in two titanic world holocausts generated in the life of the peoples dominated by this inhuman code; the final violent repudiation and abandonment of the unconscionable cult by at least two of the leading races long subjected to its tyranny, and the silent rejection of it by a large majority of the people even in countries where it still holds its superficial or nominal dominance. He sees almost universal lethargy toward its claims of unction even in its own temples; and he sees general uncertainty and questioning and challenge in the ranks of its own leaders and supporters. "This beneficent code of religion" is now being revealed as far from beneficent. It is true to say that it has sadly perplexed the mind of every catechumen that ever sat at the feet of a minister of its instruction and, as emancipated thousands now testify, warped their young eager minds awry into a persuasion of acceptance of unintelligible gibberish that could be swallowed only by a total silencing of the critical faculty and its dialectical urgings. People without number come forward now to say that the Sabbath School inculcations of its scheme of theology and the rendition of its Biblical supports as given out by Christian effort, have warped their minds through all the period of youth and wasted half their lives in futile incomprehension.

These multitudes say that it was not until they had seen enough of life and truth on their own account to enable them to throw off this yoke of mental enslavement that they began to gain some balanced sense of the meaning of the Scriptures and things in philosophy and religion. Gladly, then, they have turned away from this befogged center of illusion. Almost a complete roster of those children who come up through this pattern-mill of indoctrination and then go off to higher study, drop quickly everything they were taught. And almost all of them report having to go through the often severe process of tearing their minds loose from the psychological allegiances by which they were bound to the childhood faiths, when later study reveals the untenable nature of the early implantations. So, as a matter of sheer fact, here is a religion which is registering constant failure to hold even its own children the moment they can break away, study and think for themselves.

Yet in a way that Milman did not dream of and which should have struck him with humiliation and dismay, could he have realized it, the "simple religion" of Jesus (assuming again his historic existence) does "stand completely alone in the history of our race." But Milman would not like to hear us say *how* it has stood alone. It all too truly stands alone in that no other matches it for irrationality and unintelligibility of appreciable pertinence to the realities of the human problem. Certainly no other code of theological ideas in a civilized society has ever left its protégés so disastrously uninstructed on true meanings as has this simple system. It has from the start consisted of a set of persuasions foisted upon the acceptance of groups lacking the critical genius to challenge them. It was made up of a list of specific principles of faith pushed upon the attention of the lower orders, and since they lacked the acute discriminatory powers of educated minorities, accepted by them through mass hypnotism.

Milman admits much in saying that the character of Christianity advanced or receded *pari passu* with the vacillations and vicissitudes in the character of the populations among whom it was spread. Instead of reclaiming low-conditioned groups or ages to higher level, Christianity was itself transformed by the innate good sense of humanity to purer form. It seemed never able to rise higher than its human level. It did not come down as a gift from heaven to lift people up; people had to lift it up.

It is not true, therefore, to assert that no human conceptions could have produced Christianity. Not only was Christianity—meaning of course the counterfeit Christianism that Milman thinks was true Christianity—produced by human conceptions, but, as we assert and believe we have conclusively demonstrated, produced by the *lowest* and *poorest* of human conceptions. Better human conception produced other religions far superior to Christianity. The base Christianism, like most popular religionism, came from the bungling efforts of ignorant zealots to make something out of the debris of the wreckage of former high systems. The immemorial *true* Christianity that Augustine mentions was not of human conception; Milman is right if he is thinking of *that* Christianity. It *was* handed to early man by gods, demi-gods or humans developed to near divinity. But the Christianism that Milman is lauding to the skies was *not* this body of wisdom in its purity. It came to form entirely through the blundering efforts of purely human stupidity working over and utterly misshaping the former true religion. The Christianity of history, then, was indeed a human, all too human, product. It won the world—**not** of intelligence (it never has won that) —but of rabid mass emotionalism, by spreading a body of illusions aptly fitted to agitate the mediocre level of mentality.

Milman makes the point that the preachment of Christ was far beyond his own age. But what is there of notable significance in this? The high philosophies of Plato, Aristotle and Plotinus are still far beyond the capabilities of the generality of men. Even after two thousand years of Christian illumination their marvelous revelations of consummate wisdom gather dust in library alcoves.

And one more gesture of emphasis is needed on the hackneyed theme of the characterization by such historians as Milman of the faith of Christianity as "simple." This pious assumption is so flagrant a misrepresentation of fact that its continuous flaunting by Christian pietists perpetuates popular delusion. It has often been declared so simple that any child can grasp it. Well then, the many Church Councils, especially those of the fourth century including the fateful one at Nicaea that turned the Christian world into a madhouse, should have been conducted by children, for the most learned of Christian theologians could reach no acceptable conclusions as to the basic doctrines of the faith, and the Arian controversy over the Trinity ran on with incredible rancor for two hundred years, and no one has ventured to pronounce a final judgment on it to this day. One hundred and thirty-seven delegates to a council that elected Pope Damasus were left dead after the battle over his election. And Gregory Nazianzen, when invited by Theodosius to attend a church Council, answered: "I will not sit in the seat of synods while geese and cranes confusedly wrangle." The "simplicity" of the Christian system was utterly unrecognized by the theological controversialists. Perhaps Milman and others mean that the turning of abstruse allegory and symbol into alleged "history" simplified understanding of what the Scriptures were descanting upon. If it is "simplification" to turn an abstract principle of truth into a man, then Christianity has "simplified" matters. But this one step has thrown the entire structure and pattern of true meaning completely out of focus and introduced inextricable confusion and irrationality into the system. This is the simplification that has resulted in eternal befuddlement. The greatest seminaries can not dispel the fog of bewilderment over the doctrinal meanings to this day.

Perhaps this is the fitting place to introduce the matter of the eternal attitude of reproach and contumely that the Christian Church has heaped endlessly upon the Roman Emperor Julian, nephew and successor of Constantine, upon whose head the Christian hostility has branded the stigma of enmity to the faith of Christ by fastening upon him the epithet of "the Apostate." In the minds of Christian children this monarch has been painted in the figure of a monstrous ogre, who savagely turned Christianity out after its victory and brought back the gods and idols of heathenism. A few writers, whom we shall quote, have taken a fair attitude toward this man, but on the whole the Church has not lifted a finger to correct a foul canard respecting this courageous and high-minded and gifted ruler of Rome. In few things has the narrow bigotry of Christian temper shown itself so viciously as in regard to this man and his effort to save even Christianity itself from the trend it was taking in the direction of supreme disaster.

The item can be introduced by the path that Farrar (Vol. I, 702) takes to open the discussion. He says it may be asked how it could be possible for a prince so able and so wise to have become so mastered at the age of twenty-four by a passion of hatred for such a faith as Christianity, and to undertake the "absurd" effort to bring back the temples and reinstitute the Pagan worship. (There are thousands of young college men and women today who have at the age of twenty-four developed a passion of hatred for Christianity; it was even easier for Julian in his day.) And Farrar supplies a not inconsiderable part of the answer when he says that it is not hard to see how little a man of his philosophical tastes would be attracted by the professed religion of such a man as his uncle, Constantine, through whose political conniving Christianity had been elevated to security and state sanction. For the record of this monarch had been blackened by the murder of the closest members of his family and a series of other crimes. Nor would Julian's acquaintance with Eusebius, Farrar adds, tend to inspire love for the new religion which that scheming prelate had so intrigued with Constantine to promote. Then Farrar ventures a mild exoneration of Julian by stating that "the character of Christianity had never been rightly presented to him." "The Christianity he had come to despise, the only Christianity he knew,—was mainly associated with a superstitious martyr-idolatry and a groveling relic-worship." (One might think that no further reason need be sought.) He quotes Julian as saying that the Galileans "abandon the worship of the gods to worship the moldering remains of the dead. They have filled everything with tombs and cenotaphs." "Bone-worshippers," he dubbed them. Eunapius had written: "These are the gods whom men worship nowadays, men called martyrs before whose bones, salted and pickled, the monks and the bishops lie groveling in the dust." The Christianity that Julian had to witness around him, Farrar continues, had already become degenerate. Its demoralization had kept pace with its prosperity. And, ever ready to whitewash Christianity and blacken Paganism, this great Christian authority has of course to transfer all blame back to Paganism: "Heathen influences had tainted its purity. It was infected with worldliness and corrupted by superstition." Julian, he says, despised the self-maceration of turbulent pretenders to saintliness, who in "proportion to their ignorance" were always convinced of their infallibility—the invariable picture.

"What especially disgusted him—the sin which then weakened and disgraced the Church, as it has weakened and disgraced it ever since—was the furious partisanship, the unscrupulous animosity, the savage hatred kindled among Christians by theologians and frequently by unimportant Christians. In vain he exhorted the Christians to tolerance and the mutually respected exercise of their religious freedom. He left it as his expression that 'the deadliest wild beasts are hardly so savage against human beings as most Christians are against each other.' "

But, fearing that he had damned Christianity too severely, the Canon has to redeem the situation by a renewed fling at Paganism,—still referring to Julian:

"He was not wise enough to see that Pagan women could not be like Christian women whom all admired, nor Pagan priests like the nobler portion of the Christian clergy, nor Pagan sophists like such men as Ambrose, Gregory and Basil. And thus he spoilt the whole meaning of his life by trying to overthrow the religion of eternity and to revive an idolatry so false, so empty and so deep that even in the grove of Daphne on the high festival of Apollo, in his most famous and enchanting shrine, no one was found to bring an offering to the God of Day except a single priest who brought a single goose."

Answer to this is that the thing that "spoilt the whole meaning of" Julian's life was an arrow shot into his chest no doubt by a Christian bigot while he was leading the Roman army heroically in battle, and which put an end to the young Emperor's magnificent effort to lift the Roman government out of foul political corruption by means of far-reaching and statesman-like reforms, by which he had already in the less than two years of his short reign made fine progress. Here would have been the world's supreme chance (even better than with the Stoic Marcus Aurelius) to try Plato's doctrine that the state should be ruled by philosophers. For Julian was a profound student and a genuine lover of the great Greek esoteric wisdom. Several works of his on philosophy sufficiently attest that.

The truth of this situation should be seen. Julian was not out to restore Pagan superstition; he was bent to restore philosophical understanding and end superstition, whether Pagan or Christian. He would naturally have been deeply grieved at the decay of the old religion through loss of competent understanding. He was well aware that the worship of the gods and the vogue of the myths had drifted lamentably far away from grasp of the lofty principles of true spiritual science and occult knowledge which alone can lend sound meaning to the rituals and symbolic representations of the old religion that Rome had inherited. How to revive not simply the outward forms and usages of the Pagan system, but to revitalize them with their deeper esoteric import to inspire educated worshippers, was unquestionably the heavy task and the earnest desire of this young Emperor-philosopher.

His death, instead of being fiendishly gloated over by Christians ever since and vengefully interpreted as the expression of the wrath of God against him for his apostasy from "the religion of eternity," should be sincerely mourned as indeed one of the most fatal losses in all history. His untimely death certainly was one of the most crucially decisive events in history, fully as critical as any of the ten great decisive battles, such as Marathon, Waterloo, Gettysburg and others. What can be said is that almost certainly Julian would have reestablished the Greek Academies, to reeducate an intelligentsia in the esoteric background of the Pagan religious rites and symbols, the annual festivals with their dramas. This would have restored, not Pagan idolatry, but the same true foundations of the primal Christianity that will now have to be restored if the system masquerading under the name of Christianity is to be redeemed to its true identity and made a power to benefit mankind. Julian was certainly saddened by the spectacle of the superstitious way in which the old Mystery dramas had been degraded to mechanical performance, devoid of the sanctity and cathartic power which the keen perception of the esoteric significance of every rite and symbol can alone impart to religious ceremonial. When Julian looked out from his throne and saw what was happening on both sides, the abject degradation of the old system into sheer bleak meaningless ritualism—the shell without the live kernel—and the frightful frenzy of the converts to the new wild cult of a personal Savior, he had to make a choice between the two and formulate a policy designed to bring the best results. Hope stirred in his mind of reenlightening the philosophical students first, then the upper ranks, and through them the populace, to the true meaning of the Pagan forms, to reform and respiritualize the great systems that he knew still held the germs of mighty truth. The rabid fury of unintelligent Christianity no doubt certified to him the hopelessness of gaining anything by compromise in that direction. Pagan deficiency might be corrected and redeemed; with Christian fanaticism nothing was possible but to try to stop it and let it die. He turned his hand to the salvation of the truth that lay obscured in Pagan religion.

It was beyond all argument the wisest, the only, course he could have taken, being the philosopher that he was. No one can say how well this noble effort would have succeeded if he could have held the Emperor's scepter for the seventy years of a normal life. It might have redeemed all subsequent history from a blackness that darkens the spirit merely to read it. But with a prescience born of dogmatic pomposity and self-preening arrogance, all Christian writers who have ventured a prediction based on the possibilities of Julian's having lived to carry through his restoration of Paganism, have not hesitated to paint the consequences for the world in the most lowering and portentous colors. It would have been direful, they say, beyond anything imaginable.

One must ask how it could possibly have been as evil as the actual course of events that has been written in Thoth's eternal record of human action by the "victory" of a deformed, debased and debasing Christianism. We know *that* record; what the other might have been we can only speculate. A mind unbiased and equipped to speculate intelligently can hardly believe it could have been half so wicked as the history that Christianity wrote from the third to the twentieth century.

Driven surely by evidence of abuse and venality, Julain forbade the clergy to exercise their rights "which it must be confessed they had abused" (Farrar) of drawing up wills and receiving legacies. He would not allow Christian teachers to instruct children in the classical literature. He gave his reason as this:

"To us belong eloquence, the arts of Greece, the worship of the Gods; to you nothing but ignorance and rusticity. Such is your wisdom."

Bishop Wordsworth said years ago that

"It was the worldliness, the pride, the ambition, the malignity, the craftiness and cruelty of some in high places in the Church which helped to make him an apostate."

And Farrar adds (I, 705):

"His chief hatred was concentrated, not upon the ordinary mass of Christians, but on their great leaders, such as Basil and Athanasius."

Niebuhr considered Julian's work *Misapogon* to be "one of the most elegant works which Greek literature produced in the period of its second life."

But Christian jealousy could not let Julian off with any ultimate judgment that would be fair and true. He had to be stigmatized and pigeon-holed in the category of enemies of the true faith and made to bear the slander. So Farrar says:

"He was brave, self-denying, indefatiguable; except toward the Christians he behaved with clemency and justice."
"But the Christians could not forgive him for turning the world upside down in pursuit of a pestilential chimera."

This utterly blinks the actual fact that it was a combination of decaying Pagan intelligence and obliviousness to the meanings of their own formulations (which can be no worse than the failure of Christian mentality to understand *their* own creeds and doctrines and Scriptures even now) with the supreme violence of Christian bigots that had turned the world upside down and Julian was only aiming in the wisest way to set it right end up once more. For any one to designate his noble aim as the pursuit of a pestilential chimera is but to advertise ignorance.

"He wished to displace the religion which had brought into the world its holiest ideals and noblest progress and to bring it back to the worship of phantoms and demons who had been the patrons of every vice."

This again is pious bombast, utterly contradicted by the truth of history, if that can be given a hearing. But Farrar concludes:

"His unfortunate conception of substituting for Christianity a reformed Paganism, swathed in the illusionated mist of Neo-Platonic philosophy rendered unavailing alike his talents and his labors. Nothing could be achieved by that moonlight phantom."

374

With a crude and fanatical Christianism now being sentenced with the verdict of two thousand years of ugly history, and a long-slandered Pagan philosophy, including principally this same Neo-Platonism, now once again being reconstituted in all its sublimity and splendor of luminous intelligence, perhaps it is a moot question which of the two will ultimately be declared the "moonlight phantom." Practically every honest and capable scholar who has made close acquaintance with *both* has given his verdict of superior excellence to the Pagan philosophies.

Gregory, the Church Father, remorselessly thrusts the soul of Julian into hell, while he summons from heaven the soul of the contemptible Constantius, "the most devout and Christ-loving of Emperors," to load him with praises. At Julian's death, over which all Christendom should be heavily ashamed,

"The theatres proclaimed the victory of the Cross amid their impure spectacles, and the churches and memorials of the martyrs were profaned by unseemly dances."

One must think that could Julian's spirit have witnessed this and commented upon it, his observation would likely have been: So they run true to form; they behave just like Christians.

Whether true or only another imaginative concoction of Christian vindictiveness, it is reported that Julian on his deathbed had uttered a prophecy that the Galilean would conquer, or that he had conquered. Fuller (*History of Philosophy,* 327) comments on this in connection with his statement that with the passing of Damascius and Simplicius Greek religion and philosophy died, and with its death the Judean fanaticism that so vexed him with its endless wranglings would go on unchecked, its only corrective having expired. If Julian uttered such a prophecy it can readily be seen as being the expression of the despair of his last moments in view of what would happen when his power to reform a world gone both degenerate and fanatical was withdrawn. Few champions of humanity in the line of history would have passed out so overwhelmed with the realization that their passing spelled infinite calamity to the world. He must have suffered the keenest anguish of regret that his end had come so prematurely. And Christian gloating over it ever since represents the base venting of the bigoted passions of mean souls wrought to hatred by distorted thinking. For *true* Christianity Julian's death was an infinite tragedy.

CHAPTER XVII

THE REAL GHOST OF HISTORY

It is deemed desirable to incorporate in the work at this point an assemblage of evidence indicating the non-historical character of the ancient Scriptures. This insertion is made at the expense of space that might be used to present more pertinent material. But it is regarded as essential for many reasons. It will be impossible to break the hold of false Christianism upon the mass mind as long as the Bibles are believed to be actual history. And minds can not be changed without the presentation of evidence. Let it be said promptly, however, that the data included here is but an infinitesimal fraction of all that could be gathered. A thousand pages would not be sufficient to spread out the material that lies in our notebooks alone, and that has come from only limited reading. That the conclusions set forth on the basis of this evidence fly straight in the face of all orthodox belief will not be wondered at. But that fact will not invalidate the evidence. The significant thing is that the evidence is unwelcome and will be fought.

The chief body of non-historical material affecting Christianity is of course in the New Testament. But as that grew out of and is founded on the Old, it is well to look first at the situation there. We have already presented from the *Encyclopædia Britannica* passages that state clearly the non-historical character of Hebrew Talmudic, Midrashic, Haggadic and general religious literature including the Old Testament.

Benjamin Bacon, Yale theologian, in his *Jesus and Paul* (p. 164) says that

"Haggadic teaching, whether Jewish or Christian, has no restrictions in the use of fiction save that it bring home the religious or moral truth intended. Its one rule is: 'Let all things be done unto edification.' "

And again (207) he says:

"Just as in modern times we are conscious that truth may be conveyed in many cases more effectively by fiction than by fact, so with the ancient world, *but in much higher degree.*"

The "higher degree" being that the knowing ones held keys by which to differentiate between the outer allegory and its inner core of meaning, and the uninitiated did not. The knowing ones, said Massey, kept back in secrecy the esoteric explanation of the myths, to let the crude belief in the supposed history take root among the ignorant.

A weight of cogent testimony is carried by the statement of Eusebius (*Ecclesiastical History,* Bk. II, Ch. 17) in which he quotes Philo's comment on the ascetics in Egypt:

"The whole period from dawn to eve is for them a religious exercise; they study the sacred Scriptures and expound their rational philosophy by allegory, for they regard the literal interpretation as symbolic of a concealed reality indicated in what is beneath the surface. They have also some writings of men of old, who were the founders of this sect, who left many memorials of the meaning allegorically expounded, which they use as models and copy their method of treatment."

Eusebius comments on the above as follows:

"This seems to have been said by a man who had listened to their expositions of the sacred scriptures, and it is perhaps probable that the writings of men of old, which he says were found among them, were the Gospels, the writings of the apostles and some expositions of prophets after the manner of the ancients, such as are in the *Epistle to the Hebrews* and many other of the *Epistles* of Paul."

This is significant testimony and the reference to the *Epistle to the Hebrews* would seem to be likely truth from what Jerome, according to G. R. S. Mead (*Fragments of a Faith Forgotten,* p. 128), says of a *Gospel according to the Hebrews.* This, he says, is the same as the *Gospel of the Twelve Apostles* and the *Gospel of the Nazarenes.* Then Mead states that "it should be remembered that these Nazoraeans knew nothing of the Nazareth legend which was subsequently developed by the 'in order that it might be fulfilled' school of historicizers."

A most revealing fact it is that fragments of the original Egyptian mythos, which is a system of cosmo-evolutionary laws and *archai* based on the eternal principles of being as they are reflected in nature, and which the Egyptians detected as no other people have done, crop up prolifically in the Haggadoth, the Kabalah, the Talmud and other Hebrew writings. It was this type of material that entered so largely into Philo's elucidations. The distillation of true inference from this is that this same matter had been known to the Jews themselves and known in the same category of understanding, that is, as non-historical.

So that again it is proved that Biblical "history" has been mainly derived from misinterpreted theology.

An instance—out of hundreds—comes to hand at the moment in what is said in the *Classical Journal* (Vol. 17, p. 264, T. T. Massey) to the effect that the 600,000 warriors of the Israelite multitude that reportedly came out of Egypt in the Exodus are 600,000 inhabitants of Israel in the heavens, according to the Jewish Kabalah; and the same scenes, events and personages that appear as mundane in the Pentateuch are celestial in the *Book of Enoch*.

In another work we have presented the demonstrable conclusions of Gerald Massey's study, that among ancient peoples the localities, names and character titles of kings, heroes and others, were all taken from the original zodiacal or astrological charts of the heavens and transplanted to the maps and the earthly histories and personages of national renown. History and geography were alike framed over the pattern shown in the mount, the pattern of the heavens. This universal ancient custom is the key at once to all the mythic religion of the past and the conclusive seal of the non-historical character of the Scriptural narratives.

It has been the nearly universal assumption that all mythology emerges from veridical history, or that it all had some history for its background. Massey labors with data and logic to demonstrate that the reversal of the process is the truth: the myth was first and the (alleged) history arose from it, being the rash interpretation put upon it by popular thought which can not comprehend the subtleties of the mythical message. Massey brings the *Book of Enoch* into this category. He says that one of two things is sure: either the *Book of Enoch* contains the Hebrew history in allegorical form; or the celestial allegory *is* the Hebrew history. The parallel is perfect, he affirms. Instead of being history turned into allegory, as the common opinion of scholarship has had it for centuries, it is allegory that has been turned into "history." The *Book of Enoch* certainly does contain the same characters as the sacred and secret history of the Jews; and as the *Enoch* cosmograph surely pertains to the astronomical allegory, there is established the strongest possible presumption that the material is mythical or typical in the Pentateuch. There can be no doubt that the *Book of Enoch* is just what its title claims it to be: the book of the revolutions of the heavenly bodies, with no relation to earthly human history.

The staggering fact forced upon Massey by the data he unearthed in Egyptian study is that every trait and feature which enters into the picture of the Christ as divinity, and every event or circumstance considered as pertaining to the human personality of the Christ, was pre-extant and pre-applied to the Egyptian and the Gnostic Christ figures, who never could become flesh. Massey then specifies some twenty features of character description of the Gospel Christ, and matches every one with identical items from Horus and Iu-em-hetep, the Egyptian Christ characters. The first of these recites the fact, of which all Christian minds are so oblivious, though it stands in their own Bible, that like the double-sexed Horus and other deities, the Christ of *Revelation,* who is the Alpha and Omega of the creational allegory, is represented as epicene, with female breasts.

Again Massey says that the noble full-flowing river of old Egypt's wisdom ended in a quagmire of prophecies for the Jews and a barren wilderness of desert sands for the Christians, and on these shifting sands the Christians reared their temple of the eternal which is giving way at last because it was not founded on the solid rock of the wisdom expressed in mythic and allegorical figures.

Higgins in his great *Anacalypsis* quotes Bryant in a remarkable discerning paragraph:

"Besides it is evident that most of the deified personages never existed; but were mere titles of the Deity, the Sun, as has been in a great measure proved by Macrobius. Nor was there ever anything of such detriment to ancient history as the supposing that the gods of the Gentile world had been natives of the countries where they were worshipped."

The attempt to render these fables of the gods into ostensible history misled, he says, Bishop Cumberland, Pearson, Petavius, Scaliger and numberless other great men, and among the foremost the great Newton.

Higgins asserts that the work of every ancient author without exception has come down to us badly corrupted by the skulduggery of Christian editors. He says that he suspects that "the vulgar" were taught to expect a new divine person every six hundred years.

It is as plain as day that allegory is woven into the narrative from such a fact as that Philo speaks of a character in the sacred story, "a man whose name is East." This must be held a strange appellation if it had been intended to refer to a human. But, continues the commentator, if the name be an allusion to the Incorporeal Man, who is the rising expression of the divine in human nature, it can be seen that "East" is a most appropriate name, as he is the re-orient man of the resurrection.

Allan Upward takes all significance off the field of history and roots it in its rightful place in the subjective consciousness of all men when he writes that in the early true Christianity of the Gnostics, "the redemption of the sinner is not so much the historic transaction consummated on the material cross of Calvary as it is the work of the Christ within." "An extraordinary licence was accorded in his age to the preacher to employ allegory, myth, symbolism, legend, parable, whatever he will, in the interest of religious edification."

One of the most challenging bits of testimony to the allegorical character of ancient Biblical writing is before us in a remarkable statement of the Christian Father Origen in his *Contra Celsum* (IV, 171, Spence). After making a comparison between the Gospel resurrection of Christ and the Greek resurrection of Dionysus, he remarks in a tone of apology tinged with bitterness:

"Or, forsooth, are the Greeks to be allowed to use such words with regard to the soul, and speak in allegorical fashion (*tropologein*) and we forbidden to do so?"

"Thus clearly declaring," adds Mead, "that the 'resurrection' was an allegory of the soul and not historical." This exceptional touch of resentment on the part of a learned Christian against the crude limitations imposed on his mind by Christian narrowness is most revealing. Now as then any mind illumined by the lofty philosophy of the Greeks had a hard time accepting the crudities of Christian faith and its literal restraints on intelligence.

On the subject of Old Testament historicity it is surely of great significance that the father of "real history," Herodotus, has made no mention of the world's wonder of architecture at the time he lived, the temple of Solomon at Jerusalem. A writer notes that not even the Masons claim the actual existence of Solomon. Kenealy shows that he is not noticed by Herodotus, nor by Plato or any writer of standing. It is most extraordinary, says Kenealy, that the Jewish nation, over which but a few years before the mighty Solomon had reigned in all his glory, with a magnificence scarcely equalled by the greatest monarchs, spending nearly eight billions of gold on a temple, was overlooked by Herodotus in writing of both Babylon and Egypt and in visiting both places having to pass quite close to the great capital of the Jewish nation. Kenealy even asserts that there are no proofs of the actual existence of the twelve tribes of Israel, and adds that Herodotus, the most accurate of historians, who was in Assyria when Ezra flourished, never mentions the Israelites at all. He was born in 484 B.C., when the Israelitish history, according to the Old Testament, was running its course. How, asks Kenealy, can Herodotus' silence (like Paul's, we add) be accounted for? Only on the ground, so indubitably established by Massey and others, that Old Testament writing, as even Josephus hints, is not history but sublime allegory.

Higgins draws attention to the notable fact that such an astonishing event as the crossing of the Israelites from Egypt on the dry lane through the parted waters of the Red Sea, and the overwhelming of the Egyptian hosts in the waters, was not mentioned by such historians as Berosus, Strabo, Diodorus or Herodotus. That these men should not have heard of such incredible events either from the Egyptians or the Syrians, Arabians or Jews is unaccountable on any assumption that the events really occurred. Likewise it is odd—if it is history—that the same series of occurrences took place when the Afghans or Rajapontans, shepherd tribes, invaded South India and conquered Ceylon, and were driven out over Adam's bridge. Their pursuers were similarly overwhelmed.

Massey affirms that the catacombs of Rome are crowded with Egypto-Gnostic types which had served to Roman, Persian, Greek and Jew as evidence for the non-historic origins of Christianity. The Jesus of the Gnostic Scriptures says that when he came into the world he brought with him the twelve powers; "I took them from the hands of the twelve saviors of the treasure of light"; that is, from the twelve who are called Aeons in the cosmic astrology. These twelve are the distinctive radiations of divine power that are to be gathered up by the Christ Aeon as it circles the twelve signs of the zodiac, appropriating one from each, and finally unifying them all in himself. They have been humanized and personalized when the allegory was forced into Procrustean "history."

There is another mighty book of historical record that maintains a silence profound and perplexing on what has been universally taken to be history in the Old Testament—the residence of the Hebrews in Egypt for four hundred years and their exodus therefrom. This scroll of history which speaks so eloquently by its very muteness is the mass of records on Egyptian tombs, temples, tablets, monuments and papyri. The astute Egyptians committed the events of their history to these indelible slates. Some claims have been put forth that one or two records seem to mention the name of Jacob-El as a divinity, one on a scarabaeus; and it is believed that Petrie found one reference to the name of "Ysirrael." This is too scant for historic evidence of all the chapter of Israel's connection with Egypt, which, had it been of veridical nature, would have been recorded voluminously. The going down of twelve orders (tribes) of angelic spirits into the Egypt of the flesh on earth to win evolutionary guerdon in the bondage of spirit to flesh, is the grand universal myth of the descent of souls to mundane life, and too clearly expressed in allegory to be mistaken for history by any except the most imbecile. A beautiful poetic fantasy is not made historically real by being misbelieved by a million million deluded minds.

Then there are the several "captivities" of the Hebrews in Persia, Babylon and Assyria beside the "bondage in Egypt." In *Jeremiah* (52:27-30) the total number of Israelites carried into captivity by Nebuchadnezzar is given as four thousand six hundred. This is hardly volume enough to be considered as the captivity of a whole people. There is evidence also that these displaced persons were allowed practically full personal liberty in their new home, as were many such groups of Hebrews that were from time to time settled by various monarchs about the Eastern lands to guard the trade caravans against the perpetual raids by desert brigands. Allan H. Godbey, in his monumental work, *The Ten Tribes a Myth,* has assembled incontestable evidence to all this, reducing the theological implications of the Biblical record almost to nonsense. We can not omit Massey's splendid summarization of all this pseudo-historical "captivity" and "bondage" suffered by the Israelitish Sons of God:

"It is a captivity that never was historical in a land of bondage which may be called Babylon, Egypt or Sodom; but, as *Hosea* shows, it was a bondage from which the prisoners were set free 'after two days' "—

that is, in the spiritual resurrection of the soul buried in flesh during the "three days" of its pilgrimage through the mineral, vegetable and animal kingdoms, or various other symbolizations of three, such as the three winter months or the three dark days of the moon, or the three watches of the night preceding the "fourth watch" or dawn, "night," like "winter," embleming the period of incarnation.

Massey traces the *Chr* (*Kr,Cr,Khr*) stem of the word *Christos* back to Egyptian origin and, in spite of the skepticism with which the scholar's philological work is regarded academically, it seems as if he could not be in error on this point. It comes, he says, from the Egyptian *Kher,* meaning the "Word," "Voice" or the Logos. As the Christians identified the Christ with the Logos or Word, there is sound reason to credit this origin as correct. The Greek *Ch* (our X) and the Greek *Rho* (R, but resembling our P) together form the cross in the circle, or cross and circle combined. The circle is the infinity of spirit and matter, and the cross is spirit and matter in conjunction. The combined figure, or *Chr* is thus emblematic of the entire story and meaning of all life in both its expressive and its latent phases. The power that manifests in all creation is in the cosmos the Logos, or *Kheru,* and in man it is the *Christos.* In the cosmos it is the universal voice; and in man it is the fragment, germ or seed of infinite mind that can come to conscious function in the brain-cell mechanism of a mortal body.

According to Philo the Word could not become incarnate in corporeal form and certainly not in one corporeal unit. Massey says that Philo knows no more of a Christ that could be made flesh than he knew of a Jesus in human form; and he was *exactly* contemporary with Jesus if the latter lived in reality. He is the one writer whose word about Jesus would have carried the weight of authentic testimony had he vouchsafed a single paragraph. But, no; there is not a word. Like Paul, only a little later, he never heard of the man.

Allegory and not history is again obvious in old legends that the cross of Christ represented the four cardinal points, and in Christian tradition was alleged to be composed of four kinds of wood, palm, cedar, olive and cypress, these no doubt being meant to signify respectively north, west, east and south; and these in turn typing the four elements in man's psychic constitution, sense, emotion, thought and spiritual intuition.

Again in the symbol of the Fish for the Christos power there is further evidence of allegory, pointing away from history. When two such stalwart adherents of the new faith as Augustine and Tertullian refer to Christ as the Great Fish, and his followers as the minnows, there is symbolic reference to non-personal Christly attribute, under purely zodiacal (Piscean) emblemism. The sign of Pisces is both the house of bread and of fish, *the two foods* on which the many are fed in the Gospels, symbolizing the one the food of earth, the other the food from the sea or water, and thus typifying sense and emotion, in one aspect of its reference. A historical man would have no ground of reality in being *called* a fish. In allegory the fish symbol (elaborated elsewhere) yields amazingly pertinent relevance and meaning.

Likewise the legends of Christ's birth in a stable, or in a cave, are quite definitely not in relation to history. But they immediately take on splendid significance in the myth referring to the body as the stable in which an animal nature is housed for the winter or night of incarnation, or the cave of earth (the first man is of the earth, earthy)—again indicating the body.

Neither Basilides nor Valentinus, philosophical Gnostic Christians, acknowledged any historical personage as the founder of Christianity. Gnostics generally would stand on this same ground as to the purely spiritual essence of Christhood.

A most telling and challenging item comes to light in the name of Bethany, where Jesus raised Lazarus, with two sisters present. Both Massey and later researchers, notably Wendell Harris of England, have adduced the patent fact that Bethany is a compound of the Hebrew beth, "house," and the An, or On (Egyptian Anu, Greek *Heliopolis*), city where the *sun,* symbol of the divine Christ in man, went to its death and later resurrection. It is by now recognized that Jesus is Horus, Lazarus is his "dead" Father, Osiris (El-Asar-us), and that Mary and Martha are the *Meri* and *Merti* (alternate names for Isis and Nephthys) of the Egyptian cult. Since this story is given *only* in that one of the four Gospels that is admittedly least historical of all, and by some regarded as entirely non-historical, there is every presumption that the allegorical nature of the Lazarus incident is established, especially since it is clearly derived from documents of ancient Egyptian origin. And an amazing corroboration is added by the fact that Anu is described in old Egypt as "the place of multiplying bread." At Beth-any (the "u" becomes "y" in English always) Jesus multiplied bread—and fish!

And in the Egyptian *Book of the Dead* the two Meris, Isis and Nephthys, likewise plead with their "dead" brother El-Asar-Us to arise and come forth to comfort them.

Pagan representation of abstract truth exalted the mothers of the sun-Christs to the rank of goddesses. None are human. Christianity fell into the allegory, or fell *for* the allegory when it took Mary (Maia, Maya, Meri, Moira, Myrrha, Miriam, etc.) to be a human girl. It has vainly tried to correct the error by deifying her.

Higgins records the presence of the Mosaic myths all over the known world at dates of great antiquity, with a reduplication of place names, hero names and dramatic figures.

Even the symbolism connected with the age of twelve years is found elsewhere than in the New Testament. Lundy (op. cit., p. 241) says that St. Ignatius calls Daniel the Wise, and says that at the age of twelve he became possessed of the divine spirit.

According to Benjamin Bacon (*Jesus and Paul*), Marcion, Cerinthus and the Docetic Gnostics had no difficulty with a Christ-emanation assuming temporary embodiment. "What they could not tolerate was a real flesh and blood Leader, a High Priest and King of humanity." Just so. The Pagan world had this sort of Messiah in every Roman Emperor, as Japan had in its Mikado. But then Bacon flies off into inanity when he finds he must not let the statement stand without the invariable slur on Gnostic idealism. For he says that surely the mythical interpretation of the gospel record has little to contribute to the science of religion, since science of any kind must deal with objective historic fact. The larger the basis in concrete reality the better. A science of mythology is possible, he admits; but a record of life in real moral union with the Father is a better basis for the scientific study of religion.

It seems hopeless to expect that Christian theologians can ever be brought to see that the mythological interpretation of those Gospels is the one and only way by which the dynamism of the spiritual truth depicted there by allegory can be transferred from those pages and that alleged personage over to the millions who read it now in vain. To take it as history leaves the Christ-power standing back there in Judea; to take it as allegory of the soul in every man brings its power surging back into the individual reader. This is the final answer.

When Christian people can at last be educated to read the Gospel narrative as the allegory of a divine reality *tremendously concrete and objective in themselves,* the Christian religion will be born anew.

Another stern challenge lurks in the fact that such capable minds as Marcion, Valentinus, Cerinthus and the Docetic Gnostics refused to accept Jesus as a living man. Why should these educated men deny, or debate and doubt the existence of Jesus if the man actually had lived? Their doubt indicates that no evidence of his existence was known in their day.

Even Spinoza says that it is not necessary to know Christ after the flesh; yet it is quite necessary that we should know that eternal Son of God, the wisdom of God, which has manifested itself in all things, but chiefly in the mind of man and in certain men risen to Christhood. This is the true Christian theology.

Another arresting datum is the surprising fact that, as Massey points out, the early Christians assigned two birthdays, three months apart, the one at the winter solstice, the other at the vernal equinox. These can have no other foundation than the two birthdays of the "double Horus" of Egypt, Horus the Elder, dying in the autumn and at his lowest point at the winter solstice, being reborn and resurrected at the vernal equinox as Horus the Younger.

Stellar typology was beautifully woven into the allegory. When the birthplace was in the sign of Taurus, the star that was rising in the East to herald the new birth was the Orion cluster. In this group, in Orion's belt, are the "three kings," representing the three aspects of divinity; and so standing behind the Gospel legend of the journey of the three Magi from the East to welcome the divine Babe. Allegory is everywhere behind and before the history; and allegory should have become "history" in no other way than as clarified conception in human brains.

Massey brings out that the Mohammedans, tracing usage away back to ancient custom, celebrated the birth of the babe in the cave or subterranean sanctuary, from which the Priest issued, saying: "The Virgin has brought forth: the light is about to begin to grow again." Is it not significant that non-Christians can celebrate this "Christian" festival with "Christian" customs, yet not recognize the Jesus birth and history?

The Arabs celebrated the birth of deity in the cave; the Persians marked the birth of the sun, symbol of the deity, in the cave of Mithras at the winter solstice; and the Greeks commemorated the birth of the sun-god in the stable of Augias, which Hercules, performing the twelve labors of the symbolic zodiac, had to cleanse. The stable was, of course, the physical body of man, the source of pollution to the purity of the soul resident in it for a cycle.

Klausner thinks that it is far more difficult to explain how certain Jewish writers, the evangelists, invented such a wonderful character as Jesus than it is to admit that they were describing a man who really did live. But this only testifies to Klausner's unacquaintance with the whole spirit and methodology of ancient sacred writing. They did not have to invent a fictitious character or pick up and exalt a real living entity. For never was there not at hand in esoteric literature and in the Mysteries the universal type-figure of man divinely perfected and radiant in Christly virtue. This mythos personification was never absent from the literature, the ceremonial, the art, the drama, the myths and the general thought of intelligent Pagans. One does not have to invent what is there and omnipresent.

And so it is not necessary, as many Theosophists and Rosicrucians postulate, to have recourse even to such problematic prototypal figures as the living Apollonius of Tyana (born about the year 2 A.D.) or the certainly mythical or typal figure of Jehoshua ben Pandira, nebulous Talmudic character, asserted to have lived about 115 years B.C. Ignorant wild belief, ever prone to concretize and historicize spiritual allegory, kept looking for the Messiah-light in human form and picked on now this, now that historical personage as the embodiment. Many Fundamentalist Christians of various sects are still doing the same thing. And this stupid blindness persists in spite of the Scriptural declaration that the Kingdom of Heaven cometh not with observation, lo here, or lo there.

Well does Benjamin Bacon in his *Jesus and Paul,* speaking of *Mark,* make the astute observation that, do what he will to emphasize the miraculous powers of Jesus and the marvel of his wisdom and prophetic foresight,

"It is of course impossible for him to make it at the same time the story of a real man under real historical conditions, and also the story of the superhuman being who steps down from the 'Heavenly Places' of the post-resurrection Christology. The combination is, however, attempted even in this earliest-known record of the sayings and doings of Jesus, and it is in this attempt that the influence of Paul, however indirectly, is most clearly seen."

Comment here should accentuate what Bacon so frankly avers, that *Mark* found it impossible to make a celestial allegory sound realistically like a human biography; because that was in reality what he was attempting. It is what the debased Christianity has all along been trying to do, and by now it should know that its effort has finally failed. The centuries of harlequin efforts to force the typal Jesus Logos-figure down into the frame of a personal life have constituted, all unwittingly, the consummate serio-comic farce of all time.

Most noteworthy again is Bacon's forthright asseveration that Paul, "our earliest witness," gives no evidence of knowing a "Christ after the flesh." Obviously Paul needed to make no soul-searching decision, because he had never heard of the existence or work of such a man. It is unthinkable that he would not have mentioned him if he had known him to be the founder of the esoteric faith he had himself so ardently espoused. And Bacon most truly and startlingly adds:

"Had he done otherwise, Christianity would not have survived his generation."

A string of exclamation points could not overemphasize this observation. Let the theologians ponder it.

In the Apocryphal books, such as those of which a fragment was found at Oxyrhyncus, entitled the *Logoi,* or *Sayings of Jesus,* it is obvious that a man born early in the first century could not have been the author or originator of what is there headed "the Wisdom of Jesus." Phrases common to the Ritual of old Egypt extant thousands of years earlier are found in these preserved remnants. The utterances so long assumed to be those of a speaker in the first century are definitely the lines spoken by the dramatic figures in the age-old Mystery recitals. They were long stock phrases in the speeches of the actors in the great drama.

Another item of allegory converted into assumed history turns up in the narrative of Jesus' trial before Pilate. The crowd to whom Pilate turned to throw the decision off his own conscience yelled to him to crucify Jesus and release Bar Abbas. Klausner very sagaciously and with obvious truth records a discernment of scholarship here that is very important. He scrutinizes the point that the populace demanded not Jesus, *"bar Amma"* (son of the Mother), but Jesus *"bar Abba"* (son of the Father). Klausner does not see the deeper apocryphal significance of this, but his Hebrew terminology betrays the cryptic clue to that recondite sense. In the human constitution there are the two conflicting (until they are reconciled and "marry") natures, the man of flesh, born of woman (son of the Mother, *mater,* matter), and the man of spirit (son of the Father, spirit). In the ritual dramas the mob, the hordes of lower passions in man, were dramatized as shouting their demand to crucify the Christ, as it is said in fourth *Galatians,* "he that was born after the flesh persecuted him that was born after the spirit." This relationship was appropriately dramatized in the scenario. And this is the perfect representation of what the rabble of low sense motivations cry out against the Christ man in us all the time. If anything could more plainly clinch the proof that the trials and crucifixion of the Jesus figure in the Gospels is sheer allegory and drama, and not history, it would be hard to find.

The justly famous and beautiful fifty-third chapter of *Isaiah,* the so-named Chapter of the Suffering Servant, has perplexed the theological mind no end. No one has been able to decide who is this character suffering for our trangressions and bearing the whole world's sins in his own body. Fidelity to set habitudes and modes of exegesis in Christianism require that it be equated with the Nazareth Jesus. But he wasn't alive in Isaiah's time to be the world's scapegoat for sin. Never has it been seen that it is the one universal Christ-spirit or divine principle that in all men takes upon itself the sufferance of sin that such a position and evolutionary function entails, to perform its aeonial work in the divine scheme. What is definite is that it can not be the historical Jesus, even in prophecy.

The myths had been at last converted into ostensible and half-plausible "history" and republished as such, and everything else was suppressed or pressed into the mold of the fraud. Christology was founded on the Christos who is mythical in one phase and mystical in another, and forever real in human consciousness. He was Egyptian and Gnostic in both phases, but historical in neither. The Christ was a title and a type that could not become a person,—but could be personified in a drama. One has but to turn to the second book of *Esdras* to learn that the Jesus Christ of the Gospels was both pre-historic and pre-Christian, derived from ancient Eᴏᵥᴏt. As Massey puts it,

"The true Christ, whether mythical or mystical, astronomical or spiritual, never could become a historical personage, and never did originate in any human history."

Those who did know the inner truth, whether Jews, Samaritans, Essenes or Gnostics, entirely repudiated the historical interpretation and refused to become "Christians,"—and were the best of true Christians for it! "They could no more join the ignorant fanatical Salvation Army in the first century than we can in the nineteenth," protests Massey.

The foundations of the whole "Christ biography" were already laid in entire independence of any supposed Founder of Christianity. They were cosmographs of eternal principles of truth, representing the verities of higher consciousness, and were later transferred to earth and translated into a human story which never "happened," but all the same is the pith and marrow of all that does happen.

The famed first international legalist, Grotius of the Netherlands, had evidently seen the non-factual basis of Christian or Biblical "history" so clearly that he goes the length of saying in outright fashion that

"Ecclesiastical history consists of nothing but the wickedness of the governing clergy." (*Epistolae*, p. 7.)

Amongst a lengthy list of forgeries may be mentioned that of the document known as the *Acts of Paul and Thecla*. Tertullian says of this piece that it was forged by a presbyter of Asia, who, when convicted, confessed that he did it out of respect for Paul.

It may be a bit off the side of pertinent discussion, but perhaps not entirely irrelevant to the main theme, to look briefly at the traditions of the wonders of divine prodigy alleged to have appeared in the sky when Constantine was fighting the battle of the Milvian Bridge, the victory in which gave him the imperial throne. The apparition of the cross with the Latin *In Hoc Signo Vinces* (In this sign thou shalt conquer) has been accepted by the credulous, but denied by the more critically disposed. The *Catholic Encyclopedia* (VIII-718) says that the *labarum,* or monogram of Christ had been a familiar symbol prior to Constantine's conversion. Eusebius says nothing of the cross incident, though he writes fulsomely of the providential intervention in the Emperor's favor in battles.

Militating against the historical view of the Gospel Jesus is that most strange duality of opinion which prevailed amongst the earliest Christian writers as to the personal form and appearance of the man of Galilee. Of a living person it is next to impossible that there should be two almost diametrically opposed views as to such items as form, figure and personal comeliness. Yet there are two distinct and contrary opinions on this score, the one holding that the Savior of mankind was of radiant beauty in form and feature; the other that he was ugly, deformed and repellent in aspect. An analysis of this confusion given in our work, *Who Is This King of Glory?* can not be repeated here. But that the divergent opinions had their natural origin in the two characterizations of the Egyptian Horus the Elder, old, wizened and disfigured, and Horus the Younger, shining with the beauteous glow of youth, is obvious. Yet the fact is a circumstance of the utmost singularity in Christian annals. There were of course no portraits of Jesus or his mother, as Augustine testifies. Each artist, he says, represented the Lord's face according to his own ideal conception.

Lundy's fine study of *Monumental Christianity* has found that there was no trace in art or literature of the infamous "Slaughter of the Innocents" by Herod's soldiery until about the close of the fourth century, by which time Christian imagination had begun that licentious sweep of its power to reconstruct in concreteness a history that had existed nowhere else save in overwrought minds.

There is scarcely space to elucidate capably the next point; but it is of far greater moment than will be appreciated by the readers of the brief reference here made to it. It has to do with the symbolic meaning of the terms "mount," "desert" and "wilderness" in the arcane Scriptures. Not alone Jesus of the Gospels but heroes of the Old Testament retire again and again into the "mount" and the "desert" or "wilderness," for purposes of retreat, refreshment, rest or renewal. In turning cosmic mythopoeia into actual earthly history these mounts and deserts, like the rivers, seas and lakes, must be localized on the map. But it has been given as yet to few to see how completely the alleged veridical history of the Scriptures is shot into inane gibberish the moment it is realized, as in the end it must be, that the "mount" is a hieroglyph in the archaic language of ideograms, which means just *this earth* itself; that mount in the midst of space on which all spiritual transaction for a soul in evolution takes place. "Desert" and "wilderness" are variant types of the same mundane locality. The earth is itself that "high mount" on which the temptation, the transfiguration and the crucifixion of divine soul in mortal body alike take place. It is where the ark lands after the flood of dissolution washes away all forms to begin a new cycle. And it is the secret mount on which man in his Mosaic state of development climbs aloft to commune with Deity in his tabernacle of flesh. The devastation which the rediscovered connotation of this single word works in fundamentalist conception and theology is complete and bewildering.

This is seen in all its glaring luridness when it is found used by the ancient Egyptians in connection with that other recent disclosure of buried esoteric meaning in the words "death," "the dead" and "to die." All Scriptural meaning is turned quite "downside up" by the reconstruction of theology with the aid of the clues these words furnish. It is now revealed that ancient mythicism considered and named those souls incarnated in earth life "the dead." "To die" was to incarnate; "death" was the depressed, deadened condition of conscious being while soul inhabited the "tomb" of the flesh. As the "mount" was the earth, there emerges in tremendous vividness the hidden meaning of such a phrase as is found in the Egyptian books: "The dead are those who are on the mount."

Charles B. Waite, in his *History of the Christian Religion to the Year 200*, asserts that *Luke's* Gospel had its origin in an earlier Gospel of Paul; *Mark's* in an earlier *Gospel*, or *Recollections of Peter;* and *Matthew's* in the *Oracles*, or *Sayings of Christ*, as Massey claims throughout. But, says Waite, in none of these prototypal sources is there found anything like the miraculous conception or the material resurrection of Christ; or accounts of the miracles; or references to any book containing such accounts or teachings of either of these doctrines. Nor do the Apostolic Fathers, Clement of Rome, Ignatius and Polycarp, make any mention of the miracles of Jesus or of the resurrection. These chief of Christianity's second-century spokesmen make no reference to either of the four Gospels nor to the *Acts of the Apostles,* nor are there any quotations from this literature except such as evangelical writers concede may have been taken from other sources. As Irenaeus says, there was a multitude of Gospels extant in his day.

Waite also says that it can not be denied that the evidence of the existence of the canonical Gospels was unkown to Justin Martyr, and that this lacuna in early Christian literature is well-nigh conclusive as to the non-historicity of the Gospel material. Justin's sketchy references and quotations are obviously from other sources; which again reveals that there *were* other sources out of which material in the four canonical writings could be taken. What those other sources were is the great unsolved problem which Christian scholarship has never faced or even recognized, and it is the one central point of issue on which the solution of the entire muddled problem of Gospel origination ultimately rests.

As so much of Christian evidence for the historicity of evangelical tradition has been made to rest on the *Ecclesiastical History* of Eusebius, who with Constantine convened the epoch-making Council of Nicaea, it is worth noting what Waite has to say as to the reliability of this writer's work:

"No one has contributed more to Christian history, and no one is guilty of more mistakes.

"The statements of this historian are made, not only carelessly and blunderingly, but in many instances in falsification of the facts of history. Not only the most unblushing falsehoods, but literary forgeries of the vilest character darken the pages of his apologetic and historical writing."

Another writer cited by Waite asserts:

"Eusebius had a peculiar faculty for diverging from the truth. He was ready to supply by fabrication what was wanting in historical data."

Many scholars have concurred in these opinions. It is well known on what foundations of falsehood and forgery this great world religion actually rests.

A score or more of passages could be assembled out of Paul's

Epistles, such as several in which he says that we are waiting for the appearance of our Savior, the Lord Jesus Christ, which become ridiculously incoherent if they refer to the earthly bodily coming of one who, according to all Christian claim, *had just been there!* One does not look for the coming of a person who has just been there, finished his mission and departed.

But we face now a sheaf of testimony from one of the very earliest of the Christian Fathers, which, whether the argument be pro or con, constitutes a severe shock to all Christian claims as to the historicity of the Gospels and the Jesus figure in them. The eminent Church Patriarch who gives us this datum is Irenaeus, Bishop of Lyons, Gaul (France). This fierce champion and Papias appear to be the only second-century Christians who refer to the four canonical Gospels at all. What they have to say is therefore of great importance and decidedly argues for the non-historicity of the Christian foundation.

Beginning with chapter ten of Book III of his work, Irenaeus' text bristles with names and direct quotations from all four Gospels. Before this part of his work he had mentioned only two of the Gospels, *Luke* and *John.* It seems a fair inference from this that these other Gospels had come to his knowledge between his writing the latter part of his Book II and the beginning of his Book III. This might carry the inference that these others had either just then come into existence, or had just come to his knowledge about that time. Certainly it is plausible to suppose that the whole four Gospels could not have been in existence and in circulation very long before they would have come to the eager hand of the active and prolific Irenaeus, who had only recently come from the tutelage of his aged friend Polycarp in Smyrna, "the disciple of the Apostle John." Polycarp had sent Irenaeus to Lyons. He likewise gives no evidence of acquaintance with the Gospels.

The astonishing fact, then, is that in recording his first reaction to the new Gospels of Christianity, Irenaeus launches into an immediate and fierce attack upon their historicity, charging them with error and "heresy" in *the vital points of the crucifixion and early death of Jesus!* He directly refutes the "heresy" that Jesus died and was crucified so early in life as his thirty-third year.

"It is not true," he asserts, "that Jesus Christ died as early in life and after so brief a career." "How is it possible," he demands, "that the Lord preached for *one year only?*"

He bases his authority on the oral testimony of John the disciple himself, along with the "true Gospel" and "all the elders." This latter source is notable, since Irenaeus asserts that what he then reports came to him from "the elders," some of whom in their early childhood had themselves heard the truth direct from the lips of the beloved disciple! Irenaeus proceeds with the story:

"For he came to save all through means of Himself, all, I say, who through him are born again to God—infants and children and boys and youths and old men. He therefore passed through every age becoming an infant for infants; a child for children; thus sanctifying those who are of this age; a youth for youths, and thus sanctifying them for the Lord. So likewise he was an old man for old men, that he might be a perfect Master for all, not merely as respects the setting forth of the truth, but also as regards age, sanctifying at the same time the aged also, and becoming example to them likewise. Then at last he came to death itself, that he might be 'the first-born from the dead.' "

"They, however, that they may establish their false opinion regarding that which is written, 'to proclaim the acceptable year of the Lord,' maintain that he preached for one year only and then suffered in the twelfth month. [In speaking thus] they are forgetful to their own disadvantage, destroying His work and robbing Him of that age which is both more necessary and more honorable than any other; that more advanced age, I mean, during which also as a teacher He excelled all others."

"Now that the first stage of early life embraces thirty years and that this extends onward to the fortieth year, every one will admit; but from the fortieth and fiftieth year a man begins to decline towards old age, which our Lord possessed while He still fulfilled the office of a Teacher, even as the Gospel and *all the elders* testify, those who were conversant in Asia with John, the disciple of the Lord, [affirming] that John conveyed to them that information. And He remained among them up to the times of Trajan [reigned A.D. 98-117]. Some of them, moreover, saw not only John, but other Apostles also, and heard the very same account from them, and bear testimony as to the statement. Whom, then, should we rather believe?" (Iren. *Adv. Haer*, Bk. II, Ch. xxii, secs. 3, 4, 5; *Ante-Nicene Fathers* I, 391-2.)

Yea, verily, whom shall we believe? Irenaeus or the Gospels? Irenaeus speaks from the background of possibly creditable history; the Gospels speak from the uncertain ground of mutilated myth, allegory and drama. Irenaeus' word is pertinent to the historically known data available at his time; the Gospels pertain not to objective history but to spiritual edification gone awry, relative to no time, but to all time.

The citation of this passage at length is momentous for the reason that it has at times been adduced as one of the most robust of all extra-

Gospel or secular evidences of the historicity of Jesus and the disciples. That it lends some strength to the thesis of the existence of a cult and a cult founder (who may well have been Apollonius of Tyana, for which seemingly arrant supposition there is some plausible evidence) in those days is perhaps cautiously to be admitted. But that it adds strength to the case for the historicity of Jesus and the authenticity of the Gospel narratives, is a rash and rank presumption. On the exact contrary it practically smashes that entire construction to bits! On the assumption that Irenaeus' tradition direct from the elders who had in childhood contacted John is true, there is an end to the whole fabrication of the Gospel story, roof, walls and foundation. For at one stroke the crucifixion, death, resurrection and ascension of the Lord are turned into a hoax! "If Christ be not risen, then is our faith vain," shouts the Apostle Paul. And if Irenaeus' story is true, there was no resurrection, because no death at age thirty-three; and Christianity is reduced to the emptiest of myths! The story, coming from one of the outstanding Fathers of the early Church, even more positively negates the historicity of the Gospels than does the thunderous silence of St. Paul. And if Jesus actually lived to an advanced age, as Irenaeus positively asserts, the fact makes the complete silence of all secular history on all of his life except a little span of three years (or one, as Irenaeus strangely claims!) all the more inexplicable. Even Irenaeus' claim that Jesus lived to great age carries with it no ring of history, for it reads like anything but factual reality. He says that he lived to age because then he could minister to people of every age. This is the argument used so much in religion, that a thing was so because it would so nicely fit into a preconceived hypothesis. Again if Jesus lived to the time of Trajan (his birth now being placed as far back as the year 12 B.C.), that would have made him to live to age one hundred and ten at the very least! This discloses in what a dilemma the Church now finds itself: it must, to save its tradition, discredit the veracity of Irenaeus, one of its rocks of reliance, Eusebius being already heavily discounted. Thus its historical foundations are collapsing at every turn.

In rounding out this collation of evidence indicating the non-historicity of the Christian bases, it is deemed worth the time to present in the briefest possible form a series of determinations recorded by a Christian proponent of the existence of Jesus, Joseph Warschauer, writing in a work, *The Historical Life of Christ*. His views are fairly representative and so it can not be charged that he is presenting a warped personal opinion. His conclusions are adduced here in support of the assertion on our part that Christian scholars are more and more discrediting the Gospels as sheer historical fact.

The reader of his book and many much like it can not fail to note a constant run of expressions which prove that New Testament exegesis rests almost entirely on surmise, guess, conjecture and supposition. We list some of these as succinctly as possible:

"Indeed the whole romantic story of the circumstances attending the Baptist's death is open to the gravest doubts, being, among other circumstances, palpably modeled on well-known Old Testament stories of kings and queens."

Concerning the baptism in the Jordan he says:

"Now, quite apart from any question of the miraculous—the Spirit appearing in bodily form, an actual voice from heaven uttering human speech—the account given by *Matthew* and *Luke* carries its own refutation. For it is inconceivable that Jesus could ever have met with unbelief and opposition if his Messianic kingdom had been thus visibly and audibly attested at the very start of his career before a large concourse of people who would ever have borne witness to what they had seen and heard."

He thinks the voice was an inner psychic experience of Jesus, not an objective fact.

He discredits the truth of the instances of Jesus' casting out devils from demoniacs. "Some sacrifice of historical accuracy is obvious." "That in the present instance . . . we are not holding to history at all, should need no detailed demonstration." The temptation is modeled over Old Testament prototypes. (This is his conclusion in a score of items.) "Any answer that might be attempted will be open to the charge of being purely conjectural." In one place he speaks of a "remarkable feat of textual manipulation." *Luke*, he says, gives the birth story on the model of Old Testament births of heroes and Christly figures.

"The hymn ascribed to Zacharias is in form a Messianic psalm . . . but the remainder of the story is an example of that *haggada* or fanciful religious narrative in which late Judaism delighted."

He believed that it is unlikely that Jesus' parents would have proceeded three days on their homeward journey from the Passover visit to Jerusalem before they missed their young son of twelve years, who had stayed in the temple to argue with the doctors of divinity.

He comments on the great unnaturalness of the supposition that one who was a simple obscure artisan one week should the next week realize himself to be the personalized "expectation of all nations," the cosmic Christ-Aeon, dazzling and glorious beyond all human conception. This observation is commended to all who can think.

Jesus' calling of the twelve "bears the stamp of legend and not of history." "There is no reason to assume that, if it belongs to history, it happened at this juncture,"—*in re* the cleansing of the paralytic let down through a hole in the ceiling. He attributes some of the cures of Jesus to what modern psychology calls "suggestion," or powerful emotion,—not miracles at all. Unless uttered in irony, he says, Jesus' calling not the righteous but sinners to repentance "is not likely." "The credibility of this cure need not detain us." "*Mark* tells us with what one may judge a type of exaggeration." "If they are authentic utterances of the Lord's." "We may hazard the guess . . ." "We are here moving reverently and hesitatingly in the region of surmise." "*Mark*, with whom geography is not a strong point." "*Mark's* statement is open to serious doubt." ". . . may possibly be attributable . . ." "*Mark*, though he is mistaken as to the name of the locality . . ."

And regarding the raising of Lazarus, he quotes from E. F. Scott that it is inconceivable that a miracle of such magnitude, performed in the one week in our Lord's life of which we have a full record, and in the presence of crowds of people in a suburb of Jerusalem, and a miracle which was the immediate cause of the crucifixion, should have been simply passed over by the other evangelists without mention. "We are almost compelled to the conclusion that the narrative is in the main symbolical." To which we add that Egyptian study now conclusively proves that it is just that, the names Lazarus, Bethany, Mary and Martha all being Egyptian. He quotes Prof. Burkett that for all its dramatic setting it is impossible to regard the Lazarus story as a narrative of historical events.

"These verses read like a later elaboration." But Warschauer steps for a moment into the focus of true perspective when he pauses to enumerate that not in the conquest of the outer elements or the elements of the human frame, but in the conquest of human hearts, in the power to revive dead souls and to lead them up to a perception of God's glory—there we behold the true essence of all miracle, which is ageless and ever enacted afresh. When all Christendom can let go the chimerical objective "historicity" of its Gospels and fasten solely upon their subjective historicity, all will be better for mankind.

"Seem to us of doubtful authenticity." "Perhaps not a historical feature." "The true order of events can only be conjecturally established

397

under the sole guidance of probability." "*Matthew* made a most happy conjecture of his own." ". . . evidence against his supposed birth in Bethlehem." The statement that Jesus laid his hands on a few sick folk and healed them "has the air of an interpolation." He doubts the authenticity of the "Whom do men say that I am?" utterance. "*Mark*, with a certain pettiness guesses, because the disciples needed a holiday after their recent exertions." An item "which *Mark* certainly places altogether out of its natural surroundings." "The truly desperate task of reconciling the Synoptic with the Johannine tradition." This remark has our full approbation and Warschauer our sympathy. "Clearly such an arrangement is too artificial." "The four short treatises known as Gospels are so far from being biographies that they have been not altogether unjustly described as 'records of the Passion extended backwards.'" In discharging so difficult a task as wrestling with the "life" of Jesus, the historian "will often have to content himself with something far short of certainty; weighing probability against rival probabilities, surmise against counter-surmise . . . arriving often at no more than provisional conclusions."

Space forbids giving Warschauer's sensible remarks on the unreliability of the several genealogies of Jesus. He rightly asserts that if the evangelist wished to prove Jesus' divine ancestry, they would have given us Mary's, not Joseph's, lineage! For "David's line" was broken right at the Messiah's immediate fatherhood, Joseph, David's descendant, being pushed aside so that the Holy Ghost might give the child divine fatherhood. And the genealogies—which Paul warns the believers to shun—differ widely from one another.

Easton is quoted as saying that *Mark* and the parables are allegorical. The location of the "mount" on which the "Sermon" was preached is put down as a senseless theme of endless and fruitless debate. Indeed Easton says that as an actual discourse the Sermon on the Mount was never delivered at all, and the "Mount" is a mere rhetorical or theological decoration. (We have earlier shown that is a symbolic term for the earth.) It is in *Matthew*, he claims, only a Christian counterpart of Sinai. (Our thesis again finds corroboration.) Easton (*Christ in the Gospels*) declares the miracles are a *non liquet*. He enumerates one item after another as not historical, but poetic legend. Warschauer asks what is to be made of the existence before Christian times of the document known as *Jesus, Son of Sirach*. Easton asserts that both Jewish and Christian literature from B.C. 250 to A.D. 250 simply teemed with pseudepigraphs of all sorts. And he asks if we are to class the

398

writings of *Daniel, Enoch* and *II Peter* pointblank as dishonest fabrications.

The answer, now to be given in full confidence of its correctness, is that such tomes were compiled from the floating residue of ancient written wisdom and were not considered dishonest because they were never (until ignorant Christianity took hold) considered to be objective, but only subjective, history, or allegories of history. They can be charged with dishonesty only from the standpoint of claiming to be what they never were claimed to be. We can conclude this long and perhaps boresome, but nevertheless instructive chapter with Easton's statement that "whatever was John's purpose, it was assuredly not to write history, as we understand history."

Let it be remembered, however, that this is by no means the "case" for the non-historicity of the Scriptures and the bases of Christianity. It is but a minor fragment of that "case." That, in any reasonable measure of fulness and completeness, has never been presented. It is beyond the scope of this undertaking.

CHAPTER XVIII

HIGHER CRITICISM

A portion of the mental devastation wrought by the acceptance of the fallacious foundations of Christianity is brought under observation when investigation is undertaken in the field of Biblical textual research. It is believed that strength will accrue to the conclusions of our study if a section is devoted to the presentation of a brief critique in this forbidding domain. To do anything comprehensive or conclusive upon this topic in one chapter is of course out of the question. The aim in touching upon it at all will be to present some items collated in our reading that will at least approach the matter from a somewhat new angle, or rather will base a new critique upon grounds of fact and data that will introduce entirely new principia of judgment into this badly muddled province. These new elements of criticism will prove vastly revolutionary in the main, since they rest upon a series of deductions from historical data that have been almost completely slighted in scholastic study hitherto. If these new principles of Bible criticism are generally valid, they will, in a word, be found powerful enough to overthrow all previous deductions and render to a very large degree obsolete all the previous work of Bible critics. For the new view proceeds from the standpoint from which the lay and scene of the whole field to be investigated is utterly transformed by the magic influence of a staggering new understanding of the origin of all Scriptural material. In short, the foundations on which the material itself under observation is to be based are in the new view removed out of the world of time and significance dimension in which they have been adjudged to exercise their function of meaning, and elevated to a wholly different realm of relevance.

It must already have occurred to the alert reader that if the Bible literature is—or was originally—wholly allegorical and dramatic symbology, a body of poetic representation of mystical realizations, the quantum of critical work done in the past on the basis of the assumed historicity of Old and New Testament writings must have completely missed the mark of true reference and true explication. In brief, on the premises laid down by the evidences that confirm the allegorical and non-historical character of the Bibles, all the work of criticism of the past is at one stroke reduced to the sheerest mental moonshine. It will be the purpose of this brief chapter to present in the field of textual critique some points which will contribute their meed of testimony to the validity of the allegorical bases of all study of the Bible.

The first ponderous consideration in the purview is the datum now well established that the material content of archaic books of wisdom is chiefly allegorical, with variations in the form of myth, drama, number graph and pictorial astrograph. More and more, as the previous chapter demonstrated, Christian students are segregating large portions of hitherto assumed historical occurrence in the Bible out of the category of history and placing it off on the side of poetry, legend and tradition. Well, then, if material once believed to be history is no longer taken as such, a critique based on its relevance as objective fact becomes at once so much empty froth and the hollowest mockery of determinative sense. It turns out to be entire illusion; and the vast volume of such critique becomes as futile as one's voice carried away by the wind over lonely places. It is seen to have been a mighty huffing and puffing to blow upon a house that never existed. It is part of the most asinine blunder of all time.

When the gaze that saw the Scriptures as history becomes readjusted to the discernment of the same material as sublime allegory of the essential and eternal verities, then and then only does the enormity of the misjudgment loom before the mind in all its incredible proportions. It would take a volume to reorient the meaning from the connotation into which it has been contorted as history over to what it truly signified in the non-historical approach. (This has been done already as exhaustively as could be done in six hundred pages in our work, *The Lost Light*.) The Scriptures must be completely turned inside out. For only the outside or surface has been looked at, all the while the true intent and the vital message have been hidden inside. The meaning of every item must be lifted out of its supposed historical milieu and reference and reallocated all afresh in the world of consciousness. The significance, in fine, must be moved up from the locale of earth to the domain of mind, from the objective to the subjective world. For all Scriptural "events" are fictitious portrayals of true events in man's inner world, of which outer events are but the shadows. The

401

outer is the garment of the inner. Before this adamant truth all future Bible interpretation must bend as inexorably as life bends to evolution or a reed to the wind, or water to gravity. That it has been unrecognized for many ages bespeaks the inner crassness of all Christian mentality.

The first step in this metamorphosis of Scripture must be taken along the path of the completely honest and newly intelligent reinterpretation of the Bible in full correlation with an enlightened study of comparative religion, not to omit comparative mythology, folk-lore, poetry, philology, including all symbology, allegory and drama. Humiliating as it may well be to vaunting Christian pride, the stern necessity of the case demands that Christian scholarship now go back to the Paganism it scorned and reviled without stint to pick up the lost keys which alone will open its way to the mutilated inner sense of arcane writings of old. The effort for long centuries has been to interpret books written in a form and language utterly inconsonant with our modern literature on the same plan and method as if they were modern products. This has made indigestible hash of the Bibles. Now must be adopted those methods of exposition which will render the sense at once more piquant, more succulent and completely nourishing to the mind. The method simply involves, first and foremost, the treatment of the material as allegory, not as history; or to read it as the paralogue of man's subjective history, having ended forever the gross blunder of mistaking it for particular occurrence. Says Nils W. Lund in a work shortly to be referred to in a very important connection, *Chiasmus in the New Testament,* "the study of folk-lore is especially valuable, for it offers a similar line of development as that of the Gospel tradition."

From the study of comparative systems of arcane thought must and will arise the reconstruction of philosophy, which, dismembered into fragments tossed out of all relation to each other and the whole structure, must now be reintegrated into its primal "unity of apperception," Kant's noble phrase fitting the concept here with great nicety. As Albert Pike shows in his *Morals and Dogma,* the mystic shows and performances were not the mere reading of a lecture but the deployment of a problem. Requiring research they were calculated to arouse the dormant intellect. They implied no hostility to philosophy, because philosophy is the final solvent of symbolism. Then Pike adds the most revealing truth, that the ancient interpretation of symbolism was often ill-founded and incorrect, as it has been ever since.

The alteration from symbol to dogma is fatal to both beauty and sense, and if incompetently made, leads to error, intolerance and assumed infallibility, says Pike. This is true, but must be taken carefully. Symbol indeed must be transposed over into dogma, if by dogma we mean precise recognitions of truth that can be explicitly set forth under faithful representation. The transferal must be made in a way that enhances, not vitiates, both the beauty and the sense. Pike's assertion that error and its sad consequences flow from the incompetent manner of the transposition from myth to truth adumbrated by it, is quite correct. This ineptitude led to the fatal misstep that opened the door to the quick and easy descent of the human mind to the dark Avernus of mental fog in which it has groped in wretched blindness for so long and out of which it is now to emerge at last.

Nothing is truer than that philosophy is the expounder of symbolism, while symbolism is at the same time the pointer to philosophy. It is that domain of mental activity in which symbolism heads up in final meaning. A symbol is the outer road sign pointing to where the soul will find entertainment and refreshment in the city of final understanding. Philosophies devised symbols as indices lying outside in the world of sense by which the traveling and bewildered mind might be helped to find its way to something analogous or homologous to it in the inner world where values finally must be found. Therefore symbols are semantic of verities and realities lying deep in the conceptual area of consciousness, that is, in philosophy. Like sacraments, they are outer visible signs of inner invisible realities, that to a cultivated inner eye are as realistically sensible as an object of physical sight.

Matthew Arnold declared that culture disintegrates for want of a consistent world view. Hocking of Harvard, we have already seen, makes a total grasp of world meaning basic for sound mentality. Stanley Romaine Hopper states that, to be stable, a mind must be thrust back upon philosophy, where it may acquire a foothold on the real and so renew creative satisfactions. For man is ennobled finally only by reflection and the love of wisdom. From waywardness and wandering man may return to his home of blessed assurances only by the path of wisdom. How infinitely essential it is, then, that for that comprehensive understanding of the Scriptures which will feed the deepest hunger of the God-mind fragment in man, the mind must truly know how these Scriptures form an integrated structure of meaning that is veritably the bread of life to starving souls. And this rests finally upon the correct, not the muddled and erratic, reinterpretation of symbolism and allegory into the luminous and intelligible presentments of truth. Hopper well says that we are obliged to renew the meaning of life and absorb its import. This, we maintain, is what the arcane myths were expressly devised by consummate genius to help us do. He likewise says that the individual soul is the true analogue of destiny. In it resides our failure and our hope for new achievement in the world. It is of tremendous import, then, that the Scriptures be rescued from an irrelevant reference to old characters who never lived as people, since they are clearly typal figures, and realigned with its vital pertinence to man's own soul. The Christian error that took the meaning of Scripture away from man's immediate individual (and collective) experience and isolated it upon one or a few fabled personages in "history," is responsible for the failure and the lack of hope in the world today. Well does this author of *The Crisis of Faith* say again that our world today exhibits everywhere a reduction from truth to absurdity, to the preposterous, the ironic, the cynical, or to the terrible pathos of the present conflict which seeks resolution in vain. The crisis of our times is of the intellect, the intelligence. It is a crisis of perversion arrived at through the malevolent despotism of a set of pseudo-categories which have tyrannized over and badly determined our choices. Their compelling power has been unbreakable because it has been concealed in the hidden premises of our period's assumptions and standards, which we have inherited from stultified tradition and accepted without adequate criticism. It can be added to this very sound observation that those accepted assumptions are the age-old sediment of conceptions that took form when early Christianity debased beautiful allegory into absurd "history." We are now still enthralled by the insuperable power of inherited and transmitted fallacies, from which the tyrannous power of ingrained "sacredness" of tradition prevents our liberating ourselves.

In this connection it is pertinent to say that the fixed canons of Scriptural exegesis laid down by Jerome, according to Archibald Duff (*History of Old Testament Criticism,* p. 78), established a theological tyranny for one thousand years.

Conybeare in his *The History of New Testament Criticism,* very well paraphrases Origen's position on the myths and allegories: with the utmost study and pains we must strive to enable every single reader with all reverence to understand that in dealing with the contents of the sacred books he handles words which are divine and not human. Yet Conybeare is found wrestling with the same question that perplexed Johannes Weiss and many another Christian exegetist, how the early Christians could have heard of the Pagan gods, whom scholars claim were the ante-types (but whom Massey says were then taken for anti-types) of the Christ figure in the Gospels. Conybeare writhes in a torment of mental irritation at the charge made by so many scholars that the Christ-story in the Gospels was a rescript of many antecedent allegorical biographies of Pagan cult-gods, such as Cybele, Attis, Isis, Osiris, Horus, Helena, Dendrites, Krishna, Janus, Apollonius, Aesculapius, Heracles and Oceanus, Saoshyant, Mithra and Buddha. Referring to these mythical deities and their legendary "lives," he says:

"Prick them with a pin and out gushes their lore in a copious flood; and every item is supposed to have filled the heads of the polymath authors of the Christian Gospels. Every syllable of these Gospels, every character in them, is symbolic of one or another of these gods and heroes, Hear, O Israel: 'The Christians borrowed myths of all lands from Paganism.'"

This is sardonically ironical, but it chances to be the truth! This critic of New Testament criticism then gives vent to an outgush of exasperation over the claims of such scholars as Robertson, Smith and Drews that the Christ figure in the Gospels was just the perpetuated copy of a cult-god under one or another name, but particularly that of Joshua (the Hebrew equivalent of Jesus) that was worshipped in the regions surrounding Judea or in Judea itself.

For the sake of grappling resolutely with the serpent of Christian hostility to the obvious and crucial involvements of the study of comparative religion, it is desirable to subject this scholar's position to more detailed scrutiny. It is necessary to meet and refute this stubborn recalcitrancy of Christian scholars to the truth that confronts them in volume, but which they have dodged and parried by the most arrogant methods of intellectual subterfuge and insincerity imaginable, or honestly missed by an obtuseness which is next to incredible.

He follows the passage above cited by saying we must suppose, on the Joshua cult-god theory, that the Gospels were a covert tribute to the high standing and worthy character of Pagan mythology and religious dramas, Pagan art and statuary. Again we may pause to interject that a statement made to ridicule Pagan religion, does in fact pay it high and deserved praise. If, he continues, we adopt the mythico-symbolic method of analysis, these Gospels can have been nothing else than Pagan productions. (Again he is unwittingly right.) Then he challenges this view's sponsors to explain the alchemy of mind by which the ascertained rites and beliefs of early Christians were distilled from these antecedents. The effect and the cause are so utterly disparate, he asserts, so devoid of any organic connection, that one would like to see more clearly how this relation worked out. At one end of it we have a hurly-burly of Pagan myths; at the other an army of Christian apologists inveighing against everything Pagan and martyred for doing so. Then he says with sarcasm that he only hopes that the orthodox will be delighted to learn that their Scriptures are a thousandfold more wonderful and unique than they appeared to be when they were merely inspired by the Holy Spirit. This latter, forsooth, is not half so wonderful as Pagan mythic symbolism. We have discovered a new literary genus, unexampled in the history of mankind. You rake together a thousand *irrelevant* thrums of mythology, picked at random from every age, race and clime; you get a "Christist" to throw them into a hopper and turn a crank, and out come the Gospels. In all the annals of the Bacon-Shakespeare debate we have seen nothing like it, he concludes.

Conybeare feels that this ironical vehemence of his disposes with finality of the entire movement to establish the mythico-symbolical character of the Gospels, as preposterous tommyrot and fol-de-rol. It must be calmly asserted in rebuttal, however, that his position is the one that has to be described as fatuous and insupportable to the last degree of stupidity. That a critical Christian scholar of eminence can refer to the mythical foundations of ancient literature as some weird and bizarre concoction of deluded children or barbarians, not to be seriously considered in relation to the genesis of later religions, exhibits most glaringly the bleak nescience and barrenness of modern academic or Christian genius. When the eye of a scholar can scan the field of ancient religious literature and then come away from the view with the opinion that the one element, that he must see is ubiquitous and voluminous in that domain of research, can be given no place of influence in the formation of a new creed that arose in the very milieu of that element, there is ample reason to suspect that such a vision is myopic if not totally blind. In this field of research one finds almost nothing resembling history of the objective sort; but instead endless myth and allegory. Yet Conybeare asserts that it is fatuous to take ancient religious literature as mythical material, but wholly sound to take it as history. It is the canon of scholarship to base determinations on evidence. Yet it is the "mythicists" who *have* based their opinions solidly upon massive heaps of evidence, and it is Conybeare who has paid so little heed to this evidence that he stands convicted of narrow bigotry. He is so little conversant with the mountainous data of comparative religion that he damns it all with a sneering phrase, "a thousand irrelevant thrums of mythology." Answer to this is that the thousands of mythic representations, obvious fictions as they are, constitute an organic body of such significant import that to them man must look still for his supreme enlightenment. Scholars like Conybeare have never mustered the mental insight to penetrate their outer disguise of fiction and reveal their inner core of meaning, and they continue therefore to classify it as primitive rubbish. Irrelevant thrums they most assuredly are not, but the sublimest formulations ever devised by near-divine wisdom. This critic thinks that a collection of them "picked at random from every age, race and clime" constitutes a rubbish heap of superstitious junk. Sir James Frazer's collection of them in *The Golden Bough* has been an epochal event in the history of religion. Can it mean nothing in contravention of Conybeare's argument that a thousand scraps of mythology, picked either at random or with design from every land and time, when brought together and compared in the mental atmosphere free from scornful Christian prejudice, yield an absolutely convincing evidence of their being integral parts of a stupendous system of the profoundest and most consistent organic philosophy extant in human thought? This critic has never trodden the path of long and patient search, and with a free mind, in the field of comparative mythology. No scholar with mind set to look fairly at what he finds can graze long in this interesting and fruitful pasture without at length being overwhelmed with the evidences of either the virtual identity or the organic unity, or both, of the material found in the most diverse quarters. Christian minds alone resist the force of this evidence and remain impervious to its revelations. Conybeare is sure that Robertson, Smith and Drews, not to mention Renan, Strauss, Massey, Higgins, Brandes and Mead, are fanciful enthusiasts hallucinated by some speciously alluring theory. It is quite beyond him to realize that these men, like the present writer, have come to conclusive opinions relative to the mythical nature of the Scriptures only when their minds have had to succumb to the force of the massive evidence. He does not meet and refute their position with contrary or more weighty evidence, but in exasperation simply calls them addle-pated.

But scholarship does not decide crucial points by vehement protestation; it decides on the evidence. The final word, then, is that when scholars will once look at the massed data through the new lens of a clearer resolution of symbolic and mythic signification that is now available, they will find Conybeare's irritation and his sarcasm baseless and his error costly. Massey alone lists some one hundred and eighty points of identity between the long antecedent and entirely mythical Horus of Egypt and the Gospel Jesus. Frazer, Newberry and others draw practically endless parallels between Attis, or Tammuz, or Bacchus (Dionysus), Mithra, Sabazius, Zagreus, Apollo, Hercules, Krishna, Witoba and other Pagan Sun-god deities and the Gospel Jesus. To Conybeare this weight and volume of evidence is so much moonshine of deluded theorists. But by now the trickle of evidence through the tiny hole in the dyke of Christian mental obduracy has widened to torrential volume and the dyke is fast crumbling to ruin. The day of sneering at the mythical character of the Gospels is at its sunset at last.

It is a point of great weight surely which William A. Heidel puts before us in his monumental study of ancient festivals, *The Day of Yahweh* (p. 95 f.), when he says that Bible commentators have so often pointed out the existence in the text of "recurrent motives," such as the passing over of a body of water, an outward and a return journey, and others. He then says that the first impulse of thought is to regard it as a childish resort on the part of the Bible narrator, "because it has all the appearance of a trifling play on words; but so to regard it were a grave mistake." To do so would not only be to miss valuable hints, he says, but also to treat with scant respect what to the Hebrews was certainly sacred. Still more significant is the datum that in the religious rite or sacred drama these repetitions likewise occur. Scholars have tried to explain this by asserting that the rite was based on the Scriptural narration. "But this natural assumption is clearly wrong, the rite here also *antedating the sacred story.*"

This is indeed a point of great weight and it bespeaks something other than history. When the same, or similar, or analogous incidents occur to one hero after another, as for instance the number of women, Sarah, Hannah, Elizabeth and some others all giving birth to their divine sons in old age, one can not avoid the conviction that these are not historical "coincidences." So strong and compelling is this feature, repeated in scores of items, that if people were free from religious fixations, hardly a person could read the Old Testament and maintain the belief that he is conning veridical historical event. The feeling of dealing with something quite unearthly, quite eerie as history would be overwhelming if natural reaction had its free play. Who can really believe that the waters of the geographical Red Sea parted to let the Israelites cross dryshod, and then rushed in to drown the Egyptians? Who can honestly believe that angels sang to shepherds, that a rod turned into a serpent, or that a star left its orbit to stand over a stable? The "Red Sea" at any rate *can* no longer be believed in, as it is no longer in the corrected translation. It is now the Reed Sea, meaning the human blood.

As to these recurrent themes, which as history become amazing prodigies, but as allegory are readily understood as items of cryptic truth-telling repeated again and again for emphasis or by copying, the advocates of an incontestable historical rendering must themselves swallow and ask all others to swallow, a series of endless coincidences in the stories of one figure after another; as for instance that Lot and Elkinah, the former in the nineteenth chapter of *Genesis* and the other in the *nineteenth* chapter of *Judges,* both undergo the identical experience of being demanded by a mob of rough fellows outside the house where they were overnight guests, and both offer their daughters to the violence of the mob as appeasement. And Jephthah pledges his daughter to work out of a difficulty likewise. Yes, endlessly recurrent theme and even a run of detail rises to offer serious challenge to the historicity of the Old and New Testaments alike.

Another indication of mythical character in the Scriptures is found in the countless analogies between natural phenomena and spiritual science. The life of the soul is depicted and analyzed over the correspondences found to subsist between it and the living principle in nature. Fundamental in this area is of course the one ubiquitous phenomenon of the periodical death and resurrection of vegetation, paralleled by the winter hibernation and spring revivification of animals, reptiles and insects. So recurrent is this feature in the archaic writings that some students have ventured to believe that the death and resurrection of the Christ—pretty nearly the whole central axis of Christianity—was nothing but a human application of the so-called "corn-myth." These suggestions have naturally drawn the fire of scornful rejection from the protagonists of the historical view. One who speaks out on this theme is Johannes Weiss, leading scholar in the group of high German critics in his great two-volume work on *Primitive Christianity* (p. 491). He says that the Christian position is "once and for all opposed to the fantastic notions of those who would make the death of Christ a particular instance of the story of the vegetation gods who die and come to life every year. Were there nothing else, it would appear strange that not only the resurrection but also the death of Christ should be placed in the spring of the year. In the earliest period we find no indication whatever of a yearly celebration of the death of Christ; rather it seems that the Lord's Supper was celebrated weekly."

Correction of this—and a hundred similar observations—is to be made through the clarifying fact that first and fundamentally the ancients did *not* believe that any personified forces of nature such as "vegetation gods" died and came to life every year. They saw that *vegetation* died and rose again annually; and to them that was an analogue and parallel of something of superlative interest and concern for all human knowledge, namely the comparative yet very real "death" of the soul of Christliness that in each incarnation in flesh went down into and through its winter-time of dormancy and rose again from out that sleep of inertia in the continuing springs of each evolutionary cycle or "year." Nature furnished an analogue by which the truth and meaning of *man's* life on earth, as body and soul conjoined, could be more graphically portrayed and vividly comprehended. All that ancient sagacity intimated by the constant reference to the corn-myth was that this annual round of death and resurrection in outer nature perfectly typified the analogous periodic "death" and resurrection of the soul of divinity within man himself. As Emerson says, the outer reflects the inner, and from contemplation of the visible sign a deeper realization of the invisible reality can be won.

"Once for all," we say, there is nothing fantastic about this. It is the one thing that prevents religious thought from becoming fantastic, as it has done in Christian miscalculation of what the Scriptures are dealing with. If the knowledge that the sacred writings were designed to keep man in intellectual harmony with truth and reality had not so frightfully miscarried under Christian mishandling, the utterly fantastic misconception of them as history instead of natural analogy of divine-human experience and spiritual science would not have been precipitated into world consciousness.

As to the argument of Weiss that the Christians placed both the death and the resurrection of "Christ" in the spring, what this reveals is astonishingly interesting indeed. What has to be said here is that the Christians became hopelessly entangled in the varied forms and natural bases of symbolic representations employed by the Pagans, lost the understanding necessary to avoid mistakes in seasonal datings of festivals, and ended by placing the death of "Christ" in the wrong season of the year! They placed it in the spring, when it always belonged, by every intimation of analogy, poetically and symbolically, in the autumn, to be in keeping with the death of nature. This will be contradicted, of course. But there is no argument. Just as certainly as a symbolic festival of rebirth and resurrection belongs in the spring, one commemorating death belongs in the autumn. The great ancient festivals at which the "death" of the Sun-gods was memorialized, *were* celebrated always in the fall. One, but only one, among scores of witnesses to this is the Jewish festival or series of festivals held in the month Tishri, our September. The Jewish New Year is still celebrated in September. But it was a New Year in the sense of the beginning of a new cycle of soul's immersion in the life of body, which the ancient savants poetized as the soul's "death." The similar "death" of the sun, eternal soul symbol, in the autumn was the natural basis of the spiritual or evolutionary analogue. In the fall the soul had a new birth in or into matter (figured as its "death"); in the spring it had also its rebirth from matter back to spirit, involving the death of the body but the rebirth of the soul out of its entombment in mortal flesh. Both seasons, six months apart, figured a rebirth, one from the point of view of the body, the other from that of the soul. So closely intertwined are these two ideas of rebirth that the ignorant Christians got them confused, and for three and a half centuries they celebrated the *birth* of their Lord and Savior on March 25, only transferring it to the December 25 date of the winter solstice in 345 A.D. by decree of Pope Julian II.

But a period of forty days, indicating the length of time spirit is incubated in matter before it regerminates to rise again, was fixed in ancient days as one form of festival celebration. The period began with the death of soul and ended with its resurrection. The Pagans began the period on September 21, the date of the autumn equinox, or the Passover from spirit into body and ended it on October 31, the date of the still surviving All Souls' Day, or Hallowe'en. If one kept the meaning clear it was possible also to set the same forty-days festival in the spring, placing the "death" date forty days before the glorious day of resurrection fixed for the conjunction of sun and moon after the vernal equinox, the Passover from flesh back to spirit. The fall celebration emphasized the death, the spring one the resurrection. Both are appropriately timed for those who know it all as symbolic and in what specific ways the meaning is poetized by the seasons.

But if this balance of understanding is lost and the ritual meaning is replaced by an alleged murder and fantastic bodily resurrection of a man instead of a divine principle in all men, then the celebration of the death as an objective occurrence on a given spring day on a cross of wood becomes both a symbolic anachronism and a travesty of human sense past all belief. And the celebration of the gruesome rites of Good Friday and Passion Week by maudlin Christians *in the spring* is, in the stark form of historical realism in which it is misconceived, the most awful miscarriage of sanity in human history. It is to cause millions to gloom over the idea of divine death at the very moment when life is chanting on every side its vernal hymn of victory over the bonds of wintry death.

The correctness of all this is found in the fact, among other things, that for three and a half centuries the Christians did not know whether the Christ was born, or should be commemorated, in the spring or in the dead of winter. *Had a babe been born,* surely some historical data could have been preserved. And the fact that all religions place these "births" and "deaths" at one or other of the four cardinal points in the year, zodiacally considered, is of itself sufficient attestation to any mind but one sold in slavery to chimerical pietism that the birth and death of the Christ were not historical events.

And it is time now to insert the next consideration, of overwhelming force, that to attempt to carry on Bible exegesis in total disregard of ancient astrological symbolism, expressly the zodiacal emblemism, is a fool's madness. *The zodiac is the primal key to the Scriptures!* A thousand allusions and figurations in the text can be brought out to clear sense only by reference to the marvelous and as yet only imperfectly fathomed depths of cryptic significance embodied in that sphinx-riddle circle of twelve signs and constellations. The sun in passing periodically through these twelve regions of the heavens prefigured the divine soul of man as passing through and assimilating unto itself twelve aspects of deific mind power that in the total and in the final synthesis will constitute in perfected man the perfected Christ-in-man. The first chapter of *Luke* can not be interpreted in its inner esoteric sense without reference to the zodiac, since the six-months period between the birth of John the Baptist and that of Jesus is only to be understood as the six months between the opposite signs of Virgo and Pisces, the first or natural man, the forerunner, being born in the sign of the Virgin, and the second or spiritual man being born in "Bethlehem," the "house of bread" and of *fish,* which is the sign of Pisces.

On top of this comes the next item, equally essential for true Scriptural exposition. It is numerical symbolism. As Pythagoras said, the world is built on number and the harmony of numbers. Christian ignorance has gazed like a bumpkin with open mouth at the numbers one, two, three, four, six, seven, eight, ten, twelve, twenty-four, thirty, forty and seventy (in particular forty), found recurring endlessly in its holy book, and has never yet uttered a single syllable indicating intelligent comprehension of what they signify in Scripture. Yet the total of clear meaning is finally to be found compressed in these numbers. Revival of Pagan wisdom is at last disclosing what these cardinal numbers mean, and Christianity must resort to that long-reviled and despised "heathenism" to learn after twenty centuries what its own Bible is actually talking about. There is a greater release of understanding of Bible writing in simple arithmetic of four plus three equals seven, and four times three equals twelve, not to mention seven plus three equals ten, and four times seven equals twenty-eight (the days in a moon cycle) than in all the dead dissertations on Bible "history." For these numbers refer to the component elements in man's divine-human constitution, four in the human side of his dual being and three in the divine side. We are condensing a complete manual of soul-science here in a few sentences. The four cardinal elements in nature, earth, water, air and fire, typify the four bodies constituent of man's basic fourfold composition, symbolizing respectively his four departments of consciousness, sensation, emotion, thought and spiritual will. Any one attempting to grasp Bible sense all through without knowing these positive anthropological references is eligible for the dunce-cap and the title of nincompoop. It can not be done. They are essential keys. Omitting only *earth,* John the Baptist says that his baptism is of *water,* while that of the higher principle, the Christos, is of *air* (Latin: *spiritus*) and *fire.* Jesus said he came down to scatter fire, i.e. divine spirit over the earth. Yet Christians glorify Christ and sneer at Prometheus. And out of Lucifer, the firelight bringer, they have made their anthropomorphic Satan.

Back in the seventeenth century in England there flashed out momentarily in the perceptions of two eminent Biblical commentators so clear a realization of the true status of Scriptural material that it deserves to fall with great surprise and amazement for the reader into the context of this work. It appears that Anthony Collins (1676-1729), a scholar at Eton and King's College, Cambridge, and Thomas Woolston (1699-1731), who wrote a work called *Discourses on the Miracles,* of many editions (London, 1729), at about the same time but independently arrived at the conclusion that the Bible can be properly interpreted only as allegory! Among other items Collins announced that the *Isaiah* prophecies of a virgin bearing the Christ babe referred to a young woman in Ahaz' time and could not refer to the mother of Jesus seven hundred years later. Also he declared the *Book of Daniel* was a forgery of the age of Antiochus Epiphanes. Says Conybeare (op. cit., p. 53): "This brilliant conjecture which modern inquiry has substantiated, of itself suffices to place him in the foremost rank of critics." Collins asserted that the Bible was primarily allegory, that in fact the only way to save it from nonsense was to allegorize the prophecies and take them in a secondary sense different from their obvious and literal one.

"In no other way, he urged, can they be adapted to the belief in the spiritual Messiah, who is yet to appear; for the prophecies must have been fulfilled, or the Christian faith which they evidenced is false. Since they were demonstrably enough fulfilled in their literal sense, Collins argues that the pointing of the Hebrew text must be altered, the order of words and letters transposed, words cut in half, taken away or added—any procrustean methods in short employed in order to force the text into some sort of conformity with the events."

We may be pardoned for the thought that this excerpt alone justifies the production of our book, since it lays bare, in all the gross crudity of conniving ignorance and weak human duplicity the very trick and conspiracy that we will be challenged to prove in support of our claim that the Scriptures were "doctored" and altered in order to make allegory read like ostensible history. In spite of his ignorance as to the actual non-fulfillment of ancient mythicism (misinterpreted as objective prophecy), this man Collins saw clearly what had had to be done to bring over the Gospels into the category of history. What more need be said? Massey had not studied Egyptology long before he saw as plainly as any fact can be seen that the "literalizers of the Gospel" and the "carnalizers of the Christ" had tampered with the text of Scripture to solidify the "evidence" for their historical theory. At least two hundred pages of data in our note-books alone could pile up evidence to support this accusation. But Conybeare himself comes right up to our elbow with a statement that puts the seal of veracity on our own assertion and what the additional mass of testimony would adduce. We need therefore only to cite his passage, which in effect and in essence is the proof we will be challenged to produce (op. cit., p. 46):

"With rabbinical ingenuity, *thousands of passages* were torn from the living context which gave them sense and meaning, and distorted, twisted, mutilated, misinterpreted, in order to fit them in as predictions of Jesus, the Messiah."

We have asserted that the ancients reflected their astrological symbologies in their national histories, and in their topical geography. This will be scouted as rank insupportable assertion. But let us listen as Heidel (op. cit., p. 222) speaks out:

"The Hebrew text represents Meribah and Massah as place-names. How ancient this attempt to *convert ritual into geography* may be we have no certain means of determining."

Then there was Woolston. Conybeare states the general position of this writer on the miracles related of Jesus, that they are so unworthy of a spiritual Messiah (could this be a new thought for pietists?) that they must one and all, *including the resurrection,* be set down as never having happened at all, and be explained allegorically as types and figures of the real, or spiritual alone. This is remarkable, surely. Here was a man seeing the thing lucidly at last. He falls back upon the early Fathers, instancing Origen as saying that whatsoever Jesus did in the flesh was but typical and symbolical of what he would do in the spirit; and that the "bodily diseases" he healed were no other than the infirmities of the soul that are to be cured by him, as an immanent spirit. (Let us pause to reflect that for the enunciation of this same sublime truth Origen was anathematized not three hundred years after his death.) As to the miracle of turning water into wine, Woolston affirms, the Fathers were so sensible of its "absurdity, abruptness, impertinence and senselessness . . . according to the letter" that they had recourse to a mystical and allegorical interpretation, as the only way to make it "consistent with the wisdom, sobriety and duty of the Holy Jesus." He cites Hilary, Augustine, Origen and Jerome as looking upon the whole story of the resurrection as emblematic of Christ's spiritual resurrection "out of the *grave of the letter* of the Scriptures in which he had been buried about three days and three nights according to that mystical interpretation of prophetical numbers which I have learned of them. . . . By the three days, St. Augustine says, are to be understood three ages of the world." He is resolved, he says, to give the letter of the Scriptures no rest so long as God gives him life and abili-

415

ties to attack it. The acceptance of the text as history implies "absurdities and nonsense." And this man then asks a question that should hit every reader of this work with the keenest appreciation of its pertinence. He asks how this battle against the crude historical reading of Scripture is to be won. By "a grave, sedate and serious manner"? "No, I think ridicule should here take the place of sober reason; as the most proper and effectual means to cure men of their foolish faith and absurd notions." It would be good odds to lay a wager that Woolston has the right idea. He at any rate finds unexpected confirmation from a popular modern expert in the art of producing laughter. Says Mark Twain:

"Power, money, persuasion, supplication, persecution, these can lift at a colossal humbug, push it a little, weaken it a little, century by century; but only laughter can blow it to rags and atoms at a blast." [The first chapter of our *The Lost Light* has the caption: *Tragedy Dies in Laughter*.]

A choice excerpt from the venerable *Zohar* of the Hebrews falls in here with aptness:

"R. Simeon said: 'Had I been alive when the Holy One, blessed be He, gave mankind the *Book of Enoch* and the *Book of Adam,* I would have endeavored to prevent their dissemination, because not all wise men read them with proper attention, and thus extract from them perverted ideas, such as lead men astray from the Most High to the worship of strange powers.' "

That this calamity did befall and that it has been the cause of world dementia is the inescapable conclusion of studentship. Had all wise men read the arcane books "with proper attention" to their artfully concealed significance and located their meaning on the plane of consciousness instead of on that of history, there could not have been the consuming fires of rancor and persecution that have cast such a lurid glow upon the pages of history.

A consideration given expression by Conybeare that should have instructed that scholar in a better view of the personal Messiah is worth noting. Speaking of another critic named Evanson, he states that he saw clearly how insufficient is the evidence of the Gospels to bear the strain of the vast superstructure the theologians have built upon them. This is a keen discernment, to which theologians generally have been blind. What has been loaded upon the ostensible foundation of a few ancient documents wrongly believed to be books written by divine dictation in a literal sense, is veritably a whole cosmos of meaning. Surely no simple carpenter and a dozen "fishermen" could by any circumstance be made to be the prime generators of a movement launching a message that embraced earth and man in their cosmic relations, unless the fanatical hypnotization of millions of people poured their psychological fervor into the delusion.

Conybeare next gives Joseph Priestley's contribution to Scriptural critique. His main heresy (for which he nearly lost his life at the hands of a Tory mob)

"was the entirely correct opinion that the earliest Christians neither knew anything of Trinitarian doctrine nor deified Jesus after the manner of Athanasian doctrine. He denied that the Apostles could have discerned God Almighty in the man of flesh and blood with whom they familiarly consorted. 'I am really astonished,' he wrote to Horsley, 'how you really entertain the idea of any number of persons being on this even footing, as you call it, with a being whom they gradually believe to be maker of themselves and all things, even the Eternal God himself.'"

This opens the way to our saying what has often pressed for statement, a thing which, if it could ever be given a half minute of full consideration, would shake millions of sensible but credulous Christians out of their childish dream of the historical Gospels and their Christ personage. One has but to take the Gospel story *as* history and then picture a hundred aspects of what it presupposes, reconstruct them on the basis of realistic actuality, to see how completely impossible it all is. One needs but to ask how countryside peasants could have acquired the specialized education assuredly needed to enable them to "spot" a cosmic Logos when they saw one in the form of a neighborhood carpenter! That ages of searching study could have faced this necessary feature of Christian theological assertion and never seen the preposterousness of its obvious implications marks the whole record of Christian pietism as a thing of doltishness beyond credence. And millions of persons at this day are possessed with the assumption that if the same Galilean came walking down the street now, any one looking at him would know that he was the Cosmic Lord and Co-creator of the universe with the Father. But no theologian has ever told *how* one would be able to differentiate this human being from the order of common humanity. And Conybeare himself admits that the Galilean fishermen knew nothing about a way to identify one of the three members of the cosmic Trinity.

A sidelight of considerable value is thrown upon the great controversial situation in the fourth century by a comment of Farrar on the arguments of Arius on the non-identity of the Son with the Father in the Trinity. Farrar says that Arius was forced by his doctrinal stand to "sever Jesus" (Greek: *luei Iēsoun*) and reduce the whole work of redemption to an interior process. The Ebionites, says Farrar, had denied Jesus' full divinity; the Docetists had likewise denied his humanity. But it was reserved for the Arians at once to affirm and nullify them both. They evidently accomplished this logical legerdemain by affirming his divinity as a *spiritual principle,* while denying his humanity as a person of history. It all came from the incredible blunder of conceiving that the Logos or Word of God could be a man of flesh on earth. Arius saw clearly enough that he had to "sever Jesus" the man from the cosmic or creational Aeon, coequal with the Father, if only to save Christian doctrinism from committing itself to a preposterous imbecility of thought.

Nature symbolism and analogy, mythical forms embodying mystical intimations and universal truths, astrological pictography based on the zodiacal chart and the thirty-six constellations, numerological significance and the four elements must all be reinstated in the workshop of Bible interpretation as tools of competent elucidation. But there remains another device that has lurked undiscovered in the Scriptural construct for lo these many ages, which must now be brought out and used to throw a still clearer light upon the dark obscurity that still enshrouds this field. This completely lost open sesame to an unsuspected source and range of meaning in the Bible lies wholly on the form side of Bible structure, having nothing directly to do with the verbal content. Perhaps it might be said that it expresses meaning through form and arrangement, not through language. But it does involve number and in most startling fashion.

Nothing so glaringly emphasizes modern Christian deadness to all true significance in its Bible as the demonstration of dullness in its failure to respond with any least show of recognition of the importance of just about the most momentous discovery of a cryptic structure in its literature in two thousand years, when a few years ago a book was published which should have swept all Christendom with a wave of intense interest and led to a new envisagement of the Scriptures. The book, entitled *Chiasmus in the New Testament,* was produced by a Chicago theologian, Nils Wilhelm Lund. It announced and by abundant citation from both Old and New Testaments alike amply demonstrated the fact that the writing in both books was adjusted to fit into a frame of structure based amazingly on the key number of our universe,—seven. It is difficult to illustrate without a diagram, but "Chiasmus" is a structure made over the outline of the Greek letter *Chi,* which is approximately the English "X." It pervades the Bible throughout in surprising regularity. There will be found a series of four statements in a line of sequential development or relation, which might be lettered A, B, C, D, or numbered 1, 2, 3, 4. But when the fifth is added it is found to *repeat* C or 3; the sixth repeats B or 2; and the seventh and last repeats A or 1. It thus runs the sequence of A, B, C, D, C, B, A, or 1, 2, 3, 4, 3, 2, 1. The development of the thought or statement takes four steps forward, then seemingly turns and retraces the three steps of the initial movement and returns to where it began. There is enough material in the Bible that Lund has collected to illustrate the pattern to fill the more than three hundred pages of his book This obviously proves the device to be a definite scheme of sacred composition.

Perhaps the book and its astonishing revelation of a new element of meaning in Holy Writ failed to create more of a stir because the author himself, while having done a magnificent piece of analytic work on the text to exemplify the principle, closes his treatise with never a gleam of comprehension of the equally astonishing purport of this strange design. Without this elucidation of its meaning his study remained merely an interesting and, as we would say, curious phenomenon, and dented theological perspicacity not an inch.

Had he or his fellow-exegetists had the slightest inkling of what this chiasmus structure indicated, it might have caused a ruction in theological quarters indeed. The period of time that Jonah should have been mythically held in the whale's belly, and that Jesus should have remained in the bonds of hell and the grave, *is not three, but three and a half.* This correct number is found three times in the eleventh and twelfth chapters of *Revelation.* It represents or diagrams the exact half of the seven stages which life units must pass through on their way to full involvement in matter's realm, which are of course followed by a return through the same three and a half planes to the starting point in the empyrean. Life takes three and a half steps downward or outward into the toils of matter and then retraces its steps to return to the Father. It "descends" through the atmic plane to the mental, then to the emotional and finally lands on the physical. The physical plane is thus the nadir of the downward movement or involution, and so becomes the turning point where the return is begun. In Old Testament allegory Sinai is the word that marks this plane of the return, because it is derived from the Egyptian *seni,* meaning "point of turning to return." This etymological revelation could itself alone effect a turning of Bible exegesis to return to sane bases and edifying, instead of stultifying conclusions. It is itself a great point in evidence that the Old Testament is not history or geography.

This entire elucidation will be received with vehement protestation of its unsoundness. But it is the key to the chiasmus form of the Bible, and there is no other key to this otherwise entirely enigmatic structure.

And how can orthodox dullness remain forever inert to the illuminating implications of what all this lights up? Staring it in the face is this "peculiar" form device, which carres the imputation of divine dictation even more strongly than words can tell it. The Scriptures were constructed with such transcendent genius that not only does the language speak its elevated meaning, but it falls into such a form that this itself dramatizes or reconstructs the very figure-graph of the life movement. This is a stupendous announcement, which stupefied fundamentalists will probably go on blandly ignoring for several hundred years more. At any rate there stands the phenomenon, and whether Christianity slumbers on in its mental torpor or awakens to newness of life depends largely on whether it will take heed to this strange discovery or not.

And not only does chiasmus present its extraordinary challenge to intelligence, but a perhaps still greater wonder comes to light in the further fact that almost every verse, all key words, many chapters as a whole, and even books, in the Hebrew and Greek, come out, through the number value of the letters of those alphabets, to total seven or a multiple of it. A man named Panin, who spent forty years counting these aggregates, reveals that there are some fifteen words and combinations of words in the first verse of *Genesis* that total seven or a multiple. To begin with the verse has seven Hebrew words. This numerical value runs all through the Bible. If one will reflect on these facts, the Bible will appear as remarkable for its sheer form as for its meaning. And Christians, disdaining to learn or copy from Pagans, have never seen the basic significance of the great "magic" number seven. It is Philo who says that it is doubtful if any one can adequately celebrate the marvel of the number six, which is crowned with completion of its work in the number seven. All cycles run through seven stages. God wrought at his creation six "days" and consummated it on the seventh. A Hebrew slave, says *Numbers* (21), was to work in bondage six years and go free in the seventh. It was commanded that fields should be worked six years and go unworked the seventh. This can not be history; it is allegory.

We can come now to the briefest possible survey of the Bible books, more particularly the four Gospels and *Revelation* of the New Testament, in the more immediate sphere of textual criticism. To enter this field with any attempt at thoroughness is out of the question, as it would involve a large work in itself. The purpose in touching it at all is to point out some obvious elements in the case which appear to have been neglected in all the massive study devoted to it. Scholars have labored over comparison of texts and manuscripts with the greatest care and with even a display of ingenuity of the highest degree. Yet it would seem as if their noble effort has gone almost completely for nought, because of their stubborn recalcitrancy to the large basic factors in the case, by neglect of which they have missed sound conclusions at every turn. To the six or seven fundamental corrections already announced in this chapter must now be added another, the implications of which will vastly reorient the whole scheme of Scriptural study. The new plank in the platform structure must rest firmly on the sub-structure fact that the Gospels and Bible literature generally are based on old Egypt's now readable literature and are themselves rescripts of old, old books of the Essenes or other cults preserving the arcane books from remotest antiquity. Support for this revolutionary statement has already been adduced. It seems incontestable. If criticism can now be based on this new datum, a thousand perplexing and virtually insoluble questions resolve themselves at once into clear sense. A wholly new envisagement of the material can be gained and a complete new set of conclusions arrived at.

Taking up the four Gospels it will be clear at once that all the tomes that have been devoted to *guessing* when *Matthew, Mark, Luke* and *John* were written and by whom, are at one stroke rendered obsolete and reduced to rubbish by the alteration of the dates from somewhere allegedly between the years 50 and 120 A.D. to an unknown date at least some thousands of years B.C., possibly ten thousand. As long as these four documents were stubbornly held to be biographies of a man who was claimed to have lived from about 1 A.D. to 33 A.D., their composition had perforce to be dated within a measurable period following the year 33 A.D. Had the knowledge prevailed, however, that the character in them known as Jesus the Christ was not a man of flesh, but the ritual-dramatic figure personifying the Christ-in-man, a principle of higher consciousness, there would have been no need to fix their date of composition at any specific time. Eusebius' statement and hundreds of suggested intimations of data strengthen the conclusion that they were of immemorial antiquity. Therefore there was at no time any necessity to tie them in with the life of a man in the first century.

Our discussion of this point has brought out the new principle of criticism or of determination that the Gospels were *not* written in the late first or early second centuries, but, already in existence for thousands of years (with Jesus in them!), were *for the first time in history brought forth out of esoteric custodianship* and *spread,* with all the danger of misinterpretation (which at once happened) *among the populace at large.* We have cited in our first pages the challenging statement of Augustine that the *true Christian religion* had already existed from the beginning of man, that in his age it began to be called Christianity, and that at Antioch, not at Jerusalem. This gives rise to a consideration that has never even been thought of, much less accorded its natural and decisive weight in the problem. It is of stupendous consequence in the debate on textual criticism. It is that, if the one true Christian religion had been in existence for ages antecedent to the first century A.D., it must have had its assumedly full complement of supporting literature, or Scriptures, to preserve its creedology and doctrinism and to carry its gospel. It is absolutely unthinkable that the whole world was permeated with this hoary religion that Augustine speaks of and that the immense body of sacred literature found in all nations far back in time was wholly unrelated to this true Christianity, but that a true Christianity existed all by itself in total isolation from the main or universal corpus of religious literature everywhere extant. On this point logic speaks out in thunder tones that shake the unsteady edifice of post-third century "Christianity" to its foundations. For however the premises are arranged, logic asserts that the vast range of ancient Hindu, Persian, Greek, Hebrew, Egyptian and Norse religious literature was *true Christian* literature—if Augustus and Eusebius (and others) spoke truly. (And if they have falsified, their untrustworthiness shakes the house of Christianity violently again.)

Christianity here faces a fateful dilemma. If it upholds its founders and early historians, it tears down the very foundations on which it rests; if it repudiates these spokesmen, it likewise jars its stability. It has kept its course between this Scylla and Charybdis up to now by obscuring the troublesome data. Its only chance of survival lies in the continued ignorance of its following. It had its inception in ignorance and only by sufferance of ignorance has it continued. It rejoiced in the ignorance of its adherents from the start and this fatal delight set the norm for its policy ever since. Hear Milman (p. 331):

"While they swept in converts indiscriminately from the palace and the public street, while the Emperor and the lowest of the populace were alike admitted on little more than the open profession of allegiance, they were satisfied if their allegiance in this respect was *blind and complete.*"

Following upon this cataclysmic new canon of criticism is another, that which has to do with the inclusion of *four* Gospels covering in general the same narrative in the Christian Bible. If any other notable or influential tome in the world had reprinted the same lengthy narrative of ostensible history four times over, it would have been held to be a matter of brainless idiosyncrasy. But when fanatical pietism is the dominating force in any movement, reason and balanced judgment go into complete abeyance. Irenaeus explained that there had to be four Gospels because there were four points of the compass and four winds. The odd thing is that all four winds in the Christian Gospels blow the same way and carry the same breezy message,—except when in scores of big and little points they directly contradict each other. When they blow in opposite directions they have created tempests in the brains and books of the cloistered exegetists.

And that lands us right in the midst of the eternal debate as to the authorship of these four books selected for the canon. What it is possible to say now should end this aeonial controversy short off. One of the blind spots blocking out a critical view of the palpable realities of the case has been the incredible obtuseness of judgment which permitted all the hosts of textual critics to go on assuming for centuries that these four Gospels were actually the separate and original writings of four different writers, each writing in his own distinctive fashion and style of diction an account or record of ostensibly the same set of historical occurrences, containing a run of the same sermons and discourses uttered by one or more characters in the story, and all four, in large measure, actually repeating almost whole sections and chapters in the same identical words! It is past all plausible supposition to claim that any four persons in history would or could sit down in their own libraries and compose documents describing a given epoch in history with all detailed events, and come out at the end with four books of about equal length and more or less exactly identical wording verse by verse! This is a phenomenon that has been blindly accepted by all Christian thought in the field of documentary study. It is quite on a par with the dominant legend handed down about the authorship of the Septuagint translation: that *seventy* translators were shut up in seventy separate cubicles in a monastery, each with a copy of the Hebrew MS, and with no exchange or communication during their entire period of labor, all seventy at the end emerged with precisely the same Greek wording of every verse! Well has it been claimed that Christianity has been built upon miracles. That four independent narrators should have come up with four almost identically-worded books of considerable length is the "miracle" on which the whole fabric of this Christianity rests. Now this grotesque fabric is tottering to its fall, shaken and shattered by the sane reflection at last that the four documents can be nothing other than four slightly varying copies of a common tradition, long only oral, but finally written, which the Council of Nicaea decided to incorporate in the official canon to give cumulative weight to a fiction they knew already rested on the weakest foundations, and also perhaps because each one contained some minor portions not included in the others.

Conybeare puts the idea just enunciated in pretty much the same way. He says that a "common element" is evident in all three (Synoptic) Gospels to any one who reflects how impossible it would have been that three independent writers should remember a long and complicated body of incident and teaching in the same way and transfer it to paper page after page in almost identical words.

Theological critics have a few times been driven close to recognition of this clearly inescapable resolution of the problem. Several of them have indeed hinted at the possible existence of a "common document," an "original document," now lost, lurking in obscurity behind all the four, and which all four have copied! Some of these glimmerings of sanity must be commented upon. Conybeare says (*History of New Testament Criticism,* p. 69) that a certain Mr. Smith, of Jordanhill, in a *Dissertation on the Origin and Connection of the Gospels* (Edinburgh, 1853) argued that oral tradition, the alleged personal knowledge the Gospel writers had acquired by experience or hearsay, was not adequate to explain the identities of word and event which are evident in the Synoptic Gospels. Conybeare comments that *John* is unaffected by the circumstance that *Matthew* and *Luke* both copied *Mark,* instead of all three having—as was supposed by Mr. Smith— "copied common but now vanished ulterior documents."

It is important to note that, as Conybeare writes, a tradition preserved by Papias (A.D. 120-140) states that Matthew "composed the *Logia,* or oracles of the Lord in the Hebrew tongue,—i.e. in the Aramaic patois of Palestine and that various peoples subsequently rendered these *Logia* into the Greek as best they could." Many scholars believe today, says Conybeare, that *Matthew's* Hebrew *Logia* were a selection of prophecies of Jesus Christ culled from the Old Testament. So here once more is cogent evidence that the Gospels were material long extant before Jesus ever could have lived.

Conybeare continues: in any case our first Gospel is *no* translation of the document attested by Papias; for, as Dean Robinson remarks,

"Our *St. Matthew* is demonstrably composed in the main out of two *Greek* books," so that we must "conclude either that Papias made a mistake in saying that St. Matthew wrote in Hebrew, or that if he wrote in Hebrew, his work has perished without leaving a trace behind it."

Some more of this discussion is introduced here to give readers an idea of the inextricable labyrinth of floating conjectures and traditions one becomes entangled in when entering upon the study of Bible criticism. So Conybeare continues: there is furthermore a statement in Irenaeus (about 170-180) to the effect that Matthew published his gospel among the Jews in his own tongue at the time that Peter and Paul were preaching the gospel in Rome and founding the Church. This statement seems to be independent of that of Papias, as most certainly is the story *related by Eusebius* about Pantaenus, the catechist of Alexandria and teacher of Clement and Origen. This story runs that about the year 180 Pantaenus visited India and found the natives using a *Gospel of Matthew* written in Hebrew, which Bartholomew had conveyed to them. Origen and Eusebius equally believed that our *Matthew* was the work of the Apostle originally composed in Hebrew.

Is it pertinent to ask how the natives of India could make use of a Matthew Gospel written in Hebrew, when for centuries of the Middle Ages there was hardly a native in all southern Europe in the countries west of Greece who could be found to teach the Renaissance scholars the Greek tongue, so as to read the great Greek classics and Aristotle's works then being brought out to the light.

It is not immediately incidental to the point at issue, but still is not too far removed from bearing upon the whole theme of Bible writing that Conybeare lets another fierce cat out of the bag when he concedes

425

that it is practically certain that the John of whom Irenaeus heard Polycarp say that he had known him in his boyhood, was *not* the Apostle John, but the Presbyter John! The exclamation point is fully justified, as with this there flies out the window another cherished bit of tradition converted into alleged reality by Christian fiction-mongering, in which its devotees were most adept. Irenaeus, as Conybeare, claims, had confused the two Johns.

Even now among the best educated Anglicans there is a tendency, says Conybeare, to give up the fourth Gospel (*John*). Dean Robinson says of it that it is *not history* in the lower sense of a contemporary narrative of events as they appeared to the youthful onlooker; not an exact reproduction of the very words spoken by Christ or to him. He says also that the old man (John) could not be expected to remember the events of the life of Christ in detail, especially the exact language of the discourses! The story is rather a drama that is enacted, he says, "in which every incident tells, or it would not be there. The record moves not on the lines of the ordinary succession of events so much as on the pathway of ideas." This, let it be said, is a true discernment, and adds more grist to the mill that grinds the flour of final conclusion that the Gospels are dramatic rituals of spiritual ideas and nothing else.

But so gripping is Conybeare's dissertation on the authenticity of the *Gospel of John* that it would be a deprivation not to notice it. He writes that for seventeen hundred years the theology that elevates Jesus of Nazareth out of and above human history, transforming him into the Word of God, which triumphed at Nicaea and inspired Athanasius, was based on this fourth Gospel more than on any other book of the New Testament. It now at last appears, from such admissions as that of Dean Robinson and others, that this entire theological fabric was woven in the mind of an Apostle meditating in extreme old age on the half-forgotten scenes and conversations of his youth. Such, says Conybeare, is the best case which can be made out for orthodox theology. We are left with the roofless ruins of a stately edifice which sheltered orthodox theologians of the past. And even these ruins are crumbling further down.

All this is astonishing enough. But to save our readers from gathering an erroneous impression it needs to be said that *John's* Gospel was most assuredly not the (original) fabrication of any John or other man in his old age. For if one thing in all this tangle of misguided conjectures is solid fact, it is the truth that many documents of the general kind called *Logia,* or *"Sayings of the Lord,"* dramatized as spoken on the Mount (of earth!) by the divine Personage in man to the natural man for his wise guidance, were extant in all the Eastern lands at that and earlier times. "John" did not need to fabricate such a conception of the Logos, or such a document expressing it. For, as Irenaeus testifies, hundreds of such books were floating about in his day, the second century. And only ignorance mistook the Jesus in them for a living man.

Conybeare ventures the assertion that as regards these many other gospels, such as that according to Peter, and the *Gospel of the Egyptians,* the Church did well to exclude them from its canon. How does he know? How can he say this? It is sheer prejudice and assumption. The presence of the *Gospel of the Egyptians* in the canon might have gone far to shatter the false accretions of ignorance and wild belief about the historicity of material that was never other than allegorical, and thus saved millions of Christians from being duped by "history" concocted out of beautiful fiction. This conclusion is well founded if only on the fact that this gospel so clearly revealed the purely allegorical nature of Scripture that the orthodox party saw to it that it was completely obliterated.

Newberry in his fine work, *The Rainbow Bridge,* says it is probable that even such stories as the creation legends of Persia and that in *Genesis* originated from a "common document." And Conybeare comes up with a remarkable statement that no one now contends that *Matthew's* Gospel is other than the work of an unknown writer, who compiled it out of *Mark's* Gospel and "Q," the *common document* of *Matthew* and *Luke.* And what is this "Q" document? A hypothetical fabrication of the minds of scholars who hit upon the one really rational idea that has occurred to them in all this search and speculation. As in science, so here; the mind is confronted by data; it seeks a plausible hypothecation that will account for them. And the existence of a *common document* was hypothecated to account for links of connection and traces of similarity that could find no rational explanation otherwise.

Our assertion is that this "common document" is the correct tack of speculative criticism at last. But the hard fact for orthodox partisans to swallow in accepting it is the necessity going with it of conceding that it was not a Christian but a Pagan document! And what also will have to be taken in is the fact that this "common document" was not just one individual book standing alone in literature, sharply distinguished from all other writings, and alone furnishing a basis for the four Gospels canonized, but instead was "common" in the sense that it was, in one variant or another, a common possession of all the world of the East then and a long time before. This "common source" was not at all in any sense to be regarded (as Christian commentators do) as the original conception or product of a single writer's brain or pen, a literary creation produced as a modern author generates a book out of his knowledge or imagination. It was the composite sum-total of the primordial true Christian revelation (of Augustine's description), or literary deposit of wisdom expressed in formularies long or short, in formations expressing numerical foundations as in the chiasmus, given to early humanity by developed giants in intellect, and handed on for ages purely by oral tradition, but finally here and there becoming consigned to written books. The many rescripts of such basic "rudimentals," so to say, of sapient philosophy and moral and spiritual truth, cosmology and anthropology, were extant, but secretly cherished for ages. About the late second and early third centuries the ignorant Christians got hold of some of them floating about and brought them out to public accessibility. The Gospels were, as Eusebius testifies, *not* composed, originated, written after the first century to detail the biography of a man living fully two hundred years before they first appear. The solution of the whole immense mystery of the Gospels and the origin of Christianity founded on them is now revealed in the simple statement that the Gospels, though not written at that time, *were released from secrecy to common accessibility* about the second century. And as Mead has so well shown, it was this release of these documents and the mob's frightful conversion of their esoteric spiritual meaning into assumed history that produced the madness that has engulfed a third of the world ever since.

Here—at last—is the true story and the true basis of all textual criticism.

CHAPTER XIX

THEN IS OUR FAITH VAIN

The purpose of this work is to present evidence that the religion
known as Christianity was based on fallacious foundations and then
to trace the disastrous consequences of a faith so wrongly based. The
material of the present chapter must be considered surely as constituting one of the most devastating exhibits of that evidence in the entire
field. To the ordinary intelligent Christian devotee, with a mind resting confidently on the assurances provided in never-failing volume and
certitude by the priests of orthodoxy, the data here adduced to undermine the historical authenticity and credibility of the resurrection of
Jesus of Nazareth must come as indeed a most shattering explosion
of the proverbial bombshell. For, as Paul says and theologians have
seconded, the one final axis of support on which Christianity rests is
the *physical* resurrection of the crucified Galilean from his hillside
grave.

Of course, if the over-all contention is either admitted or demonstrated past controversy (as we claim it is) that the Gospels are
what the vast body of evidence now flowing in from Egyptian research
proves them to be, it is a labor of supererogation to disprove the historical authenticity of any "event" in the entire Gospel narrative, or
in the "life" of Jesus. If he did not live at all, all such "events" are
interdicted as history.

But the presentation now to be made of material pertaining to the
alleged bodily resurrection of Jesus will be made on the basis of the
assumed actuality of the man's existence. The matter can not be argued
on any other basis. The point to be established is that even if he lived,
his resurrection can by no means be accepted as having occurred in the
way that common belief asserts that it did. Again it must be remarked
that the testimony of a few scholars here presented can be only a
minor fraction of what could be collated. Indeed it may not even be

the strongest that might be available. But that which is given must be seen to be formidable in all conscience.

But the birth, the temptation, the baptism, the anointing, the election as Messiah, the exaltation to Logos status, the transfiguration, the crucifixion, the burial, resurrection and ascension are all involved in this conglomerate of data and resolution of their meaning. If one falls from history to drama, the rest fall with it. So it is important to note what Warschauer has to say as to the transfiguration (*The Historical Life of Christ,* p. 192.):

> "But that core, the true character of what took place on that occasion, is hidden beneath thick layers of legendary and mythological matter, and it is only by patiently applying the solvent of cautious criticism that we shall arrive at what is historical, a most important result . . . unless we can accept this whole complex of miracles as fact, we shall have to try and explain what it is, other than fact, other than history."

This understanding and approach of Warschauer in this instance should have been the discernment, objective and working method of scholarship all along. His last sentence states the entire problem in a nutshell. Since the reality of these "miracles" is fast fading from the realm of fact and of history, the important business of the Christian system should have been, and must now be, to ascertain *what they are other than fact, other than history*. We have unfolded their *other* character in previous works and are continuing the revelation in this one. The everlasting difficulty and obstacle to success in this matter is the fact that not since Plato's day, or the days of ancient Egypt, perhaps, has any one been able to persuade the scholars that these hoary graphs and glyphs depicting the form and manner and meaning of all human history are themselves something other than history. They are the typal intimations of what all objective history deposits or builds into the human consciousness. They are the outward pictorial portrayals of all the mighty realizations, insights, knowings and understandings which take form in innermost awareness from man's total historical experience. They are this and nothing more. That scholarship has not seen and held them as such, but has mistaken them for only the mere ripple of action of a few humans, has been the supreme catastrophe of all the world, and the parent of unending evil and suffering. The obfuscation of the mind of half the world has been the cost-price of that failure of insight, that dearth of sagacity, that sloth of the herd instinct.

There is presented here exactly what Warschauer prescribes as the solvent of what to him seem like insuperable riddles,—"cautious criticism." As far as our reading has gone, this is the only instance in which we have noted the employment of criticism on the part of orthodoxy that is "cautious" enough to envisage a way out of confusion to land on sane ground. The critique we shall here introduce is not our own, but that of a scholar whom Conybeare in his own history of criticism rates as perhaps the greatest of modern theological critics and exegetists. He is the German Johannes Weiss and our excerpts are taken from his two volumes on *The History of Primitive Christianity.* We paraphrase Weiss' pages of text with the utmost care to give his conclusions with exactitude.

There is not a single trace, he writes, in St. Paul of the now common idea derived from the Gospels and the *Book of Acts* that through his resurrection Jesus returned to the conditions of earthly life, not one trace of the idea that he ate and drank with his disciples; or that he arose in and as the same body of flesh which he had occupied before the crucifixion. When Paul speaks of the resurrection he is not talking at all of a purely physical resuscitation, as of a drowned or deceased person returning to the same life in the same body. For the Apostle Jesus' resurrection carries the identical significance of his glorification and exaltation, which are processes of *spiritual* transfiguration in the inner consciousness, affecting the body by charging it with a higher dynamic, but in no wise taking it out of its sphere of existence in the area of natural law. His occasional reference to the resurrection without the remotest allusion to a physical resurgence of a deceased corpus points to this idea.

That the words translated "raised," "rose again," "made alive again" by act of God, "rose up," "stood up," "came forth from their graves" to return once more to life upon earth, carried in the general mind of antecedent time the connotation of a resurrection of the physical body after death, is clearly established by Weiss. This meaning, he says, is the essential feature in the *popular notion* of the resurrection. So the people looked upon Jesus as John the Baptist risen from the dead, who had now resumed his work upon earth with renewed vigor (*Mark* 6:14). The popular conception was that a Messianic figure—even a Lazarus raised from the dead—having passed through the halls of death and overcome its power, would live and reign upon earth for a thousand years, as *Revelation* (20:4) states the idea. When this common concept of the resurrection was now likewise applied to Jesus, one might expect that it would be carried further to the idea that he should remain upon earth and here establish his Messianic kingdom.

Weiss then inserts in a note that if there ever was a pre-Christian Jewish doctrine of the death and resurrection of the Messiah, it can only have looked forward to some such continuation of his life upon earth—"but this was suppressed by the Christians in view of the historical facts," Jesus having tarried only forty days on earth after his translation to spiritual state. This indefinite continuation on earth after his exaltation, says Weiss, is just what did not happen. Jesus did not remain on earth. Hence the *popular concept of the resurrection does not apply really to the case of Jesus.* This is a momentous pronouncement put forth by an eminent Christian theologian. It is a telling blow straight at the heart of the Christian faith.

It is the *Book of Acts* which recognizes and removes this disharmony, Weiss continues, when it states (1:9 f.) that after forty days of earthly life the Risen One ascended upon the clouds towards heaven. Thus a second miracle is added to that of the resurrection. It is certainly noticeable that Paul has heard nothing from the primitive community about the ascension as a special miracle in addition to the resurrection; for him the two are one, because both are the inner subjective consummation of the apotheosis of the human mind in its final union with the Divine. Indeed, says Weiss, "strictly taken, resurrection and exaltation are mutually exclusive ideas." To be sure they are, if "resurrection" is made to refer to a physical reanimation of a corpse, and "exaltation" is a psycho-spiritual regeneration. These two things are worlds apart. What Weiss is saying is that as Paul and *Acts* speak of them, they are not thus differentiated, but are in essence one and the same thing. Take "resurrection" in its obvious non-physical sense, and it reads "exaltation."

Weiss says it is significant that the resurrection narratives in the Gospels know nothing about an ascension; only *John* (20:17) states that the risen Lord had not yet gone up to the Father, though even here nothing is said of this final exaltation. On the contrary, a conception is reflected in the stories of *Matthew, Luke* and *John* which is fundamentally incompatible with the idea of resurrection: Jesus appears as the one who is already exalted. In *Matthew* (28:20) and elsewhere Jesus' manifestations are described in terms which imply that he is no longer confined within space and time, but is a spirit free from the burdens of the physical, rather than merely a person who has returned to life. The implications are all metaphysical and none of them physical. He appears suddenly among his own, passes through

432

closed doors, disappears as suddenly again; will not permit any one to touch him, and breathes upon his disciples like a bodiless spirit. In these features of the narrative is reflected the early idea that Jesus "appeared" to his disciples as the Heavenly One, visible only for brief instants.

A footnote here calls attention to the fact that in the oldest texts it reads simply that "he parted from them," whereas in later texts there have been added the words "and was carried up into heaven." Weiss adds in another note that the Passion and Resurrection narratives in *Luke* have been more "touched up" and "revised" by harmonists than the earlier chapters have been. Here is seen the work of those Christian hands that had to scratch about in a hurry to make allegory read like history. It is important to note this. The evidence of this literary skulduggery is hidden, of course, but Weiss, like Conybeare, here testifies to it. The manipulation can be traced in thousands of deletions, interpolations, changes, twisted translations.

Then the learned German scholar recalls the passages in which the disciples, Thomas especially, are convinced of Jesus' actual corporeality. In explanation of this apparent contradiction with the indications of his purely spirit-form status, he adduces that these passages were "probably added by the redactor." Peter's sermon (*Acts* 10:40 f.) emphasizes the complete restoration of his former corporeality; "these are properly the resurrection narratives, whose motive is to defend the disciples against the charge of having seen a 'ghost.'"

The first group of narratives, Weiss conceives, spoke out spontaneously and exuberantly the reaction of the disciples and the women to the marvel and miracle of what they had borne witness to. A second group, however, reflected a sober prosaic "second thought" about it all, and endeavored to put it all back on a footing of positive actuality. So Weiss is forced to say that the great question is precisely whether or not the "appearances" proved what they were supposed to do.

Popular ideology about the spirits of the departed would credit the disciples with having witnessed a series of phantom apparitions of their deceased Master. Therefore, Weiss thinks, the writers of the resurrection narrative set themselves to refute these interpretations that would prevail roundabout; and so they placed special emphasis upon the items accentuating Jesus' physical realness. Hence Weiss characterizes the resurrection recitals as apologetic survivals of the controversy over the question whether or not a miracle like the resuscitation of a dead person was possible. It was a play to add to the great reputation of

Jesus as a miracle-worker by the climactic miracle of effecting his own return from the grave. The Jews would not have regarded it as extraordinary or unnatural for the spirit of Jesus to have reincarnated; but for the Hellenistic populations this explanation would have been difficult, says Weiss, and *Acts* (17:31 *f*.) expresses this difficulty. "Accordingly these massive resurrection stories must first have originated upon Hellenic soil, for the purpose of missionary apologetics," is the great scholar's conclusion.

Then he argues the point that the failure of the women to report to the disciples what the angel sitting in the empty tomb had told them —"He is not here; he is risen"—constitutes a datum of weighty significance, as it indicates the existence of a faith in the resurrection of Jesus "without any reference whatever to the empty grave."

The likelihood that the disciples could come and steal the body of Jesus from the tomb while it was guarded by the Roman sentries is discounted by Weiss. He credits this story to outright "tampering with facts." The story, he says, was expanded as a legend in the spirit of the times, and *accretions were gradually made to the original narrative.* A long account taken from the *Gospel of Peter,* going into detail as to a very different series of events at the resurrection, is given by Weiss. His conclusion is that the whole story in *Matthew* is one of an overworked imagination, sweeping traditional imaginative embellishments up to a veritable paroxysm of fanciful elaboration. He says it is the creation of unfettered fancy, with a specific apologetic motive. Even though, he argues, it may be true that some experience of the excited women, particularly Mary Magdalene, gave the first impetus to this further development—the empty tomb—"it is nevertheless clear that we are here dealing with a legendary and unreliable tradition." These are momentous words to come from a leading Christian commentator. They put all Christianity in jeopardy.

He then builds a new and different thesis of the resurrection upon a quite possible and plausible interpretation of the word "risen." We have now seen, he expounds, that from the "appearances" it by no means follows that the "Jesus is risen" cry of the angel in the tomb has to refer to the revivification and disappearance of the physical body. It can, and far more probably does, refer to his exaltation to spiritual heavens, which Paul would make equivalent to the ascension. It bespoke his transfiguration, his glorification in a world of transcendent being.

Then, says Weiss, and very pertinently, a further and final conclusion forced upon us is that the doctrinal statement, "on the third day he rose again," does not rest upon fact, but reflects a theory which was originally simply added on to the fact of the appearances. Where did it come from, he inquires. And the statement itself gives clear answer: "according to the Scriptures" Jesus must have risen on the third day. Now that Jesus had appeared to his disciples, they recalled the various Old Testament "prophetic texts," which said that the Messianic redeemer would arise from death on the third day. For a long time now it has been suspected, declares Weiss, that this phrase "on the third day," instead of being derived from facts of experience, really rested upon entirely different considerations, chiefly upon the general expectation, based on immemorial mythical tradition, that a resurrection would naturally take place on the third day. (That Weiss is completely correct in this reasoning is incontestably established by volumes of scholarly testimony, but most of all by a great work dealing with ancient festivals, *The Day of Yahweh,* by William A. Heidel.) The instant a veritable survival or reappearance of a figure believed to be the Messiah seemed to be asserted or at any rate bruited about as a fact, it would be taken as dogmatic certainty that it was a fulfilment of the ancient prophecy, and the third day would inevitably be made the time of his arising. And so it came about that this time period was included in the earliest creed, even though it did not strictly accord with the experience of the disciples, the time being in the assumed historical case of Jesus only two days. "That we have to do with a doctrinal statement rather than an incontestable matter of fact is evident from" this "third day" phrase in the story.

Why was the inclusion of this phrase so imperative that it was applied to Jesus, "even though properly it did not relate to him at all?" Weiss again asks.

"For not only did he *not* 'rise again' in the real sense, i.e., to take up his earthly life once more, nor did this take place either 'on the third day' or 'after three days.' Where did it originate? Since everything took place according to the Scriptures, as St. Paul says, it is to the Scriptures that we must turn."

And then he cites its location in *Hosea* 6:1 *f.*

It can be added here that the phrase not only is found in the Hebrew Old Testament, but that it was extant in the general field of ancient religion and always in an allegorical reference.

Accordingly, Weiss continues, some writers have supposed that the early Christians were following a popular tradition, not found in the Old Testament, but perhaps in some Apocryphal writings or merely in oral traditions (why not in both?), and thence read it into the passage in *Hosea*. The same scholars have pointed out that in the neighborhood of Palestine at the time of Jesus there was a widespread cult and myth of a dying and rising god known among the Babylonians as Tammuz, among the Phoenicians as Adonis, among the Egyptians as Osiris and among the Romans as the Phrygian Attis. Weiss ventures the daring suggestion that "it is really an extraordinary parallel that according to Plutarch (*De Iside et Osiride,* 13:39) the day commemorating the death of Osiris was the seventeenth of Athyr, the day of the recovery the nineteenth—that is, the third day; and that the Roman observance of the death of Attis came on the twenty-second of March, his restoration on the twenty-fifth (three days). These parallels and their congruity with the passage from *Hosea,*—and also with the earliest Christian creed—are scarcely accidental.

(We pause to say that here, from a Christian writer, is the full answer to Conybeare's challenge as to how a Pagan god-cult could have influenced early Christianity. Further evidences of a similar nature are to be found everywhere. Coming from a fellow-Christian critic, it should have weight.)

The simplest explanation, Weiss goes on, is that in all these references the three days merely designate the briefest possible period of time. This matches in childish naiveté and ignorance the many other guessing evasions of Christian writers as to the meaning of the several numbers repeated in the Bible. For the sake of exhibiting the utter imbecility of even the best Christian scholarship in regard to Pagan systematism, especially in their employment of numbers to designate the most basic cosmic processes and relations, it is well to cite Weiss' sentences in which he glaringly advertises his lack of all true understanding:

"Accordingly the three days were never more nor less than a popular expression for a very brief interval of time, only during which the resurrection could take place; and if the same period is presupposed in the myths of Attis and Osiris (perhaps once likewise in that of Adonis?) it was for exactly the same reason."

This is the most astonishing absurdity, and coming from nearly the most eminent of Christian scholars, it reveals what the effort to rebuild true conceptions has to combat. As before briefly hinted, the three days in the tomb of "death" are the Pagan mythicization of the period during which the sparks of divine consciousness are buried in a condition termed "death" in and under the limiting deadening thraldom of matter, inhibiting while giving implementation to its higher diviner powers and faculties. The Scriptures state that God sends down to death and he raises up again, and that he does this in three days. Could Weiss have been unmindful of such a passage as this one?—"As Jonas was three days and three nights in the belly of the whale, so must the Son of Man be three days and three nights in the bowels of the earth." The three "days" really in cosmic reference allude to the three long aeons spent by the soul of life in peregrinating upward through the mineral, the vegetable and the animal kingdoms, the fourth bringing it to the human in man. Is it too much to ask that eminent Christian thinkers should give some rational evidence that they know the simplest rudiments of the true interpretation of their own Scriptures?

Weiss is so far "liberal" in his mood that he thinks the Galilean disciples of Jesus could even have known something of the Adonis or the Osiris cults!

"Hellenistic cults of this sort—for example in Byblus, where a center of the Adonis cult was to be found—lay, so to speak, before the very doors of Galilee. But it is doubtful if they would have had sufficient interest in these cults and in the ideas they enshrined to use them in explaining their own faith. It is much more likely that they would have gone out of their way to avoid such analogies."

We have no way of knowing how rabidly a group of ignorant peasants in Galilee might by this time have reacted to the mythical-mystical forms of Pagan expressions of lofty cosmic and human truth, which it can safely be presumed had long ago been turned by popular stupidity into outlandish literal fol-de-rol. But that they could have been standing almost entirely detached from and untouched by the cult representations and cult systems that, instead of being sporadic and occasional, were quite universal (esoterically) in those days, is another of the follies that obsess Christian minds. But Weiss continues:

"Now that Jesus was dead and had appeared to his followers, the teaching was transferred to him, its fulfilment was recognized in his career, and as a consequence the whole tradition of the empty tomb took form. But rather than assume the existence of this hypothetical secret tradition, it would seem wiser to suppose that the early Christians found in the passage from *Hosea* a prediction of the death and resurrection of the Messiah, and then *spun out from this the whole doctrine of the resurrection."*

This singular mélange of partial truth and clinging mistaken view practically admits the basic premises of our work. Such authors as Weiss and others representing Christian view are cited in quantity in these pages, not so much for what they know as for what they admit, what slips out from them in unwary moments. For us to print herein the blank bald statement that the early Christians concocted, fabricated the story of the resurrection out of elements of ancient Pagan tradition, and that indeed there was no *physical* resurrection at all, that the entire legend was the product of the excited fancy of some Galilean peasants who, witnessing some spiritistic phenomena, to save face in the community then wove the narrative of a supernatural event that was to electrify sixty generations of world life, would bring down upon us the virulent condemnation of the orthodox Christian world. But what will that Christian world do when it finds this very same statement pronounced by one of its own leading expositors? Such products of modern liberated criticism catch the Christian system on the two horns of the great dilemma: it must either repudiate its own grounds and supports, or repudiate its best spokesmen. And in either case it stands weakened, if not mortally wounded.

Concluding the case Weiss says that whatever view one may hold of the source of the phrase, it is of first importance to recognize that "raised again on the third day" was not the original language of the Christian faith, *nor did it rest upon historical facts, but was afterwards added* to the earlier accounts of the appearances, and then in time produced the whole series of Easter stories.

So we have out of the mouths of Christianity's own most studious commentators at last an admission of what must now be seen to be the truth, that the very corner stone of the edifice of this great religious persuasion is a tale as empty of historical reality as the tomb it invented for the story, a fantastic fiction "spun" out of material wholly imaginative and never based on fact. And even the fabrication of the canard is admitted to have been perpetrated with fraudulent intent and for purposes of deception. So at last we may know that the alleged crowning event in all history, the world-transfiguring miracle of Easter, stands revealed in all its naked poverty as a shrewdly concocted miracle designed to hynotize the credulous minds of ignorant millions.

Weiss' final conclusion as to the true character of the "appearances" of Jesus after the "return from the grave" must not be omitted. Put in brief form, it is that the disciples and the women saw not any actually rearisen physical body of the Lord, but the wraith of his spiritual body. We have the testimony and often the evidence of both Spiritualists and non-Spiritualists to the effect that in thousands of instances the spirit-form of deceased people, in dress, feature and action fully like the persons while in life, appeared to them, talking and even revealing facts of vital importance known only to them but proved true by eventualities, and appearing through closed doors and as miraculously vanishing.

In March of 1942 there appeared in the daily issue of the *Atlanta* (Georgia) *Constitution* a brief news item stating that a citizen of that town had been murdered; that no clues could be located; but that a week or so after the event the little eight-year-old daughter of the murdered man came down to her mother in the morning saying, "Mother, Daddy came and stood by my bed last night and told me who killed him." She revealed the names of two men only slightly known to the family; the police called them in and upon grilling they confessed and implicated a third man. This obviously true event can be matched by thousands.

If Weiss is correct in his elucidation of what he conceives to be true in the resurrection story in the Gospels, then there occurred in Atlanta, Georgia, on a March morning in 1942 an event *fully as important and as momentous* for all human history as the alleged first Easter miracle of the year—unknown. For this modern event and that ancient one were completely identical. Some people back there reported they saw a spirit-form of a recently deceased person; the Atlanta girl reported the same thing, and, moreover, adduced evidence which under test corroborated the reality of her vision! In this respect her experience stands as even more veridical and trustworthy than that in ancient Galilee. Weiss has spent much of a lifetime trying to find proofs of the reality of the Judean report, and apparently came off rather discomfited.

In the finale, the mountain of exuberant Christian faith which labored to bring forth the consummative event in all human history, ended by producing a mouse in the shape of just another commonplace instance of a phenomenon repeated almost daily in the seances of the semi-despised Spiritualism. A dozen magazines over the last century have been filled every month with generally well-attested cases of the same kind. Camille Flammarion, some forty years ago the world's leading astronomer, spent over fifty years of his life in collecting data now contained in three volumes of authentic cases of the utmost remarkable character in this field. The upshot of the matter is that the Gospels, the rock of the Christian faith, are left with no more reality to them than appertains to a wraith. They become the ghost of an alleged salvation.

His investigations, honest if somewhat distorted in points, evidently shook Weiss' own confidence as a Christian. For he sees the possibility of a fearful realization that our own resurrection may go out with that of Jesus! "But does not our own resurrection depend upon the Easter miracle? According to the belief of Paul and the early Christians it does." Jesus' rising again ended for us the fearsome power of death (*Col.* 2:15).

"For the first time one went down to the realm of Hades who could not be held there (*Acts* 2:31); henceforth his power was broken and would be forever destroyed at the end of the age (*I Cor.* 15:26)."

(All this of course is to be seen in revised light if the spiritual-body view of the resurrection is taken instead of the corporeal one. If, as Paul says, the soul is "sown" in a natural body and raised in and as a *spiritual* body, resurrection thus rationally understood is a certainty for all, and no one need be alarmed about what happened or did not happen back in Palestine in the long ago. But we must stay with Weiss on the ground he works from.)

So he hedged from the view of Christian gullibility and erroneous imagination to a sane retrenchment of his own faith in the meaning of Easter:

"But as for ourselves we must admit we can no longer think in such terms. To be exact, the majority of Christians at the present time do not really believe in a resurrection of the flesh on the last day. . . ."

This is astounding, for its utterance points to a Christianity that faces the decline and fall of its sway in this world. Christianity, as constituted for seventeen hundred years, stands or falls with the resurrection, and that conceived in the special sense of the corporeal rearising from death of a man, Jesus, on a given morning about the year eight, or ten or twelve B.C. Now, as Warschauer did for so many of the Gospel incidents, Weiss comes along and wipes away the resurrection in precisely that special sense, its corporeal reality. He reduces it to the category of what can be ordinarily seen to occur in a vast run of phenomena following death—the visible appearance of the spirit-body. If, then, Christianity is to survive, it must do so by conforming its basic phenomena and claims to that which is normal, dropping that which is abnormal, miraculous, supernatural. But this again is just what Weiss affirms it can not do. For he says:

"Once more, however, the old objection arises: we must avoid placing the eternal life of Jesus on a level with that of other departed souls. He can not be thought of as one among many." [Yet how effusively, to nausea sometimes, the writers play up the divine Master's being so wonderfully "human," so like unto us in all respects, save sin!]

"For him, some one will say, there must be reserved a special place. Had we no other evidence of his victory over death than that of our own departed, the whole thing would fall into uncertainty. This objection really touches the essential point. If his immortality is no different from ours, it can scarcely be used any longer as proof of our hope for the life to come. The situation must in fact be reversed: if and in so far as we believe that we shall live after death, though we, too, like him must die, then and to that extent we can believe in his continued existence. And this, for many persons, is simply not enough. They demand objective irrefutable proof that there is an eternal life. Hence they go back to the old view, that the tangible irrefutable miracle of the physical resurrection of Jesus provides the indispensable support both of their own faith and that of Christendom generally. *Unfortunately* it is to be feared that this support will never again appear as firm and immovable as it did to our forefathers. In some form or other, even among the most ardent believers, doubt has begun to undermine the narratives of the Gospels. And when we are admonished that we must 'believe' these narratives, the admonition lacks sense and meaning today. The word 'believe' is misused in such a connection. It is simply misapplied to a fact in the past. Either a fact is established beyond all doubt—in which case there is no need to 'believe' it; or else it is uncertain—in which case to believe it, that is, to suppress and silence doubt, would be dishonorable. In this case it would be especially perverse to attempt to base a conviction of one's own eternal life upon a 'faith' in certain facts, when, although faith had been wrested from doubt, the facts seemed forever insecure. Alas, how easily the structure may collapse and how frail it really is, even for many who think they hold the true faith. Our belief in life to come, if it is to have permanence, must have other foundations than some narrative of events full of contradictions and impossibilities. But even were the Gospel narratives far less contradictory and far more reliable than they are, our faith could not be based on such a foundation. For in so serious a question as this, one can decide and believe only upon the basis of his own experience and conviction, not upon that of the strange and—so far as we are concerned—unexaminable experiences of others long ago. What St. Paul and the Gospels really tell us, in the end, is only this: That the disciples were certain that the Lord was still alive; and that their experiences were so overwhelming and convincing that they based their whole lives henceforth upon them."

(Yet thousands of people today, just as sincere and in general far more intelligent than those hypothetical or mythical Galilean fishermen, testify to experiences of the identical sort that are just as overwhelming and convincing to them, and orthodox Christianity puts them down as crack-brained enthusiasts and denounces them in a thousand sermons and books.)

And then, if we can take Weiss' words for what they logically connote, we see him tearing down not only the supports of the resurrection, but those of the two other events that are of equal significance to Christian schematism, the crucifixion and the birth itself. For he says that, although the many divergences or contradictions found in the stories in the Gospels may be explained as perfectly natural and characteristic of human testimony in general, it may be worth noting that in quantity, range and variety "there is more evidence for the resurrection of Jesus than for his death—not to mention his birth." Having shown how meager in fact is the evidence for the resurrection, how much less substantial must then be the credibility of the birth and the death stories!

Further disenchantment of the whole fairy belief in the resurrection arises from his conclusion on the statement that at the same time certain ideas reflected in the Gospels, as for example that of *St. Luke* (24:39), where Jesus asks the disciples to behold his hands and his feet, "for a spirit hath not flesh and bones as ye see me have" (unless, Weiss adds, in a note, this is one more interpolation!), "will have to be simply abandoned. The defenders of the traditional ecclesiastical view have no alternative but to choose one or the other of these two conceptions, for there is no unity whatsoever in the Biblical teaching on this point," i.e. whether Jesus rose in the flesh or only in spirit.

That there is indeed no unity whatsoever in the Biblical teaching is amply evident if one reads Weiss' own listing of the discrepancies, divergences, contradictions and inconsistencies in the Gospel accounts of the resurrection. We cite some of these for the sake of opening the eyes of readers—or rather of non-readers—of the Bible to the unreliability of the resurrection story as given to certify the alleged climactic event in world history. Weiss writes that the reader

"will therefore scarcely recognize the contradictions between narratives— e.g. that according to *John,* Mary Magdalene alone came to the grave, and that according to the other Gospels there were three women present; or that according to *Mark* the women made no report to the disciples, while according to *John,* Peter and the beloved disciple ran to the grave

442

as soon as they were called; or that according to *Luke* the disciples did not believe, while according to *Matthew* they did just as they were bidden by the women; or that according to *Luke* and *John*, they remained in Jerusalem, according to *Matthew* they returned to Galilee; or that the presence of a watch at the grave, related in detail by *Matthew*, is simply excluded by *Mark*, *Luke* and *John*; or that the angel is absent in *John*, while *Luke* has two of them—and so on."

"The risen Lord appears in one passage as completely incorporeal, though not invisible, while in another he is represented as eating and drinking; and then once more he becomes spirit-like again, untouchable, emerging suddenly out of invisibility and as swiftly disappearing"—

precisely as all wraiths of deceased persons do at the conventional seances of Spiritualists, or as in the well-established case of the deceased wife of the eminent Dr. Russell H. Conwell, founder of the Baptist Temple and Temple University in Philadelphia, who saw and conversed with his departed but very present wife Sarah every morning for six months in succession, the apparition revealing to him in two instances the whereabouts of his Civil War discharge papers and his gold pen which he had had another person hide in a place unknown to him, to test her.

It is submitted here that this array of contradictions in the stories of four narrators seriously invalidates the authenticity of the event basic for Christianity's existence. What credence can be put in a recital of alleged facts as jumbled as this? A great Christian expositor gives up in despair.

We hold that the general intelligence and accuracy of the critique of this eminent Christian exegetist virtually rings the death knell of a Christianity that is built on a thousand untenable conceptions. He undermines the one uniquely vital and essential foundation of the Christian system. The one thing it claimed to offer humanity that no other system ventured to hold forth was the historical reality of God who had himself come in the person of his only Son to demonstrate and certify to mankind the conquest of death, in all its *physical* realness, through his rising again bodily out of the grave. On this platform of asserted veridical demonstration the Christian faith was founded and has drawn the allegiance of untold millions over twenty centuries. Now a keen-minded scholar, himself of the faith, looks discreetly over the evidence and finds that, in the form so long claimed and asseverated, *this demonstration never occurred!* Unless this great German scholar's piercing determinations can be overruled and shown to be erroneous, the result of his searchings means nothing less than the end of any claims to uniqueness by Christianity among religions. It logically means the end of Christianism, known as Christianity.

But in one sense, ironically enough, the resurrection stories in the Gospels do prove the uniqueness of Christianity, indeed its very exceptional uniqueness. It was catastrophically unique in that it alone of religions translated the universal ancient allegorization of the rising again of the soul that was represented, like the seed in the earth, as going to its death in its incarnation in the grave or tomb of the body and rising to a new cycle of life in its springtime, in the unthinkably stupid sense of the physical arising of the human fleshly body after death from a rock-hewn grave on a Judean hillside. This is the uniqueness of Christianity that earned for it the sublime contempt of every man of rational intelligence when it was propagated among the dull-minded rabble of the Roman Empire. This is the uniqueness of a Christianism that could survive only by virtue of the hypnotic inculcations of a designing priestcraft in the uncritical minds of the millions down through the Dark Ages. And it is the uniqueness of a Christianity that, as light is born again and intelligence can be asserted to dominate the public mind, will be most heartily ashamed of its galling notoriety for having fallen into the most fatal of all blunders in history. Christianity is the one unique religion of all time, the only one to mistake the Christ's exaltation and transfiguration in inner consciousness for a physical resurrection and ascension.

It must be indeed insufferable to Christian "pride" and presumption that Weiss has the bluntness of honesty to stand forth and say, in the finale, that "if only one could see into the hearts of men, and if every one did his best to get his ideas fully clarified, it would probably turn out that no one really" believes in the physical resurrection of the personalized Christ anyway. And so it eventuates that the world, according to hundreds of Christian books, has been saved from Pagan heathenism, from Stygian spiritual darkness and from a welter of moral depravity by the power of a doctrine, based on alleged historical reality, which turns out to have been an unfounded hoax from beginning to end. This is the picture of history, as claimed by Christian zealotry on the one side and then analyzed by Christian mentality and honest scholarship on the other. Christian thinkers, using the liberty of conscientious criticism that was itself wrested from tyrannous ecclesiasticism at the cost of oceans of blood, have now come along and knocked down the structures of ignorant assumption set up by purblind zealots toying with a truth they could not understand. At

444

no time has this arrogant impostor, Christianism, been consistent or harmonious with itself. It has ever been a welter of elements diverse and discordant, and has lived only by the suppression of its discrepancies, its inconsistencies and its falsities.

If we were asked to point out an aspect of Weiss' presentation that displays in most flagrant form the weakest element in the Christian conceptions he deals with, perhaps the central weakness in all Christian theory, we would point to the sentences in which he says that the Christian can hardly stomach the acceptance of the appearances of the risen Jesus as "on a level with that of other departed souls." His survival and visible appearance from the grave "can not be thought of as only one among many." For him there must be reserved a special place and a special and unique form of immortality, which common man does not share. Other souls of deceased people have come back to talk with those left behind. But this will not do for the Christian, whose only satisfaction must be nourished and fed upon the unchallenged uniqueness and superiority of his system, and its Christ, over all others. The Christian must see his belief and its demonstrations declared and acknowledged the paragon, the one alone crowned with complete perfection. Jesus must stand as the nonpareil among Messiahs and his resurrection must be nonpareil among phenomena.

To our mind nothing so baldly reveals the essential smallness and basic error of Christian attitudes and set of mind as this blindness in regard to such a central dogma as the resurrection. To us it advertises the total unbalance and eccentricity of the fundamental postulates on which it rests. When a cult philosophy leads its followers for many centuries so far off the track of normal understanding as to indoctrinate or hypnotize them with the idea that a scheme of elucidation designed to enlighten and exalt mankind loses all its virile and beneficent power because it brings and applies its meaning-references within the range and sphere of phenomena attainable or demonstrable in man's own normal area of accomplishment, that teaching, it is submitted, has twisted the human mind awry to follow an errant trail. Again, a religion that conditions the minds of its hallucinated devotees to the idea that for a demonstration to command the awe and reverence and obedience of mankind, it must manifest a power to work miracles whole worlds removed above the level of human achievement, that it degrades itself in human estimation by deploying these powers on the level on which man lives his common life, must be convicted of an erroneous principium of both psychology and practical theology at one stroke. It is a question of the localization of pragmatic values, whether an exemplary demonstration of miraculous, or at any rate divine power is made operable on the level of man's experience and attainment, or raised to inaccessible dimensions above his reach.

Christianity has felt that it has had to keep its unique Son of God so much a paragon, so far above the level of humanity, that to speak of man's being on the same plane with it is to besmirch and blaspheme the holy majesty of it. Morbid and maudlin psychologizations from the start, habitually reanimated in every generation of Christian manipulation, have saturated the Christian mind with the thought that if the personal Christ demonstrated only what man can himself demonstrate, all the romantic halo of heroic glory is at one fell stroke disenchanted in a deflation of the Gospels to just common experience we all have or may have. Right here, if we can grasp and hold it, is the nub of the great crucial question of the historical blessing or scourge of the Christian system. The crucial point lies right in the discernment that the psychological blessedness of the system, or any system, inheres in its indoctrinating the mind with the idea that the supreme excellence of a divine examplar resided in its demonstration or exemplification of the very thing that *was* attainable or demonstrable by man! A divine Savior who came to dazzle man with the demonstration of supernal powers and excellence far beyond man's possible reach left man standing agape with awe, but hopeless. To show him the glorious unattainable is to tease him with the proof of his own inferiority. The religion that will grip and arouse him to hopeful achievement is that which will present to him for his emulation an ideal of beauty and splendor as his own attainable goal. Weiss could not see, as the others could not see, that the supreme utility and beneficence of the Christian system would be enormously enhanced in the world if any historical certitude could be adduced to support the Gospel narrative that the actual spirit-form or spiritual body (which St. Paul says we all have) of the crucified Jesus appeared to the disciples and to Paul in absolute living demonstration of the survival and reality of his soul from out the tomb of annihilation. And they can not see that the glory and the worth of this proof would lie directly in the fact that it took place not in any super-cosmic or supernatural fashion, but precisely in the way that it could be expected to occur to all of us. Weiss thinks its power over the human imagination would lie in its total and utter uniqueness as of a thing far above the experience of ordinary humans. The truth is that its dynamic weight for humanity would in-

446

here precisely in its promise of identity with our own attainable experience. Man will be allured to higher life by the revelation and demonstration of the glory that is *open to him;* he will gape coldly at the glory of the unattainable. Christianity robbed him of his birthright all through. It gave all to Jesus, leaving common mortals standing in poverty. This false religion took the path of immeasurable calamity for the West when it instilled the general idea that the resurrection, as also the transfiguration and the exaltation, was anything other than the survival in elevated ranges of consciousness of the divine soul, the Christ, that till death inhabits the mortal body of every son of earth. It opened the path to this calamity when it took that mode of interpretation of its Scriptures which made the allegories of experience, universal to all men, referable to only one historical figure. This blunder made the experience, dramatized in all old Scriptures, Judean and isolated, not universal and ecumenical. It must be put down in the most forthright terms that, beyond any other religion on earth Christianity has afflicted its devotees with the direst poverty of spirit, of lively incentive and of cheering hope, by stealing from the consciousness of its people the one ideological factor of supreme value,—the knowledge that the Christ demonstrated for us not *his* life as infinitely remote from ours, but *our* life lived by him in its finished perfection. When Weiss and all Christians can come to see that the glorious truth of the original truly Christian resurrection lies in the fact that the glory of Easter is precisely the *same* glory that we shall demonstrate in the continuity of the soul's life out of the body, clothed in its shining vesture of spiritual light, then will a transfiguring motive begin to exercise its beneficent sweetness through the offices of a regenerated Christianity. The strength and living dynamism of the Easter allegory will only begin to work as the spiritual leaven in the lives of humans when it is again seen, as the ancients saw it, that the dramatized Christ resurrection was typal of the divine resurrection of the soul of every man. Humanity will begin to reinaugurate its Golden Age when it is realized that the essential crucial point of all present history is not whether Christ was resurrected in ancient Judea, but whether he is being resurrected in human consciousness today, in humanity collectively. Christianity of today misses the point and focus, or the locale, of vital reference by some two thousand years. Its power will stream forth again to irrigate the conscious desert of mortal life when it is known factually, empirically that the Jesus resurrection was exactly the model set by sage dramatic art to quicken our understanding of

447

that very mode of resurrection and return to the Fatherland of a higher kingdom which we will experience following bodily demise. Its supreme magnificence of inspiring meaning must be found precisely in the fact that Jesus' resurrection was right on the level of our own prospective experience. Thus only can it have exhilarating, thrilling significance—for us.

In *II Timothy* Paul warns the brethren to beware of false teachers, especially Hymenaeus and Philetus, "who concerning the truth have erred greatly, saying that the resurrection is past already." Here was Christianity's clue in its own Scriptures to the truth of the resurrection doctrine, could it have thrown off the bondage of old traditional falsities and warped ideations long ingrained in theology. Paul's statement repudiates the historicity of the Gospel resurrection, as Weiss also has done. The Apostle says it is wrong to think that whatever may have happened on the first Easter morn fulfills the meaning of the doctrine of the resurrection. For humanity in the mass the resurrection is an aeonial transformation, a veritable transfiguration of the soul; and it is not past, but tragically still to come. The demonstration of any Ensampler is to awaken man to the realization of what he has still to consummate within his own history. It is a gross mistake to think of the resurrection as past; it is still to come. How world history would be changed if it was in any measurable degree near its attainment! Weiss—and Paul—are right: the historical view of the resurrection in Christian doctrinism is practically meaningless.

Only the new view, reoriented on the lines of the ancient Pagan allegorical understanding and representation, will avail to hasten the time when the world may in sober earnestness turn its hand, as Voltaire suggested, to the serious business of resurrecting its long and still crucified Christ.

CHAPTER XX

DEMENTIA IN EXCELSIS

It was intimated at the outset that the movement of so-called Christianity perverted the stream of ancient spiritual teaching that flowed onward among the esoteric groups by flinging it out openly to the masses, for whose narrow range of mystic sensibilities and intellectual comprehension the allegorical representations had to be exotericized into ostensible factuality and thus reduced to literal nonsense. It was also indicated that the study would undertake to show how such an obscuration or perversion of the truth that alone liberates the human mind from bondage to blind superstition had resulted in the implantation in the Western consciousness of ideas and conceptions in the field of theology and Bible meaning twisted far askew from sane significance, and finally had operated over the centuries to distort the mentality of Europe into weird and frightful extravagances of dementia. This portion of the assignment is now approached, but with grave misgivings as to the possibility of dealing in any more than sketchy fashion with what again would demand a whole book for any treatment that pretended thoroughness. Only a few of the more glaring features of Christian dementia can be examined in the limited space remaining. These are chosen with the hope that they may prove suggestively illustrative of a larger range of kindred aberrations in the human narrative of Christianity's influence.

Voltaire has been cited as saying that men's hearts are cruel because their minds are dark and that they will continue to commit atrocities as long as they continue to believe absurdities. The same observation applies also to the commission of abnormalities and eccentricities, unnatural and inhuman practices that do not quite fall into the class of atrocities in the more barbaric sense. The inevitable consequences of its corrupted philosophies and theological absurdities came to open manifestation in most flagrant and most repulsive form in one great lamentable chapter of Christianity's history, running from as early as the third century on down almost to the present twentieth century, and indeed still casting its morbid shadow athwart the sunshine of this modern day. This outburst of twisted Christian theory into ungainly practice can be denominated by the general term of Christian asceticism. All in all, it pictures an exhibition of human action under the mental lash of atrociously misconceived canons of spiritual morality that falls little short of matching the fiendish cruelties inflicted in the Inquisition. An odd difference between the two enormities lies in the fact that while the slaughters of the Inquisition were wreaked upon the enemies of the Church, the singular barbarities of asceticism were vented by the Christians upon themselves.

It is a chapter of idiosyncrasy little known to either the Christian or the non-Christian public and, like so much else needing to be recorded, next to unbelievable. How such a vicious malpractice, driving its victims, the holy monks, by the thousands into the self-infliction of sadistic tortures won its dominance in Christian thought, will be the pressing inquiry of all readers. How such a quixotic enormity arose and swept to wide prevalence in the religion proclaimed to have dispensed the blessing of divine benignance and sanity to mankind is indeed a question needing a lucid answer at this time.

Many historians have given the nub of the answer, since it is not hard to locate. In so far as it is still in some measure considered virtuous and in continuing vogue, it is ascribed directly to the moralistic principles of the Christian faith. But when its outrageous excesses and unrestrained profligacies of conduct demand that it be held up to condemnation, its rise and spread are attributed to the influence of Oriental, Persian and Hindu religious philosophies that crept in and sadly corrupted the pure Christian faith with exotic tendencies.

Milman, von Mosheim, Farrar and indeed most Christian scholars speak at length of the adulteration early in Christian history of the pure stream of Christian teaching by the influx of Oriental doctrinism with its emphasis on certain elements of religious psychology. Especially did the Persian Zoroastrian doctrine of the dualism of all life, pitting the two polar forces of light and darkness, or spirit and matter against each other in a struggle for the aeonial mastery of the world and man, infiltrate into Christian thought. The Hellenic, the Alexandrian, the Jewish, the Chaldean, the Egyptian all more or less directly represented the world as the battle-ground between these two forces, and Christianity could not help but imbibe the influences of so wide-spread a doctrinism. The less was it able to do so when, after the second century the writings of St. Paul had become well known in the pale of the Church. For these *Epistles*, too, accentuate the war between the law of the flesh and the law of the mind of Christ in man. When he wrote that he felt a law of his members warring against the law of his mind, and seeking to drag him away from the love of Christ, he cried out in despair of being saved from "the body of this death," which he says consists of being carnally minded and subject to the lusts of the flesh. There was ample text in the Scriptures themselves to start the drive toward the crucifixion of the flesh on behalf of the salvation of the soul. Early and with full vehemence, nay with fanatic abandon, the madness was on. The plunge of Christianity into ascetic morbidity to endure many centuries was taken. History can but record the lugubrious chronicle. The annals of the wrestling of the human mind with the philosophical problem of the duality of the life force constitute one of the most intriguing, yet withal one of the most pathetic chapters in all the history of thought. It is inextricably intwined with the still more engrossing problem of the origin of "evil." For, in briefest possible form of exposition, evil arose from the opposition exerted by matter, the negative pole of the duality, against spirit, the positive pole. Spirit was haloed with all the attributes and characteristics of "good," while matter was loaded with all the obloquy of "evil." Spirit, divine mind planned and worked to lift creatural life to the level of pure conceptuality of reason and the good; matter opposed, blocked, thwarted and defiled this effort, hence was evil.

Milman in his analysis of the influence of Oriental religionism upon Christianity again and again reverts to the phrase, "the malignity of matter." This sets the idea in bold outline. It sharply defines the philosophical ground-source of asceticism. Matter is conceived as being hostile to spirit. It is the enemy, the evil power, the devil. As the Christian Science creedology expounds the same idea today, "matter is the parent of all evil." Annihilate the concept of matter from human thought and you will rid the world of evil. Its power is only in your (erroneous) thought; your belief in its reality alone gives it power to afflict you. Destroy your thought of it and you have destroyed its power.

To this thesis the answer is that matter has a way of demonstrating its real existence whether minds deny it or not. You can think yourself into veritable hypnotism and utterly annihilate your concept of matter. But you awake and matter is still there, performing its divine function. It was here before you came and will be here when you, the asserted creator of it, are gone. It mocks you while you are thinking it out of existence. It proves to be real, sure enough. It does not depend for existence upon your hypostatization of it. It is by no means commensurable with your thought of it. If Christian Science was right, matter would come into and go out of existence with every affirmation or denial of its being. But it remains obstinately and calmly the same.

It is as real as spirit, and real because spirit is real, for it is spirit itself, but spirit concretized by what might be called a reduction of cosmic or divine "temperature." To argue that spirit is alone real, matter utterly unreal, is to contend that water vapor, or water itself is real, but ice unreal. For matter is but the iced form of spirit. Modern physical science has at last destroyed the delusions of wrong philosophical thinking about matter. It has found that under the terrific force of electric energies matter can be "melted" or dissolved back into spirit, as under heat ice can be melted back to water and water into invisible vapor. Matter is just the visible crystallization of invisible spirit. And in every language spirit has been designated by the very words for breath, wind, vapor, air. Spirit and matter are but the forms taken by the ultimate essence of being under high or low temperatures or pressure states of cosmic energy.

But calamitous consequences have flowed from the failure of this knowledge in human thinking. False conceptualism arose out of the inability of thought to make the necessary distinction between the idea of *polar opposition* in the duality of spirit and matter, and that of the *ethical character* of that opposition. The opposition of *polarity,* positive against negative or *vice versa,* was misconstrued into the opposition of good against evil and evil against good. The disaster of thought came from the false characterization of spirit as solely good and of matter as absolutely evil. It was a question of taking *relative* values for *absolute* ones. Only in a *relative* sense are the two ends of the polarity to be characterized as either good or evil. In the final or *absolute* sense both are good, or perhaps, as Nietzsche put it, beyond good and evil. This may seem to be a profitless abstraction, too remote to influence human happiness. Far from it; it is a concept of such tremendous practicality and constant relevance to all human thought that it becomes at last the philosophical determinant of most human happiness or failure of it. It assuredly makes a world of difference in this human life of ours whether we are deluded into conceiving that the world itself—the matter of it—is against our felicity or amicable to it. The one alternative in the dual possibility can make us think and act as wretched creatures being plagued with "the malignity of matter"; the other can bless us with the assurance that all things, including matter, body, sense, work together for good to those that love the Lord's visible creation, and cease despising the visible to gain promised bliss in the invisible worlds.

It was just this misconception that has afflicted countless millions of victims of bad philosophical logic, who were beaten down to the low state of counting themselves wretched creatures being tortured by the devil of matter. Spirit, having become enshrined in unbalanced theory as alone good, centuries of mesmerized intellection of millions finally so stamped its thought-deformity upon the very body of man that the responsive effort of fanatic Christian zeal to combat and beat down the detested flesh carried this expression of a simple error of conception to the most frightful excesses ever known in the world of the West. The manifestations even overmatched, if that were possible, the similar excesses in India, where the exaltation of spirit over matter had been a vicious development from the same egregious misconstructions of philosophy.

The body of man is to his soul as the horse is to the rider. It is never, to be sure, to be permitted to dominate and drive the rider against his sane wishes and purposes. It must be subdued if fractious and made docile, obedient and serviceable. But—and here is the abyss of difference that well analogizes the nub of the entire philosophical problem—by no means is this horse to be beaten into helplessness, abused, injured, crippled, nay, even mentally despised and flouted. He is to be maintained indeed in the fullest vigor of his bodily powers and kept as lusty as his nature gives him the right to be. This simple and sane recognition, the application of this analogy to the problem of the "evil" of matter and the body, could have beautified a brutal and ugly Christian European history. And Hawthorne's *Scarlet Letter* might not have had to be written,—though to lose it would have been an inconsolable misfortune. Puritanism could have relaxed its social sternness,—as it has had to do since.

The ascetic Christian attitude toward the body stands as one of the supreme cultural afflictions and miscarriages of all time. The evil psychological consequences which it generated have been and still are incalculably vast and iniquitous. It has brooded like a blight or a plague over the collective consciousness of Western mankind, injecting the insidious poison of its erroneous ideation into the body of social life at all times. It has leavened the social consciousness with a thought chemicalization that induces a general sickliness into all human life. It has eaten like a canker into the core of all human happiness, engendering unhealthy conditions in the very blood of human nature. And from the vitiation of the inner life stream every sort of abnormality, the sores and boils of corrupted life currents, has erupted upon the surface of the common life of the individual and the mass. At long last, what we call modern science has unearthed the subterranean lair of this insidious corrosion, and a new science is born. Little as it is yet known, and erroneous as are some aspects of its technique, the Freudian discovery of the critical role played by the traditional obsession of the concept of the inherent evil nature of man's sexual functions is one of the greatest findings in world history. It is not a wholly new discovery, for the ancients had knowledge of it; and one of the worst of the defections of Christianity from high Pagan truth was that which turned from the wholesome and salutary Pagan regard for the human body to the ruinous misconception of the body's evil character. That change and its consequences are the theme of this chapter.

Through new clarification of vision a new phase of the historical clash between Christianism and Paganism is destined now to transpire. Oddly enough, as one of the acts of what the Greeks called Fate or Nemesis, we shall now witness, indeed are now witnessing, the vindication of Paganism over Christianity in the turn of the tide in civilization's arrival at a greater sanity, as the result of the development of the new science of Psychoanalysis. Through the findings of this study the world has now of necessity to repudiate Christian attitudes and return once more to the saner and loftier moralities of Pagan wisdom. Christianity must now repudiate its own philosophy of the body's "evil" nature and reinstate the noble concepts of that Greek philosophy which, instead of befouling the flesh with dishonor and sin, rendered it beautiful beyond the attainment of any other people in the earth. This brings the reflection that in a word Christianity so *mentally* disfigured the physical body of man that a *physical* disfigurement came to actuality as the result. It is that which cometh out from within that defileth the man. Philosophical condemnation of the body in Christian ideation finally emerged as bodily ugliness. The Greeks substituted a mentally lovely concept of the body and out to the surface came physical beauty. But Christianity, poisoned at the mental core, even held it a sin to have a beautiful body, or to delight in it. This is true. Love of beauty

454

came to be held a deadly Christian sin; and some shadows of this terrible debasement of mind still linger in certain recesses of both Catholic and Protestant teaching.

The age-long prevalence of Christian attitudes has finally resulted in giving to the word "pagan" the special meaning of that which takes a friendly or glorified view of the body, its fleshly instincts and its sense pleasures or expressions. To practice a "pagan" philosophy is considered in Christian thinking to be the devotion of primary interest to the life of the body, as in many ways contradistinguished from the life of the spirit. It is a loud modern cry from religious circles that modern life is reverting to pagan status, because so large a portion of time and concern is being expended upon purely physical outlets of energy, to the exclusion of devotion to spiritual interests. This specific secondary connotation has been fastened upon the word because it has been used so generally in connections and contexts which throw upon it the implication that Paganism, as a religious system, is thus charged with having limited its central drive to the gross concerns of the body, while Christianity rose immeasurably above that low engrossment to center primary interest upon the holier life of the spirit. Naturally this impression can easily be given, if a propaganda which decries the body as irremediably evil holds up to criticism a system which gives the body its due and rightful place of importance and rank in true understanding of anthropology. To say anything good about the body becomes a criterion of baseness to a cult that considers the body the devil's foul creation. Who can estimate what this terrible error of judgment has cost the Western world?

It would seem to be a proposition standing before the open mind of rational men as worthy of unreserved approbation that if man would hold his body in higher esteem, he would indubitably be inclined to treat it with the greater consideration. This is simply to say that if he honors it in his mind, he will honor it with better treatment. At any rate an intelligent Paganism paid it higher honor, and the result was seen in its still thrilling beautification. The body's beauty faded out under Christian conceptualism and treatment.

The verdict of centuries of history is in; that judgment is recorded in incontestable factuality. Christian ideologies stamped themselves upon history, and the imprint, ugly or beautiful, stands like fossil remains, shaped in solid fact. We are pointing unobservant eyes to those indelible prints where ugliness writes the judgment of time, the actual reality of error generating deformity in the world. The calmer clearer judgment of later times can now profit by the longer view in retrospect and discern the arrant error of unenlightened pietistic violence. And Christianity must face its record fossilized in history. And that record shows the words "tragic error" written over most of the specific features, claims and institutes of the religion called Christianity.

The practice of asceticism covered the long period in Christian history from the third century nearly to the present. It was in the early centuries, however, that it was exploited in its most invidious forms. The testimony of one or two of the leading Christian historians must be called in to place the enormity of this unseemly excrescence upon the body of Christianity in its full light of actual truth.

Kershner (*Pioneers of Christian Thought,* p. 87) writes that it was the persuasion of young women in the Christian communion that by retiring to a convent and remaining aloof from the world of humanity, they would become the brides of Christ; and equally it was the belief of young men, founded on many promises, that they would be given to enjoy the unspeakable beatitude of Paradise as reward for their voluntary crucifixion of all human pleasures and desires. Kershner denominates this "a singularly abnormal philosophy."

One of the greatest practitioners of asceticism in the fourth century was Martin of Tours. He instituted a whole school or movement that drew hundreds to enlist in his regime of austerities and mortifications of the flesh to glorify the spirit. Farrar, in speaking of this feature, says that we read with sorrow the story of their self-maceration. It shows, he points out, the *danger and evil of a false ideal even when it is followed with perfect sincerity.* "The monks of Martin were swept away by the tide of triumphant superstition, and helped swell its overwhelming violence." The biography of the saint became the most popular book of the day. At Rome the booksellers made fortunes by it, and amanuenses could not copy it fast enough for the demand. In Africa also among the monks of the desert and in great cities like Carthage it was in all men's hands; and at Alexandria, so the author himself tells us, nearly all the people had it by heart. The miracles in which it abounded constituted its chief appeal to the multitude of readers, and they were so generously supplied as to include no less than three instances of raising men from the dead. The monks of Marmontier pressed Severus not to omit the narrative of even one prodigy, although he admits that some of them were too absurd even for their strong credulity. "May the opinion never prevail in the Church of Christ," wrote Julius Africanus, "that any false thing can be fabricated for

Christ's glory." (Staid historians, as we have seen, have shown how the entire structure was erected on fictions and forgeries fabricated for Christ's glory.) In Vol. II (p. 220) of his *Lives of the Fathers,* Farrar stigmatizes asceticism in such fashion as this:

"It taught the world the infinite value of the individual soul. [This can be challenged as very questionable.] But the *errors on which the whole theory was based* produced a crop of terrible evils. Nature avenged herself on those who violated her laws. The indolence of morbid speculation; the perpetual sickness of self-introspection undisturbed by the paltry industry of weaving palm leaves into baskets; the glorification of dirt; the confusion of sanctity with abhorrent self-mortifications; the daring disruption of natural and sacred ties; the violation of the innocent laws of human intercourse; the expansion of selfishness to infinitude,—these were prolific of disastrous consequences. *God branded the ambitious attempt with sterility and failure.* Men who aimed at making their life better than that which Christ had taught, or the Apostles preached, sank into a condition which was often worse than that of the beasts which perish. . . . The self-degraded body reacted on the enfeebled mind. No faith became too revolting, no maceration too frightful, no contradiction of the natural affections too violently extreme. It is impossible to read without pity and horror of the foul condition to which the stylites and grazing monks reduced the image of God, as though Christ were to be pleased by the wildest exaggerations of the Phariseeism which he so burningly denounced. . . . The impulse which filled the deserts of Egypt with anchorites and monks and nuns became in time an unmixed evil. The motives which led to it were not only mistaken, but even in many cases cowardly and insincere. . . . It seemed an easier thing to fly from the world than to face its perils and miseries. . . . It was one of the evils of desert monasticism that it filled the pure atmosphere of Christianity with a miasma of gross superstition, which was fed with a crop of lying legends. . . . It darkened the lives and consciences of millions, who, living in the world, were taught to believe that they were only aiming at an inferior sanctity, and would only receive a second-rate or dubious reward. It altered the perspective and center of gravity of the Christian life. Macarius prayed one hundred times a day; Paul the Simple three hundred times, which he counted by pebbles; and he was greatly distressed to hear of a virgin who prayed seven hundred times a day. A spectator once saw Simon Stylites make twelve hundred and forty-four genuflexions—and then stopped counting."

We are not surprised, he adds, to learn that conditions so unnatural produced shipwreck of mind as well as of body. The weakened brains of the hermits were disturbed by visions of hellish monsters and their sleepless nights were affrighted by hideous sights and sounds. All too frequently they found that their desertion of the common life of men only ended in a state of demoniacal possession. They often imagined that they worked prodigious miracles. Many were turned virtually into hypochondriacs. We learn from stories in Cassian that monks and hermits sometimes committed the most terrible crimes which, under the influence of demoniac delusion they took for heroic acts of virtue. Nilus and Pachomius, unexceptionable witnesses, testify that many monks ended their careers in lunacy and suicide, which took the form of ripping themselves open and hurling themselves over precipitous ⌐ocks or into wells. Ambrose says that many drowned themselves, and Gregory Nazianzen speaks also of deaths by hanging. Heathens even gave to Christians the taunting name of *Biothanatoi* (self-murderers).

But the saddest fact of all, says Farrar, is that even those monks and solitaries who were sincere increased instead of diminishing the moral difficulties which they sought to avoid. The effects of compulsory celibacy of the clergy proved in countless instances to have resulted disastrously. This is substantiated by a volume of testimony of which every item may be derived, not from Reformers or Latitudinarians, but from Popes, Bishops, monks and canonized saints of the early and Medieval church. From the first it led to the gross scandals connected with the spiritual sisters (*Agapetae, Adelphai, Suzugoi, Suneisaktai, Subintroductae*) against which so many Fathers gave their warning and so many canons of Councils were passed in vain. The biographies of monks and hermits show decisively that their temptations to sloth, pride and impurity were sorer and more continuous than those which ever occur amid the beneficent and well-regulated activities of a Christian life lived in accordance with Christ's example and God's demands.

George Hodges (*The Early Church*, p. 151) paints a lurid picture of the ascetic fever:

"The philosophical reason for monasticism was drawn from the theory that the body corrupts the soul. Matter being essentially evil, and the body being the source of all sin, our proper procedure is to make the body weak. Only by the ascetic practices may we attain the victory of the spirit. The idea first appeared as heresy, being the doctrine of the Gnostics and Neoplatonists, but it took possession of the general mind. Especially in the East it poisoned the souls of the saints. At its worst it brought into being the mad monks—the grazing saints, who went about on their hands and knees and ate grass; the pillar saints, like Simon Stylites; the chained saints, so fastened together that when one lay down to sleep the other was pulled up to pray. At its best it made religion morbid, defying nature, contradicting the revelation of God in the body of man, and glorifying hunger and thirst, rags and celibacy and dirt, driving the saints into the desert."

The sainted Jerome, writing to a prominent Christian woman convert by name of Eustochium, adjured her to "let your companions be women pale and thin with fasting." The historians cite this same Jerome's unblushing confession of the burning lusts of the mind amid the burning heat of the desert. This great Father is cited as saying:

"I then who from fear of hell had condemned myself to such a prison, a comrade only of scorpions and wild beasts, was in imagination among dances of girls. My face was pale with fasting, yet my mind was heaving with desires in my frigid body, and before a man already prematurely dead in the flesh, the fires of concupiscence alone were bursting forth."

So he used to lie at Jesus' feet, watered them with his tears, wiped them with his hair and "subdued my resisting flesh with a seven-days fast."

(Farrar suggests that some at least of the passages referring to fasts in the New Testament are interpolations due to the ascetic predilections of the early scribes.)

Farrar's further descriptions can not be omitted (Vol. II, p. 232):

"Grossly ignorant, hopelessly superstitious, brutally fanatical, the monks of Egypt became as a body the vilest instruments of the worst character in ecclesiastical history."

Heading the list of such monsters was the Patriarch Theophilus of Alexandria. The infamies of the Council of Robbers were chiefly due to the turbulent opinionativeness of these outrageous incendiaries. Monks murdered Hypatia and supported the notorious Cyril in his ambitious terrorism. Monks worried and vexed the official life of Basil. Monks attacked the refuge of Chrysostom, troubled his sickness and assailed his life. Their morose pride, impenetrable ignorance and sullen bigotry made them a terror to the civil government, to which they paid no tax and rendered no service.

"Mariolatry, saint-worship, relic-worship, terrors of demons, dream divinations, lying legends, invented miracles and every form of crude superstition acquired strength from their support. The ever-increasing multitude of vagrants and bigots, whose squalid virtues were repaid by a sort of adoration, denuded the Empire of its natural defenders and left it a prey to the barbarians. Valens was more than half right in rescinding the immunity from military service which constituted for so many the temptation to monasticism and in sweeping thousands of these sturdy idlers from Egyptian deserts into the ranks of his army. He called them without any circumlocution 'the followers of laziness' (*ignaviae sectatores*). Synesius speaks of them as barbarous, indolent, brutal. Salvian shows how much the monks were hated, and the fury with which Pagans like Libanius, Eunapius, Zosimus and Rutilius speak of them is explained, if it be not excused, by the scathing pictures drawn by all the greatest of the Fathers of the Remoboth, the Massalians, the Gyrovagi and other classes of criminals and hypocrites who lived under the shelter of the monk's cowl. Hermits, monks and even nuns lived in a state of revolting dirt, which they regarded as one proof of their piety. They left a most unfavorable opinion on the cultivated heathen. Eunapius speaks of their 'swinish life,' their tyrannous self-assertion, their neglect of public decency, their filth and nakedness."

Were there space, it would be informative to introduce the whole story of Melania, a Christian convert, daughter of the consul Marcellinus. Her companion and spiritual adviser was none other than Jerome. So floridly and garishly were the sanctities of the Holy Land, where Christ had walked and talked, healed and suffered, died and risen again, painted in the imaginations and fancies of the Christians at Rome that all were stricken with the unconquerable yearning to visit those scenes on pilgrimage. Jerome persuaded the infatuated Melania, reluctant to leave her little son behind even for so holy a purpose, to undertake the trip, even though it meant turning over the child to the precarious custodianship of the city praetor.

And this Jerome wrote to Heliodorus, a priest, when a question arose as to sacrificing the sacred ties of kinship and love for the sake of Christ:

"Lo, the adversary in thy breast endeavors to slay Christ. . . . Though thy little nephew should hang about thy neck; though with hair dishevelled and rent garments thy mother should show thee the breasts with which she nurtured thee; though thy father should lie on the threshold, trample over his body with dry eyes and fly to the standard of the Cross. On a matter like this, to be cruel is the only true filial affection."

Comments Farrar:

"This extraordinary rhetoric had an immense fascination for the ladies of Rome. Fabiola, many years afterwards, could repeat the letter of Jerome by heart, and such exhortations induced the noblest matrons to fling away every human affection with unnatural callowness and to abandon the duties to which God had called them, for others at once less necessary and less blessed."

Farrar (Vol. II, 255 ff.) describes the luxury, pomp, aloofness, superciliousness, coldness and dress of the clergy. "They appeared abroad in magnificent apparel and worldly pomp, lolling in lofty chariots."

"The heathen must have secretly exulted as they watched the scandals" of the Church.

Milman, Farrar, Guignebert, Fisher, Kershner and others speak out flatly as to the corruption, deception, dishonesty, venality and immorality of the priests and bishops in almost every age. It is purposeless to load up our treatise with the multiplied testimony on this doleful theme with which the Christian histories abound. It is there in endless quantity and lurid color, if the reader wishes to add further verification. Even the *Catholic Encyclopedia* does not dissemble or cloak the true facts in this field.

It is, however, worth a paragraph to emphasize the by no means fantastic theory that Christianity was a materially contributory force to the undermining of the Roman Empire, leading to its fall. In his great volume Gibbon gives over four hundred pages to the influence of Christianity on the fortunes of the great world empire. Farrar speculates on the theme also. He says it has often been a question whether Christianity must be reckoned among the causes which overthrew the Latin strength.

"That such was the case can hardly be doubted. It exercised on the sway and the institutions of Paganism a benumbing and disintegrating force. Men who had once felt confident in the protection of Mavors (Mars) and Romulus and Victory were now profoundly disheartened. The anchor of their old polytheism was rudely torn up and they drifted on the open sea of doubt. The general indifference to all things earthly caused by too predominant and exclusive a love for the world beyond the grave, tending ever to multiply the inert masses of monks and solitaries, was another weakening influence."

Farrar's comment on Augustine's *City of God* includes the statement that it reveals how the Christian fixation of primary interest upon the anticipated rhapsodies of bliss in the community of heaven undermined all their virtues as citizens of the Empire. These subjective interests and proclivities, entirely superseded their interests in the welfare of the mundane state. So Farrar says that "all the moral energy which remained in the civilized world was turned towards pious contemplation, and yielded the Empire to the barbarians."

For the sake of what it may mean in the direction of a correction of common notions of Christian people as to the sanity, purity and lofty moral fineness of the early Christians, it is worth citing what Farrar gives us in a quotation from the fourth-century Basil, one of the leading Fathers:

461

"Every one walks by the will of his own heart; wickedness is immeasurable; the people are lawless; their religious leaders have no boldness of speech."

And speaking of Gregory of Nyssa, Farrar writes:

"He does not attempt to conceal the fact that the self-delusion and pride of monkish 'virgins' had become an open scandal. . . ." Certain things named "reveal the error in which he and most of the Fathers of that age were disastrously entangled."

Gregory of Nyssa speaks of the Christians of Babylon in terms of utter disgust and despair, dwelling especially upon their brutality, barbarism and their habitual lying. As to Jerusalem even Cyril was unable to cope either with the heresy or the gross immorality of the holy city. Then, as in so many ages, it was a sink of wickedness, and that wickedness was increased by the demoralization which ran riot among the bands of promiscuous pilgrims. The citizens of Jerusalem were like wild beasts thirsting for blood. So writes Gregory after his visit there.

Farrar does not spare vehement language in saying at one place that "such is the purblind fury and mendacity of party zeal, even when it assumes the championship of the most stainless Christianity."

In tracing the sad consequences of false conceptions upon Christian conduct it is imperative to notice—all too briefly—the attitude of the Christians of early and Medieval times toward woman. Much has been said about the pompous claim of the religion that it was the first and only one to establish the worth and dignity of the individual. Certainly not true on any intrinsic basis, it is a screaming farce or travesty of truth when it applies to women individually, or even to woman as woman. For the position to which the early and later Church demeaned women belies every assertion ever put forth on this subject. By Christian philosophy women were degraded to the lowest rating in the scale of acknowledged value to which it is possible to reduce any creature. They were regarded as the evil seducers of men from the life of the spirit and the monks fled from them as from a plague. In his *History of European Morals* Lecky presents the features of this picture in glaring colors.

The beauty of woman was a thorn in the flesh of the monks aspiring to sainthood, a torture of temptation which they could only escape by fleeing to the solitude of the desert. Even there the apparitions of the Eve temptress haunted the monkish imagination, as Jerome has etched it for us. We forbear to quote the slanderous frothings of hypocritical

462

contempt in which the harassed priests and anchorites of God affected to condemn womanhood for embodying the lure of love which attracts the male human to his mate for purposes far holier than any served by monachial pietism.

Our essay is designed to prove the falsity of Christian principles by pointing in such particulars to the historical consequences which these principles precipitated in many centuries of actual operation. Certainly here is another in the long list of abnormal influences let loose in the moral life of millions over ages. Need greater evidence of outrageous error of doctrine be adduced than this testimony which certifies the eventuation of philosophical dogma—in this case the evil of matter and the human flesh—in such a distortion of sanity as the persuasion that womanhood is evil *per se,* because it lures male man to parenthood, and incidentally to the highest expression of his real spiritual nature? What must be the verdict against a set of moral principles which turned one sex of the human duality in frightened flight from the other, or arrayed itself theoretically on the side of the good, while consigning its opposite pole to the category of Satanic evil? No little measure of the inferior secondary position in human and legal rights in even the freest of democratic countries which women have had to occupy in helpless submission and privation is unquestionably due to the degraded moral rating which an absurdly contorted philosophy of the evil nature of the body—and especially a beautiful feminine body —in Christian hands had fastened upon them. Not even Protestant churches will honor them with a place in the pulpit. Yet without their adherence in a wondrous spirit of almost blind devotion, the Church they support could hardly have maintained its existence.

In this connection the morbidity of Christian attitude toward wholesome delight in life is not to be forgotten. Probably taking their cue from the fact that there is no record of Jesus' having laughed, but heavy emphasis on his having wept, merriment, enjoyment, gaiety, happiness itself was taboo. With lightsomeness went beauty also. Romance and love were sin. In the Middle Ages Bernard of Clairvaux was scandalized by the love affair of Abelard. He suppressed his own sinful tendency in this direction by plunging into an icy pond, and later crushed and wrecked Abelard.

What a world of hidden significance underlies the statement of Farrar (Vol. II, 222) that "mistaken views of duty and a *mistaken estimate of sin* were an intolerable and needless burden to the individual, and in many instances tended to hinder rather than promote the spiritual life!"

This chapter calls for a summary survey of the disastrous consequences of the horrid misconception of the Christian doctrine of "sin." Christianity has made of this dogma the veritable Frankenstein monster of mental torment for the whole body of Christians for ages. Out of a principle of the moral life which could have been represented in its lawful place of beneficent influence in the normal understanding of human action, if envisaged with sound balanced philosophical judgment, this Christianism made a monstrosity of psychological entification, turning it mentally into a haunting spirit of remorseless malignity. If any sin in the psychological realm is unpardonable, it is that of stamping upon the helpless mind of childhood the frightening presence of a personified force such as the Christian concept of sin and its personal embodiment have been made into. The embellishment of the idea of divine punishment with every sort of the most lurid and darksome frightfulness, and the citation of misapprehended Scripture of equally dire portent for human dereliction, has accomplished a blighting of natural wholesomeness of mind in the West that stands unparalleled anywhere on earth. It has killed the natural instinct of the human part of man to exult in the boundless gift of life itself. For millions of sensitive but unintelligent souls it has turned what might have been a life of joyousness into a nightmare of dread and delusion. And of Christian history it has made a jagged horror of murder and torture. It has darkened and harried the minds of millions with the haunting fear of post-morten hell and purgatorial fires, all of which an intelligent Paganism understood rightly was an allegorical picturization of the life lived here.

Speaking of the first murders committed by the Church in the very first century in which the sword of persecution had been lifted from the necks of Christians—the slaughter of the Priscillianists (for holding some independent views on the canon, and for practicing the same austerities as those of St. Martin!)—Farrar gives us a felicitous passage to emphasize the recital:

"And for the first time the axe of the executioner was reddened with the blood of Christians, shed by Christians to avenge a difference of opinion. That bloodshed, like the beginning of sin, was indeed as a letting out of water, and the crimson stream was destined in after ages to roll for many a furlong, bridle deep."

And lest the modern man assume too confidently and complacently that all this is past history, and that the reddened snowball of human madness has well melted down and is no longer a threat to roll ahead again to perilous proportions, let us glance at the sober statement of a modern like Aldous Huxley, *in re* the claim of Christianity to have abolished slavery:

"We have witnessed, first of all, the wholesale revival of slavery in its worst and most inhuman forms—slavery imposed upon political heretics living under the various dictatorships, slavery imposed upon whole classes of conquered populations, slavery imposed upon prisoners of war. Next, we note the increasing indiscriminateness of slaughter during wartime. Area bombing, saturation bombing, rocket bombing, bombing by atomic missiles—the indiscriminateness has steadily increased throughout the Second World War, until now no nation even makes a pretence of observing the traditional distinction between civilians and combatants, innocent and guilty, but all devote themselves methodically and scientifically to general massacre and wholesale destruction."

The temptation is strong to comment on Huxley's last sentence. The extension of war from formal and uniformed combatants to promiscuous populations, if viewed in the light of the Greek conception of Fate and Nemesis, or the Hindu principle of Karma (essentially the same thing), it can well be argued that this development must be in harmony with the divine law of righteousness and the decree of Providence. For it brings the penalty of wrong action, or failure to act, back upon those responsible for the wars in the first place. Young men can always ask, and *are* asking more vehemently, why *they* must be singled out to bear the horrid brunt of war, while the lazy and inert populations of their elders can remain in security at home. It is beyond argument that wars are caused by the inertia, the greed, the unheroic conservative immobility and base complacency of whole populations. The male youth must be heroic in war in order that non-combatant millions may live most unheroically in so-called "peace." It need not be the spleen and rancor of a vindictive temper, but indeed the calm expression of a justly judging humanitarian view, that as long as whole peoples—those lolling in luxurious ease, comfort and self-indulgence in many vices—will so conduct themselves as to incite the wars, it is but right that they should have the legitimate consequences come home to them. Perhaps this late horrendous development of barbarism in the *Christian* countries of the world is needed to awaken whole citizenries, or democracies, to *their* need to live with such justice as will not require the periodic heroism of the male youth to preserve the privilege of sheathing the sword of righteousness during those periods when the causes of wars are smoldering and selfishness or folly precludes the will to adjust incipient hatreds before they burst into open fires of war.

The folly that smothered the beneficent influence of the ancient Pagan esotericism and drenched later Western generations with rivers of blood can have its evil consequences brought to an end only by the rectification of the incredible philosophical or theological blunder in misconceiving the interrelation of soul and body in the cosmic duality of all life as expressed in man's constitution. A relation misconceived as enmity must be envisaged as one of utmost beneficence. As husband and wife stand opposite to each other, but surely are not hostile, opposite poles but wedded for life and blessedness; so soul and body stand related in opposite polarity, but are to be wedded for felicity. Here is the resolution of the deplorable conflict in the human brain, fought in wretched ignorance through Christian stupidity. Says John Dewey: "The antagonism between the actual and the ideal, the spiritual and the natural, is the source of the deepest and most injurious of all enmities."

CHAPTER XXI

PRAYER AND HEALING

Reserved for the end of the study are two aspects of Christian inculcation that have been perhaps the two chief elements of influence by which the maudlin religion of Christianism has maintained its grip on the Occidental mind for ages. Much of what has been presented here is of more immediate interest to theologians than to the common man. But these two items now to be considered do touch the general life very closely. So strong indeed is their influence that their critique here expounded will have close to epochal value if it be found based on truth and sound reason.

First to be scanned is the great religious ritual practice which in a variety of forms falls under the general designation of prayer.

It must be prefaced that by no means is prayer a distinctively Christian formulary. With likely truth it can be said that all religions have used and exalted prayer as an integral element in their systems. Indeed prayer is hardly even to be limited to religion as an interest disparate from secular life. It may be said to be a common or universal human resort or psychological expression. It comes out as a natural and spontaneous manifestation of man's sense of his relation of dependence upon the force or forces rated as beneficent that order the life of the cosmos. So long as man conceives his life to be the responsible concern of a Power greater than himself, a view that the general course of his experience constrains him to take, he is impelled by the strenuosity of conditions at times to cry aloud to this Power for aid, consolation, succor. It is but natural that man the creature should be moved by the impulse to seek communion with the Power conceived to be his Parent. It is understandable that God's earthly children should be moved to carry to this King of Life their deepest desires, cares and woes. The natural involvements of man's situation constrain him to turn in varied degrees of realistic earnestness to this source of blessedness.

It is therefore not of prayer as distinctly a Christian usage, but rather as a general mood of human motivation that the critique here is set forth. It is a broad effort to institute an examination of the whole rationale of prayer, in the interests of a deflation of much of the provable superstition that attaches to it, and of an appraisement of its place and value in the life of religion balanced by philosophical intelligence.

But the word itself needs succinct definition at the outset, lest the discussion keep missing the mark of precise reference. Like many words in the dictionary it has several shades of meaning. It certainly has a formal meaning and an informal one. Formal prayer would of course be the class of prayers uttered in the formality of religious services, or under some institute of formal procedure, or spoken in set forms of language. This form of prayer might be and usually is made in a public service, but could be, and often is, the utterance of an individual in privacy. It is spoken according to a formula, premeditated or extemporaneous.

Then there is another kind of prayer which will fall closely within the orbit of the connotation of the word chiefly to be considered here. It might be called the informal prayer, a free spontaneous outspeaking, either orally or silently, of the inner feelings of the individual; a voluble or silent call of the human mind and heart to the deific powers conceived to be disposed to hear and respond to such an entreaty. It may not even come to outspoken utterance at all; it may be only a welling up in consciousness of the unformulated aspirations of the Ego. It may indeed even so lack explicit formulation as not even to be well defined in the mind of the one thus praying. Prayer in this sense may reach out and embrace a very large segment of a person's entire activity in life, and it virtually does so in the case of people of whom it is heard said often that their whole life is a prayer.

In both senses, or definitions, prayer has been declared to be a communion of man in mortal life with the Supreme Power conceived to have generated his existence, and religiously believed to be keeping a beneficent oversight over human affairs, as well as being credited with the ability to interpose its will in the stream of mundane history. This definition of prayer applies very widely, and is part of the general religious theory of many of the so-called modern spiritual cult systems. Prayer is thus defined to be the communion of the spirit of man with the mind or spirit of Deity. It is of course instituted or initiated by man at his lowly station and addressed by him to the All-Father.

Many applications of its meaning in this higher form of definition run out into such diffuse vagueness as to render difficult of sensible discussion certain items of the critique. For example, in the case of many splendid humanitarian and very truly spiritual persons who do not engage in any ostensible exercise of prayer at all, it would by no means be true to say that they do not pray, if the more expanded definition of prayer is considered. In this wider spread of the word's connotation they may be the truest prayers of all. Their own spiritual minds may be silently in closer and more productive harmony of consciousness with the Cosmic Mind than would be the case with those who professedly devote themselves to formal praying.

It can be said at this point, then, that if the sense of the word "prayer" is confined to this broadest reference of the term, this critique can have no stricture of a negative sort to offer. In this its loftiest connotation prayer becomes a name for the expression of the highest aspiration of mankind, his most consecrated disposition to attune his mind, heart and soul to the will of the Supreme. As this disposition is the most worthy, the most holy of any of which man is capable, there is no occasion or foothold for derogation. Considered as the human being's most reverent and conscientious approach to the Power of beneficence in charge of the world, it stands haloed in the most sanctified of man's upward reachings. If people express their prayer in their lives, and if this is the ultimate summation of the meaning of the term, prayer must be considered a noble form of the expression of man's vital relation to a diviner world.

But there is a very justifiable critique of prayer when it is considered as a formal and express utterance, either spoken or silently meditated, of a person's address to the anthropomorphic God of conventional ideation in religious practice. This restriction of definition would still leave it covering all ecclesiastical or churchly prayers, or those in the home, or the "closet" of the individual. It embraces all prayers formally addressed to the God power, those in the Prayer Book, or the Daily Devotion Manual, or lifted up from the pulpit or at the bedside or family table. This form of prayer constitutes a part of every conventional religion's service, the other portions being a tribute of praise in song, a Scripture reading and a hortatory sermon. Of this form of prayer there is the ground for a very justifiable and very sharp citique.

Such prayers, it can be said with little chance of refutation, are prayers of appeal, of petition for blessings, of asking for the direct beneficent attention of Supreme Being to the special pleas and enumerated gifts or dispensations in behalf of those praying, or others mentioned by them. To be sure they generally postpone the begging portion until a few sentences have generously been devoted to expressing the pleaders' gratitude for life itself and its manifest blessings and opportunities. Then the humble petitioners invoke divine Goodness that they be granted pure hearts and blameless lives to merit the boundless benevolence of Providence. The listening Deity is then assured that we are willing to let him make us wiser, nobler, more seriously consecrated children, more worthy to receive his unending care and love. Then the door is wide open to send up the special pleading for lists of favors and blessings which he is told he has the power, if he but have the will, to dispense in our direction, "to usward," as some one has put it. If only the formal petition be uttered with the requisite fervor and unction, it is felt that the ear of Divine Beneficence has effectually been reached and there is a good chance of a gracious dispensation in response to our humble devoutness.

When one reflects—as any honest mind must reflect—that this sort of thing has been the unchallenged habit of religions from remote times and the undeviating custom of practically all Christians through the long run of their history, and then add the consideration, as we do now, that a moment's sane envisagement of it reduces it all to the veriest essence of irrational folly, it becomes one of those items here aggregated to substantiate the charge that Christianity has subjugated the human mind under the power of an atrocious imbecility.

For in the form crudely expounded the practice must face the implications of ridiculous illogicality in the very nature of the phenomenon under observation. In the first place there is the basic asininity of our presuming that our voiced petition will reach the attention of the Deity to whom it is addressed, at any rate in any way or manner at all approximating our naive presumption that "He" is standing by with listening ear. The very form, occasion and spirit of our address carry the suggestion that this God is some Being in the absurd form and dimensions of the old anthropomorphic God of the past thought of uncritical devotees. One does not have to raise the—as it will seem—irreverent or scurrilous question of how this one God of crude conception can listen to, reflect upon and adjudge, not to add act upon, the millions of circumstances necessarily involved in making his response to the myriads of prayers addressed to him at one and the same time. The critique simply leaves the matter at the point of the utter naiveté of mind which counts with certainty that a Being competent to hear and answer the millions of petitions is actually giving minute attention.

The explanation of the pleaders is that God is spirit and that Infinite Spirit is everywhere present, and is able to hear and respond. Few indeed rise to this more abstruse exposition; but even this is vague, uncertain, problematical. It rests indeed finally only on the assertions of Scripture that God hears and answers prayer. What "He" is, how "He" is present, and how "He" can hear and answer are questions left all in the basket of faith. No one stops to take a realistic view of what the simple belief that God hears and answers prayers necessarily involves.

A second stricture is even more glaring in its testimony to childish crudity of thought. This is the item of the absurd persuasion that it is devoutly befitting for men to address formal requests for benisons which on any of the established presuppositions in the case, the divine Being addressed *must* be presumed to know all about infinitely better than the postulants themselves can know. If anything could be more puerile in its irrationality than the presumption of lowly mortals to speak up and instruct Omniscient Deity in precisely what ways he should be best advised to bless his children, it would be hard to find even in the field of irrational religion. Indeed many prayers include in their exordium the flat statement: "O Lord, thou knowest all our needs better than we can know them." What, then, in the name of all logical sense is the good of turning and directing the divine Mind toward the exact methods to be used in assuring us of the blessings we think we ought to have? All this is so highly ridiculous that it is past belief indeed to realize that the sanity of ages has not caught up with it and banished it to its proper limbo of oblivion.

Along with this goes the kindred reflection that "He" not only knows both what we would ask for, what we need and what we should have, better than we can possibly know these things ourselves, but that there has never been a moment in our lives when "He" has *not* been both ready and eagerly watching for every opportunity to advance to us every single blessedness which, in the just dispensation of love and beneficence it is possible or fatefully permissible for him to vouchsafe to us. The average prayer of Christians puts them in a position of ridiculousness quite analogous to that of a small child who would come every day to his school-teacher and devoutly plead that she be good and generous enough to exert herself to pour knowledge and understanding into him,—in spite of his stupidity and inattention.

471

And this holds up in high light the exact ineptitude of the general prayer. From this angle of consideration it is all supremely inane. What must "God" be thinking of his children when they show themselves still so dull and "dumb" that they go on century after century failing to realize that he has organized the cosmic situation and the hierarchical order in such a way that in almost automatic fashion every creature of his Providence will duly receive that highest possible meed of blessing that he has qualified himself to appropriate, and that God himself can not pour in more than the vessel will hold? If fancy might be permitted a moment's fling in the anthropomorphic spirit, one is sanctioned in believing that God himself might grow weary, possibly justifiably exasperated (the Old Testament says that he waxed wroth!), in being called upon to listen to these incessant pleadings from his people, to whom he has without end in his inspired Scriptures given the rock assurance that not a sparrow falls without his notice, and that he has already provided for attention to their every impulse of need, by sending into their very own hearts and minds the power of the Holy Spirit, the Comforter. What can it be but the most perspicuous sanity to suggest that "God" would feel like saying to the army of pleaders: Run along now; don't keep continually bothering me—I have cosmic work to do. Look within and without, and you will feel my spirit watching to help you at every turn, at every instant. Until you do this there is little I can do for you; you must awaken the seed of your own power that you permit to slumber within you before my beneficent will can bring you the larger life you ask for. I have planted my spirit within you, so that you can not fail to find its ever-present help and blessing. If you will not find and use the power I have delegated to you, you can not benefit by any other bounty I can allocate to you. You must absorb the smaller rills of my living stream of power before you can be filled with the mightier tides.

But now comes the most deplorable item, one which goes beyond mere ridiculousness to positive harm of the costliest sort for humanity. This point registers a charge against Christianity of such gravity that it places that religion henceforth under the onus of admitting its erroneous position with due humility, or receiving the brunt of a heavy condemnation from all minds awakened to right perception. It is the charge here laid before the court of a more enlightened human opinion, that Christianity, through its chimerical misconception and misapplication of the force of prayer, has precipitated into the organic body of general thought a virus of intellectual error that has done more to paralyze the spontaneous initiative of the divine powers struggling to come from latency to active function in humanity than any other single influence generated in the religious life. This is a grave accusation and must be accompanied by supporting data.

The particulars of the charge are to be found in the basic fact that prayer of the kind sketched above, inflicts upon the human soul a veritable palsy. How, it will be flung back, can this severe accusation be substantiated? Simply, the answer is, by the very conditions of the activity involved. In this common form of prayer the soul of the suppliant is put in such a relationship to the divine Power that its own independent initiative is crippled, being afflicted with the consciousness of its own impotence and dependence. The prayer itself dramatizes and tremendously reinforces the sense of the helplessness of the divine fragment in man, and rivets upon consciousness the lamentable hypnotization of its own self-generative genius. In such prayer the outer intelligence of the petitioner puts itself in the position of a sycophantic servility, renounces, so to say, its own inherent prerogatives of self-initiated action and stands before the divine throne as a naked suppliant. It perpetrates upon the human consciousness the greatest of all psychological crimes, inasmuch as it slays the sole incentive to the growth of the seed-divinity in man, namely the outer man's sense of the need to awaken the slumbering god within his own bosom. It keeps the nub and focus of the job to be done up in heaven (or over in Judea), when the work is to be accomplished in the individual's home.

The prayer attitude totally ignores this call upon the innate powers of immanent deity in the person's own subjective life, blocks any reliance upon them and deflects any and all attention of the outer mind from the only power that is actually available, that lying unused within and provided by God for just such usage. Prayer thus is a reaching out of the personal energies to call in the aid of a power exterior to the individual consciousness and not regarded as operable by the human agency; and by this very fact it commits against the individually deific power the crime of disinheritance of its incarnational birthright.

The divine soul is in the human constitution precisely for the evolutionary purpose of undergoing an experience that will push it to the deployment of its energies under the stress and strain of the exigencies of its incarnation in these fleshly bodies in the world milieu. It is for a long time as though dead, suffering death, enduring the death of a

473

sort inflicted upon it by the inertia of matter under whose power it descends, lying dormant in the tomb of death—the physical body. From this wintry torpidity it must be awakened. In the long run of incarnational experience events themselves will finally arouse it to awareness of the meaning and the teaching power of all that happens to it. But all is a haphazard, a chance hit or miss run of affairs, until at last the intelligence of the outer mind instructed by adequate philosophy becomes well oriented to the knowledge that for the methodical and successful, if not more rapid, progress of the soul's grasp on evolutionary rationale, the direction of the outer mind inward upon its own activities is a requisite and an advantage of unsurpassed benefit.

As long, then, as the outer mind leaps over the latent intelligence within the man himself and looks to and calls upon a supposed power exterior to his own resources, man is committing a costly malfeasance against his own soul. Thus is built up the gravest of the accusations against Christianity. It is almost indisputable, if rightly estimated, that the mental fixations superinduced upon the consciousness of the Christian millions over the centuries by the egregious hallucinations of the prayer vogue have produced one of the most shocking wastes of psychic energy in the long course of human life.

Prayer of the begging sort is bad enough as a fatuity itself, but it becomes positively heinous in its being pushed forward to take the place of something else which should be the truer expression of man's spirit under the stress of testing. For it obtrudes and becomes a substitute for an *activity* of the spirit on its own part that constitutes in all cases the only chance for victory. However futile it may appear in itself, it becomes infinitely hurtful through its holding off any real effort of the soul to come awake to its mightier prerogatives, which it thus lets die of atrophy for want of stimulation and challenge. This is the supreme charge against prayer for blessings: it lets the deity within man atrophy for lack of exercise.

It is the nature of that deity that, lying long asleep within the inner depths of consciousness, it can be awakened only by the knocking on the outer door from outside. It takes the shocks and jolts, the vicissitudes and exigencies of the outer man's experience in the actual world to arouse it from slumber. The god lying in "death" in the tomb of physical man can be roused for his resurrection only by the severity of the experience of the outer personality. When the eventualities of fortune threaten the outer self with actual hardship, loss or suffering,

474

then the superficial mind of man is driven to seek the resources of its inner but mostly silent partner in the duality. Man's extremity is his god's opportunity. Put more philosophically, the outer man's need and suffering are the inner god's call to awakening and action. Here, incidentally, is the philosophical rationale of the need of suffering and indeed that likewise of the existence of so-called evil.

But as long as the outer mind is deluded by the belief that help is to be sought and obtained from a predicated source of power once localized in a man in history, or still wielded by an omnipotent God above the heavens, the pressure that could be exerted upon the slumbering deity within the man himself is never brought to bear. An influence that could bestir torpid or unborn divinity to conscious activity in the actual range of man's own initiative is diverted away from its proper locale of operation and spent in total futility out upon a historical fiction, or an empty region of the cosmos, while the power that is to be trained to function is held in longer slumber. Prayer directed to a power transcending man's own reach or exercise perpetrates the tragedy of holding the divinity in man fast bound in the arms of "death,"—the death of spirit on the cross of matter. Of all tragedies this is the most grievous, the most woeful.

Then there is the consideration which it seems incredible the Christian mind has not seen and obliterated from the situation. It has to do with the base sycophantic attitude so manifest in the prayer motive. It has most direct reference to the prayers that ask for lavish blessings —and how few do not! We speak of the debasing psychological effect of the eternal posture of begging, pleading, imploring. It is frightfully aggravated nearly always by the additional emphasis in God's ear of man's wretched status as miserable sinner and worm of the dust. To win God's greater pity the human feels he must begin with an exaggeration of his own foulness and unworthiness. The more wretched we can make ourselves to be in God's sight, the more may God be disposed to "have mercy upon us, miserable sinners."

Had not the wholesome natural strength of man's belief in himself been shattered or overpowered by the religious insinuations as to our inherent baseness (through Adam's first sin), prayer of the pleading sort could never have gained a mass vogue. For nothing but such a dire perversion of natural human feeling could have kept forever in abeyance the instinctive sense of the ignominy of begging. When has begging ever been held honorable in secular human life? On the contrary it has ever been despised as ignoble and the mark of human failure and baseness. Yet Christianity and other religions have given it a place of honor. Whether we agree with Nietzsche or not, it is readily possible to appreciate the solid ground of his anathemas against Christianity as "slave morality." It is the exaltation of human wretchedness as a claim on Deity. It colors with the pink hue of a virtue the very lack of virtue. It sanctifies weakness and failure.

So far has this bent of ideology gone in Christianity that it has perpetrated the kindred crime of categorizing in despicable light the very best of man's righteous exertions. An oft-repeated dictum from the pulpits is that man's highest human nobility is in the sight of God as filthy rags. And then a Christian world affects to be surprised when the righteousness of man's actions fails from sheer feebleness, and a world is engulfed in the maelstroms of rash unrighteousness. What can Christendom expect after eighteen centuries of teaching that man's earnest endeavors are worthless in God's sight? The evidence thus accumulates that false Christian prepossessions have been responsible for world debacle.

If God could be dramatized as disposed to tell his children to run along and not weary him with endless supplications, also he might be pictured as adding: Do stop groveling at my feet and pleading for mercy. I did not make you to crawl in shame in the dust. I made you to stand up and make a fight of it. I can't awaken your divinity until you do battle on your own account. Nothing but *your* effort will unchain the sleeping giant of my power within you. If you will arise from the dust and fight upon your feet, you will be surprised to find that the resources I have provided and buried in your own constitution come forth for your help at just the right time. Do you expect to have beneficence fed to you as you lie supine or grovel in the dirt? Up off your knees and to the fight! A blessing given to you without your winning it could not even be held. I have not generated you for a race of marionettes, but to be gods in your own right. Up and cease this miserable groaning! You, my sons, are soon to be gods; and gods do not grovel in the dust.

On its record for eighteen centuries Christianity must go down in history as the religion that deprecated human goodness and raised to universal honor and dignity the base human instinct of beggary. If it can be charged that any religion on earth has ground the spirit of mankind down in the dust of the consciousness of its meanness, the religion that must bear the onus of that accusation is Christianity. The chief psychological measure used in Christian propaganda of the evangelistic sort has been to throw the hapless prospective proselyte helpless in its arms by first paralyzing his human resistance with the obsession of the sin consciousness. Nearly all Christian evangelism—renewed and accentuated in the very Cathedral of St. John the Divine in New York City as this is written—has aimed to drag down the healthy spirit of humans by the stupefying narcotic of the exaggerated self-accusation of sin. Christianity finds it hard to win new converts without reducing them emotionally to such wretchedness of self-depreciation that they surrender the last remnants of reason and human worth and throw themselves in abject abasement on the promised mercy of God. With all our searching we can find nothing in Paganism to match this sin against the Holy Spirit, man's basic rational intelligence. Language will exhaust itself in vain to characterize properly the enormity of this perversion of right human ideation, but it may not be untrue to say that infinitely worse than any reputed slaying of the Son of Man upon a wooden cross in the long past is the unending crucifixion of the divine Christ in the present lives of Christian believers.

The word "surrender" crept naturally into one of the sentences just written. This, too, comes in for its share of the strictures on prayer. It is a natural accompaniment of the prayer motive and technique. One can hardly descend to the prayer motive without having surrendered his own sense of initiative and divine prerogative. If one asks a higher Power to pick one up out of the mire, one must have let go of all grip on oneself. The incessant evangelical cry has been the need of the sinner to "surrender" to God. In this word has been embalmed another measure of the abject beating down of the human spirit. Self-abasement was not enough; the last step is surrender. With this the ruination of the human integrity is complete. Man has quit. He has thrown up the fight. He has cast himself on the mercy of God; and one may well wonder what God can do with a creature who will not fight for the values he has been promised, but which are his for the winning. The Old Testament represents Deity as losing all patience with his Israel children who will not fight the good fight, and railing out upon them with the hot fury of his anger. For even man's groping logic assures him that beneficence can not be held or enjoyed by the creature without the initial exertion to develop the qualities by which alone its enjoyment can become a reality.

Surrender! A man in his natural sanity would logically presume that surrender is the last thing God would wish his creatures to do with

477

any power or faculty generated in the course of evolution to carry man onward to his goal. Only on the very limited and of course permissible sense of letting go or renouncing evil tendencies on the purely brutish side of the duality is the word legitimately to be introduced into the spirito-ethical purview. A man does well, obviously, to "surrender" his selfishness, his remnants of animal ferocity, his narrow besotted addictions that have accrued and clung to him from the animal stage of his evolution. A drunkard does well to "surrender" himself to a more manly aspiration for self-control. A miser does well to surrender his gloating over mere gold, and let the sweet tides of human charity and fellowship inundate his soul.

But "surrender" in its Christian evangelical sense is not saved by any reasonable limitation to this acceptable usage. One is implored to let go one's human grasp on the whole supervision of the life process, and relax every effort that the mind would normally conceive to be conducive to the well-being of the individual. Surrender here means ceasing to make a further fight of it with the instrumentalities ordinarily believed to be the proper ones for the ends of all living. And again enters the damning factor of a paralysis of self-endeavor on the part of the individual. As in the case of "sin," it is all an emphasis on the negative side, whereas all accentuation should be laid on the grasping of the positive elements as the instruments of uplift and salvation. It is enough to insist that evil should be given up. God has insisted that the creature must turn from his evil way to gain eternal life. All rewards are promised to "him that overcometh." But when this due understanding is emotionally overmagnified into the egregious persuasion that man must cease fighting with the powers of reason and judgment and will which he finds he must use to solve the problems of his earthly life, it is going to ridiculous and disastrous lengths of false assumption. Instead of the misunderstood urge to surrender, it would be far saner and more wholesome to urge the unawakened person to take a better grip on himself. For God is not going to save any of his earthly creatures from the necessary and salutary exertion of saving himself. The very economy of the cosmos is based upon every creature's ultimate control over the forces and powers which evolution sets before him the task of bringing under intelligent direction. The divine self in man is to become the conscious king over the "seven elementary powers" of the purely human creature. These lower and more physical energies are to be administered by humans risen to mastership of every agency in the repertoire of powers. "Know ye not," Paul reminds us, "that we are to manage angels, let alone mundane things?" The cosmic intelligence can not use weaklings, incompetents, grovelers in the dust, pleaders for mercy, beggars for favors. Therefore it puts its recruits for service in its higher work through a fairly rigorous school and program of training, calling for the exercise and development of the powerful forces to be wielded by the future lords of angelic hierarchies in the mighty work of creation. For all God's creatures are to become conscious coworkers with him in his vast and endless labor. Christianity has been for centuries quite out of harmony with the spirit and temper of this enterprise. Instead of inspiring its multitudinous devotees to face up to the effort with courage and resolution, it has afflicted them with the miasmatic obsession of unworthiness, of helplessness and surrender. From the start its votaries thought it more glorious to be thrown to the lions or burned at the stake than to fight a living battle. For they not only succumbed to it as dire injustice and brutal tyranny, but wildly sought and provoked it when it might have been obviated.

The final word in the critique of prayer comes to utterance in the statement that it has deadened man's own initiative. It has been used as a craven excuse and self-deluding justification for cowardly shirking of the obligation to *act*. It is the retreat and refuge of souls who lack the proper knowledge and the divine heroism needed to solve difficult problems and dangerous situations by forthright action. It is the attitude and the spirit of children running to their parents or elders for help when trouble threatens. It is so much easier and safer to sit at home and pray that God will interpose to adjust international antagonisms and impasses than to take hold and with the exertion of the divinest resources within our own control reach just decisions. Nothing can be more pitiable than to see the head of a great or a lesser religious community call upon his adherents over the earth to unite to pray for the righteous settlement of grievous wrongs or difficulties, when the divine power of initiating righteous action has been placed within human control and lies there inert and undeveloped until called upon for just such exertion. The loving parent will safeguard his child as long as it has no abilities developed to make his own way. But as these abilities unfold in their due order, the wise parent puts the child on its own resources and devices. To continue doing its work for it would be to stunt its growth. Such is the Father's relation to his children on earth. If man does not solve his own problems, he will remain the child. Prayer is the evidence that he is afraid to let go the Father's hand and apply his own resources and bring out his own powers. Prayer is the resource of a soul still lingering in childlike dependency, the fledgling still afraid to trust its own wings. When resorted to by those who could and should act, it is the recourse of cowardice. Beyond calculation is the volume of human suffering and tragedy of every sort that has had to be endured by the substitution of inaction and prayer for resolute exertion on the physical plane. The mistaken notion that prayer can be substituted for courageous action has afflicted humanity with untold calamity.

Christian apologists have stoutly insisted that Christianity was undermined and bled of its more virile temper by the stealthy and insidious infiltration into its primitive motivations of the enervating currents of negative and passive ideology assimilated from India. There could be some substance to this complaint. The Hindu religions inordinately stressed denial of the value of this physical life, proclaiming all blessedness as springing from the total renunciation of the interests that hold life in the body. Hindu philosophy had no sympathy with a doctrine that localized true wealth in the earthly experience. Surcease of human woe in unconsciousness and the lulling call of the dreamy bliss of Nirvana stupefied Hindu zest for the physical life, in which the magnificent Greek philosophy had localized its supreme values—until the fatal "failure of nerve." India may be largely responsible for all this. Greece herself possibly succumbed to the lethal seduction, and turned her effort from earth to heaven. It is the sign of the beginning of the decay of a religion unenlightened by philosophy. It must be true that God wants us to graduate from the kindergarten stage of dependence and prayer and evolve our own resources through the exertion of the germinal divine power he has endowed us with. "When I was a child I spake as a child, but when I became a man I put away childish things." There are really few people who believe that "God" hears and answers prayers. But there would be few who on reflection would not think that he must take due note of heroic action. In the end, therefore, there is only one effective form of prayer, and that is action. The *Zohar* of the ancient Hebrews says again and again that the powers *above* bestir themselves to action only in response to a stirring on the side of the powers *below*. God can not be sure of your *full* sincerity until you act. It is God speaking through Emerson's pen when he says: Your actions (or failure to act) shout so loudly that I can not hear what you say—in prayer.

In the same general category of weaknesses exhibited and inculcated

480

by Christian forms of ideology must be mentioned the singular doctrine of the forgiveness of sins and the vicarious atonement. They are twin progeny of the same doctrinal leaning. All arose out of the misconception of the basic elements in the doctrines that effect the final harmonization of the two long conflicting natures in man's dual constitution. Man, says Plato, is the union of a god's mind with the physical elementary powers of an animal body. "Through body it is an animal; through intellect it is a god." A long conflict ensues from the beginning of their copartnership in the physical existence, growing out of the animal man's inability to transform his selfish instincts quickly to the altruistic or cooperative function of the god-soul germinating within. But as the outer man gradually unfolds his own powers of intelligence and finally grasps the rationale of the plan for perfect unification of its forces with the divine order of a higher creation, the two warring elements are reconciled and make a mutual rapprochement of their efforts. This is theologically called the reconciliation, the atonement. As it was the initiative and control exercised by the higher soul that engineered the successful outcome of this eventual "marriage," it was the soul that was given credit for the work. So from the standpoint of the human level it was vicarious for the physical man.

Properly held in this rationale, the doctrine of vicarious atonement can be, and is an item of true understanding. But twisted out of sensible relation and misapplied to false personal "history" and in the wrong world, it has wreaked havoc with sane intelligence. It worked over finally, in the lowest levels of mentality, into the idea that a man was sent to earth to save mortals the effort to save themselves. This divine emissary obligingly took upon himself the onus and labor of relieving man of the natural consequences of his blind blundering. Man's sins were washed away in the red blood that flowed forth— two pints or thereabouts of it—from the wounded side on Calvary!

But what was washed away by the doctrine thus outrageously misinterpreted was the rational sanity of millions of hapless victims of bad thinking. The words of the doctrine can remain as beautiful poetry, but become ruinous if taken for personal biography. The atonement, the reconciliation between God and man in the latter's constitution, the marriage of the spirit from above and animal soul from below, is effectuated through the suffering, the sacrificial oblation of the descending unit of divine mind. And the transformation of animal soul into spiritual immortality could not be achieved without

481

the immolation of the god-soul on the altar of matter, or its "death" in the tomb of body.

A mortal is enlightened by knowing these teachings of the arcane science relative to his life effort. But to mistake the sense in so unconscionable a way as to think the doctrine means the salvation of the mortal wholly without reference to his own accomplishment of the felicitous outcome by exertions initiated and persisted in under the severest trial is to slay again the spirit of self-responsibility that alone can avail to win the crown. If the perversion of meaning works to the mental conclusion in the general mind, as precisely it has done, that a sheer affirmation of "belief" in the man Jesus will bring the magical result without further struggle by the individual, it sinks the mind into delusion and stultification of its faculties. And this has been the outcome of Christianism's misteaching.

. . . .

If prayer and its corollary psychological influence have steeped the Christian mind in delusion, even more atrociously has the same thing been done by the Christian prepossession in the matter of "healing." Again a theme that would require a whole treatise in itself must be compacted within a half-chapter.

It is a common idea that Pagans rested their faith in the beneficence of life on what the Greeks called *physis* or *nature,* while Christianity presented the knowledge and operable science of the higher principle of divine soul or God's spirit, brought to earth for the first and only time by the incarnation or epiphany of Jesus of Nazareth. The notion is utterly false, but it well serves the purpose of introducing the brief dissertation here presented on the matter of Christian healing.

The vogue of Christian healing was launched through the mistaken belief that the Gospels were a biography of a living individual. In the Gospels the man Jesus (assuming he lived) performed a run of "miracles," mostly in the field of physical healings. And when "he" said that we shall do even greater things than those recorded of him, the whole Christian mind was set off on the wild pursuit of miracle-working. Only in the modern day has there been the carrying of this implication of religious theories about bodily healing into its wildest exploitation in the fantastic assumptions of Christian Science; but something little short of this extreme delusion has been fermenting in Christian practice over the centuries. Indeed so prominent a place has healing made for itself in Christian motivation that no individual propagation of a new evangelistic movement or message could hope to win a hearing unless it was able to add to its preachment the psychological stimulus of reputed cures of all maladies. If his message led to healings, it was thus divinely certified. If his preaching was attended by miraculous manifestations, it was of God. No dissertation is needed to remind us how pitiably eager and excitable the common people are over the report that a healer is repeating what Jesus did. It is one of the most pathetic of human manifestations, repeated time and again in all religious history. The study of the tides of fervor and frenzy that have swept over the populace in Christian history is one of the most eerily fascinating, if dispiriting, of pursuits.

And again it has to be declared that Christian practice and belief have plunged millions into wild hallucination, contorting a thing otherwise beautiful and ennobling into an instrument of outlandish folly. The tragedy was fastened hard on the Christian mentality by the reputed historicity of the Gospel "miracles." As long as these "incidents" were held, as Origen held them, to be dramatic representations of the power of the immanent Christ spirit to heal all men's imperfections and maladies, and so taken as only *types* of inner purifications, they served the splendid end of inciting men to let the divine ferment work its benign influence upon their minds and eventually upon their bodies. This understanding directly promoted the culture of the higher Self in all right-minded and thoughtful and earnest persons. It engendered the efficacy of spiritual religion at its best. It awakened the slumbering infant god within and challenged or provoked the exercise of his powers.

But the moment the intelligent view was misplaced and the gross physical meaning was substituted, the door was open to the entry of a host of preposterous assumptions, all eventually ruinous to balance and wholesome influence. And with this development Christianity thrust its people into one more of the long list of its imbecile infatuations and went madly careening after another of its illusive mirages.

The investigation of religious healings is a most fascinating one, too vast for any competent treatment here. But a cursory scanning of its main features may yield much profit along with our general survey. Nearly every one of hundreds of cult movements has come into being through remarkable manifestations in the category of spiritual cures of illness and functional disease. "Miracle" can lay claim to a vast body of ostensible evidence of the most extraordinary character and generally valid authenticity. "Cases" of miraculous cure and recovery in a wide variety of maladies run into great number. There is no intention here to deny a record of vast proportions and of challenging nature. On a shallow view of this record the case for the actuality of healing and for the substantiation of the claims advanced might be thought to be impregnably established. But what is here posited is the assertion that a deeper and more scientifically oriented insight quite thoroughly invalidates all the common presuppositions in the case. A more competent knowledge of the divine-human psyche in man yields an explanation of the phenomena that decidedly negates the common beliefs and the theoretical assumptions on which they are based.

Popular views are hardly ever based on more accurate technological knowledge on any matter, but persist in spite of such default. They are generated by the most naive conceptions and only slowly give way to correction as bits of technical detail filter out from fonts of true scientific discovery. The subject of healing is just now in process of being liberalized by new findings in the scientific aspects of the study. Common belief is being forced to a change of view. As the new light increases it will effect an emendation of unsupportable beliefs in this field. And a prodigious chapter of wretched human gullibility, deception and fanaticism in religion will happily be brought to its finis.

As is ever the case when crude belief or naive supposition is replaced by more accurate knowledge, the boundless area of "miracle" and the "supernatural" is reduced by so much, and what was believed to lie over in that territory is brought down into the familiar ground of the natural and the explicable. Much of the "romance" of religious excitability is thus lost, and religion does not take too kindly to this dismantling of its airy castles and roseate paradises of faith.

But fact, however disillusioning, is both more salutary and more intrinsically romantic in the end. The romance of truth is always more thrilling than the romance of dream or illusion. For it is dream actualized. No magic of the supernatural can overmatch the magic of the natural or the actual. Religion has all too largely tended to become the lure of the supernatural, the miraculous and the magical, when the real power and expansion of life is only to arise from the love and cultivation of the natural. Man must extract his blessedness from the constant, the regular, the normal. For here is where the laws that work for his beneficence operate. Man's happy ongoing comes through his obedience to law. Miracle excites because it ostensibly violates or transcends law. The human mind has stood wrapt in wonder before "miracle," which can bring it little general good, while ever standing callous and lethargic in the presence of that everyday miracle of life and nature through the agency of which alone is true benison to be won.

But whether it is emotionally acceptable to Christian pietists or not, the findings of a more empirical psychological science offer an explanation of the whole run of "miraculous" phenomena that at one stroke strips the entire range of such manifestations of all its former aura of magic and miracle and reduces it wholly to the level of a natural function. Cures may still appear wonderful, but not more wonderful than that mysterious, though now common phenomenon constantly handled with growing scientific skill, which offers the key to knowledge of what law is in operation,—the phenomenon of hypnotism.

"Miracles" matching in variety and marvel those recited in the history of healing cultism can be, and are being duplicated every day now in the clinical laboratories of psychiatrists. Without the fanfare and sensational emotionalism of the evangelical procedure, cures and transformations of mind and character are daily being wrought by the practitioners of the cultus of the "unconscious." At last the lid of the conscious mind is being lifted long enough to enable observation to be made of the effective operation of the great Overmind, as well as the Undermind, both of which function at levels out of range of the normal waking consciousness. In these strata or worlds of consciousness are found the forces that work the supposed "miracles" of faith. And "faith," after all the ages of blind belief that it could command the offices of God's benevolence and power, is now found to be nothing but a predisposing agency of self-hypnosis. Ever since T. J. Hudson's *The Law of Mental Medicine* and *The Law of Psychic Phenomena* and Freud's discovery of the "unconscious," the miraculous aspects of the age-old religious healing phenomena have been doomed to dissipation in the light of common knowledge and a perfectly understood rationale. The day of miracle in this field of superstition and human credulity is happily at an end. There is at hand a law that explains it, and in the domain of the natural. It is the law of suggestion; the law of hypnotism. One hypnotizes oneself by the intensity of a single suggestion or by constant repetition of a suggestion; and once hypnotized, the individual is capable of many a demonstration of wonder-working that we formerly were wont to assign to the agency of the gods. And once more Christian belief in a divine power *outside* the individual is dispelled as a rank error, a construction of ignorance, and the mind is forced to acknowledge the active factor of causation as a power resident and operative within the human constitution, not in

485

remote Judea or in cosmic heavens. And it is remarkable how this consideration dramatizes the entire fallacy of Christian belief: it has placed practically all the potent values of theology outside the human house, and has had man looking everywhere *but within himself* for the location of those powers which effectuate his salvation. At last empirical science, whose findings can not be gainsaid or withstood, breaks down the last rampart of theological superstition in Christianism and demonstrates in the laboratory that the Christ who heals the soul and body of man is a power submerged deep in the constitution of man himself, and is not one that could in the remotest way be dependent upon the historical coming of a Son of God in the flesh of one man at any time.

Hypnotism need not be induced by overt manipulation or by an operative; one can hypnotize oneself. And the agency can be a suggestion, a philosophy, a persuasion, a conviction, a belief, an infatuation, a book, a sermon, a piece of music, a personality, an addiction of any kind. Hold a conviction long enough and it ends by holding you. A habit is something which you say a person has (from *habeo,* Latin, I *have*). In reality it is something that has the person. Faith, great lauded virtue of the Christian system, is now found to be but the surrender of the conscious critical mind to the hypnotizing tendency of an idea or belief of some kind. But woe to the one surrendering his critical mind to any idea but one that is in full accord with truth and reality! Surrender your mind to a belief that is chimerical, and you have surrendered yourself to a demoniacal obsession. Psychoanalysis is the science of unseating those demoniacs from their control of a mind.

The burden of this book is that the supreme charge against Christianity is that it has caused the obsession of untold millions of minds with a series of fatuous beliefs which have motivated centuries of human actions perpetrating a body of follies, fanaticisms, cruelties and inhumanities unmatched in all history. And the instructive difference between Christianity and, let us say, Greek philosophy, is now seen in startling clarity, as the difference between surrender of the mind in Christianity to a series of wild and chimerical fancies in no wise based on any correspondence with truth and reality; while Greek philosophy was a system of intellectual propositions based on a complete harmonization with the known realities, the forces and elements of man's constitution and the laws of the cosmos.

From the day on which it was demonstrated that a manipulator of hypnotism could run a darning needle through the forearm of a mesmerized subject without his feeling any pain, and that hypnotism could be employed in surgical operations instead of anaesthetics, it should have been clear that the secret law that produced religious "cures" was in our possession. It only remained to demonstrate the identity between the various processes of suggestion subjectively administered and the actual physical manipulation of the mesmerist to prove up the solution of the mystery. Religious hysteria is now at last unmasked. Its outer aura of emotional excitability, assumption of the presence and activity of divine power and interposition of the hand of God himself are all now rudely dispelled, and the human at last, after centuries of the grossest belief in the play of Providence or of demons or spirits, can face the known realities of his own consciousness. He can be shown that the most startling manifestations in the realm of his own conscious life can be explained as just the consequences of his own ill-understood and ill-controlled mental activities. No longer need mortals be tossed emotionally about by the weirdest fancies of superstition or belief in agencies working in the great realm of the unknown, to alarm, frighten or delude the ignorant mind of the human. We stand at last liberated from twenty centuries of religious nightmare that is not to be charged solely to Christian nescience, being common to the strata of ignorance in all humanity, but at any rate a nightmare that ran to horrifying extremes under Christian sway.

It is nearly incredible, too, that there has never been in Christian thinking the clear insight to discern a glaring flaw in the philosophy which countenanced and perpetuated the vogue of healing, the true bases of which now reveal the non-divine and non-sanctified character of the phenomena. So romantically were the manifestations cast in the realm of the miraculous that there was inevitably granted to all such proceedings the rank and character of divinely accredited occurrences. No one ever stopped to question the moral legitimacy of the seemingly providential cures. If a diseased person could reach a healer and be healed, there was no question but that it was the will of God that he be healed. No one stopped to think what that presupposition did to the *moral law*. On the one side stood the more rational Christian recognition of the universal reign of law in the spiritual as well as in the natural world. If there was no other witness to this, there is at least Drummond's book, *The Natural Law in the Spiritual World*. Kant was certainly not unchristian or anti-Christian; and his two eternal sources of wonder were, as he said, the starry heavens above him and the moral law within. Christianity's incessant boast of its superiority over the heathen philosophies was that it recognized and related human conduct to the play of the moral law; whereas the Pagan world could not envisage such an abstraction of the subjective processes. Therefore it can be affirmed that Christianity regarded the moral law as God's mode of righteous rulership of the world.

So here is the postulation of the moral law as the norm of righteousness and justice on the one side of Christian philosophy, and a belief of miracles of healing on the other, with the possibility of a clash between the two imminent at any time. The implications inseparable from the belief in miracle fly straight in the face of the postulations inherent in the moral law.

For how do physical illness, disease, infirmity come? By a whimsical, random, wanton dispensation of a Providence that can perpetrate no injustice? No Christian would so ascribe ill fortune. Christianity, a bit uncertainly indeed, still clings to the concept of causation under divine law. Therefore people's diseases and cripplings, such as rheumatism, gout and the functional disorders of the body and toxic pollution of the blood, must be attributed to unintelligent and unwise and unnatural habits of living. Perhaps if simple truth was recognized, some ninety percent of all such maladies are engendered by the single item of wrong addictions in the eating habits. People habitually eat too much, or too frequently, or wrong combinations, or use devitalized foods. At any rate this is a prominent aspect of the situation and will serve to illuminate the argument. It is real and demonstrable enough to give valid force to the assertion that the afflictions for the cure of which people flock *en masse* to a healer have been brought upon them by their own violation of the moral law, in this case the law of moderation and correctness in diet.

Well, then, a mind that looks to see the righteous play of the moral law will have to ask the question (that will of course shock minds hypnotized with piety): what right does a habitual violator of the moral law have to be healed by the touch of a person wielding some form of magnetic power currents in his dynamic person, when there is not on the part of the suppliant the intimation of a single item of change from the course that superinduced the evil condition? What becomes of our reverence for the moral law if we can see it flouted and the evil consequences of its violation swept away from the breaker of the law without his mending his way in the slightest degree? The Jesus figure himself in one case made the relief or cure of illness dependent on repentance and "sinning no more." This at least maintains regard for the ineluctable rule of the moral forces. But in the furore that has always accompanied the demonstrations of faith healings no one has paused to reflect on the question how and why the obvious violators of the laws of life, established for beneficent evolutionary purposes and safeguarded in that beneficence by having inevitable suffering attendant upon their violation, were entitled to escape, by the intervention of some healer's offices, from the natural consequences of their breaking the law, with no prerequisites of repentance or correction of bad habits, or even the intention or the promise to cease the practices causing the disorder. Life does not distribute its largesse in indiscriminate disregard of the moral law. And what moral right does a healer have to go about dispensing manipulations that amount in effect to the enablement of people to escape, apparently and temporarily at any rate, the natural salutary effects of their violation of the laws of eternal justice? Or what right have the people to flock to grasp the aid of such a manipulator, to escape the very thing that alone will warn them off continued violation?

The sane philosophy of pain and suffering is that they are ordained under the law of beneficence to warn us away from the courses of violation in which we stupidly and obdurately persist. The uses of pain and evil hap are divinely ordered for their pedagogical utility. Pain teaches man when nothing else will. If he can violate law and escape the pains, he will plunge on to his ruin. Pain is the divine brake on the wild car of man's wilful waywardness. If anything steps in to deprive him of the full play of this teaching element, he will be bereft of the one factor that can save him from worse tragedy. And obviously the healings, as commonly manifested, do thus interpose to obviate the natural consequences of violation of the great law of good.

The likely possibility in the case is that such seemingly efficacious cures are only hypnotizations at any rate and will not last. Indeed the record largely reveals that they "wear off" in a short time, precisely as a hypnotizing force does. The conclusion is that they have been vastly overrated in significance all down the centuries. But that Christian ideation can have been so blind for two millennia to both the psychological nature and the moral connotations of this matter of faith healing is a sad attestation again of the puerile numbness to which erroneous beliefs can reduce the human mind.

So we have the doctrines of salvation, of prayer, of the forgiveness of sins, of the vicarious atonement, and finally of the traditional belief in healing, all raised in Christian polity to a place of great power in the life of devotees, and all contributing with never-failing force to hypnotize the believer with the persuasion that he can sin and escape the consequences. It is as clear as anything can well be that Christianity is thus responsible for the general spirit of lawlessness so evident throughout all Christian history, and so extremely menacing to all cultural control at this present. Whatever may be alleged to the contrary and whatever may be the failings and aberrations of sane wisdom in other lines among non-Christian faiths, in none of them has there been so manifest a disregard of the inviolability of the moral law as has been demonstrated in all ages under Christianity. The Greeks had their Fate, or Fortune, or Nemesis; the Egyptians their Thoth making an indelible record in the book of life and weighing the good and evil deeds of the soul in the scales of the balance; the Hindus had their Karma; the Mohammedans their Kismet. Christianity nullified its asseverated law of cause and effect, or reaping in the exact measure of the sowing, by the exaggerated and misapplied doctrine of forgiveness and by asserting that the rigor of the moral law of the old dispensation—an eye for an eye—would be softened by the love and mercy of the Christ interceding for erring men at the throne of God.

We hear much of religion and philosophy, art, music, poetry being hugged to the bosoms of multitudes of people as mechanisms of escape from the rough commonplace of actuality into realms of romantic idealism. It is submitted here, on the evidence adduced, that of all religions serving as sheer modes or channels of such escape motivation, Christianity must be reckoned as, though in a different way and on a different side, about equal to the lethalizing religions of India. And the infinite tragedy of Christianity is that it has been an escape not from dispiriting realism into romantic idealism, but an escape from reality into infatuation and delusion. For the pall of false historical and literal acceptance under which the orthodox Christian mind lives has hallucinated that mind with eerie forms of unreality, so that the Christian lives in a world in which reality is minimized to irrelevance and imagination is stimulated to seek real values in a set of utterly unreal theological postulates. This is not an escape; it is a fall into dementia.

CHAPTER XXII

THE NIGHT IS LONG

In dropping the curtain on this intellectual scenario it seems desirable to undertake a presage of the immediate future, pivoting on the point of the present from our fairly close view of the past to prospect on the outcome of the forces still at work in the field of religious culture. It was stated at the outset that it was impossible for any one to grasp the rationale of the present world situation without a knowledge of what eventuated in the cataclysmic third century. For the forces of mental blindness and crafty duplicity which then overmastered the minority powers of philosophical balance and sane intelligence, are the same forces that have perpetuated themselves in weighty influence down to their straining activity at the present moment. And now, forced to relax their hold upon the more northern lands of Europe by the powerful rebellion of the Protestant movement in the sixteenth century, they are stretching every nerve of their slowly increasing might to regain the political dominance they haughtily exercised over the political fortunes of Europe through the middle centuries of the Christian era. For a recovery of that mastership is tantamount to rulership of the entire globe. Now as then the aims, attitudes, methods and prime characteristics of the monster force of popular nescience and low-pitched intellectualism are recognizable as the same unchanged and unchanging earmarks of that fatal third century debacle of sanity and triumph of a baneful mass inferiority.

But now the forces that were then largely the spontaneous and unorganized, the loose but massive expression of low-grade intelligence, asserting themselves in ponderous resentment against the dominance of an esoteric philosophical hegemony itself reduced at the period to a somewhat less noble standard than before, are no longer loose and unorganized, but massively unified and directed by perhaps the most astute psychological craftiness in the history of mankind. After ages of a career of repeated loss of power and prestige from lack of an all-controlling central authority, this giant engine of mass mediocrity of intellect and the blind persuasions of faith that are its congenial by-products, has through the driving force of its own aspirations for survival and for power, learned to discipline itself to the extreme degree of resigning all individual independence into the hands of a centralized organ of rulership. It is aimed to achieve success through the avoidance of the crippling influences of purely democratic division and fragmentation of power. So that, as Guignebert so handily phrases it, a movement that sprang into being out of the impulse of free individuals to escape what was considered a tyranny of generalized traditional systems of the Pagan world and to take a stand for an unfettered faith in the native motions of the human spirit itself, came in the end to be enchained by the organic systematism of a psychological tyranny unmatched in the annals of religion.

What has occurred, of course, is better understood in the light of common appreciations, when it is simply recognized that a smart and alert thinking group within the movement, taught by observation and analysis of past failures and weaknesses in its career, saw at last the dire consequences of unfettered freedom of religious impulses and mystical extravagances, and resolved to obviate these annoying dispersals of strength springing from democratic liberalism by clamping upon the entire movement the bans and bands of a supreme authority that no individual or group would dare, as in the middle centuries, to disregard. For the most part the loyalties inspired by blind faith were strong enough to hold the entire corporate unit together in spite of the abrogation of personal liberties of thought, so that the desired solidarity was acquired without too serious expression of rebellious dissent. And once this imperious domination and command of instant obedience and subservience was attained, there was developed and perfected the most ingenious polity of mental sway over the stolid masses of adherents ever to be manipulated by any oligarchy of leaders in known history.

The terms of this astute polity were dictated by the findings from a study of human psychology unparalleled in its shrewdness and deftness. The constitution of the regime was framed of the principles observed in operation over the years. Within the frame and spirit of a movement ostensibly religious there was built up a machinery of governance even more rigidly mechanical in its running than the corporate enginery of any secular government. And with all power wielded by the unchallengeable head of the hierarchy, there thus exists in the modern world this monstrous embodiment of unbounded political ambition wielding as its sword of power the enslaved but docile adherence and psychological loyalties of the massed populace of the middle and lower classes.

These elements of the population, numerous as always, it strategically aims to increase rapidly by the sanctified preachment of the godliness of large families and obstruction of the modern propaganda of birth control. Precisely as in the days of its first fanatic upspringing it appeals to and fastens its grip upon the lower classes. These it aims to hold by conditioning their minds, particularly in childhood, through the inculcations of teaching and the motivations of fear, as well as through the rituals and pageantries so impressive to the young. Critical questioning and challenge are met and generally silenced by the resources of "explanation" unbelievable in its speciousness and subtlety. Much of the unpalatable history of the movement is touched up for better appearance, deftly recolored, artfully ignored or openly denied. Among major items of this policy program is, of course, the vast overestimate of the number of Christian martyrs under the Roman persecutions, and the unconscionable softening down and mild palliation of the unspeakable inhumanities and tortures of the Spanish Inquisition, the slaughter of the Albigenses and all that record of unthinkable horror. Indeed the history that touches the movement itself has been almost entirely rewritten to conduce at every point to the enhancement of the reputation of this organic entity and to redound in subtle ways to the discredit of its opponents. Its inner board of strategic polity keeps vigilant watch upon every turn of event in the world, indeed upon every vein of cultural development in science, philosophy and education, and concocts measures both aggressive and defensive calculated to turn every such significant incident to its advantage.

As ignorance was its mother and the source-spring of its world power, it is bound to cherish ignorance as its patron saint and monitor forever, for the breath of knowledge would wither it away. Therefore it keeps its clientele ignorant, conditioning what it is pleased to call its educational system with just those elements which tend to make the reception and retention of its principles enduring. As it forcefully blocked the European mind from the privilege of thinking freely for over fifteen centuries, it fights every new discovery of secular knowledge, since new light and truth promises generally to prove inimical to its traditional fixations. The damaging impact of new knowledge must be held to a minimum.

493

As it arose out of the spirit of envy, resentment and hatred of esoteric philosophy as purveyed by the Mystery Schools of the ancient
world, it runs true to character by standing in inveterate hostility to
the groups which, surreptitiously during the Middle Ages and now
again openly in the modern period, have aimed to restore the dissemination and culture of the ancient metaphysical sciences in the domain
of free religious and philosophical culture. Hence it is the sworn
enemy of Masonry, Theosophy, Rosicrucianism, Anthroposophy,
Protestantism and Humanism. It must oppose its power to these cultures because they essay to include the offices of intellectual or rational
philosophy in their several systematic approaches to the progress of
spiritual science. To the extent to which they succeed in intellectualiz-
ing religion with philosophy, they reduce in their lives the predominance of the religious influence and increase that of the rational principle. As this procedure proportionately disarms the power of sheer
faith and fortifies the spirit of critical rationality, the consequences
would always be menacing and fatal to the control which is so much
more smoothly maintained over minds swayed by faith alone.

And this is basically true in spite of the effort of no mean subtlety
put forth by the Christian theology to utilize the deepest sophistries
of the rational faculty to accredit the reign of faith. This reduced the
situation to a paradoxical and quizzical status of using rational
processes to fasten ever more firmly the clamps that hold immovable
a posture of mind based on faith, the antithesis of reason. Even this
paradox is given the semblance of rationality by the subtle definition
slipped illegitimately into the word "faith," to make it carry the essence of intuitional certitude. In the airy spiritual or mystical strato-
sphere of human consciousness there is indefiniteness enough to permit intimations of this sort to maintain a claim of some validity. The
central impulse and moving spirit of the Christian movement must
ever be generated from the side of faith and religion, as distinct from
the mainsprings emanating from the side of intelligence, knowledge
and philosophy. It fights the warfare of faith against the spirit of
search for truth; of religion against philosophy and science. If it could
have had its way, science as the world knows it since the seventeenth
century would have died a-borning. For it did make every effort of
its scourging power to crush it. Science and rationalism ever menace it.

There emerges from all this staggering truth the cheering reflection
that it was only when this monstrous gag of pious faith on the free

494

use of the mind was removed and the stifling pressure of "holy Church" was loosed that the Western mind began to move forward to the achievement of more progress in knowledge and the development of power to ease the burden of physical effort than had been attained in the endless centuries of religious domination. The issue has proven beyond all cavil that the religion of faith fastened ruthlessly upon the West by the fanatical zealots of the third century has lain like a blight upon the human mind over all the period, until the unconquerable spirit of free investigation forced the horrid tentacles of the octopus to relax its clammy grip in the seventeenth century.

But even the loosening of the death-hold of pious faith by the young giant of physical science has not by any means assured the future predominance of culture over ignorance. The power of ignorance can reach out and subvert science as it once quenched philosophy. It also can convert science slyly to its own ends. Radio, television, atom power can be turned to the service of evil conceptions. Water can not rise higher than its level, and science can only put into the hands of common low humanity the more ready instruments for the ribald revel. One of the immediate results of the perfection of television is that five million people spend their evenings watching young men pound each other's heads where ten thousand only could do so before. Marvelous inventions do but scatter the lowest forms of tawdry cheapness over a wider area. They therefore drag mediocrity still lower.

The measure of culture is in man, and as man is either base or noble, he converts all he touches to base or noble uses. Ignorance, the admitted essence and genesis of all human evils, will win its victories as long as men do not bestir the latent divinity within themselves and rise out of dullness into intelligence. To hold its own seat on the throne, to perpetuate its own reign, ignorance must block interest and progress in the cultivation of philosophy, that final culture of the soul of man which enlightens him as to what use to make of all other knowledge. For even knowledge itself, as pure mental acquirement, is not of much more utility to man than are the things produced by science. Both science and knowledge are morally neutral; they are not either good or bad in themselves. As the ultimate criterion of good or evil is to be localized in the interior of man's conscious being, *things* become good or bad only in the moral consequences which accrue from the uses to which men apply them. A base man may use either a marvelous invention or a wonderful bit of knowledge, as of the effect of poison, for the most beastly of purposes.

It is philosophy, "divine philosophy," as the Greeks called it, which in the end gives the human mind both the light by which it can discriminate between the good or evil use of things. When the high pursuits or the innate love of philosophy are in eclipse, the world sinks into the lower levels of baseness and evils multiply. And the religion that holds its loyal adherents to a level less elevated than their possible attainment is the foulest of all treacheries and betrayals. "To your faith add virtue, and to virtue knowledge" is still the motto of a true Christianity that has been flouted for eighteen centuries by an ignorant and now insolent Christianism. The eclipse of high Pagan philosophy by Christianity in the third and fourth centuries still stands as the direst fatality in the life of the world.

The Protestant Reformation of the sixteenth century must, in spite of terribly serious reservations, be regarded as the most important and right-motivated development in Western history. It saved the West from complete demoralization; it saved for humanity the chance to regain its freedom to study philosophy and to develop science. But— expressing a whole volume in a sentence or two—it stopped lamentable leagues short of its real goal. It took one step or two, when it should have taken ten to its true objective. The Reformers did not lack courage; they boldly attacked a scorpion whose sting was death. But they did lack the knowledge of what had been thrown away in the third century, and what therefore had to be restored to make a thorough job of their valiant effort. Tragically they did not then have the benefit of the translations of the mighty spiritual lore of old Egypt, and lacking this they could only approach the Scriptures, which they wisely made the authoritative guide of the moral and spiritual life of Christians, with blind eyes. Had they possessed the Egyptian backgrounds and basic principles of divine philosophy, they could have gone back and refurbished and illuminated with brilliant light the great work of Philo first, then of Origen, in rehabilitating the Scriptures in the full true splendor of the esoteric meaning which they still hold, but which has been a light beyond the range of their limited vision, an ultra-violet too high pitched for them to catch.

If the debacle of lofty spiritual intuition in the third century was the infinite tragedy of early Christian influence, the failure of the Protestant Reformation to go its full length in repairing the damage done in the initial catastrophe was the hardly less serious tragedy of later Christianity. It was neither radical nor thorough enough, lacking the recapture of the true norms of judgment and interpretation, which are only now coming out to clear discernment in the more competent reading of Egypt's books, to bring to an end, but could only weaken and baffle for a time, the dismal forces of ignorance and the sly manipulation of its dupes by designing ecclesiastical authority. And without the full clear light of esoteric understanding and the restored mystical reinterpretation, far beyond what Origen could make of it, the available intelligence of Luther, Zwingli, Calvin and Melanchthon was not adequate to carry the movement the far further lengths it would have had to go to complete the reconstruction of the mangled theological doctrinism and fortify it to maintain its position against counter attack. Nor was there then, nor, lamentably, is there now, the acumen or the genius on the part of Protestants to accept the drastic revolution in their own order of theological science still clearly necessary before a rehabilitation of Christianity to its pure pristine status can be achieved. For the very potentiality of adequate acumen or genius needed not only to restore "Origen's allegories," but to carry their light and their release of understanding far beyond where he left them clear on to the apex of their splendid shining in minds expanded to power to glimpse the brilliance of inspired philosophy has been blunted and deadened in all Christian minds by centuries of obscurantism and an erroneous approach.

The reawakening and reconditioning of that obtuse mind, still lulled to somnolence by the hypnotic influence of ages of arrant tradition, and prolonged by its narcotizing of the sensibilities of each generation's childhood, is going to be a nearly hopeless expectation. Yet the future of civilized man depends upon its success. If the new Reformation does not quickly set in and move forward this time to complete renovation of modern religion, lifting it from an infamous past to the culture of the emotions stabilized by philosophical intelligence, infinite further catastrophe appears inevitable for the race. Religion must be rewed to philosophy. For religion, as pure emotional content, functions only as devotion. But devotion uninstructed as to its wholly right and beneficent objective, or devotion to what, has proven to be close to the most infernal force, capable of endless infamy and inhumanity, known to history. Religion separated from philosophy always stalks abroad as a potential but eventually actual menace to all the interests of higher good that must be stabilized by sound knowledge. The element of human consciousness, then, that is the ultimate factor indispensable for good, is the intelligently discriminating intellect.

Only when the present leadership in religion will muster the wis-

dom and the courage to place Christianity back again on those fundamental *archai* of cosmological and anthropological truth of that arcane
system from the primal spring of which it first flowed forth, only to
be polluted by the muck and mire of the channels of low human
mentality through which it had to make its course out into the low-
lands of history, will any organic motif under the name of Christianity be empowered by the law of divine sanction to function toward
the evolutionary apotheosization of the race. Then and then only can
the blind man's tapping staff of "faith" be exchanged for the open-
eyed vision of the path illuminated by the bright lamp of instructed
intelligence.

Mankind is admittedly today facing a crisis considered the most
dangerous in its history. Civilization, so-called, confesses itself menaced
with imminent possibility of eradication. An analysis of the world
situation in its outer appearances should at any rate present to ordinary
understanding the lay-out of the forces at work as they fall under
open observation. Such a sketch should fortify the mind with the
primary principles needed to be studied and applied.

Lying immediately under the eye, then, of any one who will be
observant, are seen to be two predominant forces of personnel, purpose
and policy, embodied in the activities of two strong and intensely
vigorous groups of partisans. Both are distinctly bent upon the purpose of dominating the entire world. As, quite understandably, any
group harboring a plot aiming at world control would not *dare* proclaim or let slip its real intent to common knowledge, the first strategy
of such a predatory motivation is to disguise its real drive under the
name, style and semblance of a high-sounding and broadly generalized
romantic ideality, or utopian humanitarianism. Every such bold scheme
will show itself masquerading behind a cloak or front of this sort.
This stratagem has been openly proclaimed by a publicist of one of the
two parties as the routine formula of successful deception to attain fixed
goals. It is even more patent, if unattested, in the constant moves and
ruses of the other of the two parties.

The party of the first part in this sketch is the political bureau of a
bakers' dozen men, which is concealing its actual motives behind the
mask of the idealistic politico-economic dream known as Communism;
the party of the second part is the ecclesiastical organization perpetuating the system herein called Christianism, and hiding its grasping
ambitions behind the skirts of "holy religion." Both render sham and
temporizing homage to democracy; but democracy will disappear com-

pletely if either gains final control. Democracy is instantly wiped out by the first party when it gains power; democracy has been hardly a reality at any time in any land dominated by the religious grip of the second party. An observation of a friend in casual conversation ventured the assertion that any country long dominated by the religion of Christianism and indurated under the ecclesiastical power of pietism, is in any true sense incapable of democracy. If either of the two parties wins total control, all democratic liberties will vanish.

It is most significant and interesting to note that, all too short and wholly incomplete as was the Protestant Reformation, its results have provided modern civilization with its only stalwart bulwark of defense and its only robust promise of salvation. For a survey of the world situation reveals that of those nations which yet stand together, so to say, in the breach to stem the tide of disintegration hurtling madly against its walls, the ones that furnish the only appreciable hope of holding the ground successfully are those five or six whose populations are still predominantly Protestant. The United States, Canada, England, Holland, Luxemburg, Norway, Denmark,—these six or seven peoples are left to save the gains of individual freedom from total abrogation by either of the two parties under discussion. Even these, in so far as they are insidiously infiltrated and undermined by influence from either or both the two parties, are weakened in their position on the side of liberty. The treacherous sapping and sabotaging of France's strength in the Second World War, under the domination of the religion which is the second party's mask, is a notable instance of the specification here made. Tersely it can be said, with little chance of refutation, that in the contemporary "cold war" being waged for the absolute rulership of the world, and in the possible actual war believed so imminent, the side that will fight for the essentials of true democracy and civilized freedom on this globe will be those Protestant populations; and they will have to wage this life and death struggle with little substantial help from those nations long and still conditioned to ignorance, blind belief, superstition and poverty by a Church striving desperately to regain the political power it once held and so frightfully abused. All the countries of Central and South America, Spain, Portugal, Italy not only can not be counted on to lend any considerable help in the crisis of war, but on the other hand will even have to be supported and defended by the power and effort of the Protestant countries. France alone is a question-mark; it is an uncertain quantity. The Protestant spirit has still some weight in its councils. But self-interest, inward corruption and the insidious Fascist bent inherent in the dominant ecclesiastical establishment that still has the French under its thrall, render it extremely undependable in the conflict to save human liberties. It was the collapse of France internally in the Second World War that permitted events to shape up into the outline of supreme peril for human society.

If, as the Papal encyclicals endlessly reiterate *ad nauseum*, the Christian religion of faith and piety is the one rampart of human society and the one sword of conquering might, and the old first form of organization of Christianity is the one true embodiment of that redoubtable Christian power, why should the naive mind not expect that it would be that true Christian Church and its warriors of the spirit that would be standing at the point of danger, all powerful to avert disaster? Instead it is the godless rebels, the lost souls of Protestants, who alone stand to make the fight and save Christian civilization. And again history speaks in the bluntest of tones to belie the unctuous claims of this degenerate pietism, this "ersatz" Christianity. This same putrid corruption of human sanity, as history now records, rose up to smother the interior light of man's divine self in the early centuries. It ran its brutal course and dragged its blood-stained trail of slaughter and ruthlessness down through the centuries. And still the same blind force, though not now blindly directed, it is gathering its strength to make another supreme effort to stifle the free spirit of mankind under the blanket of its imposed doctrinism and its regimented faith.

The New Reformation may under Providence be in time to avert this ineffable horror. The old knowledge that Christianism suppressed is now once again, and this time in competent understanding, available to restore Christianity to its true bases. The Reformers had not the help of the Rosetta Stone. But it is here now; and through its hieroglyphic lines we are able again to hear the voice of old Egypt's sapiency. Listening to that oracular voice, that *logos* of the wisdom out of which grew the primal true Christianity, a wiser world will rebuild the philosophical religion of the divine soul in man.

It remains only to epitomize in a few final words the two or three outstanding features in the indictment of this religion on the charge of having afflicted the minds of humans with the most heinous of hypnotic delusions. The work here being concluded has enumerated, charted and analyzed the nefarious influence of a host of minor *errata* in the dogmatic program of this institution. They are all ancillary to several others that are central and basic.

As Nietzsche said that the dictionary failed to supply him with words competent to register his utter detestation of the "slave morality" of this "Christian" faith, much the same accusation has to be entered here. The mind finds the strongest superlatives falling blunt and dull upon the paper in its effort to present the true picture of the havoc wrought in the conscious life of the world's citizenry by the impregnation of what Jung calls the "collective unconscious" of half the world with prepossessions of a weird and irrational list of indoctrinated ideas that in the end turn into the most corrosive obsessions and unseat the reason. It is not in the least degree an exaggeration to proclaim that the Christian religion, in the forms and conceptions in which it has been put forth or preached and expounded for sixteen centuries, has demented Western man. This general declaration is what the work has undertaken, as far as a gargantuan project could be achieved within the restricted number of its pages, to support by massed data.

The gross charge that is entered against this system of faith is that of having fastened upon the collective mind of the Occident first the idea that the salvation of the individual and the world from evolutionary catastrophe was effectuated only by the advent to earth, the personal life, the teaching of a new dispensation, and finally the suffering and death of one certain man in history; and, second, of having likewise fastened upon this general body of thought the prepossession that at the death of the body the eternal destiny of the surviving consciousness, or soul, would be lived out in one or other of two regions, the one a place of ineffable bliss, the other a limbo of unbearable but never-ending torment of body and soul.

These two impositions of an authoritative religious dictatorship have demented and derationalized the Western mentality through a process of mass hypnotization staggering in its extent and its depredations in the sacred field of conceptual life.

It should require no elaborated dissertation to establish the recognition that the predication of the human existence of the Christos principle as a man of flesh has forged in the collective acceptance of Christendom the most fatal of all misunderstandings. Crime committed in ignorance is still catalogued as crime, whether violating the civil or the moral law. In whatever of the two categories obtaining, the crime of which this work accuses Christianity—the crime of the third century—

501

must forever rank as the most corroding and devastating of all crimes which can be committed against the divine soul of man: the crime of having deprived the outer mind of humanity of the knowledge that the saving power in life is a power central and operative *only* in the interior region of man's own conscious being. For long it has slumbered in a deathlike trance; but later it is to be awakened by the impingement upon it of the actual experiences, the pains and joys of the outer personality, the body and its senses. The greatest crime that can be perpetrated against the mortal on earth is to deceive people with the fairy tale or the Santa Claus myth that a man was born, lived and died two thousand years ago, whose sufferings, death and resurrection have achieved the opening of the gates of Paradise for all men who will mentally be hypnotized with the story.

How can language paint in realistic hues the psychological monstrousness and deadliness of this gigantic deception? To slay a man's mind is to murder him. The worst feature of such psychological murder is that the hypnotization veils off utterly from the conscious man the knowledge of the presence and potential kingship in his own life of the babe of Christhood slumbering in his cradle in each mortal.

In summation, then, the indictment takes the form of the charge that Christianity has committed the greatest of all possible crimes against the human being, in that it has caused to be lost to the outer mind of men the supreme blessedness of conscious knowledge of the divinity within its own sphere of agency, while wasting in utter futility the awful mass of sentimental devotion of that outer consciousness upon the intimations tied up in a myth. To have mistaken the fictitious outer veil of the myth for actual occurrence and thus to have diverted the saving power of psychic effort and devotion away from the place of focus within the individual's own center of being, where alone regenerative work can be effected for each life, is again the commission of the direst of perversions. This most disastrous of all deadly crimes Christianity has committed. And this according to its own exuberant asseverations.

For, ironically enough, the one supreme claim on which it bases its allegations of superior excellence and power is precisely the thesis that it gave in the person of Jesus of Nazareth the one solid support on which the mind of a mortal can rest in irrefragable assurance that a divine principle has been brought to man on earth. This essay asserts that the claim thus announced is the one thing that not only has *not* made divinity available to any man, but has sharply and blindingly cut him off, by a fatal hypnotization, from the living possibility man always has had of finding divinity ever available to him in a place infinitely nearer than Judea and closer than 33 A.D.,—namely in the unexplored recesses of his own consciousness. The Christian allocation of the Christos, as the power with which man is to effect an intimate relation of atonement and union, outside the human breast and brain, in a remote episode in history (as to which there is yet not a shred of authentic evidence), must stand as the crowning sin of a civilization calling itself cultured. The Christian system has loosed and perpetrated this consummate enormity.

And of companion status is the second accusation: that Christianity has caused its billions to be haunted through life by the fear of suffering an endless torture in a horrid limbo known as hell when earth life is done, as a consequence of some indiscretions or unwisdom of human conduct,—if not bought free of the dire penalty for thirty or more pieces of silver. Again language admits its inadequacy to depict the psychological havoc wrought upon the mass mind by this phantom bogie of theological dementia. This haunting dread of endless suffering in hell, with even the pursuing malignity of a hypothecated and entified Devil in every moment of life—so that even the emancipated Luther threw his ink-well at him—is the twin psychological crime this monstrous engine of ignorance has wreaked upon its countless victims, who, hypnotized by faith when not by fear, dance in tune to every sophism the crafty manipulators pipe out. The demoralization of the Christian nations by these two hypnotizations stands at the head of all historical infamies. These might well be said to be the two arms of the cross of infamy and death upon which the *real* Christos, awaiting his recognition in the breast of every man, is being crucified by Christianity. Doubtless it is apt enough in the unconscious ironies that history itself shapes out, that Christianity is the religion that has made actual the crucifixion of the Christ in two distinct senses: the one in the false belief of the historical death of an actual man-Christ on a wooden cross in Judea, A.D. 33: the other in the portentously *real* crucifixion, in mystical consciousness, of the Christ-spirit on the cross of human mental crudity and neglect.

And at the sharp summit of all human refinement of fiendish criminality stands the consummate charge brought by history against this foul schematism that cloaks ulterior purpose under the mantle and mask of holy religion. In the court of common intelligence it has been decreed over and over again that the one crime that must carry the foulest stigma of all is that which deliberately aims to exploit the most sacred motivations of the human psyche, in the expression of which man is both holiest and noblest and at the same time most easily victimized by designing cunning,—the forces that make man a religious being. The conniving shrewdness of implacable human ambition to dominate the earth, which has evolved the colossal machinery invented to catch and enchain the divinest motions of the human spirit, for the express end of enslaving the masses in a mental (and economic) bondage to its Juggernaut of ecclesiastical power,—this, if recognized for what it truly is, should be branded as the foulest of all foul things. Even the most wretched crimes of passion or ignorance find some measure of extenuation. But the crime of plotting to use the sacredest aspirations of life as the tool with which to build world empire,—this is the nadir of the despicable in all human consensus. Christian historians themselves have had ample justification in characterizing this or that period of ecclesiastical governance in Christian history as a veritable sink of iniquity, a putrid cesspool of infamy. No words of ours could surpass in luridness their frank descriptions.

If the masses of "dumb driven cattle" thus exploited by cloaked deviltry can not be awakened to rise in their collective might and, directed by better intelligence, cease to lend themselves, and to sacrifice their hapless children, to this soulless Moloch, there will be another two thousand years of Dark Age Christianism. The world faces that situation and that choice now.

Heathen darkness, then Christian light, has been the cry of the founders and perpetrators of the "Christian" faith. This work for the first time presents the truth as the exact reversal of this order: Pagan light, then "Christian" night. And anxiously, with the annual recurrence of the Christmas festival as these words are being written, comes the phrase from the Christmas hymn heard in the church of our boyhood days: "Watchman, tell us of the night." The Pagan light is smothered in dire and apparently dawnless darkness of the Christian night. With infinite anxiety the world should be sending up the cry to the watchman on the heights of prophetic vision: What of the night? "What its signs of promise are?" Can he descry any first faint gleams of returning dawn? Will the long spiritual night and winter of human spiritual genius come to an end at last? Will the ineffable radiance of the divine message of Hermes, Orpheus, Plato and Zoroaster, even of Pythagoras, Aristotle, Plotinus, Proclus and Plutarch, of Philo, Clement, Origen, Dionysius and Erigena, and those

504

who kept the candle of philosophical knowledge and recondite esotericism burning in subterranean grots during all the centuries when
the ecclesiastical monster beat down every effort to set its light again
on the hilltops, even quenching finally the glorious outburst in the
fourteenth century Renaissance of the Platonists in Italy,—will the
long-buried light arise to irradiate the human mind again with the
joyous exuberance of rational delight? Can the ancient mountain
spring of high truth be cleared of the muck of accumulated ignorance
so that the living waters of intelligence can gush forth again to wash
away the dams of hypnotic indoctrination of false theses and irrigate
thirsty souls once more with the delectable drink of divine philosophy?

Within hours after the last paragraph was written, in which was
used the poetic figure in the Yuletide hymn, *Watchman, tell us of the
night,* our daily perusal of the *New York Times* brought under the
eye a brief notice of a newly published religious book under the title:
Watchman, What of the Night?, by the Archbishop of York, Cyril
Garbett. A nine-line summary of it reveals that it is a tract for the
times based on four convictions. If these four convictions are the concise epitome of the place and function of Christianity in the world of
1950 by so eminent an ecclesiastic as the Archbishop of York, they
may well serve as a brief for a concluding synthesis of our work.
The four theses are: first, that the world is in revolution; second, that
Christianity has now become the religion of no more than a minority;
third, that its gospel is definitely supernatural; and, fourth, that this
gospel will alone overcome the dangerous evils that threaten mankind.

On the first thesis—the world in religious revolution—what can
any sane man conclude from this but that after two thousand years
of its complete dominance of the Western world by this endlessly proclaimed one true and saving religion, that world has ceased regarding
Christianity as its savior and has turned in violent revolt against it?

On the second thesis—that it is held only by a minority, and, he
might have added, that minority composed in its bulk of the less
thoughtful section of the populations, those who let "leaders" do their
critical thinking instead of thinking for themselves, and who are in
the churches by force of tradition and social pressure—what again is to
be concluded but that the one true religion has failed? Only one question arises: Has it failed because of its intrinsic demerit and inadequacy, or because the majority of Western humanity has failed it? Has
the religion failed the men of sixty generations, or have the men failed
it? If the latter answer is snapped up to spare Christianity the ignomin-

505

ious verdict of nearly total failure, then the age-old debate as to the comparative worth and efficacy of one religion as against another has been an empty and aimless waste of words. For this would relegate the decision finally and incontrovertibly to the side of the men and exonerate the religion. The ultimate resolution of the debate would be that it is not religions that succeed in making men better beings, but always men that succeed in making religions better. Splendid humans can make a splendid religion out of even an erroneous set of doctrinal ideas, rising superior even to wrong influences; low humans can and always do tear down a pure, high and true religion to basest failure.

But it is Christianity and its apologists and protagonists that have forever held and bandied the claim that the heathen religions had lowered and degraded their votaries, while loudly vaunting that the Christian faith had proved its truth and superiority by the fruits of its influence upon the West. It is therefore Christianity that must, on the basis of its own principle of criticism, holding the religion, not the men, responsible for historical outcomes, accept the conclusion now that this religion has finally demonstrated its failure. If the spurning of a religion that has had infinite time to prove its value by a large majority of those who should by now have been lifted to near-divine beatitude by so lofty, so true, so deifying a religion, is not the conclusive evidence of its failure, one asks what greater marks are demanded?

On the third point—that the Christian gospel is definitely supernatural—let the briefest possible comment be complete assent. This work has endeavored to establish that Christianity was doomed to failure precisely because it *was* supernatural, and therefore not adapted to benefit man, who must live his life in the environment of nature, and must find his highest good in the harmonization of his life with natural law. A religion that despises the natural, as Christianity has flagrantly done (particularly in its debasement of the body) and implants in men's minds the notions that their greatest exaltation and blessedness is to be won by catching up at a supernal power in the hope that it will lift them above the ordained provenance of natural law, is destined at once and continually to cut man off in disordered eccentricity and derationalization from the play of the normal evolutionary offices of his relation to nature.

Man's natural powers are gradually, of course, to be entwined with the mental and spiritual energies deployed into his life by the Paraclete, which flow from within or "from above," as Paul says. Precise delimitations on the meaning of "natural" and "supernatural" must be stated here, else there is confusion everywhere. Christian teaching has always erred in giving a false connotation to "supernatural," making it refer to forces of magic and miracle which it has dissociated entirely from the prerogative and conscious control of man himself. Christianity took the supernatural—which should never be considered in any other sense than is expressed by the better word "supernormal"— and placed it up and outside of man's own domain, and only to be begged for as by a poverty-stricken suppliant, when all the while it should have been declared a potential function of his own nature and always within the reach of his own aspiration. No religion can render man the one prime service religion should supply unless it instructs him in the knowledge that nothing is more marvelous, magical and miraculous than the laws of beneficence that regulate and support his entire life, be it on the physical or the spiritual side. He must be taught that two widely separated and diverse vibration rates and frequencies of cosmic intelligent power are lodged and operative within the province of his bodily life, and that the one is commonly denominated "natural," in Greek terms, "physical," while the other is designated "spiritual" or "divine." But the woeful disservice that misinstruction can render the human, thus constituted, is to hypnotize his reason with the false notion that only the natural is himself, and the supernatural (supernormal) or spiritual is something or somebody else,—a god or God.

So it has eventuated that this religion has misused the term "supernatural" in such a way as to deprive its adherents of the one and only saving knowledge possible for man as a potential culturist, that the saving divinity, or spiritual vibration, is a force resident within and available to the personality of man at all times.

A religion teaching such a perversion of crucial knowledge set the seal of its own failure and doom upon history and human evolution. Christianity essayed in blind philosophical ignorance to convert man to God, but bound man's intellect to the notion that God was to be found only in Jesus of Nazareth.

The final, consummate catastrophic error of Christianity that destined it to supreme fatuity lay in its inculcation of the idea that man was to be converted to the Deity resident somewhere else than in himself. Speaking of Paul's conversion on the road to Damascus, which incidentally he says, since Paul's account and that in *Acts* differ so widely, must be concluded to be a "literary" and not a "historical" story, Dr. Robert Norwood remarks in his *The Heresy of Antioch* (p. 39):

"No other conversion is genuine. Only as we find ourselves can we enter the Kingdom of God."

Man has found neither God nor himself in Christianity, except in instances where the irrepressible divinity in individuals was powerful enough to dissolve the encrusting armor and shackling influences of false theology, because he was taught by Christianity to look for God in the vacuous spaces of heaven, and thus missed both the God who is in the heaven of man's own higher consciousness and the God of cosmic infinity. For the God in his own upper area of realization is his own Higher Self, a fragment of the infinite Godhood. The Pagan religious philosophies stressed abundantly the element that could be called "supernatural"; but they did not deprive man of the supreme benison of knowing that the divinity that could be invited or incited to lift man above his common level was integral within himself. Man's genius is a divinity, declared Heraclitus; and Plato asserts we are divine on the mental side.

As to the fourth item—that the gospel of Christianity will alone overcome the dangerous evils that threaten mankind—here is the millionth parrot reiteration of that purely stereotyped and mechanical confident assertion that Christianity can not be conceded any possibility of failure, and still uttered in blind disregard of the historical failure now being evidenced as never before. What sound reason can the Archbishop advance to support the claim that a gospel that has written the ghastliest record in blood and insanity across the pages of twenty centuries of history will alone save humanity now? If it has not saved mankind in so long a period, with complete opportunity, what grounds are there to think that it can do any better now? There are none that one can see. The argument seems to be that since Christianity after a long age in human history is now held by only a minority, is fantastically supernatural, and humanity is revolting against it, therefore it is the sole savior to which we can turn. That is the logic one finds in the Archbishop's four points.

Well indeed may we anxiously query the watchman: What of the night? For we are still enshrouded in the deep shadows of Christian darkness, and one of the most ominous signs on the still unstreaked horizon is the wretched miscalculation and the egregiously false assumption found in books put out by Christian spokesmen.

The Christianity that we have had since the third century is decidedly *not* the sole power by which the world will overcome its menacing evils. Christianity has itself killed the nuclear core of the saving power that it may once in some measure have possessed. No influence from the side of religion save the power that comes from the certain knowledge that man can call upon the potentially infinite source of wisdom lying as yet largely untapped within his own constitution will avail to save him *from* the misleadings and hallucinations of the most bizarre fetishism ever to befuddle men capable of better thought. No religion but one that will place deity universally back in the conscious recesses of man's own nature will be potent enough to save him. And even that potency can not be stirred to action and development of function until the outer earthly man *knows* that the power of salvation must be worked by himself and from within himself. A religion that puts the least block in the way of all men's knowledge that the only deity that can save them from ills fostered by their own ignorance is the infant god who must be recognized, cared for, loved and brought to growth by the exercise of its fledgling powers within themselves, must be seen for what it is,—a scourge of the earth.

The always and finally crucial question is whether men can acquire from any religion the rudiments of higher knowledge and apply them with consummate wisdom to the definite diminution of the savage instincts brought up in the subconscious from the past stages of animal evolution and to the corresponding expansion of the superior mind of the immanent god. The god only conquers and takes his seat on the inner throne as the personality "lets the ape and tiger die" out of his consciousness. The "dying daily" unto the flesh and the world is Paul's way of stating this. The interests of the flesh mean "death," says the Apostle, while those of the spirit mean life and peace. But for man to pray to some power outside himself to give those interests a shove forward and galvanize them into function, and to stand waiting until that supposititious external power turns on the current for him, is to invite the final stultification and paralysis that a false religion can afflict man with.

The vital question is not whether a given religion can save mankind; for this very framing of the matter implies that man is a puppet and rises or falls by the character of the religion he happens to be born into. The final test is whether man can implement the verities and motive springs of influence in his religion so as to assimilate and incorporate their salutary powers into his own history. In the end man's salvation lies in and with himself. God in his unerring wisdom has dowered man with the energies and faculties requisite to effect his own salvation. Indeed any vicarious salvation would disorder the operation; would throw the factors in it out of proper collaboration with each other; and let the evolving intelligence that needs the exercise of self-reliance for ultimate victory stand deprived of its indispensable training for godhood.

The Christian preachment that man is to be saved by Infinite Goodness or by sheer mental assent to the historical implications of the literalized Gospels must be set down, when at last sanity can register in the human brain, as the most colossal ineptitude and costliest tragedy of the ages. Alongside it the Christian conception that the human family is to be redeemed by a power that was implemented through its incarnation in only one person in history, must finally be recognized as the most chimerical fantasy of delusion that ever infatuated mankind. There is nothing to match the imbecile notion that the power that is to uplift the race from animal savagery to love and graciousness could have been made available for all men through its sole incorporation in the flesh of one single man. That all men should have to look to this one man as the author and finisher of their salvation is beyond all words the coronal fatuity of all time. No doctrine in all the realm of ideal conception could be half so fatal as this.

That a Christ-*principle* was made available to work for the salvation of mortals from the hell of unregenerated animal propensity here on earth,—that is a doctrine sane and cheering. For this principle would be equally distributed to all men potentially, and would be found standing in time of need at every man's side. It can be established on firm philological ground that neither the term "Lord," nor "Jesus," nor "Christ" ever had been taken as referring to a living person until the debacle of all intelligence in the third century of the Christian movement opened the door to such an untoward blunder. Christianity has never been able to offer so much as a line in answer to the question a ten-year-old child will ask, why God let eons of time pass by before he despatched his only Son to the planet to provide for man the one and only hope of escape from certain perdition. The sheer idea of the implementation of human deification through the agency of any one man, walking in body like other men, at a given moment in history, is itself the most preposterous of suppositions. The thought that a religion which broadcast so bizarre an idea to the world should have been swept on to a dominating position in that part of the world assumed to be the summit product of human civilization, is a phenomenon as inexplicable as it is portentous and dispiriting.

While it is true that man does not stand in relation to a religious philosophy as a mere marionette, to be made good or bad as he is influenced by a good or bad religion, nevertheless the issues of life are mightily determined by the ideology that haunts and possesses any brain. If man is to implement a religion to its highest beneficence, instead of being merely implemented by it, it is still a matter of immense moment what religion he becomes addicted to for the building of the house of his life. Even the tilling of a farmer's field depends largely upon the efficiency of the plowing instrument. So the perfectibility of life, which rests always and ultimately upon the strength of the spirit and the intelligence of the mortal chiefly concerned, nevertheless can be vastly aided, or as disastrously thwarted, by the true fitness of the philosophy resorted to.

It happens that man is himself both the plowman and the field he is plowing. It becomes tenfold more important, then, whether he uses for self-cultivation a philosophy that works well or one that will thwart healthy growth. A philosophy serves his mental and spiritual bodies—for he has such, as Paul assures us—much as food serves his physical corpus. All alike thrive on suitable food and suffer from wrong feeding. This essay has endeavored to show beyond all dispute that the mental and spiritual segments in the life of the West have for long ages been fed upon a supposed diet of surpassing religious quality, which turns out to be totally indigestible and productive of severe illness in those partaking of it. The psychological health of the Occident during those centuries has been ruined by a diet of improper ideological nutriment provided by Christianity. The symptoms of the disease have been bigotry, hatred, separativeness, failure of brotherhood, violence, ignorance, greed, laziness, corruption, falsity, political chicanery, immorality, superstition, eccentricity, fanaticism, forgery, insanity, persecution, war and slaughter.

While there has been a great measure of fruit of better quality, intermixed with the depravity that stands as the record of this disease, it can be attributed to the fact that it has inevitably enlisted many of sterling native character, whom even so eccentric a theology could not corrupt. Strong and impeccable Christians have at times almost made the religion one to be respected, as they attached the credit of their own virtue to its practice. Christianity did retain the shell of Pagan constructions of truth, and vigorous characters could revivify the dynamic force of the original sense, as their own lives gave meaning to the dead formularies. And this says that there is a certain modicum of Pagan wisdom still active in aspects of the system. Truth is still powerful, no matter how caricatured. The true lineaments of the original beauty can at times be glimpsed through the present distortions.

So the dissertation closes with the note on which it began,—the clarion call to the modern world to return to the primitive Christianity which the founder of Christian theology, Augustine, proclaimed had been the *true* religion of all humanity *before* the execrable wantonness of impiously pious religionism in the third century laid desecrating hands upon its beauteous light and befouled it with smoke and smudge of bad oil. But that *true* Christianity is also true Egyptology, true Hellenism, true Zoroastrianism, true Hebraism, true Hinduism, true Buddhism, true Platonism and Neo-Platonism, true esotericism in all religions. When that true religion is taken up again, man will have recovered the necessary intellectual basis of world brotherhood.

Only then will the long shadow of the third century be dispelled as the strong light of the restored true Christianity rises on the modern day and illumines the world universally with the benignant rays of the primeval revelation of truth to mankind.

INDEX

Birth, The Virgin, 175
Book of the Dead, The, 22, 154, 302, 308, 384
Breasted, Wm. H., 111, 140
Buddha, The, 147, 149, 241, 405
Buddhism, 193, 512
Budge, E. A. W., 112, 154-5, 315, 322-3

C

Carpenter, Edward, 169, 311, 313
Case, Shirley J., 322, 324-5
Cave, The, 375, 385-6
Celsus, 110, 127, 130-1, 151, 165, 168, 174, 197, 206, 208, 222
Cerinthus, 338, 385
- Chiasmus, 402, 418 *ff.,* 428
Christ, The, 52, 55, 59, 78, 98, 102, 121, 126, 155, 177, 195, 198, 212, 239, 243, 259, 272, 293, 299, 306, 313, 317, 331, 333-4, 365, 379-80, 397, 445, 501, 510
Christianism, 13 *ff.,* 21-2, 24, 43, 55, 63-4, 66, 101, 120, 133, 226, 230, 236-7, 255, 298, 323-4, 328, 358, 363, 368, 373, 376, 387, 389, 443-5, 454, 464, 482, 486, 496, 498, 500, 504
Christianity:
  Apology for, 21
  Apostolic, 43, 123, 126, 244, 275, 327, 330, 330-7
  Bias of, 11, 290, 407
  Bigotry of, 21, 293
  Brought nothing new, 19
  Brought the Dark Ages, 6
  Changed its character, 14, 40
  Conspiracy of, 9, 11-3, 291, 298, 313, 414
  Copied from Paganism, 20, 65, 132, 156, 271
  Corrupted truth, 167, 209, 226, 245, 248, 268
  Corruption in, 118-9, 461

Christianity (Cont.)
  Deception in, 9, 11, 19, 219, 266, 278, 290-3, 349, 363, 390, 392, 438, 461
  Degeneration of, 60, 176, 180, 230, 255, 268, 286, 371
  Dementia of, 293, 344, 348, 416, 449 *ff.,* 501, 503
  Derived from Paganism, 211, 225, 236, 246, 273, 276, 281, 317, 323-5, 421, 436
  Destroyed truth, 5, 6, 226, 283
  Disintegration of, 76, 282
  Europe never had it, 1 *ff.*
  Failure of, 280, 298
  False claims of, 8, 19-20, 25, 33, 35, 118, 213, 224, 258, 264, 298, 302, 309, 311, 315, 353, 456, 503
  Falsehood of, 7, 25, 396
  False teachings of, 7, 8, 67, 402
  Falsified history, 15, 19, 134
  Fanaticism of, 179, 197, 227, 229, 236, 256, 259, 297, 300, 336, 373, 375, 484, 511
  Frauds in, 123-4, 174, 180, 197, 290-2, 300, 363, 389, 414-5
  From Egypt, 157, 308, 421
  Hatred of philosophy, 6, 38, 46, 50-1, 54, 66, 85, 120-1, 141-2, 163, 176, 181-3, 208, 224, 283, 340, 347
  History of, never written, 4, 15
  Hypnotizing power of, 190, 194, 241, 257
  Ignorance in, 56, 58-9, 66-9, 83, 98, 103-4, 121, 151, 155, 164, 171, 224, 243
  Intolerance in, 180
  Its history subjective, 11, 461
  Low level of, 218, 221, 229, 306, 341-2, 358, 431
  Military, 60
  Not the first true religion, 4
  Obsessions of, 10
  Origins of, 7, 12, 15-6, 20-1, 25-7, 32, 36, 77, 102, 134, 138, 155, 235, 241,

514

OTHER BOOKS BY THE SAME AUTHOR

THEOSOPHY: A Modern Revival of Ancient Wisdom. The Academy Press, 227 Murray Street, Elizabeth 2, New Jersey. 2nd Edition, 1944. 351 pp. Index, Bibliography. $3.00.

This work, issued under the imprimatur of Columbia University, New York City, stands as the only accredited academic work dealing with the great renaissance of ancient Oriental Esotericism in the Western world in modern times. It was the author's thesis presented for the degree of Doctor of Philosophy in Religion and Philosophy and was the second volume of a projected series of publications undertaken by the Philosophy Department of Columbia University under the title of *Studies in Religion and Culture,* designed to present a luminous history of every religious denomination, cult or movement in the United States. It is regarded by both Theosophists and non-Theosophists as perhaps the most judicial treatment of the subject yet presented. Its digest and analysis of the great principles of the Esoteric Wisdom of antiquity has been lauded by discerning students as the clearest and most perspicacious so far given.

THE LOST LIGHT: An Interpretation of Ancient Scriptures. The Academy Press, 227 Murray Street, Elizabeth 2, New Jersey. 1940. 611 pp. Extensive Bibliography and Index. Second Edition 1948. $3.00.

This work is regarded by many, among them leading clergymen and university teachers, as the one true and correct interpretation of the Christian and other Scriptures made at any time. With keys drawn from ancient Egypt's wisdom it pierces through the outer veil of Bible literalism and alleged history and reconstructs the long-lost structure of sublime arcane meaning, retranslating the "lost language of symbolism" in which the books of archaic wisdom were written.

The author's enlightened insight and amazing scholarship have combined in this work to establish the epochal fact that the Christian religion can no longer be considered a product of Judea in the first century A.D., but is of remote Egyptian origin. The correlation made between the Christian Bible and the long antecedent religious literature of Egypt is a scholarly achievement of absolutely epochal significance. It is the virtual documentary proof of Augustine's statement that "that which is called Christianity existed among the ancients and never did not exist

523

. . . from the very beginning of the human race . . . until it was called Christianity in our day." The evidence amassed demonstrates beyond cavil that the Bible is a reprint of old Egyptian texts, whose meaning can not be grasped without the keys of understanding discovered by the author in the Egyptian writings.

It is not too strong an assertion to state that it floods the entire area of hitherto dark and dubious interpretation of Bible meaning with a veritable radiant light of clear comprehension. It appears destined to become soon the indispensable handbook for Bible reading and the cornerstone of the "religion of the new age" or the "one-world religion" so devoutly prophesied and longed-for.

WHO IS THIS KING OF GLORY?: A Critical Study of the Christos-Messiah Tradition. The Academy Press, 227 Murray Street. Elizabeth 2, New Jersey. 1944. 492 pp. Index. $3.00.

As *The Lost Light* reveals *what* was lost, and restores it, *Who Is This King of Glory?* tells the thrilling story of *how* and *why* the Light was lost. And this revelation of the truth of history that has never before been made common knowledge constitutes undoubtedly the most significant and gripping story ever told in the history of religion. More than that, this story becomes the key to the understanding of the world situation in religion today. This book is the narrative of what happened back in the third century of Christian history, when the Christian movement passed over from the hands of the Philosophers of the Greek world into those of the unphilosophical and worldly-minded Romans and suffered thereby the total extinction of its original light of esoteric spiritual meaning, the historical result of which was the sixteen centuries of the Dark Ages.

The book is dedicated to the thesis that the saving divinity, the Christos, is a spiritual principle within the heart and mind of man. The whole great and immemorial tradition of Messiah's coming to redeem fallen humanity is in this work handled with a historical perspective, with an impregnable array of scholarly data and with a consummate insight into the truth that will rank this volume as the crowning work of sanity in religion.

Back of the great world wars of modern times are the mighty clashes in religious ideology. Unquestionably what is happening now is but the long shadow of what transpired in that fatal debacle of spiritual truth in the third century, and this incredible story is told for the first time in this work. The book is the natural companion of *The Lost Light*. The two make a mighty team, pulling together to lift the car of religion out of the mire of superstition and bigotry onto the highroad of intelligence and luminous meaning.

SEX AS SYMBOL: The Ancient Light in Modern Psychology. The Academy Press, 227 Murray Street, Elizabeth 2, New Jersey. 1945. 345 pp. Index. $3.00.

This work was undertaken by the author when he became aware that his grasp of the fundamentals of the ancient Science of the Soul had put into his hands the keys that opened wide the doors of understanding of the whole complicated and confused groping in the field of modern Psychoanalysis since Freud's discovery of the so-called "Unconscious." It was obvious that the ancient Sages had covered this entire field with consummate intelligence. There was needed only the application of the basic principles of their perfected knowledge to resolve all the problems baffling the modern psychologist. Sex As Symbol therefore stands as the first work clarifying Psychoanalysis with the radiant light of ancient wisdom.

Then the modern inclusion of sex in the motivation of human behavior demanded exegesis. It is in this field that Sex As Symbol outranks all other works on Psychoanalysis in the modern day. The prominence of phallic symbols in high ancient religious systems has never before been understood, much less sanely expounded and vindicated as something transcending gross sensualism. It is not too much to assert that in this work sex is given its truly lofty place and rated at its exalted character for the first time in religious literature. The achievement of this task with the authority of truth has justly won for the book the accolade of being the most luminous work yet produced in the field of modern Psychoanalysis. For not only is sex revealed as the truest key-symbol of the supreme significance of human life itself, but it is brilliantly analyzed as to its place and function in the individual human's program of evolution, his sanity, balance, mental health and happiness.

If it is possible for one book to lift sex from low and base regard to a veritable pinnacle of purity and nobility in the light of its true character, this book will do it.